21

PERSECUTION AND TOLERATION

PERSECUTION AND TOLERATION

PAPERS READ AT
THE TWENTY-SECOND SUMMER MEETING AND
THE TWENTY-THIRD WINTER MEETING
OF THE
ECCLESIASTICAL HISTORY SOCIETY

EDITED BY

W.J. SHEILS

PUBLISHED FOR
THE ECCLESIASTICAL HISTORY SOCIETY

BY

BASIL BLACKWELL

1984

British Library Cataloguing in Publication Data

Sheils, W. J.
  Toleration and persecution.—(Studies in
  Church history; v.21)
  1. Persecution—History
  I. Title   II. Series
  272   BR1601.2

ISBN 0-631-13601-0

Zoo29292

272

Printed in Great Britain by
T.J. Press Ltd, Padstow

CONTENTS

Preface   *page* ix

List of Contributors   x

Introduction   xiii

Religious Toleration in Classical Antiquity   1
PETER GARNSEY

'To Flee or Not to Flee': An Assessment of Athanasius's
De Fuga Sua   29
ALVYN PETTERSEN

Popular Violence and Popular Heresy in Western Europe
*c*1000–1179   43
R. I. MOORE

The First Crusade and the Persecution of the Jews   51
JONATHAN RILEY-SMITH

The Language of Persecution: John of Salisbury and the
early phase of the Becket Dispute (1163–66)   73
JOHN McLOUGHLIN

The Mohammetan and Idolatry   89
JENNIFER BRAY

The Possibility of Toleration: Marsiglio and the City
States of Italy   99
DIANA M. WEBB

Infidels and Jews: Clement VI's attitude to persecution
and toleration   115
DIANA WOOD

Reginald Pecock: a tolerant man in an age of intolerance   125
ROY M. HAINES

Mission and Inquisition among *Conversos* and *Moriscos* in
Spain 1250–1550   139
JOHN EDWARDS

CONTENTS

Persecution and Toleration in Reformation Europe   153
N. M. SUTHERLAND

Persecution and Toleration in the English Reformation   163
(Presidential Address)   163
G. R. ELTON

Anglicans, Puritans and American Indians: Persecution
or Toleration?   189
H. C. PORTER

Toleration and the Cromwellian Protectorate   199
BLAIR WORDEN

The Enforcement of the Conventicle Acts 1664–1679   235
ANTHONY FLETCHER

Sir Peter Pett, Sceptical Toryism and the Science of
Toleration in the 1680s   247
MARK GOLDIE

The Politics of 'Persecution': Scots Episcopalian Toleration
and the Harley Ministry, 1710–12   275
D. SZECHI

The Persecution of the French Jesuits by the Parlement of
Paris 1761–71   289
D. G. THOMPSON

'No Law Would be Granted Us': Institutional Protestantism
and the problem of Catholic poverty in England 1839–42   303
GERARD CONNOLLY

Bishop Alexander and the Jews of Jerusalem   317
PATRICK IRWIN

Pope Pius IX and Religious Freedom   329
PETER DOYLE

Tolerant bishops in an intolerant Church: the Puseyite
threat in Ulster   343
S. PETER KERR

Persecution and Toleration in pre-colonial Africa:
nineteenth-century Yorubaland   357
JOHN ILIFFE

CONTENTS

Toleration and Persecution in colonial Natal   379
J. B. BRAIN

The religious background to Max Weber   393
NORMAN STONE

Intolerable tolerance: the Canadian bishops and the
1912 'Appeal on behalf of Christian Unity'   409
RICHARD E. RUGGLE

The persecution of George Jackson: a British Fundamentalist
Controversy   421
D. W. BEBBINGTON

The Pope and the Jews in 1942   435
OWEN CHADWICK

Religion and Social Control in the Soviet Union 1945–1964   473
GAVIN WHITE

Abbreviations   481

PREFACE

'Persecution and Toleration' provided the theme of the 1983 summer conference and the subsequent winter meeting of the Ecclesiastical History Society. These gatherings, held at Magdalene College, Cambridge and King's College, London respectively, were presided over by Professor G.R. Elton, whose choice of theme it was. The two concepts, embracing as they do the two extremes of Christian, and indeed of non-Christian, attitudes to differing belief-systems and competing forms of churchmanship, proved a popular one with the Society and produced a very full programme of papers. The papers published here represent but a selection of those delivered at Cambridge and London, and serve to indicate the wide range of topics and periods discussed at the conference.

Once again the Society is indebted to the British Academy for the generous financial assistance it has given towards the cost of publication.

W. J. Sheils

CONTRIBUTORS

G. R. ELTON *(President)*
Regius Professor of Modern History in the
University of Cambridge

D. W. BEBBINGTON
Lecturer in History, University of Stirling

J. B. BRAIN
Associate Professor of History, University of
Durban-Westville

JENNIFER BRAY
Research Officer, History Department, Birkbeck College,
University of London

SIR OWEN CHADWICK O.M.
Regius Professor Emeritus of Modern History,
University of Cambridge

GERARD CONNOLLY
Kent

PETER DOYLE
Principal Lecturer in History, Bedford College of
Hgher Education

J. H. EDWARDS
Lecturer in Medieval History, University of Birmingham

ANTHONY FLETCHER
Senior Lecturer in History, University of Sheffield

PETER GARNSEY
University Lecturer in Ancient History and Fellow of
Jesus College, Cambridge

MARK GOLDIE
Lecturer in History, Churchill College, University of
Cambridge

ROY MARTIN HAINES
Professor of History, Dalhousie University, Nova Scotia

CONTRIBUTORS

JOHN ILIFFE
Reader in African History, University of Cambridge, and Fellow of St John's College

PATRICK IRWIN
Research Student, Pembroke College, University of Cambridge

S. PETER KERR
Tutor in Church History, Lincoln Theological College

JOHN McLOUGHLIN
Research Student, Trinity College, Dublin

R. I. MOORE
Senior Lecturer in History, University of Sheffield

ALVYN PETTERSEN
Chaplain, Clare College, University of Cambridge

H. C. PORTER
Lecturer in History, University of Cambridge

RICHARD E. RUGGLE
Research Student, Trinity College, Toronto

JONATHAN S. C. RILEY-SMITH
Professor of History, Royal Holloway College, University of London

NORMAN STONE
University Lecturer in Modern History and Fellow of Trinity College, Cambridge

N. M. SUTHERLAND
Reader in Early Modern History, University of London

D. SZECHI
Research Fellow, University of Sheffield

D. G. THOMPSON
Associate Professor of History, University of New Brunswick, Canada

DIANA M. WEBB
Lecturer in History, King's College, University of London

CONTRIBUTORS

GAVIN WHITE
> Lecturer in Theology and Church History, University of Glasgow

DIANA WOOD
> Lecturer in History, University of East Anglia

BLAIR WORDEN
> Fellow and Tutor in Modern History, St Edmund Hall, University of Oxford

INTRODUCTION

Religions spring from faith, and faith, endeavouring to maintain its own convictions, cannot permit the existence of rivals or dissenters. Thus religions organized in powerful churches and in command of their scene persecute as a matter of course and tend to regard toleration as a sign of weakness or even of wickedness towards whatever deity they worship. Among the religious, toleration is demanded by the persecuted who need it if they are ever to become triumphant, when, all too often, they start to persecute in their turn. A highly unsubtle interplay of persecution and toleration thus conveniently sums up the millenia of religious and more especially of ecclesiastical history. To say this is not cynicism but sobriety of judgment, and the commentator should remember that the gods, if they exist, do not necessarily share the zeal of their followers. This truth holds for all religions. Even the ancient Greeks, so often in the past misrepresented as worshipping only reason, thought it desirable (as Garnsey shows) to seek the favour of their guardian deities by protecting them energetically against rivals and preserving them jealously for themselves; even Africans (as Iliffe shows) knew the virtues of persecution before they made the acquaintance of Christianity.

In practice, religions have usually felt most violently intolerant not of other religions but of dissenters within their own ranks. However much Muslims enjoy hitting Christians, they get far more mileage out of the sectarian strife inside Islam. And of all religions the Christian, being the most sophisticated and therefore that productive of most variety, has worked out most thoroughly the principles and practice of destroying the heretic—as several papers in this volume demonstrate. It should cause more disquiet than one commonly encounters that a faith whose founder seemed resolved to transcend the denominational boundaries should have taken so enthusiastically to the rooting out of deviation. Even the experience of being itself the victim of persecution, which filled the first 300 years of its existence, seems only to have sharpened its capacity to do unto others as it itself had been done by. At any rate, it is certainly fascinating to discover that a faith which created the most remarkably complex theologies ever invented should also have given so much deep thought and positive action to the cleansing of a hearth which really only its passion for philosophy had dirtied in the first place.

Of course, not all persecution arises from a clash of faiths: such mundane things as politics and diplomacy could play their part. Anti-Catholicism in Max Weber's Germany (Stone) owed less to protestant zeal than to the rivalry of two powerful secular institutions—*Kaiserreich* and Vatican; hostility to Christianity in Soviet Russia (White) springs less from the manifest efforts of Marxism to play at being a religion than from a political desire to remove a competitor for men's allegiance to the all-powerful state. There is a sort of moral problem here: do we regard persecution as better or as worse when it results from truly religious conviction? The man who (with Thomas More) believes that failure to persecute heretics endangers his own and other people's salvation testifies to his faith, but it is a faith which turns a supposedly benevolent God into a relentless judge. The man who allows persecution to happen because to take a stand against it might threaten his own or other people's fortunes on earth at least does not place the burden of the deed on his god.

Among the adherents to religion the Jews have been, in a sense, most fortunate in that most of the time they have been deprived of the chance to persecute. Notoriously they have been the standard victims, for reasons which scholars (and others) have been learnedly analysing over the centuries without realizing that those too weak to defend themselves will always find willing persecutors, whatever particular smokescreens those persecutors may erect to justify their actions to themselves and to the world. The Jewish experience altered hardly at all between the age of the Crusades (Riley-Smith) and the age of Hitler (Chadwick). This last case is especially interesting because it brings out the collaboration of convenience and faith, though this is my reading of the event, not Chadwick's: when the papacy failed to interfere with the Nazi persecution, it acted from both political calculation and a well-entrenched anti-semitism. The observer may decide for himself which motive he finds the less displeasing. But the Jews' apparent avoidance of acts of persecution does not elevate them above their fellow-men: given the chance, however rarely, they have proved as eager and able as anyone to stamp on the heads of dissenters and to smite the Philistines. At least they have been frank enough about it: the Jehovah of the Old Testament lacks tolerance as manifestly as the God of the New seems to favour it. Yet since their God so consistently saved them from being able to persecute, the Jews should perhaps realize that they may have misjudged his views on this touchy subject.

In the mass, toleration has been proclaimed almost always by those who needed it to survive at all and by those who cannot bring themselves to elevate any form of religion to an importance weighty enough to justify killing for it. Toleration is the preserve of the persecuted and the indifferent—and those who become indifferent to religion generally find some other manifestation of a faith which enables them to become intolerant again. However, this is true only of the mass. Individuals do not have to abandon their religion in order to abandon the hunting of other men. Enough people of that rarer sort wander through the pages of this book to relieve the predominant gloom. And in fairness it must also be said that though Christianity has been the most consistently persecuting religion yet seen in this world, it has also produced the largest number of men and women who could faithfully serve their God without thinking it necessary to persecute anyone in deed or in word.

G.R. Elton

RELIGIOUS TOLERATION
IN CLASSICAL ANTIQUITY

by PETER GARNSEY

I

TOLERATION IMPLIES disapproval or disagreement coupled with an unwillingness to take action against those who are viewed with disfavour in the interest of some moral or political principle. It is an active concept, not to be confused with indifference, apathy or passive acquiescence.[1] In this paper I reexamine, in the light of this strong definition of toleration, the contrast commonly drawn for the world of classical antiquity between a tolerant paganism and an intolerant Christianity. Toleration implies a degree of acceptance as well as a degree of disapproval. In evaluating the attitudes of pagans to other pagans in antiquity we must satisfy ourselves, first, that ancient polytheistic systems were as open and inclusive as is often assumed, and second, that where mutual acceptance might be said to have prevailed, this was not merely casual acceptance, but entailed compromise between competing gods and rituals. Again where religions can be seen to have been seriously at variance with each other, as were the sundry pagan cults with

---

[1] I employ the definition of B. Crick in 'Toleration and tolerance in theory and practice', *Government and opposition: A journal of comparative politics* 6 (1971) pp 144–71; cf. P. King, in the same volume, 'The problem of tolerance', pp 172–207, and *Toleration* (London 1976). I have not however found it useful to reproduce their distinction between toleration and tolerance.
The literature on persecution in antiquity is large, whereas that dealing with toleration is insubstantial—which gives me a justification for adding to it. But see A. Momigliano in S. Humphreys, *Anthropology and the Greeks* (London 1978) pp 179–93; [J. A.] North, 'Religious toleration [in Republican Rome', *Proceedings of the Cambridge Philological Society* n s 25 (1979)] pp 85–103. Other relevant work that I have read with great profit includes [P.] Brown, ['Religious coercion in the later Roman Empire: the case of North Africa', *History* 48 (1963)] pp 283–305; 'St. Augustine's attitude [to religious coercion', *JRS* 64 (1974)] pp 107–16; *Augustine [of Hippo* (London 1967)]; [H.] Chadwick, 'Gewissen', [*Reallexikon für Antike und Christentum* 10 (1978)] pp 1026–1107. I am grateful to G. E. M. de Ste Croix for adding to my collection of references to toleration from his vast knowledge of the literature of late antiquity. My debt is substantial to these and other scholars, especially Richard Gordon, and to Myles Burnyeat and Moses Finley who showed me ways of improving an earlier draft of this paper.

Judaism and Christianity, where therefore toleration was at least in principle a possible option, we must ask how far pagan authorities and (in so far as this can be discerned) ordinary pagans were inclined to choose that option. A pertinent issue is whether any general arguments for toleration or religious freedom were produced from the pagan side before Christianity became the religion of the emperor. The existence or absence of a 'literature of toleration' may legitimately be taken as a pointer (no more) to religious attitudes and policies. The Christian church, for its part, stands accused, and convicted, of intolerance towards pagans, Jews and nonconformists within its own ranks (heretics, schismatics). But it is appropriate to ask how speedily and comprehensively the principle of religious freedom, advanced first by Tertullian at the turn of the second century AD, was abandoned once Christianity captured the throne.

II

Ancient religions, with the exception of Judaism and Christianity, were polytheistic.[2] In response to the mysterious forces of nature the ancients summoned up a throng of deities, with various, sometimes overlapping, competences. The gods were looked to by the community for protection against nature and against man. Misfortune was an infallible sign of the displeasure of the gods and the failure of men to propitiate them; few held that the gods were uninterested in men and their affairs; even fewer that the gods did not exist at all. The reality of the gods of another community was similarly taken for granted. The very existence of that community was proof not just of the existence of its gods, but also of their general satisfaction at the attentions they were receiving from the people whom they were protecting.

But the case for a tolerant paganism cannot rest on the mere recognition of and respect for gods of other communities. What counts for more is the attitude of a community to religious dissension and non-

---

[2] On Greek religion see [E. R.] Dodds, [*The Greeks and the Irrational* (Berkeley 1951)]; [M. P.] Nilsson, [*Geschichte der griechischen Religion* (3 ed München 1967)]; W. Burkert, *Griechische Religion der archaischen und klassischen Epoche* (Stuttgart 1977). On Roman religion, see [K.] Latte, [*Römische Religionsgeschichte* (München 1960)]; J. Le Gall, *La religion romaine* (Paris 1975); J. H. W. G. Liebeschuetz, *Continuity and change in Roman religion* (Oxford 1979); [R.] MacMullen, [*Paganism in the Roman empire* (New Haven 1981)]; [J. A.] North, ['Conservation and change in Roman religion', *Papers of the British School at Rome* 44 (1976)] pp 1–12.

conformity at home, and to the intrusion of new religious influences from outside.

Democratic Athens was responsible for the death of Socrates in 399, charged with corrupting the youth, introducing new gods and showing disrespect for the old. Moreover, the democracy may have (the tradition is suspect): passed a law against 'impiety' on the proposal of one Diopeithes and prosecuted among others the philosopher Anaxagoras and the sophist Protagoras for impiety—all in the late 430s. Protagoras' treatise began with the agnostic sentence: 'Concerning the gods, I am not able to know either that they do exist or that they do not exist, for many are the obstacles that impede such knowledge, notably the obscurity of the question and the brevity of human life.' The democracy certainly in 415 punished with exile or death a number of Athenians accused of mutilating the Herms and parodying the Eleusinian mysteries, and, in a separate but roughly contemporaneous incident, expelled Diagoras of Melos for mocking the mysteries. 'The Great Age of Greek Enlightenment', wrote E. R. Dodds, 'was also, like our own time, an Age of Persecution.'[3]

Two things should be said in explanation, though not exoneration, of the Athenians. First, it was entirely logical for a pagan political community in antiquity to be intolerant of nonconformity and protective of its gods. The polis protected its gods because the gods protected the polis. Religious deviance was dangerous in principle because it prejudiced the good relations between gods and men on which the safety of the state was held to depend. Second, the acts of intolerance listed above (there were a few other isolated incidents) are concentrated in the period of the Peloponnesian war and its immediate aftermath, a critical period for Athens and Athenian democracy. To consider only the last and best known incident, a defeated and humiliated Athens found a scapegoat in Socrates. Its choice of victim was explicable. Quite apart from the embarrassment which this 'diabolic needler'[4] had brought to individuals in public or private debate, he had played an important role in the education of traitors like the arch-oligarch Critias and the maverick Alcibiades. This last issue is alluded to in the charge of corrupting the youth. It is only an

---

[3] Dodds p 189. For references and source-criticism see K. J. Dover, 'The freedom of the intellectual in Greek society', *Talanta* 7 (1976) pp 24 seq Cf. the wide-ranging article of G. W. Clarke, 'Books for the burning', *Prudentia* 4 (1972) pp 67–82. Best on Socrates is [G. X.] Santas, [*Socrates* (London 1979)].

[4] Santas p 6.

allusion because the amnesty oath, taken after the Thirty Tyrants (led by Critias) gave way to a restored democracy, precluded a direct attack; the accusers fell back on charges not overtly political. The actual charges did however have strong political overtones, for secular and sacred, patriotism and piety, were inseparable in antiquity. Their gravity is not in doubt: no less an issue was at stake than the health and prosperity of the community.

Of the two religious charges, which are connected, that of introducing new deities holds a special interest for our subject. If Athenian, or Greek, religion was for whatever reason a closed system, then religious strife and compromise—toleration in fact—become possibilities, at least in principle. If on the other hand Athenian polytheism was supple and inclusive, then toleration is, strictly, an irrelevant concept. It is this latter view of ancient paganism which is normally held.

The history of pagan communities shows a pattern of change as well as continuity in the character and content of religious practice. But there never was an open-door policy, and at least in some periods strict limits were set to the willingness of any given community to receive and assimilate foreign gods and rituals. The civic cult of Athens in the classical period, for example, was expanded only in response to crisis, when a sharp downturn in the public fortunes of the community appeared to necessitate a religious innovation.

In fifth century Athens, the entry of Bendis,[5] a non-Greek deity, into the Athenian pantheon by decree is without parallel. Even the admission of the cult of the Greek hero Asclepius from Epidaurus in 420 was a rare event. The first steps in Asclepius' introduction were taken as early as 430–29, the year in which the decree for Bendis was passed. These are the years of the great plague. Asclepius was to be admitted into the Roman state cult in 293 in similar circumstances: his was the quintessential cult of crisis. Bendis, a Thracian Artemis worshipped with orgiastic rites, is the more unlikely arrival.

The well-known penchant of ordinary Athenians in the years of the Peloponnesian war for mystery religions of an orgiastic character with origins in the north and east provides only part of the explanation.[6] A political element in the decision cannot be ignored. In 433

---

[5] W. S. Ferguson, 'Orgeonika', *Hesperia* Suppl. 8 (1949) pp 131; Nilsson pp 833–5 (Bendis), pp 806–8 (Asclepius).

[6] M. P. Nilsson, *Greek popular religions* (New York 1940) pp 84–101.

some Thracians received permission from the Athenian assembly to acquire a site and place on it a shrine of Bendis. It was in this year that an alliance was struck between the Athenians and the Thracian king Sitalces. The timber reserves of Thrace and the proximity of the kingdom to the trade route from the Black Sea made Sitalces a highly desirable ally for Athens, a naval power dependent on grain and timber imports. The upgrading of Bendis a few years later points to the value placed on the alliance by the Athenians in the early years of the war. But without the plague Bendis would never have received a public cult. And the treatment of Bendis was exceptional.[7]

That a charge of religious innovation should have been levelled (however unjustly) against Socrates, then, becomes intelligible. The state religion of Athens *was* exclusive. In theory at any rate the pantheon was complete, and the gods of Athens did not ordinarily tolerate intruders. The promotion of Bendis by decree of the assembly was carefully prepared for by an official visit to the oracle of Dodona. Divine approval had to be won. Even the earlier concession of 433 required similar measures: it was not a trivial event, then, perhaps the first of a limited series.[8]

To return to the original question: is the language of toleration appropriately applied to the religious climate of classical Athens? I do not think so. The Athenians actively defended their gods against, as they put it, impiety (*asebeia*). The private performance of foreign cults, which could not in any case be kept out of a cosmopolitan city such as Athens was, was not attacked. But then to many or most Athenians it was quite acceptable and not felt to subvert the worship of the official gods. The 'conservative opposition's' disdain for popular religion—as witnessed for example in the banishment of Sabazios and the other foreign cults in Aristophanes' *Horai* or in the ridicule that Demosthenes heaped on Aeschines for his youthful participation in the rites of Sabazios at the side of his priestess mother[9]—

---

[7] The introduction of the Egyptian God Ammon by the 370s BC is a superficial parallel. But Ammon had an oracle (Delphi was frequently in the hands of enemies of Athens), he had Greek intermediaries (the Cyrenaeans), and he was closely identified with Zeus. See H. W. Parke, *The Oracles of Zeus* (Oxford 1967) pp 217–19; S. Dow, 'The arrival of Isis at Athens', *Harvard Theological Review* 30 (1935) pp 184.

[8] *IG* II² 1283, a third century inscription, refers back to the Athenian decree of 433 which fulfilled an oracle from Dodona. *IG* II² 337 (333–2 BC) is a decree giving traders from Citium, Cyprus, area for a shrine to Aphrodite, just as the Egyptians have one to Isis.

[9] Cic., *de leg*. 2.37, cf. Aristoph., *Wasps* 9 seq, *Birds* 875; Dem. 18. 259–61; Nilsson pp 836–7.

was essentially a manifestation of class and cultural snobbery. In any case the 'official' position could always be restated at the expense of an individual or a group whose activities had earned the public displeasure.[10] Similarly, the 'exclusiveness' of the state religion was not based on any idea that the Athenian religious heritage was incompatible with or 'truer' than that of any other community. Finally, there is no hint of a debate about toleration. Notoriously Socrates, whom many would like to see as the prototype conscientious objector, did not offer a plea for the liberty of conscience. It is a fact that no doctrine of active rights made an appearance in the ancient world.[11] The interests of the individual were not entirely neglected—in particular as citizen he was allowed the passive right of protection against the arbitrary acts of magistrates and judges—but it was taken for granted even by democratic theorists and spokesmen that the best interests of the individual would coincide with those of the community as a whole. Coincidence of interests did not mean parity of interests. The citizen was not so much encouraged to exert his individuality as reminded of his duty to abide by the customs and laws of the community. At his trial, and indeed by standing trial rather than running away, Socrates announced his submission to the authority of the city and its laws and courts.

III

Roman religion has the reputation of having been decidedly receptive to and tolerant of alien influences. Did not the Romans in the third century BC alone introduce, among other things, the Greek cults of Ceres and Asclepius, Venus Erycina from Sicily, the Magna Mater from Asia Minor, the first Secular Games for Dis Pater and Proserpina—king and queen of the underworld—and the first human sacrifice. One scholar has even seen a resemblance between Roman 'openhandedness' in religion and in the political sphere, between the adding of new gods and cults and the adding of new citizens.[12]

The admission of new gods was characteristically a consequence of the expansion of Rome. Some gods, for example those of states

[10] Dem., 19.281 (execution of Ninos, priestess of Sabazios)
[11] R. Tuck, *Natural Rights Theories* (Cambridge 1979) ch 1; cf. M. I. Finley, 'The freedom of the citizen in the Greek world', *Talanta* 7 (1975) pp 1–23.
[12] North p 11. For innovations in general, Latte pp 213–63.

whom the Romans were bent on destroying, were simply annexed. The Romans were skilful at inventing institutional mechanisms to defuse the issue of god-snatching. One such was the quaint ritual of *evocatio*.[13] The gods of an enemy were 'summoned out' of the besieged city; their 'abandonment' of the community they were supposed to protect, in response to the offer of 'the same or even more splendid worship among the Roman people', sealed the fate of the city. This rite, which took the form of a contract between the Roman attackers and the gods, more particularly the tutelary god, of the doomed city, was turned against cities in Tuscany, notably Veii, the city in southern Etruria which blocked Rome's advance to the North; it may also have been brought into service against other Italian communities; it was certainly revived for the final, spectacular, destruction of Carthage in the middle of the second century BC. Other stratagems were developed for other situations. One was *exoratio* by which gods were induced to change sides but not homes. It suited the Romans to afford some defeated opponents continued existence and a measure of autonomy. Local cults and rituals were permitted to continue. The religion of a defeated state could do no harm for like the state itself it had lost its sting. In favoured cases the Roman state cult was expanded to accommodate it.

Another setting for the admission of foreign cults is familiar to us from the Greek context. In times of emergency the Romans were driven to religious experiment under the direction of the Sibylline books and their official interpreters. The invasion of Hannibal led to an extraordinary series of innovations, designed to restore the *pax deorum*.[14] The climax came in 205 when the Decemvirs discovered an oracle in the Sibylline books to the effect that 'if ever a foreign foe should invade the land of Italy, he could be driven out of Italy and defeated if the Idaean Mother should be brought from Pessinus to Rome'. This was the Great Mother of the gods, or Cybele, a Phrygian goddess whose worship was marked by ecstatic dancing culminating, at least when practised at the cult centre of Pessinus, in self-castration. One would like to know how much advance knowledge Roman senators had about the cult which they so clearly coveted. When the goddess arrived they quickly banned Roman citizens from her procession and the attendant ceremonies, which were

---

[13] See R. Ogilvie, *Commentary on Livy I–V* (Oxford 1965) pp 674 seq. Citation from Pliny, *hist. nat.* 28.18.
[14] Latte pp 251–62; citations from Livy 29.10, Dion. Hal. 2.19.5.

shorn of their more extreme elements. 'So cautious are they', wrote Dionysios of Halicarnassos, 'about admitting any foreign religious customs and so great in their aversion to all pompous display that is wanting in decorum'. Concerning the manner of the removal of the goddess from Asia Minor there is doubt on several points, in particular on the part played by Attalos king of Pergamum, friend but not official ally of Rome, and the circumstances surrounding his handing over to the Romans of the black stone, apparently a meteorite, which represented the goddess. There are echoes here of *evocatio*, especially as a feature of that rite appears to have been the physical removal of the cult statue of the deity who was held to have changed sides.

Livy's account implies that Roman senators made a connection at the time between this case and the summoning of Asclepios from Epidaurus at the time of a prolonged epidemic in Rome in the late 290s.[15] On that occasion the Roman ambassadors brought away (no doubt together with the rest of the cult apparatus) a serpent which passed for the god himself. In later times the story that the god came of its own free will achieved popularity: understandably, since the voluntary accession of a god was confirmation of Rome's greatness. Contemporary Greeks presumably saw the affair as a straightforward act of *Machtpolitik*.

Thus far in discussing the attitude of Romans to foreign cults there has been no temptation to introduce the concept of 'toleration'. Roman-style polytheism was disposed to expand and absorb or at least neutralize other gods, not to tolerate them. The admission into the state cult of a captive and tamed Magna Mater does not break the pattern.

The Romans remained deeply suspicious of exotic mystery cults. The brutal attack on Bacchic rites in 186 BC—less than two decades after the importation of Magna Mater—was not out of character.[16] Bacchus was not a recent arrival in Rome and Italy. But the worship of the god had taken on new elements which were bound to attract the hostile attention of the state authorities: it was not merely the orgiastic rites, described and no doubt embroidered by an indignant Livy, which offended, but also and more importantly the cell structure, marked by an oath of membership, a common treasury, a broadly-based following and a hierarchy of lay officials as well as a priesthood. The whole organization was in effect autonomous, re-

[15] Latte pp 225–7.
[16] North 'Religious Toleration' with bibliography

moved from the supervision and control which the state expected to exert over religious activities. It is hardly surprising that it was regarded as subversive and that the rites of Bacchus were only allowed to survive in an emasculated form.

The Bacchanalian affair can be regarded as a turning point in the religious history of the Roman state. It marked the appearance within the Roman community itself of the first of a succession of specifically religious organizations devoted exclusively to religion, culminating in Christianity. None of these (basically oriental) cults were invited guests—there was, significantly, no successor to Magna Mater for a long period—but on the other hand there was no way in which their entry could be barred. What was the Roman response?

One option that was in principle available was systematic persecution. It was not taken up. A lapse into active persecution was always a possibility as is demonstrated by the periodic expulsions of Chaldaeans, Isis-devotees, Christians and Jews—even Jews, who at least from the period of Julius Caesar's ascendancy enjoyed a privileged status in Rome. But for the most part, religious organizations that were unauthorized, that were viewed as out of step with the *mos maiorum* or just illegal, were 'allowed' to exist because there was no way of excluding them or stamping them out. 'Toleration by default' would seem a possible, if charitable, description of the attitude of the Roman authorities. It would be more in line with our definition of toleration to say that governments showed by their inaction an appreciation of the limits of their power or a passive acquiescence in the presence of cults which they could not control. The Jews are the exception that proves the rule. In a letter of Julius Caesar to the city of Parium quoted by Josephus, the dictator instructs the Parians to permit the Jews resident in their city to carry out their traditional rites and practices, pointing out that he himself had excused only Jews from his general ban on *thiasoi*, religious associations, in Rome.[17] As to Christians, Trajan's famous ruling[18] that they were not to be hunted down (*non conquirendi sunt*) did not create a privileged status for Christianity, and certainly does not amount to a policy of toleration. Christianity was never an authorized religion—

---

[17] Jos., *Ant. Jud* 14.213; cf. Suet., *Div. Iul.* 42.3.
[18] Pliny, *Ep.* 10.97. For the position of Christianity with relation to the state see G. E. M. de Ste Croix, 'Why were the early Christians persecuted?' in M. I. Finley ed *Studies in Ancient Society* (London 1974) pp 210–49; *The Class Struggle in the Ancient Greek World* (London 1981) pp 396–405; 419–41, etc.

religio licita, in Tertullian's phrase;[19] in fact simply being a Christian was an offence. The claim that theirs was the one true religion, their active proselytism and their obstinate refusal to participate in the imperial cult meant that Christians were always vulnerable to the charge of disloyalty to emperor and state.

But at least we can use the term 'toleration' in good conscience with respect to the Jews. The Jewish religion was disliked by Romans of Caesar's class and generation,[20] it was incompatible with the *cultus deorum*, but it was nevertheless given official sanction. The Roman *beneficium* to the Jews, however, was not secure; it had to be renewed with every change of government. Moreover, those Romans who were friendly to the Jews were guided primarily by political considerations, not moral principles. And the initiative always came from the Jewish side.

Toleration for the Jews had its origin in the attempts of the Jews of Judaea to free themselves from Seleucid control, and specifically in the approach of Judas Maccabee to the Romans in 161 BC in the aftermath of the persecution of Antiochus IV, culminating in the attempt to convert the temple of Yahwe into a temple of Zeus. Interference in the ancestral cults of a nation on this scale was 'unheard of in the Greek-speaking world from immemorial times'.[21] The Roman senate received the Jewish envoys and agreed to a declaration of friendship. The senatorial decree, a copy of which went back to Judaea, was engraved on bronze tablets and set up in the Capitol. Jews and Romans were drawn together by strategic considerations, which on the Roman side consisted in a desire to embarrass and weaken Syria. The pattern was repeated in the following century in the civil war period, when first Julius Caesar and subsequently Octavian (later Augustus) received valuable military assistance from the Jews. Caesar cashed in on Jewish resentment at Pompey's outrageous conduct in violating the Holy of Holies after besieging and taking Jerusalem; while Herod moved faster than most after the

---

[19] Tert., *Apol.* 21.1.

[20] e.g. Cic., *pro Flacco* 67–9.

[21] A. Momigliano, *Alien wisdom* (Cambridge 1975) p 100, and in general, pp 97–122; E. Schürer, *The history of the Jewish people in the age of Jesus Christ (175 B.C.–A.D. 135)* (rev. edn. G. Vermes, F. Millar, M. Black Edinburgh 1973–79). Other work on the Jews and Romans includes J. Juster, *Les Juifs dans l'Empire Romain: leur condition juridique, économique et sociale* (Paris 1914); E. Mary Smallwood, *The Jews under Roman rule* (Leiden 1976); A. M. Rabello, 'The legal condition of the Jews in the Roman empire', H. Temporini ed *Aufstieg und Niedergang der römischen Welt* II Principat 13 (1980) pp 662–762.

battle of Actium to join the winning side. The reward was a series of official edicts and letters instructing their recipients—Greek cities in the East—to allow the Jews resident in their cities to live in accordance with their traditional customs and laws.

Three points are worth noting about the documents. First, they came about as a result of Jewish initiative. Shrewd, energetic and on the whole effective diplomacy, built on a close personal relationship between Jewish and Roman leaders, is a striking feature of the hundred years from Caesar to Claudius, carrying the Jews through even the crisis years of the reign of Gaius—when the Jews were compelled to play their last card, a threat to lay down their lives *en masse* in defence of their religion and way of life. Second, the documents are numerous—and presumably Josephus' dossier is not complete— and repetitious. But this is an indication of not so much Roman enthusiasm as Greek hostility. The letters and edicts of Caesar, Augustus and Claudius were a direct consequence of anti-Jewish sentiment and activity in provincial cities in the Greek East. Toleration rested on an ephemeral foundation if it had to be constantly reasserted. Moreover, Jewish credit inevitably wore thin, as rulers who had been the private beneficiaries of Jewish support gave way to others who lacked cause for gratitude and were more inclined to see Jews as trouble-makers. Third, the documents regularly acknowledge that the Romans are extending privileged treatment to the Jews because of services rendered. And that is all. No further motivation or justification is offered. There is an absolute lack of any apologia for religious pluralism or religious freedom. The Jewish right to their ancestral customs is not built up into a general principle applicable to every *ethnos* (people) let alone every individual.

Nor does anything of the kind surface in pagan literature as a whole. It is particularly noteworthy that the philosophical sceptics were barren of ideas in this area, unlike some of their successors in the sixteenth or seventeenth centuries, who developed rationalistic arguments for toleration on the basis of the uncertainty of religious knowledge.[22] Cotta, who acts as the spokesman of the Academic Sceptics in Cicero's *de natura deorum*, energetically refutes the sundry philosophical proofs of the existence of the gods and the various dog-

---

[22] The main classical texts are Cic., *de natura deorum* and *Academica*, and Sextus Empiricus, *Outlines of Pyrrhonism* (*P. H.*). For later sceptics see R. H. Popkin, *The history of scepticism from Erasmus to Spinoza* (Berkeley 1979); [Q.] Skinner, [*The Foundations of modern political thought* (Cambridge 1979)] esp vol 2, pt 3, ch. 8.

mas about their character, but then falls back upon the assertion of an undogmatic belief in the Roman ancestral religion, which he announces himself fully prepared as a pontiff to uphold.[23]

Cotta's position finds an echo in pre-Cartesian sceptics such as Montaigne. Montaigne's sceptical attitude to proof in the area of religious belief coexisted with a firm and conventional Catholicism. The liberal humanists of a sceptical bent were in general sincere believers. On the issue of persecution they typically equivocated. Montaigne, for example, was a supporter of religious unity but an opponent of persecution. The ancient sceptics make no statement about persecution and toleration. Cotta's stress on his obligation as a religious official to protect the state religion implies, among other things, a readiness to limit the religious choices of Romans, or at any rate those of Romans of Rome and Italy. Disapproval of atheism is similarly implicit in the references in the same treatise to the sentences passed on such as Protagoras and Diagoras and the attack on Epicureanism for undermining religion. But atheism was a peripheral phenomenon in antiquity.[24] Oriental cults, indeed all non-Roman cults, are largely ignored in the de natura deorum and also in the work of Sextus Empiricus, the main source for Pyrrhonian as opposed to Academic Scepticism. Sextus notes that local sacrifices and ritual practices are diverse, but this is merely to prepare the ground for the sceptical decision to suspend judgment 'as to the natural existence of anything good or bad or (in general) fit or unfit to be done'.[25] He can be said to have tacitly accepted but not openly advocated religious diversity. Roman government attitudes, as we saw, were no different. The emperors in their edicts showed a disinclination to lay down general principles. In the absence of such statements, it is permissible to attribute to Rome's leaders nothing more grandiose than an appreciation of the distinctness of the different peoples who made up their empire, combined with an implicit recognition of their inability to control their subjects beyond a certain point and the unwisdom of rousing local passions.

---

[23] Cic. de nat. deorum 3.5–9; cf. Sex.Empir., P.H. 1.16–17.

[24] Cic., de nat. deorum 1.63, 115; 3.5–7; cf. Sex.Emp., c. Phys. 1.51; A. B. Drachmann, Atheism in classical antiquity (London 1922).

[25] Sex.Empir., P.H. 3.235.

IV

Arguments for religious toleration, when they do emerge in antiquity, are part of a response to active or threatened persecution or intolerance from those under attack. Jewish apologetic is not very creative in this area. It sets for itself the limited objective of gaining protection for Jewish religion and culture, and employs to this end specific arguments relating to the nature of the Jewish religion, its piety, high moral standards and ancient origins, and to the record of Roman recognition and favour and Jewish support and loyalty. Only one writer puts forward arguments of broader significance—Josephus. In a speech[26] given by Josephus to Nicolaos of Damascus before Augustus' lieutenant Agrippa, the platitude 'for each community (*ethnos, polis*) its own ancestral customs' is transformed into a prescription which an imperial government could not ignore without jeopardizing not only civil order (for the Jews will fight to the death) but also the prosperity of the whole empire. The index of prosperity which Nicolaos offers is precisely the ability of every community to follow its ancestral traditions without harassment: 'And the happiness that the whole human race enjoys, thanks to you, we measure by the fact that it is possible for people in every country to live and prosper while respecting their own traditions'. This prosperity moreover has a divine underpinning, it is a reward for those who tolerate. As Nicolaos goes on to say: 'For if the Deity delights in being honoured, it also delights in those who permit it to be honoured.' Agrippa was ultimately persuaded by more tangible factors, in paricular, Herod's friendship and the calculation that confirming Jewish privileges would not 'cause the Roman government any trouble'—the ultimate criterion. Yet it would be a mistake to underrate the appeal of Nicolaos' argument. This was a world in which all alike, pagans, Jews and Christians, thought that the fortunes of men and states were dependent on divine goodwill.

The argument of Nicolaos is bold but slippery; it depends on the premise that religious freedom for Jews and their enemies (Greeks) could be put on the same level, that in each case it was a *beneficium* (privilege or favour) which was revocable. This is false. The local cults (and especially the civic cults of the poleis) were not at risk, unless as in the case of the Druids they offended against Roman sacrificial rules. And the Jews did present special problems, both abroad,

---

[26] Jos. *Ant. Jud.* 16.31–57.

where they breached the unity of the polis, and at home, where they sought to exclude all other religions. In a later passage[27] Josephus, this time speaking in the first person, again glosses over the 'awkwardness' of the Jews, but this time argues for mutual tolerance by pleading shared moral values. It is not differing customs that truly divide men, that are the essence of 'foreignness', but contrasting moralities. Josephus is optimistic: 'goodness (*kalokagathia*) is common to all men and alone enables society to endure'. The tactic is not unlike that employed by Castellio, Professor of Greek at Basle and opponent of Calvin in the mid-sixteenth century, when in the anonymous treatise *de haereticis* he made a plea for toleration between Christians on the basis of the common ground that they all shared, 'the gold coin which is everywhere acceptable, no matter what the image'.[28] Josephus' idea lacks a precise parallel in ancient thought, and in so far as he is ascribing virtue to ordinary humanity, it is decidedly anti-philosophical.

Early Christian apologetics has as its standard themes the unique truth of Christianity, the harmlessness and innocence of Christians, the folly of pagans, and the iniquity of Jews. When the injustice of persecution is brought up, the argument quickly disintegrates into a threat of divine judgment.[29] Tertullian, an African of the late second and early third century AD, breaks new ground. In the *Apologeticus* 24.5 he writes:

> Look to it, whether this may also form part of the accusation of irreligion—to do away with freedom of religion (*libertas religionis*), to forbid a man choice of deity (*optio diuinitatis*), so that I may not worship whom I would, but am forced to worship whom I would not. No one, not even a man, will wish to receive reluctant worship.

and in the *ad Scapulam* 2.2. we read:

> We worship the one god whom you all know through nature; it is his thunder and lightning at which you tremble, his blessings in which you rejoice. The rest you think are gods, but we know are demons. Nevertheless it is ordained by both man-made and natural law that each person may worship whatever he wishes, nor does one man's religion either injure or benefit the next

[27] Jos., *Ant. Jud.* 16.174–78.
[28] S. Castellio, *Concerning heretics: whether they are to be persecuted*, (trans R. H. Bainton New York 1935) at p 130; Skinner 2 pp 245–8.
[29] e.g. Justin, *Apol.* 1.68.

man. It is however not for religion to compel religion, which is something to be taken up voluntarily not under duress. Sacrifices are demanded only of those willing to perform them. You will render no real service to your gods by compelling us to sacrifice. For they can have no desire for sacrifices from the unwilling, unless they are animated by a spirit of contention, which is a thing altogether undivine.

About a hundred years later another African, Lactantius, reacted to the Great Persecution of Diocletian with an expanded version of Tertullian's statement.[30] This is a summary of his arguments:

1. Religion is not something that can be imposed: 'There is nothing so voluntary as religion.'

2. Persecution is a violation of both human and divine law.

3. There follows a moral/linguistic argument: persecution is bad; religion is by definition about the good: *Necesse est bonum in religione uersari, non malum.* It is, as it were, a contradiction in terms to persecute, to do evil, in the name of religion.

4. Persecution is not good for the persecuting religion, in three ways:

    4.i The gods won't welcome the sacrifice that is forced out of the unwilling, because it is in effect a curse, *execratio*, not a sacrifice.

    4.ii If you try to defend religion by bloodshed, torture, evil, it will be polluted and violated, not defended.

    4.iii Those who persecute will receive their just deserts. God, to whom it falls to punish those who despise him (for that is not our job), will do so, just as surely as he will avenge the toils and injuries of us his servants. (This is spelled out in grisly detail by the same author in *de mortibus persecutorum.*).

5. There is another way. It is to talk things out, to use debate (*oratio*) and persuasion (*hortamenta*). The debate might well be public. Let us call the pagan priests to a public meeting (*contio*) and give them the chance to urge us to take up their religion. We will listen. We don't want anyone to worship our god, the god of all, against their will; and if anyone refuses, we don't get cross. They ought to be like us: out style is to die rather than kill, to be patient rather than cruel, faithful rather than criminal.

None of this sounds very sophisticated to modern ears. We have a bald statement of principle, the beginnings of an empirical argument—persecution is bad for the persecutor—and an alternative

---

[30] Lactantius, *Inst. Div.* 5.19.9–24; 5.20.7–10; *Epit.Inst. Div.* 47 (52).3–49 (54).7.

strategy—argue it out. It is however a fresh start. The sources of Tertullian are an unsolved and probably insoluble problem. Tertullian's 'no one, not even a man, will wish to receive reluctant worship' recalls in Josephus 'They are not grateful for honours conferred under compulsion and constraint' (referring to Roman emperors).[31] But Tertullian has turned an empirical observation into a general principle and in so doing coined a phrase: *libertas religionis*. His 'religious liberty', moreover, is an attribute of individuals, not the exclusive possession of an *ethnos* or *polis*.[32] The breeding ground of this idea is perhaps the tension, which receives its first exposure in St Paul's writings, between the authority of individual conscience and the wisdom of the Christian community.[33] At any rate, it does seem to be a breakthrough that only a Christian could make, because the Christian, notoriously, had abandoned his ancestral tradition and embraced a supranational universal religion. Finally Tertullian has firmly rooted his doctrine in both human and natural (or divine) law; compare Nicolaos' tentative suggestion that the free exercise of *ta patria* has divine approval. There seems no escape from the hypothesis that the mind at work was in fact Tertullian's. This is not as unsatisfactory a solution as it may sound, since his work as a whole is full of novel argumentation, even if the quality is variable.

The Christian contribution to toleration theory peters out with the cessation of persecution and the upturn in the Church's fortunes. For example, Ambrose is capable of mouthing the precepts that religion is not to be forced and that everyone has the right to defend and practise his religion, but the remarks are intended merely for the ears of a raw fourteen-year-old emperor, Valentinian II, it is *his* 'right' to stand by his Christian faith (and by extension, to uphold his brother Gratian's anti-pagan actions) which Ambrose claims to be defending (*Ep.* 17.7). Ambrose's aim is to persuade Valentinian to *reject* the option of toleration—for which, incidentally, his favoured word is *dissimulatio*, pretence. Themes introduced by Tertullian and Lactantius

---

[31] Jos., *c. Apion* 2.73.
[32] I emphasise 'exclusive'. Tertullian was of course capable of employing the familiar argument more appropriate to Jewish apologetic that all others (who turn out to be *provinciae* or *civitates*) are permitted their gods; e.g. *Apol.* 24.7–10; cf. Athenagoras, *Embassy* 1. Both Geffcken's criticism and Crehan's defence of Athenagoras miss the point. See J. H. Crehan, *Athenagoras: Embassy for the Christians* (Trans and comm London 1956) at p 123. The standard works on Tertullian do not appear to notice the innovation which I have signalled above.
[33] Chadwick, 'Gewissen' pp 1066 seq.

were also utilized by Donatists.[34] In particular, they stated much more clearly than their predecessors had done that to advocate and practise coercion was to fly in the face of traditional Christian doctrine. Their criticism of the church establishment not only for favouring persecution but also for calling in the legislative and coercive arms of the state provoked Augustine into developing a doctrine of 'just persecution'. Donatists were not averse to appealing to imperial enactments for their own purposes, specifically, to justify their suppression of the Maximianist schism in 393–4, and their main tactic against orthodox coercion was not argument but violence. Insofar as they resorted to argument, they were mainly concerned to press their claims to be the Catholic Church, and were not much inclined to fall back on the essentially defensive strategy of setting up a debate on toleration. This can be said of all Christian sects in this age of religious fervour and fanaticism. Few Christian writers reveal a non-sectarian spirit. We might single out Socrates the ecclesiastical historian, who frequently expresses distaste for bigotry and strife, which is contrary to the spirit of Christianity and disturbs the peace of the Church and the world;[35] or Salvian, bishop of Marseilles, who excuses barbarian heretics (they were Arians) on the grounds of ignorance and inferior instruction, and even suggests that they may not fare badly on the day of judgment;[36] or the shadowy Pseudo-Dionysius the Areopagite who argues in the sixth century for instruction rather than punishment for those in ignorance and error, basing his case on the mildness and mercifulness of Jesus.[37] These are, however, peripheral figures compared with Ambrose and Augustine who dominate the debate with pagans and dissenting Christians in the crucial late fourth and early fifth centuries AD. Meanwhile it is worth pondering the fact that our three conciliatory authors, and other Christians who take a similar line, were writing after the Christian church committed itself irrevocably under Theodosius I to a policy of persecution in alliance with the state.

[34] Donatist arguments are mostly buried under the massive weight of Augustinian scholarship. But see the useful reconstructions of P. Monceaux, *Histoire littéraire de l'Afrique Chrétienne* (Paris 1920) 5 pp 309–39. The best discussion is in P. Brown, *Augustine of Hippo* (London 1967) chs 19–21, esp 21. W. H. C. Frend, *Donatist Church* (Oxford 1952) remains a classic; see ch 20.

[35] Socrates, *HE* 7.15; 1.23.

[36] Salvian, *De Gub. Dei* 5.2.5–11.

[37] Ps.-Dionysius, *Ep.* 8.5 (MPL 3.1096C–7B). Translation by R. F. Hathaway, *Hierarchy and the definition of order in the letters of Ps.-Dionysius* (The Hague 1969) 148–9.

17

From the preceding age, between the collapse of the persecution of Christianity and the inauguration of the persecution of paganism, a period when Christian emperors on the whole pursued a policy of toleration, no justification of this policy survives beyond that offered by Constantine (and Licinius) in the so-called 'Edict of Milan' of 313.[38] Of special interest in the Edict are the fleeting evocation of an eirenic motive for toleration:

> Your Devotion understands that to others also freedom for their own worship and cult is likewise left open and freely granted, as befits the quiet of our times.

and the assumption—which seventy years later Ambrose would resoundingly reject—that toleration would be pleasing to God and would guarantee the prosperity of the realm:

> Our purpose is to grant both to the Christians and to all others full authority to follow whatever worship each man has desired; whereby whatsoever Divinity dwells in heaven may be benevolent and propitious to us, and to all who are placed under our authority.

In a second pronouncement of 324[39] issued after the defeat of Licinius, Constantine has abandoned his respect for non-Christian worship, and is now openly contemptuous of the error of those who practise it. But they are still free to do so:

> With regard to those who will hold themselves aloof from us, let them have, if they please, their temples of falsehood: we have the glorious edifice of the truth. We pray, however, that they too may receive the same blessing which thou hast given in accordance with thy nature, and thus experience that heartfelt joy which unity of sentiment inspires.

This prayer for the salvation of the pagans contrasts strangely with the dark threat of imminent heavenly medicine in the document with which the emperor wound up his fruitless persecution of the

---

[38] See Eusebius, *HE* 10.5.1–14 with Lactantius, *De Mort. Pers.* 48.1–12.

[39] Eusebius, *Vita Const.* 2.56. T. D. Barnes, *Constantine and Eusebius* (Cambridge Mass. 1981) pp 209 seq, has recently revived the contention that Constantine had earlier in 324 revoked the policy of toleration in an edict which among other things banned pagan sacrifice. He rests his case on Eusebius, *Vita Const.* 2.45. A. H. M. Jones, *Later Roman Empire* (Oxford 1966) 1 pp 91–2, also believes in this law, but is unimpressed by the Eusebius text, preferring to argue from *CTh.* 16.10.2, 341 (Constans and Constantius II). On the other side, H. A. Drake, *In Praise of Constantine* (Berkeley 1975) pp 65–6, attacks only the text in the Code. It would be easier to believe Eusebius, and the sons of Constantine, if the alleged law had been quoted, and if it could be reconciled with the friendlier document issued subsequently.

Donatists three years earlier.[40] For Constantine heretics and schismatics were wicked and criminal, pagans merely in error. Here he was merely echoing conventional ecclesiastical wisdom. *Hairesis*, a neutral word meaning, in relevant usages, 'school of thought', received in a Christian context the derogatory sense of a school of thought which deviated from the orthodox line dictated by the Church. Pagans could never have given the word this twist; their religion was a matter of ritual and worship, not doctrine. Heresy was from New Testament times regarded as a stain on the image of the Church, even if there was little agreement on what heresy was.[41] The readiness of Christians to dispute amongst themselves over matters of doctrine and discipline was noticed and exploited by pagan apologists from Celsus onwards, and Augustine in a moment of candour acknowledged that Christians in North Africa could learn something from the cohesiveness of the pagan communities.[42] He did not it seems make the deduction that tranquillity could be achieved through mutual toleration. Similarly, Origen, who is found candidly admitting in his reply to Celsus that in matters of morality and religion unanimity was impossible, in another work ranks orthodoxy above piety. Ironically, Origen was not himself considered a model of orthodoxy.[43]

To return to Constantine: there was not felt to be any contradiction in his persecuting dissenters within the Church and tolerating pagans. There had been no practical possibility of persecuting heretics before. A Christian emperor had the means to repress, and had no choice but to repress, to preserve the unity of the Church, to assert the indivisibility of the body of Christ. The suspension of persecution of Donatists in 321 was a tacit acknowledgement of the limits of power; it did not lead to a policy of toleration, let alone reconciliation. A renewal of persecution was always in prospect.

Paganism, however, was tolerated in the period from Constantine to Gratian. Emperors were tolerant in deed, if not always in word.

[40] Optatus, *de schism. Don.* 9.
[41] Chadwick, 'Gewissen' pp 1098–9. On intolerance within the Christian (and Jewish) community, see G. Forkmann, *The limits of the religious community; expulsion from the religious community within the Qumran sect, within Rabbinic Judaism, and within primitive Christianity* (Lund 1972). On *hairesis* see J. Glucker, *Antiochus and the Late Academy* (Göttingen 1978) pp 166 esp 167–8, 184–7.
[42] Origen, *c. Celsum* 3.10–12; 5.61; cf. Julian in Amm. Marc. 22.5.3–4; Aug., *de util. jejun.* 9, *PL* 40.712–3.
[43] Origen, *in Mt. comm. ser.* 33, Chadwick, 'Gewissen' p 1098; cf. Tertullian, *monog.* 2.3 (another heretic).

Constantius issued general prohibitions of sacrifice but did nothing to have them enforced; it was as if merely by issuing anti-pagan legislation he had salved his conscience and appeased God.[44] The essential fact is that the pagan priesthoods of the state cult, the augurs, flamens and vestals, continued to receive their subsidies, Christian emperors bore the official pagan title of *pontifex maximus*, and the worship of dead emperors was allowed.

It is often assumed that a degeneration of pagan-Christian relations was inevitable: an aggressive monotheistic religion would inevitably descend to active persecution once it had convinced itself of the likelihood of success, once it had persuaded the political authorities to turn the full coercive apparatus of the state against its rivals. Ambrose is usually branded the villain of the piece, the powerful bishop of Milan of whom it was said even the devil was afraid, who intimidated weak emperors, forcing them to disestablish the pagan cults and then suppress them. But what of the emperor Julian, at least the equal of Ambrose in fanatical zeal and strength of personality (to the chagrin of the moderate pagan historian Ammianus Marcellinus), whose shortlived pagan reaction put the wind up the Christian establishment? Until the reign of Julian peaceful competition with paganism had seemed a winning strategy, and justifiably: with the authority and financial resources of the emperor behind the Christians, the contest had been unequal.[45] Julian, to be sure, professed to be uninterested in persecuting Christianity: 'It might be proper to cure them, even against their will, as one cures the insane, except that we concede indulgence to all for this kind of disease. We ought I think to teach, but not punish, the demented' (*Ep*. 36 Wright). And again, Christians 'have strayed rather from ignorance than of set purpose'. They are suffering enough already, and there is no need to add to their burden: 'We ought to pity rather than

---

[44] Constantius: *CTh*. 16.10.2, 341; 16.10.6, 356. But cf. 16.10.3, 342; Symm., *Rel*. 3.7; '*nihil ille decerpsit sacrarum uirginum priuilegiis, repleuit nobilibus sacerdotio. Romanis caerimoniis non negauit inpensas . . .*' Valentinian I was unambiguously for toleration: *CTh*. 9.16.9. 371 (referring to earlier law); cf. Amm.Marc. 30.9.5. Gratian issued an act of toleration after the disaster at Adrianople, see Socr., *HE* 5.2.1; Soz., *HE* 7.1.3; it was rescinded on 3 August 379, from Milan: *CTh*. 16.5.5. For Gratian's measures against paganism, see A. Cameron, 'Gratian's repudiation of the pontifical robe', *JRS* 58 (1968) pp 96–102.

[45] Cf. P. Brown, 'Aspects of the Christianization of the Roman aristocracy', *JRS* 61 (1971) pp 1–11. On the role of Ambrose, see J. F. Matthews, *Western aristocracies and imperial court A.D. 364–425* (Oxford 1975) ch 8, esp pp 186–92. Ambrose was particularly upset by the edict on teaching. See *Ep*. 17.4, on *CTh*. 13.3.5, 362 with Julian, *Ep*. 36 (Wright); cf. Amm. Marc. 22.10.7; 25.4.20.

hate men who in matters of the greatest importance are in such a bad way. For the greatest of blessings is reverence for the gods, just as irreverence is the greatest of all evils. So those who have turned aside from the gods to corpses and relics pay this as their penalty. We suffer in sympathy with those who are afflicted by disease, while rejoicing with those who are being released and set free by the aid of the gods' (*Ep.* 41 Wright). Julian did not launch a persecution, but the signs were ominous. His reign was sufficiently disturbing to persuade the Church to strike for a quick victory.

Julian was not the man to produce novel arguments in favour of toleration. His sentiments, if we disregard the Platonic colouring, resemble those of the reluctant tolerators, Constantine and, on the pagan side, Maximin Daia.[46] This was the contribution of Themistius, philosopher, rhetorician and courtier, who though a pagan had served Christian emperors and had been passed over by Julian.[47] A plea for toleration forms a substantial part of an oration delivered to Jovian on 1 January 364, in the hope that the new emperor, succeeding shortly after the death of Julian, could be steered into enacting laws of toleration. Almost at once Themistius lays down the axiom that moral and religious matters lie outside the sphere of legislation. This is an astonishing statement coming from an avowed champion of Hellenism. In ancient Greek thought the authority of the polis was held to be total. Unfortunately Themistius does not develop this highly promising line of argument, but he turns instead to the more conventional notion of the impotence of legislation. Laws can produce only apostasy and opportunism. He who changes his religion at the drop of a hat will change it back again with equal facility when the government is captured by the other side. This proposition is backed up with some homespun psychology: you cannot win support from someone who has not chosen to

---

[46] Maximin Daia: Eusebius, *HE* 9.9a.1–10: not persecution, but persuasion.

[47] Themistius, *Orat.* 5, ed G. Downey, *Themistius* (Teubner 1965), 1 esp 67b–70c. See [G.] Dagron, ['Empire romaine d'Orient au IVᵉ siècle et les traditions politiques de l'hellénisme: le témoigne de Themistius', *Travaux et mémoires du Centre de recherche d'histoire et civilisation byzantine* 3 (Paris 1968)] pp 1–242, at 163–72 (transl. and discussion); L. J. Daly, 'Themistius' plea for religious tolerance', *Greek, Roman and Byzantine Studies* 12 (1971) pp 65–79. A lost *Orat.* 12 (AD 375–6), see G. Downey and A. Norman, *Themistius* (Teubner edn 1974) 3 pp 137–44, was held by several Christian commentators to have persuaded Valens to moderate his persecution of the Nicenes. See Dagron p 13 and n 73, pp 22, 186–90. Themistius is omitted in the otherwise useful B. Croke, J. Harris, *Religious conflict in fourth-century Rome: a documentary Study* (Sydney 1982).

give it to you in his heart. The same point is made more pungently by the pagan rhetorician of Antioch, Libanius, in his *pro templis*:[48]

> If they tell you that some others, in response to these measures, have been converted and now share their faith, don't be deceived, for they are talking of conversions that are apparent and not sincere. They say they have changed their beliefs; but they have not. This is the truth. They haven't abandoned their ancestral gods to worship new ones, but rather are cheating their persecutors. They go to their services, mix with their congregations, follow their other practices; they look as if they are praying, but they call on no one unless it is their own gods. It is wrong that they should be doing it in those surroundings, but all the same it is their own gods they are addressing. Just as in a tragedy, the man who plays the part of a tyrant is not himself a tyrant, but he who wears the mask of a tyrant, so each of them has remained himself; the change is merely apparent.

This is a powerful argument, drawing credibility from recent happenings when Julian put the clock back, but only momentarily.

Legislation is impotent and impermanent. In addition, the legislation of intolerance is out of step with the law of god, which states that every man must choose his own route (*hodos*). The existence of this law is confirmed for Themistius not by theological argument, but by an appeal to the nature and experience of man. On the one hand, as Homer says, 'Everyone sacrifices to a different god' (but it is a truth that is older than Homer), and God approves of this; on the other hand, anyone with a deep understanding of human nature knows that competition, 'a healthy rivalry in piety', brings out the best in men. There follow two similes. The first is of a race, in which all the competitors are striving toward the same goal, but not by the same route. The second is a comparison with the imperial army, which is not monolithic but consists of various elements with various functions and at various distances from the emperor—but all are devoted to him. The section ends with Themistius' vision of three principal cultures engaged in healthy competition: Syrian (that is, Christian), Hellenic, and Egyptian. The contrast with Julianic doctrine is marked: what Julian had seen as a fundamental conflict of religions

---

[48] Libanius, *Orat.* 30.28 (AD 386); R. Van Loy, 'Le "Pro Templis" de Libanius', *Byzantion* 8 (1933) pp 7–39, 389–404 (transl. and comm.); P. Petit, *Libanius et la vie municipale à Antioche au IVe siècle après Jésus-Christ* (Paris 1955) pp 191–216. Libanius is attacking the destructive activity of monks in the train of Cynegius, Praetorian Prefect of the East (384–6).

(Christianity versus Hellenism) Themistius reduces to the more manageable problem of the contiguity of rival civilisations. Themistius is prepared to draw a discreet veil over the religious side of Hellenism, to sever culture from religion, in the interests of survival.

We come finally to the well-known exchange between the Roman aristocrat Symmachus and Ambrose, bishop of Milan.[49] Symmachus was no more inclined to theological argument than Themistius. He was responding to a concrete issue, the disestablishment of the *cultus deorum* by Gratian, and he addressed himself to the political role of the old religion and the social consequences of its neglect rather than to matters spiritual. The ritual observance of the state religion was the means of victory over the barbarians and the basis of the glory of Rome for some 1,200 years. When the *cultus deorum* was abandoned, disaster followed: 'While the vestals and priests were treated fairly, things prospered. When their emoluments were taken away, universal famine followed'. There was in fact a food crisis in Rome in the following year, 383.

So far the argument is solidly conventional and based on the *mos maiorum*. But Symmachus also uses the argument from tradition to clinch the case for religious diversity. Tradition told him that the mystery of godhead was not brought within man's understanding by any one means. Hence the form of religious observance could and should vary: 'to every man his own custom and his own ritual' (*suus enim cuique mos, suus ritus est*). The gods were known by the benefits they conferred, and they have sent man more ways than one in which to express themselves; there was no one way to so tremendous a secret.

Ambrose was prepared to debate the origin of Rome's greatness. It was not, he retorts, the worship of the gods which made Rome great, as for example the capture of the emperor Valerian by the Persians showed. Ambrose then boldly contradicts the assertion that the repudiation of the gods by Gratian had produced natural disaster: 'everything since then has progressed for the better'; there was no universal disaster—some provinces experienced ample harvests— and no punishment for sacrilege. In fact the bumper crops of the following year may be seen as a reward for faith. The two men, it is

[49] Symm., *Rel.* 3, ed O Seeck, *MGH Auct. Antiq.* 6.1 (1883) pp 280–3; R. H. Barrow, *Prefect and Emperor* (Oxford 1973) (with transl); see also M. Lavarenne's Budé edition of Prudentius vol. 3, (3 edn 1963), where the *Relatio* and the reply of Ambrose, *Ep.* 17–18 may be found together, and also Prudentius, *c. Symm.*

clear, had a similar idea of the role of religion in the world; they agreed that the security of the empire rested on the goodwill of the divine power or powers. Again, each accepted that the foremost issue between them was political, the safety of the state, Symmachus defending the guardianship of the traditional gods of Rome against Ambrose's conviction that in Christ the best insurance policy could be found. Against the argument from tradition, which Ambrose could not employ—his sensitiveness in this matter is shown by his talk of the pervasiveness of change—Ambrose pressed the claims of revelation. Thus on the issue of the toleration of dissent—for the state had now adopted the ideology of Catholic Christianity—Symmachus' assertion of a god-given diversity of forms of worship was met by Ambrose's retort that God revealed to man in Christ was an exclusive doctrine. God was a jealous god and had to be worshipped alone. Thanks to Scripture, his identity was clear—in contrast with that of the *numen multiplex*, the pagan supreme unknowable divinity in its various manifestations—and a Christian emperor could not condone idolatry. 'A Christian emperor has learned to honour the altar of Christ alone.' In a word, Ambrose's position was that the safety of the empire could be secured only by the exclusive worship of the Christian god.

V

Paganism in Graeco-Roman antiquity was not one religion, but a plethora of cults varying with the countless ethnic and political communities which made up the ancient Mediterranean world. No community claimed privileged or exclusive access to the divine, none denied the reality of another's gods or their viability for that other community. Each community, however, was proud and protective of its indigenous cults and in normal circumstances was not disposed to supplement them or permit them to be undermined or subverted from within. The trial and death of Socrates and the suppression of the Bacchanalia give an indication of the way the charge of subversion might be applied. The usual picture of civic cults as supple and receptive to foreign influences is a distortion of the truth. In any case, toleration is not synonymous with inclusiveness. In the case of Rome neither term seems to direct us to the essential point, which is that this was an expanding community bent on subjecting foreign peoples and their gods. Gods were treated as booty to be destroyed, transported, selectively assimilated, or simply left behind, defeated gods in defeated communities. It has been said of the Roman empire when the process of expansion was complete that it was 'completely tolerant, in heaven as on earth'—with acknowledged partial or total exceptions, notably Jews, Christians and Druids.[50] This is simply a misuse of terminology. The gods in question had been made subject together with the communities to which they were attached; the Romans had nothing to fear from them and cannot be said to have extended to them that combination of disapproval and acceptance which is toleration. To be sure, it suited Jews and Christians to argue that they were or should be on the same footing as the mass of pagan cults and rituals, but the argument is totally unconvincing.

The Roman state tolerated the Jews, at least from time to time, but hardly anyone else, certainly not the Christians. Toleration of the Jews was sporadic because their loyalty to the empire was an uncertain factor, dependent on close relations marked by exchanges of *beneficia* between individual leaders. Even from the most friendly Romans the Jews secured no more than *ad hoc* pronouncements supporting their freedom to practise their traditional rites and customs on grounds that were avowedly strategic and therefore ephemeral. The Roman authorities never committed themselves to a general statement on toleration. If they possessed the concept—and no doubt they did implicitly—they kept it to themselves.

Toleration theory was a byproduct of persecution and came from those in a position of weakness. The Christians proved more fertile in this area than the Jews, partly perhaps because they lacked most of the Jews' assets and bargaining points. It must be stressed, however, that very few out of the many Christian apologists contributed to the 'toleration debate', such as it was. Again, theoretical arguments for toleration were not a crucial weapon in the battle of paganism against Christianity.

As for the arguments themselves: Jewish, Christian and pagan apologists alike elevated the principle of religious autonomy and diversity into an argument for toleration—it was precisely this move which the leaders of the pagan establishment under the early empire failed to make. Conversely, there were individual moments of inventiveness when a breakthrough was made against the whole weight of classical tradition: Josephus' idea of common goodness,

[50] MacMullen p 2.

25

Tertullian's doctrine of *libertas religionis* and Themistius' glimpse of a political community in which personal morality and religion are not tampered with by legislation, are cases in point. The ancient 'literature of toleration' though unimpressive in bulk contained promising ideas which in some cases were to be elaborated and extended in later periods.

This paper has discussed policy and attitudes of governments and members of the elite. The impression has perhaps been created that ancient society was marked by intolerance at all levels, at any rate from the time when exclusive monotheistic religions became active in the communities (particularly urban) of the Mediterranean basin. Ordinary people did not always follow the lead of their social, political and ecclesiastical betters, insofar as a lead was given; and even where the wish of the authorities was unmistakable, it did not follow that official policy would find willing and effective executors in the localities. The argument works both ways: people might be less tolerant or more tolerant than they were expected to be. But at least we can avoid blanket generalizations, for example, that pagan Greeks and Christians alike were actively hostile to Jews as a matter of course. This assumption must be qualified in the light of, first, a decree of the early 40s BC which reveals that Jews had at one stage established a particularly strong position in the city of Sardis with the cooperation of the city authorities,[51] and second, a letter of the early fifth century AD, which shows that Jews and Christians had coexisted peaceably on the Balearic island of Minorca prior to the arrival in 417 or 418 of the relics of St Stephen which inspired the bishop Severus, author of the letter, to smash the synagogue and forcibly convert the Jews.[52] Again, the inefficacy of imperial pronouncements is demonstrated by, for example, the survival in fifth century Spain of the heresy of Priscillianism with the connivance of secular as well as ecclesiastical officials,[53] and—a rather different case—the existence of pagan practices, including the frequent consultation of soothsayers, astrologers and exorcists, among Augustine's own congregation in North Africa. Time-honoured

---

[51] *Jos., Ant. Jud.* 14.259–61, referring to 'many great privileges' in the past and present concessions, including a site presumably meant for worship or communal purposes, and the provision of 'suitable food'.

[52] *Epistula Severi ad omnem ecclesiam, PL* 41.821–32; P. Brown, *The cult of the saints* (London 1981) pp 103–5; E. D. Hunt, 'St. Stephen in Minorca: an episode in Jewish-Christian relations in the early 5th century AD', *JTS* 33 (1982) pp 106–23.

[53] *CSEL* 83 (1981) *ep* 11 (ed J. Divjak). On Priscillian, see H. Chadwick, *Priscillian of Avila* (Oxford 1976).

pagan remedies continued to command the respect of ordinary people, despite the promulgation of *Christiana lex* and the presence of a bishop prepared to enforce it.[54] 'In the later Roman Empire religious coercion in some form was one of the "facts of life" for a provincial bishop.'[55] Another 'given', it might be suggested, was a greater degree of coexistence, compromise—in short, toleration—between pagans and Christians than the ecclesiastical establishment would have liked.

Jesus College, Cambridge

[54] See Brown, *Augustine* p 247; cf. Chadwick, 'Gewissen' p 1074, citing Ps.-Clem. *Rom. hom.* 1.5; Ambrosiast., *quaest.* 115.51. See G. Fowden, 'The Platonist philosopher and his circle in late antiquity', Φιλοσοφια 7 (1977) pp 359–83 on the coexistence of pagan and Christian intellectuals at Alexandria in the early 3rd century A.D.

[55] Citation from Brown, 'St. Augustine's attitude' p 107.

'TO FLEE OR NOT TO FLEE': AN ASSESSMENT OF ATHANASIUS'S *DE FUGA SUA*

by ALVYN PETTERSEN

THE VERY question 'to flee or not to flee?' strikes the historian of the early church as an unusual question. For neither the martyrologies nor the histories of that persecuted body seem to entertain such. The death of Polycarp at Smyrna seems to rule out the possibility of flight for subsequent confessors of Christ; and the events of Maximian's reign (AD 306–13) confirm that identity with Christ, even in death, was the true vocation of the faithful. Eusebius, an eye witness of some of the events of that reign, records examples of weakness and apostasy, but only to set off what was the real character of the Christian church at the time, namely constancy and defiance in the face of persecution. Yet not only does he allude to that constancy, but he records it:

> and we ourselves also beheld . . . many, all at once, in a single day, some of whom suffered decapitation, others the punishment of fire; so that the murderous axe was dulled and, worn out, was broken in pieces, while the executioners themselves grew utterly weary and took it in turns to succeed one another. It was then that we observed a most marvellous eagerness and a truly divine power and zeal in those who had placed their faith in the Christ of God. Thus, as soon as sentence was given against the first, some from one quarter, and others from another would leap up to the tribunal before the judge and confess themselves Christians; paying no heed when faced with terrors and the varied forms of tortures, but undismayed and boldly speaking of the piety towards the God of the universe, and with joy and laughter and gladness receiving the final sentence of death; so that they sung and sent up hymns and thanksgivings to the God of the universe even to the very last breath.[1]

The laudatory tenor of the history commends the acceptance of persecution as strongly as do the martyrologies.

---

[1] Eusebius, *Ecclesiastical History* (trans. J. E. L. Oulton) viii.9.2. Compare *ibid.* vi.41.11–13.

29

Nor indeed does Athanasius himself seem beyond commending the action of martyrs who willingly suffered death at the hands of persecutors, rather than betray the truth for which they stood. In his early work, the *De Incarnatione*, he recalls in words similar to Eusebius's[2] how

men . . . weak by nature, rushed to death . . . with ready spirit defying it, . . . rather preferring, for the sake of Christ, the zeal for death to this present life.[3]

Women and young children were to do the same thing, 'eagerly rushing to death for their devotion to Christ'.[4] In his festal letter for Easter 341, Athanasius encourages the afflicted churches of Egypt:

being insulted, we should not be disturbed, but should give our cheek to the smiter, and even bow the shoulder . . . But let us, knowing that we suffer for the truth, and that those who deny the Lord smite and persecute us, count it all joy . . . knowing that the trial of our faith worketh patience.

Indeed, in this affliction, the bishop asserts, the Church enters into the passion of Christ:

our Saviour did not redeem us by ease; but he abolished death by suffering for us. And respecting this, he intimated to us before, saying, In this world you shall have tribulations . . . So we, when we are tried . . . will not separate ourselves from the love of God.

It is not therefore without significance that the troubled churches of the Alexandrian's diocese are encouraged in this paschal letter to be 'mindful of him who was sacrificed in the days of the Passover'.

Certainly the arguments used in the *De Incarnatione*, and which reoccur in the *De Vita Antonii*, are but traditional proofs, and that in the festal letter quoted, sent incidentally not by a bishop who courted martyrdom but who was exiled to Rome, stresses but the need to be true to the Christian faith. Yet there lies behind both these the conviction that it is proper to side with the crucified Saviour, whose salvation is experienced even amidst the terror of persecution. Not to side with the crucified Saviour in all circumstances is to betray his trust and to be unfaithful to the suffering God. Given therefore this understanding of allegiance to Christ, it is not surprising that

---

[2] *Ibid* ii.17.10.
[3] Athanasius, *De Incarnatione* 29.
[4] *Ibid* 29. A similar commendation of the life of martyrdom occurs also in his later work, the *De Vita Antonii* 79–80.

An Assessment of Athanasius's De Fuga Sua

Athanasius was accused of lack of faith and of cowardice when he fled his Arian persecutors in cAD 357, nor that he felt obliged to write an *apologia* for his flight.

Athanasius justified his flight from the Arians on both political and theological grounds. The political reasons are more specific, and relate to Arian policy. The theological justification is more general, arising as it does from the concrete situation of his flight.

The bishop's political apology is more colourful than impartiality for the truth required. The Arians are charged with being ignorant and unscrupulous: for they are ignorant of the Scriptures whence Athanasius believes he finds justification for his beliefs and action;[5] and they are unscrupulous in their behaviour. They were they who were disturbing the peace of the Church, 'on no pretence whatsoever except that (various bishops of the Church) would not unite themselves to the Arian heresy';[6] and they were they who were seeking to kill Athanasius and his presbyters, using the magistrates as tools of their wickedness,[7] and to no other end than that they might stop Athanasius opposing their impiety and confuting their heresy. Certainly, according to Athanasius, their charges against him were not 'for the sake of virtue'.[8]

That, however, is not the end of the bishop's case. For according to him, the very accusations of the Arians against him do indeed bring blame against the Arians themselves. For, firstly, irrespective of whether flight is right or wrong, flight itself points to the wickedness of the persecutors. 'For no man flees from the gentle and humane, but from the cruel and the evil minded'.[9] Secondly, if it is wrong to flee, a crime of which the Arians accuse Athanasius, it is yet worse to be the cause of that flight, especially when that flight is from murder, an evil explicitly condemned by Scripture. In this second argument, however, it must be noted that Athanasius does not allow the accusation of cowardice to stand. The conditional 'if it is wrong to flee' is allowed but for the purpose of his case. 'If, as the Arians allege, it is wrong to flee, then', argues Athanasius on the basis of the Arian allegation, 'it is yet worse to be the occasion of that flight.' This interpretation of the conditional is indeed confirmed both in this chapter and elsewhere. In this chapter the bishop states that in

---

[5] Athanasius, *De Fuga Sua* 2.
[6] *Ibid* 4.
[7] *Ibid* 3.
[8] *Ibid* 2.
[9] *Ibid* 8.

31

being put to flight by the Arians, he has in fact been sent forth by them as a monument of their iniquity. To that end Athanasius is not being cowardly, but is being courageously faithful in his witness to true innocency of godly life.[10] Elsewhere Athanasius tells of his escape from the hands of his persecutors.[11] His laity was keeping a night vigil preparatory to a communion on the morning, when Syrianus entered, accompanied by soldiers and Arians. Yet their bishop did not flee immediately. He first sent his people away, and only then was dragged away by the monks and clergy. Events again, he felt, clearly demonstrated his courage in the face of the Arian violence.

The account of his withdrawal was not seen, however, in simply a political manner. That Athanasius was able to escape despite the presence of a large contingent of soldiers and Arians, both inside and outside the Church, was read as evidence of divine guidance and protection of the bishop, in the face of which it would have been highly ungrateful of him towards his divine Saviour to have surrendered himself into the hands of those who sought him. The divine protection of him who withdrew confirmed the propriety of his flight on that occasion.

Athanasius's theological justification of his flight from the Arians truly begins however with a few general remarks. Persecution, Athanasius asserts, is a device of the devil, before which flight is only inappropriate if virtue is served by standing firm, as it was during the outrages of George of Cappadocia. Then many were killed, and their bodies were spirited away. Yet virtue was served in that other Christians were encouraged by their loyal confessions, and in that the persecutors were therein seen to be guilty of impiety and cruelty.[12] In short, evil was not to be tolerated in a passive manner, but was to be received and transformed in such a way that good sprang from that evil.

Within that context flight was not seen as wrong on every occasion. To establish this, Athanasius cited Old and New Testament figures whose flights were not seen as contrary to the will of God; he refers to the Jewish cities of refuge, whither refugees fled for security; he quotes New Testament texts which advocate flight: 'but when they persecute you in this city, flee ye into another.'[13] Most

[10] *Ibid* 21.
[11] *Ibid* 24–25.
[12] *Ibid* 7, compare *ibid* 2, 10.
[13] Matthew 10:23, compare *ibid* 24: 15.

importantly, he recalls the withdrawal of Christ from danger, both during his infancy, to Egypt, and during his public ministry, from the threatening public gaze of the Jews:

> the Logos himself, being made man for our sake, condescended to hide himself when he was sought after.[14]

Of interest here is the idea of 'condescension'. Flight, when appropriate, was in accordance with the divine will; trust and humble courage were then needed to align the human will with the divine. Only empty bravado and pride could then stay that humility and condescension which accepted the divine will, and which forbade the selfish challenging of the persecutor that often resulted in suicide, a martyrdom in witness not to God but to egocentricity. Variously therefore the Logos of God, both before his incarnation and during it, set an example, showing that flight was not always wrong.

If however flight was not always wrong, it was not always right. According to Athanasius, there is a time allotted by the Creator to every man, a time to live and a time to die. This was true even in the case of the Christ. For the divine Logos of the Father, who became man, measured out 'time . . . to his own body'.[15] Thus, when he was sought before his time, he hid himself,

> but when (the Logos) has brought on that time, which he himself has appointed, at which he desired to suffer in the body for all men, he announced it to the Father, saying, 'Father, the hour is come; glorify thy Son'. And then he no longer hid himself from those who sought him, but stood willing to be taken by them.[16]

Living thus, he shewed to all men 'that the life and death of man depend upon the divine sentence';[17] and being obedient to this divine sentence in both life and death, he glorified the Father, and so lived a glorious life and an honourable death. Similarly the saints knew that a 'time' had been allocated to each of them, and lived in the light of this knowledge. However, unlike the Christ, the saints did not know the end of the time which Providence had appointed to them. They therefore were unwilling at once to deliver themselves into the power of those who conspired against them. Rather than possibly

---

[14] Athanasius, *De Fuga Sua* 12.
[15] *Ibid* 15.
[16] *Ibid* 15.
[17] *Ibid* 15, compare Matthew 5: 36; 10: 29.

acting rashly, in contrast with the will of God, they would flee and hide. So they hid:

> until either the appointed time of death arrived, or God who had appointed their time spoke unto them and stayed the designs of their enemies, or else delivered up the persecuted to their persecutors, according as it seemed good to him.[18]

Flight therefore seems to have been the norm.[19] For such made allowances for human ignorance concerning the hour of one's death, and safeguarded one from rashly losing one's life in what would have amounted to suicide. Despite this norm, there was yet for Athanasius the possibility of the persecuted rightly giving himself to his persecutor:

> when the Spirit spoke to them, then as righteous men they went and met their enemies. By which they also shewed their obedience and zeal towards God.[20]

In short, men were not to tempt God by rashly anticipating—or indeed prompting—their own death. Equally, however, they were to be ready, when the time of their death did approach, to contend for the truth even unto death.

Initially Athanasius's analysis of persecution and of the appropriate response to it seems rather deterministic: the time of life and death is laid out, and it is but the person's duty to fulfil that time. Yet the initiative lies with the persecuted person to fulfil such. For it is he who must flee; it is he who must be ready to face death for the sake of the truth; and it is he who, in the light of divine revelation, must go and meet his enemies. Selfless devotion to divine providence is that to which the persecuted is called. In meeting this vocation, whether in hiding or in death, the persecuted finds himself a martyr, a witness to the truth of the divine will.

Nor was this witness in flight any less difficult or less demanding than that of standing to face death. For flight which was rightly undertaken was not a flight from death through cowardice, but a submission to the conflict and war against death. It bravely resisted the temptation to offer oneself up without reason to one's pursuers, a self oblation which would have been selfish suicide rather than godly martyrdom. It courageously renounced the acceptance of an untimely death as an easy escape from the tribulations of flight. Thus in

---

[18] *Ibid* 16.
[19] Compare *ibid* 22: 23.
[20] *Ibid* 17, compare *ibid* 22.

selflessly esteeming death lightly and in accepting the hardship of flight, the persecuted were tried like 'gold in the furnace' and were found worthy of God. In their tribulations they found patience; in their deliverance they found salvation. Thus Athanasius can conclude:

> they therefore whose course was consummated in their flight did not perish dishonourably, but attained as well as others the glory of martyrdom.[21]

Given this analysis of flight in the face of persecution, there seems to be a rift between the attitudes in the *De Fuga Sua* on the one hand, and those in the *Festal Letters* and the *De Vita Antonii* on the other. Both the *Festal Letters* and the *De Vita Antonii* advocate the training of the self, lest one fall when faced with trials and tribulations. *Festal Letter* 13, for example, urges the preparation of the mind by meditating upon the difficulties connected with godliness, and of the body by keeping it under discipline. Thus, 'when trials come, (one) may be able to bear them easily, as having been exercised in these things'. The *De Vita Antonii* meanwhile warns against arrogance and carelessness in the face of trials. Rather, through stringent practices the Christian is to discipline the weaknesses of the body, therein making it more able to cope with future trials.[22] Being so prepared, the Christian is to resist all trials, being confident that God will deliver him from that which seeks to overwhelm faith and godliness. Yet nowhere does Athanasius suggest in the *Festal Letters* that this deliverance will come in the form of flight. Indeed, letter 13 seems to stress this resistance:

> when the enemies are set against us, we should glory in affliction; and . . . when we are persecuted, we should not be discouraged, but rather press after the crown of the high calling in Jesus Christ our Lord.

Thus, in the very resisting, salvation will be found. In short, to resist is to be true to Christ by identifying with him in his saving passion, whereas to flee is to identify with those who deny the Lord, and so crucify his body. Yet, if flight is not truly considered in the *Festal Letters*, it seems excluded in the *De Vita Antonii*. As a general rule, not being false to Christ involves resisting all trials. Hence 'each of those who truly struggle can say, "It is not I, but the grace of God which is in me"'.[23] This point is made more clearly in two accounts

---

[21] *Ibid* 17.

[22] Athanasius, *De Vita Antonii* 7, compare *ibid* 18; 19.

[23] *Ibid* 5.

of the devil attacking Antony through the guise of animals. In the first the monk is threatened by a pack of hyenas, and in the second by a beast, half man, half ass. As each hyena came forward to bite him, he said,

> if you have received authority over me, I am prepared to be devoured by you. But if you were sent by demons, waste no time in retreating. For I am a servant of Christ.[24]

In the second account the monk signs himself with the cross and says,

> I am a servant of Christ. If you have been sent out against me, look, here I am![25]

This willingness to resist, even to the point of death, is then given a Christological basis in an account of a discourse between the monk and some Hellenists, where Antony stresses that 'to confess a cross . . . is a signal of courage and evidence of disdain for death' and that it is preferable 'when a plot is introduced by evil men, to endure the cross and not to cower in fear before any form of death'.[26]

For all this, there may however be the beginning of a change in attitude in the account of Antony's visit to Alexandria during the Maximian persecutions.[27] There is still reference to martyrs as 'contestants', who in and through their deaths were 'perfected'. According to the account Antony wanted to share in these deaths. For 'he yearned to suffer martyrdom'. Indeed, to that end Antony almost seems to have courted martyrdom. For it happened that he amongst others used to render service to the confessors. To stop this, the secular judge ordered the monks not to appear in the law courts, nor to stay in the city at all:

> all the others thought it wise to go into hiding that day. But Antony took this so seriously that he washed his upper garment and stood on the next day in a prominent place in front, to be clearly visible to the prefect.

The next day the prefect and his escort passed by and saw Antony standing there, 'calmly demonstrating the purposefulness that belongs to us Christians'. Yet, despite this incident looking to all intents and purposes like the courting of the martyrdom for which Antony prayed, and which the writer relates to the purposefulness

---

[24] *Ibid* 52.
[25] *Ibid* 53, compare *ibid* 79, where the same despising of death on account of the Truth incarnate is seen, but this time in the willingness of martyrs to die in persecutions.
[26] *Ibid* 74–75.
[27] *Ibid* 46.

which belongs to 'us Christians', we must yet notice the desert father's unwillingness 'to hand himself over' to the persecuting authorities, despite his desire to be a martyr.

Yet, for all this possible change in attitude, the account of the death of Antony himself probably summarises the approach of the *De Vita Antonii* to death—albeit in this case a natural death, 'when (Antony) learned from providence about his death, he spoke to his brothers . . . "now it is time for me to perish."'

At this the monks were upset. But not Antony:

he, like one sailing from a foreign city to his own, talked cheerfully and exhorted them not to lose heart in their labour nor to grow weary in the discipline, but to live as though dying daily.

Providence has 'allocated' to him his time of death; for this he had trained daily, by living as though on the point of death. He was not therefore unready for his death, but in fact looked forward to it as a welcome liberation to the presence of God. This last scene of the *De Vita Antonii* acts almost as an epitaph, which bears the Pauline legend, 'to live is Christ, and to die is gain'.[28]

A significant factor in effecting this resistance to evil, whether in the form of temptation or persecution, is an otherworldly perspective. Some of the consequences of persecution that are mentioned in the *De Fuga Sua* are found in the *Festal Letters* and in the *De Vita Antonii:* patience, fortitude and long-suffering are effected through this probation of a virtuous life. A witness to the divine truth is therein accomplished. Yet the motive given in the *Festal Letters* and the *De Vita Antonii* for enduring these trials and tribulations is missing from the *De Fuga Sua.* Future heavenly goods cause the present temporal events to pale into insignificance: 'Christians', Athanasius asserts in festal letter 13, 'should not look at temporal things, but fix (their) attention on those which are eternal'.

The same thought pervades the *De Vita Antonii:* the ephemeral things of this life are to be sacrificed for the heavenly. For Christians are not to consider 'when we look at the world, that we have given up things of some greatness. For even the entire earth is itself quite small in relation to all of heaven'.[29] It is not surprising therefore that death, properly understood, is likened to a 'sailing away from a foreign city to (one's) own'.[30]

[28] Philippians 1: 21.
[29] Athanasius *De Vita Antonii*, 17, compare *ibid* 45, where the same thought is couched in terms of the devoting of time to the soul rather than the body.
[30] *Ibid* 89.

Two major differences therefore seem to exist between the attitudes shown to trials and persecutions in the *De Fuga Sua* on the one hand and the *Festal Letters* and the *De Vita Antonii* on the other. Firstly, there is the matter of whether or not it is permissible to flee persecution. For both the *Festal Letters* and the *De Vita Antonii* seem to presuppose that one ought not to flee, whereas the *De Fuga Sua* allows for flight in certain circumstances. Even then, however, it must be admitted that what is primarily being sought in the *De Vita Antonii* is not resistance at all costs and in all circumstances, but loyalty to the truth, even if that loyalty eventually ends in death. Hence, for example, Antony is unwilling to hand himself over to the persecutors in Alexandria. Related to this fact is the idea, matched incidentally in the *De Fuga Sua*, that there is a time allocated for death. The desert father thus knows of the inappropriateness of handing himself over to a probable death when in Alexandria during the Maximian persecutions, but does recognise the time of this death when it comes. The other major difference relates to the otherworldly emphasis of the *Festal Letters* and the *De Vita Antonii*, which does not feature in the *De Fuga Sua*. Admittedly, we must be cautious of such an argument from silence. Yet the dualistic emphasis of the former two, manifest in the subordination of the earthly world to the heavenly, and of the body to the soul, so contrasts with the incarnational stress of the *De Fuga Sua*, revealed both in the centrality of Christological thought to its argument and in its consequently positive attitude to matter—and especially to flight, which in itself is neither good nor bad, but which can be used either well or badly—makes the absence of the otherworldly stress from the *De Fuga Sua* telling.

Why, however, there is this shift in theological stress is not entirely clear. A plausible hypothesis can however be devised. A 'Coptic' spirituality is present in the *Festal Letters* until at least the letter for Easter 341; it is also present, although with slight qualifications, as we have already noted, in the *De Vita Antonii*. This work dates from A.D. 356–57.[31] By middle or late 357, when the *De Fuga Sua* was written,[32] this spirituality had been superceded by a more Hellenistic theology. This change is abrupt. Nor is it possible to re-

[31] See J. Quasten, *Patrology* (Antwerp 1966) 3 p 39. Compare L. W. Barnard and B. R. Brennan, in *Vigiliae Christianae*, Vols. 28 and 30.

[32] See A. Robertson's preface to the *Apologia de Fuga sua* in P. Schaff and H. Wace, edd *A select library of Nicene and post Nicene Fathers of the Christian Church*, Second Series 4.

duce the abruptness of this change by arguing that the *De Vita Antonii* is a life of Antony and not a dogmatic work of Athanasius. For while the *De Vita Antonii* is a life of Antony, it is yet a life which portrays a theology and spirituality which Athanasius strongly supports.[33] To explain this sudden change in theological emphasis we need to seek for a critical event. This is readily supplied by the bishop's flight from the harrassment of the Arians. Not only the flight itself would force a change in his theological outlook, but also his having to write an *apologia* for that flight would effect that change being publicly stated. How critical this flight was to Athanasius is indeed to be seen in that, as a result of it, he found himself defending himself before both his enemies, the Arians, and his diocese, the Catholics. For he, as the representative of orthodoxy, was called to defend his action in the face of the charges of the heterodox Arians; and he, as the bishop whose theological leadership was sought not only by the Catholics of the Delta but also by the more ascetic Coptic Christians of the hinterland, had to justify an action which might have appeared to have betrayed his previously given spiritual direction. In the absence of information in any other direction, we may suppose then that the flight from the Arians was the major cause of this change in theological perspective regarding behaviour when persecuted.

While the change in theological outlook seems to have been abrupt, there are certain factors which help to explain the different positions which Athanasius held regarding trials and persecutions. These factors extend beyond the fact that the pastoral contexts of the *Festal Letters* and the *De Vita Antonii* make the norm of not fleeing in the face of trials and persecutions explicable, and the situation in which the *De Fuga Sua* was written makes the norm of flight understandable. For, on the one hand, letters exhorting their readers to remain true to the faith are hardly to advocate flight, and the *De Vita Antonii*, portraying the saintly life which all may imitate, is equally unlikely to propound fleeing before trials and tribulations. On the other hand, a work, which is an *apologia* for a flight which has already occurred, is likely to have a different emphasis.

Factors which may have coloured the theological attitudes found in the *Festal Letters* and the *De Vita Antonii* are the matter of martyrdom and the use of Scripture. Martyrdom was seen by the Christians in Egypt, and especially by the Copts there, as part of their duty of

---

[33] Compare Athanasius, *De Vita Antonii*, preface.

destroying the symbols of pagan civilisation. For they were citizens of a theocracy. Thus, where the two cultures, religious and secular, confronted one another, the religious man was called to die a martyr's death for the truth. Within the *Festal Letters* this entailed the resisting of the Arian attempt to stop the celebrating of the religious feast of Easter, and in the *De Vita Antonii* the rebuffing of the pressures of Greek sophists and Arian heretics. The attitude to the world, as witnessed in such resistance, may indeed have been strengthened by the radical dualistic theology of the Manichaeans, which was introduced into Egypt in the 280s,[34] and which found a responsive echo amongst the Copts, and by the strong example of the loyal martyrs, the large number of whom is suggested by the fact that in AD 308 parties of more than one hundred each of Egyptian confessors were being sent north to work in the mines of Cilicia and Palestine, as though there were sufficient in those of the Thebaid.[35] The matter of the use of Scripture corroborated such resistance to secularity. Biblical literalism was the understanding of the Bible generally espoused by the desert fathers of Egypt. Antony, for example, was no exception to this biblical method. His ascetic life was wholly inspired by the Bible, whose pages were sufficient for all instruction:[36] he had indeed 'sold all' in order to follow Christ. These desert fathers, as the *De Vita Antonii* itself witnesses, were great influences upon the Christian attitudes in Egypt generally, and coloured the thought of many.

There were, however, also factors which made possible Athanasius's change in theological attitude in AD 357. The otherworldliness and anti-materialism found in Coptic theology was balanced in Catholic theology by a strong incarnational theology, as is found in the anti-Arian writings of Athanasius himself. For all this, Athanasius can, however, combine, albeit in a not too happy union, both this otherworldliness and an incarnational theology when speaking of martyrs in his *De Incarnatione*.[37] Again, the readiness of the Christians to die for their faith was being altered gradually by the ideas of Platonic contemplation. This was irreconcilable with martyrdom. For union with God through gradual self-purification was a ladder of ascent, which demanded a long life, and not a sudden death. In the light of this the Catholic church was coming to accept

[34] Compare Alexander of Lycopolis, *De Placitis Manichaeorum* 2. PG.18.413.
[35] See Eusebius, *Palestinian Martyrs* 8.13.
[36] Athanasius, *De Vita Antonii* 16.
[37] Athanasius, *De Incarnatione* 29.

the taming of the human passions through asceticism as a substitute for martyrdom. In Egypt this thinking was strongest in and around Alexandria, where contact with the wider Hellenistic world was greater. Biblical literalism was also under challenge then. Philosophical theology, as represented by Clement, Origen and Dionysius[38] was steadily relegating the literal word of Scripture to second place, in favour of the truer significance of the text, to be discovered through analogy and allegory based on an understanding of Scripture as a whole. Hence the Lord's commandments concerning the duty of taking up of one's cross and following him could be and were allegorised into meanings which required not death for its own sake but asceticism and contemplation, whereby the soul advanced towards communion with the Divine. Within this method, it was easier to see that flight on all occasions was not always wrong. What was important was faithful witness to the truth. In this sense one was to be a 'martyr' or 'witness'.[39] This allegorising of the scriptural demand for martyrdom was no doubt also confirmed by the general thinking within the Church that one was not to surrender oneself to persecutors in order to become a martyr,[40] and by the general shift in ecclesiastical thought in which 'red martyrdom' was giving way to 'white martyrdom'. Within such, trials were as dangerous as persecutions. For both could 'kill' the spiritual man. To avoid such a death one might in certain circumstances turn away from the source of temptation; similarly one might, in the appropriate circumstances, turn away from persecution. Within this context, however, it should be noted that while an allegorical interpretation of Scripture did render flight a possible option for the persecuted, Athanasius did not in fact interpret scriptural demands for martyrdom allegorically in his *De Fuga Sua*. Rather he used proof texts such as Matthew 10:23 and 24:15, and quoted proof cases of Old and New Testament figures who justly fled their persecutors. The Hellenistic climate made Athanasius's *apologia* a possibility. Yet at heart he himself was not really so far from the literalism of the Coptic Christians.

---

[38] See H. Chadwick on Clement and Origen in A. H. Armstrong, ed *Cambridge History of Greek and early Medieval Philosophy* (Cambridge 1967) pp 168–195.

[39] Athanasius, *De Fuga Sua* 17.

[40] Compare *The Martyrdom of Polycarp* 4. Also see Council of Elvira, Spain. AD 305. Overzealous Christians whose provocative actions involved the smashing of idols were not to be regarded if apprehended and punished as martyrs.

As one might suspect, and as has been noticed elsewhere,[41] Atharasius is not the proponent of a static theology. His theology calls upon both the thinking of the Copts and the understanding of the Greeks. The resultant theology then relates and reacts to immediate events. Thus, in this case, Athanasius's attitude to trials and persecutions is that in which one is called to 'take up one's cross and follow Christ'. Variations occur however in the degree of the literalism with which this injunction is understood, a variation especially dictated by the retrospective self-justification of his flight from the Arians in the late 350s.

Clare College, Cambridge

---

[41] W. H. C. Frend, 'Athanasius as an Egyptian Christian Leader in the fourth century' in *Religion, Popular and Unpopular in the Early Christian Centuries* (London 1976).

POPULAR VIOLENCE AND POPULAR HERESY IN WESTERN EUROPE, c1000–1179

by R. I. MOORE

IN GENERAL modern writers on popular heresy in the high middle ages have shared the opinion of contemporary observers that the capacity of dissident preachers to attract a popular following, stimulate sentiments of intense devotion and loyalty, and canalise resentment of clerical exaction and abuse, constituted a significant threat to the authority of the Church. Hence, more or less explicitly, the extension of the theory and practice of coercion in the twelfth and thirteenth centuries has been seen as a defensive reaction designed (with the emphasis according to the preference of the historian) to protect clerical privilege and spiritual authority. There are, however, distinguished exceptions. In one of the few passages in his writings where religious persecution is discussed, Southern accounts for it thus:

> . . . those who bore authority in the church were agents with very limited powers of initiative. They were not free agents. Doubtless they were responsible for some terrible acts of violence and cruelty, among which the Albigensian Crusade holds a particular horror. But on the whole the holders of ecclesiastical authority were less prone to violence, even against unbelievers, than the people whom they ruled.[1]

From there it is a short step to the judgements of Hamilton's excellent account of the Inquisition that heretics 'aroused intense feelings of fear among the mass of the people', 'the attitude of the clergy was shaped by the society in which they lived, which regarded the persecution of heretics as normal', and the Inquisition 'substituted the rule of law for mob violence in the persecution of heresy.'[2]

It would be easy to multiply less refined expressions of those assumptions. Their implications for the function of religious conviction and of religious orthodoxy in western society in the high middle ages, and for the nature both of secular and ecclesiastical power, and

---

[1] R. W. Southern, *Western Society and the Church in the Middle Ages* (Harmondsworth 1970) p 19.
[2] Bernard Hamilton, *The Medieval Inquisition* (London 1981) pp 25, 33, 57.

the relationship between those who exercised it and their subjects, are far too extensive to pursue here. My present object is the more modest one of considering the nature of the evidence upon which those judgements rest, as it is provided by the history of popular heresy in the eleventh and twelfth centuries. The decrees of the Third Lateran Council of 1179 and the bull *Ad abolendam* issued by Lucius III in consort with Frederick Barbarossa at Verona in 1184 committed the Church fully to the detection, investigation and extirpation of heresy at every level, and adumbrated a comprehensive, though still imperfect, mechanism for doing so. Evidence of popular pressure for persecution would need to date from before this time. Apart from the difficulty of estimating thereafter the extent to which popular expressions of hostility to heresy reflected the sentiments and consequences of those acts and of subsequent coercive legislation, it becomes increasingly difficult to know when the illegality of heresy and the existence of active machinery for repressing it were being exploited for sectional or material ends.

In the two centuries before 1179 we have some record of about thirty cases of popular heresy from western Europe.[3] For the present purpose we can dispense with the tedious definitions which the specification of a more exact number would involve. Leaving aside mere expressions of anxiety by the authors of the sources I find some indication of popular support for the heresy in question in about half of these, varying in intensity and unambiguity from the necessity which Bishop Gebuin of Châlons-sur-Marne felt to 'recall the partly deluded people from heresy'[4] after the death of Leutard of Vertus in 1016 to the dramatic, broadly-based and in some measure violent enthusiasm that enabled the Patarenes to disrupt Milan for two decades after 1056, or Henry of Lausanne to seize control of Le Mans for a few weeks in 1116. It is unnecessary here to do more than reiterate the conclusion of every recent discussion of the question that those who were attracted to the heretical sects in this period, whether as casual observers or to the point of martyrdom, appear to conform to no simple delineation of their motives or origins, and were drawn from every social class, both clerical and lay.

It is now a truism that in the pursuit of heresy the secular magnates of western Europe were no less determined than the ecclesiastical,

---

[3] Except for direct quotations, references to sources translated in R. I. Moore, *The Birth of Popular Heresy* (London 1975) and to discussion in R. I. Moore, *The Origins of European Dissent* (London 1977) are not given here.
[4] Bouquet 10 p 23.

and in this period often more effective and more ruthless. While this fact may lie behind some assertions of 'popular' hostility to heresy we need not suspect either Southern or Hamilton of equating the populace with the laity: Southern's reference to 'the people whom they ruled' and Hamilton's to 'mob violence' show that the pressure towards persecution to which they refer came from below, from the unprivileged who did not hold office or institutional authority. It is not, therefore, exemplified by the *majores* of Milan who insisted against the protests of Archbishop Aribert on burning the heretics whom he uncovered at Monforte in 1023,[5] or, still less, by the Emperor Henry III who at Goslar in 1052 hanged those who refused to eat a chicken. Nor should we accept as clear evidence of popular detestation of religious deviance instances where its only manifestation is said to be that the heresy was detected as a result of its having been reported to the authorities by some public-spirited citizen: we must remember that heresy to be condemned had to be publicly avowed as well as privately espoused. The *Publicani* who came to England in 1163 and were, according to William of Newburgh 'tracked down by men curious to know to what foreign sect they belonged'[6] and their co-religionists (in all probability) who 'came to Cologne secretly from Flanders' in the same year, and were burned after their neighbours reported their failure to go to church,[7] were the victims rather of xenophobia and zealous authority rather than of popular hostility to heresy *per se*.

The first suggestion of popular violence against heretics is in the account of the synod of Orléans in 1022. After the examination of the accused had been completed in the church of St. Croix, and their condemnation pronounced, 'Queen Constance stood before the doors of the church to prevent the common people from killing them inside the building and they were expelled from the bosom of the church.'[8] As it happens, the only violence which befell them on their way to the flames to which they were consigned was at the hands of the queen herself, when she struck out the eye of her former confessor Etienne with her sceptre. The apprehension of popular violence was not fulfilled. In any case, now that Bautier has detected

[5] Landulf Senior, *Historia Mediolanensis* II, *MGH SS* 8 pp 65–6. Hamilton p 25, mistakenly attributes this action to 'the people'.
[6] *Historia Rerum Anglicarum* 2 p xiii: *Chronicles of the Reigns of Stephen* etc., ed R. Howlett (*RS* 1885) 2 p 133.
[7] *Chronica Regia Coloniensis, MGH SRG* 18 p 114.
[8] *Gesta synodi Aurelianensis*, Bouquet 10 p 539.

political faction and court intrigue behind this whole affair[9] (which, you may recall, was inaugurated by the infiltration of the knight Aréfast into the ranks of the allegedly heretical sect as an agent provocateur) it could hardly provide a basis for any further generalisation. On similar grounds little significance can be attached to the hostility demonstrated against Pierre Maurand by the crowd which witnessed his questioning and condemnation by the papal mission at Toulouse in 1178. As Mundy has shown so well, that mission had been precipitated by Count Raymond V in the hope of recovering his political control over that thrusting and rebellious city, and released a variety of tensions and antagonisms within it; many of them were directed against the wealthy moneylender Maurand, who was indeed a Cathar perfect, but not necessarily against the heresy itself, as Henry of Clairvaux's account of the state of the city and of the blasphemous gibes and graphic gestures with which the citizens greeted him and his fellow legate makes clear.[10] Prudence also requires us to classify as *sui generis* the death of Pierre de Bruys, c1138, 'when', in the words of Peter the Venerable which constitute the whole of our knowledge about it, 'the faithful at St. Gilles avenged the flames of the holy cross which he had set alight by burning him with it.'[11] There is little scope here for speculation, but it is fair comment not only that both Pierre and Henry of Lausanne had apparently preached both safely and successfully in Provence for long periods, but that if the citizens of St. Gilles du Gard displayed exceptional ferocity towards the great mocker of relics and holy objects it would have been readily understandable at a time when a lucrative pilgrimage trade was bringing substantial returns on the investment represented by their basilica, then in the course of its magnificent rebuilding.[12]

There remains only a handful of episodes of which the surviving accounts contain plain indications of popular violence against those accused of heresy. They do however include some which are both well known and dramatic in character, and may have contributed

[9] R-H Bautier, 'L'hérésie d'Orléans et le mouvement intellectuel au début du xie. siècle. Documents et hypothèses.' 95e. *Congrés des Sociétés savantes*, Reims 1970, *Section philologique et historique* (1975) 1 pp 63–88.

[10] Henri de Marcy in *PL* 204 cols 235–40. J. H. Mundy, *Liberty and Political Power in Toulouse*, 1050–1230 (New York 1954) pp 53–62; 'Noblesse et hérésie. Une famille cathare: les Maurand', *Annales* 29.5 (1974) pp 1211–4.

[11] *Tractatus contra Petrobusianos* ed. James Fearns, *CC Continuatio Mediaevalis* 10 (1968) p 5.

[12] K. J. Conant, *Carolingian and Romanesque Architecture* (Harmondsworth 1974 edn) p 253.

disproportionately to the process of generalisation. The first is the case of Ramihrdus of Cambrai, the preacher against simony and incest who was arraigned by the bishop of Cambrai in 1076 and answered impeccably when he was questioned on matters of faith, but refused to affirm his answers by taking communion, on the grounds that all of the priests present were so corrupt that to accept it from any of them would be contrary to papal decrees. Thereupon the meeting denounced him as a heresiarch and adjourned, but 'certain of the bishop's servants, with many others, led him out and took him to a hut which they set on fire.'[13]

Some forty years later Guibert of Nogent assisted in the interrogation of Clement and Everard of Bucy at Soissons. After they had been put to the ordeal by water and condemned Guibert and Bishop Lisiard left them in prison and went to seek the advice of the prelates then in council at Soissons about what to do next. 'But in the interval the faithful people, fearing weakness on the part of the clergy, ran to the prison, seized them, placed them on a fire outside the city, and burned them to ashes.'[14]

When, at Liège in 1135, an unspecified number of heretics did not deny charges against them 'the people wanted to stone them, but they were frightened and took flight during the night. Three of them were captured and imprisoned, of whom one was burned at the stake while the other two made a confession of faith and returned to the Church.'[15] Ten years later when more heretics were convicted and confessed in the same city 'an angry crowd seized them and wanted to burn them, but by God's mercy we [the canons of the cathedral, whose letter to Lucius II is the source for this episode] were able to save almost all of them from immediate death.'[16]

The last, and perhaps the best known, of these cases is that of the two sects of heretics detected at Cologne in 1143 whose disputes with each other enabled Eberwin of Steinfeld to provide us, through his description of their doctrines to St Bernard, with the first evidence of the appearance of Byzantine Bogomilism in the west. After extensive examination they 'were seized by the people, who were moved by great enthusiasm (though we were against it), put to the stake and burned.'[17]

[13] *Chron. S. Andreae Cameracensium, MGH SS* 7 p 540.
[14] *PL* 156 cols 952–3.
[15] *Annales Rodenses, MGH SS* 16 p 711.
[16] *PL* 179 cols 937–8.
[17] *PL* 182 col 677.

It is otiose to remark that these incidents are not only few in number but strikingly similar in character, and appear in a relatively restricted area at a relatively clearly defined period. If that in itself limits the extent to which they may support generalisations of the kind with which we began, closer consideration of them will do so even further. For it is perfectly clear that in these cases we are confronted with the operation of a traditional judicial procedure, that of trial by ordeal. Both at Soissons and at Cologne (according to St Bernard,[18] though Eberwin does not mention it) the accused were put to the ordeal by water, and the requirement that Ramihrdus, as a priest, should take communion was of the same character. Both in 1145 and in 1135 the confessions of those accused at Liège obviated the necessity of the ordeal itself, but the public character of the proceedings which the brief accounts we have of them imply places them within the same juridical framework. The trials and examinations of those accused of heresy in the eleventh and twelfth centuries are clearly distinguishable between those which took place in public and those which were conducted by, and only in the presence of, ecclesiastical or secular office holders. In all of those in the first category, and in none of those in the second, the accused were required, if they denied the charge, to expose themselves through ordeal or through the taking of a solemn oath on relics or gospels to divine judgement or sanction.[19] Thus at Orléans, where you will recall that the people were admitted to the church only after the conclusion of the hearing, there was no attempt to test the assertions of the accused, whereas at Arras in 1025 their interrogation before the assembled people was preceded by their confinement for three days and by fasting and prayer on the part of the clerks; these were the ordinary preliminaries of trial by ordeal, and when the accused proclaimed their acceptance of the items of faith declared by the bishop they were required to confirm their statement by an oath, and sign a written confession of faith with a cross. We may note that three days was the period for which the accused at Cologne in 1143 withstood interrogation before the people took the law—quite literally in my contention—into their own hands.[20]

It hardly needs stressing nowadays that in many parts of northern Europe at just this period trial by ordeal was under attack by both

---

[18] *Serm. in cantica* lxvi, *PL* 183, col 1100.
[19] Moore, *Origins of European Dissent* pp 258–9.
[20] *PL* 182 col 677.

ecclesiastical and secular authority, in principle as they saw it because it was irrational and barbarous, and in fact, as Brown has shown so well,[21] because it represented authority rooted in tradition and the community and was therefore an obstacle to central power. What the ordeal tested was not the truth of the accusation but what the community thought about the accused. When Clement of Bucy 'was thrown into the vat and floated like a stick' the unbounded joy with which the assembled people pronounced the sentence may have owed at least as much to his association with the cruel and rapacious Count John of Soissons as to his views on baptism.[22] And when the bishop went off to consult his fellows instead of carrying out the sentence he flouted the verdict of the community, which defended its traditional procedures in the same way as the people of Liège and Cologne in the same circumstances. The case of Ramihrdus is perhaps less clear, but since his refusal to take communion was tantamount in these terms to an admission of guilt the underlying rationale appears to be the same.

The ordeal certainly produced an expression of popular sentiment, but it did not invariably condemn heresy. At Trier, c1120, the priest Frederick William took communion to support his avowal of innocence when he was charged with heretical preaching, and lived if not to tell the tale at least to confirm his wickedness some time later by being taken in adultery; that Albero, the priest of Mercke near Cologne who was dismissed some time around the middle of the century for preaching that corrupt priests could not give true sacraments, asked to defend himself with the hot iron perhaps reflects the popularity which he was admitted to have won among his parishioners; and though one of the Deonarii—probably the same sect as the Publicani whom we have already mentioned—charged at Vézelay in 1167 was condemned by the ordeal by water which they had themselves requested, another was saved by it.[23]

In conclusion, then, I am unable to offer any clear evidence from these years of popular hostility to heresy, or to heretics, as such. Cer-

---

[21] P. R. L. Brown, 'Society and the Supernatural: a Medieval Change', *Daedalus* 104 (1975) 133–51, now in P. R. L. Brown, *Society and the Holy in Late Antiquity* (London 1982) pp 302–332. Even if the remarkable characterisation of 'Superstition and Science: Nature, Fortune and the Passing of the Medieval Ordeal' proposed by Charles M. Radding, *AHR* 84 (1979) pp 945–969, were plausible in itself it would not invalidate the suggestion of tension between the two forms of justice postulated by Brown and above.

[22] I owe this point to Dr. Janet Nelson.

[23] *Historia Viziliacensis Monasterii*, Bouquet 12 pp 343–4.

tainly some heretics incurred it, for particular reasons which may or may not be visible now, and certainly there might be danger in being different, and perhaps especially in being a stranger in a small community. We are still some way from a clear view of the relationships between popular heresy, violence and authority in the twelfth-century west. But it does seem that as we seek to form it one of the entities which need not be superfluously postulated is a Durkheimian conviction of communal abhorrence of diversity in religious practice and belief.

Sheffield University

THE FIRST CRUSADE AND THE PERSECUTION
OF THE JEWS

by JONATHAN RILEY-SMITH

ETWEEN DECEMBER 1095 and July 1096 there took
place the first pogrom in western European History, a series
of events so distressing to the Jewish people that rumours of
them reached the Near East in advance of the First Crusade, inspiring
the communities there with messianic fervour, while dirges in
honour of the martyrs are recited in the synagogues to this day.[1] The
first outbreaks seem to have occurred in France soon after the preaching of the crusade and the first evidence of them is a letter written by
the French communities to their Rhineland counterparts, warning
them of the impending threat.[2] It is possible that persecution was
widespread in France, even though the details of it are lost, apart
from a reference to an anti-Jewish riot which broke out among men
gathering to take the cross in Rouen.[3] Much more evidence is available about events in the Rhineland. On 3 May 1096 the storm broke
over the community at Speyer, where a crusading army of Rhinelanders and Swabians under Count Emich of Leiningen had
gathered.[4] Emich's army marched north to Worms, where the

---

[1] J. Prawer, *The Latin Kingdom of Jerusalem* (London 1972) pp 234–5; S. D. Goitein,
'Geniza Sources [for the Crusader Period: a Survey', *Outremer*, edd B. Z. Kedar,
H. E. Mayer and R. C. Smail (Jerusalem 1982)] p. 308. The most detailed treat-
ments of the subject are still those in T. Wolff, *Die Bauernkreuzzüge des Jahres 1096*
(Tübingen 1891) and [J. W.] Parkes, *The Jew [in the Medieval Community* (London
1938)] pp 58–89. For a recent attempt to date the Hebrew sources, see A. S.
Abulafia, 'The interrelationship between the Hebrew chronicles on the first
crusade', *Journal of Semitic Studies* 27 (1982) pp 221–39.

[2] 'Mainz Anon[ymous', trans S. Eidelberg, *The Jews and the Crusaders* (Madison
1977)] pp 99–100. For the date of this letter, see [P.] Riant, 'Inventaire critique [des
lettres historiques des croisades', *Archives de l'Orient latin* 1 (1881)] p 111.

[3] Guibert of Nogent, *De vita sua* ed E.-R. Labande (Paris 1981) pp 246–8. See
Richard of Poitiers, ['Chronicon', Bouquet 12] pp 411–12; Geoffrey of Bruil,
['Chronica', Bouquet 12] p 428.

[4] [Solomon] Bar Simson, ['Chronicle', trans Eidelberg, *The Jews and the Crusaders*] p
22; [Eliezer] Bar Nathan, ['Chronicle' trans Eidelberg, *The Jews and the Crusaders*]
pp 80, 91; 'Mainz Anon' pp 100–1; Bernold of St Blasien, ['Chronicon', *MGH
SS* 5] p 465; [H.] Hagenmeyer, *Chronologie [des la première croisade* (Paris 1902)]
pp 19–20. For the dates of the massacres and the names of the dead, see also S.

51

massacres began on the 18th,[5] and then to Mainz, where it was probably joined by more Swabians under Count Hartmann of Dillingen-Kybourg and by an army of French, English, Flemish and Lorrainer crusaders. Between 25 and 29 May the Jewish community at Mainz was annihilated.[6] The movements of the crusaders, at no point very clear, now become impossible to trace with certainty. Some marched north to Cologne, where the Jews had already been dispersed into neighbouring settlements. Throughout June and into early July they were hunted out and destroyed: at Wevelinghoven, Ellen, Neuss, Dortmund, Mörs, Geldern and Xanten; only at Kerpen were the refugees saved.[7] Another band of crusaders seems to have marched south–west to Trier[8] and then to Metz,[9] where the massacres continued. During May a separate crusading army, probably that of Peter the Hermit, forced almost the whole community at Regensburg to undergo baptism.[10] The communities at Wessili and Prague also suffered, probably from the attentions of an army of Saxons and Bohemians led by a priest called Folcmar.[11] This terrible sequence of massacres has attracted a good deal of attention from historians, but it is my opinion that more could still be said on one fairly

Salfeld, *Das Martyrologium des Nurnberger Memorbuches* (Berlin 1898) pp 97–8, 101–19, 133–4, 137–41, 143, 151; A. Neubacher, 'Le Memorbuch de Mayence', *Revue des études juives* 4 (1882) pp 10–11, 14.

[5] Bar Simson pp 23–4; Bar Nathan pp 81–2, 91; 'Mainz Anon' pp 101–2; Bernold of St Blasien p 465; 'Annalista Saxo', [*MGH SS* 6] p 729; Hagenmeyer, *Chronologie* pp 20–1.

[6] Albert of Aachen, ['Historia Hierosolymitana', *RHC Occ* 4] pp 291–3; William of Tyre, ['Historia rerum in partibus transmarinis gestarum', *RHC Occ* 1] pp 66–7; Bar Simson pp 23–4, 28–49; Bar Nathan pp 82–5, 91; 'Mainz Anon' pp 99–100, 105–15; Ekkehard of Aura, 'Chron[icon', *MGH SS* 6] p 209; 'Annalista Saxo' p 729; 'Annales Brunwilarenses', [*MGH SS* 1] p 100; 'Annales Corbeienses', *MGH SS* 3 p 7; 'Annales S Albani Moguntini (Wirziburgenses)', [*MGH SS* 2] p 246; 'Annales Hildesheimenses', [*MGH SS* 3] p 106; Hagenmeyer, *Chronologie* pp 22–4.

[7] Bar Simson pp 49–61; Bar Nathan pp 85–91; Albert of Aachen p 292; William of Tyre p 66; 'Annalista Saxo' p 729; 'Annales Brunwilarenses' p 100; Hagenmeyer, *Chronologie* pp 16–18, 19, 23–5, 26–30.

[8] Bar Simson pp 62–7; Bar Nathan p 92; 'Gesta Treverorum', [*MGH SS* 8] pp 190–1; Hagenmeyer, *Chronologie* pp 25–6.

[9] Bar Simson pp 62, 67; Bar Nathan p 92; Hagenmeyer (*Chronologie* p 18) placed this earlier.

[10] Bar Simson pp 62, 67; Bar Nathan p 92; Ekkehard of Aura, 'Chron' p 208. The events of Regensburg were dated by the Mainz Necrology to 23 May, which seems to fit with the probable dates of Peter the Hermit's passage through Bavaria. See Hagenmeyer, *Chronologie* pp 21–2.

[11] Bar Simson pp 62, 67–8; Bar Nathan p 92; Cosmas of Prague, ['Chronica Boemorum', *MGH SS* 9] p 103; 'Annales Pragenses', [*MGH SS* 3] p 120;

narrow topic: the relationship between them and the crusade itself.[12] That there is a close relationship is beyond doubt. Although the Jews in the Rhineland had already been subjected to spasmodic ill-treatment, they had not felt under threat before the crusade was preached. They were protected to a certain extent and as tension increased the head of the Mainz community, Rabbi Kalonymos, sent urgently for help to the emperor Henry IV, who was then in Italy. Henry's prohibition against harming them came too late to save them, but on his return to Germany he toured the affected areas and tried to restore something of the *status quo*. In his General Peace of 1103 the Jews were singled out for protection.[13] They seem to have felt themselves to have been fairly well integrated into the towns in which they lived. The great community at Mainz responded coolly to the warning from France, replying that it felt no fear.[14] Its insouciance seemed at first to have been justified by the fact that some of the townspeople took its side; but after an armed engagement in which a crusader was killed, both bodies of Christians turned on the Jews, who were blamed for dividing them;[15] in fact the physical destruction at Mainz seems to have been greater than elsewhere.[16] When the news of the pogrom reached Worms, the Jews entrusted their valuables to their gentile neighbours;[17] at the first signs of trouble at Cologne they sought refuge with their gentile acquaintances.[18] In every town except Cologne and Trier the massacre began with the arrival of the crusaders, although townspeople and villagers also took part, and the hunting of Jews through the settlements around

---

Hagenmeyer, *Chronologie* pp 16–18. For an apparently slightly later outbreak, see 'Annales Cameracenses', *MGH SS* 16, p 510.

[12] Compare H. Liebeschutz, 'The Crusading Movement and its Bearing on the Christian Attitude towards Jewry', *Journal of Jewish Studies* 10 (1959) pp 97–111; A. M. Shapiro, 'Jews and Christians in the Period of the Crusades—A Commentary on the First Holocaust', *Journal of Ecumenical Studies* 9 (1972) pp 725–49; A. Waas, 'Volk Gottes und Militia Christi—Juden und Kreuzfahrer', *Miscellanea Mediaevalia* 4 *Judentum im Mittelalter* (Berlin 1966) pp 410–34.

[13] Bar Simson p 25. See Ekkehard of Aura, 'Chron' pp 208–9; Parkes, *The Jew* pp 79–81, 105–6. In the 1060s Archbishop Everard of Trier tried to expel all Jews who would not be baptized. His death was attributed to Jewish witchcraft. 'Gesta Treverorum' p 182.

[14] 'Mainz Anon' pp 99–100.

[15] 'Mainz Anon' p 106; 'Annalista Saxo' p 729.

[16] 'Annales S Albani Moguntini (Wirziburgenses)' p 246; 'Annales Hildesheimenses' p 106.

[17] 'Mainz Anon' p 102.

[18] Bar Simson p 49; Bar Nathan p 85.

Cologne may have been largely the burghers' work.[19] A short time before the outbreak at Trier Peter the Hermit had preached in the city on his way to the East.[20] Several armies, containing crusaders from all over Europe, took part in the pogrom. It was crusaders, or those about to take the cross, who persecuted the Jews in France.[21] Emich of Leiningen's Rhinelanders and Swabians[22] were, as we have seen, joined by another band of Swabians under Count Hartmann of Dillingen-Kybourg[23] and by an army of French, English, Flemish and Lorrainer crusaders.[24] Peter the Hermit's army consisted of French, Swabians, Bavarians and Lorrainers[25] and Folcmar's probably of Saxons and Bohemians.[26] It should be stressed that, although these early armies disintegrated in the Balkans or were defeated by the Turks soon after crossing into Asia Minor, they were not contemptible. There is a tendency to consider them to have been made up of undisciplined hordes of peasants. It is true that contemporaries were inclined to explain their excesses and lack of success in terms of the large numbers of ordinary people, poor, women and children, in their ranks.[27] They may well have included more non-combatants than the armies that departed later and there were certainly disreputable elements in them,[28] and the adherents of strange sects, like the group following Emich which venerated a goose believed to be filled with the Holy Spirit.[29] But they were not nearly so unprofessional as they are assumed to have been. We know very little, it is true, about Folcmar's army.[30] Peter the Hermit's strikes one as being an old-fashioned armed pilgrimage, with a strong ecclesiastical contingent

[19] See Bar Simson pp 27–8, 30, 59; 'Mainz Anon' pp 99, 100, 101–2, 103, 107, 112–13; Albert of Aachen, p 292.

[20] Bar Simson p 62.

[21] Guibert of Nogent, De vita sua pp 246–8; Richard of Poitiers pp 411–12; Geoffrey of Bruil p 428.

[22] Bar Simson p 70; Albert of Aachen p 292; [H.] Hagenmeyer, 'Etude [sur la Chronique de Zimmern', Archives de l'Orient latin 2 (1884)] pp 75–6.

[23] William of Tyre p 66; 'Chronique de Zimmern', [ed H. Hagenmeyer, Archives de l'Orient latin 2 (1884)] p 23; Hagenmeyer, 'Etude' pp 74–6. See Albert of Aachen p 299.

[24] Albert of Aachen pp 291–2; William of Tyre p 66.

[25] Albert of Aachen p 276.

[26] Ekkehard of Aura, 'Hierosolymita', [RHC Occ 5] p 12.

[27] See for instance Guibert of Nogent, 'Gesta [Dei per Francos', RHC Occ 4] pp 142–3.

[28] Albert of Aachen p 291; Bernold of St Blasien p 464; William of Tyre p 66.

[29] Guibert of Nogent, 'Gesta' p 251; Ekkehard of Aura, 'Hierosolymita' p 19; Albert of Aachen p 295; Bar Simson p 27.

[30] Ekkehard of Aura, 'Hierosolymita' pp 12, 20.

The First Crusade and the Jews

in it. Peter had great difficulty in controlling his forces in the Balkans and in Asia Minor,[31] but his later career on the crusade was to show that he was far from being simply an incompetent rabble-rouser.[32] His captains, Godfrey Burel of Étampes,[33] Raynald of Broyes,[34] Walter fitzWaleran of Breteuil[35] and Fulcher of Chartres,[36] all seem to have been experienced knights; Fulcher was to end his days as a great lord in the County of Edessa.[37] Attached to Peter's army, moreover, was a strong force of Swabian nobles under the Count Palatine Hugh of Tübingen and Duke Walter of Tegk.[38] Emich of Leiningen's forces were not negligible either. Emich was a major south German noble. So was Count Hartmann of Dillingen-Kybourg. They were probably accompanied by the Counts of Rötteln, Zweibrücken, Salm and Viernenberg and the Lord of Bollanden.[39] The army of French, English, Flemish and Lorrainer crusaders which met Emich at Mainz was, according to one report, large and well-equipped.[40] It was under the leadership of a remarkable group of men, Clarembold of Vendeuil, Thomas of Marle Lord of Coucy, William the Carpenter Viscount of Melun and Drogo of Nesle.[41] After the break-up of Emich's forces these men joined Hugh of Vermandois, the brother of the King of France, and continued their journey to the East. Clarembold of Vendeuil[42] and Thomas of Marle had distinguished crusades and Thomas had a

---

[31] Albert of Aachen pp 272, 276–89 passim.

[32] Gesta Francorum [et aliorum Hierosolimitanorum, ed R. Hill (London 1962)] pp 33, 66–7, 94; Peter Tudebode, [Historia de Hierosolimitano itinere, edd J. H. and L. L. Hill (Paris 1977) pp 68–9, 108–9, 144–5, Raymond of Aguilers, [Liber, edd J. H. and L. L. Hill (Paris 1969)] pp 79, 111; Fulcher of Chartres, [Historia Hierosolimitana, ed H. Hagenmeyer (Heidelberg 1913)] pp 247–8; Albert of Aachen pp 314, 470, 491–2.

[33] Albert of Aachen pp 277, 278, 281.

[34] Ibid pp 277, 281.

[35] Ibid pp 278, 281.

[36] Ibid pp 281, 283.

[37] [J.] Riley-Smith, 'The motives [of the earliest crusaders and the settlement of Latin Palestine', EHR 98 (1983)] pp 721–36.

[38] 'Chronique de Zimmern' pp 22–9; Hagenmeyer, 'Etude' pp 69–72, 77–9.

[39] Hagenmeyer, 'Etude' pp 74–7.

[40] Albert of Aachen p 291. See also Ekkehard of Aura, 'Hierosolymita' p 20. The combined armies under Emich's leadership had a substantial body of knights. Albert of Aachen p 294.

[41] Ibid pp 293–5, 299; William of Tyre p 66.

[42] Albert of Aachen pp 304–5, 398; Herimannus, 'Liber de restauratione monasterii S Martini Tornacensis', MGH SS 14 p 283; William of Tyre pp 80, 218; Robert of Rheims, [Historia Iherosolimitana', RHC Occ 3] p 833; La Chanson d'Antioche, [ed S. Duparc-Quioc 2 vols (Paris, 1977–8)] 1, pp 69, 440, 450, 451.

colourful and violent career before he died in 1130 as Count of Amiens.[43] William the Carpenter, who had already fought in Spain, was panicked into flight from Antioch but he eventually settled as a fief-holder in the Principality of Antioch.[44] Drogo of Nesle, of an illustrious French family, joined Baldwin of Boulogne, following him to Edessa and then to Jerusalem.[45] These captains must all have witnessed or taken part in the persecutions, as did William, a son of the Count of Eu, who saved the life of a Jewish child during the riot in Rouen.[46]

It is not possible, therefore, to adhere to the comforting view that the massacres were perpetrated by gangs of peasants. Most were carried out by armies containing crusaders from all parts of western Europe, led by experienced captains. So what were the crusaders' motives? There is evidence for the wish to get supplies by extortion and looting, for attempts to convert the Jews by force and for a desire for vengeance on them. I propose to deal with these in turn.

A near contemporary who, like most educated churchmen, found the events abhorrent, was in no doubt that at their root was greed. Writing of the disasters that beset so many of the early crusaders in the Balkans, he commented

> This is believed to be the hand of the Lord working against the pilgrims, who sinned in his sight with their great impurity and intercourse with prostitutes and slaughtered the wandering Jews, who admittedly were contrary to Christ, more from avarice for money than for the justice of God.[47]

In fact most of the examples of avarice described in the Hebrew sources were attributed by the Jews not to crusaders but to bishops, their officials and townspeople, who took bribes in return for promises of protection, which they then failed to carry out.[48] In many cases the promises made were probably sincere and the break-

[43] Albert of Aachen pp 315, 332, 422, 464, 468; William of Tyre pp 46, 134, 263, 352; La Chanson d'Antioche 1 pp 69, 94, 155, 156, 160, 171, 307, 441, 451, 526; Robert of Rheims p 833. See Dictionnaire de Biographie Française 9 cols 867–8.

[44] Gesta Francorum pp 33–4; Peter Tudebode pp 68–9; J. Riley-Smith, 'The motives' pp 731.

[45] Duparc-Quioc, La Chanson d'Antioche 2 p 229; Riley-Smith, 'The motives' pp 736.

[46] Guibert of Nogent, De vita sua pp 248–50.

[47] Albert of Aachen p 295. See also Bernold of St Blasien p 466. Albert's account obviously influenced H. E. Mayer (The Crusades (Oxford 1972) pp 43–4), but not N. Cohn (The Pursuit of the Millenium, 2 ed (London 1962) pp 49–52) nor J. Prawer (Histoire du royaume latin de Jérusalem 2 vols (Paris 1969–70) 1 pp 181–90).

[48] Bar Simson pp 28, 44, 59, 62–4; Bar Nathan p 89; 'Mainz Anon' p 107. See also Cosmas of Prague p 104. For a refusal to take a bribe, see 'Mainz Anon' p 101.

ing of them reluctant, but there were examples of mixed motives. At the first sign of trouble, for instance, the members of the Mainz community were encouraged to bring all their possessions into the courtyard of the archbishop's palace and to make over a sum of money to Archbishop Ruthard himself. Ruthard fled before the mob broke in. Although it is probable that he had originally wanted to protect the Jews, his relatives were later accused of stealing from them and in 1098 he was forced out of the city by the emperor.[49] It is certain, however, that crusaders made financial demands of Jewish communities in the cities on their line of march and it is apparent that these were extortions backed by threats of force. When Peter the Hermit reached Trier in early April 1096 he brought with him a letter from the Jews of France asking their co-religionists everywhere to give him provisions; in return, it said, Peter promised to speak kindly of Israel. His arrival and preaching terrified the community at Trier, which suggests that there was an anti-semitic tone to his sermons.[50] Godfrey of Bouillon apparently threatened to eradicate Jews before accepting bribes in appeasement from what must have been the remnants of the communities of Cologne and Mainz.[51] The Jews of Mainz had earlier hoped in vain to pacify Emich of Leiningen by offering him money and letters, obviously like that carried by Peter the Hermit, which he could have presented to the communities he came across on his march.[52] And perhaps in the erroneous belief that canon law permitted the expropriation of the goods of infidels,[53] crusaders joined the local inhabitants in looting Jewish property in the towns where the massacres took place;[54] at Mainz the Jews delayed their enemies for a while by throwing money out of the windows to distract them.[55]

Grasping as the crusaders appear to have been, they acted in this way not in response to theory but to necessity: the needs of their armies—of any army—on the march. Extortion and looting were

[49] Bar Simson pp 23–4, 28, 30; 'Mainz Anon' pp 106, 107, 109; Albert of Aachen p 292; Ekkehard of Aura, 'Chron' p 209; 'Annalista Saxo' p 729.

[50] Bar Simson p 62. For the date, see Hagenmeyer, *Chronologie* pp 18–19.

[51] Bar Simson pp 24–5.

[52] Bar Simson p 29; 'Mainz Anon' p 107. See also 'Mainz Anon' p 100.

[53] See 'Notitiae duae Lemovicenses [de praedicatione crucis in Aquitania', *RHC Occ* 5] p 351; Geoffrey of Bruil p 428; Sigebert of Gembloux, ['Chronica', *MGH SS* 6] p 367; 'Anon[ymi] Florinensis [brevis narratio belli sacri', *RHC Occ* 5] p 371.

[54] Bar Simson pp 35, 50; 'Mainz Anon' pp 110, 112; Albert of Aachen pp 292–3; 'Annales S Disibodi', [*MGH SS* 17] pp 15–16.

[55] Bar Simson pp 34–5; 'Mainz Anon' p 110.

linked to crusading to the extent that crusade preaching was responsible for the departure on a long march of large numbers of men and women without proper logistical planning or any system for provisioning and, in the case of the armies with which we are primarily concerned, at a time of food shortage without even waiting for the harvest which, when it came in 1096, was a good one.[56] Provisions and animals—horses and beasts of burden—came to be at the forefront of their minds from dawn to dusk. When in touch with Christian suppliers they had to pay often exorbitant prices. To meet these costs they had to rely on alms from Christians[57] and on subventions: from Jews, as here, and later from Muslims.[58] Often they had not enough cash; they met with reluctant merchants and unsympathetic officials;[59] and for most of the time they were to be out of contact with friendly suppliers. Plundering became a normal and necessary occupation, which explains the quarrels over booty, the occasional orders against turning aside for spoil in battle and the carnage and sacking that accompanied the fall of Jerusalem. Historians who argue that the crusaders had materialistic motives on the grounds that they were so often concerned with loot should try to explain how otherwise these armies would have been kept supplied.

Everywhere attempts were made to force Christianity on the Jews, who had heard that the crusaders intended to offer them the choice of conversion or death[60] and that they desired to 'cut them off from being a nation':[61] a Christian writer confirmed that the aim of the crusaders was 'to wipe out or convert'.[62] Synagogues, Torah scrolls and cemeteries were desecrated.[63] At times the Christians employed terror-tactics: during the persecution at Mörs they covered their swords with the blood of animals to frighten the Jews into thinking that killings had already taken place.[64] In every settle-

---

[56] Fulcher of Chartres p 154; Guibert of Nogent, 'Gesta' p 141.
[57] See, for example, Albert of Aachen pp 278, 283. It is noteworthy that the early armies entered the Balkans loaded with cash, pp 281, 289–90, 293.
[58] See *Gesta Francorum* pp 83, 84, 86; Peter Tudebode 127, 128, 132; Raymond of Aguilers pp 103, 107, 111, 112, 125.
[59] For the early stages, see above all Albert of Aachen pp 274–312; *Gesta Francorum* pp 2–13; Peter Tudebode pp 32–48; Raymond of Aguilers pp 35–42; Fulcher of Chartres pp 168–76.
[60] Bar Simson p 22; 'Mainz Anon' p 99.
[61] Bar Simson p 47; 'Mainz Anon' p 102; Bar Nathan p 80.
[62] Ekkehard of Aura, 'Hierosolymita' p 20. See 'Annales S Disibodi' pp 15–16.
[63] Bar Simson pp 37, 41, 50, 61, 62–3; Bar Nathan pp 81, 85; 'Mainz Anon' pp 112–13. For what was to be a typical charge against Jews, see 'Mainz Anon' p 102.
[64] Bar Nathan p 89.

ment subjected to the persecutions Jews were slaughtered when they refused to convert and so desperate did they become that they died at their own hands or at those of members of their communities to avoid defilement.[65] Those who submitted to baptism were spared:[66] Guibert of Nogent's autobiography contains the story of a learned monk, whose life began as a young Jewish boy in Rouen. He was saved by a son of the Count of Eu, who took him to his mother, Countess Helisende. She asked the child if he desired baptism and when he was too frightened to demur had him immediately christened. He was given the name of William and sent as an oblate to the monastery of Fly to prevent him returning to his parents.[67]

One factor in this campaign of forced conversions may have been eschatological expectations. A passage on Emich of Leiningen in the chronicle of Bar Simson has attracted a good deal of attention.

> [Emich] concocted a tale that an apostle of the crucified one had come to him and made a sign on his flesh to inform him that when he arrived in Greek Italy [the crucified one] himself would appear and place a kingly crown upon his head, and Emich would vanquish his foes.[68]

The French historian Alphandéry suggested that this was a distorted reference to the popular phophecy of the last Frankish or German king in occupation of Jerusalem before the Last Days: it was believed that in the reign of this last king the Jews would be converted to Christianity.[69] This legend had also been the basis of Benzo of Alba's advice of c1085 to Henry IV of Germany to proceed to Jerusalem and rule there, and it is also to be found reflected in Guibert

---

[65] Bar Simson pp 22–3, 35–44, 45–7, 50–8, 60, 65–7; Bar Nathan pp 80–1, 83–90; 'Mainz Anon' pp 102–5, 107, 109–14; Albert of Aachen pp 292–3; Ekkehard of Aura, 'Hierosolymita' p 20; Ekkehard of Aura, 'Chron' p 208; Bernold of St Blasien p 465; 'Notitiae duae Lemovicenses' p 351; Geoffrey of Bruil p 428; 'Anon. Florinensis' p 371; Cosmas of Prague p 103; 'Gesta Treverorum' p 190; 'Annalista Saxo' p 729; 'Annales Augustani', *MGH SS* 3 p 139; Sigebert of Gembloux p 367; 'Sigeberti Continuatio Auctarium Aquicinense', [*MGH SS* 6] p 394, 'Annales S Disibodi' pp 15–16.

[66] Bar Simson pp 23, 39–41, 67, 68; Bar Nathan p 84; Ekkehard of Aura, 'Chron' p 208; 'Notitiae duae Lemovicenses' p 351; Geoffrey of Bruil p 428; 'Anon. Florinensis' p 371; 'Annalista Saxo' p 729; 'Annales S Albani Moguntini (Wirziburgenses)' p 246; 'Annales Hildesheimenses' p 106; 'Annales Pragenses' p 120; Sigebert of Gembloux p 367; Sigeberti Continuatio 'Auctarium Aquicinense' p 394; 'Annales S Disibodi' pp 15–16; 'Annales S Pauli Virdunensis', *MGH SS* 16 p 501.

[67] Guibert of Nogent, *De vita sua* p 248–52.

[68] Bar Simson p 28.

[69] P. Alphandéry and A. Dupront, *La chrétienté et l'idée de croisade*, 2 vols (Paris 1954–9) 1 pp 74–6.

of Nogent's version of Urban II's proclamation of the crusade at Clermont, in which the pope was made to argue that the occupation of Jerusalem by Christians was a necessary precondition for the appearance of Anti-Christ and therefore a step towards Dooms-day.[70] It has recently been pointed out that the evidence for wide-spread eschatological fervour is not copious.[71] There is enough, however, to lead one to suppose that eschatological ideas had a cer-tain currency and that they did find some echo in Bar Simson's account of Emich's motivation, although all that we know of Emich suggests that he had no intention of travelling to the East by way of southern Italy.

Other elements in Bar Simson's story, however, ring true. That Emich had visions is confirmed in the account of the German abbot Ekkehard of Aura. 'Emich . . . like another Saul, called, so it is said, by divine revelations to religious practice of this sort [the crusade].'[72] Visions and dreams were taken seriously at the time and such an in-spiration to crusade does not appear to have been unusual.[73] The most famous vision associated with the early stages of the crusade was said to have been experienced by Peter the Hermit, who claimed to have seen Christ and to have been handed a celestial letter of com-mission by the archangel Gabriel.[74] Nor was it unusual for visionaries to display brandings, usually of the cross, which they claimed had appeared miraculously on their flesh. The most no-torious was abbot Baldwin, Godfrey of Bouillon's chaplain. Baldwin financed his crusade out of oblations made by the faithful, who were led to believe that he had been marked on the forehead by

[70] Benzo of Alba, 'Ad Heinricum IV . . . libri', *MGH SS* 11 pp 605, 617; Guibert of Nogent, 'Gesta' pp 138–9.

[71] B. McGinn, 'Iter Sancti Sepulchri: the Piety of the First Crusaders', *The Walter Prescott Webb Lectures: Essays in Medieval Civilization*, ed R. E. Sullivan *et al.* (Austin 1978) pp 47–8, 66–7.

[72] Ekkehard of Aura, 'Hierosolymita' p 20.

[73] For visions during the preaching of the crusade, see Albert of Aachen pp 415–16, 486–8; Ekkehard of Aura, 'Hierosolymita' pp 38–9; Caffaro di Caschifellone, 'De liberatione civitatum orientis', ed L. T. Belgrano, *Annali Genovesi* 5 vols (Genoa 1890–1929) 1 pp 100–1, 106. For visions in the course of the crusade, see various works by J. Riley-Smith: 'An Approach to Crusading Ethics' *Reading Medieval Studies* 6 (1980) pp 12– 13; 'The First Crusade and St Peter', *Outremer* edd B .Z. Kedar, H. E. Mayer and R. C. Smail (Jerusalem 1982) pp 53–6; 'Death on the First Crusade' [*The end of strife* ed D. M. Loades] forthcoming.

[74] Albert of Aachen p 273; 'Historia peregrinorum [euntium Jerosolymam', *RHC Occ 3*] p 169; William of Tyre p 35; Ekkehard of Aura, 'Hierosolymita' p 40; *La Chanson d'Antioche* 1 pp 21–2, 32–3, Riant, 'Inventaire critique' pp 96–9, 110–11, 714.

an angel. In the course of the crusade he confessed and reformed and he later became the first abbot of St Mary of the Valley of Josaphat in Jerusalem and the first Latin archbishop of Caesarea.[75] In fact reactions to the preaching of the cross seem often to have been hysterical. At this distance Emich looks as though he was very unstable: this is certainly suggested by Ekkehard's comparison of him to Saul. To the Jewish chroniclers he was merciless and wicked,[76] and at least one Christian contemporary seems to have thought the same: even before the crusade he was 'notorious for his tyrannical behaviour'; and after his death in 1117 his ghost was believed to haunt the region of Mainz imploring alms and prayers from the faithful so that he might be released.[77] One cannot state with certainty that he was motivated by eschatological beliefs, but it seems likely that he shared in the general hysteria and manifested it more strangely than most.

Eschatological myth may help to explain Emich's attitude, but there is little evidence that it convinced many. And anyway forcible conversions were directly contrary to the clear injunctions of canon law, obeyed on the crusade, incidentally, by Bohemond of Taranto who, on 28 June 1098, promised the soldiers of the garrison of the citadel of Antioch who did not wish to convert safe-conducts into Muslim territory.[78] For centuries it had been a repeatedly enunciated principle that infidels, and particularly Jews, should never be forced to the faith but could only be persuaded by reason. For instance, in 633, in a decree that passed into the collections of canon law, the Council of Toledo had stated

> The holy synod orders concerning the Jews that no one be forced into belief. *When God wants to show mercy he does, and when*

[75] Guibert of Nogent, 'Gesta' pp 182–3, 251; William of Tyre p 423. For other examples, see Raymond of Aguilers p 102; Fulcher of Chartres pp 169–70; Baldric of Bourgueil, 'Historia Jerosolimitana', *RHC Occ* 4 p17; Guibert of Nogent, 'Gesta' pp 250–1; Ekkehard of Aura, 'Hierosolymita' p 19; Bernold of St Blasien p 464; 'Historia de translatione sanctorum magni Nicolai . . . alterius Nicolai, Theodorique', *RHC Occ* 5 p 255; Orderic Vitalis, *Historia aecclesiastica* ed M. Chibnall, 6 vols (Oxford 1969–79)5 p 30.

[76] Bar Simson p 28, 70; 'Mainz Anon' p 107.

[77] Ekkehard of Aura, 'Hierosolymita' p 20; Ekkehard of Aura, 'Chron' p 261. For his death, see *ibid* p 253; Otto of Freising, *Gesta Friderici* [1. *Imperatoris*, ed G. Waitz (Hanover 1912)] p 29.

[78] *Gesta Francorum* p 71; Peter Tudebode pp 113–14; Robert of Rheims pp 835–6; Baldric of Bourgueil p 79; Guibert of Nogent, 'Gesta' pp 207–8; 'Historia peregrinorum' p 206; Orderic Vitalis 5 pp 116–18. For a correct distinction between the just war against pagans and the use of force against heretics, see a letter from the leaders of the crusade. [H.] Hagenmeyer, [*Die*] *Kreuzzugsbriefe* [*aus den Jahren 1088–1100* (Innsbruck 1901)] p 164.

he wants to harden someone's heart he does so (Romans 9: 18). Such men are not saved against their wills, but willingly, so that the pattern of justice may be perfect.[79]

As statements in the Christian accounts of the pogrom demonstrate, educated churchmen were in no doubt about this matter. To Albert of Aachen,

God is a just judge and orders that no one be brought unwillingly or by force under the yoke of the catholic faith.[80]

According to Cosmas of Prague,

[the bishop of Prague] seeing that [the forcible baptisms] were against canon law and led by zeal for justice, tried vainly, because unaided, to forbid them lest the Jews be baptized against their wills.[81]

In fact most of the bishops made some effort to protect the Jews, although with varying degrees of success, taking them into their fortified palaces and, at Speyer, Mainz and Cologne, dispersing them in their villages in the countryside.[82] The bishop of Speyer was outstandingly successful: he made no effort to interfere with the Jews' religion and he took strong measures against his townspeople.[83] The bishop of Prague also took a strong line, but with less success.[84] The archbishop of Mainz began well, but he weakened in the face of the mob, as we have seen.[85] He then tried to exploit the Jews' fears to convert them,[86] as did the archbishop of Trier, whose performance also left something to be desired.[87] Individual priests at Mainz and Xanten also tried to take advantage of the situation to gain converts,[88] although that is obviously not the same thing as holding to the idea of baptism by force.

The senior clergy, however powerless they proved to be in practice, knew their church law. It is unlikely, therefore, that any respon-

---

[79] For a concise account of these prohibitions, see F. Lotter, *Die Konzeption des Wendenkreuzzugs* (Sigmaringen 1977) pp 34–8.

[80] Albert of Aachen p 295.

[81] Cosmas of Prague p 103.

[82] Bar Simson pp 28–9, 44–5, 50; Bar Nathan pp 83–4, 86; 'Mainz Anon' pp 101, 106. For the protection of a local civil authority, see Bar Simson pp 67–8.

[83] Bar Simson p 22; 'Mainz Anon' p 101.

[84] Cosmas of Prague p 103.

[85] Bar Simson pp 28–30; 'Mainz Anon' pp 106, 107, 109.

[86] Bar Simson p 45.

[87] Bar Simson pp 63–5; 'Gesta Treverorum' pp 190–1. Compare the behaviour of an earlier archbishop of Trier. 'Gesta Treverorum' p 182. For Worms, see Bar Simson p 23; 'Mainz Anon' pp 101–6.

[88] 'Mainz Anon' p 114; Bar Simson p 57.

sible crusade preacher ever suggested to the faithful that they were embarking on a war of conversion, although it is possible that popular preachers were not so restrained: we have seen that Peter the Hermit may well have been indulging in dangerous rhetoric. But there was an idea around which was ambiguous enough to be interpreted by the ignorant or careless as supporting the concept of a missionary war. Odd asides in the histories of three educated and theologically-minded French churchmen suggest that in the highest circles the crusade was being protrayed as a war for the expansion of Christianity. Robert of Rheims made Pope Urban II preach at the Council of Clermont:

> May the stories of your ancestors move you and excite your souls to strength; the worth and greatness of King Charlemagne and of Louis his son and of others of your kings, who destroyed the kingdoms of the pagans and extended into them the boundaries of Holy Church.[89]

Baldric of Bourgueil referred to God in the context of the crusade as the 'propagator of Christian expansion'[90] and Guibert of Nogent called crusaders 'the propagators of the faith'.[91] It is not surprising that when combined with contempt for the validity of pagan rule this idea was reflected during the crusade in attitudes not far removed from those in favour of forcible conversion, even if they could technically be distinguished from them. From Nicaea in the summer of 1097 the leaders sent envoys to the Fatimid caliph of Egypt offering him Christianity or battle;[92] and much the same choice seems to have been put by Peter the Hermit in an embassy to the Muslim general Karbuqa in the summer of 1098.[93] Raymond of St Gilles refused to make a treaty with the emir of Tripoli unless he was baptized.[94] The success of the crusade led to wild talk of a Christian conquest of Asia.[95] It may be that the persecutions in the Rhineland were partly set off by careless references to the expansion of Christianity, especially since many crusaders found it difficult to make any distinc-

[89] Robert of Rheims p 728.
[90] Baldric of Bourgueil p 9.
[91] Guibert of Nogent, 'Gesta', p 213; see also p 139.
[92] 'Historia peregrinorum' p 181.
[93] *Gesta Francorum* p 66; Peter Tudebode p 108.
[94] *Gesta Francorum* p 83; Peter Tudebode p 128; Robert of Rheims p 853; Orderic Vitalis 5 p 146. Corrupt version in 'Historia peregrinorum' p 210.
[95] See Raymond of Aguilers pp 131, 136; *La Chanson d'Antioche* 1 p 215. See J. Richard, *The Latin Kingdom of Jerusalem* (Amsterdam 1979) pp 20–1.

tion between Jews and Muslims as enemies of the faith. In France crusaders were reported saying that

> it was unjust for those who took up arms against rebels against Christ to allow enemies of Christ to live in their own land.[96]

At Rouen men who had come to the city to take the cross began to say

> We wish to attack the enemies of God in the East, once we have crossed great tracts of territory, when before our eyes are the Jews, more hostile to God than any other race. The enterprise is absurd.[97]

And the German Jews knew that such views were current in France.[98] Jews were held to be internal enemies of the Church[99] and it was this which presumably led a later writer to comment of the south Italian Norman crusaders that they 'held Jews, heretics and Muslims, all of whom they called enemies of God, equally detestable'.[100]

Now, the suggestion that the crusaders misconceived their rôle to the extent that they thought they were fighting a war of conversion in which they made no distinction between Muslim and Jew would be convincing were it not for a remarkable fact. It is not generally realized that this group of incidents is almost unique. Although they suffered badly enough, Jewish communities in the Near East do not seem to have been subjected to the treatment meted out to the Rhinelanders. Professor Goitein has shown that the traditional picture of the persecution of the Jews in Palestine by the crusaders should be modified. Caught up in the sack of the cities, the communities suffered loss of life and in Jerusalem the synagogue and Torah scrolls were destroyed and a Karaite library taken. Many Jews were sold into slavery. But most seem to have been ransomed; and at least part of the Karaite library was sold back. While on occasion conversion to Christianity was offered, there is no evidence that refusal meant death. Although the Jewish community in Jerusalem was wiped out, Professor Goitein has recently commented that 'the

---

[96] Richard of Poitiers pp 411–12.

[97] Guibert of Nogent, *De vita sua* p 246–8.

[98] Bar Simson p 22; 'Mainz Anon' p 99. At the time of the Second Crusade much the same sentiments were expressed by Peter the Venerable, although he wanted to tax the Jews, not kill them. Peter the Venerable, *Letters*, ed G. Constable 2 vols (Cambridge Mass. 1967)1 pp 328–30.

[99] Ekkehard of Aura, 'Chron' p 208.

[100] Orderic Vitalis 5 p 44. See Raymond of Aguilers p 115.

crusaders liquidated a Jewish community already in a state of liquidation'.[101] Indeed, if we leave aside a slightly different case of the involuntary reception of the faith, the practice of Christian priests of baptizing dying Turks as they lay on the battlefield,[102] there are in fact only two examples outside Europe of forcible mass conversion in the sources for the First Crusade and one of them almost certainly did not occur. The doubtful reference is to be found in Robert of Rheims's account of the taking of al-Barah in Syria by Count Raymond of St Gilles in late September 1098. According to Robert

> The count ordered that all should be enchained and that those who would not believe in Christ as saviour should be beheaded . . . No one from such a great multitude was saved unless he willingly confessed Christ and was baptized. And so that city was cleansed and recalled to the worship of our faith.[103]

That seems plain enough. But Robert of Rheims was not on the crusade and his assertion is to be found nowhere else, although all contemporary accounts agree that there was great slaughter, a display of deliberate ferocity in a region with an already strong indigenous Christian presence before the establishment of the first Latin bishopric. Raymond of St Gilles's chaplain Raymond of Aguilers, who was present at al-Barah, reported that many of the inhabitants were killed or sold into slavery in Antioch, but that those who surrendered in the course of the fighting were set free. This looks like a case in which resistance was punished by the razing of the town and the destruction of the inhabitants. It is noteworthy that some manuscripts of Raymond's *Liber* have the word '*crediderant*', which does not really make sense in the context, substituted for '*reddiderant*',[104] and it may have been some such textual variant that persuaded Robert of Rheims to write as he did. At any rate it is unlikely that there was an attempt to convert by force at al-Barah.

The other case is, however, well documented. In the middle of July 1098 a south French knight called Raymond Pilet, who seems to

---

[101] S. D. Goitein, 'Geniza Sources' p 308; see pp 306–14; S. D. Goitein, 'Contemporary Letters on the Capture of Jerusalem by the Crusaders', *Journal of Jewish Studies* 3 (1952) pp 162–7; S. D. Goitein, *A Mediterranean Society*, 3 vols (Berkeley 1967–78)3 p 356.

[102] Fulcher of Chartres p 227. See also the story in Albert of Aachen (p 319) of a Muslim scout, whose captors suspected that fear rather than conviction was responsible for his conversion.

[103] Robert of Rheims p 840.

[104] Raymond of Aguilers pp 91–2. See also *Gesta Francorum* pp 74–5; Peter Tudebode p 117; Baldric of Bourgueil pp 82–3; Guibert of Nogent, 'Gesta' p 210; 'Historia peregrinorum' p 207; Orderic Vitalis 5 p 134.

have acquired substantial loot, financed a large expedition which he led into the countryside south of Antioch. On 17 July he reached a fortified place east of Ma'arrat-an-Nu'man called Tall Manas, which was held by Syrian Christians, and on the 25th he took a nearby fortress which he had been informed was full of Muslims. All those in it who refused to be baptized were killed. Two days later his force, supplemented by local Christians, was bloodily repulsed from Ma'arrat.[105] Robert of Rheims, who, it will be remembered, was never on the crusade, reported that Raymond Pilet had an especial hatred of Turks,[106] but a reading of the sources suggests to me that he had become involved in the complex inter-religious rivalries of the region and that his alliance with a group of local Christians was responsible for what happened.

The fact that there are so few cases of forcible mass conversion and no parallels with what happened in Western Europe leads one to wonder whether a commitment to missionary war was really prevalent in the crusading armies. At this stage it is worth considering a third motive. There is strong evidence for a desire for revenge upon the Jews for the crucifixion, which one contemporary understood to be a purpose of the crusade, and this idea was referred to often enough in both Jewish and Christian sources for one to be led to suppose that it was fairly prevalent.[107] It does not, therefore, come as a surprise to learn that crusaders in the well-equipped army of French, English, Flemings and Lorrainers, which met with Emich at Mainz, claimed that the pogrom was the start of their service against the enemies of the Christian faith[108] or that German crusaders announced their intention of clearing a path to Jerusalem which began with the Rhineland Jews: a count called Dithmar was reported as saying that he would not leave Germany until he had killed a Jew. The Jews had heard that it was believed that killing them would gain indulgences and that their co-religionists were slain in the name of Christ.[109] Residual feelings of vengeance may even have been manifesting themselves towards the end of the crusade, although, as we

[105] *Gesta Francorum* pp 73–4; Peter Tudebode pp 115–16; Baldric of Bourgueil pp 81–2; Guibert of Nogent, 'Gesta' p 209; Robert of Rheims p 838; 'Historia peregrinorum' pp 206–7; Orderic Vitalis 5 pp 130, 132; Kamal ad-Din, 'Chronique d'Alep', *RHC Or* 3 p 584. For date, see Hagenmeyer, *Chronologie* pp 179–82.
[106] Robert of Rheims p 838.
[107] Bar Simson pp 22, 25–6, 30; Bar Nathan p 80; 'Mainz Anon' pp 99, 102; 'Annalista Saxo' p 729.
[108] Albert of Aachen p 292. See 'Annales Blandinienses', *MGH SS* 5 p 27.
[109] 'Mainz Anon' p 100; Bar Simson p 39.

have seen, the Jews in Palestine were not treated as badly as their confrères in Europe had been: they were no longer an alien minority and feelings of animosity towards them must have been overshadowed by fears of the Muslim powers. But it was reported that the South Italian Norman leader Tancred chose to ransom them for 30 pieces of silver each.[110] It is clear that in respect of the desire for vengeance a significant number of crusaders did not distinguish between Muslims and Jews and could not understand why, if they were called upon to take up arms against the former, they should not also persecute the latter. In order to explain how they came to think this it is necessary to touch briefly on the justifications of the crusade. Pope Urban called for a war of liberation with two purposes. The first was the freeing of the eastern churches in general and the church of Jerusalem in particular from the oppression and ravages of the Muslims;[111] the second was the freeing of the city of Jerusalem from the servitude into which it had fallen.[112] So one aim was the liberation of people, the baptized members of the Church; the other was the liberation of a place. Urban put both goals within the context of Christian love. Love of neighbour would find expression in the help given to one's suffering brothers, even at the risk of one's own life; love of God would find expression not only in such an act of charity to God's own children, but also in the liberation of God's own city, the focus of divine interventions in the world, hallowed by the presence and blood of Christ.[113] It was the goal of Jerusalem that almost certainly led Urban to introduce for crusaders the wearing of the cross, reflecting contemporary preoccupations with the cross as a devotional symbol,

[110] Baldric of Bourgueil p 103 note.
[111] R. Somerville, 'The Councils of Urban II: 1. Decreta Claromontensia' *Annuarium Historiae Conciliorum*, Suppl. 1 (1972) p 74; Conciliar decree in 'Historia peregrinorum' pp 169–70; Hagenmeyer, *Kreuzzugsbriefe* p 136; [W.] Wiederhold, 'Papsturkunden [in Florenz', *Nachrichten von der Gesellschaft der Wissenschaften zu Göttingen*, Phil.-hist. K1. (Göttingen 1901)] p 313; P. Kehr, *Papsturkunden in Spanien. I. Katalonien* (Berlin 1926) p 287.
[112] Hagenmayer, *Kreuzzugsbriefe* pp 136, 137; Wiederhold, 'Papsturkunden' p 313; Urban II, 'Epistolae et privilegia', *PL* 151 col 478. The view put forward by C. Erdmann (*The Origin of the Idea of Crusade* (Princeton 1977) pp 355–71) that help to the eastern Christians was Urban's priority and that to him the goal of Jerusalem was secondary is untenable. See especially H. E. J. Cowdrey, 'Pope Urban II's Preaching of the First Crusade' *History* 55 (1970) pp 177–88.
[113] Hagenmeyer, *Kreuzzugsbriefe* p 137; Clermont decree in 'Historia peregrinorum' p 169. See also Kehr, *Papsturkunden* p 287; Baldric of Bourgueil p 15; J. Riley-Smith, 'Crusading as an act of love', [*History* 65 (1980)] pp 177–8.

with the crucifixion and with the duty of men to follow the way of the cross. [114] Jerusalem and the Holy Land, moreover, were, in an interpretation of Psalm 79, Christ's personal possession—'God, the pagans have invaded your heritage'—and their occupation by the Muslims was an injury to Christ himself. I have pointed out elsewhere that in an age of vendettas appeals to west European knights to go to the aid of their Christian brothers and their spiritual father, who had lost his patrimony, would remind them of their obligation to avenge injury to their kin or feudal lords. [115] There can be little doubt that the crusade was on one level a war of vengeance. The leaders, writing to the pope in September 1098, informed him that

The Turks, who inflicted much dishonour on Our Lord Jesus Christ, have been taken and killed and we Jerusalemites have avenged the injury to the supreme God Jesus Christ. [116]

Baldric of Bourgueil gave in his *Historia* a version of a sermon preached beneath the walls of Jerusalem in the summer of 1099. Of course the words are those of the learned French bishop himself, writing seven or eight years later, but the sentiments might well have been those of less distinguished crusade preachers.

Rouse yourselves, members of Christ's household! Rouse yourselves, knights and footsoldiers and seize firmly that city, our commonwealth! Give heed to Christ, who today is banished from that city and is crucified; and with Joseph of Arimathea take him down from the cross; and lay up in the sepulchre of your hearts an incomparable treasure, that desirable treasure; and forcefully take Christ away from these impious crucifiers. For every time those bad judges, confederates of Herod and Pilate, make sport of and enslave your brothers they crucify Christ. Every time they torment them and kill them they lance Christ's side with Longinus. Indeed they do all these things and, what is worse, they deride and cast reproaches on Christ and our law and they provoke us with rash speech. What are you doing about these things? Is it right for you to listen to these things, to see these things done and not to lament them? I address fathers and sons and brothers and nephews. If an outsider were to strike any of you down would you not avenge your blood-relative? How much more ought you to avenge your God, your father,

---

[114] See Clermont decree in 'Historia peregrinorum' p 170; Hagenmeyer, *Kreuzzugsbriefe* p 164. Riley-Smith, 'Death on the First Crusade' forthcoming.

[115] Riley-Smith, 'Crusading as an act of love' pp 190–2.

[116] Hagenmeyer, *Kreuzzugsbriefe* p 161.

your brother, whom you see reproached, banished from his estates, crucified; whom you hear calling, desolate and begging for aid.[117]

The response of so many crusaders now becomes explicable. If they were being called upon to make good and avenge injuries to Christ which included the occupation of his land four and a half centuries before, why should they not also avenge the crucifixion, an injury to Christ's person? The Jews reported that French crusaders argued that

> We are going to a distant country to make war against mighty kings and are endangering our lives to conquer the kingdoms which do not believe in the crucified one, when it is actually the Jews who murdered and crucified him.[118]

In the minds of the crusaders the crucifixion and the Muslim occupation of Palestine could become confused. In an extraordinary scene in the *Chanson d'Antioche*, the greatest of the vernacular epics of the First Crusade, Christ was pictured hanging on the cross between the two thieves. The good thief commented

> 'It would be most just, moreover, if you should be avenged
> On these treacherous Jews by whom you are so tormented'.
> When Our Lord heard him he turned towards him:
> 'Friend', said he, 'the people are not yet born
> Who will come to avenge me with their steel lances.
> So they will come to kill the faithless pagans
> Who have always refused my commandments.
> Holy Christianity will be honoured by them
> And my land conquered and my country freed.
> A thousand years from today they will be baptized and raised
> And will cause the Holy Sepulchre to be regained and adored.
> .... know certainly
> That from over the seas will come a new race
> Which will take revenge on the death of its father'.

---

[117] Baldric of Bourgueil p 101. Other references to vengeance. Vengeance on behalf of God: Raymond of Aguilers p 134; Orderic Vitalis 5 p 4; William of Malmesbury, *Gesta regum Anglorum*, ed W. Stubbs 2 vols (London 1889) 2 p 429; *La Chanson d'Antioche* 1 pp 20, 22, 23, 30, 34, 36, 53, 56, 148, 473, 513, 517; and see the references in note 119 below. Vengeance on behalf of eastern Christians and pilgrims: Robert of Rheims pp 728, 805; Baldric of Borgueil p 28; Orderic Vitalis 5 p 40. Vengeance on behalf of fellow-crusaders: Albert of Aachen pp 384, 411; Baldric of Bourgueil p 50; *La Chanson d'Antioche* 1 p 331. Divine Vengeance: *Gesta Francorum* pp 17, 54–5; Guibert of Nogent, 'Gesta' pp 192–3, 229; Bartolf of Nangis, 'Gesta Francorum Iherusalem expugnantium', *RHC Occ* 3 p 501; Robert of Rheims pp 830, 868.

[118] 'Mainz Anon' p 99; also Bar Simson p 22; Bar Nathan p 80.

It has been suggested that this scene was added to the *Chanson* in *c*1180 by the poet Graindor, who went on to write of the destruction of Jerusalem by Titus and Vespasian as an earlier act of vengeance for the crucifixion, an idea that echoed the eighth-century legend incorporated in the twelfth-century poem, *La Venjance Nostre Seigneur*.[119] But it was certainly linked to the First Crusade by contemporaries, for the Roman destruction of Jerusalem as an act of vengeance was referred to in a barbarously forged papal encyclical, a piece of crusade propaganda which seems to have emanated from the south French abbey of Moissac.[120] Further evidence for the idea, although in this case sharply distinguishing the crucifixion from the Muslim occupation of Palestine, is provided by the Jewish chronicler Bar Simson, who reported crusaders saying to Jews

> You are the children of those who killed the object of our veneration, hanging him on a tree; and he himself had said: 'There will yet come a day when my children will come and avenge my blood'. We are his children and it is therefore obligatory for us to avenge him since you are the ones who rebel and disbelieve in him.[121]

The Church had an answer, but it was inadequate to deal with the forces it itself had unleashed. As early as 1063, at the time of the planning of a Christian advance on Barbastro in Spain, Pope Alexander II had been obliged to write to the Spanish bishops, forbidding attacks on Jews.

> The reasons (for the use of violence against) Jews and Muslims are certainly dissimilar. For one may justly fight against those who persecute Christians and drive them from the towns and their own sees. The Jews are prepared to serve Christians everywhere.

This letter was included in the canon law collections of Ivo of Chartres and Gratian[122] and its message was developed by later canon lawyers.

---

[119] *La Chanson d'Antioche* 1 pp 25–9, 68, 79, 223, 363, 383. For Graindor's interpolation, see *La Chanson d'Antioche* 2, pp 100, 125, 143. See also L. A. T. Gryting, *The oldest version of the twelfth-century poem, La Venjance Nostre Seigneur* (Michigan 1952).

[120] See A. Gieysztor, 'The Genesis of the Crusades: the Encylical of Sergius IV (1009–1012)', *Medievalia et Humanistica* 5 (1948) pp 21–2; 6 (1948) pp 29–30, 33–4.

[121] Bar Simson p 25.

[122] Ivo of Chartres, 'Decretum', *PL* 161 cols 824–5; Ivo of Chartres, 'Panormia', *PL* 161 col 1311; Gratian, 'Decretum', C. XXIII, q. 8, c. 11. See also Jaffé 1 nos 4532–3.

We ought to persecute Muslims because they exert themselves to invade us and ours, but by no means ought we to persecute the Jews, because they are ready to serve us. In general terms we say that we ought to persecute both Muslims and Jews when they are in revolt. But after we have conquered them we ought not to kill them or force them to the faith.[123] In 1146, when the preaching of a Cistercian monk called Radulph led to more anti-Jewish riots, forced baptisms and massacres in the Rhineland, again against the background of a crusade and calls for vengeance,[124] Saint Bernard tried to make good the damage, arguing that the very existence of the Jews witnessed to the success and therefore the truth of Christianity and that violence was only justified in response to force.[125] These points were repeated over a century later by the Dominican Minister General Humbert of Romans.

There are others who say that, if we ought to rid the world of the Muslims, why do we not do the same to the Jews? . . . I would reply that it has been prophesied that in the end the remnant of the Jews will be converted; as far as the conversion of the Muslims is concerned, no one has any reason to expect it, according to the judgement of Hell, because no man can reach them to preach the Gospel to them. Again, the Jews are so abject, because they are in our power and are our servants and cannot molest us as the Muslims do. Also, if they were removed from the world, what the scriptures say about their rejection would not be so clearly apparent as it is now; and so their existence is an aid to our faith. Therefore they must be tolerated because there is hope that they may be converted, just as one does not immediately cut down a tree from which there is still hope of fruit; because of the fact that we must take care that we are not cruel, and we would be acting very cruelly if we were to kill people subject to us when they were not rising up against us; and because of the help their existence gives to the Christian faith, all of which factors are absent as far as the Muslims are concerned.[126]

[123] *The Summa Parisiensis on the Decretum Gratiani*, ed T. P. McLaughlin (Toronto 1952) p 40. See E.-D. Hehl, *Kirche und Krieg im 12. Jahrhundert* (Stuttgart 1980) p 239.

[124] See Ephraim of Bonn, 'The Book of Remembrance', trans Eidelberg, *The Jews and the Crusaders* pp 121–33; Otto of Freising, *Gesta Friderici* pp 58–9, 63.

[125] Bernard of Clairvaux, *Opera*, edd J. Leclercq *et al*. 8 (Rome 1977) pp 316–17, 320–2.

[126] Humbert of Romans, 'Opus tripartitum', ed E. Brown, *Fasciculus rerum expetendarum et fugiendarum* 2 (London 1960) p 195.

So strictly speaking force could only be used to meet present injury, and that injury had to be apparent and material: military aggression, the occupation of Christian property or revolt. Past acts were relevant only in so far as their consequences still constituted such an injury: the occupation of Jerusalem by the Muslims in 638 was relevant only because Muslims still held it. The crucifixion was clearly not in this category. But in their eagerness to arouse the faithful to what was of its very nature a voluntary exercise—not subject to the demands of feudal service or conscription—preachers, even, it seems, senior ones, were prepared to make use of the idea of vengeance, which they knew would be attractive to their audiences. The trouble with the use of the notion of vengeance was that it involved an abstract injury, 'shame' or 'dishonour', to which any past action, however distant, contributed. The vengeful do not forget; and if called upon to remember the dishonour to Christ of the occupation of Jerusalem 450 years before they were also reminded of the dishonour to Christ of the crucifixion, over a thousand years before. It was useless for churchmen to dwell on the criterion for Christian force of present injury when at the same time they drew the attention of their listeners to their obligations under the custom of the vendetta.

Royal Holloway College University of London

THE LANGUAGE OF PERSECUTION: JOHN OF SALISBURY AND THE EARLY PHASE OF THE BECKET DISPUTE (1163–66)

by JOHN McLOUGHLIN

MEDIEVAL CHURCHMEN who became involved in ecclesiastical disputes or in disputes with secular authority, had access to a rich 'language' of phrase and imagery with which to strengthen their case. This 'language', drawing on Scriptural sources and on standard interpretations of Scripture,[1] could be used to depict almost any dispute as a struggle between good and evil, as the persecution of pious men by the impious, as the renewed persecution of the Church Universal, as a latterday trial and passion of Christ, or as an assault on church liberties.

To polemicists the advantages of this 'language'—a 'language of persecution'—were that it was highly emotive and that it touched on deeply ingrained religious values. It could be used to simplify issues which were in reality highly complex or very unclear. It could transform personal and political disputes into disputes over fundamental principles. This polemical use of the 'language of persecution' can be observed in the earliest phase (1163–64) of the Becket dispute. At that stage Becket's episcopal colleagues, though sensitive to the canonical issues at stake (the trial and punishment of criminous clerks, the dangers of agreeing unconditionally to recognise the customs of the kingdom, appeals to the Holy See), nevertheless regarded the dispute between Becket and the king as a personal one.[2] Alan of Tewkes-

---

[1] By 'standard interpretations' is meant those interpretations which most educated churchmen would have known and accepted. The interpretations which would have been familiar to John of Salisbury and his readers are those contained in the *Glossa ordinaria*, which is discussed in Beryl Smalley, *The study of the Bible in the Middle Ages* (Oxford 1952) pp 46–66. The edition of the Gl[ossa] ord[inaria] which will be cited here is *Biblia sacra cum glossa ordinaria . . . opera et studio Duacensium emendatis* 6 vols (Douai and Antwerp 1617).

[2] The episcopate was divided on most aspects of the dispute. For the debates which took place among the bishops at the councils of Westminster (on the issue of 'criminous clerks') and Clarendon (on whether they should accept unconditionally the customs of the kingdom) see [David] Knowles, [*The*] E[piscopal] C[olleagues of] *Archbishop Thomas Becket* (Cambridge 1951)] pp 57–8, 61–2.

73

bury[3] tells of how the bishops met during the Council of North-
ampton (November 1164) and debated whether Becket ought to
resign. The canonical issues seem to have been discussed but the prevailing view was that expressed by Bartholomew bishop of Exeter,
who argued that the attack by the king was directed at Becket and
not at the rest of the Church.[4] Bartholomew's recommendation
was that Becket should resign for the good of the whole Church.

One of the most urgent tasks facing Becket and his advisers was to
combat this view, not just in the English Church but also in the papal
curia. Throughout 1163 and 1164 Becket sent a series of letters to
Pope Alexander III, emphasising the fundamental issues involved
and making use of themes of persecution. In the letter *Littere con-
solationis* (written after 1 October 1163)[5] Becket developed the
themes of Christ's passion, the comparison of Becket with Christ
and exploited the images of shipwreck and storm, which were to become recurrent motifs in pro-Becket polemic.[6] Writing to the pope
in November 1164, Becket emphasised the theme of assault on the
libertas ecclesiae,[7] identified his own predicament with that of the
pope (who was then in conflict with the emperor Frederick Barbarossa),[8] and then drew a stark contrast between himself and his
fellow-bishops, who, he says, conspiring with the prince and
placing more value on their worldly obligations than on their
spiritual ones.[9] About the same time Becket received a letter from
one of his advisers.[10] In this the themes of tribulation and persecution

---

[3] M[aterials for the history of Thomas] B[ecket Archbishop of Canterbury . . .] edd J. C.
Robertson and J. B. Shepherd 7 vols (RS 1875–85) 2 pp 326–9.

[4] MB 2 p 328: '*Temporis instantia id requirit, maxime cum non sit generalis sed personalis
haec persecutio. Satius est igitur unum caput in parte perclitari, quam totam ecclesiam
Anglicanam inevitabili discrimini exponere.*' For the trustworthiness of this account
note Knowles, *EC* p 72.

[5] MB 5 ep 29. For dating of letters from *MB* I have followed the provisional dating
given in the appendices of Anne Duggan, *Thomas Becket: A textual history of his letters*
(Oxford 1980). For dating and discussion of the letters note Index 2 (Incipits), *ibid.*

[6] The Christ themes: '*multiplicantur injuriae, non nostrae sed Christi—immo quia Christi, eo
magis nostrae*', *MB* 5 p 48; '*Eripitur Jesu Christo quod sanguine suo comparavit; in ipsam Ejus
sortem potestas saecularis manum extendit*' ibid. For an image which combines storm and
shipwreck: '*succendentibus sibi invicem more fluctum procellis, solum nobis videmus
imminere naufragium, nec . . . "Domine salva nos, perimus"*': ibid.

[7] MB 5 ep 74 (*Ad audientiam tuam*) p 138.

[8] Ibid p 138 where Becket hopes *eam vel solam vel maximam meae persecutionis causam
attendas, quod exemplo tuo usus sum.*

[9] Ibid pp 140–1: *Quid etiam si in universam ecclesiam cum offenso nobis principe con-
spirationem fecerunt? Et te, pater sanctissime, suspectio ista poterat attingere.* '*At*',
inquient, '*regis tenebantur ex debito domini.*' Sed illi corporaliter, mihi spiritualiter.

[10] MB 5 ep 59 (*Legitur Constantii principis*), November– December 1164.

74

are fully developed and we can see some of the *loci*[11] which were later to recur throughout the dispute: the Lord will punish those who desire evil; He will bring to nought the 'counsel of Achitophel'; Becket is identified with the 'innocent David', a Scriptural figure for Christ; the king's persecution of the Church is likened to the attack by Antiochus against the Maccabees.

What I intend to do in this paper is, using the 'language of persecution', to show how John of Salisbury was drawn reluctantly into becoming a leading exponent of Becket's cause. John's relationship with Becket has seemed ambivalent to historians.[12] At first John worked as an adviser and agent to Becket, playing an important part in Becket's campaign to obtain the canonisation of Anselm in 1163[13] and then acting as Becket's agent in France at the turn of 1163/64.[14] There is also some evidence that by early 1164 John was regarded as an influential and very formidable adviser to Becket.[15] However, at some point in 1164 or 1165 John withdrew from Becket's household and made vigorous efforts to gain a personal settlement with Henry II.[16] Why should John have distanced himself thus from Becket? One explanation which has not usually been considered is that John, like

---

[11] Divine vengeance: *ibid* pp 107–8: '*Inimici Filii hominis gladii accinti et ad nocendum preparati.*' For the 'counsel of Achitophel' and the 'innocent David', *ibid* p 107: '*consilia Achitophel consociorumque eius adversus David innocentem infatuet.*' For the attack on the Maccabees, *ibid* p 107.

[12] This problem is discussed by Anne Duggan in *The world of John of Salisbury* (Oxford 1984). Duggan's article was still unpublished when this article was written. While she argues for a coolness between John and Becket in the opening phase of the dispute, she does not go so far as to suggest that they differed on policies or tactics. Note also Brooke: 'For reasons which can be guessed, but not fully explained, John refused to be one of Becket's companions' in *The Letters of John of Salisbury* [hereafter *JS Epp.*] edd W. J. Millor and C. N. L. Brooke, 2 vols (*OMT* 1955, 1979) 2 p xix. The best account of John's relationship with Becket is to be found in chapter 4 of [Beryl Smalley, *The*] *Becket conflict [and the schools*] (Oxford 1973)]. Smalley takes a view differing in emphasis from that expressed in this paper: 'That John suffered unwillingly does not prove that he dissented from Becket's cause', *ibid* p 103.

[13] John's role in drafting the *Vita Sancti Anselmi* (*PL* 199 cols 1009–40) and the significance of the campaign to canonise Anselm is discussed by R. W. Southern, *Saint Anselm and his biographer* (Cambridge 1963) pp 336–43.

[14] Note *JS Epp* 2 ep 136 written in early 1164.

[15] William FitzStephen says that John of Salisbury and John of Canterbury were removed from England by Henry to prevent them from giving counsel and aid to Becket (*MB* 3 p 46). Placed in the context of the Council of Clarendon this passage must be incorrect; see *JS Epp* 2 p xx. However it may be that FitzStephen is recording the vague recollection that very early in the dispute the two Johns were seen as closely identified with Becket.

[16] For the withdrawal from Becket's household see *JS Epp* 2 ep 139 (probably 1164–65) p 23 end: '*sciatisque pro certo quia michi propositum est ut non sim de cetero curialis; et*

the English bishops, regarded the dispute as 'personal', in the sense that it was a breakdown in relations between archbishop and king, and that although there were fundamental issues involved—such as *libertas ecclesiae* and the authority of the pope—nevertheless other churchmen should not be dragged in. John expresses the idea in the *Historia pontificalis* which was probably written between 1164 and 1166.[17] In a thinly veiled attack on Henry II, John suggests a contrast between Archbishop Theobald's two periods of exile and Becket's exile:

> On neither occasion, though he [Theobald] numbered the king and his counsellors among his bitterest enemies, was one of the archbishop's friends or supporters proscribed or driven into exile rather than remain in their own country. The archbishop alone suffered the miseries of exile and the pains of proscription; his friends were free to come and go as they wished and even, if they chose, to bring him material assistance for his needs.[18]

In his attack on Henry, John reveals his view that the dispute ought to be a 'personal' one and that the archbishop alone ought to bear the brunt of the struggle.

My suggestion is that as the dispute escalated in 1166 John was compelled to abandon this view and to commit himself fully to the Becket cause. At the conference of Angers (Easter 1166) John's attempts to gain a personal reconciliation with Henry were sharply rebuffed and it became clear to John that there was no realistic chance of a settlement for himself.[19] In the summer of 1166 Becket polarised the dispute by threatening to excommunicate Henry and by actually excommunicating several of his officials.[20] Becket's actions forced English churchmen to opt for one side or the other. The bishops, under some royal pressure, opted for the king, while John, re-affirming his basic loyalties and his commitment to the liberties of the Church, opted for Becket.

hoc ipsum bene novit dominus Cantuariensis, a cuius me subtraxi consortio, sed nec fidem subtraho nec caritatem.' John's search for a personal reconciliation can be seen in epp 137–9, 150–1.

[17] *Historia pontificalis* ed Marjorie Chibnall (London 1956). For discussion of the dating see pp xxiv–xxx.

[18] *Ibid* p 42. Cf Herbert of Bosham's account of the mass expulsions: *MB* 3 p 359.

[19] For John's comments on the failure of the conference at Angers see *JS Epp* 2 ep 164 (?May–June 1166) pp 84–7, and ep 167 (early June 1166) p 99 (*in profectione versus Andegavim . . . simile subire dispendium.*) Cf *JS Epp* 2 p xxvii.

[20] For John's account of excommunications at Vézelay and the appeal by the bishops see *JS Epp* 2 ep 168 pp 108–115.

The language of persecution

This interpretation would account for John's efforts to gain a personal settlement, as well as accounting for the scraps of evidence which suggest that John was offering advice which differed sharply from that of Becket's closest advisers. In the early phase of the dispute John seems to have been more concerned with safeguarding the privileges and possessions of Canterbury than with fighting the Constitutions of Clarendon.[21] In a well-known letter written to Becket in January 1165 (Ep. 144), John urged Becket to stop vexing himself with the legal aspects of the dispute and, instead, to pray, meditate and to read the Psalms and Gregory's *Moralia*.[22] As Beryl Smalley[23] has pointed out, John went further: he entreated Becket towards the end of the letter to pay more attention to protecting the possessions of Canterbury from encroachment by other bishops and he suggested that Becket obtain from the pope 'letters patent that no encroachment upon the church of Canterbury at this crisis can harm it in time to come'.[24] Six months later (in the late summer of 1165) John was once again touching on the Canterbury theme.[25] After discussing the crisis facing the universal church and identifying Becket's situation with the pope's, John suddenly switched direction:

> If the protectors (*patroni*) of the holy Church of Canterbury are with you—and it is well to keep them always in our minds—under God this storm will be duly stayed . . .

If we look at the *Historia pontificalis*, an essential source for John's attitudes at this period, we find evidence of the same concern with Canterbury's interests. In describing the conflict between Theobald and Stephen in 1148–49,[26] the focus of John's attention was not on the rights of the papacy or on the general *libertas ecclesiae* but on the failure of the English bishops to make the king restore confiscated goods to Theobald and provide compensation of the injuries suffered by him.

---

[21] John's concerns with the interests and possessions of Canterbury would have been sharpened by his years in the household of Archbishop Theobald. Note John's role in drafting letters for Theobald in 1160–61 when Theobald—then seriously ill and close to death—was seeking to put his affairs in order. (See *JS Epp* 1 the series of letters epp 116–135; see *ibid* Appendix 5) For an interesting presentation of John's loyalties to Canterbury, see Hans Liebeschütz, *Mediaeval Humanism in the life and writings of John of Salisbury* (London 1950) pp 101–03.

[22] *JS Epp* 2 pp 32–5.

[23] *Becket conflict* p 103.

[24] *JS Epp* 2 p 35.

[25] *Ibid* ep 152 pp 56–7.

[26] *Historia pontificalis* pp 45–6.

To argue my interpretation I shall compare the letters written in 1164 and 1165 with those written in 1166. The sample used consists of all John's letters which can be dated to between early 1164 and 1 October 1166. The initial date is that of the earliest dateable letter (Ep. 136) which John wrote during the Becket dispute. The final date is that of a letter (Ep. 184) to Gerard Pucelle. As a cut-off point it is somewhat arbitrary and has been chosen simply because John's shift in view had already occurred by that stage. There is an imbalance in the surviving evidence: only nine letters can be assigned to the period 1164– 65,[27] while twenty-seven belong to the year 1166.[28] The imbalance means that particular care has to be taken in assessing shifts in John's attitudes. It also means that detailed attention will have to be paid to the earlier set of letters. In addition to these we have also to consider twenty-six letters to which no certain date can be assigned.[29]

The letters 1164–65

Of the nine letters which can be assigned with reasonable assurance to the years 1164–65, five are concerned mainly with John's efforts to obtain a personal reconciliation,[30] three are addressed to Becket[31] and one is to John's half-brother, Robert son of Egidia.[32]

In the 'reconciliation letters' John naturally avoids the 'language of persecution'. The one allusion he does make to persecution is entirely neutral. In a letter to Robert, prior of Merton, he expresses the hope that the Lord 'may soften the anger of the king who has persecuted me and still persecutes me without occasion.'[33] There is no reference here to general persecution of the Church.

As we might expect, John's letters to Becket are rather different in viewpoint. Though distancing himself from Becket, John accepted that Becket was struggling for *libertas ecclesiae*. At the beginning of 1164 John wrote to Becket saying that in looking for support in the papal *curia*, 'It is in your favour that you are afflicted (*tribulamini*) for the liberty of the Church.'[34] But within the letter this remark is iso-

[27] *JS Epp* 2 epp 136–9, 144–5, 150–2.
[28] *Ibid* epp 158–84.
[29] *Ibid* epp 141, 146, 156, 202–4, 210 and the letters listed in nn 46–7 below.
[30] *Ibid* epp 137–9, 150–1.
[31] *Ibid* epp 136, 144, 152.
[32] *Ibid* ep 145.
[33] *Ibid* ep 151 p 51.
[34] *Ibid* p 11.

lated and is unsupported by any of the themes from the 'language of persecution', such as divine vengeance, the persecution of the Church, or the passion of Christ.

In the next extant letter from John to Becket the 'language of persecution' is also absent but there is an emphasis on personal tribulation. This is the well-known Ep. 144 mentioned already. Here John depicts the period of adversity as a spiritual test, a means of self-improvement.[35] A few months later (summer 1165) John makes the same point when writing to Bartholomew of Exeter: 'the exile has undoubtedly been profitable to the archbishop of Canterbury both for his learning (*ad litteraturum*) and his character'.[36]

It is in Ep. 152, written to Becket in the late summer of 1165 that we catch a glimpse of the persecution theme. But even this is very circumscribed. After outlining the successes of the emperor Frederick Barbarossa against the papacy, John suddenly makes comments that apply with equal force to the papacy and to Becket:

> In such a storm I consider nothing more salutary for us than to fly to Christ's mercy, who, even if He is a second time crucified, is not killed, but will have his executioners more fearfully crucified in vengeance for His dove.[37]

This is the earliest extant reference to the themes of crucifixion and divine vengeance and is linked to the notion that Becket is fighting for fundamental principles. For a few lines later John remarks that 'we' have stood for the practice of divine law (*lex divina*). It is conceivable that John was already elaborating these themes in letters now lost. But it seems unlikely. In the first place, John introduces the themes of crucifixion and divine vengeance in the context of the crisis facing the entire Church: the schism and the struggle between emperor and pope. John had not yet reached the stage of applying persecution themes directly to Becket. Secondly, about the same time John was writing to Bartholomew of Exeter,[38] depicting the exile entirely in terms of adversity and personal tribulation and not in terms of persecution.

There is however a letter which may have been written in 1165 and which contains an elaborate treatment of persecution themes. This

---

[35] *Ibid* pp 32–5. The idea of persecution as a spiritual and beneficial test was a commonplace; thus Jerome: *Persecutio non ad negationem credentium, sed ad probationem pertinet et coronam* (*PL* 24 col 187).

[36] *JS Epp* 2 ep 150 pp 48–9.

[37] *Ibid* p 55.

[38] see n 36 above.

letter (Ep. 145) to John's half-brother Robert is dated by Brooke as 'probably 1165' though it may well have been written as late as the summer of 1166.[39] The uncertainty about the date is tantalising but cannot be resolved. In the letter John thanks Robert for sending him a gold ring set with a sapphire and carrying the inscription: *Christus vincit, Christus regnat, Christus imperat.* The words are drawn from the *Laudes regiae*[40] used in the coronation of emperors and kings and they immediately arouse the suspicion that the 'gift' with its topical inscription might be a fictional device to criticise the enemies of the Church: Henry II and Frederick Barbarossa. John's criticism of the emperor is explicit and trenchant: Frederick is not truly emperor but a schismatic 'striving by force and fraud' to overthrow God's designs and to take the imperial dignity from Christ.[41] 'He is eager to abolish the name of Christ from the Empire but as the inscription of your gift tells us, Christ's name alone endureth for ever.'[42] In contrast the criticism of Henry is much more vague. John draws on the 'language of persecution' to make comments that apply with equal force to the pope's predicament and to Becket's. Commenting on the phrase *Christus regnat* he says:

> it has . . . attributed to Christ His kingdom, so as to teach those who have been through the hazards of strife and hardship with Christ that they will reign with Him; and that his adversaries, when justice is turned to judgement, are to be destroyed with double disorder and destruction.[43]

There then follows what could possibly be interpreted as a critical contrast between Christ the King and Henry:

> The King's [Christ's] honour loveth judgement and his eyes (since they love it) look upon equity; for where our love is, there is our eye.[44]

If this is indeed an attack on Henry II its vagueness would have been dictated by John's sense of caution. The interception of a letter explicitly attacking Henry would have placed Robert in great danger, especially if it were sent in 1165, a year of massive expulsions and widespread intimidation of Becket's supporters, their friends and

---

[39] The letter mentions '*fraterculus*', evidently John's brother Richard who was probably in England until May or June 1166; see *JS Epp* 2 p xxv.
[40] *JS Epp* 2 ep 145 n 1.
[41] *Ibid* p 41.
[42] *Ibid.*
[43] *Ibid* p 39.
[44] *Ibid.*

families. It is arguable that in more favourable circumstances John might have expressed his views more forcefully. But this argument cannot be taken for granted, for even in Ep. 152 written to Becket John avoids making a direct attack on Henry, preferring to suggest parallels between Becket's situation and the pope's.

John's Ep. 152 and perhaps his letter to Robert—if it was written in 1165—indicate that John thought of the dispute at this stage in terms of Christ offering succour to the exiles and bringing vengeance on Becket's enemies and on the enemies of the Church Universal. But these are themes of consolation and tribulation, very different to the Christ themes which John was to use during 1166. For then John compared Becket's adversity with the trial and passion of Christ and identified Becket's cause as Christ's cause.

The letters without an exact date

The twenty-six letters[45] to which no exact date can be assigned do nothing to challenge the impression which we have gained from the letters discussed above. Of the undateable letters, seventeen make no reference to the 'language of persecution';[46] two contain Christ imagery but not in relation to the Becket dispute;[47] one gives a glimpse of the 'language of persecution' when John refers to himself as 'an exile for God and the freedom of the Church.'[48] The remaining six contain more significant allusions to persecution.

In Ep. 146 to Robert son of Egidia, John alludes to 1 Peter 4: 15–16, which he was to use twice again in the spring and autumn of 1166:

> You know St Peter's saying: 'If any man suffer as a Christian, let him be not ashamed, but let him glorify God' . . . You are assured, I take it, that our little brother is not 'suffering as a murderer or a blasphemer or a seeker after other men's goods'[49]

Likewise in a letter to Master Ralph de Beaumont (Ep. 210) John makes a passing allusion to Christ imagery. After several oblique references to the Becket dispute, John expresses his hope that Ralph

---

[45] See n 29 above.

[46] *JS Epp* 2 epp 140, 142, 147–9, 153–5, 195, 201, 208–9, 211, 267, 268. (Brooke does not assign a date but there is reason to think that it was written in 1166 or later—I intend to discuss the dating of this and other letters in my dissertation, *The friendship circles of John of Salisbury* Trinity College Dublin) pp 270–1.

[47] *JS Epp* 2 pp 206–07.

[48] *Ibid* p 27.

[49] *Ibid* pp 41–3.

will not lose faith (*non diffidis*) in the kingdom of Christ (*de regno Christi*).[50]

In Ep. 156 to Robert prior to Merton, John uses a string of allusions to tribulation and persecution:[51]

> I am beaten with these scourges, and sharper scourges still—and I know not the cause of the beating.

> If it means that God of His mercy would have me suffer for justice's sake, I esteem myself most happy

> I profess I have kept faith with God's Church, have faithfully obeyed my archbishop.

Three letters to Master Ralph of Lisieux (Epp. 202–4) contain sharper and more polemical references to persecution. In Ep. 202 John depicts the exiles as fighting for church liberties, justice and the law of God.[52] Later in the letter the Christ imagery is brought out:[53]

> Let them say what they will: let them boast that they have prevailed over the Lord's anointed in their vanity . . . The ears of those who hissed and laughed at Christ's poor shall ring with the hisses and outcry of the faithful.

In the passage which contains these two excerpts, John deploys two other themes from the 'language of persecution': vengeance against the enemies of God and the vision of the world as transitory and vain:[54]

> Destruction is waiting at the gate for those whose joy is for a moment, whose glory is fire, dung and a worm.

In Ep. 203, to Master Ralph, John depicts the exiles as 'the household of faith (*domesticis fidei*) . . . the scattered children of Israel'.[55] In the third letter to Master Ralph (Ep. 204) John draws a sharp contrast between those who suffer for the word of Christ (*pro verbo Christi*) and the evil men who, fawning on the world (*adulantium mundo*) prefer to 'rule in the counsel of the wicked with earthly princes'.[56]

Of the twenty-six undateable letters, only those addressed to

---

[50] John contrasts (*ibid* p 338–9) those 'whom the world, showing no gratitude to God, persecutes without cause' and 'those who seemed to be the pillars of the church . . .' The reference to the kingdom of Christ: p 340–1.

[51] *Ibid* p 63.

[52] *Ibid* p 297: 'But He who sought out the mean and sick and permitted us to make profession of justice and witnesses of the law . . . He gives us boldness to hope'.

[53] *Ibid* p 299.

[54] *Ibid.*

[55] *Ibid* pp 300–01.

[56] *Ibid* pp 304–5.

Master Ralph of Lisieux show a trenchant and polemical use of the 'language of persecution'. There seems to be no way of dating these three letters, but in tone they differ greatly from the letters which we can assign with certainty to 1164–65; they have more in common with those written in 1166.

The letters of 1166

The sudden increase in extant letters which occurs in 1166 appears to reflect John's growing commitment as an adviser to Becket. It seems likely that, with the upsurge of political activity in the summer of 1166, John was actually writing more letters than before. But even if this were not so, he was at least taking greater care to preserve them. The detailed and sometimes very lengthy letters sent to Bartholomew of Exeter and Becket[57] suggest that he was now fulfilling the role of active adviser and apologist for the Becket circle.

Of the twenty-seven letters written at this stage, all but six contain some reference to persecution.[58] Sometimes the reference is very slight. Thus in Ep. 170 (late June 1166) John writes to Baldwin archdeacon of Totnes and speaks of the misfortunes of exile and the abandonment by people whom John had regarded as old friends. At the end of all this, John asks Baldwin to pray

> that our faith fail not, that we do nothing under this storm to offend the Lord, but, as He alone can, make profit even out of temptation. Indeed, He has made a beginning: He has granted us a zeal in suffering for justice.[59]

More often the themes of persecution receive greater elaboration, and in some letters (for instance Ep. 168 to Bartholomew of Exeter) the whole text is keenly polemical and infused with the 'language of persecution'.

The bulk of letters from 1166 were written during the summer, after Becket had passed sentence of excommunication against several of Henry's officials and after the English bishops had lodged their appeal against Becket. The polemic in these letters is directed mainly against the bishops and to a lesser extent against the king.

What then were the main features of John's polemic? The most dramatic and most often quoted aspect of his polemic is the series of

[57] To Bartholomew: *ibid* ep 171 and the lengthy epp 168 and 174. To Becket: epp 173, 179 and the lengthy 175–6.
[58] The exceptions are *ibid* epp 158, 160, 162, 166, 170, 182.
[59] *Ibid* p 123.

attacks against Gilbert Foliot, bishop of London.[60] By identifying Gilbert as Doeg the Edomite, who instigated the attack on Nob, the village of the priests (I Kings (I Samuel) 22), John casts Gilbert into the role of persecutor of the priesthood.[61] There is also the implication that Gilbert is the enemy of Christ, for the standard interpretation of *Doeth Idumaeus* was that as an adversary of King David he prefigured the enemies of Christ: Judas and Antichrist.[62] Further, by describing Gilbert's political activities as the 'counsel of Achitophel' John seeks to portray Gilbert as a false friend and adviser.[63]

However the core of John's polemic is not the colourful and occasional attacks on Foliot, but the more sustained presentation of Becket's cause as Christ's cause, the equation of Becket's adversity with Christ's passion and by extension the presentation of Becket's opponents as the perfidious Jews who crucified Christ.

Medieval writers had two main ways of defining and describing persecution: first in terms of the ten great persecutions waged by the Roman emperors against the early Church;[64] secondly, in terms of the passion of Christ. John used only the second, the Christ-centred method,[65] which, as we have seen, was already being exploited by Becket in 1163 and 1164.

The Christ theme is most highly developed in the letters to Becket. In advising and consoling him, John speaks of 'our enemies . . . or rather the enemies of Christ and the Church'.[66] In Ep. 176 John draws a graphic picture of the followers of Christ standing up to the threats of tyrants . . . the cowardice of a judge . . . the

---

[60] For instance David Knowles, *Thomas Becket* (London 1970) p 114.

[61] *JS Epp* 2 ep 175 pp 152–3, 156–7; ep 181 pp 202–3.

[62] Note for instance Cassiodorus: *Quapropter per nomen Doech Idumaei jure Antichristus intelligitur . . . (PL* 70 col 373 A)

[63] *JS Epp* 2 ep 175 pp 152–3, 156–7.

[64] Thus Orosius in *Liber Historiarum* 6.26: *Decem persecutiones a Nerone usque ad Maximianum Ecclesia Christi passa est (PL* 31 col 1130A). Cf Gerhoch of Reichersberg *In Psalmum XXXIX: deinde in passionibus martirum, quibus a Nerone usque ad Maximianum et Diocletianum decies repetitis quasi per X cornua bestia illa fuit terribilis,* MGH Lib 3 p 435 lines 12–4. Cf Gerhoch *In Psalmum XXIX, ibid* p 418 lines 10–12.

[65] During the entire Becket dispute John makes only one reference to persecution by a Roman emperor: 'Peter and Paul would have escaped Nero's sword, and not even made him their enemy, if they had not preached against men's pleasures and wrongdoings.' (*JS Epp* 2 ep 187 pp 246–7). There is one indirect reference to Henry II as being like the emperors Titus and Vespasian, who were not among the persecutors of the early church but who had repressed the Jewish people with great cruelty. See ep 173 pp 136–7; the allusion to Psalm 79: 14–15 (80: 13–14) and the *Gl ord* on this.

[66] *JS Epp* 2 ep 175 p 165.

avarice and inconstancy of those who seek at every turn what is their own—that is the things of the flesh, not the things of Christ Jesus.[67]

In the same letter John alludes to Psalm 2: 2, saying:
Has the king ever abandoned intercourse with the excommunicate? Have not the bishops and almost all the clergy stood by him against the Lord and His anointed (*adversus Dominum et adversus christum eius*).[68]

Psalm 2 was traditionally given a Christological interpretation. The *Glossa Ordinaria*, quoting the Pseudo-Bede,[69] notes that in the early part of the Psalm the prophet speaks *de Iudaeis propter Christi passionem*. In the glosses on Psalm 2, the *reges terrae et principes* who stand against the Lord, are variously interpreted as the persecutors of Christ (Herod, Annas and Caiphas, Pilate) and as 'those kings who stand up against the Lord'.

In Ep. 179 there is a passage linking Becket with Christ:
He [Christ] is still prepared to die for the humble and carry the shame of the Cross. This seems to be the right course because those who persecuted you and Christ in you are said to have lost some of the king's favour . . . Christ will triumph.[70]

The image of the Church as the bride of Christ is found also. In Ep. 180 to Walter de Insula it is linked to a cluster of Christ-references.[71] John notes that if the 'king returns to himself he will appease his Lord, the church's bridegroom'. Then there follows a warning: if the king despises the *exules et proscriptos Dei* because they are poor, he should remember that Christ protects such men (*talium patronus est Christus*). After listing several persons who were destroyed by God, John asserts in an echo of I Peter 4: 15–16, that the Becket exiles suffer not as criminals but as *Christiani*. The image of Henry waging war on Christ is brought out in a letter to Bartholomew: 'cares chafe him on every side but he presses on with the war which he wages on Christ and the Church.'[72]

---

[67] *Ibid* p 167.
[68] *Ibid* p 175.
[69] *PL* 93 col 489. For the identification of the Pseudo-Bede as Manegold of Lautenbach see the general remarks and references in Smalley, *Study of the Bible* pp 48–9.
[70] *JS Epp* 2 p 191.
[71] *Ibid* pp 194–5.
[72] *Ibid* ep 168 p 109.

The counterpart of the Christ theme was to depict Becket's opponents as the persecutors of Christ. For this, however, the references are fewer and less explicit. The English bishops are occasionally described as 'high priests' (*principes sacerdotium*).[73] There is a curious reference in which Becket is likened to the 'penitent thief' who was crucified alongside Christ and who was mocked by the *perfidi Iudaei*.[74] The 'penitent thief' must be an allusion to Becket's role in making exactions from the Church for the Toulouse campaign in 1159. For during 1166 this was one of the topics raised by Becket's opponents to discredit Becket's stance as a defender of church liberties.[75] The *perfidi Iudaei* are, John indicates, Becket's enemies within the English Church.[76]

In Ep. 173 to Becket, John speaks of the English bishops as cheering every wrong done to the churches, *dicentes 'Euge, euge'*[77]—an echo of Psalm 34(35): 21 which reads: *Et dilataverunt super me os suum: Dixerunt Euge, Euge! viderunt oculi mei*. In the *Glossa Ordinaria*, the word *dilataverunt* is defined as 'openly crying "Crucify, crucify."' The *Glossa* also contains a cross-reference to Matthew 27: 42 where the priests, scribes and elders jeered Christ, challenging Him to descend from the cross if He were truly the King of Israel.

The identification of Becket with Christ and of Becket's opponents with the Jews, is complemented by the array of other themes drawn from the 'language of persecution': divine vengeance;[78] the identification of Henry with Frederick Barbarossa[79] (and the accompanying implication that Henry and the English bishops were attacking the Church Universal just like the German schismatics); setting

---

[73] *Ibid* ep 178 p 186.

[74] *Ibid* ep 163 p 84: '*Ridet ad haec prudentia carnis, et perfidorum vocibus Iudaeorum insultat et maledicit ei qui cum Christo pendet in ligno.*'

[75] John counteracts these accusations: 'Someone will say that the imposition of the tax and harrying of churches is to be laid wholly at the door of the king's chancellor . . .' *ibid* ep 168 pp 105–7.

[76] *Nunquid enim clerus institutus est ut comedens* etc, *ibid* p 84.

[77] *Ibid* p 134.

[78] For instance, *ibid* ep 169 pp 118–9: 'But wait awhile, and in time they will be held in regard (*in tempore erit respectus eorum*).' This reference to Wisdom 3: 6 is explained in *Gl ord* as *in diei iudicii*. The next sentence in John's letter is more direct: 'In the meantime there is no peace for the wicked' etc.

[79] For instance *JS Epp* 2 ep 181 p 201: 'The king puts his trust in the Emperor and in the hope that he will capture the pope as is foretold to him by the prophets of Baal, who see false things and foolish, because they speak not from the Lord.'

The language of persecution

In the summer of 1166 John crossed some kind of boundary in his relations with Becket. From the start he had always been sympathetic to Becket's struggle for *libertas ecclesiae*; but he had taken the view that the struggle should be fought and settled by Henry and Becket; he withdrew from Becket's *familia* and proferred advice that was very different from that which Becket was receiving from his own aides. It was during the intense months of 1166, when churchmen were being forced to declare their loyalties, that John opted for Becket and began to exploit the 'language of persecution' to console and counsel the Becket circle, to reprove the English bishops and to encourage sympathisers, like those in Exeter, to stand firm.

Trinity College, Dublin

---

[80] For instance, *ibid* ep 174 pp 144–7 are combined the themes of divine vengeance and historical scale. After listing Cain, Pharaoh, Adoni-bezek and Ham as examples of the dictum 'Wherewithal a man sinneth, by the same also shall he be punished.' John remarks: 'in every age and in every race, if one considers the history of divine providence, one will clearly recognise that there has always been some similarity between crime and punishment.'

[81] The blessedness of suffering for justice, a *locus* drawn from Matthew 5: 10 and I Peter 3: 14 is to be found in *ibid* ep 161 pp 78–9: *patimini propter iusticiam beati eritis* and occurs at a later stage in ep 273 p 572 and ep 298 p 696. The theme of *pro iusticia pati* (with no mention of beautitude) is found at pp 250, 258, 296, 302–3.

THE MOHAMMETAN AND IDOLATRY

by JENNIFER BRAY

THE ANACHRONISTIC ascription of membership of the Moslem faith to the persecutors of Christians in the period before the Peace of the Church appears in Anglo-Norman hagiography in the late twelfth century, or early thirteenth,[1] and in English lives later in the thirteenth century.[2] It may be, at least in part, the result of the corruption in meaning of a derivative of the word *Mahomet*, found in Anglo-Norman as *mahumez* in the early twelfth century[3] and in English by the end of the same century in the form of *maumez*,[4] idols. The confusion in identification was made possible by the attribution of the rôle of the Roman officials to the Moslems—both groups martyred Christians in large numbers—and by an association of practices and qualities based on the opposition, real or alleged, of both Romans and Moslems to the Christian faith.

Accusations specifically of idolatry were of little importance in official crusade propaganda as it is recorded.[5] The early accounts of the words of Pope Urban at Clermont include references to the appropriation of Christian land by the Moslems, the destruction and defilement of churches and the death or forced apostasy of Christ-

---

[1] Chardri, *La Vie des set Dormanz*, B. Merrilees, *Anglo-Norman Text Society* 35 (London 1977) pp 7, 41.

[2] ['St Katherine,' *The] S[outh] E[nglish] L[egendary*, C. D'Evelyn and A. J. Mill,] *EETS OS* 236 [(London 1956 reprinted 1967)] pp 539, 541, 542.

[3] Philippe de Thaon, *Le Livre de Sibile*, H. Shields, *Anglo-Norman Text Society* 37 (London 1979) p 78.

[4] *Seinte Marharete, [þe Meiden ant Martyr*, F. M. Mack, *EETS OS* 193 (London 1934)] p 2. The period of composition most recently suggested for this work is 1190–1200, possibly a few years later: E. J. Dobson, *The Origins of 'Ancrene Wisse'* (Oxford 1976) p 166. The same word, in the form of *mahomet*, is found with the same meaning in medieval French, and examples of the same confusion of Moslem and Roman persecutors exist within the same period: 'La Vie de Sainte Catherine d'Alexandrie as contained in the Paris Manuscript *La Clayette*,' H. A. Todd, *PMLA* 15 (1900) pp 19, 62; 'Les Vies de Sainte Catherine d'Alexandrie en ancien Français, 2, La Vie du MS. 948 du Tours,' E. C. Fawtier-Jones, *Romania* 58 (1932) p 212.

[5] 'The beliefs and customs of the infidels' do not appear to have been a matter of acute concern to ecclesiastical authorities in the early stages of crusade propaganda. Compare C. M. Jones, 'The conventional Saracen of the Songs of Geste,' *Speculum* 17 (1942) pp 203–4.

ians,[6] points also found in the letter of the Emperor Alexius to Robert I of Flanders.[7]

The early chronicles of the first two crusades are remarkable for the lack of interest evinced in the beliefs of the opponents.

This is true, and nobody can deny it, that if only they had stood firm in the faith of Christ and holy Christendom, and had been willing to accept One God in Three Persons, and had believed rightly and faithfully that the Son of God was born of a virgin mother, that he suffered, and rose from the dead and ascended in the sight of his disciples into Heaven, and sent them in full measure the comfort of the Holy Ghost, and that he reigns in Heaven and earth, you could not find stronger or braver or more skilful soldiers.[8]

It was enough that the Moslems were not Christian.

The name of the prophet is found in various recognisable forms— *Machumet*,[9] *Mathomus*[10]—and so is a later, derivative form of his name for his followers,[11] but neither is common and the latter is rare. Specifically sectarian terms are much less frequently used than terms of racial identification,[12] like 'Turks, Arabs, Saracens,'[13] which do not appear to be differentiated, or expressions of disapprobation; *pagani*,[14] *gens prorsus a Deo aliena*,[15] *barbaræ nationes*.[16]

There are general references to polytheism in the early chronicles. An example of this is found in the speech attributed to the amir after the defeat of his forces at the battle of Ascalon. This was clearly popular for it is found in several compositions. 'O spirits of the gods!

[6] R[obert the] M[onk, *Historia Iherosolimitana*,] *RHC Occ* 3 p 721; F[ulcher of] C[hartres, *Historia Hierosolimitana (1095–1127)*, H. Hagenmeyer (Heidelberg 1913)] pp 33–4; D. C. Munro, 'The speech of Pope Urban II at Clermont, 1095,' *American Historical Review* 11 (1906) pp 231–42; J. Riley-Smith, *What were the Crusades?* (London 1977) pp 22–3.

[7] *Die Kreuzzugsbriefe aus den Jahren 1088–1100: Eine Quellensammlung zur Geschichte des ersten Kreuzzuges*, H. Hagenmeyer (Innsbruck 1901) pp 130–6.

[8] G[esta] F[rancorum et aliorum Hierosolimitanorum, R. Hill (London 1962)] p 21.

[9] *GF* p 96.

[10] *RM, RHC Occ* 3 pp 788, 877.

[11] W[illiam of] T[yre, continuation, *Historia Rerum in Partibus Transmarinis Gestarum*,] *RHC Occ* 2, p 524.

[12] G. Constable, 'The Second Crusade as seen by Contemporaries,' *Traditio* 9 (1953) p 213 n 2.

[13] *GF*, p 19. See also *RM, RHC Occ* 3 p 788; Ekkehard of Aura, *Hierosolimita*, H. Hagenmeyer (Tübingen 1877) p 79.

[14] *FC* p 143.

[15] *RM, RHC Occ* 3 p 721.

[16] B[audri of] D[ol, *Historia Jerosolimitana*,] *RHC Occ* 4, p 13.

The Mohammetan and Idolatry

... I swear by Mohammed and by the glory of all the gods that I will never raise another army . . .!'[17] Robert the Monk's account of the invocation is more elaborate and the infernal gods are also included.[18] The freedom with which changes were made in the powers allegedly invoked suggests that the section appealed to chroniclers because it was felt to be dramatically appropriate, not because it furnished precise information on the nature of Moslem belief. There was probably no clear distinction between polytheism and idolatry: the second was often but not always assumed to be implied by the first.

A definite statement that the opponents venerated idols, *simulacra*, is to be found in one of the accounts of Urban's speech.[19] There is also an incident involving an image of Mahommed in a later work, an incident which occurred when Tancred entered the Temple. Inside the building he saw an idol of gold, richly adorned. When he was informed by Moslem bystanders that this was an image of Mahommed he urged his men to join him in hacking it into the pieces which he then distributed to them: '*de vili factum est pretiosum*'.[20] This is closer in content and spirit to the *chansons de geste* than to the early crusade chronicles.

More frequent and at least as dramatic are the references to polytheism, idols and idolatry in the *Chanson de Roland*, now dated about 1100.[21] In the first laisse one finds the association of *Mahumet* and *Appolin*,[22] later frequent companions, and the breaking and defiling of the idols[23] which became a standard feature. The *Chanson de Guillaume* does not make the same indubitable references to idols but does list numerous gods.[24]

The theme of martyrdom is constantly reiterated in the chronicles. In the references to the sufferings of the eastern Christians at the hands of the Moslems, found in accounts of Urban's speech, in the

[17] *GF* p 96.
[18] *RM, RHC Occ* 3 pp 877–8.
[19] The clearest example of this is to be found in *BD, RHC Occ* 4 p 13. See also [L. and J. Riley-Smith, *The*] *Crusades: Idea and Reality*, [(London 1981)] p 50.
[20] Tudebod, imitated and continued, *Historia Peregrinorum euntium Jerusolymam ad Liberandum Sanctum Sepulchrum de Potestate Ethnicorum, RHC Occ* 3 p 222.
[21] [*The Song of*] *Roland* [*: An Analytical Edition*, G. J. Brault, 2 vols (London 1978)] 1 pp 5–6.
[22] *Ibid* 2 p 2.
[23] *Ibid* 2 pp 156–8.
[24] [*Recherches sur la Chanson de*] *Guillaume* [*: Études accompagnées d'une Édition*, J. Wathelet-Willem, *Bibliothèque de la Faculté de Philosophie et Lettres de l'Université de Liège* 210, 2 vols (Paris 1975)] 2 pp 955, 1045. References are to the critical text.

'*angarias patitur indignas genus electum*',[25] there is a suggestion that their deaths were those of martyrs, but in the exhortation to those present to go to the defence of the Holy Land this is explicit and unmistakable: '*Pulchrum sit vobis mori in illa civitate pro Christo, in qua Christus pro vobis mortuus est.*'[26] They will either return victorious '*vel sanguine uestro purpurati, perenne bravium adepiscemini.*'[27] The *Gesta Dei per Francos* refers to those who fell in the Holy Land as having received the gift of martyrdom.[28]

The *Chanson de Roland* is similarly imbued with the sense of martyrdom. When Turpin addresses the Christian knights before the battle he states:

> Asoldrai vos pur vo3 anmes guarir.
>
> Se vos mure3, estere3 sein3 martirs,
>
> Sieges avrez el greignor parëis. [29]

Roland, when death is near, remarks, '*Ci recevrums martyrie*'.[30]

Here, I would suggest is the causal connection between the Moslem of the crusaders and the Roman of the hagiographer. Mass martyrdom, particularly that of the Diocletian persecutions, was associated with idolatry, which is linked to polytheism, and the suffering of the martyrs was usually portrayed as the direct result of their refusal to honour the idols. The martyrdom of the occasional individual by the Norsemen or the Germanic tribes—I omit Ursula and the eleven thousand virgins—or the Jews did not make the same emotional impact or create the same associations. My hypothesis is that the Roman persecutions, through the veritable idolatry of the polytheistic persecutors, created a lasting association between widespread persecution for the faith and the practice of idolatry, the essential point of conflict in the *legenda*, and that the beliefs and practices of the Moslems were automatically assumed to be idolatrous

[25] *WT, RHC Occ* 1i p 40.

[26] *BD, RHC Occ* 4 p 15. See also *GF* pp 1–2, and Riley-Smith, *What were the Crusades?* pp 32–3.

[27] *BD, RHC Occ* 4 p 15.

[28] *Historia quæ dicitur Gesta Dei per Francos, RHC Occ* 4, pp 159, 205.

[29] *Roland* 2 p 72.

[30] *Ibid* 2 p 118. The other early *chansons de geste* do not follow 'l'exemple épuré et exceptionnel de la sévère *Chanson de Roland*': J. Horrent, *Le Pèlerinage de Charlemagne: Essai d' Explication littéraire avec des Notes de Critique textuelle, Bibliothèque de la Faculté de Philosophie et Lettres de l' Université de Liège* 158 (Paris 1961) p 75. In two of these *chansons mal martire* and *malvais martire* are found, applied in each case to the enemies of the speaker and implying that the death desired for the opponents is death in a wrongful cause: *Gormont et Isembert*, A Bayot, *Les Classiques français du moyen âge* (Paris 1914) p 6; *Guillaume* 2 p 1029.

because of their association with the mass martyrdom of Christians. It was made possible, in spite of experiential knowledge to the contrary, by the lack of interest in what the Moslems did believe and by the assumption that no abomination was too horrible to be attributed to the enemies of Christ.[31] It was long before more informed works, which were unfavourable but did not perpetuate the grosser misconceptions,[32] affected the depiction of the Moslem in English works.

The identification of Moslems with idolatry is so complete by the end of the twelfth century in England that *maumez* is used for the idols of the Romans and this is found again in the early thirteenth century.[33] The use of the same word in the same way in these works, the lives of Saints Margaret and Katherine, is not, by itself, evidence for the widespread use of the word, for both works were written in the same monastery and possibly by the same author,[34] but in an Anglo-Norman work not later than 1230–40 there occurs an early and extreme example of the identification of the two groups of persecutors. In *La Vie de Saint Auban* the word *Sarazin* is used throughout the work for non-Christians: it is applied to Alban himself before his conversion and to his opponents after it;[35] the pagans invoke '*Phebum, Mahum et Tervagant*',[36] although some Roman divinities, besides Apollo, are mentioned.[37] All this occurs in the passion of a Romano-Briton, beheaded at Verulamium according, as the author noted, to Roman law,[38] a work written, moreover, at St Albans and attributed by some to the chronicler Matthew Paris.[39] By the late thirteenth century the Romans are said to worship Mohammed in an English work which was widely disseminated. When the Emperor

---

[31] 'It is safe to speak evil of those whose malignity exceeds whatever ill can be spoken': Guibert of Nogent, quoted from, R. W. Southern, *Western Views of Islam in the Middle Ages* (Cambridge Mass. 1962) p 31.

[32] James of Vitry, *Lettres*, R. B. C. Huygens (Leiden 1960) p 95: William of Tripoli, *Tractatus de Statu Saracenorum et de Mahomete pseudopropheta et eorum lege et fide*, H. Prutz, *Kulturgeschichte der Kreuzzüge* (Berlin 1883) pp 573–98.

[33] *Seinte Marharete* p 2; *Seinte Katerine*, S. R. T. O. d'Ardenne and E. J. Dobson, *EETS SS 7* (Oxford 1981) pp 4, 24, 92.

[34] R. M. Wilson, 'A Note on the Authorship of the "Katherine Group",' *Leeds Studies in English and Kindred Languages* 1 (1932) pp 24–7. Dobson, *The Origins of 'Ancrene Wisse'* p 115.

[35] [*La Vie de*] *Seint Auban*[: *an Anglo-Norman Poem of the Thirteenth Century*, A. R. Harden, *Anglo-Norman Text Society* 19 (Oxford 1978)] pp 2, 11, 16.

[36] *Ibid* p 48.

[37] *Ibid* pp 31, 35.

[38] *Ibid* p 21.

[39] *Ibid* pp ix–xiii.

Maxentius laments the defection of his trusted commander to Christianity he

> þo gan drawe his her. & sore sike & grone
> Mahoun he seide hou schal ich do. schal ich bileue alone.[40]

This continues to appear throughout the fourteenth century. In the Auchinleck 'Seynt Katerine' the religion of Maxentius is emphasised and he has undergone the racial metamorphosis of the persecutors of Saint Alban.

> Mahoun he held for his god:
> He trowed in þat fals lay;
> On Jhesu Crist no leued he nouȝt,
> Þat lord is & god verray.
> Sarrazin he was ful strong,
> Wiþ cristendom he seyd nay,
> For alle þat leued on Jhesu Crist
> He stroyd hem boþe niȝt & day.[41]

In the later life of Saint Katherine associated with the *Northern Homily Cycle* Maxentius is a devotee of *Mahown*,[42] and in the curious and violent life twice edited from the Cambridge manuscript[43] he worships 'Tarmagaunt and Apolyne'[44] and is a 'false, cursyde sarasyne'.[45] His devotion to Islam is made even more clear by the religion imputed to his followers[46] and by the words of his wife:

> 'Mahounde and the y forsake'.[47]

For the fifteenth-century author, but not for all readers, the persecutor abandons his association with Islam, although his practice of *mawmentrie* continues.[48]

[40] *SEL, EETS OS* 236 p 541.
[41] *A[lt]e[nglische] L[egenden,] n[eue] F[olge,* Carl Horstmann (Heilbronn 1881)] p 242.
[42] *Ibid* p 165.
[43] *Ibid* pp 260–64; *The Life of St Katherine: the Tale of the Knight and his Wife: and an Account of the Magical Manuscript of Dr. Caius,* J. O. Halliwell (Brixton Hill 1848) pp 1–19. There is also a handsome facsimile edition: *The Cambridge University Library MS. Ff.2.38,* introduced by F. McSparran and P. R. Robinson (London 1979). It is possible that the life may be very early fifteenth-century, but the existence of an early fifteenth-century Welsh manuscript containing a translation of this work and showing evidence of corruption in translation or transmission, suggests fourteenth-century composition: *Vita sancti Tathei and Buched seintly Katrin,* H. I. Bell, *The Bangor Welsh MSS Society* 1 (Bangor 1909) pp 31–99.
[44] *AeL, nF,* p 260.
[45] *Ibid* p 262.
[46] *Ibid* pp 261, 262, 263.
[47] *Ibid* p 262.
[48] [John] Capgrave, [*The Life of St Katherine of Alexandria,* Carl Horstmann, *EETS OS* 100 (London 1893 reprinted 1975)] p 274.

The Mohammetan and Idolatry

I have drawn my illustrations for the identification of the Roman and Moslem persecutors, with few exceptions, from the lives of the one saint, Katherine of Alexandria, although the same anachronism exists in the English lives of other saints, among them Christina and Lawrence.[49] Lawrence, who was martyred in Rome, has, like Alban, no connection with the Middle East, so the association is not simply the result of their persecutors' operating in the same area, an interpretation which might be sustained if it occured only in the lives of Saint Katherine.

The lives in her honour in which the Emperor Maxentius is depicted as a devotee of *Mahoun*[50] are based on an eleventh-century latin work known as the 'Vulgate',[51] or on the *Legenda Aurea*,[52] in which the emperor, although he displays the devotion to his idols and the wild rage required of a tormentor,[53] is a much more complex and sympathetic figure than is usual for his type and is certainly not connected with Islam. This suggests that the recurrence of the association of Mohammed with the idolatrous late Roman tyrant reflects popular prejudice and was not a concept continually renewed simply because it was embedded in the common written sources.

The fifteenth-century vernacular lives, which are based, directly or indirectly, on the same sources, do not make a Moslem of Maxentius. One of the authors was a learned man who held a doctorate from Cambridge[54] and a second may have held the same degree.[55] Of the writer whose life was inserted into the *Gilte Legende*[56] nothing is known except that he probably wrote in a dialect of the London area.[57] He was not the 'discrete maister' who was responsible for combining the conversion of this work with a

[49] *SEL, EETS OS* 235 p 320; *ibid* 236 p 363.

[50] *Ibid* 236 pp 533–43; *AeL, nF* pp 242–59; *ibid* pp 165–73; *ibid* pp 260–4.

[51] The most recent edition of this is in *Seinte Katerine, EETS SS* 7 pp 144–203.

[52] Th. Graesse (1890 reprinted Osnabrück 1965) pp 789–97.

[53] H. Delehaye, *Les Passions des Martyrs et les Genres littéraires* (Brussells 1921) pp 245–6.

[54] This was John Capgrave: see A. de Meijer, 'John Capgrave, O.E.S.A.,' *Augustiniana* 5 (1955) pp 400–40; *ibid* 7 (1957) pp 118–48, 531–75.

[55] The statement that Bokenham held a doctorate is found in the colophon to the unique manuscript of his lives: Osbern Bokenham, *Legendys of Hooly Wummen*, M. S. Serjeantson, *EETS OS* 206 (London 1938) p 289.

[56] 'The Life of St Catharine of Alexandria in Middle English Prose,' (A. Kurvinen unpub. D. Phil. thesis Oxford 1960).

[57] *Ibid* pp 1–126. *Three Lives from the Gilte Legende*, R. Hamer, *Middle English Texts* 9 (Heidelberg 1978) p 34.

passion translated afresh from the 'Vulgate';[58] his work is notable for the sureness of its style rather than for the display of learning. Caxton, who made some alterations to the Gilte Legende text, did not introduce associations with Islam.[59] The author of the unpublished 'Lyf of Quen Kateren' appears, from some of his references, to have been a man of some learning, even if his grasp of geography is uncertain.[60] Capgrave and Bokenham, the known authors, both with some claim to be called historians, knew better than to associate a Roman of the early fourth century with Islam, and probably enough about Islam to dissociate it from the practice of idolatry. This may have been true of the anonymous writers as well. That it was the authors and not the public who were responsible for this may be seen in the fact that earlier lives containing the anachronism exist in fifteenth-century and even late fifteenth-century copies:[61] they were still being read and reproduced, even though they were no longer being written.

The learning of these fifteenth-century hagiographers contrasts with the absence of indications of erudition in the thirteenth- and fourteenth-century vernacular lives which contain examples of the confusion. The life in the *South English Legendary* was almost certainly by a clerk,[62] but the unknown author of the Auchinleck life seems to have adapted his style to that of the romance of *Guy of Warwick*, which is found in the same manuscript,[63] and it is possible that it was to the composition of works of this genre that he was more accustomed. The lives are vigorous and the emphasis is on the

[58]Cambridge MS Gonville and Caius College 390/610, f 56ᵛ. The text was edited from another manuscript which cannot now be located and which did not contain this information: *The Life and Martyrdom of Saint Katherine of Alexandria, Virgin and Martyr*, A. G. H. Gibbs, Roxburghe Club (London 1884).

[59]The text consulted was the 1483 (?) edition of *The Golden Legende* ff 384ʳ–390ʳ.

[60]Longleat MS 55, ff 55ʳ–65ʳ. The author appears to have believed that Alexandria was in Greece: *ibid* f 55ʳ⁻ᵛ.

[61]The reference to *Mahoun* is retained in the latest of the *South English Legendary* manuscripts, MS Bodley 779, f 112ᵛ, which is dated c1450: M. Görlach, *The Textual Tradition of the South English Legendary*, Leeds Texts and Monographs, New Series 6 (Leeds 1974) pp 75–77. Cambridge MS Gonville and Caius College 175–96 is fifteenth-century; M. R. James, *A Descriptive Catalogue of the Manuscripts in the Library of Gonville and Caius College* 2 vols (Cambridge 1907) 1 pp 199–201. Cambridge MS, University Library Ff.II.38 is dated late in the reign of Henry VI: F. E. Richardson, *Sir Eglamour of Artois*, EETS OS 256 (London 1965) p xii.

[62]Th. Wolpers, *Die englische Heiligenlegende des Mittelalters: eine Formgeschichte des Legenderzählens von der spätantiken lateinischen Tradition bis zur Mitte des 16. Jahrhundert* (Tübingen 1964) pp 209–46.

[63]*The Auchinleck Manuscript National Library of Scotland Advocates' MS.19.2.1*, introduced by D. Pearsall and I. C. Cunningham (London 1977) p x.

events rather than on psychological or theological niceties. While the authors are obviously literate and, as their sources indicate, able to read Latin, the works do not suggest an interest in, or grasp of, history any more than they suggest a concern for theology.

Earlier learned lives were in Latin[64] and in them a number of pejorative terms were used for the objects of pagan devotion, none of which had any intrinsic connection with Islam.[65] I have not found the identification of the two groups of persecutors in a Latin work. The Latin life of Saint Alban, which was incorporated into the chronicle which usually goes under the name Matthew Paris, was not his own composition,[66] although, presumably, acceptable to him. It contains none of the references to the Moslem 'Trinity' or to Saracens which are so marked a feature of the Anglo-Norman life of the saint which he also copied, but did not certainly compose.[67] Matthew, if, in spite of his knowledge of Moslem practices,[68] he was the author *La Vie de Seint Auban*, is exceptional among learned authors in perpetuating this anachronism.

Other developments also affected the union imposed on the two races and its dissolution. Interest in the crusades was strong during the thirteenth century and continued intermittently into the fourteenth,[69] and so the depiction of the Moslem as persecutor and opponent of Christianity might be expected to gain a response. But the Moslem was increasingly replaced as the enemy of the Church by the heretics, against whom crusades had been declared since the end of the twelfth century.[70] With the diminishing importance of the Moslem as the enemy of the Faith the psychological obstacle to the acceptance of more nearly accurate information about Islam was at least diminished. The attitude expressed in some Lollard works towards the Moslems was related to that of Peter the Venerable, for whom they were heretics, very important heretics:[71] to the Lollards

[64]Examples of this are: *Passio Sancte Katerine* by an unidentified Richard, Cambridge MS Corpus Christi College 375, ff 1ʳ–54ʳ; Bodley MS Laud Misc. 515, f 109ʳ–116ʳ.

[65]*Simulacra* was favoured, as the word for idols, by Richard, Cambridge MS Corpus Christi College 375, f 11ʳ⁻ᵛ, but the author of the passion in Bodley MS Laud Misc. 515 prefered periphrastic expressions: '*Statuasque precantur Supplicibusque putant inflectere marmora verbis*': ibid f 110ʳ.

[66]M[atthew] P[aris, *Chronica Majora*, H. R. Luard, *RS*, 7 vols (London 1872–83)]1, pp 149–54.

[67]*Saint Auban* pp xii–xiii, xvii.

[68]*MP* 3 pp 352–361.

[69]Riley-Smith, *Crusades: Idea and Reality* pp 19–34.

[70]*Ibid* p 34.

[71]Southern, *Western Views of Islam in the Middle Ages* p 38.

they were heretics, but only heretics like many others who deviated from what these writers considered Christian.[72]

The Lollards themselves were a matter of greater and more immediate concern than the Moslems. One of the objects of Lollard and Wycliffite attack was the veneration of images, which may be found designated by the term *mawmetry* in works attributed to Wyclif himself, or more generally ascribed to Wycliffites and Lollards.[73] From the late fourteenth century and on into the fifteenth idolatry became a matter to be treated with some caution.[74] It was not that idolatry was considered less heinous but that it became necessary to distinguish between idolatry and the permissible veneration of one's own images. The frequent use of the word *mawmetry* by critics of the Church to describe the practices of the Church, and by the Church to describe such non-Christians as the Romans, weakened the association of the word with the faith from which it was derived. The images it conjured up depended on the particular religious associations of its users, and might be the images of a saint in an English church or the images of Venus and Apollo for which that saint had been martyred for refusing to honour.

The persecution of Christians by Moslems, I have suggested, was a major factor in the identification of the latter with the idolatry of the Roman persecutors, who were then depicted as Moslems in some passions in those languages into which a word derived from *Mahomet* was introduced as a term for idolatry. This bizarre association dissolved when Moslems lost their pre-eminence as the enemies of Christ, 'mawmetry' developed new associations, and the learned applied themselves to vernacular composition.

University of London
Birkbeck College

[72] A. Hudson *Selections from English Wycliffite Writings*, (Cambridge 1978) p 107.
[73] *Ibid* pp 19, 23; John Wycliffe, *Two Short Treatises, against the Orders of the Begging Friars*, T. Iames (Oxford 1608) p 12.
[74] J. Russell-Smith, 'Walter Hilton and a Tract in Defence of the Veneration of Images,' *Dominican Studies* 7 (1954) p 200.

THE POSSIBILITY OF TOLERATION:
MARSIGLIO AND THE CITY STATES OF ITALY

by DIANA M. WEBB

IN THE course of his lengthy arguments in the *Defensor Pacis* against the right of the priesthood to exercise coercive jurisdiction over men in this life, Marsiglio of Padua deals with the problem of the persecution of heresy, pausing in one place to remark:

> By these considerations, however, we do not wish to say that it is inappropriate that heretics or those who are otherwise infidel be coerced, but that the authority for this, if it be lawful to do so, belongs only to the human legislator.[1]

The conditional clause, *si liceat hoc fieri*, seems to have irritated both d'Entrèves and de Lagarde. Both emphasised the possibility that it was an addition of 1328 to the 1324 text, as if that consideration would diminish its force,[2] and both argued that Marsiglio's obsessive concern with the unity of the state must have entailed in him the acceptance, indeed the advocacy, of religious coercion.[3] Gewirth was somewhat more cautious; agreeing that Marsiglio's prime concern was to ensure that the authority to persecute rested with the secular power and not with the clergy, but pointing also to Marsiglio's use of the conditional mood in his pronouncements on the subject, and contrasting the standpoint that this seems to imply with Aquinas's much more definite position that 'heretics must be compelled to hold the faith' and 'can justly be killed'.[4] Clearly, if the people decide to make religious error an actionable offence, there can be no doubt of their right to do so. 'Hence' Marsiglio writes, 'either this position must be taken in communities of believers, or else individuals must be permitted to teach what they wish concerning the faith, as Hilary seems to have thought in his epistle to Constantius.'[5]

---

[1] *Defensor* [*Pacis*] II. v. 7. Text: [*The Defensor Pacis of Marsilius of Padua* ed C. W.] Previté-Orton (Cambridge 1928). Translation: [A.] Gewirth, [*Marsilius of Padua, The Defender of Peace*] 2 vols (New York 1951–6) 2.

[2] Previté-Orton p 154; for the mss. pp xxvi–xliii.

[3] G. de Lagarde, *La Naissance de l'Esprit Laique au Declin du Moyen Age, 2: Marsile de Padoue.* (Saint-Paul-Trois-Châteaux 1934) pp 279–80; A. P. d'Entrèves, *The Medieval Contribution to Political Thought* (Oxford 1939) pp 77–9.

[4] Gewirth 1 pp 160–6 also 2 pp lix–lxv.

[5] *Defensor* II. xxviii. 17.

Marsiglio, it has been plausibly suggested, 'is not certain whether effects on the community's religious interests require coercion.'[6] The difficulty of establishing an incontrovertible interpretation of Marsiglio's views on this matter seems in large part to rest on the fact that he envisages two possible situations and leaves the power to choose between them to the human legislator.

> Now if human law were to prohibit heretics or other infidels from dwelling in the region, and yet such a person were found there, he must be corrected in this world as a transgressor of human law, and the penalty fixed by that law for such trans-gression must be inflicted on him by the judge who is the guardian of human law by the authority of the legislator . . . But, if human law did not prohibit the heretic or other infidel from dwelling among the faithful in the same province, as heretics and Jews are now permitted to do by human laws even in these times of Christian peoples, rulers, and pontiffs, then I say that no one is allowed to judge or coerce a heretic or other in-fidel by any penalty in property or in person for the status of the present life.[7]

Religious diversity, whether or not it is desirable, is seen here as a practical possibility. Now it has been widely acknowledged that the political problems and constitutional practices of the Italian city states were much on Marsiglio's mind as he wrote the *Defensor Pacis*.[8] It has also been widely recognised that the religious life of these cities exhibits certain features which diverge from what is often taken to be the medieval norm. Might it not be fruitful to ask whether this aspect of city state experience too was among the in-fluences which went to the making of the *Defensor*?

In a paper given to this society some years ago, Alexander Murray argued that there was abundant evidence for the existence in thirteenth-century Italy of scepticism, indifference and ignorance in the matter of religion. Elsewhere, he has drawn on similar evidence

---

[6] [E.] Lewis, ['The Positivism of Marsiglio of Padua'], Speculum 38 (1963) p 579 n 147; and see generally pp 572–82 on the divine law.

[7] *Defensor* II. x. 3.

[8] [N.] Rubinstein, ['Marsilius of Padua and Italian Political Thought in his Time'] in *Europe in the Late Middle Ages* eds J. R. Hale, J. R. L. Highfield and B. Smalley (London 1965) pp 44–75; [Q.] Skinner, [*The Foundations of Modern Political Thought*] 2 vols (Cambridge 1978) 1 pp 53–65.

to come to similar conclusions about thirteenth-century France.[9] There is nothing too surprising about this, once one has taken the mental step of abandoning the concept of an implausibly unanimous medieval 'age of faith', and it is possible to suspect that a similar picture could be drawn from the strictures of preachers and the laments of the church's champions and the church's critics alike for every corner of Christendom. It is hard to believe that the indifferent and the sceptical, or many of the simply ignorant, were enthusiastic about the imposition of a compulsory religious orthodoxy, and it might even be a rash assumption that all of the devout favoured the actual persecution of dissent. That heretics did not alarm or antagonise all medieval Europeans is clear. To quote a recent view, 'Within a generation of the arrival of the first Cathars, the people of Languedoc and Lombardy had found that the heretics were not a threat to their society at all.'[10]

The fact remains that, whatever the disposition of the populace, orthodoxy was imposed in Italy (and in the Languedoc, of course) as elsewhere. From the late twelfth century onwards the laws not only of the Church, but of the states of Europe, including one by one the city states of Italy, made provision for the persecution of dissent. Were these laws the reflection of a popular religious sentiment welling up from underneath, or are we rather to see at work the alliance, not always a harmonious one, of the clergy, as proponents of a clear view of the purposes of earthly life, with the effective rulers of society? Powerful men consented to identify themselves with clerical interests, up to a point which proved to be by no means a fixed one, and used their power to impose orthodoxy. There is no question of denying that members of the ruling classes, of the clergy and of the Christian populace were sincerely convinced that the existence of religious dissent polluted society and endangered the eternal salvation of its members, but the actual embodiment of that conviction in secular law and the development of the persecution of heresy look very much, as Boswell has suggested for the development of the legal persecution of homosexuality, like an aspect of the growth of

[9] A. Murray, 'Piety and Impiety in Thirteenth-Century Italy', *SCH* 8 (1971) pp 83–106; 'Religion among the Poor in Thirteenth-Century France: the Testimony of Humbert des Romans', *Traditio* 30 (1974) pp 285–324.
[10] B. Hamilton, *The Medieval Inquisition* (London 1981) p 26.

government itself, the assertion of the more detailed control of the rulers of society over the life of society.[11]

That struggles between contenders for power within a given society might affect the progress of persecution is clearly demonstrated by the history of several Italian cities in the thirteenth century. At Verona, one of the major north Italian centres of Catharism, Fra' Giovanni da Schio intervened in 1233 to act as mediator between the factions of Ezzelino da Romano and the count of San Bonifazio. As part of the settlement he contrived, sixty heretics were burnt *ex melioribus* of the city. Later in the century, the Franciscan inquisition was able to begin functioning regularly at Verona as the Scala dynasty established itself in control of the city. In June 1278 Nicholas III congratulated the Scala on their devotion to the Roman Church, including their recent help in extirpating a notable nest of heretics at Sirmione, and rewarded them with the grant of a castle which had once been fortified by Ezzelino.[12]

It is possible that the alliance of the clergy and the secular power, in the Italian cities as elsewhere in Europe, had the effect of supplying society with an ideology which could, so to speak, expand with the expansion of territorial and legislative powers, while more localised loyalties and interests were reduced in importance and autonomy. The cult of the patron saint, whose relics or shrine were under the guardianship of the cathedral clergy, might be studied as one expression of this alliance. To read the detailed regulations for the feast of the Assumption that are laid down in the statutes of Siena or of Parma is to be in no doubt that, whether or not spontaneous popular sentiment was involved, these occasions were above all displays of civic discipline, of the right of the commune to command demonstrations of obedience, symbolised by the offerings made at the altar of the Virgin, from its citizens and from the dwellers in its wider territory.[13] A delicious flavour of small-town life in the age of the

---

[11] J. Boswell, *Christianity, Social Tolerance, and Homosexuality* (Chicago 1980) pp 270–1. Ch. 10 generally contains interesting material on the vexed problem of the part played by 'popular' and 'official' pressures in fomenting persecution of minorities.

[12] [C.] Cipolla, ['Il Patarenismo a Verona nel secolo XIII'], *Archivio Veneto* 25 (1183) pp 66–7, 287, 81.

[13] For Siena: *Il Costituto del Comune di Siena volgarizzato nel MCCCIX-MCCCX*, ed A. Lisini, 2 vols (Siena 1905) 1 pp 64–8. This vernacular recension represents the Sienese statutes as they had been redacted through the later thirteenth century. For Parma: *Statuta Comunis Parmae* [*digesta anno*] *MCCLV* [ed A. Ronchini (Parma 1856)] pp 200–3. These regulations were repeated and amplified in subsequent recensions.

triumph of orthodoxy emerges from the chapter of the statutes of Parma in 1255 which lays it down that four *Fratres Poenitentiae* (that is, Franciscan tertiaries) are to have the monopoly of making and selling the candles for the feast of the Assumption.[14] The Church sought a grander monopoly. It is a fair contention that individuals and communities needed the assurance that they stood well with supernatural powers and that they would seek that assurance by whatever means seemed most effective, be it Catholic, Cathar or quasi-pagan. It was the Church's business to ensure that the orthodox path was the one taken, while secular authorities approved of an orderly and visible regulation of civic religious life, themselves doubtless deriving reassurance from it. Heretics and their *fautores*, those sometimes powerful men whose groups of retainers and political affiliations inside and outside the commune could make them dangerous, seem to belong in a framework of loosely associated groups of friends and kinsmen, neighbours and clients, who acknowledged grudgingly if at all that their membership of the commune meant submission to a common legal, social and political discipline. One Cathar belief seems oddly symbolic of this anarchism, if it may so be called. In the *Summa* which he wrote in 1250 the former Cathar turned Dominican inquisitor, Ranier Sacchoni of Piacenza, listed among Cathar beliefs the following: 'Secular powers sin mortally if they punish heretics or evildoers *(malefactores)*'[15] His fellow-townsman Salvo Burci had already in 1235 devoted a section of his treatise *Supra Stella* to this same belief, under the heading *De gladio temporali*. As it was axiomatic that God had created the world, so he intended it to be in good order, 'but without secular justice no order can be maintained'.[16] It is hard to imagine any proponent of civic government who would not have agreed with this contention. The whole of the *Defensor pacis* might be described as a celebration of it. Whether the run of Cathar believers actually constituted a threat to public order, or whether they were perceived to do so by their neighbours, would be different questions.

---

[14] *Statuta Comunis Parmae MCCLV* p 203.

[15] F. Sanjek, 'Raynerius Sacchoni O.P., Summa de Catharis', *AFP* 44(1974) p 43; R. I. Moore, *The Birth of Popular Heresy* (London 1975) p 133.

[16] P. Ilarino da Milano, 'Il "Liber supra Stella" del Piacentino Salvo Burci, contro i Catari e altre correnti ereticali', *Aevum* 19 (1945) p 325. For this belief, and professions of it at Bologna in the late thirteenth century, see [E.] Dupré-Theseider, 'L'eresia [a Bologna nei tempi di Dante' in *Studi Storici in onore i Gioacchino Volpe*, 2 vols (Florence 1958)] 1 pp 408, 421–2.

Something like an affirmation of an older, looser view of society's essential bonds seems to emerge from the oft-quoted words of a *miles sagax* conversing with the bishop of Toulouse early in the thirteenth century and reported by Guillaume de Puylaurens. The bishop asked the knight why, if he and his people conceded that the Roman Church had such excellent answers to the heretics, they did not expel and persecute them. 'We cannot', replied the knight, 'we were brought up with them; we have kinsmen among them, and we see them leading honourable lives.'[17] Clearly this *miles sagax* did not think that the sky was going to fall on his head because he and his did not shape their views of how society worked solely according to clerical criteria. Kinship, friendship and neighbourhood counted for much, as did a decent life as ordinary men thought they understood it. If the sky did proceed to fall, it was in the shape of the Albigensian Crusade, which we are now perhaps more inclined to regard as the result of human contrivance rather than as the spontaneous explosion of the wrath of God, much as Puylaurens wished his readers to believe that it was in fact the latter.[18] Is it possible to form some idea of how Italians in the thirteenth and fourteenth centuries conceived the vital bonds of society, how deeply what we may loosely call the clerical view had penetrated the consciousness of laymen?

The annals of the period from the late twelfth century on are full of the refusals of civic governments to receive or implement anti-heretical legislation. Shortly after the promulgation of the decree *Ad Abolendam* against heretics at Verona in 1184, Lucius III was complaining that the newly-elected *podestá* of Rimini had been prevented from taking an oath to observe it,[19] and in 1199 Innocent III reported that the men of Treviso were refusing to receive a legatine decree against heresy for the admirably simple reason that they reckoned themselves the enemies of the apostolic see.[20] The appearance of the Inquisition resulted in frequent outbursts of hostility, as at Piacenza in 1233, where it may well be that the riot was stage-managed by the powerful local *fautores* of Catharism; but later in the century, as at Parma in 1279 or Bologna in 1299, the burnings of heretics seem to have caused genuine popular unrest.[21]

[17] G. de Puylaurens, *Chronique* ed J. Duvernoy (Paris 1976) pp 48–51.

[18] *Ibid* p 22: '*Dei iudicia, quibus propter peccata populi decrevit terras miseras flagellare.*'

[19] L. Tonini, *Della Storia Civile e Sacra Riminese* 6 vols (Rimini 1848–82) 2 pp 589–90.

[20] *PL* 214, cols 555–8.

[21] Dupré-Theseider, 'L'eresia' pp 418–21 for a list of incidents; and for heresy in the social and political setting of the communes generally, *idem*, 'Gli eretici nel mondo comunale italiano', *Bollettino della Società di Studi Valdesi* 114 (1963) pp 3–23.

The Possibility of Toleration

In these incidents a number of motives were at work, among which positive sympathy for heresy or any sentiment of toleration may well have played a very minor part. In the first place there was opposition to any intrusion of episcopal, papal or imperial jurisdiction into the area that the architects of civic autonomy were trying to stake out. The suppression of heresy evidently did not seem, by comparison, a very urgent matter. Later, there was clearly much simple dislike of the power, prerogatives and methods of the Inquisition, reinforced by increasing suspicion of the motives of the inquisitors. In the late thirteenth century posthumous burnings, accompanied of course by the confiscation and sale of the goods of the deceased, aroused much adverse comment, as at Bologna in 1299 when the bones of one Rosafiore were exhumed and burnt. A riot resulted, which was subsequently investigated by the Inquisition.[22] The rioter who asked what harm Rosafiore's remains could do anyone had clearly not got the message that the heretic, alive or dead, polluted Christian society; and the ritual character of the transaction had escaped the hard-headed sceptic who asked, somewhat disconcertingly, how the inquisitors could be sure that they had got the right remains. It was alleged, further, that the principal motive of the condemnation had been to get hold of a castle which had been Rosafiore's property.[23] For the rest, simple criticism of the excessive power enjoyed by the inquisition and the frequently encountered attacks on the avarice and immorality of the friars predominated. Dupré-Theseider concluded from his study of the Bolognese material that there was little evidence of resentment of heretics among the populace; he was, on the other hand struck by 'the criticism, sometimes pretty virulent, against the Church seen as an entity which regulated the collective life of believers and as such sought to interfere as much as possible in the most varied aspects of their practical behaviour.'[24] This popular indifference to heretics might, in his view, help to account for the long periods of time over which Cathars who were ultimately, even if posthumously, brought to book, had been able to practise their faith. It becomes still more interesting if, as he contends, Bologna was not notably productive of native heretics, for the most part importing them, by way of trade and business, from such centres as Verona, Ferrara, Mantua or

[22] Dupré-Theseider, 'L'eresia' pp 414–17.
[23] *Ibid* p 410.
[24] *Ibid* p 395.

Florence. Insofar as they were aware that they were living cheek by jowl with heretics, the good folk of Bologna seem not to have been over-perturbed by the intelligence.

What, however, of the rulers of the communes? There were good reasons, both internal and external, why in the course of the later thirteenth century the imperial and papal directives against heresy were received in one city after another. The interaction of internal power struggles with the peninsula-wide struggle between the papacy and the Hohenstaufen was obviously crucial. No commune lived in such cosy isolation that its rulers could afford to disregard the possible build-up of an alliance of powers, including probably its own exiles, against it. Fear and resentment of Frederick II aided the papacy in its quest for allies within the cities, while the mendicants endeavoured to put down roots in urban society. In 1233 the Franciscan Fra Gherardo Boccabadati was called in to settle the quarrels of the citizens of Parma. The result of his activity was not only a spate of reconciliations and pardons, but numerous laws, against heretics, adulterers, soothsayers, sorcerers and other offenders against Christian decency. The accession to the papacy of Innocent IV, who had been a canon of the cathedral of Parma and whose family were powerful in the area, then went far to effect the shift of this particular city from its imperial loyalties.[25] More generally, the death of Frederick II and the final defeat of the Hohenstaufen helped to set the seal on the process whereby the initiative in the communes passed to those who were prepared to accommodate the Church's essential demands. The late thirteenth-century codes of Parma, Bologna, Verona, Siena or Marsiglio's own Padua all accepted the procedure which must have seemed so objectionable to Marsiglio: the *podestà*, as executive head of the government, bound himself to accept unquestioningly the judgement of the Church as to who was a heretic and to use his powers to bring them to justice.[26]

The existence of these anti-heretical laws did not however mean

---

[25] *Statuta Comunis Parmac MCCLV* pp v–ix. For the orthodox offensive at Parma and elsewhere, see also [N.] Housley, ['Politics and Heresy in Italy: Anti-Heretical Crusades, Orders and Confraternities, 1200–1500', *JEH* 33 (1982)] pp 193–208.

[26] For Parma: *Statuta Comunis Parmae MCCLV* pp 269–72. For Bologna: *Statuti [del Comune] di Bologna [dall' anno 1245 all' anno 1267* ed L. Frati 3 vols (Bologna 1869–77)] 1 pp 67–8, 446; 3 p 408. For Verona, Cipolla pp 71–3. For Siena: L. Zdekauer, *Il Constituto del Comune di Siena dell' anno 1262* (Milan 1897) pp 53–4; also idem, 'Il frammento degli ultimi due libri del più antico constituto senese', *Bollettino Senese di Storia Patria* 2 (1895) p 318. For Padua, *Statuti del Comune di Padova dal secolo XII all' anno 1285* ed. A. Gloria (Padua 1873) p 423.

that these same secular authorities were not going to wage war on the fiscal and jurisdictional privileges of the clergy. There were attacks on the immunity of criminous clerks and attempts to levy taxes on the Church.[27] Marsiglio's view that a piece of property possessed by an ecclesiastic or a criminal act committed by one could not be accorded a specially spiritual character was clearly widely endorsed by the rulers of the communes, even where they had set their face against what they were prepared to regard as doctrinal error.[28] Marsiglio perceived and described the anomalous internal situation of the commune, with its competing and overlapping jurisdictions, as one who sought to correct familiar institutions by reference to a model which seemed to him to have timeless validity: the state, the self-subsistent unity, of Aristotle. His contemporaries who resented clerical jurisdiction and immunities, and their predecessors who had resisted the intrusion of an anti-heretical jurisdiction which represented episcopal, papal or imperial interference within the commune, may not have seen their societies in Aristotelian terms, but they were upholding what at bottom was the same ideal, the autonomous secular state.

A peculiar interest attaches, in this connection, to the testimony of a contemporary who could not, in all essentials, seem more different from Marsiglio: the Florentine chronicler Giovanni Villani.[29] Villani's Guelf orthodoxy is not in question. He was interested in the civic cult, in relics, saints and miracles; he was furthermore deeply persuaded that to do the will of God was the only way for Florence to ensure earthly prosperity, and that to uphold *santa Chiesa* was to do the will of God. It is, in itself, perhaps unimportant that he does not mention heresy in his account of thirteenth-century Florence. The activities of Peter Martyr and the organization of the Catholic faithful in the middle of the century have left no mark on his version of the building of the popular commune.[30] What is striking is the supreme importance to him of the ideal of the commune itself. In the earlier days of the Guelf-Ghibelline split, he believes, there were those who favoured the empire, and those who favoured *santa Chiesa*, but all

[27] Rubinstein pp 47–8; [J. K.] Hyde, [*Padua in the Age of Dante* (Manchester 1966)] p 239. For an example of a statute against criminous clerks, *Statuti di Bologna* 1 p 421.
[28] *Defensor* II. ii. 5–7.
[29] [G.] Villani, [*Cronica*] ed. F. Dragomanni 4 vols (Florence 1845).
[30] Housley pp 198–9; J. N. Stephens, 'Heresy in Medieval and Renaissance Florence', *PP* 54 (1972) pp 28–9, with further references.

were at one in devotion to the commune.[31] It was the great merit of the *popolo*, as the nobles plunged ever deeper into faction-fighting under these labels, that they held fast to the commune.[32] It emerges gradually that the communal ideal is best upheld by those who love *santa Chiesa*.[33] We can take it therefore that the commune is going to be orthodox and that Villani took for granted, and approved, the persecution of heretics that he never mentions. What is of more interest is that the all-important commune is conceived in essentially secular terms. We may think of the solemn figure labelled *Bonum Comune*, alternatively the 'Good Commune' or the 'Common Good', who is enthroned in the middle of Ambrogio Lorenzetti's fresco of Good Government, painted at Siena in the 1330s.[34] These frescoes themselves represent as well as any text the existence of a secular vocabulary in which the ideals of earthly governance could be expressed.

Villani does not have much to say about heresy at any time. He mentions Fra Dolcino,[35] but his first mention of the *inquisitore de' paterini* at Florence is in connection with the burning of the astrologer Cecco d'Ascoli in 1327.[36] He records the furore over the absolute poverty of Christ and John XXII's condemnations of the Visconti and Lewis of Bavaria as heretics.[37] These notices remind us that, like Marsiglio, Villani lived in an age when the term 'heretic' was attaching itself to new groups and becoming more freely used in political contexts. From Marsiglio's standpoint it was an urgent matter that the definition of heresy and the power to pronounce a man a heretic were not left in the hands of a corrupt hierarchy.[38] Villani does not seem similarly concerned, although, as the years pass, a note of dis-

---

[31] Villani I pp 220: '*pure era parte tra' cittadini nobili, che chi amava la signoria della Chiesa, e chi quella dello 'mperio, ma però in istato e bene del comune tutti erano in concordia.*'

[32] *Ibid* p 253: '*Il popolo e comune di Firenze si mantenea in unitade, e bene, e onore, e stato della repubblica*'.

[33] On the death of Frederick II in 1250, the Florentine Ghibelline leaders refused to take part in an expedition against Pistoia, resenting the rule of the popolo, '*e per lo passato tempo erano usi di fare le forze, e tiranneggiare per la baldanza dell 'mperadore.*' On the successful completion of the expedition the leading Ghibellines were expelled from the city and '*il popolo e gli guelfi*' remained in charge (*ibid* p 268).

[34] N. Rubinstein, 'Political Ideas in Sienese Art: the frescoes by Ambrogio Lorenzetti and Taddeo di Bartolo in the Palazzo Pubblico', *Journal of the Warburg and Courtauld Institutes* 21 (1958) pp 180–9.

[35] Villani 2 pp 116–17. What worries him most about the Dolcinians is that they live '*a comune a guise di bestie*'.

[36] *Ibid* 3 pp 41–2.

[37] *Ibid* 2 pp 239, 247; 3 p 22.

[38] E.g. *Defensor* II. xxvi. 8, 9.

illusionment with the materialistic and political Church of his day begins to obtrude. In 1345, nonetheless, he condemned the Florentine government, dominated at the time by what he regarded as unworthy elements from the lower guilds, for passing certain laws against the liberty of the Church.[39] This did not prevent him from expressing himself strongly and at length on the subject of the action taken by the Franciscan inquisitor, Piero dell' Aquila, 'a proud and avaricious man', in March 1346.[40]

Appointed to act as proctor for a cardinal who was claiming twelve thousand florins from the failed banking firm of the Acciauioli, the inquisitor had Salvestro Baroncelli, a partner in the firm, arrested as he was leaving the palace of the priors. The government took immediate umbrage at this insult to its *signoria e franchigia*, and exacted savage punishment from the citizen messengers who had physically arrested Baroncelli on the inquisitor's behalf. The ambassadors to Avignon who bore the republic's appeal against the interdict that the inquisitor now predictably laid on the city took with them a dossier of complaints against him. In two years he had exacted more than seven thousand florins in fines for heresy. Villani wished posterity to know that there were not enough heretics in Florence to realise that amount. 'But in order to make money, he exacted large fines, according to the man's wealth, for every little idle word that anyone wrongfully said against God, or for saying that usury was not a mortal sin.' The government responded to this challenge by forbidding the inquisitor to take actions outside the scope of his office and forbidding also the payment of fines for heresy. If a heretic was found, he was to be burnt. The inquisitor was denied the use of the communal prison, and forbidden to have more than six servants licensed to carry arms. Simultaneously the bishops of Florence and Fiesole were also restricted in the number of *famigli* they could have armed. 'It was said', Villani reports, 'that Fra Piero the inquisitor had licensed more than two hundred and fifty citizens to carry arms, and made almost a thousand florins a year, or maybe more, out of it; similarly the bishops didn't lose by it, and they acquired friends to their advantage, and to the detriment of the republic.' In this respect at least Villani approved the action of the government in stemming the growth of a little state within the state.

---

[39] Villani 4, pp 74–5.
[40] *Ibid* pp 95–7. Cf. [M.] Becker, ['Florentine Politics and the Diffusion of Heresy in the Trecento' *Speculum* 34 (1959)] esp pp 63–5.

Villani was also obviously sure that he knew, that everyone knew, what a real heretic was; and neither a casual blasphemer nor a usurer qualified. Whether or not it was for lack of 'real' heretics to prosecute, the Florentine inquisition paid increased attention to usury in the fourteenth century, much to the annoyance of the businessmen who ran the government. In this respect, if in no other, Villani and his respectable Guelf fellow-guildsmen might have acknowledged kinship with the Giovanni da Matro who in 1305 suffered posthumous condemnation at Verona. Giovanni's offences included not only the standard ones of visiting and doing reverence to Cathars and giving them aid and comfort, but also denying the resurrection of the body and the sinfulness of usury. If a man could receive rent for his house, Giovanni allegedly believed, he could receive money for making a loan.[41] Men who would have no truck with what they understood to be doctrinal error were irritated not only by the various privileges claimed by the clergy as a body, but by interference with everyday business practices. It was only in the later part of the fourteenth century that the Florentine authorities, fearing that the Fraticelli might really be a subversive influence among the lower classes, permitted the Inquisition once again to function effectively.[42]

There might then be little sentiment of toleration for doctrinal divergence, although there is some evidence to suggest that among the Italian populace at large there was widespread indifference on the matter and some opposition to persecution, if only because of the ugly face it displayed when it was carried out. In 1279 it was the execution of an innkeeper's wife at Parma which sparked a riot in which the Dominican convent was attacked, and a contributory cause of the disturbances at Bologna in 1299 was the refusal of the sacrament to one of the condemned who asked for it.[43] Posthumous condemnations provoked a sceptical and hostile reaction, while the secular rulers of society had their own reasons for disliking the actual mechanism whereby persecution was carried out, if only because they did not feel entirely confident of their ability to control it and ensure that it attacked only the right people. Marsiglio's demand that if persecution was to be carried out it must be done by the state itself, with the clergy reduced to the role of expert witnesses, was one logi-

[41] Cipolla pp 274–5.
[42] Becker pp 73–4.
[43] Dupré-Theseider, 'L'eresia' pp 413– 419.

cal response to this situation. Although his formulation of it may be extreme, he represents an ideology to which, in its basics, the good Guelf Villani also subscribed: the ideology of the commune itself, the format afforded to social, economic and political life by the autonomy of the city-states. This community, in most men's minds, had an essential spiritual dimension. Villani and many others would argue that it was vital to the commune's temporal health that it be orthodox and obedient to the Visible Church; Marsiglio had to argue that this aspect of the community's interests, like all others, would be best served by the unified authority of the human legislator.

If then we postulate with Marsiglio a completely self-determining state, with no cause to fear the intervention of any external power in its affairs, can we believe that he, in 1324, can have envisaged the possibility that its rulers would forego the power to persecute religious dissent? As we have seen, he accorded them the power, indeed the exclusive power, to persecute if they thought fit. The extent of that permission is the more striking if we consider the remarkable passage in which Marsiglio comes closest to declaring that the persecution of religious dissent is in fact absolutely impermissible:

> According to the truth, therefore, and the clear intention of the Apostle and the saints, who were the foremost teachers of the church or faith, it is not commanded that anyone, even an infidel, let alone a believer, be compelled in this world through pain or punishment to observe the commands of the evangelic law, especially by a priest.[44]

Why, we cannot but ask, 'especially by a priest'? If the prohibition on coercion is so categoric, it must apply equally to all earthly powers. If we move from the realm of pure principle into that shadowy area where considerations of justification and of practical necessity overlap and where rulers make their policy calculations, we may ask what Marsiglio thought persecution, if it were to take place, would actually achieve. His contention that coercion was of no value for the salvation of the unbeliever himself was of course no novelty,[45] but he was prepared to acknowledge that the unbeliever, or the sinner in a more general sense, might be held to contaminate the faithful and that measures might therefore be thought necessary against him. In general however he seems less perturbed by this danger than by possible abuses of the power of excommunication;

---

[44] *Defensor* II. ix. 7.
[45] *Ibid* II. v. 6; II. ix. 2, 4.

this too must be brought under the control of the community.[46] Villani, we have seen, believed that there were few real heretics in fourteenth-century Florence. Perhaps Marsiglio too thought them too few to be any danger in this world or the next, or perhaps he was aware of a popular indifference towards them which made them less rather than more infectious. All that is clear is that whatever his own calculations, the human legislator was entitled to make what dispositions it would.

How many Italians in the early fourteenth century shared Marsiglio's belief that Christ alone was the true judge of breaches of the divine law and that he would inflict penalties solely 'for the status of the future life'?[47] Before we dismiss these professions as so much cynical contrivance designed simply to undermine the Church's earthly authority, we might glance at the most illustrious of all Marsiglio's Italian contemporaries. It has been remarked that 'It was always characteristic of Dante's religious outlook to view the Christian faith precisely in function of, in relation to, life after death', and that (in the *Convivio*) 'neither church nor sacraments are represented as having any relevance to man's moral life in this world . . . The reader is left wondering whether Dante regarded them as important *only* in view of the afterlife.' In the *Monarchia* and the *Inferno* as well as in the *Convivio*, Dante could work on an ethical scheme which was in essentials derived from antiquity rather than from Christianity, while it was his intense personal need to believe in the immortality of the soul which made him choose the Epicureans as his representative heretics in hell, even though 'he had all the aberrant Christian sects to choose from.'[48]

If Marsiglio and Villani, with all their profound differences, yet had in common some fundamental ideas on the autonomy and dignity of the commune, Marsiglio and Dante also display a kinship which derives from the vigour and complexity of Italian intellectual life in the age of the rediscovery of Aristotle and the cultivation of the poetry and moral philosophy of the ancients.[49] Such secular cultural interests, like the political, social and economic activities which were open to the upper classes of the Italian cities, imparted to earthly life a seductive self-sufficiency which posed obvious problems of har-

---

[46] *Ibid* II. vi. 12, 13. Cf. Lewis p 579 n 147, with further references to the *Defensor Minor*.

[47] *Defensor* II. ix. 1.

[48] K. Foster, *The Two Dantes* (London 1977) pp 238–9, and ch 10 *passim*; p 11.

[49] Skinner 1 pt 1 *passim*; Hyde ch 10.

monisation with the claims of the Church to regulate secular activity and thought for the sake of a heavenly reward. It was the age also of the Franciscan crisis, when the Church's apparent failure to honour the claims of poverty and spirituality to its loyalties discredited it in the eyes of many of the faithful. Spiritual Franciscans, like Cathars before them, could look more convincingly holy. Marsiglio, Dante and Villani, in different degrees and combinations, all underwent these mingled influences. Marsiglio represents one intelligible permutation of them; and that he may have contemplated the possibility of toleration does not seem to lie beyond the bounds of the conceivable.

University of London
King's College

INFIDELS AND JEWS: CLEMENT VI'S ATTITUDE
TO PERSECUTION AND TOLERATION

by DIANA WOOD

C LEMENT VI was a pope who appeared to face both ways. This impression is confirmed by the fact that some historians have hailed him as a humanist pope, if not the first humanist pope,[1] whereas his conception of the Christian society and of papal sovereignty followed thoroughly traditional and authoritarian lines. A glance at his best known political sermon, that preached in 1346 to approve the future emperor Charles IV as king of the Romans, would suffice to show this.[2] His attitude to infidels and Jews also appears paradoxical, for he persecuted the one and tolerated the other, and this despite the threat presented by both to the purity of the Faith. This is not to suggest that Clement was the only pope to exhibit this dichotomy, for it was a common enough one: it was just that his views on infidels and Jews were more extreme than those of others, and the contrast therefore more pointed.

The questions to which Clement addressed himself when voicing his views on infidels were twofold. Firstly, could infidels rightly have any dominion in the world, or should they be destroyed just because they were infidels? Secondly, was there a case for forcible conversion of infidels to Christianity? The answers are to be found mainly in a *collatio* the pope preached when he created Louis de la Cerda, a great-grandson of Saint Louis of France, king of the still-pagan Fortune Islands, in the vain hope that he would conquer them for the Holy See.[3]

The classic discussion on the position of infidels during the late-medieval period was that of Innocent IV. Clement VI followed him

[1] P. Fournier, 'Pierre Roger (Clément VI)', *Histoire littéraire de la France*, 36 (1938) p 220; A. Maier, 'Zu Walter Burleys Politik-Kommentator', *Ausgehendes Mittelalter. Gesammelte Aufsätze zur Geistesgeschichte des 14 Jahrhunderts*, 1 (Rome 1964) p 99; J. E. Wrigley, 'Studies in the Life of Pierre Roger (Pope Clement VI) and of Related Writings of Petrarch', (unpub Ph D Pennsylvania 1965) p liii.
[2] *MGH Const* VIII no 100 pp 143–63.
[3] [Paris, Bibliothèque S[ain]t[e] G[eneviève MS] 240, fols 336ᵛ–43ᵛ. On Louis de la Cerda see G. Daumet, 'Louis de la Cerda ou d'Espagne', *Bulletin Hispanique*, 15 (1913) pp 38–67.

only up to a point. Innocent had accorded the pope universal jurisdiction by right, but had realized that in practice it would not be recognized. All men were the sheep of Christ by creation, he explained, although not all were of the fold.[4] This sentiment formed the basis of his views. Clement VI, however, was determined to make papal universality of jurisdiction a reality by extending papal *imperium* wherever possible. The situation was particularly urgent in the fourteenth century, when the papacy had lost much of its effective power, and when the boundaries of Christendom were being increasingly threatened by the Turks, especially in the Eastern Mediterranean.[5] An extension of the practical boundaries of papal authority elsewhere might go some way towards counterbalancing Eastern losses and restoring papal prestige. Clement was therefore quite open with Louis de la Cerda in admitting that extending the Faith was the same thing as extending papal *imperium*:[6] '. . . *dico quod hic concurrit fidei et nostri imperii dilatatio copiosa vel gloriosa.*'

On the subject of infidel dominion Clement took a harder line than Innocent had done. Innocent thought that the lordship of infidels was not of itself evil, and that the pope therefore had no *prima facie* cause to destroy it: it was held without sin.[7] Starting from his premiss of the universality of papal jurisdiction, Clement explained that the whole world had once been Christian. Using St Paul's words to the Romans, he emphasised that when Christ had sent forth His followers to preach, the sound of their voices had gone out into all lands. And this meant that there was literally no corner of the world where they had not been heard. Everywhere had once been Christian, and of course infidels could have no rights in lands which had once been sanctified.[8] Clement even went to the lengths of citing

[4] Innocent IV, [*Commentaria in quinque libros Decretalium* (Venice 1578)], *ad Decretales* III, xxxiv, 8 fol 176ᵛ. For discussion on papal jurisdiction over infidels see W. Ullmann, *Medieval Papalism: the Political Theories of the Medieval Canonists* (London 1949); [M. J.] Wilks, *The Problem [of Sovereignty in the Later Middle Ages* (Cambridge 1963)] pp 413–22; J. Muldoon, *Popes, Lawyers and Infidels: the Church and the Non-Christian World, 1250–1530* (Philadelphia 1979); [M.] Villey, [L'idée de la croisade chez les juristes du moyen âge', *Relazioni del X congresso internazionale di scienze storiche* 3 (Florence 1955)] pp 565–94.
[5] See J. Gay, *Le pape Clément VI et les affaires d'Orient* (Paris 1904) pp 15–31.
[6] St G 240 fol 337ᵛ.
[7] Innocent IV, *ad Decretales* III, xxxiv, 8, fol 176ᵛ. Compare [Thomas] Aquinas, *Summa Theologiae* [Editiones Paulinae (Rome, 1962)] II, ii, q. x, art 1, p 1131.
[8] St G 240 fol 337ᵛ: '*Qui quando misit apostolos non solum misit ad unam provinciam, sed ad universam terram . . . Et deducit Apostolus ad Romanos x [18] "In omnem terram exivit sonus eorum et in fines orbis terrae verba eorum"*', and *ibid* fol 340ʳ: '"*Prima ratio est quia*

a letter of Augustine which proved that there had once been Christian monks and abbots on the islands.[9] But even without this particular example, his argument that the whole world had once been Christian would have been enough to lead him to his general conclusion that infidels could have no rights anywhere in the world, and that they merited attack simply *ratione infidelitatis*.[10]

There were two aspects to the discussion, the lordship of infidels over Christians and that of infidels over infidels. On the first Clement was able to agree with Innocent IV, and with Aquinas, whom he cited, that infidel lordship over Christians should be destroyed.[11] He pretended to be more dubious about the lordship of infidels over infidels, but his conclusion was plain enough: the *Ecclesia* could use the plenitude of power to order its destruction whenever this was expedient.[12] It was not necessarily always expedient. In the case of the Tartars, Clement's initial reaction was tolerant, even friendly, to judge from his letter to Djani-beg, khan of the Crimea. This was because the khan's predecessors had allowed Christian preachers into their territories and had protected them.[13] No doubt the pontiff hoped that the khan would emulate his forebears, and so foster a peaceable extension of papal *imperium*. Infidel lordship would become Christian lordship. It was only later in the pontificate, when the Tartars attacked the Christian kingdoms of Poland and Hungary that the pope declared a crusade against them.[14] But ultimately, as Clement warned, all non-Christian lordship merited the use of force, because all true dominion was

terre iste quandoque fuerunt Christianorum et ideo non possunt infideles ius habere. Quod autem quandoque fuerunt Christianorum videtur ex ratione generali pro auctoritatibus supra allegatis, scilicet "in omnem terram . . .". Unde Apostolus . . . reputat valde falsum quod sit aliqua pars que non audierit vocem Apostolorum et discipulorum. Unde dicit sed dicens numquid non audierunt. Hoc quidem "in omnem terram exivit sonus eorum, etc".'

[9] *Ibid fol 340^r.* Compare Augustine, Ep 48 *CSEL* 33 pp 137–40.

[10] *Ibid fol 341^r:* '*Quarta ratio est generaliter ratione fidelitatis. Forte enim infideles ratione infidelitatis merentur perdere omnem dominium, et possunt cogi ad suscipiendum fidem vel dimittendum terras quas possident'.*

[11] *Ibid fol 341^v:* '*Sed prosequendo de aliis infidelibus Thomas clare in secunda secunde q. x in corpore questionis dicit quod per sententiam vel ordinationem Ecclesie, auctoritatem Dei habentis dominium vel prelatio infidelium super infideles tolli potest, quia infideles merito sue infidelitatis merentur potestatem amittere super fideles qui transferuntur in filios Dei'.* Compare Aquinas, *Summa Theologiae* II, ii, q. x, art. 10, p 1138.

[12] St G 240 fols 341^v–42^r: '*Sed maius dubium est de dominio infidelis super infidelem. Sed hic tango aliqua conferendo. Et videtur quod per auctoritatem seu sententiam Ecclesie, que plenam potestatem habet, potest iuste statui et ordinari quod tale dominium ab eis tollatur sive in una regione sive in omnibus sicut ei visum fuit expedire'.*

[13] [O.] Raynaldus, [*Annales Ecclesiastici*] [(Lucca 1750)] caps 21–22 p 316.

[14] A. Theiner, *Vetera Monumenta Poloniae et Lithuaniae* 1 (Rome 1860) no 713 p 539.

based on virtue, and there was no virtue among infidels, merely its shadow: true dominion among them was thus impossible.[15] This view was an advance on Innocent's idea of the sinless nature of infidel jurisdiction. It was more like that of Hostiensis, and was similar to that adopted by several fourteenth-century publicists that *extra Ecclesiam non est imperium*.[16]

On the second question, that of the forcible conversion of infidels, Clement was again more extreme than Innocent IV. Innocent thought that infidels should not be compelled to embrace Christianity, but merely to admit Christian preachers. It was only in cases where they were blatantly infringing natural law that the pope could step in to punish them, although Innocent did not commit himself on what form that punishment should take. In practice, as he was driven to admit, it could be shown that the majority of infidels were breaking natural law by worshipping idols rather than the one God, the creator, which justified papal intervention.[17] The canonist at least admitted the possibility that some infidels might not be infringing natural law: Clement VI did not. As sinners against natural law infidels must be compelled by the pope, the prince of monarchs, whose duty it was, he declared, to coerce his subjects to live according to right reason.[18] The compulsion of infidels to live according to right reason was a euphemism for their forcible conversion to Christianity, so that they would live according to divine law. Clement reached this conclusion again largely through arguments based on universality. He explained to Louis de la Cerda that men are infused with the spirit of the creator. They are made in the image of Christ. If the things which are Caesar's, because they bear his image, must be

[15] St G 240, fol 343ʳ: '*Nullum dominium debet esse sine virtute. In infidelibus autem nulla est virtus sed ymago virtutis solum, ergo nec verum dominium*'. Compare this with the radical view of Aegidius Romanus, *De Ecclesiastica Potestate*, ed R. Scholz (Weimar 1929) bk ii cap 11 p 96: '. . . *nullam possessionem, nullum dominium, nullam potestatem possunt infideles habere vere et cum iusticia, sed usurpando et cum iniusticia*'. For discussion see Villey pp 570–1.

[16] Hostiensis, *Commentaria in quinque Decretalium libros* (Venice 1581) 2, *ad Decretales* III, xxxiv, 8, fol 128ᵛ: '*Mihi tamen videtur quod in adventum Christi omnis honor et omnis principatus et omne dominium et iurisdictio de iure et ex causa iusta . . . omni infideli subtracta fuerit et ad fideles translata*'. On *extra imperium* see J. Muldoon, '*Extra Ecclesiam non est imperium*: the canonists and the legitimacy of secular power', *SGra* 9 (1966) pp 551–80 esp pp 578–9.

[17] Innocent IV, *ad Decretales* III, xxxiv, 8 fol 176ᵛ.

[18] St G 240, fol 340ʳ: '. . . *ratio est quia isti peccant contra legem nature. Peccantes autem contra legem nature puniendi sunt per principem monarchie sicut est papa ad quem pertinet subditos cohercere ut vivant secundum rectam rationem*'.

rendered to Caesar, then obviously things belonging to God and bearing His image must be rendered to Him. This could happen only through the Faith.[19] Employing the familiar imagery of the Book of Daniel, the pope observed that the fifth kingdom was given to the Christian people, and that it had to crush all infidel kingdoms. Christendom had to fill the whole earth like the great mountain of the prophecy. On this basis, kings who forced infidels to embrace Christianity were to be lauded: indeed, the pope himself ought to use force against them.[20] But was this right? After all, as Clement realized, pagans should come voluntarily to the Faith. And there was no reference in Scripture to the compulsion of infidels.[21] But as so often with Clement, it was the spirit rather than the letter of Scripture which counted, and this seemed to indicate that the Church must realize its universal potential on earth. To make this point he drew on Romans, 11: 25–6: 'Blindness in part is happened to Israel, until the fullness of the Gentiles be come in. And so all Israel shall be saved'.[22] Israel in this case signified the Universal Church, and blindness was conventionally applied to unbelievers and heretics in papal writing, to contrast with those illumined by the light of truth, the light of the world. Clement was convinced that the fullness of the Gentiles should have been converted at the coming of Christ, but as this had clearly not happened they would now have to be compelled, assuming that they would not come in voluntarily.[23] By forcing them it was as if the pope were helping the fulfilment of a divine prophecy.

Traditionally the papacy's attitude to the Jews, from the time of Gregory I onward, had been one of tolerance, although often it was limited tolerance.[24] Innocent III, for example, had protected the Jews in his *Constitutio pro Judaeis*, itself partly a repetition of earlier legisla-

---

[19] *Ibid* fol 343[r]

[20] *Ibid* fols 342[v]–43[r]: '. . . *scriptum est Dan ii°* [34] *quod lapis excisus de monte sine manibus,* [*et*] *percussit statuam . . . et comminuit quatuor regna . . . Iste enim lapis excisus sine manibus est Christus . . . cuius regni . . . non erit finis. Quod regnum datum est populo Christiano, et habet comminuere omnia regna infidelium. Unde sequitur quod iste lapis factus est mons magnus, et implevit universam terram. Debet enim eius regnum, scilicet Christianitas, totam terram implere. Item ad hoc videtur facere quod reges qui tales coegerunt ad fidem, ab Ecclesia commendatur . . . Item ad hoc videtur facere quod Romani pontifices similia fecerunt'.*

[21] *Ibid* fol 339[v]: '*Sed videte quod hic concurrit unum dubium satis magnum iterum non placent Deo coacta servicia. Iterum non legimus aliquem in sacra scriptura fuisse coactum*'.

[22] *Ibid* fol 343[r]. Compare Romans 11: 25.

[23] St G 240, fol 343[r].

[24] See, in general, [E. A.] Synan, [*The Popes and the Jews in the Middle Ages* (New York and London 1965)]; [S.] Grayzel, [*The Church and the Jews in the Thirteenth Century,*

tion, but he had added a saving clause to the effect that protection would apply only to those Jews who did not plot against the Faith.[25] The Fourth Lateran Council of 1215 had imposed the wearing of distinctive clothing upon the Jews.[26] John XXII initially protected them from the fanatical Pastoreaux, but later appeared to condone their banishment from papal territories by assisting the foundation of chapels dedicated to the Virgin on the sites of former synagogues.[27] Scrupulous in guarding the purity of the Faith, he renewed the proscriptions of the Talmud issued by Clement IV and Honorius IV.[28]

In the year 1348 the Jews were accused, not for the first time, of poisoning the wells and fountains and so causing the Black Death. Thousands were massacred, and the murders were supplemented by Jewish suicides and politic conversions to Christianity.[29] Clement issued a bull protecting the Jews and their property on 4 July 1348,[30] and this was followed by a tougher one on 26 September.[31] By the following spring the papal orders had taken effect, perhaps because of their irrefutable logic that since the plague did not spare the Jews themselves, and since it raged in areas where there were no Jews, they could hardly have caused the disease.[32] A few months later, however, the massacres started again with renewed ferocity, inspired by the bands of heretical flagellants who swept Europe. These thought that they could appease the wrath of God, which had dealt mankind the punishment of plague, through their revoltingly spectacular penance of public flagellation. For good measure, they also demanded the extermination of the Jews, in the belief that God

rev ed (New York 1966)]; L. Bardinet, 'Condition civile des Juifs du Comtat Venaissin pendant le séjour des papes à Avignon, 1309–76', *RH* 12 (1880) pp 1–47.

[25] Grayzel pt 2 no 5 p 92. See his comments on the indebtedness of Innocent to earlier popes at pp 76–8.

[26] See A. Cutler, 'Innocent III and the distinctive clothing of Jews and Muslims', *Studies in Medieval Culture* 3 (Michigan 1970) pp 92–116.

[27] See John's letter to the Archbishop of Narbonne, 19 June 1320, ed A. Coulon, *Jean XXII, Lettres secrètes et curiales (1316–34) relatives à la France* (Paris 1900–61) no 1104. See *Ibid* No 1284 describing the foundation of the chapel at Bédarrides, 4 September 1321. For discussion of John's attitude see Synan pp 129–31.

[28] Raynaldus, 5 cap 24 pp 137–8.

[29] *Prima Vita [Clementis VI,* in S. Baluzius, *Vitae Paparum Avenionensium* ed G. Mollat (Paris 1914–27) 1] pp 251–2; *Sexta Vita [Clementis VI] ibid* p 306.

[30] Raynaldus 6 cap 33 p 477.

[31] [Clement VI, *Lettres se rapportant à la France* ed E.] Déprez, [J. Glennison and G. Mollat (Paris 1901–61)] no 3966.

[32] *Ibid.*

willed it.[33] Through invective and flagellation they would whip up
the people's emotion and then lead them forth to murder. Clement
VI condemned them in October 1349.[34]

Clement's attitude as evidenced by his three bulls was one of tolerance towards the people of Israel. His main accusation against the
Flagellants was that under pretence of piety they had let loose the
works of impiety. They had cruelly shed the blood of the Jews,
whom 'Christian piety receives and sustains and does not allow to be
harmed', he emphasised.[35] Certainly Clement had sustained them
the previous year. He had condemned the Jewish massacres in the
strongest possible terms, threatening excommunication to any who
harmed them. He had protected their property and had ordered
Christians to submit any quarrels they had with Jews to due process
of law.[36] Much of this repeated the *Constitutio pro Judaeis*. There
could scarcely have been a greater contrast than with Clement's
attitude to infidels. The question of forcible conversion was equally
contrasted. Clement did admit to hating the faithlessness of the Jews,
who obdurately refused to recognize the hidden meaning of their
own scriptures and prophets, and to accept the Faith and salvation.[37]
Nevertheless, again echoing the *Constitutio*, Clement forbad Christians to force unwilling Jews to baptism, though they were to accept
'without calumny' any who came voluntarily. He added that those
who were compelled to be baptised were not believed to possess the
true Faith.[38] The contrast scarcely needs underlining.

Why did Clement tolerate the Jews? Since we lack any sermon of
his on the subject it is not an easy question to answer. There is some
evidence that in his personal capacity, as a humanist and scholar,
Clement was interested in Jewish culture. In his student days at Paris
he had copied part of the Hebrew alphabet into his commonplace
book, implying that he was trying to learn it.[39] At Avignon the

---

[33] See *Prima Vita* pp 251–52; *Sexta Vita* pp 306–07. For the belief that they were performing God's will see [P.] Fredericq, 'Deux sermons [inédits de Jean du Fayt sur
les Flagellants (5 octobre 1349) et sur le Grand Schisme d'Occident (1378)' *Bulletin
de l'Academie royale de Belgique, Classe de Lettres* (Brussels 1903) nos 9–10] pp 688–
718 at p 691. In general see N. Cohn, *The Pursuit of the Millenium* (London 1962) pp
124–48.

[34] Raynaldus 6 cap 21 p 495.

[35] *Ibid.*

[36] Raynaldus 6 cap 33 p 477 and Déprez no 3966.

[37] Déprez no 3966.

[38] Raynaldus 6 cap 33 p 477.

[39] Vatican MS Borghese 247 fol 143ʳ: see A. Maier, *Codices Burghesiani Bibliothecae
Vaticanae, Studi e Testi* 170 (1967) p 298.

astronomer, Leo Judaeus, the rabbi Levi ben Gerson, dedicated certainly one, and probably two, works to Clement, and the pope then commissioned their translation from Hebrew into Latin.[40] The destruction of the Jews would have brought Clement no personal advantage. Nor would it have brought financial gain, for there is no evidence that the Avignon popes were in their debt.[41] There was also no territorial or political advantage, for the Jews lived in minority groups in Gentile domains. Clement must then have had theoretical reasons.

His conception of the people of Israel has to be pieced together from scattered letters and sermons. The sermons especially reverberate with Old-Testament citation and allegory: indeed, Clement might well be dubbed an Old-Testament pope. The traditional reason for tolerating the Jews was that of Augustine, namely that they bore witness to the truth of the Faith, more especially since they possessed the writings in which the coming of Christ was prophesied.[42] Innocent III had endorsed this in his introduction to the *Constitutio*, and although Clement did not repeat it, his remarks about the Jews' refusal to recognize the meaning of the prophets, also stated by Innocent, may be a shorthand formula for a familiar idea. Clement's friend, Jean de Fayt, a master in theology at Paris, had cited it in the sermon he preached to persuade the pope to condemn the Flagellants, in particular for their massacre of the Jews.[43]

The sole reason the pope gave for protecting the chosen people was that they were precisely that, for Christ had issued from them.[44] This, however, is a drastic abbreviation of his views. From his political *collationes* there emerges a close identification between the people of Israel and the Christian people. For example, in the piece for Charles, king of the Romans, the whole theory of papal authority and the creation of emperors and kings is based on two Old-Testament references: 'Solomon', that is, Charles, 'shall sit upon

[40] L. Thorndike, *A History of Magic and Experimental Science* (Columbia 1934) 3 pp 309–10.

[41] Y. Renouard, *Les relations des papes d'Avignon et des compagnies commerciales et bancaires de 1316 à 1378, BEFAR* 151 (Paris 1941) p 106 n 58.

[42] Augustine, *Enarratio in Psalmum 58, CC* 39 p 744.

[43] Ed Fredericq, 'Deux sermons' pp 694–708. On Jean de Fayt see *ibid* pp 688–91 and N.-N. Huyghebaert, 'Jean Bernier de Fayt', *DHGE* 16 cols 780–82. Clement VI commissioned Jean to compile three dictionaries of quotations for him from Aristotle, Augustine and Boethius.

[44] Déprez no 3966.

my throne and rule for me',[45] and, 'Not at the election of the people, but at their petition, Samuel', that is, Clement VI, 'according to the counsel of God, gave them King Saul'.[46] The whole sermon is devoted to showing how Clement was 'establishing the throne of his kingdom over Israel',[47] in the words of another quotation, and the Israelites are frequently compared with the Christian people over whom Charles is being granted universal powers. Humbert of Vienne, the captain-general of Clement's crusading expedition of 1345, was, in the words of Maccabees, made 'a leader in Israel'.[48] Then there is the identification of Rome with Jerusalem. Clement's jubilee year of 1350, which encouraged pilgrims to visit the Eternal City, had been proclaimed in accordance with the Mosaic law of Leviticus.[49] More direct is the comparison between Clement's cathedral church of the Lateran and the Temple of Jerusalem, which the pope had added to the list of obligatory pilgrimage places.[50] In 1347 the ostentatious Roman revolutionary Cola di Rienzo had ritually immersed himself in the font there. It had been fouled like the vessels of the Temple at Belshazzar's feast, Clement complained. Cola had polluted the Temple of the Lord: *templum Domini, quod est Rome*, he wrote,[51] signifying that for him the Temple of Jerusalem was the prototype of the Lateran.

The people of Israel had in fact become the prototype for the Christian people, and in a pre-papal sermon Clement had underlined the essential continuity between them. Christians were denoted as the 'heirs of Abraham': they were 'his seed for ever'.[52] For Clement the *Ecclesia* was itself a continuation of the synagogue, and the advent of Christ had effected a transformation rather than a break. Before the birth of Christ the synagogue had been limited to one people, in one land, Judea, he told Louis de la Cerda. Now, however, the

[45] 3 Kings 1: 35: *MGH Const* VIII no 100 pp 143–63.
[46] 1 Kings 8: 5–6: *MGH Const* VIII no 100 p 155.
[47] 1 Paralipomenon 22: 10: *MGH Const* VIII no 100 p 152.
[48] St G 240, fol 521^v: 1 Maccabees 2: 55.
[49] Leviticus 25: 8–13. See Clement's bull *Unigenitus Dei filius* of 27 January 1349, *Extravagantes communes* V, ix, 2 [ed A. Friedberg, *Corpus Iuris Canonici* (Leipzig 1879) cols 1304–06]. See also Clement's sermon on the jubilee year, Frankfurt Stadtbibliothek MS 71, fol 418^r. On the Old Testament jubilee see R. North, *Sociology of the Biblical Jubilee* (Rome 1954).
[50] *Extravagantes communes* V, ix, 2.
[51] *MGH Const* VIII no 376, p 420.
[52] St G 240, fols 300^v–301^r. For the idea that Abraham was the prototype of the pope see Wilks, *The Problem* pp 538–9.

Church was universally diffused throughout all lands.[53] In the New Testament, God did not speak just to the people of Israel through the prophets, but he spoke to the whole world through the son whom he had constituted the heir of all things.[54] Ultimately Clement saw Christ Himself as the essential link between Jew and Gentile. He was the mean between them, connecting and including both. As he explained, echoing the sermons of Innocent III, Christ had liked to perform all His actions *in medio*. He had been born in between two animals, the ox and the ass, signifying respectively Gentiles and Jews.[55] Christ always wished to be *in medio* so that He might, like the biblical corner-stone, unite two things equally, namely the Gentiles and the Jews.[56] Preaching five months before his election to the papacy, Clement declared that just as the ox and the ass had tarried at the manger, and Christ had offered food to both, so today both peoples are fed and refreshed in the manger of the Church.[57]

The paradox of toleration and persecution seems to have disappeared. For Clement VI infidels were a threat to the universality of papal *imperium* and to the fulfilment of the Old-Testament prophecies about Christendom filling the whole earth. Infidel lordship had to be destroyed and the fullness of the Gentiles brought in, if necessary by force. But how could Clement VI have fulfilled his role as the vicar of Christ, the corner-stone who had joined Jew and Gentile to make them one, if he had persecuted the people of Israel?

University of East Anglia

---

[53] St G 240, fol 337ᵛ: '*Unde videtur michi quod licet ante adventum Christi synagoga coartata fuisset in uno populo et in una transmigratione, scilicet in Judea . . . post mortem Christi Ecclesia non esset coartata, sed magis per totum orbem dilatata*'.

[54] *Ibid: 'Et propter hoc in novo testamento non est Deus solum locutus filiis Israhel in prophetis, sed locutus est toti mundo in filio quem constituit heredem universorum*'.

[55] Sermon on the feast of the circumcision (undated), *ibid* fol 413ʳ: '*Et ideo videtur michi quod quasi omnia facta sua voluit facere in medio. In medio duorum animalium bovis et asini, id est in medio populo gentilis et iudei nasci. Per bovem enim . . . populus Israheliticus . . . per asinum autem . . . populus gentilis*'. Compare Innocent III, *PL* 217, 509.

[56] St G 240, fol 413ʳ: '*Voluit sicut lapis angularis [Psalmum 118:22] in medio poni ut coniungeret utrumque pariter: iudeorum scilicet et gentilium*'. Compare Innocent III, *PL* 217, 811.

[57] Sermon on the feast of the Epiphany (Avignon, 6 January 1342) St G 240, fol 395ᵛ: '*Et sicut ista duo animalia in presepi iacebant et ambobus alimentum commune ihesus prebobat, sic uterque populus in presepi hodie ecclesie pascitur et reficitur*'.

REGINALD PECOCK: A TOLERANT MAN
IN AN AGE OF INTOLERANCE

by ROY MARTIN HAINES

R EGINALD PECOCK, bishop of St. Asaph and subsequently of Chichester, has surely been one of the most
misrepresented of men.[1] Condemned in his later years as a
heretic, he was grossly misunderstood by that garrulous prophet of
doom, Thomas Gascoigne,[2] who described him as this 'Pacock' who
loosed arrows at the sun, one of which by the just judgment of God
fell upon his own head.[3] John Foxe allotted him a place as a protestant confessor and Father Robert Parsons wished the martyrologist
joy of one who had [allegedly] denied three articles of the Creed and
'perjuriously abjured' against his conscience.[4] Nicholas Harpsfield

---

[1] For a summary biography: Emden (O) *s.v.*; also *DNB*; Le Neve 7 p 3. The best short
account of Pecock's life and thought is that by [E. F.] Jacob, ['Reynold Pecock,
Bishop of Chichester'] *PBA* 37 (1951) pp 121–53, repr. [idem] *Essays [in Later
Medieval History]* (Manchester 1968) pp 1–34. [E. M.] Blackie, ['Reginald Pecock']
EHR 26 (1911) pp 448–68, is still of value, though it needs to be read in conjunction
with [M.] Deanesly, *[The] Lollard Bible* (Cambridge 1920 repr 1966). The most
recent bibliography is in [J. F.] Patrouch [jr.], *[Reginald Pecock]* (New York 1970).
[2] *'Heu! heu! heu! Domine Deus desolata est domina gencium, i.e. ecclesia, quae olim fuit
domina gencium'* (*Notae Thomae Gascoigne* from Oxford Bodleian MS Auctar D iv 5):
Loci [e Libro Veritatum, ed J. E. Thorold Rogers] (Oxford 1881) p 231. The *Loci* are
extracted from Oxford Bodleian Lincoln Coll. MSS 117–8. For Gascoigne himself:
[W. A.] Pronger [Mrs Maxwell], 'Thomas Gascoigne', *EHR* 53 (1938) pp 606–26;
54 (1939) pp 20–37 (based on an Oxford B. Litt. thesis), where there are a number of
criticisms of Thorold Rogers's editorial work. However, the latter appears to have
extracted all that is relevant to Pecock.
[3] *Loci* p 218 and compare p 217. Quotations in English in the text have been
modernised.
[4] Foxe's martyrology, Parsons, Harpsfield and the *Index* (n 6 below) are mentioned
by the perspicacious author of 'Bishop Pecock, his character and fortunes', *Dublin
Review* 24 ns (1875) p 28 (based on Foxe and Hearne?). Compare [V. H. H.] Green,
Bishop [Reginald] Pecock (Cambridge 1945) p 2; 'Concerning Pecock's Opinions,
not only from Nicholas Doleman's [that is Parsons's] *Three Conversions of England* .
. .' in [Walteri] *Hemingford [. . . Historia,* ed T. Hearne] (Oxford 1731) 1 appendix pp
cli–clii [also n 6 below]; [R. Parsons or Persons], *Three Conversions of England* (np
1604) 2 pp 264–7. Foxe placed Pecock in his 'Kalender' for 11 February (1457): *[The]
Acts and Monuments [of John Foxe . . . with a preliminary dissertation by G. Townsend,* ed
S. R. Cattley] 8 vols (London 1837–41) 1 (preceding text). Townsend examines the

125

classified Pecock as a Wycliffite,[5] while the Spanish *Index Expurgatorius* of 1667 labelled him 'pseudo bishop' and, with quaint anachronism, 'a Lutheran professor of Oxford'.[6]

In the late-seventeenth century Henry Wharton incongruously adduced Pecock—in company with Aquinas, Gerson, Marsilio of Padua, Thomas Netter of Walden, and a number of others—as support for his contention that 'Scripture is the Rule of Faith'; an argument designed 'to overthrow the plea of tradition'.[7] As a *pièce justificative* Wharton provided a not very satisfactory edition of Pecock's *Book of Faith*. This was the only work of Pecock's in print when Lewis wrote a biography of him, first published in a limited edition of 1744.[8] Significantly this constituted the sequel to the author's study of Wyclif.[9] Dean Hook, in the nineteenth century, was to cite 'A bully in prosperity is generally a coward in adversity'[10] as epitomising Pecock's vainglorious confidence in his own views and his subsequent ignominious retraction of them. This time-honoured tag (*Tumidus in prosperis et timidus in adversis*) had been invoked against an earlier prelate, Archbishop John Stratford, but in a political rather than in a philosophical or credal context.[11]

By the twentieth century, though still an object of misrepresentation, Pecock was being appraised more justly. The subject of a Ph.D.

criticisms of Foxe by (among others) Parsons and Harpsfield, *ibid* 1 pp 421–38, 438–66.

[5] *Dublin Review*, p 28; N. Harpsfield ed Richard Gibbon, *Historia Anglicana Ecclesiastica: Historia Wicleffiana* (Douai 1622) pp 719–20; N. Harpsfield (under pseudonym Alan Cope), *Dialogi Sex contra . . . Oppugnatores et Pseudo-Martyres* (Antwerp 1566) pp 738–1002 (sixth dialogue).

[6] *Hemingford* 1 appendix p lxxvii n 1. Hearne adds: '*E quibus verbis, quid de Antiquariorum Hispanicorum in re critica peritia sit judicandum, facillime elici potest*'.

[7] *A treatise proving Scripture* [*to be the Rule of Faith: Writ by Reginald Peacock*] (London 1688).

[8] J. Lewis, *The Life of . . . Reynold Pecock* (London 1744 repr Oxford 1820). However, Lewis did have access to extracts from the Repressor: see *The Works of the Rev. Daniel Waterland . . .* ed W. Van Mildert 11 vols (Oxford 1823–8) 10 pp 208–74; BL Add MS 33906.

[9] The fact is acclaimed by the full title of Lewis's work. J. A. Robson wrote of his contribution in *Wyclif and the Oxford Schools* (Cambridge 1961) p 2: 'Protestant low-church Whiggery, flushed with the triumph of the Hanoverian settlement, came to the defence of Wyclif's memory in the person of John Lewis of Margate (1675–1747)'. There is an even less complimentary description in *Hearne's Collections* 10 p 128, cited Jacob, *Essays* p 4 n 3.

[10] W. F. Hook, *Lives of the Archbishops of Canterbury* 12 vols (London 1860–76) 5 p 304. Hook discusses Pecock *s.v.* Archbishops Stafford and Bourchier, *ibid* pp 178–82, 293–311.

[11] Wharton 1 pp 25–6 (Lambeth MS 99 fol 139ʳ).

dissertation at the Catholic University of America, which substantially exonerated him from the taint of heresy,[12] and, at a biographical level, of a Manchester M.A. thesis,[13] the controversial bishop also provided a topic for winners of the Arnold essay prize (1922)[14] and of the Thirlwall prize. This last was V. H. H. Green, whose excellent study of Pecock in 1945 superseded Lewis's work as the substantive biography.[15] By that time virtually all of the surviving corpus of Pecock's writings was available in print.[16] Green, however, perhaps failed to substantiate the overall importance of his subject for the fifteenth century.[17] Yet Morison, almost forty years previously in his introduction to the *Book of Faith*, had described Pecock as 'the Renaissance man in a land still content with the ancient ways and thoughts' and, more memorably, as one for whom faith was 'A little island in the ocean of reason' where 'he watched with delight the waves, as they sapped the cliffs, and slowly but surely reduced its poor circumference'.[18] For Emerson, writing in the 1950s, 'Pecock stands as an almost unique thinker', someone who could be 'at the same time an almost completely orthodox Christian

[12] [E. A.] Hannick, [*Reginald Pecock: Churchman and Man of Letters*] (np 1922) esp p 15. Compare *Dublin Review* 24 p 50: 'We think enough has been said to show that the charges against Pecock, even so far as material heresy is concerned are false, or, to say the least, not proved'. C. Babington, editor of [*The*] *Repressor* [*of over much blaming of the Clergy*] 2 vols (RS 1860) 1 pp l–lii n 1, discusses some of Lewis's statements with respect to Pecock's 'errors'.

[13] T. Kelly, 'Reginald Pecock: a Contribution to his Biography' (1945) cited by Patrouch in his bibliography and by Jacob, *Essays* pp 4 n 1, 7 n 2, 11.

[14] J. H. Buckland (née Flemming), 'Reginald Pecock: his place in the History of English Thought' (Thomas Arnold prize, Oxford). I have not seen a copy of this.

[15] Green, *Bishop Pecock*.

[16] *Repressor* (Cambridge UL MS Kk iv 26); [*The*] *Book of Faith* (Cambridge MS Trinity Coll B 14 45), edited by Wharton and reedited with a lengthy introductory essay by J. L. Morison (Glasgow 1909); [*The*] *Donet* (Oxford Bodleian MS Bodley 916) ed E. V. Hitchcock, *EETS* os 156 (London 1921), collated with [*The*] *Poore Mennis Myrrour* (BL Add MS 37788); [*The*] *Folewer* [*to the Donet*] (BL MS Royal 17 D IX) ed E. V. Hitchcock, *EETS* os 164 (London 1924); [*The*] *Reule* [*of Crysten Religioun*] (New York Pierpoint Morgan MS 519) ed W. C. Greet, *EETS* os 171 (London 1927). See Green, *Bishop Pecock*, app 2 for a list of works surviving and lost.

[17] Compare Greene, *Bishop Pecock* cap 15 pp 230–35 'Pecock's Significance' and [E. H.] Emerson, '[Reginald] Pecock: Christian Rationalist', *Speculum* 31 (1956) p 235: Green 'seems unable to decide exactly what Pecock's importance is' despite his claim that 'he was a man who, from nearly every point of view, played a significant and interesting part in fifteenth-century history and whose life and works are not unworthy of being characterized and studied'.

[18] *Book of Faith* intro p 86.

and a philosophic rationalist with a regard for reason not to be found in any other mediaeval English thinker'.[19] It is surprising, then, that Joseph Lecler in his book *Toleration and the Reformation* (1960), although discussing at some length Nicholas of Cusa, Marsilio Ficino, and Pico della Mirandola, overlooks their contemporary or near-contemporary, Reginald Pecock.[20] By contrast Henry Wharton, admittedly with an axe to grind, had expatiated upon Pecock's tolerance. 'Not only did he disown the infallibility of the Church', he claimed, 'but also disallowed and condemned the practice of burning hereticks. He desired rather to win them to her obedience by gentle methods, and thought it more noble to convince them by reasons and arguments, than by racks and fires'.[21]

Mandell Creighton's definition in his Hulsean lectures (1893–4) of a tolerant person provides an apt starting point for an examination of Pecock's position. 'The tolerant man', the bishop felt, 'has decided opinions, but recognises the process by which he reached them . . . He always keeps in view the hope of spreading his own opinions, but he endeavours to do so by producing conviction'.[22] Pecock would have had equal sympathy for John Locke's defence of toleration: 'No way that I walk in against my conscience will ever lead me to the mansions of the blessed. I may grow rich by an art that I dislike, I may be cured of a disease by remedies that I distrust; but I cannot be saved by a religion that I distrust, or by a worship that I dislike.'[23]

The English church of the late-fourteenth and fifteenth centuries had not been so concerned with the arts of intellectual persuasion as with those of officially sanctioned presentation and, where need arose, of judicial enquiry into 'false opinions' followed by recantation. The basic faith was presented to the laity; its acceptance without argument was mandatory. Even preaching, twin weapon with the confessional of the Church's didactic armament, had been restricted by Archbishop Arundel for fear that its use might do irreparable

---

[19] 'Pecock: Christian Rationalist' pp 235–6. An area beyond the confines of the present article concerns Pecock's importance in the history of English prose, where opinion has also been divided. See, for instance, *The New Cambridge Bibliography of English Literature* ed G. Watson 1 *600–1660* (Cambridge 1974) cols 665–6, 805; A. G. Kennedy, *A Bibiliography of Writings in the English Language* (New York 1961) p 175 nos 4814–6; G. P. Krapp, *The Rise of English Literary Prose* (Oxford 1915) pp 73 *seq*; Hitchcock's introduction to the *Folewer*; Hannick cap 5; Patrouch cap 2.

[20] 1 bk 2 'Christian Humanism and the Religious Divisions'.

[21] *A treatise proving Scripture* p xxxvi.

[22] *Persecution and Tolerance* (London 1895) p 123.

[23] *Epistola de Tolerantia* ed R. Klibansky trans J. W. Gough (Oxford 1968) pp 98–9.

harm in the wrong hands.[24] Such action had appalled many churchmen, Gascoigne among them, and Pecock's sermon of 1447 in defence of non-preaching bishops, so often misconstrued, riled them still further.[25] But what, one must ask, was Pecock attempting to do?

There is some danger, I would suggest, in maintaining that Pecock was intent on erecting a self-consistent system of belief to take the place of orthodox Christianity or 'right faith'[26] as then understood.[27] His works were intended to serve a two-fold purpose: on the one hand to defend the existing Church, its beliefs, its practices, its structure, its personnel; on the other, to provide a positive code of belief and practice, as of moral behaviour, orthodox in intent but which could be understood and followed by literate, intelligent laymen, and to a degree even by the less gifted.[28] Pecock was faced with a practical problem. No longer was it possible to regard discussion of religious matters, of the Christian way of life, as confined to clerics, as did some of the old-fashioned preachers.[29] Lay

---

[24] [R. M.] Haines, 'Education [in English Ecclesiastical Legislation of the Later Middle Ages]', *SCH* 7 (Cambridge 1971) pp 161–75. For Arundel's constitutions (1407) see Wilkins 3 pp 314–19.

[25] Gascoigne repeatedly returns to the question of Pecock's sermons on this theme; for example, *Loci* pp 15, 35, 39, 41, 44, 49. Jacob, *Essays* p 4 n 2, questions Mrs Maxwell's emphasis (Pronger, 'Thomas Gascoigne' p 30) on Gascoigne's fixation, pointing out his concern about Pecock's attitude to the doctors. For Pecock's defence of the 1447 sermon made to Archbishop Stafford: *Abbreviatio Reginaldi Pecok, Repressor* 2 pp 615–19.

[26] *Folewer* p 69, à propos of 'our faith': 'And þis feiþ we clepen "catholik feiþ", þat is to seie, vnyversal or general feiþ, and þe same feiþ we clepen "ortodox feiþ", þat is to seie riȝt feiþ'.

[27] Emerson, 'Pecock: Christian Rationalist' p 236, argues that what he 'confessed under pressure', that is preferring judgment of natural reason to the New and Old Testaments and the Church's determination, 'he had earlier . . . established as the ideal for which men should strive'. [G. F.] Nuttall, '[Bishop] Pecock and the Lollards', *Transactions of the Congregational Historical Society* 13 (1937–39) p 83, writes that Pecock's 'scepticism is a rational one, it is in favour of reason at the expense of the Church; and, in that by him faith and reason are brought into the closest relationship, it is at the expense of faith too, as faith was then understood'. Nuttall saw similarities between Pecock's thought and that of both Abelard and Hooker. Various writers have taken up the comparison with the latter; for instance P. Munz, *The Place of Hooker in the History of Thought* (London 1952) pp 41–5.

[28] The first part is particularly the concern of the *Repressor*, constituting a vindication of the Church against the Lollards; the second is the subject of the (inchoate) *Donet*, its sequel the *Folewer*, and of the *Reule*. The *Book of Faith* is more concerned with the 'grounding' of faith and the nature of authority in the Church.

[29] The intent of the anti-Lollard sermons which may be tentatively ascribed to the Benedictine John Paunteley is to ridicule Lollard opinions and the Lollards themselves, to assert that matters of faith and theology are for clerics alone, and to argue

men and women anxious to argue from Scripture were a fact of everyday life in Pecock's time. From his experience of London and Westminster he knew that the king's service comprised men of 'subtlety and height of wit', qualities essential for the law's interpretation. Likewise he accepted the fact that a prominent mercer must needs exercise 'high and subtle wit' in his 'reckonings and bargainings'.[30] Men of this stamp were equally capable of comprehending (rather than merely accepting) matters of religion. In divinity 'all Christian persons ought to be scholars.'[31] But preaching was no adequate means of exposition, for not all would or could catch the full and appropriate meaning on first hearing. The written word possessed the advantage of providing instruction in a form which could be studied at leisure.[32] By no means every lay person was capable of rising to such a level, but extracts and summaries of didactic material—Pecock's, of course—could be graduated in difficulty to match the varying capacity of would-be learners.[33] Ideas such as these were justification for rendering his *Reule of Crysten Religioun* in English.[34] All the same, the schoolmasterly Pecock did not consider that all theological matters came within the range of lay persons. He had a sense of professionalism;

that current miracles provide proof of the Church's 'validity'. See R. M. Haines, '"Wilde Wittes and Wilfulnes", John Swetstock's attack on those "Poyswunmongeres", the Lollards', *SCH* 8 (Cambridge 1971) pp 143–53, esp pp 148–9; *idem*, 'Church, Society and Politics in the Early Fifteenth Century as viewed from an English Pulpit', *SCH* 12 (Oxford 1975) pp 143–57, esp p 153.

[30] *Reule* p 21, compare *Folewer* p 7. For the feminine role see C. Cross, '"Great Reasoners in Scripture": the activities of women Lollards 1380–1530', *Medieval Women*, ed D. Baker (Oxford 1978) pp 359–80.

[31] *Folewer* p 13, compare *Reule* p 87. For the study of the bible in the fifteenth century see Deanesly, *Lollard Bible* esp cap 13, and for Pecock (likened in two respects to Wyclif and Purvey), *ibid* pp 360–4.

[32] 'And þerfore myche raþer mowe suche maters be left to þe peple in writyng, for as myche as þei mowe þe writyng ofte rede and þerupon studie, þerupon conseil aske and have helpyng, and so þe bettir it kunne and þe bettir kepe hem fro erryng and of it þe mysundirstonding, þan if þei schulde it heere oonly oonys or twies bi word of preching'. *Reule* p 21. Elsewhere (*Repressor* pp 88–9) Pecock distinguishes between the functions of preaching (exhortation) and of scholarly exposition.

[33] 'Meete to ech mannys mesure of receyvableness'. *Reule* p 22.

[34] *Reule* pp 17–22. Pecock suggested that his works were 'in þe comoun peplis langage' for two sorts of people. 'Oon is of hem whiche holden hem silf so stifly . . . foolili and oonli to þe uce of þe bible in her modiris langage' that they hold 'alle oþere bookis writun or in latyn or in þe comoun peplis langage to be writun into waast . . . and cumbring of cristen mennes wittes. The 'oþer soort' while reading and studying the New Testament in English and admitting the use of other books in that language 'þei apprisin so myche þo unsavery bokis' and hold them to be 'riche jewils . . . loued and multiplied abroad of alle cristenpeple'.

higher things and true understanding of Holy Scripture were for 'substantially learned clerks well learned in logic and moral philosophy and in divinity'.[35] Consequently in the *Reule* he lapses into Latin for a discussion of the Trinity and pertinent questions posed by Peter Lombard in his *Sentences*.[36] But Pecock did not advocate slavish acceptance of authority; on the contrary, his works contain numerous warnings against the uncritical adoption of the opinions of doctors, however eminent.[37]

Exposition and refutation were required in English in order to reach the laity as a whole and the Lollards in particular. In the case of the latter Pecock had not only to defend the Church's position,[38] but also to overcome a reliance on the literal interpretation of Scripture amounting to bibliolatry.[39] It is arguable that Pecock the scholastic, with his almost naïve reliance on the syllogism—which even the simplest layman might employ[40]—was a rationalist in advance of his time, who in the last resort would be thrown back on the necessity of validating reason by reason.[41] It appears, however, that it was the situation which confronted him, rather than any predilection of his own, which forced Pecock to extend the principles of the Schools to a wider sphere. Lollards, he explains, were prepared to accept only what was vouched for by Scripture; moreover, they relied upon their own idiosyncratic interpretations.[42] Pecock did controvert specific

[35] For example, *Folewer* p 7: 'And in oþire bookis whiche y write for lay men, y write maters passyng þe capacite and þe power of lay men forto þo maters vndirstonde'.

[36] *Reule* pp 88–90. He also cites Scripture in Latin, *ibid* pp 133–4, 136–8, as well as in English.

[37] For example, *Folewer* pp 11, 65–8; *Reule* pp 464–6. Pecock's *The just apprising of doctors* has been lost.

[38] In the second section of the *Repressor* Pecock attempts a vindication of the Church's attitude to images and pilgrimages; in the third he defends the clergy's revenues; in the fourth the clerical hierarchy and ecclesiastical legislation, and finally, the religious orders.

[39] For the 'Bible men' see *Repressor* p 87, where Pecock mentions diverse groups: 'Doctourmongers', 'Opinion holders' and 'Neutralis'.

[40] *Folewer* p 37, also p 10; *Book of Faith* pp 174–5; *Repressor* pp 8–9, where Pecock mentions his intention to write a treatise on logic in English; Patrouch pp 54–9.

[41] Nuttall, 'Pecock and the Lollards' pp 85–6: 'In the last resort Pecock would have had to admit that reason, by which articles of faith are to be proved, is its own intrinsic authority, which is a telling illustration of the non-rationalism of a religious conviction, to which the rationalist is eventually driven back; for he would have found it hard to defend the authority of reason by reason'.

[42] *Repressor* p 102, where the Lollard opinion is said to have been: 'If eny man be not oonli meke, but if ther with al he kepe and fulfille al the lawe of God . . . he schal have the trewe vndirstonding of Holi Scripture thouȝ no man ellis teche him save God'. Pecock summarises his view in the *Reule* p 33: 'Manye untrewe opynyouns feyned

interpretations, but his main thrust came as a bold challenge to the self-sufficiency of Scripture.[43] Insistence on the 'doom of reason' effectively removed the conflict to neutral ground. Neither Scripture nor the Church was to be advanced as the ultimate authority.

In theory this was an excellent strategy, but inevitably one which alarmed more conservatively-minded clerics. There had been a long tradition in the English church, enshrined in the legislation of the thirteenth century, that clergy at parochial level were responsible for teaching the basic articles of the faith. Such articles were not intended to promote discussion. The manuals for priestly instruction, so much a feature of the fourteenth century, vastly extended the amount of information available. Such manuals were heavily dependent on canon law, which makes but rare intrusion into Pecock's scheme of instruction.[44] It can however be said that he was in line with this didactic tradition. Indeed, a recent commentator has invoked both Archbishop Pecham's *Ignorantia sacerdotum*[45] and Myrk's *Instructions for parish priests*[46] as providing an appropriate background to Pecock as an educationalist, while rightly pointing out that whereas Pecham and Myrk were both addressing priests, Pecock's prospective audience was comprised of lay people.

If canon law was substantially absent from Pecock's authorities, so too were most of the doctors of the Church, whom he cited sparingly and on occasion mainly to point out their deficiencies.[47] Scripture and even the Apostles' Creed were placed in a historical context, and a time-honoured fiction, the Donation of Constantine, was proved to be such by arguments which have been compared favour-

---

and forged . . . wiþoute ground of sufficient resoun or holy scripture, and also þat manye oþer opynyouns taken as for foundid in scripture mysvndirstonden'.

[43] *Repressor* p 10: 'It longith not to Holi Scripture, neither it is his office into which God hath him ordeyned, neither it is his part forto grounde eny gouernaunce or deede or service of God, or eny lawe of God, or eny trouthe which mannis resoun bi nature may fynde, learne, and knowe' (the first of thirteen conclusions).

[44] But see *Repressor* p 33. Elsewhere (*Folewer* p 52) canon law is considered to be the third kind of 'prudence', that is of 'knowyng wherbi we knowen what is to be doon or to be left undoon in oure gouernauncis'.

[45] See Haines, 'Education'; Patrouch pp 109–13.

[46] *John Myrk, Instructions for Parish Priests* ed E. Peacock, *EETS* os 31 (London 1968); Patrouch pp 113–23.

[47] He challenged Jerome's statement that 'Sithen the chirche wexid in dignitees or in possessiouns, he decrecid in vertues' (*Repressor* pp 334–9); claimed that with respect to the relationship of faith and reason Gregory contradicted himself (*Book of Faith* pp 145–52); and remarked of 'the philosopher', 'Wat was Aristotil oþir þan a louer of trouþ?' (*Folewer* p 151).

ably with those of Nicholas of Cusa and Lorenzo Valla.[48] Pecock went further. In place of such minimal schemes of instruction as those promulgated by Grosseteste and Pecham, which he considered inadequate for the laity's instruction, he devised a system of his own comprising the 'Seven Matters of Knowledge' and the 'Four Tables'.[49] He also suggested revisions in the liturgy to facilitate lay comprehension and provided his own (modified) version of the Creed in English.[50]

The open-mindedness of Pecock stemmed from a quite exceptional tolerance allied to an overweening confidence in his own mental capacity. By arguments appropriate to the psychologist, anthropologist, philosopher, theologian, educationalist or historian, and by the method of the logician, Pecock strove to make his systematisation of Christian belief and practice as widely acceptable as possible. The time was not ripe for an approach of this kind. Although his works were believed to have been circulated fairly widely, it is probable that their length and prolixity, their intellectual framework and, it has to be admitted, their somewhat turgid quality, prevented their having much impact on the Lollards. Clearly his fellow clerks read them. One of his bitterest critics was Thomas Gascoigne, who in his extensive and repetitive *Dictionarium Theologicum* provides most of the biographical details we have concerning Pecock.[51] A recurring theme of Gascoigne's is Pecock's sermons in defence of bishops who did not preach to their flocks; a notion which arose *'propriis glosis'* rather than from the holy doctors of the Church. Someone who impugned the veracity of saints such as Jerome, Ambrose, Augustine and Gregory was—so it was felt—

---

[48] See V. H. H. Green, 'The Donation of Constantine', *CQR* 135 (1942) pp 36–64; A. B. Ferguson, 'Reginald Pecock and the Renaissance Sense of History', *Studies in the Renaissance* 13 (1966) pp 147–65. The latter argues (p 157) that Pecock 'never questioned the providential scheme of history' but was 'able to see the religious traditions in a new perspective, the perspective of human experience'.

[49] Patrouch pp 123–40 summarises Pecock's 'system'.

[50] In the *Reule* pp 398–408, Pecock assesses practices associated with prayer and the divine office. Compare *Donet* pp 202–14. The English version of the Apostles' Creed is in the latter, pp 103–4. A 'Long version' has not survived.

[51] Especially *Loci* pp 208–18. Gascoigne can be supplemented by the [*Registrum Abbatiae Johannis*] *Whethamstede*, [ed H. T. Riley] (RS 1871) 1 pp 279–89 (*Hemingford* pp 490–502) and by the derogatory *Brief Latin Chronicle* in *Three Fifteenth-Century Chronicles*, ed J. Gairdner, Camden Society ns 28 (London 1880) pp 167–8. For contemporary critics see Jacob, *Essays* pp 13–14. Pecock himself (*Folewer* p 226) comments on current criticism and abuse 'mych unclerkli'.

rightly reduced to shame in the presence of thousands.[52] The penitent allegedly uttered the following quatrain:

Wit hath wonder that reason cannot tell;
How a mother is maid and God is man.
Leave reason, believe the wonder;
Belief hath mastery and reason is under.[53]

Pecock was no martyr, indeed there is no reason why he should have been, for he was always prepared to yield either to superior argument or to the authority of the Church.[54] For us he cuts a pathetic figure; his life's endeavour committed to the flames, his academic reputation reduced to ashes. He was forced to declare that he had preferred his own judgment (*judicia mea naturalis ratio*) above that of the Old and New Testaments, and that he had held and taught doctrines other than those of the Holy Roman Church. The six articles of his recantation (a seventh occurs only in Whetehamstede's chronicle and is rightly discredited)[55] were wrenched from their context. His books were ostentatiously burned at that same St. Paul's Cross where he had preached in defence of episcopal conduct and also at Carfax in Oxford as part of a ceremony attended by the chancellor of the university—his *alma mater*. What happened then is uncertain, but after being forced to resign his bishopric he probably ended his days in confinement at Thorney Abbey in Ely diocese.[56]

A champion to pick up the gauntlet for Pecock's refutation had already been found, but there was no forum of debate such as the bishop had advocated. Whatever its conventional merits, John Bury's *Gladius Salomonis*—the word of God—was not designed to concede any vestige of validity to Pecock's corpus. The bishop's

[52] *Loci* p 216 (compare 214, 217). See also *Folewer* pp 66–7; *Reule* pp 464–6; *Book of Faith* pp 145–52.

[53] *Loci* p 217; *Hemingford* p 488; *Repressor* p 623. Compare BL MS Sloane 3534, fol 3ᵛ, which also has a Latin version.

[54] For example, *Reule* pp 96–7: 'He is in no synne . . . so þat he be redy to forsake his errour as soone as he may dresse hym silf bettir into trouþe'. Also *Reule* p 29, where Pecock promises submission to his 'ordynaries' (prior to his elevation to the episcopate).

[55] *Whethamstede* pp 285–6; *Hemingford* p 498; *Acts and Monuments* 3 p 733 (from Canterbury Reg Bourchier). The recantation is in Oxford Bodleian MS Ashmole 789, fol 303ᵛ (cited Jacob, *Essays* p 19 n 2); *Whethamstede* pp 286–7. See also Hannick pp 14–15.

[56] *Repressor* intro pp lvii–lviii, and for the sources of Archbishop Bourchier's instruction to the abbot of Thorney, *ibid* n 3; Oxford Bodleian MS Ashmole fol 789, fol 326ʳ (cited Jacob, *Essays* p 22 n 3). See also R. M. Haines, 'The Practice and Problems of a Fifteenth-Century English Bishop: The Episcopate of William Gray', *Mediaeval Studies* 34 (1972) pp 456–7.

writings were declared to be of greater danger to the faithful than the opinions of Mohammed, Sabellius, Arius, or even Wyclif himself; firstly because of the novelty of his teaching, secondly by reason of the position of authority which he occupied, and thirdly on account of the seductive sweetness of his errors.[57] Animadversions can be made against some of Bury's arguments and of the interpretation he placed upon his victim's words;[58] more significant is his incapacity to consider, let alone to appreciate, the legitimacy of Pecock's underlying purpose. To parody the bishop's obtrusive conceit was no difficult task. *'Mecum sapientia est, mecum prudentia, mecum virtus, immo et omnium virtutum singularis solaque gubernatrix ratio'* are the words put into his mouth.[59] Others too were not slow to ridicule the man who had once risen so high on life's wheel of fortune:

Sic deplumatus pavo fuit, et spoliatus,
Sicque sibi siluit, vox quia rauca fuit,
Sic dudum volucris, quae nomen habebat honoris,
Bubo, non pavo, dicitur esse modo.[60]

His condemnation reduced Pecock to the same level as Wyclif, whose heresies he abhorred.[61] As John Foxe was at immense pains to demonstrate, fifteenth-century England was notorious for intolerance.[62] Both in the eyes of Thomas Netter of Walden and in those of the Benedictine monk and doctor of theology, John Paunteley, a fiercely anti-Lollard preacher, Henry V had been a king dedicated to the extirpation of Lollardy, by force if necessary.[63] Such a climate still pervaded the 1450s; it was not sympathetic to the toleration implicit in Pecock's unfamiliar methods of proselytising.

[57] *Repressor* p 602.
[58] For instance, *Repressor* p 576 n 1. [J.] Gairdner *Lollardy [and the Reformation in England]* 4 vols (London 1908–13) 1 pp 238–42, concludes that Bury's is 'really a very able treatise'.
[59] *Repressor* p 606 (*Gladius Salomonis*).
[60] *Whethamstede* p 288.
[61] For Pecock's attitude to Wyclif see Parouche cap 3. In view of work on the survival of Lollards into the sixteenth century this chapter now requires revision. Green, *Bishop Pecock* pp 68–9, points out that statutory oaths were taken at Queens' and King's Colleges, Cambridge, against the 'damnable errors' of Wyclif and Pecock. The brief analysis of the former's thought by G. Leff, 'John Wyclif: the Path to Dissent', *PBA* 52 (1966) pp 143–80, provides a useful means of comparison.
[62] The theme of *Acts and Monuments* 2.
[63] For Netter's arguments in the *Doctrinale* and its two supplements: Gairdner, *Lollardy* 1 pp 186–201; for Paunteley: R. M. Haines, '"Our Master Mariner, Our Sovereign Lord", a Contemporary Preacher's view of Henry V', *Mediaeval Studies* 38 (1976) pp 85–96.

In his book, *Development of Religious Toleration in England*,[64] W. K. Jordan put forward the view that 'Some of the noblest minds in modern times have suggested that the priceless benefits of toleration rest, not upon a better understanding of the spiritual nature of Christ's teachings, but upon scepticism about the possibility of definitely and dogmatically ascertaining any body of religious truth'. From which point he goes on to make the well-worn distinction between 'indifference' and 'tolerance'. Pecock was not of this opinion: indifferent he was not, but he felt with such passion as was appropriate to a man of reason that, at a time when traditional authority was either under fire or being misconstrued, reason could provide a strong element of certainty in religious matters. The argument that 'Religious toleration was revived in the sixteenth century by the Reformers who in the early period of the Reformation advocated freedom of conscience, as well as obedience to God, as man's primary duty',[65] entirely overlooks Pecock. It is true that only a few of his works have survived, and then only in individual manuscripts, but the leaven of ideas such as his would in any case remain difficult to detect. If Foxe was 'in advance of his time in advocating religious toleration', Pecock's position in that respect is even more pronounced. Of course, like Foxe, he could scarcely have envisaged the 'permissiveness' in religious belief some half a millennium ahead.

The reader who has successfully disentangled Pecock's convoluted arguments will not be able to suppress a certain surprise, even admiration, for the apparent 'modernity' of certain elements of his work, not least his suggestions about 'social service'.[66] Nonetheless, he will probably admit that the fifteenth-century Church rightly discerned in the author an undermining influence. A laity which was encouraged to encroach to such an extent on clerical monopoly was potentially dangerous; the way of suppression was seen to be preferable. As a consequence, Pecock in the view of most of his peers stood rightly condemned as an insidious heretic who had subtly modified the accepted norms of authority and

---

[64] (London 1932) 1 p 15.
[65] V. N. Olsen, *John Foxe and the Elizabethan Church* (Berkeley and London 1973) p 197. Compare U. Henriques, *Religious Toleration in England* (Toronto 1961) p 1: 'The development of religious toleration in England was an ultimate and wholly unintended consequence of the Reformation'.
[66] *Reule* pp 389–95.

exalted human reason—'the greatest doctor this side God himself'[67]—and above all his own. To add that this approach flew in the face of the contemporary emphasis on devotional life and mysticism points to another aspect of a complex story.[68] Perhaps the final comment should be left to Babington, the editor of Pecock's most impressive work. 'He was the enlightened advocate of toleration in times peculiarly intolerant; he was the acute propounder of a rational piety against unreasoning and most unreasonable opponents'.[69]

Dalhousie University

---

[67] *Folewer* p 10. Yet Pecock warned against 'Every hasty and vnsufficientli considerid and unavisid doom of resoun' (*Reule* p 466).

[68] F. W. Bussell, *Religious Thought and Heresy in the Middle Ages* (London 1918) pp 684–7; Jacob, *Essays* pp 30–4.

[69] *Repressor* intro p lix.

MISSION AND INQUISITION AMONG *CONVERSOS* AND *MORISCOS* IN SPAIN, 1250–1550

by JOHN EDWARDS

THE EXAMPLE of co-existence between Christians, Jews and Muslims in medieval Spain should, in theory, be an inspiration to those who hope for a successful multi-faith society today. On the other hand, the expulsion in 1492 of Jews who refused baptism, and of Muslims who adopted a similar attitude, from Castile in 1502 and Aragon in 1610, implies that the Spanish example should rather be seen as a warning of the consequences of failure. The question of interfaith relations will be considered here mainly from the point of view of Christians who attempted to cope with the proximity of the other two 'religions of the book'. It will, however, be possible to look at the feasibility of the long-term existence of Jewish and Muslim communities in Spain, and at the problems faced by converts from these two faiths to Christianity.

It is necessary, for both theoretical and practical reasons, to treat the whole of the late Middle Ages, from 1250 and continuing up to 1550, as a unit, though the final expulsion of the *moriscos*, in 1610, will not be specifically discussed. The introduction to Castile of the new foundation of the Inquisition in 1478 was a significant point in a process of readjustment in relations between Christianity, the dominant religion of western Europe, and the Jewish and Islamic minorities. This shift in attitudes was largely attributable to the orders of friars, newly founded in the thirteenth century, and in particular to the Dominicans and Franciscans. In this period, as Jeremy Cohen has argued, an alternative was developed to the traditional Christian attitude to the Jews. Since the time when the New Testament texts were written, the surviving Jews, who rejected the Christian claim that Jesus was Lord and Messiah, had been regarded as a remnant, which represented the old covenant between God and Israel, one which had been good in its time, but which had been replaced, since Jesus's earthly ministry, by the new covenant of grace. Now the Church was Israel, the heir to the Old Testament

139

promises, and the Christians were the chosen people of God, but the Jews nonetheless had a place in Christendom, as a warning of the consequences of failure to acknowledge Christ, and, in due time, a sign, through their conversion, of the imminent Parousia, the second coming of Christ.[1] In the 1240s and 1250s, and particularly in France and Spain, another approach to the Jews developed, in which their conversion was given a much higher priority. The ideas seem to have come mainly from the friars, especially the Dominicans, and, with the active support of secular governments, in particular those of Louis IX of France and James I of Aragon, they were put into effect, at least in some measure, by means of a programme of missionary preaching, formal disputations between theologians, and secular legislation. The theology behind this new proselytising movement is perhaps best represented by the monumental polemical work, *Pugio fidei* ('Dagger of the faith'), which was completed in 1278 by the Catalan Dominican normally known as Raymond Martini, and which provided both a defence of Christianity against Muslims, and, above all, Jews, and ammunition for missionaries who sought to spread the faith among believers in those faiths. It first refuted the supposed objections of pagan philosophers and rationalistic Muslims to the concept of revealed religion, and then attempted to prove to Jews, from their own scriptures and rabbinical writings, quoted in Hebrew, that the Messiah had come in Jesus.[2]

Christian attitudes to rabbinical texts, the Babylonian Talmud and the Mishna, seem to have evolved rapidly between the 1240s, when Talmudic books were burnt in Paris after the 'victory' of the Jewish convert Nicholas Donin over Rabbi Yehiel of Meaux, to the argument of *Pugio fidei* and the approach adopted by Pablo Christiani at the disputation of Barcelona in 1263, in which Talmudic texts were used as a means of convincing the Jews of the truth of Christianity.[3] Increasingly, from about 1250 onwards, two kinds of Judaism were distinguished by Christian theologians and preachers. Old Testament Judaism had its place in salvation history, as the Church had

---

[1] [Jeremy] Cohen, *The friars [and the Jews. The evolution of medieval anti-Judaism* (Ithaca and London 1982)] pp 19–32.

[2] Two analyses of *Pugio fidei* in Cohen, *The friars* pp 132–56 and [Ina] Willi-Plein [and Thomas] Willi, *Glaubensdolch [und Messiasbeweis. Die Begegnung von Judentum, Christentum und Islam im 13. Jahrhundert in Spanien* (Neukirchen-Vluyn 1980)] pp 23–78.

[3] Analysis of the Paris and Barcelona disputations in Cohen, *The friars* pp 60–85, 108–28. For the surviving texts and further analysis see Hyam Maccoby, *Judaism on trial. Jewish–Christian disputations in the Middle Ages* (London and Toronto 1982).

always taught, but now, instead of talking constantly about Jews as though they were still those of biblical times, the friars and their supporters identified contemporary Jews as different. The Jews of late medieval Europe were thus seen as having no place in God's scheme of salvation. Instead, they were a blind remnant, corrupted by the teachings of the rabbis, and, in addition, the Torah itself, though once a valid Law, was no longer the basis of a valid mode of life. This new view had interesting consequences for textual criticism, in that Martini and his friends were prepared to distinguish different 'layers' of text in the Talmud, in order to identify 'valid' older texts and later corruptions, but it also had important implications for the living conditions of medieval Spanish Jews.

It is clear that both theological and social factors helped to segregate Jews from Christians in medieval Europe. In Castile and Aragon, as elsewhere, Jews were still dependent on monarchs for the privilege of existing in Christian kingdoms, and paid heavy taxes in return. Always in theory and sometimes in practice, social intercourse between the two communities was discouraged, both by Jewish dietary laws and by the restrictions imposed by the Church and secular authorities. Interlocked with religious and social pressures were the popular stereotypes which the distinctiveness and separation of Jews from Gentiles encouraged.[4] The new thirteenth-century approach to the Jews not only led to the reaffirmation at various times, for example in Aragon in the 1260s and Castile in the 1390s, of traditional restrictions, but also to the permanent addition of preaching missions to the agenda of the Church. Thus a doctrinal offensive paralleled the task of freeing all Spanish soil from infidel rule, though in both cases the theoretical demands might be ignored for long periods. It was in the late fourteenth century that pressure on Jews to convert mounted with unique force. The social and economic problems and political instability, which lay behind the Gentile attacks on Jewish communities which cut a swathe across Spain, from Seville to Barcelona, in the spring and summer of 1391, have received due attention.[5] It should, however, be remembered that the violence was accompanied, and in some degree motivated, by the missionary campaign which the friars had begun, with royal support, in the previous century. The original attack in Seville

[4] Maurice Kriegel, *Les Juifs à la fin du Moyen Age dans l'Europe méditerranéenne* (Paris 1979) pp 13–56.
[5] Philippe Wolff, 'The 1391 pogrom in Spain. Social crisis or not?', *PP* 50 (1971) pp 4–18.

appears to have resulted from the preaching to Christians of the archdeacon of nearby Ecija, Ferrán Martínez, who whipped up the residual sentiment which focused on the Jews as 'Christ-killers'.[6] After 1391, both in Castile and in Aragon, preaching to Jews accompanied the social and political aftermath of the riots. The best-known and most influential missionary was another Catalan, Vincent Ferrer. The peak of his influence was in the first two decades of the fifteenth century, when he received the support, both of Ferdinand I of Aragon and of the anti-pope Benedict XIII, who, in 1413–14, staged another formal Christian–Jewish disputation at Tortosa, in which Martini's *Pugio fidei* was used once again.[7] As a result of a combination of the pogroms of 1391, the apparent debating defeat of their representatives at Tortosa, and the preaching campaigns of Ferrer, large numbers of Aragonese Jews had, by 1420, converted to Christianity, in many cases leaving the surviving Jewish artisans and tradesmen without their social and intellectual leadership.

Both the content and the effects of Vincent Ferrer's preaching have been much studied. It is clear from the surviving sermons that the friar was an eloquent speaker, capable of eliciting emotional responses from his audiences. In one sermon, for example, he created a word-picture, in traditional style, of the Church as a beautiful countess, whom the Jews were unable to gaze upon because of their blindness. There is evidence in his works that Ferrer preached against violence towards the Jews, but he did believe that the policy of physical segregation of those who would not convert should be more effectively implemented by the secular authorities.[8] His hostility towards Jews was evidently religious, not racial, but its consequences for their social life could be severe. The nature of Ferrer's mission and its results may usefully be studied by reference to one particular town, Teruel, where the introduction of the Inquisition was to be resisted later in the century. Vincent came to Teruel twice,

[6] M. Mollat and P. Wolff, *The popular revolutions of the late Middle Ages* (London 1973) pp 214–5.

[7] The full Christian account of the Tortosa disputation is edited and studied in Antonio Pacios López, *La disputa de Tortosa*, 2 vols (Madrid 1957).

[8] R. Chabas, 'Estudio sobre los sermones valencianos de San Vicente Ferrer que se conservan en manuscritos en la biblioteca de la basílica metropolitana de Valencia', *Revista de Archivos, Bibliotecas y Museos* 8 (1903) pp 111–26, esp pp 124–5. For Ferrer's attitude to the Jews, Francisca Vendrell, 'La actividad proselitista de San Vicente Ferrer durante el reinado de Fernando I de Aragón', *Sefarad* 13 (1953) pp 87–104 and José María Millás Vallicrosa, 'San Vicente Ferrer y el antisemitismo', *Sefarad* 10 (1950) 182–4.

in April and October 1412. He organised night-time meetings, in which his sermons from a platform in the main square were preceded by torchlight processions, which included squads of flagellants. The two-fold purpose of the mission was to inspire greater faith among the Christians and to convert the Jews. Here, as elsewhere, the town council not only provided financial support for the preacher and his assistants, but also, at his urging, re-established a ghetto for the Jews who retained their old religion.[9] Teruel's Jewish community never recovered from the friar's visit. It was left, walled-in and leaderless, until, having been constrained to give damning testimony against converts by the Inquisition, the remaining Jews were ordered to leave the town in 1486.[10]

After 1420, attention, in both Castile and Aragon, shifted from the Jews themselves to the converts from Judaism to Christianity. There appear to have been several reasons for this change. The fact that many of those who converted as a result of preaching and social pressure between 1390 and 1420 were members of the social and intellectual elites of their communities meant that many of the converts quickly achieved success in careers, such as ecclesiastical and secular public office, which had previously not been open to them. Inevitably, some 'Old Christians', as those who saw themselves as being of entirely Christian stock were known, were thus excluded from jobs which they might otherwise have expected to obtain. In contrast, after the disintegration in this period of the great urban Jewish communities, such as those of Seville, Córdoba, Toledo and Barcelona, Jews increasingly became a feature of small towns and villages, a process which both brought them closer to the land and land-holding, and, at least to some extent, diverted away from them the traditional Christian animosity towards moneylenders and 'social parasites'.[11] From then on, the *conversos* (converts from Judaism) re-

---

[9] Antonio C. Floriano, 'San Vicente Ferrer y las aljamas turolenses', B[oletín de la] R[eal] A[cademia de la] H[istoria] 84 (1924) pp 551–80.

[10] Evidence of the decline in Teruel's Jewry is to be found in charters of Ferdinand I and Alfonso V in [Fritz] Baer, *Die Juden* [im christlichen Spanien, 2 vols (Berlin 1929–33 repr Farnborough 1970)] 1 pp 826–7, 836–7, 846–7. A leading convert in Teruel is discussed in Vendrell, 'Concesión de nobleza a un converso', *Sefarad* 8 (1948) pp 397–401. For the fate of Teruel's *conversos* at the hands of the Inquisition, [Manuel] Sánchez Moya [and Jasone] Monasterio Aspiri, 'Los judaizantes [turolenses en el siglo XV', *Sefarad* 32 (1972)] pp 105–40, 307–40; 33 (1973) pp 111–43, 325–56.

[11] On rural Jews, detailed studies in, for example, Francisco Cantera Burgos and Carlos Carrete Parrondo, 'La judería de Hita', *Sefarad* 32 (1972) 249–306 and 'La judería de Buitrago' *ibid* pp 34–87. A general survey in Angus MacKay, 'Rural Jews', duplicated summary of a paper delivered at Leeds Judeo–Spanish seminar, 1978.

placed the Jews as the main target of Old Christian hostility. The process which culminated in the introduction of the Inquisition to Castile was initiated in 1449, when a rebellion in Toledo against John II led to attacks on *conversos* and the promulgation of the 'Sentence-statute', named after the rebel leader, Pero Sarmiento, which barred *conversos* henceforth from public office. [12] The Castilian government enlisted the help of the Papacy in crushing this rebellion, so that, in addition to the restoration of royal authority, the years after 1449 saw a strong assertion of the rights as Christians of whose who converted from Judaism, which was achieved through the influence of, among others, Cardinal Juan de Torquemada, the uncle of the first Castilian Inquisitor-General, and which is best represented by Pope Nicholas V's bull of 1449, *Humani generis inimicus*. [13] The pope was supported by the learned works of various *converso* clerics and officials, such as Bishop Alonso de Cartagena, the *relator* of the royal council of Castile, Fernán Díaz de Toledo, Lope de Barrientos, bishop of Cuenca, and Cardinal Juan de Torquemada himself. [14]

However, the desire of the converts from Judaism to protect their own status in Christendom had one unfortunate consequence. Increasingly, in the 1450s and 1460s, *conversos*, such as the Franciscan Alonso de Espina, proposed that, as the main religious and social problem facing Castile appeared to be false converts from Judaism, the best way of curing society's real or imagined ills would be to revive the old institution which had originally been devised to repress unorthodox views among Christians in the south of France, the Inquisition. [15] Eventually, after serious rioting in Andalusia in 1473, the new rulers of Castile and Aragon, Isabella and Ferdinand, succumbed to this pressure and, in 1478, obtained from Pope Sixtus IV a bull authorising the new tribunal, which began at Seville in 1480 and spread through both kingdoms. [16] Initially, the Jews were used as

[12] [Eloy] Benito [Ruano,] *Toledo [en el siglo XV. Vida política* (Madrid 1961)] pp 34–81 and 'La "Sentencia-estatuto" de Pero Sarmiento' in *Los orígenes del problema converso* (Barcelona 1976) pp 49–98.

[13] Nicholas V's two bulls for Toledo in Benito *Toledo* pp 198–203.

[14] Alonso de Cartagena, *Defensorium unitatis christianae*, ed Manuel Alonso (Madrid 1943); Fernán Díaz de Toledo, *Instrucción del relator para el obispo de Cuenca, a favor de la nación hebrea*, in Cartagena, *Defensorium*, ed Alonso pp 343–56; Lope de Barrientos's reply, *ibid* pp 324–38; Juan de Torquemada, *Tractatus contra madianitas et ismaelitas*, ed Nicolás López Martínez and Vicente Proaño Gil (Burgos 1957).

[15] Fray Alonso de Espina, *Fortalitium fidei (1459)* (Lyons 1511) quoted in Americo Castro, *The structure of Spanish history* (Princeton 1954) p 539.

[16] MacKay, 'Popular movements and pogroms in fifteenth-century Castile', *PP* 55 (1972) pp 35–67. Manuel Nieto Cumplido, 'La revuelta contra los conversos de

witnesses against 'judaising' converts,[17] but when their usefulness was over, those who remained faithful to the old covenant were perceived to be a bad influence on the *conversos* and they were expelled, first from Andalusia in 1483, then from parts of Aragon in 1486, and finally from all the lands of the Catholic Monarchs in 1492.[18] One of the last acts in the Inquisition's campaign to persuade the Crown to order this expulsion seems to have been the notorious 'ritual murder' trial, known by the name of the supposed victim, the 'holy child of La Guardia', which took place in 1491, and involved, most irregularly, the trial of an unbaptised Jew by the Inquisition.[19] From 1492 onwards, Jews were merely fantasy enemies of the Old Christians, though *conversos* continued to cause worry through their supposed religious and racial impurity.[20]

It may be argued, therefore, that the Inquisition proved to be an effective instrument for achieving the assimilation of the great bulk of the Jewish population of Spain to Christian society. If the Jewish communities of the pre-1391 period are taken as a base, it appears that about eighty per cent of the Jews and their descendants became Christian, while the rest emigrated in 1492.[21] The inquisitorial procedure, which owed more to the priestly ministry of penance than to the practice of law courts, undoubtedly created terror and division among the convert communities, and relatively few Jews withstood the various social, intellectual and religious pressures to convert, even though the evidence of the Inquisition's trials suggests that many of them in fact devised their own individual or

Córdoba en 1473', in *Homenaje a Antón de Montoro en el V centenario de su muerte* (Montoro 1977) pp 31–49. Bernardino Llorca, *Bulario pontificio de la Inquisición española en su período constitucional (1478–1525), Miscellanea Historiae Pontificiae* 15 (Rome 1949).

[17] For cases of Jewish testimony in Inquisition trials, Haim Beinart, 'Jewish witnesses for the prosecution of the Spanish Inquisition', in *Essays in honour of Ben Beinart, Acta Juridica* (Capetown 1978) 37–46; Fidel Fita, 'La Inquisición toledana. Relación contemporánea de los autos y autillos que celebró desde el año 1485 hasta él de 1501', *BRAH* 11 (1887) p 294. Teruel cases in A[rchivo] H[istórico] N[acional] (Madrid), Sección] Inq[uisición,] Leg[ajos] 542 no. 41, 543 no. 8, 544 nos 11, 12, 546 nos 1, 4–6.

[18] Baer, *Die Juden* 2 pp 348–9; 1 pp 569–913.

[19] Fita, 'La verdad sobre el martirio del Santo Niño de La Guardia, o sea el proceso y quema (16 noviembre 1491) del judío Juçe Franco en Avila', *BRAH* 11 (1887) pp 7–134.

[20] A. A. Sicroff, *Les controverses des statuts de 'pureté de sang' en Espagne du XVe au XVIIe siècle* (Paris 1960).

[21] Miguel Angel Ladero Quesada, 'Le nombre des Juifs dans la Castille du XVe siècle', *Proceedings of the Sixth World Congress of Jewish Studies (Jerusalem, 1973)* (Jerusalem 1975) vol 2 pp 45–52.

family mixtures of Jewish and Christian belief and practice.[22] It is questionable, however, to what extent Muslim experience with Christianity paralleled that of the Jews.

In principle, all the policies which have been outlined with regard to relations between Christianity and Judaism also applied, *mutatis mutandis*, to its approach to Islam. The militant and self-confident Christians, like Pablo Christiani and Raymond Martini, who supported and attempted to implement the ideas of Raymond of Peñaforte, approached Muslims in the belief that they were on the brink of conversion, that Muslim scholars did not actually believe in the tenets of Islam, and that it was necessary to carry out the missions rapidly, as the Parousia appeared to be imminent. A school of Arabic was founded in Tunis, on Peñaforte's initiative, so that the friars could evangelise more effectively. It is hard to avoid seeing such enterprises as at best bravely outrageous and at worst comically foolish. Only eight Catalan Dominicans actually studied in Tunis, and the enterprise soon declined to extinction, but it illustrates various factors which were to be important later, in the attempts of the Church to convert the remaining Muslim populations of the kingdoms of Granada and Valencia. The main points were the sublime self-confidence of the Christians and their belief in the unique truth of their religion, the importance of a close alliance between ecclesiastical and secular authorities and personnel, and an awareness of the need to bridge a linguistic and cultural gap, if Muslims were to be converted. The thirteenth-century euphoria died down, though Raymond Lull kept it going into the fourteenth century, with support for Arabic and Hebrew studies coming from the council of Vienne in 1311, but it remains to see what happened to Muslims and converts from Islam (*moriscos*) in the age of the Catholic Monarchs and their Inquisition.[23]

The main religious figures in the early years of Christian rule in the kingdom of Granada were Fray Hernando de Talavera, the first archbishop, and Cardinal Jiménez de Cisneros, archbishop of Toledo and Inquisitor-General. The *capítulos* agreed between the Castilian Crown and the surrendering Muslim authorities guaran-

[22] Bernard Hamilton, *The medieval Inquisition* (London 1981) pp 49–59. For cases of religious mixture in Teruel, see AHN Inq.leg. 544 no. 17 and Sánchez Moya and Monasterio Aspiri, 'Los judaizantes'.
[23] Cohen, *The friars* pp 104–8, 199–225. Willi-Plein and Willi, *Glaubensdolch* pp 11–14. R. I. Burns, 'Christian–Islamic confrontation in the west; the dream of conversion', *AHR* 76 (1971) pp 1386–1434.

teed religious freedom for the remaining Muslim population, but it was assumed from the start that these people should sooner or later become Christians. Before long, the *bienes habices*, or goods used to support the Islamic cult, were transferred to the Christian clergy, while Talavera organised efforts to teach Christianity to the Moors. Even before the conquest, he and others had been catechising selected converts in Christian territory, but, once established in Granada, he set up an Arabic school and sought Arabic-speaking clergy. He is said to have tried to learn the language himself, but not to have got beyond the first nouns. This mission to Muslims should not, however, be seen in isolation. Talavera may be regarded not only as a holy man, respected by the faithful of both religions, but also as a model Tridentine prelate before his time. Even more daringly, he allowed the use of both Spanish and Arabic, in order to increase the devotion of the people. However, although there can be no doubt about Talavera's zeal and doctrinal orthodoxy, a more ruthless policy of 'baptism by numbers' was introduced by Cisneros, with royal support. One result was the Alpujarras uprising, soon followed by others in the Serranía de Ronda, and the Sierra Bermeja, behind Málaga. Before long, the captain-general of Granada, the count of Tendilla, was intervening, on grounds of the need to preserve public order, to prevent Old Christian attacks on Muslims. Talavera, meanwhile, seems to have become increasingly disillusioned and was even accused of heresy, shortly before his death, by the inquisitor of Córdoba, Diego Rodríguez Lucero.[24] There is some dispute about the role of the Inquisition in Granada before 1550. It is clear that the official introduction of the tribunal to the area took place after a Catholic council at Granada in 1526, but Meseguer has argued that Talavera himself dealt with inquisitorial cases, in the traditional manner, as diocesan bishop.[25] It is not, however, disputed that, even when it did start work in the kingdom, the Holy Office treated the *moriscos* very mildly, at least until after 1550.[26]

[24] Tarsicio de Azcona, *Isabel la Católica* (Madrid 1964) pp 547–55 and 'El tipo ideal de obispo en la iglesia española antes de la rebelión luterana', *Hispania Sacra* 11 (1958) pp 21–64. H. C. Lea, *The moriscos of Spain, their conversion and expulsion* (London 1901) pp 18–22, 47–51.

[25] [Augustin] Redondo, [*Antonio de*] *Guevara* [*1480?–1545) et l'Espagne de son temps* (Geneva 1976)] pp 272–3. Juan Meseguer Fernández, 'Fernando de Talavera, Cisneros y la Inquisición', in *La Inquisición española. Nueva visión, nuevos horizontes* (Madrid 1980) pp 371–400.

[26] Redondo, *Guevara* p 285. José María García Fuentes, *La Inquisición en Granada en el siglo XVI* (Granada 1981) pp xxx–xxxvii.

The situation in Valencia was rather different. Here, a Muslim population had remained under Christian rule since the thirteenth-century reconquest, forming a significant part of the rural labour-force. These *mudéjares* had effective religious freedom, and were allowed to lead an Islamic life by their lords, who protected them from the Church, as long as they paid their heavy seigneurial dues and labour services.[27] Thus mission was not seriously tried in the Valencian countryside until the issue had been forced by the rebellion of the Germanía in 1521. This movement of anti-seigneurial and anti-monarchical resistance also led to the compulsory baptism of many Muslims, particularly in the south of the kingdom. When the rising had been crushed, the problem of what to do with large numbers of unwilling and uncatechised converts remained. The question of the validity of these baptisms caused much agonised debate in royal and ecclesiastical circles, but the result, inevitably, was that these people were henceforth treated as Christians, though it was recognised that a massive teaching work lay ahead of the newly-strengthened clerical structure in the kingdom. The features which stand out from all the available accounts, both secular and eccesiastical, are, on the Muslim side, the determination of the *moriscos* to retain their Islamic lifestyle and for this purpose to keep their links with Muslims in North Africa and the eastern Mediterranean, and, on the Christian side, the reluctance of the lords to lose the financial benefits of their vassals' remaining Muslim, and the difficulties experienced by the Church, both in the technical communication of the gospel to the ex-Muslims, and in finding clerics to do this job effectively.[28]

In view of the amount of energy which was devoted to converting Jews and Muslims to Christianity in medieval Spain, it might be expected that the process of communicating one religion to believers in another would have received considerable attention. The militancy of Christianity, particularly among the friars, has already been alluded to, but the missionary efforts of preachers, theological disputants and parish priests undeniably failed on the great majority of occasions. If conversions from either religion took place, they were, with the exception of a few individuals, brought about by

---

[27] John Boswell, *The royal treasure. The Muslim communities under the Crown of Aragon in the fourteenth-century* (New Haven and London 1977).

[28] Redondo, *Guevara* pp 218–62. Tulio Halperín Donghi, *Un conflicto nacional. Moros y cristianos viejos en Valencia* (Valencia 1980) pp 95–118, 135–71.

social, political and legal pressures. The new problem of false converts, which was thus created, was supposedly solved by the Inquisition. The communication of the doctrinal tenets of the three faiths clearly preoccupied their respective leaders and intellectuals, but it is quite clear that on neither side of Christian–Jewish or Christian–Islamic debates and polemics was there any serious attempt at dialogue, in the sense of a preparedness to draw up the agenda for debate jointly, and to be genuinely affected by the resulting exchange of views. None of the three religions was, of course, monolithic, as each was affected by tensions between fundamentalists and rationalists, though Christianity, perhaps because of the success of the scholastics' work, appeared less divided in this way than Judaism or Islam. There was, however, little real intellectual or spiritual understanding of the opposing faith to be seen in the medieval polemics, and set-piece disputations, which affected Jews but not Muslims in this period, were not genuine dialogues but merely adjuncts of missionary activity.[29]

At the practical level, however, more understanding of the problems involved in changing people's religion is discernible in the conduct of the Church. Here, though, there is a curious difference between attitudes towards Jews and Muslims, which has wide implications. Very little seems to have been done to teach the newly-converted Jews the Christian faith. Concern was occasionally expressed about this neglect, but on the whole it was apparently assumed that an admission that Jesus was Messiah, with the addition of the baptismal water, was enough to turn the former Jews into new men and women. Theologically, this was indeed the case, as Nicholas V pointed out in 1449, but the efforts made in the fifteenth-century to separate physically the Jewish and Christian communities in towns all over Spain, together with the growing obsession with racial purity, show that theology was not enough. The Inquisition was efficient in its own terms, and the expulsion of unbaptised Jews undoubtedly assisted the assimilation of the *conversos*, but, in the last analysis, the Holy Office was trying to solve a social problem by theological means, and was thus operating in the wrong set of categories. This contradiction was highlighted by the confrontation

---

[29] For Muslim–Christian polemic, Louis Cardaillac, *Morisques et chrétiens. Un affrontement polémique (1492–1640)* (Paris 1977). On dialogue, William A. Christian, Sr, *Oppositions of religious doctrines. A study in the logic of dialogue among religions* (London 1972) p 17.

with the Muslim populations of Granada and Valencia. Very soon after arriving in Granada, Talavera realised that changing Muslims into Christians would involve detaching them completely from their old lives.[30] It was thus necessary to repress the social as well as the strictly religious activities of the former Muslim communities, in addition to publicising the attractions of the Christian way of life. Becoming a Christian thus meant that a Muslim had to change his language and dress, as well as practising Catholicism in his public and private life. The difficulty of making this transition explains both the draconian measures proposed by Charles V's advisers, such as Dr Lorenzo Galíndez de Carvajal, and the failure of the attempts, first of Talavera and later of the Jesuits, to turn *morisco* children into Catholic Christians.[31] In their desperation, the ecclesiastical and secular authorities proposed taking children away from their parents, in order to indoctrinate them more effectively, and developed a conspiracy theory to explain *morisco* intransigence. The concept of international Jewry, with a co-ordinated policy against Christendom, had gained a limited currency in the fifteenth-century,[32] but the belief that the sixteenth-century *moriscos* were a fifth column for North Africans and Turks was more credible.

Recent studies of so-called 'popular' religion are now reaching a higher level of sophistication. It is increasingly understood that the relationship between religion as believed and religion as practised is complex, for all social groups, including professional theologians.[33] However, even if it is accepted that pre-modern systems of belief were, in their own terms, as rational as explanations of life and ways of practically coping with it as are modern beliefs, it is still true, as Stuart Clark has recently admitted, that the difficult part is converting from one of these 'systems' to another.[34] This, though, is pre-

---

[30] Talavera, 'Instrucción y carta para los vecinos del Albayçín' in Ladero, *Los mudéjares de Castilla en tiempo de Isabel I* (Valladolid 1969) pp 293–5.

[31] Galíndez de Carvajal in Redondo, *Guevara* pp 275–84. Antonio Garrido Aranda, 'Papel de la Iglesia de Granada en la asimilación de la sociedad morisca', *Anuario de Historia Moderna y Contemporánea* 2 (1975) pp 69–103. For Jesuit education, Nigel Griffin, '*Un muro invisible*; *moriscos* and *cristianos viejos* in Granada' in F. W. Hodcroft, D. G. Pattison, R. D. F. Pring-Mill, R. W. Truman eds *Medieval and Renaissance Studies on Spain and Portugal in honour of P. E. Russell* (Oxford 1981) pp 133–54.

[32] Adolfo de Castro, *The history of the Jews in Christian Spain* trans E. D. G. M. Kirwan (Cambridge 1851) pp 160–3.

[33] William A. Christian, Jr, *Local religion in sixteenth-century Spain* (Princeton 1981).

[34] Stuart Clark, 'French historians and early modern popular culture', *PP* 100 (1983) p 98.

cisely what the Spanish Crown and the Catholic Church expected their Jewish and Muslim fellow-citizens to do in the fifteenth and early sixteenth centuries. Beneath the theory, whether that of medieval and early modern lawyers and clerics or that of modern anthropologists, philosophers and social historians, it is nonetheless true that, just as the Inquisition records show many Jews to have slipped rapidly, and perhaps with relief, into the majority Christian culture, the constant traffic of renegades and missing persons across the Christian–Muslim frontier[35] had shown that, as Mercedes García Arenal has asserted in the case of Cuenca, there was no reason in principle why the *moriscos* could not have assimilated too, whatever the maestro Braudel may have said.[36] Politics, and an excess of doctrinal purity, prevented this happy but confused state from being reached.

University of Birmingham

---

[35] Cross-frontier traffic is discussed in MacKay, 'The ballad and the frontier in late medieval Spain', *Bulletin of Hispanic Studies* 53 (1976) pp 15–33.

[36] Mercedes García-Arenal, *Inquisición y moriscos. Los procesos del tribunal de Cuenca* (Madrid 1978) p 117, criticising Fernand Braudel, 'Conflicts et refus de civilisation: espagnols et morisques au XVIe siècle', *Annales* 2 (1947) 397–410.

PERSECUTION AND TOLERATION
IN REFORMATION EUROPE

by N. M. SUTHERLAND

PERSECUTION IS self-explanatory, but toleration, when one starts to consider it, blurs like the recollection of a dream. To what, in the first place, does toleration refer: to deviant opinions, deviant practices, or to potentially subversive organisations? Genuine toleration has probably always been very rare—and probably still is. In the sense of complete religious liberty, it was not generally accepted until varying dates in the nineteenth century. Then it had more to do with materialism and indifference than with any generous spirit of tolerance. If, in the sixteenth century, toleration was not entirely unknown—both in theory and in practice—it must be attributed to something more compelling than 'a disposition to be patient with the opinions of others'—in the OED's rather engaging definition. For one thing, toleration was not then regarded as a particularly desirable virtue, and therefore not widely entertained as an ideal. The ideal was rather that God, in his mercy and wisdom, should reunite the Church, or churches. This was expressed, for example, in the preamble to the edict of Nantes in 1598, though one could discount it as propaganda.

The Protestant Reformation produced the most widespread heresy—in the sense of deviation from the Catholic Church— that western Christendom had ever experienced. It was also more far-reaching than previous heresies, even those which had been doctrinally similar, and the challenge to the Papacy was carried further than ever before. In the sixteenth century, Europe had been deeply disturbed by the questing and the scholarship of the Renaissance, by the spread of literacy and, increasingly, by the perils and possibilities of printing, which both produced and manipulated a new force of public opinion. New factors in the development of states were also producing conflicts and tensions which were to influence reactions to doctrinal and ecclesiastical changes. Furthermore, they enabled religion to be used as an exploitable force. Increasingly secularised 'national' churches offered, more than ever, a powerful vested interest to be defended. But, if states had moved, or were moving,

153

away from subservience to Rome, unity of religion was still assumed to be the basis of unity in the state.

Once Luther had been excommunicated, and Rome dramatically repudiated, much of the Reformation conflict came to be about church structure and government. This immediately brought it into the sphere of Church/State relations, and tended to block the way to a resolution of diversity in religion through church reform, and doctrinal reconciliation—which never proved to be possible. While doctrine might change, political and ecclesiastical authorities were still seen as supporting one another, though how authority should be apportioned became the subject of acute, new and evolving controversies, as in Geneva, or in the municipalities of Holland and Zealand. If anything, the Church then mattered to the state more, rather than less. Since it had long been axiomatic that heresy must be suppressed, the problem of persecution or toleration arose—as an aspect of authority and obedience—in every country affected by the Reformation. Where the Reformation was introduced from above, the problem naturally occurred in a different form. Eventually, where the Reformation survived, it enhanced state sovereignty at the expense of the Church. But this could not have been the case had toleration prevailed.

Diversity of religion was naturally bound to produce demands for toleration, not only by mystics, who existed in all ages, but by those who wanted their own way and challenged the right of authority to thwart them. Toleration had previously been a largely philosophical issue, since earlier heresies were relatively localised, and potentially heretical theological controversies had affected only a learned elite. During the Reformation, however, the issue of toleration could hardly be avoided when the sheer weight of numbers, their resources and affiliations, created a new problem of scale. What could not be coerced or exterminated, would have to be either endured or accommodated. If the existence of heresy had been considered a menace to ordered society in the thirteenth century, when the Inquisition became fairly extensive, it was a vastly greater threat in the sixteenth century. But, whereas, in theory, the purpose of the Inquisition was the salvation of souls, in the sixteenth century—which possessed not only printing but also firearms—it was the problem of law and order which became a paramount criterion. This may be clearly illustrated from the so-called religious edicts of the Netherlands and France. Thus the policy and procedures of persecution or toleration depended on social and political circumstances, and these were not static.

Persecution and Toleration in Reformation Europe

While religious toleration might, ostensibly, have solved various problems arising from matters of conscience and self-defence, it was actually barely possible where other quarrels already existed: where political opponents either belonged to, or briskly adopted, opposing faiths, where there were disputed jurisdictions, or where there was a struggle for power and rivalry among the nobility. Such conflicts abounded in sixteenth-century Europe, and diversity of religion augmented them, providing ideological respectability and extending their original scope. Besides, toleration could not simply be proclaimed. No government could—successfully—be more tolerant than the governed, and tolerance was emphatically not the spirit of the age. Toleration required, in other words, a degree of social and political stability which was not typical of the period, or else an exceptionally strong secular power, such as Henry IV of France. But, whether even a Henry IV could have prevailed in France in the 1560s, is an open question; nor did he ever claim to be conferring toleration, but to be enforcing peace.

There were, of course, exceptions, mainly in areas or circumstances in which public order did not depend upon conformity. Toleration existed for some time in Poland and in Transylvania—areas of weak central government in which the nobles were stronger than the prince. The emperor Maximilian II also permitted it to the nobles of his patrimonial lands, thereby securing their loyalty. Maximilian was not, in any case, an ardent Catholic and it is doubtful whether one should really classify as toleration concessions obtained by nobles who could be dangerous. In Hesse, also, the margrave Philip was tolerant, even of Anabaptists. He was, however, tolerant in the early Lutheran sense: he would not execute for religion alone, without clear evidence of other offences but he was rigorous in his control of sedition, and he helped in suppressing both the Knights' War and the Peasants' Revolt. Thus, one of the principal problems thrown up by the Reformation was the genuine difficulty of distinguishing between heresy and sedition.

Even the literary examples which testify to the conception of toleration, tend to contain caveats which amount to the distinction between heresy and sedition. Jacob Storr of Zweibrücken maintained that the prince had no power to suppress the Mass by force. But he qualified that by saying that *peaceful* subjects should be permitted freedom of religion. The inference was that the seditious must be dealt with. Martin Becanius, a Catholic theologian, also

155

favoured toleration. But he was writing later, after the experience of so-called religious wars, and really only advocated humanitarian and pragmatic expedients in circumstances of deadlock—such as arose almost everywhere.

The dice, therefore, appeared to be loaded in favour of persecution. All Catholic princes were bound by canon and civil law to oppose heresy, and were also likely to be bound by some oath of office. There was, as yet, no conception of individual liberty, and intolerance derived naturally enough from any claim, whether orthodox or heretical, to possess a monopoly of truth. Thus, persecution appeared inevitable in a society whose conception of truth was narrowly contained within church dogmas, albeit on the Catholic side still, paradoxically, ill-defined. So long as people thought, in constricted terms, of true and false doctrine, false doctrine was bound to arouse enmities, which could affect other spheres of life. It must, therefore, be regarded as dangerous.

Rome and the emperor were as quick to swoop upon Luther, once he had attracted notoriety, as their political circumstances permitted. But, while he could be excommunicated by the Church, and outlawed by the State, this did not suffice to extinguish what he had begun. Thus the circumstances in which the Reformation arose ensured that the issues of persecution or toleration were not determined on purely religious grounds, or even, in some cases, on religious grounds at all. Consequently, the initial, detached idealism of the humanists and reformers was bound to be short-lived. They were soon brought face to face with the same practical realities as the Papacy and Charles V.

It was not for Luther to seek toleration—considering himself to be right—though he was, originally, prepared to extend toleration to others. His position, however, was exceptional. In spite of his outcast state, he enjoyed recognition and protection in electoral Saxony. As a dissident, he was bound to reject the coercive power of the Church, and equally rejected the power of the State in the sphere of religion. Thus he repudiated the use of force or coercion in spiritual matters, conceiving of the dual powers of Church and State as wholly separate, though it was perfectly clear that they were not. The Church's function was to ensure piety, and that of the State was to provide peace.

Unlike Erasmus, Luther could not avoid reality. He was forced to realise that religion, in order to survive, would have to be institutionalised, and that only the prince could do it. Luther was, furthermore, deeply shaken by the Anabaptists, the Knights' War and the Peasants' Revolt—in other words, by major problems of public order. By 1526, Luther had accepted that religious liberty must be restricted where there was any danger of sedition. He agreed that, 'in order to prevent harmful revolt and other mischief,' the prince could not accept any sect or division in his territory. In the Lutheran Church of Saxony, those who could not conform were required to leave. Luther reserved the principle of religious liberty by declaring that princes did not compel faith, but only suppressed external abominations. This certainly smacks of semantic wriggling; nevertheless, insistence upon conformity—even with penalties for disobedience—was not quite the same thing as persecution for belief. It was rather the imposition of authority in the interests of law and order. If the reform, or the construction of the Church had become the duty of the prince, clearly he could ill afford to be tolerant of other churches. Opposition to the prince's religion became opposition to the prince himself, which brings us back to the teasing distinction between heresy and sedition. There was, nevertheless, around 1530, some disagreement among Protestants as to whether diversity really ought to be permitted.

If, on the one hand, toleration was virtually impossible, persecution on the other, generally proved to be impracticable. It was simply not an effective means of eradicating heresy, tending to exceed the executive power of governments. Consequently the Reformation era witnessed a variety of prevaricating attitudes and endeavours, such as eirenicism, humanitarianism, and doctrinal reconciliation. It also produced what one might call certain intermediate conditions, between persecution and toleration.

Eirenicism was mainly an attitude of the humanists who did not care to push conflicts to extremes, and it has often been taken for moral cowardice. In Erasmus, it sprang from his fear of schism and of lack of faith, both of which he unwittingly promoted. Eirenicism had no place, however, in the *realpolitik* of the 1520s, of which Erasmus had no understanding. War, after all, was not generally regarded as evil, but rather as normal and honourable. Humanitarianism is primarily a philosophical attribute, difficult to establish in public affairs. Yet, if not the basis of policy it was, nevertheless, expressed by Catherine de Medici, who had no wish to decimate thousands of Frenchmen in pursuit of the obviously impossible. In other words, the heretics in France could not, physically, be exterminated, and Catherine acted in that realisation from 1560 onwards. Queen Elizabeth, also, was humanitarian in her refusal to seek windows into men's souls, or to persecute beyond the requirements of national security.

Doctrinal reconciliation was a prolonged and practical endeavour, which really requires an extensive survey. At the outset, it was vaguely assumed that the problem of religion could only be, and must be solved by a general council. Contemporaries dared not admit that a council could neither dispose of divergent opinions, nor enforce its own decisions. Furthermore, a council required peace, and European conditions which did not obtained. One alternative, abhorrent to the Papacy, was reconciliation at a national or local level. There were a number of councils or colloquies in Germany, albeit described as diets, of which the most significant were those of Augsburg in 1530 and Regensburg in 1541. The diet of Augsburg produced its famous Lutheran confession which was, upon various occasions, considered as a basis for doctrinal reconciliation.

The other outstanding example of a national council or colloquy was that of Poissy in France in 1561. The assembly of Poissy has been seriously misunderstood and the purpose of most of the participants was actually to convert their opponents. The pope, for his part, sent a special legate and the general of the Jesuits to traverse the proceedings. Nevertheless, there was also an attempt at doctrinal reconciliation, and the cardinal of Lorraine proposed the Confession of Augsburg as a *via media*. Furthermore, a team of learned moderates, Catholics and Calvinists, did produce several possible formulae of fascinating ambiguity. But, given the current mania for precise interpretations, this was entirely wasted ingenuity. Besides, there remained, in any case, the problems of church structure and government. Reconciliation—an endeavour on the part of only relatively few leaders to end diversity and achieve some way between persecution and toleration—could only have succeeded in the absence of any authoritarian pronouncements. Yet, even after the council of Trent, which defined doctrine, the ideal continued to linger on.

In the category of intermediate conditions, one might place freedom of conscience, recognition, and licenced co-existence. Freedom of conscience, repeatedly granted in France, detached belief from conduct, and could be seen as one way of distinguishing between heresy and sedition. While belief is beyond external control, freedom of conscience was a valuable liberty, since dissenters were liable to betray themselves. In the absence of any system of conformity, liberty of conscience approximated to recognition. Recognition was generally implied rather than specified, stopping short of the legalisation of dissent. For example, the diet of Speyer in 1526 declared that estates and subjects would live in such a way as everyone trusted to justify before God and the emperor. That was neither persecution nor toleration, but it did imply a grudging recognition. One might also cite the French edict of Romorantin, May 1560, which also implied recognition, and ended persecution on purely religious grounds; its main purpose, however, was really to provide for law and order in the aftermath of a conspiracy.

Licenced co-existence is a circumlocution to cover forms and degrees of toleration brought about by expedience and deadlock, as distinct from any tolerant intentions. One could cite, for example, the religious peace of Augsburg, 1555, after the definitive loss of religious unity and the failure of reconciliation. The notorious maxim, *cuius regio ejus religio*, certainly represented recognition; the licence was for the princes rather their subjects. It was, above all, an acknowledgement of deadlock, following violence. The French edict of January 1562 went further, authorising limited, supervised protestant worship, outside the towns. This, like Augsburg, was also a deadlock expedient, but before the occurrence of violence—which it failed to avert.

If all Catholic princes began by opposing heresy, the manner and nature of that persecution varied from country to country, and the outcome was frequently affected by foreign intervention. The most common denominator was deadlock, leading to some rough compromise, or 'intermediate condition,' between persecution and toleration. The emperor, above all princes, was bound to defend religion. But his ability to do so was curtailed by the hostility of the Papacy, as well as France, and finally of his own princes. He was unable to enforce the edict of Worms, proscribing Luther, to prevent interim agreements which amounted to recognition, or to enforce adequate Catholic reforms. Thus, in Germany, deadlock following hostilities, together with foreign intervention, led to a regional solution in the peace of Augsburg. This was neither Catholic nor Protestant in inspiration, neither oppressive persecution nor effective toleration.

In his patrimonial Netherlands, Charles V instituted an Inquisition in 1522, which largely eliminated Lutheranism. But, after the rise of Calvinism in the 1550s, the severe religious edicts came to be widely opposed, even by a predominantly Catholic population. Their aversion from persecution had to do with privilege, patronage, jurisdictions and commerce; possibly also indifference. Religious problems in the Netherlands proved insurmountable. This was not because the Spanish held any monopoly of fanaticism, but because neither Catholics nor Protestants would tolerate each other. There also, deadlock following hostilities, together with foreign intervention, ultimately led to a regional solution, but one brought about by war rather than treaty or edict.

France is the principal example of licenced co-existence. Diversity in religion could not be welcome to any king of France, where Catholicism was held to be a fundamental law. Here too, licence, in varying degrees, was the outcome of deadlock, both before and after hostilities, with elements of foreign intervention. Nevertheless, the edict of January 1562 did afford humanitarian recognition, and a realistic approximation to toleration, albeit primarily in the interests of peace, law and order. No subsequent edict of pacification was ever described as an edict of toleration, although Calvinism was never again to be illegal in France in time of peace, until 1685.

England, of course, was unique. Heresy did not simply arise, calling for persecution. It was, however, possible to die for religion in Henrician and in Elizabethan England. Where conformity is required by law, and heresy is defined by law, it might be alleged that persecution exists. But, while Elizabeth required conformity, lay Catholicism was not precisely illegal, and the point at which penalisation becomes persecution is no doubt debatable. Radical Protestants, however, could also be persecuted, not for false doctrine, but for rocking the ship of state. In both cases, public order and national security were the criteria. Scotland was also unique, where Protestantism, after a long gestation, was established by revolution. Here, again, a much weakened crown was unable to persecute. It is doubtful, however, if Queen Mary really wanted to, since her sights were clearly fixed on neighbouring England.

Obviously there are no original conclusions to be drawn. The scale of the Reformation threw up new problems in the handling of heresy, which were everywhere determined by social and political circumstances. Neither persecution nor toleration could be adequately enforced. Thus, for the most part, hostilities, deadlock and foreign intervention led to a variety of intermediate conditions.

University of London
Bedford College

PERSECUTION AND TOLERATION
IN THE ENGLISH REFORMATION

by G. R. ELTON

THE CENTURY of the Reformation, in England as elsewhere, sharpened all conflicts and augmented persecution. As the unity of Christendom broke up, the rival parties acquired that sort of confidence in their own righteousness that encourages men to put one another to death for conscience sake; an era of moderation and tolerance gave way to one of ever more savage repression. To the openminded willingness which characterized the humanism of Erasmus and More as well as the Rome of Leo X there succeeded the bigotry typical of Carafa, Calvin, Knox and the English puritans; only the gradual evaporation of such passions, produced by each side's inability to triumph totally, produced a weariness with religious strife which made the return of mutual sufferance possible. That, at least, is the received story. Historians of toleration, as for instance Jordan and Lecler,[1] firmly described the history of persecution in this way. Jordan identified six developments which led to its decline in sixteenth-century England: a growing political strength among dissident sects, the impossibility of preventing splintering and preserving uniformity, the needs of trade which overrode religious hostility, experience of travel, the failure to suppress dissident publications, and finally a growing scepticism which denied the claims to exclusive truth advanced by this or that faction.[2] In other words, only two things moved men, once they had fallen away from the generosity of the pre-Reformation era, to substitute an uneasy toleration for a vigorous persecution: the external pressures of experience and the decline of religious fervour. By implication, men of power called for repression and only those who could not hope to win favoured toleration, until general exhaustion set in. It is a convincing enough picture, and much evidence no doubt supports it. But it is a picture—a general and rather schematic

---

[1] [W. K.] Jordan, [*The Development of Religious*] *Toleration* [*in England from the Beginning of the English Reformation to the Death of Queen Elizabeth* (London 1932)]; J. Lecler, *Toleration and the Reformation* (2 vols. London 1960).
[2] Jordan, *Toleration* pp 20–3.

panorama which makes little allowance for the real opinions of individuals. On this occasion I should like to test it by looking at the attitudes of two highly articulate sixteenth-century Englishmen—Thomas More, humanist and loyal son of the universal Church, and John Foxe, humanist and faithful protestant. Both, we know, were men of sensitivity and sense. How did they stand to the problem of persecution?

It may be thought that Thomas More deserves a rest: has not enough been said about, for and against (mostly for) him? He is, however, really rather central to this discussion. A major figure in that humanist and Erasmian movement in Church and society whose influence (political and intellectual) can fairly be traced in all sorts of places through the remainder of the century, he was a believing Christian who before the Reformation had offered reasoned criticism of his Church, then came to dread the Reformation, and as lord chancellor was in a position exceptional for an intellectual of having to apply his convictions in practice. Of course, he was not a 'typical' Erasmian if only because such a thing could hardly exist among those individualists whom only loose ties of shared ideals and occasional friendship held together. With respect to the treatment of heresy he may have been even less typical because he chose to stand forth as its chief opponent, to a degree that bewildered even those Erasmians who continued to adhere to the old Church. Even in (mistakenly) defending him against a charge of imprisoning suspects, Erasmus was obliged to admit that More 'hates those seditious teachings which are now so tragically shaking our world; that is something he has never disguised or wished should remain secret.' Indeed, Erasmus added in an aside which the over-active community of More-scholars has chosen to ignore, 'he is so firm in his piety that if there is to be any tilting of the balance even a tiny bit he must be said to be closer to superstition than to impiousness'.[3] In the mouth of that chief foe to 'superstition'—the form which official Christianity had taken in the later middle ages—that assessment, uttered as late as 1532, is distincly critical. Sir Thomas, it seems, had long before this made it plain to Erasmus that the problem of heresy—toleration or persecution—stood at the centre of his thought; and

---

[3] *Erasmi Epistolae*, ed. P. S. Allen X p 137: '*Odit ille seditiosa dogmata, quibus nunc misere concutitur orbis. Hoc ille non dissimulat, nec cupit esse clam; sic addictus pietati vt, si in alterutram partem aliquantulum inclinet momentum, superstitioni quam impietati vicinior esse videatur.*'

since the two men never met and rarely corresponded after 1521 his position had evidently become solid well before he started combating the Lutherans. And his devotion to the existing Church was such that to the prince of humanists it seemed appropriate to speak in terms which accused his old associate of betraying the central tenet of Christian humanism.

That More contemplated diversity in religion and the problems it posed even before Luther's irruption is, of course, well known, as are the apparent tensions between the attitude he adopted in *Utopia* and his behaviour towards Tyndale and the rest. With a breathtaking boldness which elevates a non-sequitur to the status of an explanatory epigram—the sort of boldness which marks More's devotees— R. W. Chambers jumped the gulf by saying that 'it is precisely More's tolerance that makes him, on true Utopian principles, intolerant of the Reformation'. He went on to allege that More's fury against heretics derived from his conviction that 'all religious experience is sacred': his inner beliefs were offended by the heretics only because they attacked the worship of saints and such-like practices.[4] Quite apart from the fact that More's objections to Luther and Tyndale went vastly deeper than that, we may note that Chambers does not explain why More was always so scathing about the religious experiences described by heretics. Bland and smug, this remains the level of reflection at which More-idolaters treat a very delicate problem: and it will not do. We have More's word—endless thousands of words—to testify to his belief in persecution; indeed, it has been shown that he practised it precisely by the definition of it that he himself set up in the *Dialogue of Comfort*.[5] I do not propose to go over all that ground again. '*Odit ille seditiosa dogmata*' and made no bones about it: why should we, in our post-Enlightenment squeamishness, deny his convictions and their consequences when he himself wished to make them public? But questions remain. What sort of toleration did the humanist More believe in, and what did the persecution of heretics mean to the More who preferred to appear leaning to superstition rather than impiety?

On the face of it, religious toleration prevails in Utopia. 'They count it among their most ancient principles that no one should ever

---

[4] R. W. Chambers, *Thomas More,* (London 1935) pp 252–3.
[5] Leland Miles, 'Persecution and the *Dialogue of Comfort*: a fresh look at the charges against Thomas More,' *Journal of British Studies* 5 (1965) pp 19–30.

suffer harm for his religion'.[6] Utopus had introduced this regulation
not only for the sake of peace, which he recognized would be
totally ruined by constant wrangling and implacable hatred, but
also because he decided that this rule would best serve the cause
of religion itself. He would not venture rashly to lay down the
law, feeling uncertain whether God would not prefer to have
varied and manifold forms of worship, inspiring different
people differently.[7]

This reflects the humanist conviction that, while Christianity
represented God's only truth, Jews and Moslems—and possibly
other heathens—must be allowed to regard their religion as also permitted by God, especially if they have not had the chance to learn
about the Christian revelation. We find this species of tolerance also,
for instance, in Thomas Starkey whose Lupset cited 'the opinion of
great wise men' to support the view that obedience to the law of
nature and their own civil ordinances would save Jews, Saracens,
Turks and Moors—though he added that he would have to leave it to
'the secret judgment of God' whether 'it be so or not'.[8] This special
concession to other established confessions can be found granted
occasionally through the rest of the century; it deserves a little better
than it gets in the grudging comment of Father Surtz who seems
anxious to save More from any charge of relativism or from being
thought to agree with God's preference for variety in his worship.[9]

Not pausing to wonder what Utopus would have thought of the
constant wrangling and implacable hatred that fills More's *Confutation
of Tyndale*, we note that to all appearance religious intolerance was
absent from the kingdom he founded. However, there were limits.
In the first place, More spoke of Christianity as though it was a
single, agreed and perfect doctrine: he says not one word about
heresy. Secondly, Utopian toleration knows bounds. There every-

[6] *Utopia* p 218/29–30: '*Siquidem hoc inter antiquissima instituta numerant, ne sua cuiquam
religio fraudi sit.*' All citations from More's works are from the Yale edition of *The
Complete Works of St. Thomas More*. Quotations for *Utopia* are given in my own
translation, and where necessary I have repunctuated the Latin; throughout this
paper I have modernized the spelling of English quotations.
[7] *Ibid* p 220/7–12: '*Haec Vtopus instituit non respectu pacis modo, quam assiduo certamine
atque inexpiabili odio funditus uidet euerti, sed quod arbitratus est, uti sic decerneretur, ipsius
etiam religionis interesse, de qua nihil est ausus temere definire, uelut incertum habens, an
uariam ac multiplicem expetens cultum deus aliud inspiret alij [sic: ?alios].*'
[8] Thomas Lupset, *The Dialogue between Pole and Lupset*, ed. K. Burton (London 1948)
pp 34–5.
[9] *Utopia* p 521.

body is entitled to try to convert others to his own beliefs, but only if he confines himself to quiet and moderate argument. If, finding persuasion unsuccessful, he descends to reckless verbal attacks or attempts to use actual force, he becomes liable to the ultimate Utopian punishments—exile or enslavement.[10] In view of the vocabulary which More was to acquire in his polemics, we may note that the laws of Utopus specifically condemned intemperate abuse. Utopus, we are told, dreaded the civil strife which such disagreements bring about and in particular held that verbal or physical violence was much more likely to promote the victory of a false faith: for he expected that in the course of time rational thought would discover that true religion in expectation of which he decreed toleration, and which would then be formally established. Utopian tolerance represented a holding action and presupposed the existence of a single true religion; it did not admit the right of several religions, each held to be true by their followers, to exist side by side once the real truth of God's will had become known. Thus in the last resort there was toleration in Utopia only so long as it had not turned Christian. Even so, as Christian attitudes to rival faiths went, More's Utopian fiction had some eirenic virtue.

In due course, More was to discover that it had become impossible to speak of a single Christian faith, and if in 1516 he had been honest he would even then have admitted and considered the problems of heresy and schism; if he had done so, it seems unlikely that he would ever have been thought of as essentially a man of toleration. Once he confronted heresy he had to explain his new-found violence: he did so by taking the line that Luther and his followers could not be tolerated because their noise led to civil strife and they promoted their cause by violent attacks on the existing order. Reading More's controversial writings, it is hard to believe that even if Luther had cooed as any sucking-dove More would have granted him the right to deviate from orthodoxy. However, he used the reservations contained in Utopus' scheme of things as a handy bridge to the other shore where he could forget about the possibility that God might prefer variety in his worship or that all the truth was not yet known. Submitting himself totally to the authority of the Church, he could become a persecutor. In view of his use of those Utopian limitations, his account of behaviour which was not tolerated there deserves a glance. One unfortunate man, converted by Hythloday and display-

[10] *Ibid* p 220/3–7.

ing all the zeal of the new believer, exceeded the proprieties in his efforts to persuade fellow Utopians to turn Christian. In his anger he called all other religions profane, accused their followers of blasphemy and sacrilege, and assured them that the fires of hell were waiting for them; for which reason he was tried and condemned to exile, not (we are told) because he expressed such contempt for their religion but because he was stirring up riots—though we are not told that anyone in fact rioted.[11] Zeal of this kind was frowned upon, but it had to be of the kind that condemned other believers outright; moreover, both cause and agent of the man's punishment belonged to the civil sphere. It is thus fairly clear that, given the right reactions and carefully defined allegations, Utopian toleration did not inhibit the persecution of heretics: thus More prophetically guarded his later apparent change of mind. But he did not change it because he held, with Utopus, that all forms of worship must be tolerated so long as they do not cause tumults. He persecuted heresy not (as Chambers suggested) because he treated denunciations of harmless pilgrimages as offences against the multiplicity of worship, but because he saw in it a threat to that only truth which in Utopia still needed discovery.

From about 1521, More discovered himself involved in the realities of religious strife; the speculations of *Utopia* ceased to be adequate for his purposes. At first he certainly tried to adhere to the proposition that heretics must be persecuted because they pursue their ends in violent ways which disturb the people. Killing them is a surgical form of social therapy.[12] They always started it: Augustine turned to repression only after the Donatists had resorted to violence, and the English statute under which heretics were burned resulted from Oldcastle's (Lord Cobham's) rebellion. Similarly he justified the current severity against heretics by charging them with savagery: it was 'the violent cruelty first used by the heretics themselves against good catholic folk' that forced princes to suppress them by fire and the sword, 'for preservation not of the faith only but also of the peace among their people'. More's allegations of heretical violence are very tendentious. In the *Dialogue against Heresies* he blamed the Sack of Rome on the Lutherans and ignored the part played by good Catholic Spaniards, and in the *Confutation* he offered the German peasants' war as a characteristic consequence of heresy;[13]

[11] *Ibid* p 218/21–9.
[12] *Dialogue against Heresies* pp 406–10.
[13] *Ibid* pp 370–2; *Confutation of Tyndale* pp 482–3.

yet he must have known that the onset of persecution preceded both events. In any case, he provided no proof for the connection between those disturbances and the Reformation but confined himself to emotional outcries and loud resentment at the language used by the Lutherans against the Church. Reading his own violence, one feels inclined to remind him that the Utopian preacher was exiled for overstepping the mark in advocating orthodoxy. No doubt More believed that the revolting peasants of 1525 would have remained at peace had it not been for Luther, and he may have believed Augustine's charges against the Donatists. No honest lawyer, however, should have argued that the Lancastrian heresy acts resulted from a rising of 1414 when (as he must have known) the most important of them was passed in 1401. In short, the links with Utopian principles represented by his attempts to justify persecution by the need to maintain peace in society against violent disruption are spurious; they hide convictions about the treatment of dissidents which are anchored in a genuinely persecuting temperament.

For soon More forgot that heretics caused trouble by annoying people in their settled ways and pursued them because they were only too likely to win people over. That he came to advocate the killing of heretics as a worthy end in itself emerges disconcertingly from the unbridled violence and savage contempt with which he referred to them. As he said in 1534, when debating with St German: let the adversary prove that a number of heretics consigned to the fire had suffered any wrong 'but if it were that they were burned no sooner'.[14] He persecuted worse than the orthodox bishops, as when he lambasted Thomas Hitton, a heretic apparently burned upon first conviction, as 'the devil's stinking martyr'; even Foxe's account makes it plain that his interrogators gave Hitton every chance to escape the stake but were defeated by his characteristic exalted stubbornness.[15] More would no doubt have regretted any such misplaced charity, as he did in other cases. He resented the royal pardon given to Robert Barnes and disapproved of the relative tolerance shown to Richard Bainham who nearly managed to get one too; and he never once expressed any doubt about the practice of burning men alive. His profession that the clergy burned no one but merely handed the convicted and excommunicated heretic over to the secu-

---

[14] *Apology* p 94.
[15] *Confutation* pp 13–17; John Foxe, *Acts and Monuments*, ed S. R. Cattley/Josiah Pratt VIII 712–15 [hereafter cited as *AM*].

lar arm must be read in the light of his admission that the law left that arm no option but to burn the man.[16] The mixture of lip-smacking and evasiveness in all these diatribes against individuals becomes truly nasty.

It is, in fact, idle to pretend that More's references to particular victims of the persecution have any humanity left in them. Take the case of John Tewkesbury, a wandering preacher and colporteur, in whose apprehension and trial More played an active part. In December 1531 Tewkesbury was burned as a relapsed heretic, and Tyndale expressed joy over his steadfastness at the stake. (I am not saying that More's opponents were particularly attractive either, but on the virtue of true martyrdom they were all, of course agreed. They differed only over who could claim the crown). Confronted with this joy, More could see no reason for it, unless Tyndale 'reckoned it for a great glory that the man did abide still by the stake when he was fast bound to it'. This thoroughly unfeeling remark was made about a man who had borne his awful death bravely; it was followed by allegations that Tewkesbury refrained from recanting only because he knew that his relapse made this pointless—allegations supported by the testimony of 'one James', apparently a fellow-prisoner.[17] This particular passage is interesting not only because it shows up More's attitudes and his polemical methods, but more especially because he here drops the only other 'humane' argument in favour of burning heretics that he at times advances. This is that an abjured offender who, having relapsed, is yet burned is thereby saved from changing (perjuring himself) once more: the fire destroys the body but comes nicely in time to save the soul. Thus we find More condescendingly content over an unnamed heretic who was captured with Tyndale's books on him,

> and both burned together, with more profit unto his soul than had been haply to have lived longer and after died in his bed. For in what mind he should then have died our lord knoweth, whereas now we know well he died a good Christian man.[18]

This apparently comforting notion underlies his several accounts of Thomas Bylney's fate—accounts in which he was mainly concerned to prove that the heretic had recanted at the last and thereby saved his soul, even as he died at the stake.[19] After all the abuse he had

[16] *Confutation* pp 10–11; 17–18; *Dialogue against Heresies* p 410; *Apology* pp 92–4.
[17] *Confutation* p 21.
[18] *Ibid* p 359.
[19] E.g., *Dialogue against Heresies* pp 255–8; *Confutation* pp 23–5.

heaped on Bylney, his trust that God will accept the heretic's revocation of his heresies as part-payment for 'the poor man's purgatory' can only be called unctuous. Moreover, in order to be able to maintain that recanting when being burned at the stake was better than risking a relapse into heresy during the rest of one's life, he deliberately falsified the truth of Bylney's death by ignoring or decrying the solid testimony that no such recantation had taken place.[20]

In sum, then: More believed in persecution rather than toleration, and in respect of Christian heretics he almost certainly did so before he encountered Luther. Such toleration as he permitted in Utopia could easily be converted into repression on grounds to be judged by the ruling magistrate alone and was so converted by himself from 1521 onwards. When he came to face the reality of the problem he not only himself assisted in the repression of heresy but in his writings proclaimed a consistent and relentless defence of persecution. The justifications which he provided for drastic action were no doubt sincerely felt but he supported them with such manifest deviations from the truth and wrapped them up in such volubly violent language that his real feelings are not obscured. He hated those seditious teachings and he was doing all he could to root them out by violence. We shall later say a word about the possible explanation behind this extreme reaction; for the present let it be noted that before heresy became rampant or successful in England the Christian humanist who as lord chancellor presided over English justice believed in persecution.

The second writer under consideration here, another man who had much to say about the dilemma of tolerating or persecuting dissent, is John Foxe. Foxe found it necessary to involve himself with More, especially because the chief attack on the first edition of the *Book of Martyrs* came from Nicholas Harpsfield, a leading member of the group who in Mary's reign had set about constructing Sir Thomas's posthumous fame in preparation for the canonisation they sought to obtain from Rome.[21] The chief occasion for tangling with More, quite understandably, arose for Foxe in Bylney's case.[22] After telling the story as he in his turn saw it, he went on:

But here now cometh in sir Thomas More, trumping in our

[20] J. F. Davis, 'The Trials of Thomas Bylney and the English Reformation', *Historical Journal* 24 (1981) pp 775–90.
[21] Harpsfield appears in *AM* under the pseudonym of Mr Cope.
[22] *AM* IV pp 643–52.

way with his painted card, and would needs take up this Thomas Bilney from us, and make him a convert after his sect. Thus these coated cards, though they could not by plain Scriptures convince him, being alive; yet now, after his death, by false play they will make him theirs, whether he will or no. This sir Thomas More, in his railing preface before his book against Tyndale, doth challenge Bilney to his catholic church . . . And how is this proved? By three or four mighty arguments, as big as mill-posts, fetched out of Utopia, from whence thou must know, reader, can come no fictions, but all fine poetry.

Here he makes a valid point against More, which applies not only to Bylney's case but to most of More's polemical writing: 'With the like authority as he affirmeth, I may deny the same, unless he brought better demonstration for his assertion than he doth, having no more for himself than his own αυτοσ εφη .' As he admits, he comes close to trading vituperation with More—with 'this vein of yours, which so extremely raileth and fareth against the poor martyrs and servants of Christ'. So he stops himself: 'But because Mr More is gone and dead, I will cease any further to insult upon him, lest I may seem to occur the same vice of his, "in mordendo mortuos".' However, he needs to combat More's books 'which be not yet dead, but remain alive to the hurt of many': he must do battle with More's 'book-disciples', that is to say, especially Harpsfield. It should be said that when Foxe rather contemptuously pushed aside those who held that More invariably spoke the truth—that More who 'hath cracked his credit so often and may almost be bankrupt'—he taught a needed lesson to modern scholars.

In this exchange Foxe did rather well, not so much in his arguments concerning Bylney (though he had the right of that) as in his temper. Where More ever rages, Foxe is rarely found uttering any real abuse, though he can speak very sharply about popery. That Foxe always inclined to the search for peace is well enough known, and those who have studied him have seen him expressly as a proponent of toleration. I think that in essence they were right, and I may refer myself to that work of others which I do not mean to rehearse here at length.[23] Of Foxe's eirenic temperament and preference for mildness there should be no doubt—John Foxe who even in Luther could see only the bringer of spiritual solace, the balm to 'the poor

[23] [J. F.] Mozley, [John] Foxe [and his Book (London 1940)] pp 35–6, 54–5, 86–9; [V. N.] Olsen, [John] Foxe [and the Elizabethan Church (Berkeley 1973)] ch. VI.

mourning souls of the afflicted'.[24] In all the disputes among the reformers themselves, Foxe always took the side of peace, preaching moderation and conciliation: in the Vestiarian controversy, the dispute between Whitgift and Cartwright, the usual eucharistic debates.[25] On this last issue he could speak in terms which to the committed must have sounded dangerously close to indifference. Thus when commending Luther's *Commentary on Galatians* to the reader he admitted that Luther's teaching on the Lord's Supper might upset some, seeing that it differed a little from Zwingli's views; however, he added, it differs much more from the views of the papists—so let us not fret over so trifling a difference.[26] One soon comes to recognize the tone of moderate reason—here applied to the issues which in 1529 caused the irreconcilable breach between Luther and Zwingli!—as Foxe's characteristic note. In the age of Elizabeth, when railing was still much more common than sweet reason, Foxe must be regarded as unusual in his manner, and even as More's violence had distressed Erasmus so Foxe's mildness puzzled some of his friends. When early in 1558 he expostulated with John Knox about the vehemence of *The First Blast of the Trumpet*—and thus did so while the regiment of women still included only papists—Knox admitted that he himself had begun to have some doubts; however, he wrote, 'to me it is enough to say that black is not white, and man's tyranny and foolishness is not God's perfect ordinance'.[27] Foxe lacked this kind of brutally simple certainty, and the lack made him tolerant. For the chronicler of man's inhumanity to dissenters this is no doubt a comprehensible, as it is certainly a satisfactory, state of mind.

However, while there is no need to prove again that Foxe believed in toleration rather than persecution, it is still necessary to establish what exactly toleration meant to him and where its limits lay. He habitually used opprobrious terms for the Church of Rome, but I know of no evidence that he advocated persecuting it. No conforming English protestant in the reign of Elizabeth ever called popery heretical; the term was reserved for protestant deviation and especially for sectarian dissent. Thus the question of applying the treat-

---

[24] Foxe's introduction to *Special and Chosen Sermons of D. Martin Luther* (London 1578: *STC* 16993).

[25] Olsen, *Foxe* p 203.

[26] Foxe's introduction to Luther's *Commentary on Galatians* (London 1575: *STC* 16965).

[27] British Library, Harl. MS 416, fo 70.

ment prescribed for heretics—burning at the stake—could not arise over papists, however much a man might profess to abominate the teachings of Rome. Insofar as the papists were regarded as secular enemies, as potential or actual traitors, the Elizabethan treason laws appointed secular penalties for them, and there is no reason at all to doubt that Foxe accepted the right of the magistrate to use such weapons. Yet even in this sphere he remained true to his principles, pleading repeatedly for judicious mercy rather than copying the murderous cruelty (as he saw it) of the adversary. Especially he interceded for Edmund Campion, at a time when even Elizabeth had ceased to believe that Catholic machinations could be overlooked.[28]

There was thus some high degree of consistency in Foxe's belief in toleration, though it had its limits. Interestingly enough, he drew the line at the Jews to whom (as we have seen) the humanists of the previous generation had even allowed a chance of salvation provided they obeyed their own law. For those who in his view had killed Christ, Foxe held out no hope: God of necessity must root them out. What else remained possible 'after that he was once revealed unto them for whose cause only all the commonwealth of the Jews was instituted and erected?' And he decried the Jewish pride in ancestry, for it should incline them to Christ rather than away from him:

> What may be thought of Christ himself, whom we do worship? In whom if you require who was his father, he came not indeed from man but descended from God. But if you demand of his mother: he is on his mother's side a Jew born . . . an issue of the same seed that you are . . . Why do you hate and revile your own kinsman?

He chose the baptism of a Jewish convert to preach this mixture of prejudice, naivety and appeal to better judgment.[29] It is not without interest that such sentiments distinguished him quite clearly from the characteristically deferential line taken by puritans over the Old Testament and Judaism in general.

Of Jews, who could do him and the realm no harm, he demanded conversion; from papists he expected only persecution but for them he favoured as much mercy as might be feasible. The crux of the present question touches the treatment he advocated for heretics, for those whom all the major Christian denominations—catholic or

[28] Mozley, *Foxe*, 90–1; Olsen, *Foxe*, 212.
[29] John Foxe, *De Oliua Euangelica: Sermon Preached at the Baptism of a Certain Jew* (London, 1578: *STC* 11236), sigs. B.iii^v, C.vij.

protestant—abominated and persecuted. He had to consider the problem all the time, of course, as he collected and wrote up his story of martyrdom through the ages, and in his book he consistently and predictably denounced persecution. Nor did he do so only for martyrdoms of the distant past or suffered by those whom he regarded as the founders of his own Church, but also in the cases of men and women whom he himself thought heretical. He had no sympathy with anti-Trinitarians like Joan Bocher, but nevertheless regretted that she was burned. As is well known, his faith in toleration was positively tested in 1575 when five Dutch Anabaptists were arrested and sentenced to be burned for heresy. Foxe intervened with two powerful letters, in Latin, addressed respectively to queen and privy council.[30] As for Anabaptists, he declared himself utterly opposed to their tenets and wished them converted to a better faith; yet that did not seem to him to justify the sentence. He pointed out that England was really very free of such excesses (which in 1575 was true enough) and therefore had no cause to use violence against these small groups of immigrants: it would be much better to prevent them coming in the first place. However, as he told the queen, to consign to the fire the living bodies of men whose error arose rather from blindness of judgment than wilful wickedness, struck him as very hard and more reminiscent of the Roman example than of protestant custom. '*Vitae hominum, ipse homo quum sum, faveo:*' I am for men's lives, being a man myself. Indeed, he went on, though such feelings might look foolish, he could not even pass a slaughter-house without grieving at the thought of what was happening to the cattle there: had not God in his mercy forbidden the use of such beasts as sacrifices at his altar? So, while he agreed that Anabaptists could not just be left to themselves, since they were heretics and liable to spread dangerous doctrines, he wanted to see them dealt with by other means than the stake. At this point he weakened somewhat: his other possible means included not only prison and branding but also the gallows. What above else he wanted to avoid was a rekindling of the 'pyres and fires' of Smithfield, but (as he put it to the Council) if prudence demanded that an examples be made '*non desunt, opinor, alia supplicionum pharmaca*'. However, he hoped that death was not required and asked for a month or two in which to work on those de-

---

[30] The letter to the queen is printed as App. X to Townsend's 'Life of Foxe' prefaced to the standard edition of *AM* (I, pp [27–8]); for the letter to the council see British Library, Harl. MS 417, fo 101v.

luded Dutch deviationists; it might prove possible to save them yet. As a punishment, if they remained obdurate, he clearly preferred exile—oddly enough, the Utopian punishment for religious offenders—but was prepared to accept execution if that could be carried out by means less cruel than burning. *'Vitae faveo'*—subject to the reservation *'nisi statuendum de iis exemplum iudicet prudentia'*.

Foxe's special horror of the fires of Smithfield (understandable in the historian of the Marian persecution) comes out further in a legal argument he put into his letter to the council. Had the state, he asked, in fact any right to burn anyone? If the council were relying on the act of Henry IV (he meant *de haeretico comburendo*: 2 Henry IV c. 15), he wished to point out that the alleged statute had no force since it lacked the assent of the Commons 'without which any promulgation of an act of parliament is invalid'. He reminded the council that he had proved the point in his book *'ex publicis et authenticis huius regni archivis'*; what he called 'your printed volumes of statutes' he alleged embodied a false and mendacious view 'inserted by the cunning and sophistical malice of the papists'. It would therefore be very wrong to rekindle the fires of Smithfield, long since extinguished by the queen, through a council decree which lacked the necessary authority of the law of the realm. Foxe may have thought that he had good legal opinion behind him, and he had himself looked up the roll of parliament for 2 Henry IV. However, in these historical researches Foxe unfortunately fell victim to an error which more sophisticated historians have at times repeated since: he failed to allow for the drastic changes in the structure, records and standing of parliament, and especially of the Commons as a necessary part of it, which, culminating in the proceedings of the Reformation Parliament, had produced the 'modern' institution familiar to Elizabethans. By the tests of his own day, the act of 1401 did indeed bear an incomplete and insufficient enacting clause but what was vouched in it fulfilled all the conditions of legal validity applicable at the time of its making.[31]

---

[31] For Foxe's research cf. *AM* III p 400. In the statute of 2 Henry IV none of the chapters stated an authority for this legislation; as was the custom, this was given at the head of the statute and covered all the acts contained in it. According to the formula used, the king had ordained the laws following at the prayer of the Commons and with the assent of the magnates and other lords. However, as Foxe discovered, with respect to c. 15 (the heresy act) the formula somewhat misstated the case, though no papistical malice was involved and legal validity remained unaffected. This chapter was in fact enacted in response to a request from the English clergy who begged the lay power to assist in the extermination of heresy; in reply the king *'de consensu Magnatum et aliorum Procerum Regni'* ordained certain heads of measures (including the

Nevertheless, Foxe was right in thinking that in 1575 there existed no statutory authority for burning heretics handed over by the spiritual arm: the three relevant statutes (5 Richard II c. 5, 2 Henry IV c. 15, 2 Henry V c. 7), having all been revived by 1 & 2 Philip & Mary c. 6 after their repeal in 1547, had again been repealed in the first parliament of Elizabeth (1 Eliz. I c. 1, sect. 6). However, though Foxe secured a reprieve of several weeks during which he and others tried in vain to dissuade the Anabaptists from their tenets, two of them were thereafter burned; one more having died in prison, the remaining two were let go. If the council issued a writ *de haeretico comburendo* they did so without legal authority; but the treatment by the judiciary of repealed or expired statutes remains an unexplored and mysterious territory.

Burnings for heresy grew exceedingly rare after 1558, and the fate of those two Dutchmen for that very reason made a stir. While it gave Foxe a chance to proclaim his genuine belief in toleration, it also showed that his views were not typical of his generation—rather less typical than More's had been of his, if we may judge by the use of the stake during his years in high office. Foxe, we must note, professed his views even after his side had won and controlled the machinery of repression, thus giving some sort of a lie to More's jibe that Tyndale would soon talk differently about persecution if once he were in a position to dispense rather than to receive.[32] No such double standard, it would seem, for Foxe. Faced with the first threats of division in the Church, More called for the stake. Faced with his own Church, so lately emerged from the Marian persecution, now under

duty of the secular arm to burn a relapsed heretic handed over by the Church) which were duly drawn up (probably by the judges) as an act and thus incorporated in the statute engrossed at the end of the session and in due course included in the printed volumes (*Rotuli Parliamentorum*, III pp 466–7).

[32] *Confutation* pp 789–91. The passage offers a fair example of More's polemical methods. First he constructs an imaginative and very tendentious case out of Tyndale's lament that the elect have always been persecuted, in such a way that Tyndale is made to appear ready to endorse persecution when it suits him. Next he speaks of thieves, heretics and murderers (a carefully arranged threesome) persecuting the Catholics in Switzerland and Saxony, calling up visions of killings for which he has no evidence: even the well biased modern commentary (*ibid* 1663) can speak only of severe restrictions on Catholic worship—and even that is an exaggeration at this point. More then clinches his case with one of his merry tales: about a lady who would have a man who committed adultery with his wife's maid 'hanged by the neck upon the nearest bough', but when asked what should happen to a woman who did likewise with her husband's man-servant answered that yes, the lady did wrong and should have a good talking-to. Neatly done, and in this case clever enough controversy, but a long way from being honest.

heavy attack from Rome and possibly endangered by the growth of further schismatic sects, Foxe pleaded for Campion and Anabaptists alike. However, have we here anything more than a difference between two people?

There can be no question that that difference existed and mattered. More, the public figure, civil servant, judge, the confidant of kings; Foxe, a rather private man who never rose above a canonry at Salisbury and had no place at the queen's court. There were nearly forty years between them, which fact (as we shall see) perhaps mattered most. The one thing that unites them is that they owed their fame to their pens, but even as authors these products of a humanist education differed markedly. Foxe, as we have noted, found *Utopia* worth a sneer; on the other hand, Foxe's way of conducting religious controversy by means of an historical narrative turned out to be both more attractive and more effective than More's production of strictly polemical effusions. It is odd to see how their reputations for trustworthiness have see-sawed together. Until the middle of the nineteenth century More was widely understood to have twisted the evidence a bit when attacking protestants, while Foxe was treated as gospel-truth; today most people seem to take More on trust while convinced that Foxe was quite capable of saying whatever suited his book. The earlier assessment was in fact nearer the truth and is beginning to creep back. In a variety of ways, the two men form a pair of contrasts.

The main contrast, however, lies in the psychology of their characters. Foxe's objection to persecution sprang less from calculation or reasoned principle, and least of all from a weariness with theological debate: he was and always remained an ardent protestant. Rather it reflected an ingrained passion for peace, conciliation and, as he put it, life. To the man who grieved over the fate of bullocks in the shambles nothing seems to have justified the shedding of blood, not even the cause of his faith. This point needs stressing, for it makes Foxe very exceptional even among those who were beginning to think some degree of toleration preferable to principled persecution. More similarly stands at an extreme of the spectrum, and his passionate advocacy of forcible repression arose, as I have suggested before this, from a profound apprehension of the evils caused by disobedience to the Church, the only protection for man's hope of order on this earth and salvation in the hereafter; and this apprehension in turn arose from a personal consciousness of man's helpless sinfulness which only the obedience exacted by the Church could prevent from destroying those two necessary conditions.[33] Moreover, as he proved at the end of his life, More had a contempt for man's fear of death and pain; death to him was a release which opened the door to eternal life. I cannot see that More would ever have said, '*vitae faveo*'. Exceptional in the strength of their divergent convictions, the tolerator and the persecutor embody the two possible answers to the problems raised by the Reformation in terms so stark as to be illuminating.

There was, however, one further difference between them, and a look at it takes the whole question beyond the purely personal issues. They had had very different experiences of persecution, mainly because one was born later than the other. When More attacked heresy and demanded its elimination by violence he was the man in the driving seat; his experience of persecution was that of the policeman. The story of his raid on the house of that respected London worthy, John Petyt, whom he rightly but in vain suspected of having a copy of Tyndale's New Testament, forms a splendid illustration of police methods through the ages and in any biography of More (though not here) deserves the place which has been denied to it.[34] I do not know that More ever actually witnessed a man being burned alive for the sake of his faith, though both his deeds (in pursuing heretics and their books) and his words should have been enough to allow his powerful imagination to work on the consequences for those he caught or denounced. However, he really knew persecution only from the outside, and it is notorious that as his own tribulations grew upon him he lost his passion for persecution, not because he dreaded what might happen to himself but because he came to see its irrelevance to the truths of religion or the realities of salvation.[35] Foxe probably also never attended at a burning, but he had been an exile—a victim of persecution—and the men and women who died in the fires of Smithfield included acquaintances or friends. In a very real sense, he knew what he was talking about. Thus one result of the history of religious strife was that people came to experience persecution in reality; it jumped off the page into their lives. Of course, many reacted

[33] Cf. my 'The Real Thomas More?' in *Reformation Principles and Practice*, ed. P. N. Brooks (London 1980) pp 21–31.

[34] *Narratives of the Days of the Reformation*, ed. J. G. Nichols (Camden Society 1859) pp 25–7. Foxe did not use the story in *AM*, but its truth was vouched for by Petyt's wife, herself involved in it.

[35] This is the message of More's *Dialogue of Comfort*.

with a more bitter passion and a desire for revenge, but, as Foxe showed, one could also come to recoil from it, and, as Foxe also showed, it was not only those who grew sceptical about the religious issues fought over who took that line. Are there, therefore, any signs that a preference for toleration spread more widely than the mind of John Foxe as the truths about persecution became manifest?

There were very few burnings in the reign of Elizabeth, but it is, we know, notorious that the regime pursued many of its enemies to the death. The famous debate between William Cecil and William Allen merits another look.[36] Cecil—Lord Burghley—published his defence of *The Execution of Justice in England* in 1583; in the following year Allen replied with his *True, Sincere and Modest Defence of English Catholics*. At issue stood the persecution of the Catholic missionaries in England which had been going on for about half a dozen years. Cecil maintained that the enemies of the realm were being dealt with not 'upon question of religion, but justly, by order of laws, openly condemned as traitors'; the priests were executed not under any new laws invented for their case 'either for religion or against the Pope's supremacy' but under the old and fundamental treason law of 1351.[37] (This was for instance true of Campion). Against this Allen, intent on showing that the persecution was not political but religious, at length cited the new treason legislation of 1571 and 1581 (and soon 1584 as well) which by stages made it treason in itself to be a Catholic priest, especially a Jesuit, working in England. The indignation which he and his party regularly expressed over this identification of religion with treason should perhaps be assessed against Robert Persons' proposal that the first law to be passed in an England restored to Rome should make it treason to advocate any change in the 'Catholic Roman faith'.[38] Cecil contrasted the 'mild' policy of Elizabeth's government with Mary's treatment of protestants; Allen retorted that those doings had been 'commendable and lawful'. What he meant was that if the treason act of 1351 entitled Elizabeth to execute Catholics, the heresy acts of 1401 and 1414 entitled Mary to burn protestants. Allen struck a particularly unpleasing note when he insisted that Mary did more worthily because she chose victims of

[36] The works in question are most readily available in Robert Kingdon's edition in the series 'Folger Documents of Tudor and Stuart Civilization' (Ithaca, N. Y. 1965); I shall use it here.

[37] Ed. Kingdon pp 7–8.

[38] [Robert Parsons,] *Memoriall [for the Intended Reformation of England*, ed. Edward Gee (London 1690) p 105.

no account while Elizabeth's included quite a few persons of standing, an argument which involved degrading Cranmer by calling him names; this kind of snobbery was not commonplace at the time (as Foxe sufficiently proved) and became the prerogative of the Catholic polemicists.

Both sides indeed expended much time—Cecil markedly less than Allen—in good sixteenth-century abuse of the adversary, and Allen's tract abounded with atrocity stories about the ill-treatment of priests and the horrors of execution for treason—in which he was right, even though he exaggerated the sufficiently disgusting truth. At heart, the two tracts pursued the familiar but pointless debate over the justice of deeds legitimized by statutes designed to defend respective views of public safety; they provided an unedifying commentary on Thomas Cromwell's penetrating remark to Thomas More at More's second interrogation. As Cromwell pointed out, execution for treason at the king's behest left a man quite as dead as burning for heresy at the pope's command; if one was entitled to inflict death by the law of his Church, why not the other by the law of his realm?[39] The only suitable modern comment must deplore equally the fate of heretics burned and of traitors hanged, drawn and quartered.

However, in the course of the exchange the disputants did touch upon the topic of toleration. Cecil made heavy play with the fact that many subjects of the English crown 'differ in some opinions of religion from the Church of England': yet so long as they remain loyal to the queen they will suffer neither persecution for treason nor have their consciences searched 'for their contrary opinions that savour not of treason'.[40] He pointed out that even the Marian bishops who in 1559 had refused to conform and had 'maintained the Pope's authority against the laws of the realm' had never been put on trial, being left in comfortable seclusion in private houses. In this, by the way, he exaggerated very little. Allen riposted that the only reason why Catholics had to be persecuted under the treason acts arose from the state of the law. 'You have purposely repealed . . . all former laws of the realm for burning heretics, which smelleth of something that I need not here express'—a comment either mystifying or unpleasant. Since therefore the English Church at present possessed no definition of heresy, it was compelled to persecute religion under the guise of

[39] *The Correspondence of Sir Thomas More*, ed. E. F. Rogers (Princeton 1947) pp 557–8.
[40] Ed. Kingdon pp 9–12.

treason.[41] Although he here scored a point of sorts, he really had the worse of the argument. The official doctrine of the English Church simply did not then or ever regard Roman Catholicism as heretical; because of the bull of deposition of 1570 and the papacy's avowed intent to see the bull executed, it branded the Roman faith as politically dangerous. It was not accident or some temporary insufficiency in the law which provoked trials for treason instead heresy against the priests. Later, however, Allen picked up Cecil's hint that co-existence (a species of toleration) was possible. If English Catholics, he said, 'might have obtained any piece of that liberty which catholics enjoy in Germany, Switzerland or other places among protestants', he would not complain.[42] How sincere was he in asking for the kind of co-existence which, as he put it, would have made it possible to practise the Catholic religion in England without resort to seminaries abroad and agitation from there? He certainly exaggerated the freedom permitted to Catholic worship in German protestant territories after the settlement of 1555 had divided the region into mutually exclusive religious havens. Moreover, no Swiss or German ruler was threatened with deprivation by papal edict. Allen's positive point comes out later. If England's rulers refused to return to Rome—and he suggested that only fear of losing face prevented them—they should still consider the error made in refusing liberty of conscience to Catholics 'being far the greater and more respective part of the realm'.[43] Toleration was asked for only as a preliminary stage to re-conversion.

And that, indeed, remained the position taken up by the English Catholic propagandists to the end of the reign.[44] From first to last they insisted that their religion was being persecuted in England for religion's sake and denounced the English government's allegations of treason as false. In 1580, Robert Persons went back to Thomas More by allowing the exercise of their religion to Jews and Turks but not to heretics.[45] When he, as it has been expressed, tried 'to put a reasoned moral case' for toleration,[46] he developed the theme of the inviolability of the individual conscience, though he first of all elimi-

[41] *Ibid* p 94.
[42] *Ibid* pp 261–2.
[43] *Ibid* p 265.
[44] For all this cf. T. H. Clanchy, *Papist Pamphleteers* (Chicago 1964) ch 6 'Persecution and Toleration'.
[45] *Ibid* pp 145–6.
[46] *Ibid* p 143.

nated the conscience of heretics (as More had done) on the grounds that they had been given the chance of professing the truth and had expressly and deliberately rejected it. I think he also misunderstood what conscience meant to More who had always avoided giving it that tinge of personal judgment. However, this kind of tolerance would simply allow Catholics to practise in England and leave them free to treat protestants as intolerable heretics the minute they got their chance; it was never meant to replace the real aim—total victory for Rome in England. At moments when Allen and Persons thought the omens truly propitious for the triumph of Rome they dropped all talk of even such tendentious toleration; and as late as 1596, when a Spanish victory seemed increasingly improbable, Persons returned to asking for toleration only as a convenient means for the promotion of the re-establishment of Catholic orthodoxy in England.[47]

Persons' own words are worth attention here. His real position on toleration comes out very clearly in two pieces he wrote on either side of the year 1600, as the prospects of victory waxed and waned. In 1607 he published a reply to the protestant propagandist Thomas Morton which had been in the making for several years.[48] As the title-page declared, the book meant to demonstrate 'that it is not impossible for subjects of different religions (especially catholics and protestants) to live together in dutiful obedience and subjection, under the government of his Majesty of Great Britain'. However, in 1596 he had put up a blueprint for the restructuring of England after a Catholic victory, a secret scheme which remained unpublished until 1690 when it was put into print in order to show what the country would have suffered if James II had won.[49] In chapter IV Persons discussed the treatment of three categories of subjects—Catholics, schismatics (that is, 'close or weak Catholics' who had sought peace in outward conformity), and heretics (that is, all protestants). Obviously, the first group would take over the running of the country. The second would by stages and after careful investigation be allowed back into the ruling order. As for the 'enemies, or obstinate heretics', they should at first be treated gently and have a chance to mend their ways. However, 'this toleration be only with such as live quietly and are desirous to be informed of the truth, and do not

[47] *Ibid* pp 148–51.
[48] *A Treatise Tending to Mitigation towards Catholic Subjects in England . . .* (St Omer 1607: *STC* 19417).
[49] *Memoriall* esp pp 29–34.

teach and preach or such to infect others'. What he advocated was 'a certain connivance or toleration of magistrates only for a certain time'. He very urgently did not wish to be misunderstood. He was not saying that Catholics and protestants could live together peacefully within a Catholic state:

> Yet I do give notice that my meaning is not in any way to persuade hereby that liberty of religion, to live how a man will, should be permitted to any person in any Christian commonwealth, for any cause or respect whatsoever: from which I am so far off in my judgment and affection as I think no one thing to be so dangerous, dishonourable or more offensive to Almighty God in the world than that any prince should permit the Ark of Israel and Dagon, God and the Devil, to stand and be honoured together, within his realm or country.

For Persons, toleration was only a tactic; persecution became essential if persuasion failed; and, as I said earlier, he wished to make it high treason in the secular law to speak against the faith of the Church of Rome.

One cannot imagine Persons interceding for a prisoner of the Inquisition in Spain as Foxe did for Campion. There is really no good sign that the position of Catholic spokesmen ever really changed in the sixteenth century from that taken up by More: there being but the one Church, heresy must be extinguished, and if this can be done only by violence let violence be used, whether it be the violence of the stake or the violence of armed invasion (followed, presumably, by the use of the stake). So acceptable toleration meant only provision of protection for the Catholic faction in its endeavour to restore its exclusive rule which would once more enable it to repress the protestants whom it continued to regard as heretics. I am not, of course, saying that this view prevailed among the English Catholic laity, who better understood reality, but it formed, I maintain, the unchanging teaching of its spiritual leaders. More, living while the Catholic hierarchy was still in the saddle, had not been tempted to permit even so much toleration. On the other side, the protestant case that such persecution as there was (more than enough of it) arose strictly from political perils and simply represented the right of the state to protect itself against subversion misleadingly ignored the religious passions which drove many individuals into persecuting with the weapons of the state an enemy hated as the servant of Antichrist. On the other hand, down at least to the early 1580s it represented official policy quite correctly. Even thereafter, when refusal to come to church would ruin a man and being a priest sufficed to bring him to the scaffold, it still remained true that these measures embodied not a strictly religious persecution but fear for what might happen to the outward uniformity thought essential for the survival of the English state without civil war. As we have seen, when the English government confronted what they themselves regarded as heretics—people who had offended in religion—they used the old instrument of the stake, even though in law they probably had no right to do so. The Elizabethan persecution of Catholics really sprang from secular and political motives, even though, pressed by panic, the age extended the definition of the supposed threat in a deplorably categoric fashion. But in respect of religion, their attitude did not preclude genuine toleration for varieties of the faith, whereas the attitude of the Catholics did. Everybody, of course, drew the line against those 'heresies' which stirred up the common people, everybody except Foxe—against true sectaries, though they too were not usually burned at the stake in England as they would have been in Madrid.

As J.W. Allen demonstrated long ago, budding ideas of toleration can be found among Elizabethan protestants, but they are (Foxe excepted) half-hearted and hesitant, so much so that Hooker, whom one would have expected to pronounce on the subject, avoids it with studious deliberation.[50] All that can be said for them is that they left doors open for the co-existence of more than one Christian faith in one community; they did not advocate it or ask the state to cease persecuting. Altogether, however, the thinkers we have considered do not really bear out the 'model' of persecution and toleration which I suggested at the start is pretty generally accepted. A leading member of the supposedly tolerant Christian humanist movement immediately set standards of persecuting determination which were never surpassed and rarely matched. Such signs of toleration as can be seen appearing had little to do with Jordan's six criteria: dissident sects grew no stronger though Elizabethan attacks on them were markedly less ferocious than those of Henry VIII or Mary had been; uniformity remained the ideal preached; trade and travel (dubious points) worked both ways and in the main encouraged each side to think more self-righteously of itself; censorship kept the threat of the printing press at bay; and an inclination towards tolerance grew

---

[50] J. W. Allen, *Political Thought in the Sixteenth Century* (London 1928) pp 231–46.

among believers as much as among sceptics. It has not, of course, been possible to survey the whole field thoroughly, and further research may restore Jordan's scheme, but the test cases of More and Foxe have suggested that individual character and experience had more to do with any moves towards or away from toleration than the general developments alleged which could as easily harden attitudes as they could alter them.

Nevertheless, I should like to suggest one large thought on this whole subject which goes well beyond the confines of the sixteenth century. In the last two generations or so, it has become habitual among historians to react rather violently against the excessive use of self-satisfaction and self-congratulation that prevailed among our nineteenth-century predecessors. The glorious reign of Queen Elizabeth, the virtue and mildness of her rule, have been thrust out (among other things) from our history books; much new sympathy has at the same time replaced ancient bigotry about the Church of Rome. Even though one concomitant effect has been a curious collapse of protestant confidence beyond what the case requires, much of this revision is wholly admirable—a move towards balance and truth. But the reaction against a blind admiration for the Reformation has also deprived us of one once familiar notion, and perhaps it is right that one who adheres to neither side in the wars of religion, or indeed to any form of the Christian faith, should remind you of it. I am glad to be able to cite approvingly the opinion of Charles and Katherine George with whom I otherwise find myself so often in disagreement. 'English Protestantism', they wrote, having cited William Perkins to show that by 1600 that branch of the faith could consider it possible that the true Church might appear in various guises, 'provided in the very nature of its logic a greater scope for the development and the acceptance of ceremonial, institutional, and even doctrinal variations than did Roman Catholicism;' but, they went on to say, it did not provide 'a conscious and general programme of religious toleration'.[51] To that last reservation John Foxe formed an exception. In general, however, that century did not, and in the clash of passionate convictions perhaps could not, really achieve a truly tolerant position. To that extent it is true that only the passing of passions, perhaps the growth of a sceptical indifference, could permanently guarantee the end of persecution for religion's

[51] C. H. and K. George, *The Protestant Mind of the English Reformation* (Princeton 1961) pp 376–7, 380–1.

sake. But there are flowers and there are seeds. It was in the age of religious passions that the implications of the great schism made themselves first known. As the possibility of reunion receded, true Christians of one kind came to see, by painful stages, that provided they were left alone by others they had better leave others alone too—a lesson seemingly never learned by the Catholics of that era. The powerful voices raised for true tolerance belonged to the helpless—to the likes of Michael Servetus, Michael Sattler, Caspar von Schwenckfeld. The stiller voices worked within the Church of England, among men for whom toleration was not a first condition of survival but increasingly a dictate of humanity. They observed variety and came to see true piety in various outward guises. So long as the Church of Rome adhered to its determination to rule all Christians, only protestantism offered a hope of an end to persecution.

Clare College, Cambridge.

ANGLICANS, PURITANS AND AMERICAN INDIANS: PERSECUTION OR TOLERATION?

by H. C. PORTER

I

'GO YE into all the world, and preach the Gospel to every creature' (Mark 16: 15). Modern historians find it fashionable to categorise Missions as examples of Cultural Conflict.[1] Members of the ethnohistorical school—concerned especially with the meeting and blending of Indian and European ways of life—present Conversion as a species of Persecution: an infringement of Indian human rights, an exercise in ethnocentrism or exploitative capitalism—part of the Cant of Conquest. Conversion—the colonialisation of a native belief system—means 'acculturation', 'deculturation', or tragic 'despiritualisation'.[2] Accounts of the relation between Indians and English colonists in colonial North America take a hint from the complaint of Roger Williams of Rhode Island, writing in 1654 to the authorities of Massachusetts about the destructive wars, cruel and unnecessary, against the tribes of New England.[3] Christianity means conquest, harsh and brutal. Some of this emphasis on atrocities may spring from historians' indignation at Christian activities apparently so alien to the Sermon on the Mount.[4] More of it arises from the fact that few ethnohistorians in

---

[1] Henry W. Bowden, *American Indians and Christian Missions: Studies in Cultural Conflict* (Chicago 1981).

[2] Robert F. Berkhofer, *The White Man's Indian: Images of the American Indian from Columbus to the Present* (New York 1978); Francis Jennings, *The Invasion of America: Indians, colonialism and the Cant of Conquest* (Chapel Hill 1975); Calvin Martin, *Keepers of the Game: Indian-Animal Relationships and the Fur Trade* (Berkeley 1978); Neal Salisbury, 'Red Puritans: the "Praying Indians" of Massachusetts Bay and John Eliot' *William and Mary Quarterly* 31 (January 1974) pp 27–54; Neal Salisbury, *Manitou and Providence: Indians, Europeans and the Making of New England 1500–1643* (New York 1982); Bernard Sheehan, *Savagism and Civility: Indians and Englishmen in Colonial Virginia* (Cambridge 1980).

[3] *Complete Writings of Roger Williams* VI, *Letters* ed J. R. Bartlett (New York 1963) p 272.

[4] Francis Jennings in D. B. Quinn ed *Early Maryland in a Wider World* (Detroit 1982) p 236.

the United States seem able to resist the temptation to approach early Virginia and New England by way of the Vietnam war.[5]

In the 1980s, certainly, it would be inappropriate to respond wholeheartedly to the boast in the early 1880s of the first Anglican bishop of Minnesota—that 'the Christian home, though only a log cabin, has taken the place of the wigwam: and the poor deluded Indian woman has changed to the Christian wife and mother. Where once was heard only the medicine drum and the sound of the scalp dance, there is now the bell calling Christians to prayer.'[6] But, equally, there is no call to accept without question the dogma (however popular with the World Council of Churches) that Anglo-Saxon missionary enterprise cannot be judged as other than imperialist or neocolonialist.

'I am the way, the truth, and the life: no one cometh unto the Father, but by me' (John 14: 6). As interpreted by some contributors to a book published by the SCM Press in 1961, the claim can be expanded in the following way.[7] The revelation of God in Christ is unique, distinct, superior, absolute, imcomparable; Christianity alone satisfies the needs of the soul; Christ uproots rather than supplements; all other religions are darkness, fundamentally opposed to the Truth—and what is good in them should not be stressed. Other modern Christians, while insisting that in Christ the Deity is uniquely revealed, are less narrow, accepting that other religions reflect a light of which Christ is author (and also fulfilment). Others go further still. The BBC Prayer Book, used in the Radio 4 Daily Service, insists that the Christian must show towards other faiths not only sensitivity but also humility. In 1979, in the series 'The Classics of Western Spirituality' (which includes Origen, Julian of Norwich and William Law), SPCK published *Native North American Spirituality of the Eastern Woodlands*.[8]

Arnold Toynbee, in lectures published in 1958 *(Christianity among the Religions of the World)* advised Christians to lose their 'arrogance',

[5] Richard Drinnon, *Facing West: The Metaphysics of Indian-Hating and Empire-Building* (Minneapolis 1980) ch 23 "From the Bay Colony to Indo-China'.
[6] Bishop Henry Whipple, preface to Helen Hunt Jackson, *A Century of Dishonour* (London 1881) pp ix-x.
[7] Gerald H. Anderson ed *The Theology of the Christian Mission* (London 1961). Summary from essays by Noel Davey, Gerald Anderson, Donald Miller and L. H. DeWolf, plus points from Evelyn Underhill, 'Christianity and the Claims of other Religions', in E. R. Morgan ed *Essays Catholic and Missionary* (London 1928).
[8] Edited and introduced by an anthropologist, Elizabeth Tooker.

and 'purge Christianity of the exclusive-mindedness and intolerance that follows from a belief in Christianity's uniqueness' Toynbee's tone was rather rueful, as he was aware of the theological problems and niceties. The ethnohistorians are more arrogant, dismissing statements of the uniqueness of Christianity as myopia or cultural prejudice. The claim, if expressed by English settlers in North America, becomes merely an insular blind spot.[9] Discussion deserves to be less facile.

The ideal of Conversion finds somewhat surprising modern defenders. The debate about Christianity and Judaism in the correspondence columns of 'The Times' in Spring 1983 included a letter (20 April) from Jacob Freund, who pointed out that the belief that the Jew can be converted assumes his humanity: his faith may be wrong, but not his nature or his race. The letter echoed the conclusions of the Papal Bull of Paul III in 1537:[10] the American Indians are not brute beasts without understanding, but true men, *veri homines*—because they are capable of receiving the Faith. This may seem a rather 'loaded' conception of Humanity; but the intention in the 1530s was humane.

II

From the 1490s such notions were central to European thinking about the American Indian. In England, the first mention of missionaries to the Indian was associated with the third Cabot voyage from Bristol in 1498.[11] The theme of Indian conversion continued in *Utopia*; in the play *A new interlude . . . of the iiij elementes*, written c1520 by Thomas More's brother-in-law John Rastell, who had organised an abortive expedition to the New World in 1517; in the essay on the ethics of settlement in North America written by Richard Eden as the preface to his translation, published in 1555, of *The Decades of the newe worlde* by Peter Martyr of Anghiera; in the introductions to

[9] James Axtell, 'The Ethnohistory of Early America: A Review Essay', *William and Mary Quarterly* 35 (January 1978) pp 110–44; James Axtell, *The European and the Indian: Essays in the Ethnohistory of Colonial North America* (New York 1981); Karen Kupperman, *Settling with the Indians: the Meeting of English and Indian Cultures in America 1580–1640* (London 1980); Henry W. Bowden and James P. Ronda eds *John Eliot's Indian Dialogues* (Westport Conn. 1980) pp 3–56.

[10] *Sublimis Deus* Latin text and English translation in Francis MacNutt, *Bartholomew de las Casas* (New York 1909) pp 426–31.

[11] J. A. Williamson ed *The Cabot Voyages and Bristol Discovery under Henry VII* (Hakluyt Society Cambridge 1962) p 211.

English editions in the 1560s of works by Huguenot colonists in America; and, in the 1580s, in the work of Rev. Richard Hakluyt, who invoked in 1584[12] the 'Come over and help us' appeal to Paul by the man of Macedonia (Acts 16)—a text later to be on the seal of the Massachusetts Bay Company. The theme became 'official' in the Virginia Company Charter of 1606.[13] In early Virginia the Church of England had effective missionaries in Rev. Alexander Whitaker of Trinity College Cambridge, and the layman George Thorpe.[14] Both suffered untimely deaths.

Thomas Cranmer, for one of the Good Friday Collects in the 1549 Prayer Book, and thereafter, adapted traditional prayers for Jews, heretics and infidels (*pagani*): 'have mercy upon all Jews, Turks, infidels and heretics', 'take from them all ignorance, hardness of heart and contempt of Thy word', and 'fetch them home to Thy flock, that they may be saved'. The terminology of 'pagans' and 'infidels' was not always precise: William, Cardinal Allen grouped together 'Paynims, Turks, Jews, Moors, heretics, schismatics and other infidels'.[15] But usually pagans or infidels—heathen—were considered better than heretics. Thomas More, in his *Dialogue Concerning Heresies* (1528),[16] was clear that 'heretics' and 'heathen men' were 'two divers cases'. The assumption was that the latter would welcome the preaching of the Faith of Christ, just as the native inhabitants of the New World island of Utopia had done.

Traditions of Christian thought about heathen were ultimately based on Chapter Two of Paul's Epistle to the Romans. The heathen, wrote Paul—the Gentiles—'do by nature the things contained in the Law', following 'the law written in their hearts' and 'conscience'. Roger Williams, elaborating in New England the correspondences between Paul's heathen and the American Indian, wrote of the Indian as having qualities of the Jew, the Roman and the Greek—especially

[12] Hakluyt 'Discourse of Western Planting' in E. G. R. Taylor ed *Original Writings and Correspondence of the two Richard Hakluyts* (Hakluyt Society London 1935) 2 p 216.

[13] Philip L. Barbour ed *The Jamestown Voyages under the First Charter 1606–9* (Hakluyt Society Cambridge 1969) p 25.

[14] H. C. Porter, *The Inconstant Savage: England and the North American Indian 1500–1660* (London 1979) ch 19, 'Alexander Whitaker, Cambridge Apostle to Virginia 1611–17' and ch 23, 'The Judicious Master Thorpe 1620–22'; Eric Gethyn-Jones, *George Thorpe and the Berkeley Company: A Gloucestershire Enterprise in Virginia* (Gloucester 1982).

[15] *True, Sincere and Modest Defence of English Catholics* ed Robert Kingdon (Ithaca 1965) p 257.

[16] *The Essential Thomas More* ed J. J. Greene and J. F. Dolan (London 1967) p 210.

the latter.[17] William Perkins, the Cambridge high Calvinist of the 1590s, preaching on the Romans text, stressed that 'many of the heathen have excelled in civil carriage and practice of justice, temperance, and other civil virtues', springing from 'the light of understanding', 'reasonable knowledge, proper to men'.[18] After all, the Greek classification of the Cardinal Virtues—Prudence, Temperance, Courage and Justice—had been assimilated by Augustine. The 'civil carriage' of the Indians had been noted by English observers since the settlement in 1585 on the island of Roanoke, off the coast of North Carolina. William Strachey, who had gone up to Emmanuel College in 1588, met the 'emperor' Powhatan in Virginia in 1610, and concluded that even a heathen prince could have an 'impression of the divine nature', and be seen by God as among 'His immediate instruments on earth', with a 'kind of divineness': 'infused', 'extraordinary'.[19]

The Pauline theme found a place in the controversy during the 1560s between Bishop John Jewel and the English Jesuit Thomas Harding.[20] Harding boasted of the missionary successes of the Church of Rome. Jewel retorted that the Indians had sufficient natural light to recognise the errors of their tribal religion, but not enough to withstand the lures of popery. Indeed, the popish religion much ressembled their own rites—a point confirmed by modern scholars.[21] But when the Indian was introduced to the verities of the Church of England, the heart and the conscience would satisfactorily respond. The North American Indians—to adopt an adaptation by Sellar and Yeatman—were by nature not Angels but Anglicans.

Paul also wrote (Romans 1: 20) that the heathen could understand the Power and Deity of God. The Narragansett Indians, according to Roger Williams, recognised the 'eternal Power and God-head' in sun, moon, stars and seasons.[22] Moreover, there had developed the notion, even within the puritan tradition, that something technically a 'matter of faith' might be 'well proved by the heathen by the light

---

[17] [Williams, A] *Key* [*into the Language of America* eds J. J. Teunissen and E. J. Hinz (Detroit 1973)] p 134. See Teunissen and Hinz, 'Roger Williams, St Paul and American Primitivism' *Canadian Review of American Studies* 4 (1973) pp 121–136.

[18] Perkins, *An Exposition upon the Epistle of Jude,* in *Works* 3 (Cambridge 1609) p 545.

[19] Strachey, *The Historie of Travell into Virginia Britania* ed L. B. Wright and V. Freund (Hakluyt Society London 1953) pp 60–61.

[20] *Works of Jewel* ed J. Ayre PS (Cambridge 1848) 3 pp 197–99.

[21] J. H. Parry, *The Spanish Seaborne Empire* (London 1966) ch 8 'The Spreading of the Faith' esp p 164.

[22] *Key* pp 145–46.

of reason'. The quotation is from Richard Sibbes, Master of St Catharine's College Cambridge in the late 1620s and early 1630s.[23] Roger Williams, an experienced missionary, found that Indians accept 'by reason' that the Bible is the Word of God; the process begins with their conscience reproving them 'for those sins their souls say they are guilty of'.[24] Sibbes gave, as an example of a matter of faith proved by reason, the immortality of the soul. Descriptions of Indians rarely failed to note a belief in immortality. And on the island of Utopia one of the compulsory doctrines decreed by King Utopus was the immortality of the soul: to deny it was *vitium*, error or, as the Tudor translation had it, 'heresy'.[25]

The Pauline material about the heathen had a sting in the tail. The argument ran that in spite of their natural light the heathen had *not* acknowledged the Deity. Thus they were 'without excuse', and God had rightfully given them up (Romans 1: 20). The theme was worked out by English Protestants. The heathen have abused natural reason: 'The rule of their damnation shall be the law of nature written in their hearts' wrote Richard Sibbes.[26] Moreover, preached Thomas Lever in 1550, for their abuse of reason the heathen could be punished on earth.[27] The Pauline point applied to all natural men, men outside grace. But it could be attached especially to the American Indian. Increase Mather, in the preface to *The Laws and Liberties of Massachusetts*, printed at Cambridge Massachusetts in 1648, wrote that so far as the Indians are concerned Pauline hopes of their doing by nature the things contained in the Law have proved forlorn.[28] It was a might-have-been: '*if* they had walked according to the light and law of nature . . .'. Similar thoughts puzzled Robinson Crusoe when, on the island off the gulf of the Orinoco between 1659 and 1686, he wondered why God had hidden His 'saving knowledge' from the Indians.

Others were more optimistic. For Roger Williams, Indians who sin are not as reprehensible as erring Europeans who abuse the *gospel* light. The 'proud English' should be aware of their own danger.

---

[23] Sibbes, *Works* ed A. B. Grosart (Edinburgh 1863) 5 p 467, quoted by [Sidney H.] Rooy, [*The Theology of Missions in the Puritan Tradition: A Study of Representative Puritans* (Delft 1965)] p 29. Dr Rooy's puritans are Sibbes, Richard Baxter, John Eliot, Cotton Mather and Jonathan Edwards.

[24] *Key* p 302.

[25] More, Works, *Utopia* p 222; Ralph Robinson translation in Everyman Library *Utopia* (London 1951) pp 120–21.

[26] Richard Sibbes, *Works* I p 389. Rooy p 28.

[27] *Sermons* ed E. Arber (London 1871) p 124.

[28] Sig A 2^r

Make sure thy second birth, else thou shalt see,
Heaven ope to Indians wild, but shut to thee.[29]

Thomas Hooker, in his 1631 'Farewell' Sermon to England, had been even more pessimistic about his compatriots.[30] The lapses of Old England meant that 'poor native infidels' in New England might have 'a more cool summer-parlor in hell than England shall have.' One of the missionary tracts coming from Massachusetts in the late 1640s argued that Indian response to preaching gave a warning: 'who knows but God gave life to New England to quicken Old, and hath warmed them, that they might heat us.'[31] After all, one of the aphorisms of Benjamin Whichcote, Fellow of Emmanuel in the 1630s, ran: 'The Good Nature of an Heathen is more God-like than the furious Zeal of a Christian'.[32]

III

The discovery of the New World was described by Francisco Lopez de Gomara in 1552 as 'the greatest event since the creation of the world, apart from the incarnation and death of Christ'.[33] The discovery of the American Indian had the most impact on the mind and conscience of Europe. Did the existence of the Indian encourage tolerance or intolerance in the theological reactions of Christendom? Answers to this question can appear paradoxical. A quite generous toleration of the Indian could spring from a very ungenerous conception of salvation and election. This paradox is illustrated in the writings of Roger Williams.

Williams, the founding father of Rhode Island, can be built up as a pioneer of religious liberty in North America, and as an early American democrat—in 1647 it was resolved that the form of government in Providence Plantations was 'democratical'.[34] *The Bloody Tenent, of Persecution, for cause of Conscience, discussed* (London 1644) remains a powerful (if gnarled) performance, with its basic thesis that the blood of protestants and papists, spilled in wars for the

---

[29] *Key* p 133.

[30] *Thomas Hooker: Writings in England and Holland 1626–1633*, eds G. H. Williams *et al.* (Cambridge Mass 1975) p 252.

[31] Quoted in Rooy p 187.

[32] 'Moral and Religious Aphorisms', no. 114, C. A. Patrides ed *The Cambridge Platonists* (London 1969) pp 327–28.

[33] Lewis Hanke, *Aristotle and the American Indians* (Chicago 1959) p 124.

[34] Merrill Jensen ed *American Colonial Documents to 1776*, EHD (London 1955) p 226.

claims of conscience, is not required by, nor acceptable to, Christ the Prince of Peace. 'I speak of conscience', he wrote to the authorities of Massachusetts in 1651, 'a persuasion fixed in the mind and heart of a man, which enforceth him to judge'. Again interpreting Paul, he continued: 'This conscience is found in all mankind, more or less, in Jews, Turks, Papists, Protestants, Pagans, etc.'[35] His stand in the early 1630s on the question of Indian land rights has brought him the approval (albeit modified) of the ethnohistorians. And the awkwardly titled *A Key into the Language of America*, published in London in 1643 comprised 'Observations' on the 'Customs, Manners and Worships' of the Narragansett Indians, with 'Spiritual Observations, general and particular', with a poem to round off each of the 32 chapters, and is among the most attractive English variations on the theme of the Indian Utopia.[36]

By modern liberal standards, Williams had the right ideas. But he developed them from wrong presuppositions by modern standards. This is demonstrated in the pamphlet published in London in 1645 as a supplement to the *Key*, with the subtitle *A Briefe Discourse concerning that name Heathen, commonly given to the Indians*.[37]

At the heart of Williams's thinking is an especially restricted conception of the qualifications for membership of 'a church estate, that is a converted estate'. Christ's 'true lovers are volunteers, born of His Spirit, the now only nation and royal priesthood'. The allusion is to 1 Peter 2: 9—the 'chosen generation' (*genos*), the 'royal priesthood', the 'peculiar people' (*laos*), the 'holy nation' (*ethnos*). The pattern of the true Christian—'such a convert as is acceptable to God in Jesus Christ, according to the visible rule of His last will and Testament'— is Paul on the Damascus road. There is, then, the 'holy nation': and, apart from it, 'the gentiles, the nations of the world'. Everyone not blessed with 'a true regeneration and new birth' is a gentile, a heathen. So the concept of the heathen becomes very broad: anyone who is 'unrepentant, unregenerate, natural', whether Turk, Jew, Indian—or 'unconverted and unchristian christians', Protestant or

[35] *Letters* pp 219–20. (See note 3).
[36] Eds J. J. Teunissen and E. J. Hinz (Detroit 1973). See Teunissen and Hinz, 'Roger Williams, Thomas More and the Narrangansett Utopia' *Early American Literature* 11 (1976–77) pp 281–95; Jack L. Davis, 'Roger Williams among the Narragansett Indians' *New England Quarterly* 43 (1970) pp 593–604.
[37] *Complete Writings of Roger Williams* 7 ed Perry Miller (New York 1963) pp 29–41. W. C. Gilpin is good on Williams and Indians in his *The Millenarian Piety of Roger Williams* (Chicago 1979) pp 39–43, 117–34.

Catholic. Christendom itself is largely heathen. (The main title of the 1645 pamphlet is *Christenings make not Christians*). Thus the heathen Indian is, so to speak, upgraded. In more traditional Protestant thought native peoples ranged from those worthy of hearing the Word, to those 'who have hardly anything of humanity but the outward form'; with the American Indian, 'fierce and tyrannical', somewhere in the middle.[38] But for Williams, to use the word 'heathen' in a derogatory way is to use it 'improperly, sinfully and unchristianly'. Native peoples are capable of civility.

Boast not, proud English, of thy birth and blood,
Thy brother Indian is by birth as good.
Of one blood God made him, and thee, and all,
As wise, as fair, as strong, as personal.

'Nature knows no difference between Europe and Americans in blood, birth, bodies, etc, God having of one blood made all mankind'.[39] The 'Christian' English of New England, themselves mostly heathen, had no claim to Indian land because of the Indians' assumed heathenism—nor had James I and Charles I any right to grant it. There need be no 'high opposition' between English and Indian. Williams condemns the remark he had heard from both Dutch and English colonists, that the Indian was a 'heathen dog', best killed (a foretaste of the retort of General Philip Sheridan to a Commanche chief: 'the only good Indians I ever saw were dead'). There should be no conversions 'by wiles and subtle devices, sometimes by force, compelling them to submit to that which they understand not'. (Williams was thinking of the Jesuits in Canada and Maryland). There should be no *spiritual* onslaught by 'plausible persuasions' or 'prevailing forces' on the Indians, 'many very ingenuous, plain-hearted, inquisitive'. Williams's confined conception of the true Christian led him to the position that the Indian deserves due respect.

In 1650 there were two places in the English-speaking world with written provision for religious toleration. One was Maryland. There the General Assembly had in 1649 approved 'free exercise of religion' (admittedly only for those 'professing to believe in Jesus Christ'); and noted the dangers for a commonwealth of 'the inforcing of the

---

[38] So said the German Calvinist Ursinus (1534–83), P. D. L. Avis, *The Church in the Theology of the Reformers* (London 1981) pp 173–74.
[39] Verse and prose in *Key* (1973 edn) p 133.

conscience in matter of religion'.[40] The other place was Rhode Island—or more correctly, then, 'Providence Plantations in the Narragansett Bay in New England.' No one was to be questioned or molested 'for any differences in opinion in matter of religion'; a provision confirmed in the 1663 Rhode Island Charter.[41] Williams himself used the image of a ship:[42] with 'papists and protestants, Jews and Turks' aboard. No people were 'forced to come to the ship's prayers or worship, nor compelled from their own particular prayers or worship, if they practise any'.

On three occasions Williams used his Indians as a good example to Europe, in their toleration (so he said) of the conscience and worship of others. In the *Key* of 1643 he wrote, 'They have a modest religious persuasion not to disturb any man, either themselves, English, Dutch, or any, in their conscience and worship, and therefore say: Aquiewopwauwock, hold your peace, Peeyauntam, he is at prayer.'[43] Among the pleas in *The Bloudy Tenent of Persecution* of 1644, was 'that no persons, Papists, Jews, Turks or Indians be disturbed at their worship, a thing which the very Indians abhor to practise towards any'.[44] And finally, in his 1645 pamphlet, Williams stressed the point that Christian conversion should never be by compulsion:

> so did never the Lord Jesus bring any unto His most pure worship, for He abhors (as all men, yea the very Indians, do) an unwilling spouse, and to enter into a forced bed. The will in worship, if true, is like a free vote . . . The not discerning of this truth hath let out the blood of thousands in civil combustions in all ages, and made the whore drunk, and the earth drunk with the blood of the saints and witnesses of Jesus.[45]

'America, as Europe, and all nations, lies dead in sin and trespasses'.[46] But, as a theologian concerned with the evils of persecution, Williams might have agreed that the New World had been called into existence to redress the balance of the Old.

History Faculty, Cambridge

[40] C. C. Hall ed *Narratives of Early Maryland 1633–1684* (New York 1967) p 272.
[41] *Complete Writings of Roger Williams*, 6 ed J. R. Bartlett (New York 1963) p 345.
[42] *Ibid* pp 278–79, January 1655.
[43] (1973 ed) p 193.
[44] *Complete Writings of Roger Williams*, 3 ed S. L. Caldwell (New York 1963) p 252.
[45] *Ibid* 7 p 38.
[46] *Ibid* p 37.

TOLERATION AND THE
CROMWELLIAN PROTECTORATE

by BLAIR WORDEN

TOLERATION IS a Victorian subject, a monument to Victorian liberalism. 'To us who have been educated in the nineteenth century', proclaimed F. A. Inderwick in his book on the Interregnum, 'any declaration inconsistent with religious toleration would be abhorrent and inadmissible'.[1] His sentiment would not have seemed controversial to a generation raised on such best-selling works as Buckle's *History of Civilisation in England* and Lecky's *History of the Rise and Influence of the Spirit of Rationalism.* It may be that the Victorians, enquiring into the origins of the toleration which they had achieved, were prone to congratulate the past on becoming more like the present. Yet in the late nineteenth and early twentieth centuries, when interest in the subject was perhaps at its peak, we can also detect, in the statements on toleration of a Creighton or a Figgis, a fear that the present might become more like the past: that materialism and religious indifference might destroy the moral foundations of toleration, and foster a new barbarism which would persecute Christians afresh.[2]

Like other liberal subjects, the history of toleration survived the First World War not in England but in the United States. There the 1930s produced William Haller's *Tracts on Liberty in the Puritan Revolution* and W. K. Jordan's heroic study, to which any subsequent account can be no more than a footnote, *The Development of Religious Toleration in England,* a work written under, and deeply influenced by, the shadow of European Fascism.[3] With the completion of Jordan's four volumes, the subject seems to die. Perhaps there seemed nothing more to say; but perhaps too there were changes of intellectual climate which made the evolutionary perspective of

[1] F. A. Inderwick, *The Interregnum* (1891) p 117.
[2] Bishop Creighton, *Persecution and Tolerance* (1895) e.g. pp 114–6, 124, 139; J. N. Figgis, 'Toleration', in S. L. Ollard and G. Cross eds *A Dictionary of English Church History* (1912) p 600.
[3] [W. K.] Jordan, *The Development of Religious Toleration* [*In England* (4 vols 1932–40)]. The work covered the period 1558–1660. Jordan's philosophy can be discerned in the prefaces to (and on the dust-jackets of) his four volumes, and on pp 17, 30, 41, 350 of the first of them.

Jordan and his liberal predecessors appear dated or misleading. When, now, we find S. R. Gardiner describing the seventeenth-century arguments which led to toleration as 'the lifeblood of future generations',[4] or when we observe the conviction with which Jordan awarded the adjective 'noble' to so many of the writers whom he studied, we may wonder at the sense of responsibility shown by those historians to the civilisation which sustained them; at their concern to explain the preconditions of modern freedom; and at their readiness, which rebukes the narrow relativism of a later generation, to contemplate the universal significance of the seventeenth-century arguments which they examined. Our difficulty is to dispel from the subject of toleration a faint whiff of anachronism. As we try to do so, we discover that relativism has insistent claims to make.

For more often than not in puritan England, toleration was a dirty word. It stood not for an edifying principle but for an impious policy. To grant 'a toleration' was to make an expedient concession to wickedness. The Long Parliament consistently used the term pejoratively.[5] So did most puritan divines, Independents as well as Presbyterians. Toleration was 'the whore of Babylon's back door':[6] 'the last and most desperate design of Antichrist', when His stratagems of force and violence had failed, 'to destroy Church and State'.[7] Thomas Edwards made a fair point in 1646: 'if some of those godly ministers who were famous in their time should rise out of their graves and now come among us, as Mr Perkins, Greenham, Hildersham, Dr Preston, Dr Sibs etc., they would wonder to . . . meet with such books for toleration of all religions'. How robustly, Edwards recalled, had puritans resisted toleration for Arminians in the 1620s.[8] The divines whom Edwards named had refined and inculcated the puritan scheme of salvation, in which fallen man was clay in the potter's hand, redeemable only through an inexplicable divine clemency and through an exacting process of justification and sanctification. In that scheme, 'liberty' could have nothing to do

[4] [S. R.] Gardiner, *The First Two Stuarts [and the Puritan Revolution* (1878)] p 136. Gardiner's views on liberty are boldly presented in that volume.

[5] E.g. [S. R.] Gardiner ed, *Constitutional Documents [of the Puritan Revolution* (1889)] p 219; William Haller, *Liberty and Reformation in the Puritan Revolution* (New York, 1963 repr) p 130; [Blair] Worden, *The Rump Parliament [1648–1653* (Cambridge 1974)] p 214.

[6] Christopher Fowler, *Daemonium Meridianum. Satan at Noon* (1655) p 167.

[7] Daniel Cawdrey, *Sathan Discovered* (1657) p 22.

[8] T. Edwards, *Gangraena* (1646) p 145.

with the individual dignity and self-assertion with which the modern world invests the word. It consisted in freedom from the guilt of sin, and in the release of the will from its bondage to Satan.[9] The only 'true liberty', it was agreed, was 'a power to do what we ought, not what we will'.[10]

We are now taught to regard Civil War heresy and religious diversity as expressions of social protest, and the imposition of orthodoxy as social repression. Yet warnings about the social consequences of toleration were rarely at the centre of debate. More often they were used (like the claim that toleration would be good for trade) to reinforce the appeal of an argument from theology. For the seventeenth-century discussion about toleration is principally a debate about the salvation not of society, but of souls.[11] Ultimately it is an argument between two positions: the first, that to tolerate heresy is to condemn its converts to eternal torment: the second, that to interpose human authority between God's grace and the soul is to threaten the lifeline of salvation, and to merit damnation 'as accessory to the blood of that soul'.[12] So the stakes were high. 'Thousands might curse you for ever in Hell', Richard Baxter warned the Parliament of 1654, 'if you grant such a liberty to all men to deceive them, and entice them thither'.[13] Heresy was, literally, soul-destroying. It

[9] See e.g. the Westminster Assembly's *Articles of Christian Religion* (1648: a document approved by Parliament) pp 32–3; William Strong (Independent minister), *A Treatise Showing the Subordination of the Will of Man unto the Will of God* (1657), preface and pp 45–6.

[10] Richard Vines, *Obedience to Magistrates . . . in Three Sermons* (1655) second sermon p 12; cf. e.g. the almost identical words of William Gurnall, *The Magistrate's Portraiture* (1656) p 10, and Philip Skippon's remark in [J. T. Rutt ed *The]Diary of Thomas Burton* [(4 vols 1828)] 1 p 50.

[11] Of course, the two cannot be so easily separated. But damage seems to me to have been done by the supposition that theological statements can be read as if they were merely the seventeenth-century's way of talking about the twentieth-century's sociological concerns. It is worthwhile, for example, to sit down with Thomas Edwards's book *Gangraena* and to ask how many anachronistic assumptions, and how much circular reasoning, we must deploy before we can agree with H. N. Brailsford, who wrote that the passage (on p 156) in which Edwards claims that toleration would put an end to the 'command of wives, children, servants' is 'more significant than the whole of the rest of his book': Brailsford, *The Levellers and the English Revolution* ed C. Hill (London 1961), p 42. It is fair to add that Brailsford's chapter on toleration makes perceptive points about Cromwellian policy.

[12] John Goodwin, in William Haller ed *Tracts on Liberty in the Puritan Revolution* (3 vols Columbia 1934) 3 p 42.

[13] *Humble Advice: or the Heads of those Things which were offered to many Members of Parliament by Mr Richard Baxter* (1655) p 2. Cf. e.g. [William] Grigge, *The Quaker's Jesus* (1658) preface.

was what in Christian history it always had been, a 'plague', a 'leprosy', a 'deadly poison' from which the faithful must at all costs be protected. The 'false prophets' and the 'damnable heresies' against which the Gospel had warned, and which throve upon the collapse of church discipline and the proliferation of sects in the 1640s, were 'a clear indication to us of God's heavy judgement upon this nation', certain to provoke still heavier judgements, in this world and the next, if they were not quickly purged.[14]

For the puritan clergy, the Great Rebellion was a demoralising experience. Members of their flocks, who had shared with them both the persecution of the 1630s and the apocalyptic hopes of the early 1640s, fell away to the sects, lapsed into indifference, or, bewildered by the rapid increase of religious options, succumbed to tormenting doubts about their own salvation.[15] Toleration seemed the obvious source of these evils. Behind it, puritans discerned a profoundly subversive movement: Arminianism, the philosophy of free will and free thought. In the early 1640s, identified with the Court, Arminianism was politically defeated, but it infiltrated the Civil War sects, and after 1660, in England as in protestant Europe, it achieved a slow and almost silent triumph. If we favour an evolutionary perspective and concern ourselves with the 'development' of toleration, then, as a number of historians have argued—Gardiner, Jordan and Trevor-Roper among them—it is to the Arminian reaction against Calvinist dogma that we should look for its seventeenth-century development.[16] How could puritans preserve their intellec-

---

[14] *A Testimony to the Truth of Jesus Christ* (1647) p 23. These sentiments can be widely found in the 1650s.

[15] For some eloquent complaints against this process expressed during the Protectorate, see Richard Baxter, *True Christianity* (1655) preface and p 204; Edward Reynolds, *The Peace of Jerusalem* (1657) p 34; Stephen Marshall and Giles Firmin, *The Power of the Civil Magistrate in Matters of Religion, Vindicated* (1657) pp 20, 23–4; Edmund Calamy, *A Patterne for All* (1658) pp 16–17. It is easy to forget the most obvious characteristic of puritans: their anxiety about their salvation. For an especially vivid illustration of the widespread and educated nature of this concern, see *Truth's Conflict with Error; or, Universal Redemption Controverted in Three Publike Disputations* (1650).

[16] Gardiner, *First Two Stuarts* pp 5–6, 65, 125–6, 135–6; Jordan, *Development of Religious Toleration* 2 pp 205, 280; H. R. Trevor-Roper, 'The Religious Origins of the Enlightenment', in his *Religion, The Reformation and Social Change* (1967) pp 193–236. Trevor-Roper's remarkable essay is much more subtle than the discussions by earlier writers (Buckle and Lecky among them) who connected Arminianism with the rise of toleration. Recently there have been attempts to portray puritanism as an intellectually liberalising force which effectively challenged Arminian intolerance. The more traditional view appears to receive support from the frequency with which advocates of religious liberty after 1660 appealed to the authority of

tual system against that threat? How could they beat off the principal long-term changes in seventeenth-century religion: the weakening of creeds, the decline of Hell, the retreat of the millennium, the rise of rational and practical theology?[17]

Arminianism assumed one particularly sinister form. This was Socinianism, a term which, like Arminianism, was used to describe both a doctrine and a frame of mind. The doctrine was anti-trinitarianism: the frame of mind was rational scepticism. No heresy was harder to tolerate than anti-trinitarianism. It occasioned the last public burnings for heresy in England in 1612, and was excluded from the Toleration Act of 1689. Questioning the divinity of Christ and the Holy Ghost, undermining Christ's mediation and the believer's union with Christ, anti-trinitarianism, offensive enough to Christians of most persuasions, struck at the very heart of puritan theology. 'The Trinity', explained Cromwell's chaplain John Owen, was 'the great fundamental article of our profession', 'that mystery the knowledge whereof is the only means to have a right apprehension of all other sacred truths'.[18] Parliament's draft ordinance against blasphemy in 1646, and its fierce legislation against blasphemy in 1648, were responses to the anti-trinitarian challenge; and it was in reply to anti-trinitarian literature that in 1652 John Owen framed those 'fundamental' articles of faith which were to provide the doctrinal basis of Cromwellian Church policy. From 1652 to 1654 alarm mounted at the content and the influence of the anti-trinitarian publications of John Biddle, whose offences inflamed the proceedings of the first Protectorate Parliament.

Arminians earlier in the century: e.g. Andrew Marvell, *The Rehearsal Transpros'd* ed D. I. B. Smith (Oxford 1971) pp 20, 79, 325; Henry Stubbe, *A Further Iustification of the Present War* (1673), 'Apology' p 58; Stubbe, *An Account of the Rise and Progress of Mahometanism* ed H. M. K. Shairani (1911) p 12; *The Select Works of William Penn* (3 vols 1825) 2 pp 156–7; 3 pp 47, 66–7, 84, 117, 163–4; T. E. S. Clarke and H. C. Foxcroft eds *A Life of Gilbert Burnet* 2 (Cambridge 1907) pp 323, 365; *The Great Case of Toleration Stated* (1688) pp 4–5; *The Faith of One God* (1691) p 3; A. A. Seaton, *The Theory of Toleration under the Later Stuarts* (Cambridge 1911) pp 271–2. The appeal to earlier Arminian authorities after 1660 may have owed a little, but probably not much, to political tact. The Arminian Jeremy Taylor was regarded as an established authority on religious liberty in the 1650s: e.g. John Reading, *Anabaptism Routed* (1655); Cawdrey, *Sathan Discovered*, pp 11 seq; Stubbe, *An Essay in Defence of the Good Old Cause* (1659) p 42; Jordan, *Development of Religious Toleration in England* 3 p 505.

[17] The historian of Hell is D. P. Walker, *The Decline of Hell* (Chicago 1964): the historian of the millennium is William Lamont, who has explored both the impact and the decline of millenarianism in a number of works.

[18] [William H. Goold ed *The*] *Works of John Owen* [(16 vols Banner of Truth Trust repr Edinburgh 1965–8)] 7 pp 28–9; 14 p 346.

Socinians, theologically the most subversive of the sects, were socially the least provocative of them; and Biddle was the most sober of sectaries. There was nothing to match the disturbances and the social criticisms produced by Fifth Monarchists and Quakers. Biddle's prose, like much Socinian literature, was dauntingly abstract and knotty. Anti-trinitarianism was not a village protest movement but a European intellectual movement, the secret heresy, in England, of Great Tew, and then of Milton and Newton and Locke.[19] Its biblical case, as puritans admitted, was embarrassingly 'plausible',[20] based as it was on a scriptural literalism similar to that which orthodox divines were themselves driven to advocate by the fanciful allegorical readings of other sects.[21] But there was a broader challenge, too, which is conveyed by the sub-title of Biddle's translation (condemned as 'very scandalous' before Parliament in 1654)[22] of that major work of European Socinianism, *Dissertatio de Pace*: 'wherein is elegantly and acutely argued, that not so much a bad opinion, as a bad life, exludes a Christian out of the Kingdom of Heaven; and that the things necessary to be known for salvation, are very few and easy; and finally, that those who pass amongst us under the name of heretics, are notwithstanding to be tolerated'. 'Socinians', observed the MP Samuel Gott in 1650, 'suppose him to be a good easy and indulgent God, content with anything'.[23]

In March 1654 the Council of State decided to act. John Owen, vice-chancellor of Oxford and the architect of the Cromwellian Church, accepted the government's invitation to confute Biddle's

---

[19] It can be studied in H. J. McLachlan, *Socinianism in Seventeenth-Century England* (Oxford 1951) and in McLachlan's *The Religious Opinions of Milton, Locke and Newton* (Manchester 1941). The broader intellectual significance of Socinianism is discussed by Trevor-Roper, 'The Religious Origins of the Enlightenment'; and there is a helpful account by Maurice Kelley in his introduction to *The Complete Prose Works of John Milton* (8 vols Yale 1953–83) 6 pp 47–73. Too much has been made of Owen's warning (*Works of John Owen* 12 p 52) that 'there is not a city, a town, scarce a village, in England, wherein some of this poison is not poured forth': Owen was evidently referring to a general Arminian *malaise* of which anti-trinitarianism was merely one symptom (cf *Ibid* 10 p 156, 16 p 16). It is true, however, that such evidence as we have of the existence of Socinian congregations suggests that there may have been others which have left no record. See too Keith Thomas, *Religion and the Decline of Magic* (1971) p 136.

[20] *Works of John Owen* 12 p 28; *Weekly Intelligencer* 25 June–3 July 1655.

[21] Cf. *Two Letters of Mr Iohn Biddle* (1655) pp 2–6; Biddle, *A Twofold Catechism* (1655) preface.

[22] *Journal of the House of Commons* 21 December 1654; *Several Proceedings in Parliament* 21–28 December 1654.

[23] Gott, *An Essay of the true Happiness of Man* (1650) p 267.

arguments.[24] The result was one of a series of massive works in which Owen, 'the Calvin of England', expounded and defended puritan orthodoxy. His condemnation of the 'cursed Socinians'— particularly of Hugo Grotius—was unsparing. Calvin, Owen declared, had been right to burn Biddle's intellectual ancestor, the Socinian Michael Servetus.[25] Socinianism was responsible for the 'flood' of 'scepticism, libertinism and atheism' which 'is broken upon the world', and which had advanced until 'nothing certain be left, nothing unshaken'.[26] 'The liberty of men's rational faculties having got the great vogue in the world', men were deciding 'that religion consists solely in moral honesty, and a fancied internal piety of mind towards the deity'.[27] Addressing the Parliaments of the 1650s, Owen stared the ugly modern world in the face: 'Life, heat, warmth is gone'. 'Take heed', he vainly implored MPs, 'that there rise not up a generation that know not Joseph, that knew us not in the days of our distress'.[28]

Here a voice of protest might be raised. If puritanism was so hostile to toleration, how was it then that in the Puritan Revolution so much toleration was achieved? The arrival of liberty of conscience, after all, was proclaimed by Cromwell, attacked by his Presbyterian critics, and acknowledged gratefully by some sects and grudgingly by others. The successive governments of the Interregnum, although they tried to define the boundaries of acceptable doctrine, made no attempt to impose a particular form of worship or of church government or to enforce a solution to the heated controversies of the decade about the sacraments of communion and baptism. Indeed, we know almost nothing about how most people worshipped in the 1650s.

The emergence of religious *laisser-faire* during the Puritan Revolution might seem to cast doubt on the approach which we have so far taken, and which concentrates on the theological anxieties of clergymen. Ought we not instead to be studying the facts of political life? The main reason for religious toleration in the Great Rebellion, after all, was the difficulty of stopping it. When the Presbyterians sought

[24] *Cal SPD 1654* p 3.
[25] *Works of John Owen* 12 p 41.
[26] *Ibid* 12 pp 12, 48, 61–2; 14 p 277.
[27] *Ibid* 7 pp 5–6; 15 p 76.
[28] *Ibid* 7 pp 383, 423.

to stop it, the Long Parliament proved too suspicious of clerical pretensions to make the Presbyterian settlement of 1648 compulsive. The repeal of the recusancy laws in 1650 gave recognition to practices that no one had both the will and the power to prevent. In any case, it was difficult to devise a national creed to which rival and powerful religious parties would agree. The Independents and the sects, although ready enough to forget each other's claim to liberty if they saw a chance of imposing their own *iure divino* ecclesiastical solutions,[29] were often driven together by the fear of persecution, and developed a common vocabulary of religious freedom. In the New Model Army, that vocabulary appealed to comradeship and to shared experience. Religious liberty became an integral part of the good old cause, a goal, soldiers and saints persuaded themselves, for which Civil War blood had been spilt. In the 1650s the army's wishes were not easily disregarded. And puritan divines, whatever their theoretical objections to toleration, had their own good old cause, their own Foxeian martyrology, their own memories of persecution in the 1630s, their own images of the Inquisition.

Even if we insist on the importance of ideas in the subject of toleration, ought we not at least to consider the ideas of laymen, and to move beyond the boundaries of theological argument? Should we not dwell on the radical libertarianism of a Milton or a Walwyn or a Henry Robinson, or on the Erastian anti-clericalism of a Henry Parker?[30] Were there not seventeenth-century intellectual developments, outside theology, to which toleration was the only practical solution? Were not the spread of lay education and of travel, the entrenchment of competing European faiths, and the expanding study of Church history bound to stimulate religious relativism, to cast doubt on the likelihood that truth lay where one group of divines in one country at one time said it lay? And were not the philosophical advances of the seventeenth century, which raised in pressing form

[29] That Independents, while they often pleaded for liberty for other groups, were not committed to the principle, became evident at those moments when, as in their *Apologeticall Narration* of 1644 and in the Savoy Declaration of 1658, they sought to make common cause with the Presbyterians against the sects. Owen's priorities are evident from his statement of 1649 that the problem of toleration could not be solved until Independency had been 'rightly established' in England, and 'the precious distinguished from the vile' (*Works of John Owen* 8 p 203). Jordan points out that most Independent pleas for religious liberty were made before 1649, when the Congregationalists were more often frightened by Presbyterian (or Anglican) intolerance than by the sects (*Development of Religious Toleration* 3 p 437).
[30] The religious positions of Robinson and Parker are extensively studied in W. K. Jordan, *Men of Substance* (Chicago 1942).

the question how ideas and beliefs come to settle in the mind, a further stimulus to scepticism? Theology itself, if it impinged on a broader range of ideas, was bound in its turn to be influenced by them, and to absorb something of what it opposed. Thus divines could not be oblivious to, or remain unaffected by, the gradual seventeenth-century elevation of sincerity of intention above correctness of belief. In Jeremy Taylor's words, 'an honest error is better than a hypocritical profession of truth'.[31] Even John Owen allowed that what was heresy in one man might not be heresy in another.[32] Owen, in any case, accepted strict limits to the claims of theology both in political practice and in political theory. No theocrat, he was particularly struck by one argument for liberty of conscience which appealed not to theology but to natural law: to 'that sovereign dictate of nature', 'Do not that unto others which you would not have done to you'.[33] Indeed it may seem perverse to present Owen, politically the most influential clergyman of the 1650s, as an opponent of toleration. After all, he wrote a number of works which appear to defend the principle, among them the treatise *Of Toleration* which he published in 1649.

Yet when we come to examine the formation of the government's doctrinal policies in the Protectorate, we shall find that puritan theological conservatism occupies a central place in the story. We shall also find, however, that the lessons of puritan theology did not all point in one direction; and it is to the debate within puritan theology (rather than to a conflict between theological intolerance and lay libertarianism) that we should look for the inspiration of Cromwellian policy. There were some features of puritan theology which pointed towards liberty of conscience. For to the puritan—and to the Independent more than the Presbyterian—truth lay in the spirit rather than the institution, in the power rather than the form. In this the Independents resembled the Platonists, whom they often addressed amicably across the political lines.[34] Like them, they searched for internal unity within an external diversity which might be permissible because it was not of the essence of belief. Peter Sterry, who

---

[31] Taylor, *The Liberty of Prophesying* (1647) p 163.
[32] *Works of John Owen* 8 p 60.
[33] *Ibid* 8 pp 62, 167, 195; cf. J. C. Davis, 'The Levellers and Christianity', in Brian Manning ed *Politics, Religion and the English Civil War* (1973) p 228.
[34] For the exchanges between them, see e.g. Ralph Cudworth, *A Sermon preached before the House of Commons March 31, 1647* (1647) and John Goodwin, *Redemption Redeemed* (1651) ep ded.

was both an Independent and a Platonist, and who exercised much influence at Cromwell's Court, preached courageously to Parliament in defence of the Quakers in 1656, when the Quaker James Nayler was under heavy attack from MPs.[35] For Quaker doctrine, although usually disowned by Independents, could sometimes bear a resemblance to Independent theology similar in one sense to that borne by Platonist teaching. Dr Nuttall has memorably demonstrated the affinities between the Independents' conception of the Holy Spirit and the Quakers' notion of the 'inner light',[36] affinities which give poignancy to William Sydenham's remark during the parliamentary debates on James Nayler: 'that which sticks most with me, is the nearness of this opinion to that which is a most glorious truth, that the spirit is personally in us'.[37] Might not that spirit assume more than one legitimate form?

Other characteristics of puritanism also obliged it to come to terms, in some measure, with diversity of belief. It was a religion of the ear rather than the eye, of conscience rather than ceremony. The individual believer must answer to God at the day of judgement for the stewardship of his soul. Even the stoutest champions of orthodoxy conceded that the conscience could not be forced.[38] Puritan theology, however logically expounded, was verifiable only through the believer's experience, which could not be objectively tested. The journey of the soul towards God was a long and arduous one. Different people might 'grow spiritually' at different paces, 'growing on by parts and piecemeal' according to the various lights God had given them.[39] During the pilgrim's progress, truth might, at least temporarily, be mingled with error. Even the guardians of orthodoxy might have to look to their spiritual laurels. When the

---

[35] Sterry, *The Way of God with his People* (1656) pp 14, 28 seq. Sterry had been a client of that influential Platonist advocate of religious liberty, Lord Brooke.

[36] Geoffrey F. Nuttall, *The Holy Spirit in Puritan Faith and Experience* (Oxford 1946).

[37] *Diary of Thomas Burton* 1 p 69; cf also pp 76, 86.

[38] They did, however, think that dissenters could be 'required to attend upon the ministry and dispensation of the Gospel, that they may not presumptuously exempt and deprive themselves of the means of grace and salvation' (Reynolds, *The Peace of Jerusalem* p 33; cf Marshall and Firmin, *The Power of the Civil Magistrate* p 7, and George Petter, *A brief and solid Exercitation concerning the Coercive Power of the Magistrate in Matters of Religion* (Thomason Tracts, E 885(12)) pp 41–2). For the individual's stewardship of his soul, see e.g. *Works of John Owen* 14 p 312, and Davis, 'The Levellers and Christianity'.

[39] A. G. Matthews ed *The Savoy Declaration of Faith and Order 1658,* p 161; cf e.g. *Works of John Owen* 13 p 557; Richard Baxter, *The Saints' Everlasting Rest* ed William Young (1907) pp 143–4.

Independent authors of the *Apologeticall Narration* resolved 'not to make our present judgement and practice a binding law unto ourselves for the future', they inadvertently framed a powerful argument for religious freedom.[40] As the Independent minister Timothy Armitage asked, 'Does all truth come into the world at once? And may not we persecute that which afterwards may appear to be a truth'?[41] Such persecution, risking the murder of souls, would imperil the salvation both of the persecuted and of the persecutors.

Perhaps the apparent puritan mixture of tolerance and intolerance will seem to us to exceed the average human capacity to believe contradictory things. Yet the contradictions may be illusory. They may prove, on closer inspection, merely to illustrate the surviving influence of those modern and liberal preconceptions which, in a more conscious and more confident form, inspired Gardiner and Jordan. The very word toleration has so many evaluative and potentially anachronistic connotations that, at least for the particular, purpose of exploring Cromwellian policy, it may be an impediment to understanding. For the argument within the puritan camp was not about toleration: it was about liberty of conscience. Although, in the manner of these things, men were not consistent in their terminology, there was a world of difference between allowing people to believe what they liked and permitting beliefs which were deemed to be conscionably held.[42] Liberty of conscience would allow doctrines which did not breach fundamental truths whose acceptance was essential to salvation. It would permit error, into which the believer might stumble on the path to salvation, but not heresy, Satan's chief weapon. There were, it is true, men who claimed that God wished heresies to flourish, so that the truths 'which are approved may be made manifest'.[43] But these men were not Calvinists (or at least not

---

[40] *An Apologeticall Narration, humbly submitted to Parliament. By Tho. Goodwin, Philip Nye, Sidrach Simpson, and others* (1644) p 10. Cf. Michael Fixler, *Milton and the Kingdoms of God* (1964) p 120.

[41] Quoted in Geoffrey F. Nuttall, *Visible Saints. The Congregational Way* (Oxford 1957) p 117.

[42] Owen's discourse *On Toleration* is an exception to a general rule. Speakers in the Nayler debates knew the difference between 'liberty of conscience' (or 'liberty to tender consciences'), which in principle they normally approved, and toleration, of which they disapproved. The Quakers were suspected by MPs of aiming at the latter under colour of the former. Nevertheless, there was semantic uncertainty. Often men attacked not 'toleration' but 'universal toleration' or 'toleration of all religions'.

[43] 1 Corinthians 11: 19. Sometimes this text was used to justify the toleration of error

predestinarians), and they did not shape the ecclesiastical policies of the Interregnum. The same observations may be made about those writers discussed by Jordan whose arguments are likely to sound most familiar and most attractive to a modern ear.

The goal of liberty of conscience was very different from modern liberalism. It was religious union, which persecution was held to have destroyed: the union of the believer with Christ, and the union of believers with each other. The former was essential to salvation: the latter was essential to the creation of a commonwealth fit for God's eyes. Religious division is the great anxiety of early modern Europe, as keen a stimulus to thought and guilt as class division in modern Europe. Whether we look at Renaissance hermeticism and Platonism, at the international ecumenicalism of the earlier seventeenth century, or at the Association movement of Richard Baxter in the 1650s, always we find the same yearning to end the strife in the world and in men's hearts. This was a vision especially compelling to the generation which lived through the Thirty Years War and the Puritan Revolution, the generation which was addressed by Hartlib and Dury and Comenius.[44]

The religious policy of Oliver Cromwell becomes much clearer when we see it as a search not for the toleration for which he is so often commended, but for union: for the unity of the godly party 'in the several forms of it'.[45] The letter which he sent to Parliament from Bristol in 1645, a document frequently cited to demonstrate his commitment to toleration, observed that 'all that believe have the real unity, which is most glorious, because inward and spiritual, in the Body, and to the Head'.[46] To Robert Hammond in 1648 he wrote: 'I profess to thee I desire it in my heart, I have prayed for it, I have waited for the day to see union and right understanding between the godly people (Scots, English, Jews, Gentiles, Presbyte-

---

rather than of heresy. The parable of the wheat and the tares proved to be similarly ambiguous.

[44] See H. R. Trevor-Roper, 'Three Foreigners: the Philosophy of the Puritan Revolution', in his *Religion, The Reformation and Social Change* pp 237–93. Trevor-Roper has also discussed ecumenicalism in England and in Europe, between 1590 and 1640, in 'The Good and Great Works of Richard Hooker', *New York Review of Books* 24 November 1977; in his Wiles Lectures at Belfast in 1975; and in 'The Church of England and the Greek Church in the Time of Charles I' *SCH* 15 (Oxford 1978) pp 213–40.

[45] Thomason Tracts, E 828(8), 22 February 1655, untitled, pp 7–8.

[46] [W. C.] Abbott, *Writings and Speeches [of Oliver Cromwell* (4 vols Cambridge, Mass)] 1 p 376.

rians, Independents, Anabaptists, and all)'.[47] The Cromwellian plea to the Scots for liberty of conscience in July 1650 was advanced in the hope that God would 'make all Christians of one heart'.[48] Early in 1655 Cromwell longed for 'the several interests of the people of God' to be 'healed and atoned' (that is, 'at-oned'), and commissioned a pamphlet which looked forward to 'a glorious union of the people of God, made to be of one spirit'.[49] Cromwell sought the readmission of the Jews to England for the sake not of tolerating but of converting them, and so of accomplishing the union between Jew and Gentile.[50] The main obstacle to union in the 1650s was the readiness of the sects to persecute each other. Time and again Cromwell hammered the point: 'Is it ingenuous to ask for liberty, and not to give it?' 'Where shall we find men of a universal spirit? Everyone desires to have liberty, but none will give it'.[51] He saw himself as 'a constable to part' the contending religious groups to whom he gave protection, and struggled to preserve the delicate 'posture and balance' which the Protectorate secured among them.[52]

Once we see Cromwell's purpose, we can better understand his affinity to Owen, whose own position may now appear less inconsistent. Both men wanted liberty for 'God's peculiar', not for the unregenerate. Both tolerated error, not heresy. It may be that Cromwell identified the boundary between them more through instinct than through theology, but we should not underestimate either the theological equipment or the theological orthodoxy of a man who, in conversation, could correct Fifth Monarchists on the identification of Antichrist and Quakers on the nature of the 'inner light'.[53] Displaying a consistent preoccuption with Christ's mediation which would have delighted Owen, he wanted liberty only for those who 'believe the remission of sins through the blood of Christ and free justification by the blood of Christ, and live upon the grace of God'.[54] Repeatedly in the 1650s his words suggest that 'God's

---

[47] *Ibid* 1 p 677.

[48] *Ibid* 2 pp 283–8.

[49] *Ibid* 3 pp 572–3 (cf. 3 p 119); Thomason Tracts, E 828(8); *A True State of the Case of Liberty of Conscience in the Commonwealth of England. Together with a Narrative of . . . Mr John Biddle's Sufferings* (1655) p 1.

[50] David S. Katz, *Philo-Semitism and the Readmission of the Jews to England 1603–1655* (Oxford 1982) esp p 224.

[51] Abbott, *Writings and Speeches* 3 pp 459, 547, 586; 4 p 271.

[52] *Ibid* 3 p 606; 4 p 273.

[53] *Ibid* 3 pp 373, 607–616; 4 p 309.

[54] *Ibid* 4 pp 271–2; Cf *ibid* 586, 592, 756; 4 pp 276–7.

peculiar' were to be found exclusively, or almost exclusively, within three groups: Presbyterians, Independents and Baptists.[55] Like Owen, he was appalled by the newly influential heresies of the 1650s, which he called 'blasphemous' and 'diabolical', the 'height of Satan's wickednesses'.[56] His imagination could not enter the world of the Ranters and Quakers and Socinians, whose principles seemed so different from the biblical and Christocentric radicalism he had known in the New Model in the 1640s. Confident of his ability to distinguish the people of God from 'pretenders and pretences to righteousness' and from 'men that have wonderfully lost their consciences and their wits',[57] he told a Ranter woman in 1651 that 'she was so vile a creature as he thought her unworthy to live'.[58] On another occasion he apparently left the room rather than endure the heretical statements of Doomsday Sedgwick.[59] From 1653 Cromwell was freed from the influence of Sir Henry Vane, who was committed to a much broader liberty of conscience than Cromwell's, and who now identified him as the Second Beast, 'making himself umpire of all controversies in matters of religion, and declarer of heresies, blasphemies and the like'.[60] Now Cromwell sought that 'sober liberty', mid-way between licence and tyranny, for which Marvell praised him in the *First Anniversary*, and which became the public posture of the Protectorate regime. Although he cannot be held directly responsible for all the statements of newspapers friendly to the government, he surely could, had he wished, have ended the savage attacks to which Quakers and Socinians were subjected by the press throughout the Protectorate, and which were especially vindictive at moments when leaders of those sects were threatened with the death penalty for their heresies. Quakers, portrayed as thieves and fornicators, were grotesquely caricatured and diabolised: 'you may commonly know them in the streets by their vizards'.[61]

[55] *Ibid* 3 pp 586, 607; 4 pp 272, 496. Cf C. H. Firth ed *The Clarke Papers* (4 vols 1891–1901) 3 pp 92–3; T. Birch ed *A Collection of State Papers of John Thurloe* (7 vols 1742) 2 p 67; *To the Officers and Souldiers of the Army* (1657: Thomason Tracts, E 902(4)) p 5.

[56] Abbott, *Writings and Speeches* 3 pp 586, 612; 4 p 471; cf *ibid* (e.g.) 2 p 286, and Jordan, *Development of Religious Toleration* 3 p 149.

[57] Abbott, *Writings and Speeches* 3 p 572; 4 pp 276, 719.

[58] *Mercurius Politicus* 29 May–5 June 1651.

[59] *Diary of Thomas Burton* 1 pp 103–4.

[60] Vane, *The Retired Man's Meditations* (1655) pp 368–9.

[61] *Certain Passages* 9–16 February 1655. For evident press fabrication concerning Socinians, compare the remarks about John Biddle in *Faithful Scout* 12–19 January 1655 with *Weekly Post* 6–11 March 1655 (8 March).

Toleration and the Cromwellian Protectorate

The Independent and Cromwellian preoccupation with the union of the godly people explains the otherwise puzzlingly peripheral role in the debate about religious liberty of the position of Anglicans and Roman Catholics. Anglicans, as Independents acknowledged and as modern research confirms, retained the loyalty of most of the population,[62] yet to the issue of liberty of conscience they seemed scarcely relevant. How could the godly people, who had fought the Civil War against popery and prelacy, conceive that their opponents were capable of salvation, especially while Cromwell pursued a stridently anti-Catholic foreign policy, and while the Prayer Book remained a symbol of political allegiance? It is possible that, intermittently, Cromwell believed that some Anglicans (perhaps even some Catholics) might be saved.[63] Yet in the alternation between connivance and repression visited on both denominations, it is hard to detect motives separable from the requirements of diplomacy and domestic peace. Cromwell could not be insensitive to the argument, often pressed on seventeenth-century rulers, that toleration would lead to peace and foster grateful loyalties which would strengthen the government's authority. Yet while reason of state may have modified his behaviour, it was never the foundation of his ecclesiastical policy. That foundation was the distinction between the precious and the vile.

The extent of officially sanctioned religious freedom in Cromwellian England, even if less great than is sometimes supposed, was incontestably revolutionary. The 'posture and balance' which he achieved among the saints, and in particular his success, which delighted him, in persuading the younger generation of Presbyterians to accept a position as merely one among other religious groups,[64] created a habit of ecclesiastical diversity in England which was to prove ineradicable after 1660, and which doubtless had a part to play in the subsequent emergence of religious toleration. There is no need to question the magnanimity of Cromwell's conception of an eclectic godly party, or the determination with which, as a 'Seeker' after

[62] For contemporary observation see Jordan, *Development of Religious Toleration* 4 pp 46, 173, and *Men of Substance* p 137; for modern research see J. S. Morrill 'The Church in England, 1642–9', in Morrill ed *Reactions to the English Civil War 1642–1649* (1982) pp 89–114.

[63] For hints concerning Anglicans, see Robert S. Bosher, *The Making of the Restoration Settlement. The Influence of the Laudians 1649–1662* (1951) pp 9–10; Dr. Williams's Library, Baxter MSS, Letters, VI, fols 83ᵛ, 90ʳ.

[64] Abbott, *Writings and Speeches* 4 p 272; for the younger generation, see Jordan, *Development of Religious Toleration* 3 p 316.

truth who knew that God did not customarily reveal Himself either clearly or painlessly,[65] he sought to accommodate 'mistaken' godly men who had 'the least of truth' in them.[66] Misunderstanding arises only when we confuse his policy with, or when we measure his achievements against, the principles of Victorian liberalism.

How was Cromwell's conception of liberty of conscience to be translated into practice? Here a number of problems arose, to the solution of which theology offered little if any assistance. For example, a distinction was commonly made, which sounded useful and reasonable, between the holding of a belief and the propagation of it. Stephen Marshall would allow liberty to 'men who hold dissenting opinions in lesser points', provided they were 'content to have their faith, in these, and so be quiet. I can be no advocate for such people, if they judge the spreading of their opinions to be a duty'.[67] Yet how could puritans, for whom the spreading of the Word was certainly 'a duty'—indeed, the necessary vessel by which grace was imparted—expect the sects to accept Marshall's distinction, a distinction which was made in the Blasphemy Act of 1648 and which much exercised the Parliament of 1654?[68] It was a dilemma which the sects eloquently exposed.[69] Another principle which proved less straightforward than it looked was that liberty should be dependent on peaceable behaviour. Most people would have agreed with Owen, against the Fifth Monarchists, that God would not give light to violent men, 'it being a known and received maxim that the Gospel clashes against no righteous ordinance of man'.[70] Yet even if the righteous ordinances of man could be authoritatively identified, religion and politics could not be easily separated, especially in a time of political instability. The government's reputation, and therefore its strength, were heavily dependent on its handling of the sects, in Ireland and Scotland as well as in England. In any case civil distur-

---

[65] Abbott, *Writings and Speeches* 1 pp 96–7, 416.

[66] *Ibid* 3 pp 62, 590.

[67] Marshall, *A Sermon preached to the . . . Lord Mayor . . . tending to heal our Rents and Divisions* (1653) p 31; Marshall and Firmin, *The Power of the Civil Magistrate* pp 5, 8–9. Cf *Humble Advice: or the Heads of those Things which were offered . . . by Mr Richard Baxter* p 4; Reynolds, *The Peace of Jerusalem* p 31.

[68] [C. H.] Firth and [R. S.] Rait eds *Acts and Ordinances [of the Interregnum* (3 vols 1911)] 1 p 1133; *Journal of the House of Commons* 13–15 December 1654; *Diary of Thomas Burton* 1 p cxvi.

[69] *The Protector (so called) in part Unvailed* (1655) p 75; James Nayler, *The Power and Glory of the Lord* (1656) p 6.

[70] *Works of John Owen* 8 p 165.

bance was often caused not by the sects but by mobs who set upon them.[71] It was none the less damaging to the regime for that. Again, the pattern of religious belief was bound to be affected by the pattern of government patronage. Most people, including Cromwell, believed that the magistrate had a right, even a duty, to propagate his own beliefs. But was liberty of conscience advanced if Baptists received favourable treatment in army promotions, or threatened if Quaker JPs were replaced? And did the state frustrate liberty if it allowed public maintenance only to ministers who held certain beliefs? Alternatively, was liberty offended when men were punished for refusing, on grounds of conscience, to pay tithes?

These problems, and many like them, dogged the making of religious policy under the Protectorate. But the most serious and the most urgent difficulty, of course, was to translate into practice the distinction between the precious and the vile. Cromwell's habit of vivaing candidates on the borderline could not offer a permanent or a widely applicable solution. Owen's doctrine of the self-evident truth ('Some things, indeed, are so clearly in the Scripture laid down and determined, that to question or deny them bespeaks a spirit self-condemned')[72] availed him little in controversy with so astute a biblical scholar as John Biddle. Yet circularity could scarcely be avoided. The 1650s saw a series of attempts to list essential truths, outside which salvation was unattainable and toleration therefore unthinkable. This was the purpose of the 'fundamentals' which Owen drew up, with Cromwell's evident approval, in 1652, and which were to reappear in the Protectorate.[73] In their insistence on Calvinist orthodoxy, and particularly in their laboured attempt to define and to defeat anti-trinitarianism, the 'fundamentals' were much stiffer and tighter than those alternative models—the Apostles' Creed, the Lord's Prayer and the less contentious of the Thirty-nine Articles—which formed the basis of other tests of doctrinal orthodoxy proposed during the Puritan Revolution.[74] As we shall

---

[71] E.g. *Mercurius Politicus* 2–9 February 1654; *Weekly Post* 16–23 January 1655; Ralph Farmer, *Sathan Inthroned* (1656) p 55; Inderwick, *The Interregnum* p 134; W. C. Braithwaite *The Beginnings of Quakerism* (Cambridge 1961) pp 364–5.

[72] *Works of John Owen* 8 p 60.

[73] They can be found in *Proposals for the Furtherance and Propagation of the Gospel* (1653: Thomason Tracts, E 883 (12)); *The Principles of Faith, presented by Mr Tho. Goodwin, Mr Nye, Mr Sidrach Simpson, and other Ministers* (1654: E 234 (5)); and Ralph Farmer, *The Great Mysteries of Godliness and Ungodliness* (1655) p 66.

[74] *Reliquiae Baxterianae* (1696) 1 p 198; *Humble Advice . . . by Mr Richard Baxter* pp 2–3; Taylor, *Liberty of Prophesying* p 40; Jordan, *Development of Religious Toleration* 2 pp

now find, the distinction between essentials and inessentials, the puritan version of the concept of *adiaphora*, played a significant part in the politics of the Protectorate.

The Instrument of Government of December 1653, 'the saints' civil Magna Charta',[75] appeared to make generous provision for religious freedom. The 'discovery and confutation of error' were to be entrusted to the spiritual exertions of a godly ministry, and to 'sound doctrine and the example of a good conversation'. 'Popery', 'prelacy' and 'licentiousness' were exempted from liberty, as was 'the abuse [of] this liberty to the civil injury of others and to the actual disturbance of the public peace.' Otherwise, 'such as profess faith in God by Jesus Christ . . . shall not be restrained from, but shall be protected in, the profession of the faith and the exercise of their religion'. All laws contrary to these provisions were to be 'esteemed as null and void'.[76]

The document was less straightforward than it looked. Hastily compiled and clumsily worded, it has a prominent place in that trail of ambiguity which attends Cromwell's various attempts to formulate a concrete programme for liberty of conscience.[77] He subsequently acknowledged that the Instrument 'stood in need of mending',[78] and it must be doubted whether he ever had much faith in articles 35 to 38, which contained the religious provisions of the new constitution. The provisions for liberty of conscience were silently omitted from accounts of the document by Cromwell's supporters in the days and weeks which followed the inauguration of the Protectorate.[79] Two months after the adoption of the Instrument, in a statement of February 1654 which Cromwell later endorsed, the government apologist Marchamont Nedham observed that in articles 36 and 37 'it is intimated or implied, that there is a public

147–8 (cf 395); 3 pp 91–2, 103. Cf Matthew Hale, *Of the Nature of True Religion* (1684) p 4; *Works of John Owen* 12 p 47.

[75] John Nickolls, *Original Letters and Papers of State . . . addressed to Oliver Cromwell* (1743) p 134.

[76] Gardiner, *Constitutional Documents* p 416.

[77] For the uneasy adoption of the Instrument, see [Austin] Woolrych, *Commonwealth to Protectorate* [(Oxford 1982)] pp 357–62.

[78] Abbott, *Writings and Speeches* 4 p 417.

[79] See e.g. *Mercurius Politicus* 16–22 December 1653; *Moderate Publisher* 23–30 December 1653; B[ritish] L[ibrary], Add[itional] MS 32093, fo 317ʳ, Sir Charles Wolseley to Bulstrode Whitelocke, 7 January 1654; cf Woolrych, *Commonwealth to Protectorate* p 362.

profession intended to be held forth by the magistrate, and that the profession so held forth shall extend both to doctrine, and worship or discipline'. Welcoming the implication he had spotted, Nedham remarked on 'our want of some settlement in religious matters' and on 'the spreading abroad most blasphemous opinions'. The government should 'lay a healing hand to these mortal wounds and breaches, by holding forth the truths of Christ to the nation in some solid establishment, and not quite . . . lay aside or let loose the golden reins of discipline and government in the Church'.[80] In the same month Cromwell intitiated a series of meetings in which Presbyterian and Independent divines were encouraged to frame 'a confession of faith' or a 'fundamental confession'.[81]

These moves, although bound to offend those vocal but small groups to whom the very idea of a national Church was anathema, otherwise did not in themselves offend liberty of conscience, for the Instrument clearly protected 'such as profess faith in God by Jesus Christ' from compulsion to the 'public profession' which Cromwell evidently envisaged. In any case, the clerical meetings of February 1654 may have been concerned more to secure a basis of communion among the people of God than to restrain the unorthodox. Yet in the Interregnum such ecumenical initiatives invariably produced attempts to restrict toleration.[82] This one was certain to do so, for the clergy had noticed a second and graver ambiguity in the Instrument. What precisely was meant by the words 'such as profess faith in God by Jesus Christ'? In January 1649, when the same wording had been proposed for the Agreement of the People, Ireton had immediately asked whether anti-trinitarians were excluded by it, and had received no satisfactory answer.[83] The looseness of the phrase, which might have seemed to protect dissenters, in reality exposed them to the prospect of explanatory definition. In August 1654 Richard Baxter, remarking that if the phrase meant anything it 'must comprehend every true fundamental article of our faith', and so must have been

---

[80] *A True State of the Case of the Commonwealth* (1654) pp 40–43; for Cromwell's endorsement see Abbott, *Writings and Speeches* 3 p 587.

[81] Dr Williams's Library, Baxter MSS, Letters, V, fol 199^{r-v}; VI, fol 82^{r-v}; G. M. Paul, D. H. Fleming, and J. D. Ogilvie eds *Diary of Sir Archibald Johnston of Wariston* (Scottish History Society, 3 vols 1911–40) 2 p 246; Peter Toon, *God's Statesman. The Life and Work of John Owen* (Exeter 1971) pp 91, 95.

[82] Cf. Dr Williams's Library, Baxter MSS, Letters, VI, fol 77^v.

[83] *Clarke Papers* 2 pp 171–2.

designed to suppress 'the intolerably heterodox', urged the forthcoming Parliament to set out those articles in a 'confession of faith'.[84]

So when Parliament assembled in September 1654 and was invited
to give statutory sanction to the Instrument of Government, a revision of the clauses concerning religion was widely expected.
Cromwell did nothing to dampen the expectation. While making
clear that 'liberty of conscience' was a 'fundamental' on which he
could not compromise, he hinted at his willingness to accept re-
straints on the 'prodigious blasphemies' and 'heresies' which plagued
the nation.[85] In the speech with which he dissolved the Parliament in
January 1655, he dismayed the sects by recalling that he had wished
the House to give only 'a just liberty' to 'men who are sound in the
faith', 'of the same faith with them that you call the orthodox ministry of England'.[86] His problem in 1654–5 was to persuade Parliament
to accept the distinction between error and heresy, and to provide
protection for the former while it outlawed the latter.

It was a slim hope. The Parliament of 1654, like its successor of
1656, was chosen by a new electoral system which favoured the
backwoods. Some of its ablest members were making their first
political appearances since Pride's Purge had evicted them in 1648.
Now, planning revenge for the intervening years of sectarian excess
and military rule, they formed an effective alliance with the Presbyterian machine of the City of London. In October 1654, as Parliament prepared to take the religious clauses of the Instrument into
consideration, the London Presbyterians produced a convenient list
of the heresies in circulation, the anti-trinitarianism of John Biddle
being especially emphasised.[87]

Parliament's problem, as usual, was to weave a verbal net through
which Socinians and other heretics could not slip. At first the
Commons, instinctively reverting to the eve of Pride's Purge, revived the suggestion made by the Long Parliament to the King in

[84] Baxter, *True Christianity* preface.
[85] Abbott, *Writings and Speeches* 3 pp 436, 459.
[86] *Ibid* 3 p 586; *The Petition of divers Gathered Churches, and others well affected, in and about the City of London* (1655: Thomason Tracts, E 856 (3)) p 4.
[87] *A Second Beacon Fired. Humbly presented to the Protector and Parliament* (1654); and the newspapers for mid-October 1654, listed in G. F. Fortescue, *Catalogue of the Pamphlets . . . collected by George Thomason* (2 vols 1908) 2 p 429. The Presbyterian machine had two powerful twin engines: the Stationers Company, and the London Provincial Assembly. Two leaders of the former, Luke Fawne and Samuel Gellibrand, were active officers of the latter, whose minutes can be read in a typed and annotated transcription in Dr Williams's Library.

1648 that fourteen of the Thirty-nine Articles should constitute a 'confession of faith', but after several days' debate these were found to be too broad and imprecise. Owen and the Independent ministers immediately revived their 'fundamentals' of 1652, which were now stiffened by a committee of divines named by Parliament and headed by those veterans of the campaign against Socinianism, Owen and Francis Cheynell. Anti-trinitarianism remained the principal target of the 'fundamentals', which were also aimed against anti-nomianism, mortalism, and heretical views on the authority of Scripture and on the existence of Heaven and Hell. When, in December 1654, the House eventually rejected the amended 'fundamentals', it was evidently because they were thought unworkable, not because they were too severe. Indeed they may have been thought not severe enough, for soon the House was proposing to insert into the revised Instrument a sweeping clause against 'damnable heresies'. Some MPs were concerned that so loose a proposal 'might expose the godly party, and people hereafter, to some danger',[88] but this was not an argument to deter the majority. With the army issuing public reminders of its commitment to religious liberty, Cromwell took alarm. He insisted that the 'damnable heresies' should be enumerated, and that he should have a share in their enumeration. This was the rock on which agreement between Protector and Parliament foundered, and a principal reason for the Parliament's premature and acrimonious dissolution. The Instrument had been neither revised nor statutorily confirmed.[89]

In the Parliament's debates on the Intrument's provisions for religious liberty, there was one critical moment when the House's determination to crush sectarian radicalism seems to have faltered. This was on 12 December, when the articles prepared by the divines were debated, and when 'the enumeration of heresies' was referred to a

[88] *Diary of Thomas Burton* 1 p cxiv.
[89] The complicated story outlined in this paragraph can be pieced together from: *Diary of Thomas Burton* 1 pp lix–lx, cxii–cxix; *Journal of the House of Commons*, 7–15 December 1654, 3, 9–12 January 1655; the newspapers in Thomason Tracts, E 236; R. Vaughan ed *The Protectorate of Oliver Cromwell* (2 vols 1839) 1 pp 70, 77–8, 80, 84, 101–2; Dr Williams's Library, Baxter MSS, Letters, V, fol 169ʳ; *Reliquiae Baxterianae* 1 pp 197–205; *Humble Advice . . . by Mr Richard Baxter*; *The Principles of Faith* (E 234 (5)); and 'A New Confession of Faith', Thomason Tracts, E 826(3) (MS), where the revised 'fundamentals' may be found. [W. A.] Shaw, *A History of the English Church [during the Civil Wars and under the Commonwealth 1640–1660* (2 vols 1900)] 1 p 366; 2 pp 86–92, has the best (but not an invariably reliable) secondary account.

committee. Parliament's failing ardour was revived, our sparse diary informs us, by 'a motion, which had been made often times before, against the books of one Biddle'.[90] The protracted debates about Biddle which followed are less well known than the parliamentary controversy about James Nayler in 1656 only because the latter was recorded in the rich diary of Thomas Burton. Biddle's case was no less significant than Nayler's. His books were burned, and a bill was ordered to be brought in to punish him for his 'horrid, blasphemous and execrable opinions, denying the deity of Christ and the Holy Ghost'.[91] The discussion soon broadened into an attack on the Quakers, and a bill was prepared against them too.[92] Socinians and Quakers, despite great differences between them, were often linked or confused by contemporaries, for Quakers, seeming to deny the historical Christ, threatened the centre of puritan theology much as Socinians did.[93] 'Convince any of them', wrote Owen of the Quakers, 'of the doctrine of the Trinity, and all the rest of their imaginations vanish into smoke'.[94] Nathaniel Bacon, who had drafted the proposed anti-trinitarian ordinance of 1646, complained in 1656 that the Quaker James Nayler's offence 'destroys the second person of the Trinity'.[95]

The dissolution of Parliament in January 1655 halted its proceedings against Socinians and Quakers, and Biddle was released at the end of May 1655.[96] Only weeks later he was in trouble again. Now the City Presbyterians, who supported their moves by skilful propaganda, launched a new and potentially devastating weapon.[97] The

---

[90] *Diary of Thomas Burton* 1 p cxiv (i.e. diary of Guibon Godard, published as an introduction to Burton's diary).

[91] *Ibid* pp cxv–cxvii, cxxiii–cxxx; *Journal of the House of Commons*, 15 January 1655.

[92] *Diary of Thomas Burton* p cxxvii; cf *ibid* p 169.

[93] It was widely believed, not always accurately, that Quakers (in what became the standard phrase of their critics) did not believe in 'that Christ that died at Jerusalem'. This objection appeared in Owen's 'fundamentals', and surfaced in (for example) the Nayler debates: *Diary of Thomas Burton* I pp 48, 64.

[94] *Works of John Owen* 3 p 66.

[95] *Diary of Thomas Burton* 1 p 132. Cf. (e.g.) *Nayler's Blasphemies Discovered* (1657) p 13; Jonathan Clapham, *A Full Discovery and Confutation of . . . the Quakers* (1656) pp 16–19. For Bacon and the 1646 ordinance see Jordan, *Development of Religious Toleration* 3 p 91.

[96] There is a good account of Biddle's travails in 1654–5 in McLachlan, *Socinianism in Seventeenth-Century England* pp 202–211. Cromwell's attitude to Biddle's imprisonment by Parliament was closely watched, but is hard to gauge: see *The Protector (so called) in part Unvailed* pp 26–9, 69–72; cf *Diary of Thomas Burton* 1 p 161.

[97] For the Presbyterian initiative against Biddle, see: *Cal SPD 1655* pp 224, 393; *The Spirit of Persecution again broken loose* [. . . *against Mr John Biddle and Mr William*

Blasphemy Ordinance of 1648 had never been repealed. A narrowly Presbyterian document, it carried the death penalty for anti-trinitarianism, and enjoined harsh penalties for a range of other beliefs, some of which had found shelter under the Protectorate. It had been generally assumed that the Instrument of Government had rendered the ordinance 'null and void'; but if it could be shown that Biddle did not 'profess faith in God by Jesus Christ' (a charge which he and his supporters firmly denied),[98] then it was hard to see how he could be protected by the Instrument, whose authority was in any case under challenge in the courts at this time. A chill of fear ran through the congregations, who saw in Biddle's case 'a precedent' which 'prostrateth us all . . . to punishment, and consequently destroys the [Instrument of] Government'.[99] The precedent was promptly followed, when the Cromwellian William Kiffin was threatened with imprisonment under the 1648 ordinance 'for preaching that baptism is unlawful'.[100] Well might Biddle urge Henry Lawrence, the Baptist President of the Council of State, to use his influence against 'these bloodthirsty men, whose malice, if it prevail against me, will not stop there, but extend itself to all other dissenters whatsoever, and consequently even to your Lordship'.[101] The Baptists, always torn between the attractions of a respectable political conformism which would secure them toleration, and the claims of a political radicalism which aligned some of them with Fifth Monarchists,[102] were frequently uncertain whether to distance

Kiffin (1655)]; *A True State of the Case of Liberty of Conscience* [. . . *together with a Narrative of* . . . *Mr John Biddle's Sufferings* (1655)] For Presbyterian propaganda see *An Exhortation directed to the Elders of* . . . *Lancaster* (1655); *An Exhortation to Catechising: the Long Neglect whereof is sadly Lamented* (1655) esp pp 4–5, 8, 12; Richard Vines, *The Corruption of Mind Described* (1655) esp p 13; Nicholas Estwick, *Mr Biddle's Confession of Faith* . . . *Examined and Confuted* (1656).

[98] *Two Letters of Mr Iohn Biddle* (1655) p 2; *The Spirit of Persecution again broken loose* p 4; *A True State of the Case of Liberty of Conscience* p 6; *To the Officers and Soldiers of the Army* (E 902(4)) p 2.

[99] C. H. Firth ed *Memoirs of Edmund Ludlow* (2 vols 1894) I pp 412–15; *The Petition of Divers Gathered Churches* (E 856(3)) p 2; *To the Officers and Soldiers of the Army* p 4. This fear was widely expressed.

[100] *The Spirit of Persecution again broken loose* p 20. For Kiffin's delicately ambivalent political position at this time see: *Perfect Proceedings 31 May–7 June 1655* (6 June); *The Protector (so called) in part Unvailed* p 85; *A Short Discovery of His Highness the Lord Protector's Intentions touching the Anabaptists* (1655) p 3.

[101] *Two Letters of Mr Iohn Biddle* p 6.

[102] Their historians have likewise disagreed about which of these two attitudes was the more characteristic: compare Louise F. Brown, *The Political Activities of Baptists and Fifth Monarchy Men* (1912) with B. R. White, *The English Baptists of The Seventeenth Century* (Baptist Historical Society 1983).

themselves from, or to form a common front with, theologically more adventurous sects whose members, to the Baptists' embarrassment, had often been recruited from their congregations.[103] Biddle himself had Baptist connections.[104] Confronted by the threat to Kiffin, the Baptist churches rallied to Biddle's defence.[105] So did the Arminian John Goodwin, who in the previous year had disowned 'J. Biddle's most enormous and hideous notions about the nature of God',[106] but whose own beliefs left him on the periphery of Cromwellian liberty, 'distracted between hope and fear'.[107]

Cromwell's response to the proceedings against Biddle did nothing to allay the anxiety of the sects. He refused to see Biddle,[108] and gave representations on his behalf a cool reception. 'By faith in Jesus Christ', he said when the Instrument was cited on Biddle's behalf, 'we mean such as the generality of the Protestants have'. The Blasphemy Ordinance, he affirmed, was 'in force', and the Instrument 'was never intended to maintain and protect blasphemers' against it.[109] Yet Cromwell could not afford to permit a test case which, if the prosecution were successful, would expose a significant body of the godly people to the ordinance. Taking the only course open to him, he offended both Biddle's defenders and his prosecutors. Biddle was hastened away to a long imprisonment in the Scilly Isles.

The status of the Blasphemy Ordinance was to be debated again in the Parliament of 1656, when the Quaker James Nayler, who had led his followers into Bristol in the manner of Christ's entry into Jerusalem, was summoned before the Commons. Eventually the House decided, as had the 1654 Parliament when Biddle was brought before it, to bypass the statute book and to act on its own authority.

---

[103] Richard Baxter, *The Quaker's Catechism* (1655) preface; *The True Light hath made Manifest Darkness* (1657: Thomason Tracts, E 909(4)); Grigge, *The Quaker's Jesus* pp 37, 39; *The Confession of Faith of Several Churches of Christ in the County of Somerset* (1656); *The Protector (so called) in part Unvailed* p 72; *Mercurius Politicus* 17–24 April 1656; cf. *Heart-Bleedings for Professors Abominations* (1650).

[104] *A True State of the Case of Liberty of Conscience* (E 848(12)) p 2.

[105] *A Short Discovery of the Lord Protector's Intentions touching the Anabaptists; To the Officers and Souldiers of the Army.*

[106] Thomas Jackson, *The Life of John Goodwin* (1872) p 330.

[107] *To the Officers and Souldiers of the Army* pp 3–6. Cf. Marchamont Nedham, *The Great Accuser Cast Down: or a Public Trial of Mr John Goodwin* (1657) esp p 115; *An Exhortation to Catechising* pp 12, 15.

[108] *Two Letters of Mr Iohn Biddle* p 1.

[109] *The Petition of Divers Gathered Churches* p 4; *To the Officers and Souldiers of the Army* p 2; Abbott, *Writings and Speeches* 3 p 834.

Nayler, having been threatened with the death penalty, was subjected instead to brutal and humiliating physical punishment. As in December 1654, so in December 1656, Parliament's proceedings against the blasphemer whom it interrogated belong to a context of broader religious questions before the House. For as in September 1654, so in September 1656, men looked to a new Parliament for an authoritative ecclesiastical settlement. The Presbyterians were well prepared with their own solution,[110] and Anglicans sought to join forces with them.[111] 'I know many things will be suggested unto you,' John Owen told the Parliament at its opening, 'settling of religion, establishing a discipline in the Church, not to tolerate errors, and the like'. Owen did not protest against this prospect: he merely urged Parliament to respect the Cromwellian boundary to intolerance. 'It is only the liberty and protection of the people of God as such that we plead for', he explained.[112] Cromwell, addressing the House after Owen's sermon, which his speech carefully endorsed and frequently echoed, made it clear that he too wanted 'liberty of conscience' only for 'the peculiar interest' of the people of God.[113]

In the weeks and months which followed, a series of sermons urged Parliament to legislate against the 'fanatical persons' and the 'shoals of libertines, that are every day increasing in numbers, power and malice'.[114] As in the Parliament of 1654–5, Quakers and Socinians were the principal targets. The clamour against heresy was supported by frequent demands that MPs exercise their responsibilities as godly magistrates, and be 'judges as at the first, and counsellors as at the beginning'. Dreadful punishments would afflict them, in this world and the next, if they failed to 'exercise religious severity upon the opposers of God's Commands'.[115] These exhorta-

---

[110] Dr Williams's Library, Minutes of the London Provincial Assembly (typed transcript) p 159; cf. Clapham, *A Discovery and Confutation of the . . . Quakers* advertisements at the back.

[111] *A Collection of State Papers of John Thurloe* 5 pp 598–601; Bosher, *The Making of the Restoration Settlement* pp 45–6; cf. Grigge, *The Quaker's Jesus* p 56.

[112] *Works of John Owen* 8 pp 421–2.

[113] Abbott, *Writings and Speeches* 4 pp 260, 271.

[114] *A Third Volume of Sermons preached by . . . Thomas Manton, D. D.* (1689) pp 3–4 (for the date of this sermon, see *Public Intelligencer* 22–29 September 1656); John Rowe, *Man's Duty in Magnifying God's Work* (1656) pp 23–6; John Warren, *Man's Fury subservient to God's Glory* (1657) pp 11–12; Reynolds, *The Peace of Jerusalem* pp 28–34; Matthew Barker, *The Faithful and Wise Servant* (1657) pp 15–16, 28–9. Cf. William Gurnall, *The Magistrate's Portraiture* (1656) pp 32–3; Clapham, *Discovery and Confutation of the . . . Quakers* ep. ded.

[115] William Jenkyn, *The Policy of Princes* (1656) p 23.

tions, conveying a message which MPs will have previously heard in many assize and corporation sermons, appealed to that puritan tradition of the alliance of ministry and magistracy whose pre-war character has been brought to life by Professor Collinson.[116] Speech after speech in the Nayler debates shows the continuing strength of that tradition. The Old Testament language of the discussion, and the attention paid by MPs to theological problems, cannot be dismissed as decoration. Our only intimate glimpse of the debates about religious liberty in the Parliament of 1654–5 suggests that that assembly had spoken the same language;[117] and there are signs that the pervasiveness of that language in the Parliament of 1656 might be still more evident had the diarist Thomas Burton shared the theological enthusiasms of some of his colleagues, and had he given members' speeches in full.[118] Urgent biblical issues ran through the arguments. Was the magistrate responsible for both tables of the Commandments? Were the injunctions of Leviticus in force? Was Nayler a blasphemer in the sense for which the Bible enjoined the death penalty? If he was, then MPs had not so much a right to put him to death as an imperative duty. Blasphemy was an offence against the honour of a jealous God. Speaker after speaker urged the House to 'vindicate the honour of God', as the only means 'to divert the judgement from the nation'.[119] To keep the divine wrath at bay, the heresy must be crushed before the infection spread. 'Such a leper' as Nayler 'ought to be separated from the conversation of all people'. Even MPs who urged leniency towards Nayler agreed that his prison keeper should be 'such a person as is a Quaker already, that those that have not the plague may not be infected by him'.[120]

One indication of God's intentions especially impressed MPs. It was 'a providence' that 'such an indignity to Christ should be done, sitting a Parliament'.[121] Yet when we recall the dexterity with which the Biddle case had been slipped into the parliamentary debates of 1654, we are bound to ask whether providence, in bringing Nayler's offence before the House in 1656, was not acting through politically alert agencies. As the Court party, so embarrassed by the Nayler

[116] Patrick Collinson, *The Religion of Protestants* (Oxford 1983) pp 141–188.

[117] *Colonel James Hay's Speech to the Parliament* (1655) pp 22–3, 31.

[118] Compare Bulstrode Whitelocke's speech in *State Trials* (6 vols 1730) 2 pp 273–6, with the much shorter version in *Diary of Thomas Burton* I pp 128–31.

[119] *Ibid* pp 25, 26, 34, 48, 50–1, 55, 61, 108, 110, 122, 125, 126, 132, 140, 150, 217.

[120] *Ibid* 1 pp 35–6, 39–40, 56, 71, 74, 98, 110, 124; II 131.

[121] *Ibid* 1 pp 51, 63, 70, 101, 109; cf. Grigge, *The Quaker's Jesus* pp 13, 35.

episode, observed, 'two Justices of Peace could have ended it'.[122] The Bristol magistrates who sent Nayler to London had two friends in the House who took a keen interest in Parliament's proceedings against him from the start: the experienced Bristol MP Robert Aldworth, and Thomas Bampfield, Recorder of Exeter, a city which, like Bristol, had been gravely disturbed by the recent Quaker evangelism in the West, indeed by Nayler himself. Bampfield chaired the committee which examined Nayler, and in the House virtually led the prosecution against him. The moves against Nayler were clearly a prelude to a broader attack on the Quakers, against whom petitions and pamphlets were produced with notable efficiency and shrewd timing.[123]

The legal position of Quakers, and particularly of the Quaker practice of intervening in church services, had long been unclear. The Bristol magistrates told Parliament they were 'destitute of a law to bound and restrain' Quakers, whom they had therefore been 'not able to suppress': 'we have waited long for some directions to this purpose'.[124] Bristol, 'the headquarters of this generation of Quakers',[125] had been in turmoil since 1654, and its difficulties had been widely publicised. The Quaker presence there had set the garrison against the city government, and the city government against itself.[126] The magistrates' hopes had been briefly raised by the government declaration of February 1655 which prohibited Quakers and Ranters from disturbing services, but which proved on inspection to be worded with paralysing ambiguity.[127]

In 1654 Cromwell had surprised the Bristol magistrates by supporting them against the Quakers' military patrons.[128] What would

---

[122] *Diary of Thomas Burton* I p 146.

[123] *Mercurius Politicus* 31 October, 20–27 November, 11–24 December 1656; *Public Intelligencer* 5 November, 2, 8–22 December 1656; *Journal of the House of Commons* 31 October 1656; Grigge, *The Quaker's Jesus* pp 11, 13; Farmer, *Sathan Inthroned*; *Diary of Thomas Burton* 1 pp 168–9, 171; Fortescue, *Catalogue of . . . Thomason* 2 pp 168–70.

[124] Grigge, *The Quaker's Jesus* p 34. Cf. *A True Narrative of the Examination . . . of James Nayler* (1657) p 56.

[125] Grigge, *The Quaker's Jesus* p 13.

[126] [Henry M.] Reece, ['The] Military Presence [in England' (Unpub D. Phil. thesis Oxford 1981)] pp 172–6.

[127] Farmer, *Sathan Inthroned* pp 54–5; *Several Proceedings of State Affairs* 8–22 February 1655. Cf. Braithwaite, *Beginnings of Quakerism* pp 181, 203, 445–6; Alan MacFarlane ed *The Diary of Ralph Josselin 1616–1683* (1976) p 348 (cf. p 389); Immanuel Bourne, *A Defence of the Scriptures* (1656) ep. ded.

[128] Farmer, *The Great Mysteries of Godliness and Ungodliness* ep. ded.; Reece, 'Military Presence' p 175.

he do now? Could he afford, any more than in 1654–5, to resolve the ambiguity of government policy? As in the Biddle case, the sects looked anxiously to him for protection; and as in the Biddle case, they looked in vain. On 25 December, when sentence on Nayler had already been passed and the first of his punishments carried out, Cromwell received representations on Nayler's behalf which argued, what some MPs had already suggested, that Parliament's proceedings against Nayler had breached the Instrument of Government. But Cromwell was firm. Philip Skippon, a trusted adviser of Cromwell and a Councillor of State, had already heard Cromwell state that the Instrument 'was never intended to bolster up blasphemies of this nature'.[129] Nayler, Cromwell now told petitioners on his behalf, 'asserts from the letter of the Scriptures such things as are contrary to the common principles written in every man's heart'.[130] Cromwell did, on the same day, write a mild letter to the Speaker to enquire into the constitutional and legal basis of Parliament's proceedings against Nayler, but his question, which Parliament correctly believed that it could safely leave unanswered,[131] was accompanied by an assurance that 'we detest and abhor the giving or occasioning the least countenance to persons of such opinions and practices', a view Cromwell later repeated to the army leaders.[132] His concern, as in the Biddle affair, was solely to ensure that the episode would provide no precedent for action against the people of God. As he told the army officers, 'the case of James Nayler might happen to be your own case'.[133] Later in the Parliament Cromwell gave his assent to two bills, one against vagrancy and the other for the better observation of the Lord's Day, which between them provided effective new powers against Quaker disturbances.[134] Only when the House tried to combine its sabbatarian legislation with a measure for a compulsory Presbyterian catechism, the antidote to false doctrine for which the clergy were eagerly pressing, did Cromwell demur.[135]

[129] *Diary of Thomas Burton* I pp 50, 63.
[130] *To the Officers and Souldiers of the Army* (E 902(4)) p 3.
[131] *Diary of Thomas Burton* I pp 246–70.
[132] Abbott *Writings and Speeches*, 4 pp 366, 419.
[133] *Ibid* p 417.
[134] Firth and Rait, *Acts and Ordinances* 2 pp 1098–9, 1162–70. Cf. *Diary of Thomas Burton* I pp 20–4; *Journal of the House of Commons* 31 October 1656; *Mercurius Politicus* 31 October 1656.
[135] Shaw, *History of the English Church* 1 pp 375–6; *Diary of Thomas Burton* I p 376; Reynolds, *The Peace of Jerusalem* p 33; Marshall and Firmin, *The Power of the Civil Magistrate* p 38. A similar move had been made in 1654 (*Humble Advice . . . by Mr Richard Baxter* pp 2–3, 8–10; cf. Baxter's *Catholick Unity* (1660) p 19). For the

So there is nothing surprising about Cromwell's grateful acceptance of the religious provisions of the Humble Petition and Advice, the parliamentary constitution of 1657 which is normally regarded as markedly less tolerant than the Instrument of Government which it replaced. There was to be a confession of faith, which was to be recommended to the nation but not imposed on it, and which it was to be an offence to revile. The confession was to be compiled not, as the previous Parliament had wished, by Cromwell's parliamentary opponents, but in collaboration between Cromwell and the more conciliatory House of 1657—although in the event it was never drawn up. In place of the Instrument's term 'profess faith in God by Jesus Christ', there was a long clause, progressively expanded in debate[136] and designed to define and forbid heresy, particularly antitrinitarianism. Peaceable dissenters who were not excluded by this clause were to have liberty, although to the categories excepted by the Instrument there were now added 'such who publish horrible blasphemies'.[137]

The Humble Petition and Advice, which gave statutory protection to the people of God, and which at the same time would have trapped both Biddle and Nayler, delighted Cromwell. The new constitution, he told the House, gave 'all due and just liberty' to 'the people of God': 'you have done that which never was done before'. Indeed, it was 'the greatest provision that was ever made': there had not been 'anything since Christ's time for such a Catholic interest for the people of God'.[138]

Cromwell, then, neither wanted toleration nor provided it, whether we use the term in its pejorative seventeenth-century sense or in its approving modern sense. Yet the story is not quite as simple as that. Although Cromwell's policy can fairly (if loosely) be called Calvinist, his Court was not an impregnable fortress of Calvinism. It contained men who wanted a wider liberty of belief than Cromwell allowed. There were courtiers who, while they could not condone

background to the initiative of 1657 see e.g. Vines, *Obedience to Magistrates,* third sermon pp 14–15; *An Exhortation to Catechising*; Minutes of the London Provincial Assembly pp 146, 148; Simon Ford, *A Short Catechism* (1657); *Perjury the Proof of Forgery* (1657) preface; *The Confession of Faith, together with the larger and lesser Catechisms* (1658): 'An Ecclesiastical Experiment in Cambridgeshire', *English Historical Review* 10 (1895) pp 744–53; F. J. Powicke, *A Life of the Reverend Richard Baxter 1615–1691* (1924) pp 128–32.

[136] *Journal of the House of Commons* 19 March 1657.
[137] Gardiner, *Constitutional Documents* pp 454–5.
[138] Abbott, *Writings and Speeches* 4 pp 445, 454.

James Nayler's offence, nevertheless sought to comprehend it, and with calm courage pleaded for eloquence before the House. The stance of these 'merciful men', as Burton called them, was not sectarian. None of them had been a regicide. Their influence points us to a distinctive feature of Cromwell's civilian patronage: his use for *politiques*, for men who had found it hard—or who had been too young—to choose between King and Parliament, and who would willingly serve either a Cromwell or a Stuart.[139]

Three such men lived into the Restoration to write extensively about the religious problems of their time; and we shall conclude by asking what can be learned from their writings. The first of them was Bulstrode Whitelocke, one of the most eloquent of the 'merciful men' in the Nayler debates, who in the Puritan Revolution doggedly resisted the intolerant claims of the Presbyterian clergy. He defended the Socinian MP John Fry, and regarded the eviction of Anglican ministers on doctrinal grounds as a breach of liberty of conscience.[140] After 1660 he wrote a series of manuscript treatises intended to fortify the dissenters under persecution or to persuade the government to tolerate them. They included a characteristically enormous work 'Of the Rise of Persecution', which drew heavily on Foxe to recount the history of intolerance from Cain to the Stuarts.[141]

The second figure is Whitelocke's fellow lawyer Matthew Hale.[142] Cromwell had raised him from obscurity to chair the 1652 commission on law reform which bears his name, and on which Cromwell also invited Anthony Ashley Cooper, another *politique* advocate of religious freedom, to make his political debut. The writings of Hale and Whitelocke, which have much in common (in the vapidity and the smugness of much of their prose, alas, too much in common), give an instructive impression of the lay puritanism of the 1650s and beyond: of the generation which withdrew from millenarianism, which preferred family exercises to churchgoing, and

---

[139] For the *politique* 'merciful men' in the Nayler debate, see Worden, *Rump Parliament* pp 129–31.

[140] *Ibid* p 131; Ruth Spalding, *The Improbable Puritan. A Life of Bulstrode Whitelocke 1605–1675* (1975) esp pp 96–7, 102, 243, 279; Jordan, *Development of Religious Toleration* 3 pp 68–9.

[141] It is at Longleat (Whitelocke letters, XXVII), where I have read it by kind permission of the Marquess of Bath.

[142] Hale's posthumous works can be conveniently found in T. Thirlwall ed *The Works, Moral and Religious, of Sir Matthew Hale* (2 vols 1805). Jordan has a section on him: *Development of Religious Toleration* 4 pp 61–9.

which sought, through meditation and the cultivation of a good conscience, to preserve an inward integrity amidst the havoc and the bitterness of civil war. Both men are Christian Stoics, mistrustful of externals and extremes, vigilantly taming the appetites.[143]

Our third figure is Dryden's friend Sir Charles Wolseley.[144] A much younger man than Whitelocke or Hale, his relationship with Cromwell had been much smoother, and probably much closer, than theirs. The son-in-law of Lord Saye and Sele, he came from nowhere in 1653, apparently at the age of twenty-three, to help guide the Cromwellian moderate party in Barebone's Parliament. In the Protectorate he was a consistently active member of the Council of State. Left in the cold after the Restoration, he wrote a series of books on religion in the 1660s and 1670s, among them *Liberty of Conscience . . . Asserted and Vindicated*. Whereas Hale and Whitelocke bequeathed manuscripts from the 1650s which express attitudes consistent with those of their later writings, we are left to guess at Wolseley's religious position in the 1650s, but his concern for liberty of conscience after 1660 is unlikely to have been novel.[145]

Wolseley was Whitelocke's closest ally at Cromwell's Court, despite the difference in age between them.[146] Both were men of massive—if not always well-digested—learning. Both knew Hebrew and Greek well enough to apply them to biblical scholarship. Wolseley had a forbidding command of the by-ways of classical and patristic literature: Whitelocke, like Hale, belonged to the most learned of mid-seventeenth-century circles, that of John Selden. After 1660, the careers of Whitelocke and of Wolseley can time and again be found in conjunction or in parallel. The two men collaborated with each other and with other dissenters in the literary campaign for liberty of conscience.[147] Wolseley wrote his books for

[143] Worden, *Rump Parliament* pp 131–2 (for Whitelocke); *Works . . . of Sir Matthew Hale* 1 *passim* (esp. Burnet's life of Hale); 2 e.g. pp 12, 25, 138, 159–60, 179, 211, 233, 246, 259, 286–7, 293, 415.

[144] Dryden: Philip Harth, *Contexts of Dryden's Thought* (Chicago 1968) pp 108–46, 199–200, 294–7.

[145] Cf. Woolrych, *Commonwealth to Protectorate* pp 202–3.

[146] BL, Add MS 31984 (Whitelocke's History of his Forty-eighth Year) fols 165ᵛ–166ʳ, 175ᵛ–176ʳ; Add MS 32093 fol 317ʳ.

[147] Compare (e.g.) BL, Add MS 21009 (Whitelocke, 'The King's Right to Grant Indulgence in Matters of Religion') fols 29ʳ–33ᵛ, with Wolseley's *Liberty of Conscience upon its true and proper Grounds Asserted and Vindicated* (1668) pp 52–3, 57–9; and compare both documents with e.g. *Works of John Owen* 13 p 368; Slingsby Bethel, *The Present Interest of England* (1671) pp 13–17; *Select Works of William Penn* 2 p 295.

the Whig magnate the Earl of Anglesey,[148] who published
Whitelocke's posthumous memoirs: in 1688 one of Whitelocke's
treatises on toleration was published as a contribution, supposedly
written by Anglesey, to the dissenters' campaign on behalf of James
II.[149] Wolseley committed himself to James II in the same year.[150]
Perhaps to Wolseley, who had publicly defended *de facto* politics in
the 1650s,[151] it seemed as sensible to seek liberty of conscience under
James as it had done under Cromwell. Wolseley may have been lured
into support for James by William Penn, with whom he had cooperated during the Exclusion crisis.[152] Whitelocke, too, had swum
into Penn's net. Penn supervised the publication of much of
Whitelocke's posthumous work, including his lay sermons on the
text 'Quench not the Spirit'.[153] They show how close Whitelocke
had come to the Quakers in his later years.[154]

In all three men, Whitelocke, Hale and Wolseley, we find a genuine
tolerance of mind, if by that we mean a willingness to understand
and permit beliefs based on premises very different from their own.
They were the kind of people whom Jordan liked. And in all three
men we find, in a form suitable to their troubled generation, the old
Erasmian spirit of religion: practical, rational, sceptical, tolerant. It is
the spirit that had distinguished the Arminian advocates of religious
liberty at Great Tew.[155] Whitelocke, the youthful friend of Edward
Hyde and, like Hale, the adult friend of moderate bishops, rested
much of his case for freedom of conscience on the arguments of
Jeremy Taylor,[156] just as Wolseley appealed to the authority of
Grotius and of Chillingworth.[157]

Whitelocke, for all his learning, was not much interested in doc-

---

[148] See the dedications of Wolseley's *The Unreasonableness of Atheism* (1669) and *The Reasonableness of Scripture-Belief* (1672); and *The Unreasonableness of Atheism* p 194.

[149] *The King's Right of Indulgence in Spiritual Matters* (1688) is an adaptation of BL, Add MS 21009.

[150] G. F. Duckett, *Penal Laws and Test Act* (2 vols 1882–3) 2 p 251.

[151] *Diary of Thomas Burton* 2 p 40.

[152] R. W. Blencowe ed, *Diary of . . . Henry Sidney* (2 vols 1834) pp 114–6.

[153] Whitelocke, *Quench not the Spirit* (1711; 2 edn 1715); Whitelocke, *Memorials of the English Affairs, from the suppos'd Expedition of Brute . . . to . . . King James the First* (1709) preface.

[154] This point is made by Spalding, *Improbable Puritan* p 248.

[155] See H. R. Trevor-Roper, *Edward Hyde Earl of Clarendon* (1975), and his *Religion, The Reformation and Social Change* pp 203, 216, 219, 299.

[156] BL, Add MS 21009, fols 46^r–56^r, 168^v–169^r, 190^v.

[157] Wolseley, *Justification Evangelical* (1677) p 8; *Liberty of Conscience . . . Asserted and Vindicated* pp 29, 39, 67–8; *The Reasonableness of Scripture-Belief* pp 47, 300–1.

trinal controversy. To him theology was a guide to behaviour. Wolseley and Hale agreed. Wolseley thought that 'practical sanctity is the great end of religion . . . When men confine religion to speculation, they turn divinity into metaphysics, where they dispute without end: to reduce it to practice, is to pursue its proper tendency, and to make it (as indeed it is) the great principle of union and peace'.[158] Hale, having said the same thing in very similar words, concluded that 'as the *credenda* are but few and plain, so the *facienda*, or things to be done, are such as do truly ennoble and advance the humane nature'.[159] The advancement and ennoblement of 'the humane nature' had not seemed a legitimate or attainable goal to John Owen.

All three men explored the history of the Church to try to understand the decline of Christianity into dogmatic warfare. All of them found there, in Wolseley's words, 'carnal interests and political concerns . . . twisted into the government of the Church . . . to enable the clergy, under a pretext of the power of the Gospel, to trample . . . mankind under their feet'.[160] Only blinkered human pride, Hale argued, could explain the enforcement of beliefs about free will and the Trinity, subjects which had been 'as it were industriously kept secret by Almighty God, because they are not of use to mankind to be known'.[161] Hale and Wolseley—both men with a greater capacity and a greater inclination than Whitelocke possessed to reduce a problem to first principles—investigated the claims of conscience from the starting-point not of faith but of 'ratiocination'.[162] To try to force the conscience, said Wolseley, was 'a spiritual rape'.[163] And since the understanding could not choose what to believe, imposition was also pointless.

In Wolseley's scheme of religion, Calvinist predestination is not so much refuted as forgotten. To attain salvation, he wrote, we need only 'live a sober, righteous, religious life here, such as is rationally best for ourselves, and others, and be gradually preparing for those eternal fruitions that are to come'.[164] These, as Owen's former mentor at Oxford Thomas Barlow sadly noted, were 'opinions very

---

[158] Wolseley's preface to Henry Newcombe, *A Faithful Narrative of the Life and Death of that Holy and Laborious Preacher Mr John Machin* (1671).
[159] Hale, *Of the Nature of True Religion* (1684) pp 5–6, 8, 16.
[160] *Liberty of Conscience . . . Asserted and Vindicated* pp 17–18, 20.
[161] Hale, *Of the Nature of True Religion* pp 5–6, 13, 28; cf. Wolseley, *Liberty of Conscience . . . Asserted and Vindicated* p 25.
[162] *Ibid* p 38; Hale, *Of The Nature of True Religion* pp 5–6.
[163] Wolseley, *Liberty of Conscience . . . Asserted and Vindicated* p 27.
[164] *Justification Evangelical* pp 88–9.

different from the old faith which I and, I think, the generality of our divines have held'.[165] In place of puritan theology Wolseley provided a 'rational justification' of the Christian religion, expounded in a book he called *The Reasonableness of Scripture-Belief*. The title seems to point forward to those classic works of the 1690s, John Locke's *The Reasonableness of Christianity* and John Toland's *Christianity not Mysterious*. And from the argument that Christianity is reasonable and not mysterious, it may not be a long step to the view that there are still more reasonable and still less mysterious positions than Christianity to adopt.

From an evolutionary perspective, that is no doubt where Wolseley stands. We can hardly miss the dramatic irony of his offer to abandon his claims for 'the reasonableness of Scripture-belief' if anyone could 'palpably disprove any one matter of fact in the history of the Bible'.[166] The evolutionary perspective is valuable and instructive, and without it we may become mere antiquarians, forgetful of those broad human questions about toleration which a historian's audience might fairly ask, and which a Gardiner and a Jordan strove to answer. Can we retain that perspective without succumbing to the opposite danger, of misrepresenting the past by selecting from it those features in which we see our own reflections? The writings of Whitelocke, Hale and Wolseley indicate the size of the challenge. These men like the Arminians and the Erasmians before them—and, indeed like Locke (and perhaps Toland) after them—conducted their arguments for religious liberty within Christianity, not in search of emancipation from it. Hale and Wolseley both stated that the Socinians, although they had much to commend them, took their faith in the naked intellect, and their mistrust of revelation, too far.[167] Our three writers aimed not to weaken Protestantism but to reconstruct it on a different base: a base of reason, practice and Gospel precept. They are concerned, as the Calvinists were, with the salvation of souls and with the union of believers with Christ and with each other: a salvation and a union which, they believed, theological controversy and clerical intolerance destroyed.

For to these men—as to Owen—the most alarming feature of the

---

[165] See Barlow's notes in his copy of *Justification Evangelical* in the Bodleian Library (classmark 8°C Linc. 345).

[166] *The Reasonableness of Scripture-Belief* p 195.

[167] Wolseley, *Liberty of Conscience . . . Asserted and Vindicated* ep. ded (and see *ibid*, p 304); Hale, *Of the Nature of True Religion* p 25. Cf. R[obert] F[erguson], *A Sober Inquiry into . . . Moral Virtue* (1673) ep ded to Wolseley.

age was the ubiquitous and pernicious advance of atheism and libertinism. Atheism made converts, they believed, because doctrinal rancour, clerical strife, and confessional dogmatism had discredited religion. 'Love, and charity, and even common humanity, and mutual conversation between man and man, church and church, party and party,' wrote Hale, 'is broken by the mutual collisions and animosities concerning them . . . And by this means the true life of Christian religion'—what Hale also called 'the true radical vital doctrine and religion of Christ'—'is lost or neglected by them that profess it, or disparaged among those that . . . have not entertained it . . . These men, when they see so much religion placed by professors of Christianity in these things, which every intelligent man values but as forms, or inventions, or modes, or artifices, . . . are presently apt to censure and throw off all religion, and reckon all of the same make'. Hence there 'ariseth a most fruitful and most inevitable increase of atheism and contempt of relgion.'[168] Hale began to compose 'a great design against atheism';[169] Wolseley wrote a book called *The Unreasonableness of Atheism*; Whitelocke registered his dismay at 'atheism, a wickedness increasing in these days'.[170] It is a mistake automatically to equate rationalism with religious indifference; and, as writers on religious freedom have always claimed (among them the seventeenth-century pamphleteer Henry Stubbe, who planned to write a 'history of toleration' to prove the point),[171] it may be another mistake to attribute the emergence of arguments for toleration to religious indifference. In the works of our three former Cromwellians, the development of religious toleration looks to be not evidence of a decline of religious conviction, but rather a part of the process by which the Protestant God changes his character. He becomes a friendly monitor rather than an awesome dictator, a God in whom mercy is more conspicuous than justice; and Protestantism, the religion of faith, becomes a religion of works. Once more the subject of toleration, which at first seems to beckon the past towards modernity, ends by pointing modern enquiry back towards theology.

St Edmund Hall, Oxford

[168] *Of the Nature of True Religion* pp 16, 37, 39.
[169] *Works . . . of Matthew Hale* 1 pp 36–7.
[170] Whitelocke, *Quench not the Spirit* (1715 edn) pp 52–3.
[171] Stubbe, *Essay in Defence of the Good Old Cause* 'Premonition'; Stubbe, *Further Iustification* pp 70–1. Cf. Jordan's view, *Development of Religious Toleration* I pp 15–16; 2 pp 485–6.

THE ENFORCEMENT OF THE
CONVENTICLE ACTS 1664-1679

by ANTHONY FLETCHER

THE DENOMINATIONAL writers on late Stuart dissent used to put their emphasis upon the heroism and sufferings of forbears in the faith and on cherished works of spiritual autobiography produced under restraint such as John Bunyan's *Grace Abounding* and William Penn's *No Cross, No Crown*.[1] The most important, and to my mind the most interesting, questions about persecution in this period have therefore gone unasked and unanswered. Aware of the most dramatic cases of malice and brutality, we have too readily accepted that the decades between the Restoration and the Toleration Act can be represented as the period of the 'Great Persecution'. But how far did the acts which are conventionally summarised as the Clarendon Code represent the settled mind of the Anglican gentry, whose supremacy was confirmed by the political events of 1660 and 1670? How far were these acts actually enforced? How easy were they to enforce? These are large questions, much too large for a short communication. What I shall attempt here is an analysis of the enforcement of two statutes, the Conventicle Acts of 1664 and 1670, in a limited number of counties over a confined period. By 1679 popery, the alternative bogey to dissent, was at the front of magisterial minds and the 1670 act was for the moment largely in abeyance. Greater glory for the Second Conventicle Act was yet to come, with the Tory reaction of 1682 to 1686, but that period is beyond the scope of this paper.

The story of how Anglicanism won the hearts of the English upper classes, retained their hearts through the troublesome decades from 1640 to 1660 and triumphed at the Restoration is now being fully told.[2] In the 1660s episcopacy and the prayer book became the touchstones of social conservatism, the most convenient means of identifying those who accepted the traditional order in government

---

[1] For a useful summary see [M. R.] Watts, *The Dissenters* [(Oxford 1978)] pp 227–43.

[2] J. S. Morrill, 'The Church in England 1642–9' in his *Reactions to the English Civil War* (London 1982) pp 89–114; I. M. Green, *The Re-establishment of the Church of England 1660–1663* (Oxford 1978). See also A. J. Fletcher, *The Outbreak of the English Civil War* (London 1981) pp 284–90.

and society. In the cavalier sense of priorities Church even came before King: the political tension of the reign was largely created by Charles II's determination, until the 1680s, to pursue monarchical independence at the cost of alliance with his 'old friends'.[3] The Act of 1664 'to prevent and suppress seditious conventicles' can be quite simply accounted for. Anglican insecurity remained intense: the nexus of republicanism and dissent, it was believed, still threatened the foundations of Church and State. The Act was intended, in view of neglect of the Elizabethan statute for weekly attendance at church, to check the 'dangerous practices of seditious sectaries and other disloyal persons who under pretence of tender consciences do at their meetings contrive insurrections'. Its provisions were fierce: fines of up to £100 with the alternative of transportation for a third offence, the requirement for deputy lieutenants to assist in the dispersal of dissenters' meetings, liberty for justices to break into houses on information that a conventicle was being held. But all these measures were seen as temporary expedients, since the statute was to lapse three years after the end of the current session. It did so on 1 March 1669.[4] This then was discretionary legislation par excellence, an instrument to be used briefly and as necessary against a potent but stealthy foe.

The second Conventicle Act has all the marks of a statute designed to remedy the defects of its predecessor. A single justice, instead of two justices as previously, was empowered to convict on confession, oaths of two witnesses or 'notorious evidence and circumstances of fact'. Much heavier penalties were instituted for preachers and owners of houses where conventicles were held. All fines imposed, except for a first offence by attendance, were to be levied by distress on the offender's goods and chattels, or if necessary on the goods of another member of the congregation. The provision of heavy fines on village officers and JPs who failed in their duty points to the sponsors' awareness of the difficulties that had been encountered in enforcing the first act.[5]

The bill, presented by Sir John Bramston, had a mixed reception and a rough passage. The second reading was achieved on 2 March 1670 only after long debate. The gentry's mood had shifted a good

[3] R. A. Beddard, 'The Restoration Church' in J. R. Jones, ed *The Restored Monarchy* (London 1979) pp 155–75.

[4] *Statutes of the Realm* VI pp 516–20.

[5] A. Browning, *English Historical Documents 1660–1714* (London 1953) pp 384–6.

deal since 1664. There was much more confidence about the endurance of the new regime and a corresponding uncertainty about the properness of persecuting men who accepted the social order but wished to worship quietly in their own manner. Many MPs clearly saw the need to make distinctions. Sir Robert Howard probably found assent when, while deprecating a 'general toleration' as a 'spot in any government', he declared 'he would have a party of people taken in and banish all the rest'. There were scruples about the penalties on officeholders and the powers allowed a single justice. But the main issue was one of trust. Two of the principal antagonists on 2 March were the Lancashire members Colonel Birch and Sir Roger Bradshaigh. 'A man that had no preaching near him will take it where he can', insisted Birch, drawing upon his experience of the vast Pennine parishes; 'the trading part of England is as the soul to the body. To whip them and not to be able to tell them why you do so is unreasonable'.[6] 'He excused the meetings of such conscientious people', Bradshaigh related in a letter to the Lancashire clerk of the peace the following day, 'and particularly instanced the several chapels in Manchester parish and further added that there could not be one instance produced that any such meetings had produced any insurrection or that any treason, schism or other continuance or disturbance to the government had been there hatched'. Bradshaigh countered him with all the stories of plotting he could summon, urging 'the necessity for a bill of restraint and what ways to meet with their subtle evasions'. He was sufficiently unsure of success though to press the clerk of the peace for 'more instances' to induce the passing of the bill.[7] The third reading was in fact less touch and go than he feared: the persecuting violence of the most intolerant Anglican gentry was by no means yet spent and the bill passed on 9 March by a majority of 138 to 78.[8]

How far then were these two statutes enforced? I shall confine myself in my analysis of the mechanism of persecution to eight counties spread widely across the nation: Westmorland and Lancashire in the north, Nottinghamshire and Warwickshire in the Midlands, Suffolk in the east, and Middlesex, Sussex and Wiltshire in the south. There are no quarter sessions order books or files for Westmorland before

[6] [A.] Grey, *Debates [of the House of Commons 1667–1694* (London 1763)] I pp 220–3; D. R. Whitcombe, *Charles II and the Cavalier House of Commons 1663–1674* (Manchester 1966) pp 100–1.

[7] *HMC Kenyon MSS* pp 84.

[8] Grey, *Debates* I pp 227–8.

1675 but the correspondence of Sir Daniel Fleming, that most tireless and meticulous of northern justices, affords some insight into how the acts were received there. For a man like Fleming, alert to every rumour of the fanatics' activities, the whole of the 1660s was a decade of alarms. A letter to Secretary Williamson on 21 August 1668 finds him worrying about the way others were dropping their guard: 'I observe it is now become a general policy to comply with the non-conformists; I am sure it much increases their number and I fear that it will much increase their confidence'. The following May, retailing news he had heard of the Yorkshire Presbyterians' plans to gain representation in parliament should there be an election, he stated his convictions about those who still attached themselves to 'their good old cause'. 'They will first endeavour civilly to undo us', he told Williamson, 'and if that fail then probably they will follow some martial method'. Fleming's distinctly ideological view of Restoration politics led him to become the chief proponent of the Clarendon Code in the north-east. Ironically, however, first his mention of the 1664 Conventicle Act comes in a letter to Williamson on 9 February 1670, about a year after the statute had lapsed. He had just detected 'a great conventicle' of two hundred people, which met at night at the Kendal home of 'one very active in the late rebellion'. His intention, despite the refusal of some of his fellow justices to support him, was to bind over as many as possible of the offenders to the next quarter sessions. 'They shall be all indicted,' he informed the Secretary of State challengingly, 'if we receive not in the interim orders to the contrary'. 'I know very well the boldness and numerousness of these people in this country and their great dissatisfaction to the present government both in church and state', he continued, 'therefore—so long as I am in authority—I intend to watch their actings and to help to punish them when they offend and herein I hope to receive encouragement from above'. In other words, Fleming was ready to proceed on the basis of a defunct statute, flouting the law of the land, until the government in London took action to prevent him. Moreover he was prepared to boast about his audacity. We do not know how many convictions under the Conventicle Act he had secured between 1664 and 1669, but it is evident that he secured a good many retrospective ones at Easter 1670, only a few weeks before the new Act came into force.[9]

Fleming was predictably delighted with the new Act. He was con-

[9] *HMC Le Fleming MSS* pp 58, 63, 68–9.

fident, almost complacent, when he wrote to Williamson in August 1670. Many Quakers had been convicted since the statute came into force on 10 May and the Independents had retreated from public meetings to private gatherings within the limit set of only five adults present. The powers given justices to levy by distress satisfied Fleming's ardour: 'it is as clear as the day that nothing will convince them of their errors so soon as the drawing of money from them; for a great part of their religion—notwithstanding their great zeal and fair pretences—is tied to their purse strings.' Though his claim that 'we doubt not in a short time to rout them' seems optimistic and though he subsequently abandoned his idea of bringing nonconformists to church by levying the statutory shilling fine for each Sunday's absence, the effectiveness of Fleming's policy was born out by subsequent events. Northern dissent had already lost whatever political sting it still possessed in the mid 1660s. The nonconformists were on the defensive. 'Our conventicles are at present pretty quiet', reported Fleming in November 1671, 'since we are now and then fining of them as well to let them know that we are awake and observe their actings as to remember them that the act against conventicles is still in force against them.' When the statute was suspended the following year, he wrote sourly to his friend Sir George Fletcher that he found no one pleased with the King's action and that it was regarded in his district as being 'as great a prerogative act as hath been done this good while'. Yet it was popish recusants rather than dissenters that increasingly preoccupied the activist northern justices as the 1670s wore on. He had no plans to 'further meddle' with 'our other sects of recusants' at the next sessions, Fleming told Sir John Lowther in April 1674, than 'to give the laws against them in charge'. Constables were evidently still being reminded of their duty to present conventicles in 1674 and 1675, but so far as the Westmorland bench was concerned the second Conventicle Act, swiftly enforced at the first, was a useful statute that had, for the present at least, fulfilled its function.[10]

Whereas in Cumberland and Westmorland there were at least a few other justices who were as fiercely Anglican as Sir Daniel Fleming, a much less activist mood prevailed in Lancashire. There Sir Roger Bradshaigh was something of a lone campaigner. His letter to Secretary Williamson on 21 July 1665 is full of his enthusiasm for the first Act. He had just secured a series of convictions,

[10] *HMC, Le Fleming MSS* pp 71, 86, 90, 109–10, 118.

including that of a 'stubborn Anabaptist' who had been sent to the goal for two months on his refusal to pay a ten shillings fine. He hoped to catch the same men again, believing that the transportation provision could be used 'to quit the place of them and many more'.[11] Bradshaigh, as we have seen, was a principal figure in the passing of the second Act but the lack of support he enjoyed among his colleagues is indicated by his failure to press home an attack on Gorton Chapel while he was in London in 1670. He sent up an order from the Privy Council, glossing it to convey authority for rigorous action while the new bill was still under debate. This was intended for the sheriff's table, the meeting of JPs at assizes, but it either never reached there as he instructed it should do, or it was considered and laid aside without any decision that required preservation in the clerk's order book.[12] Actually the sheriff's table at this time rarely discussed religion. The Lancashire gentry, Brian Quintrell has noted, 'pursued a fairly even handed course which reflected the moderate attitude of the lord lieutenant, Charles, eighth earl of Derby'. Bradshaigh however, having seen the new Act through, was not to be dismayed by their inertia. The rumour in the north by 1674 was that he was boasting of having levied £700 in fines through his own efforts. A full investigation of the sessions records would be needed to check that assertion, but what was done was almost certainly done by Bradshaigh virtually alone. It was not until 1683, in the very different political atmosphere of the Tory reaction, that the Lancashire bench suddenly declared a general policy of enforcing the current legislation against dissenters.[13]

We can be rather more specific about the work of Robert Thoroton, the hammer of the Nottinghamshire dissenters, than is possible, in the present state of research, about Bradshaigh's efforts in Lancashire. H. Copnall's researches into the county's quarter sessions records revealed no prosecutions under the first Act but a crop of them, all attributable to Thoroton, between 1675 and his death in 1678. Thoroton was a busy country doctor, resident at Car Colston in the Vale of Trent and on good terms with a wide circle of gentry and professional men. His papers show how these acquaintances shared his antiquarian interests and admired the industry

[11] *CSPD 1664–5* pp 484–5.
[12] *HMC Kenyon MSS* pp 84–5.
[13] B. Quintrell, ed *Proceedings of the Lancashire Justices of the Peace at the Sheriff's Table during Assizes Week 1578–1694* (Record Society of Lancashire and Cheshire CXXI 1981) pp 32–3, 145, 147; *HMC Le Fleming MSS* p 109.

which made him one of the first men to publish an account of the antiquities of his county which is still held in repute today. They had no time though for his persecuting zeal. Thoroton himself brought in convictions to sessions from all over Nottinghamshire, from Blyth and Gringley in the north, Sutton-in-Ashfield in the west and Girton near the Lincolnshire border. No one followed his lead except his friend and neighbour Peniston Whalley of Screveton, who worked with him. Thoroton was particularly severe on Quakers. It was alleged against him that he encouraged informers to roam the county on his behalf and that he urged constables to be harsh in their distraints on the goods of offenders.[14] For all this, Thoroton's impact on Nottinghamshire nonconformity was probably minimal. Routing dissent was no task for a single individual in his spare time. Some twenty of the congregations which took out licences during the period when the Declaration of Indulgence was in force were left untouched by Thorotons's campaign a few years later.[15]

The leading figure on the Warwickshire bench during the 1660s and 70s was the militant Anglican squire of Warwick Priory Sir Henry Puckering. He had settled in the county in 1654, having fought for Charles I as a young man at Edgehill. He was a conscientious administrator who drew some unpopularity upon himself for his alleged lenience to recusants and leanings towards popery. He made sporadic attempts to use the first Conventicle Act to check Warwickshire dissent but appears to have failed to persuade others to act in their own districts.[16] His account of proceedings at Warwick on the occasion of a visit by the lord lieutenant in 1666 hints at the divisions among the JPs about their policy towards dissent. 'Those who submitted on promise of good behaviour found favour', he told Secretary Williamson, 'those who were peremptory had the strictest extent of justice and refusing to pay their fines were sent to prison'.[17]

With the passing of the second Act, Puckering managed to rouse keen support from his colleague Sir John Knightley. They found some of those they convicted more than a match for them. Having

[14] H. Copnall, *Nottinghamshire County Records* (Nottingham 1915) p 141; J. Simmons, ed *English County Historians* (Wakefield 1978) pp 22–32.
[15] [F.] Bate, *The Declaration of Indulgence* [1672 (Liverpool 1908)] appendix, pp xliv, lxxv–lxxvi.
[16] S. C. Ratcliff and H. C. Johnson, eds, *Warwick County Records* (Warwick 1939) V p xxiv; *DNB*.
[17] *CSPD 1666–7* p 168.

defeated an appeal at the Epiphany sessions in 1671 by securing a loyal jury, Knightley discovered that those upon whom the bench relied for enforcement of the Act were being harried by the dissenters: 'Such is the insolence of that party and so resolved they are to fright all persons from being informers of their seditious meetings, that the court was hardly up before they arrested the informer with five several actions, the expense of which must necessarily undo a poor man—a rich one, indeed, is not able to wrestle with their untied purse'. In the same letter to Samuel Sandys, Knightley pointed out a deficiency of the Act which, to his fury, was enabling one of his victims to escape punishment. Those who drafted the statute had thought about nonconformists who might flee across county boundaries to escape distraint, but they had not considered the case of a man who removed all his goods into the next shire but remained at home himself. 'We cannot touch the man' he sighed.[18] The licences taken out under the Declaration of Indulgence and the Compton Census both declare the strength of Presbyterians, Baptists, Congregationalists and Quakers in Warwickshire by the 1670s. There were at least sixty active meetings spread around the county.[19] Judith Hurwich has suggested that there were at least 2,000 dissenting households by the early 1680s.[20] Puckering and Knightley had achieved little or nothing.

The Conventicle Acts had the potential to create division and faction on the county benches. The Suffolk squire Edmund Bohun still believed as late as 1678 that the dissenters' 'ultimate object was the destruction of the monarchy and the bringing in a republic'. Predictably he ran into trouble with more temperate colleagues. His description of an appeal against one of his convictions at the Beccles sessions in October 1673 indicates that the tide of resentment which was to sweep him off the bench four years later was already running at that time. He was fearful that, with several convicted conventiclers on the grand jury and doubts about the enforcement of the Act among fellow justices, he would lose the case. Yet on this occasion 'the whole bench fell on so handsomely that it exceeded my wishes'. The justices were swayed, it seems, by Sir Edward Turner's charge at the most recent Suffolk assizes, which had emphasised that, following the cancellation of the Declaration of Indulgence, the 1670

[18] *CSPD 1671* pp 20–1.
[19] Bate, *Declaration of Indulgence* pp lii, lxxxi.
[20] J. J. Hurwich, 'Dissent and Catholicism in English Society: A Study of Warwickshire 1660–1720' *Journal of British Studies* XVI (1976–7) pp 30–1.

Act was in full force. When the dissenters refused to take an oath that there had been no teaching at their private meeting the verdict went against them, a result that gave him 'great contentment', wrote Bohun, after he 'had first raised up the informers and then assisted them with much labour and expense'.[21] In 1675 Bohun was still recording convictions for holding conventicles in the Beccles district.[22] His dismissal two years later was engineered by Sir John Playters, who alleged he was 'wont to create disturbances among his associates'. But he took every opportunity in the following months to try and resuscitate his campaign. In September 1677, dining with the bishop of Norwich, he urged him to use his influence to pack the bench with militant Anglican friends: 'in order that these very worthy men may resist the schemes of the upstarts who, under the pretext of prudence and moderation in ecclesiastical affairs, are ruining both church and states and are lamentably endeavouring to tear them in pieces, while by certain quibbles they altogether evade and permit others to evade the execution of the laws'. The following May he was to be found discussing politics with fellow Suffolk gentry at a meeting at Halesworth about the poll tax. His own talk, he recorded in his diary, concentrated upon 'the late treasons, the puritans and their present attempts'. Edmund Bohun's record of his personal efforts to enforce the persecution of Suffolk dissenters suggests that the legacy of puritanism in that most puritan of counties was a strong sense of live and let live.[23]

An assiduous group of Middlesex justices produced what may well have been the highest total of convictions over a period of eighteen months in any single county immediately following the passing of the 1664 Conventicle Act. They set to work in Stepney on 17 July 1664, hardly more than a fortnight after the Act came into force. In all they recorded 909 convictions before the end of 1665 relating to 782 different individuals. This highly organised campaign in the London suburbs from Hendon round to Shoreditch and Stepney involved the justices in special sittings on Sundays near the places where the dissenters met. Those they convicted were taken at once through the streets to prison and kept there until their fines were paid by them or for them.[24]

---

[21] Bate, *Declaration of Indulgence* p 134.
[22] East Suffolk RO, B 105/2/7.
[23] S. Wilton Rix, ed *The Diary and Autobiography of Edmund Bohun* (Beccles 1853) pp 16–17, 37, 42, 46.
[24] J. C. Jeaffreson, ed *Middlesex County Records* (Clerkenwell 1888) III pp 340–9.

A vigorous campaign to enfore the second Conventicle Act was mounted in Wiltshire by John Eyre and Sir Edward Hungerford. Such was the connivance and inertia of constables, though, that they found it a dispiriting task. 'I wish I could give some probability of a conformity', wrote Eyre to the bishop of Salisbury in September 1670, 'but I am convinced, with many others, that there must be something more than these country officers to suppress them and their meetings'. Village officers in Wiltshire would, it seems, rather perjure themselves than present conventiclers at petty sessions and become reputed as informers. When the justices did achieve convictions, their attempts to take distresses were often stymied by communal displeasure at national policy. 'Things were offered for sale in the markets and fairs', reported Eyre, 'yet not one penny has been bid, but by way of a sneer, as sixpence or thirteen pence halfpenny for a cow and such like'. The determined refusal of Wiltshire countrymen to change their religious ways in the face of Anglican intolerance is well illustrated by an exchange between the constable and one John Hand of Culhorne. As the constable was going away with his mare, Hand's daughter remarked scoffingly that it was a wise parliament that made such a law, to which her father replied 'it was their time now but it would not hold long'.[25] But Eyre and Hungerford were not easily cast down. During 1671, with the help of some others, they succeeded in recording several hundred convictions.[26]

Sussex was another southern county where the passing of the 1670 Conventicle Act led to a burst of magisterial activity. Whereas the quarter sessions order books for 1664 to 1670 contain not a single reference to enforcement of the first Act, those for 1670 to 1679 reveal two periods of serious attention to the problem of dissent. The first ran from June 1670—three weeks after the Act came into force—to the following spring, the second, which was less intensive, from September 1673 until 1676. Here, as in Wiltshire, prosecution did not rest on the labours of a couple of individuals. At least eight justices were involved, including leading men like Sir John Pelham and Sir John Covert, , and the conventicles picked upon were widely spread across the shire.[27] Yet the Sussex campaigns clearly had little impact in a county where nonconformity, based on a well-rooted puritan

---

[25] *CSPD 1670* pp 147–8.
[26] *HMC Various Collections* I p 151; B. H. Cunnington, ed *Wiltshire Quarter Session Records* (Devizes 1932) pp 247–8.
[27] East Sussex RO, QO/EW6, fols 15ᵛ, 16ʳ, 36ᵛ–38ʳ, 43ʳ, 126ᵛ QO/EW7, fols 74ᵛ, 85ᵛ.

tradition, was strong.[28] Briefly at least they must, however, have raised the political temperature. For this was a county community in which, like in some others, the cavalier revenge of 1662 still grated in a good many manor houses. Anglicanism had come to symbolise the rule of a younger generation of gentry with new priorities.[29]

These case studies point to a tentative conclusion that needs to be tested by further research. In the countryside as opposed to the towns, the Conventicle Acts, it would seem, were not systematically enforced in the 1660s or 1670s. The story is rather one of localised battles between particular groups of dissenting congregations and either individual JPs or a few strongly motivated justices. In many cases the authorities, having taken the plunge, failed to sustain their efforts to check dissent through the period from 1664 to 1669 or from 1670 to 1679. We would like to know much more about the thinking of those who were made responsible for enforcing these contentious pieces of legislation. How far did the widespread reluctance to enforce the acts spring from an awareness of popular dislike of central interference with private worship and the potential for popular resistance to statutes that depended on informers for obtaining convictions?[30] How far did a growing sympathy with the intellectual arguments for toleration which were beginning to appear in print at this time induce inertia?[31] How far did inactivity reflect a sense that the King was at odds with his parliament, desired comprehension and disapproved of persecution?[32] These are the kind of questions which need to be answered if we are to understand the minds of provincial gentry in the 1660s and 70s. They are important questions not simply for the history of religious persecution in Charles II's reign. For current research is making it increasingly evident that the politics of the whole period from 1660 to 1690 hinged, both at Westminster and in the shires, upon the struggle between a radical movement and the alliance of Anglican gentry and the bishops intent on their own hegemony. Philip Jenkins has suggested that 'there were two distinct factions among the elite of county society' in Glamorgan and that they 'were chiefly divided by attitudes of dissent'.[33] The preservation of its political monopoly by preventing religious toleration,

---

[28] Bate, *Declaration of Indulgence*, appendix pp li, lii, lxxx–lxxxi.
[29] A. J. Fletcher, *A County Community in Peace and War* (London 1975) pp 123–4.
[30] See e.g. *CSPD 1676–7* p 210; Watts, *The Dissenters* p 246.
[31] G. R. Cragg, *From Puritanism to the Age of Reason* (London 1950) pp 190–224.
[32] See e.g. *CSPD 1672–3* p 613, *CSPD 1673* pp 120, 369.
[33] P. Jenkins, *The Making of A Ruling Class* (Cambridge 1983) p 124.

Mark Goldie has argued, was the Anglican establishment's 'pivotal' concern.[34] The Second Conventicle Act, described by Marvell as 'the quintessence of arbitary malice', was probably the most vicious of all the new penal laws. It presented justices with the dilemma faced by every ruling class possessed of the power to coerce men over their religion: whether to impose the tyranny of opinion. Their responses to that dilemma surely tell us something about the most crucial unresolved problem of later Stuart politics, the making of Whigs and Tories.

University of Sheffield

---

[34] M. Goldie, 'John Locke and Anglican Royalism', *Political Studies* XXXI (1983) pp 75–85.

SIR PETER PETT, SCEPTICAL TORYISM AND THE SCIENCE OF TOLERATION IN THE 1680s

by MARK GOLDIE

IN THE charged atmosphere of religious xenophobia in England in the 1680s it was an unusual person who could survey the state of Christendom and the zealotry of his fellow countrymen with a detached eye. Such a one was Sir Peter Pett, 'a virtuoso, and a great scholar, and Fellow of the Royal Society'.[1] His vast and inchoate book, *The Happy Future State of England*, is eirenic, Erastian and Hobbesian in outlook. It is also an exercise in the fledgling science of 'political arithmetic'. With the panoply of scientific reasoning it predicted the imminence of a secular age in which the knot of politics and religion would be untied. This paper will first sketch the background to this book, then examine its account of the state of Catholicism and dissent, and lastly appraise its claim that 'a science of politics'[2] could provide a solvent of religious persecution.

I

England's last severe religious persecution spanned the years 1678 to 1686. It began with the Popish Plot frenzy and ended when James II suspended prosecutions against the religious minorities. In its first phase Catholics were the victims. Only the year of the Armada exceeded 1679 in the numbers of Catholic martyrs. But when the Whigs exploited the Plot to try to exclude James from the succession the tide turned and the protestant dissenters suffered in the Tory revenge. In the first half of the 1680s one hundred Quakers died in jail,

---

[1] J. Dunton, *Life and Errors* (London 1818) I, p 178; see pp xvii–xviii, 194.

[2] [*The*] H[appy] F[uture] S[tate of England] (London 1688) p 185. Signature numbers will refer to the unpaginated preface written in 1685, page numbers to the main text written in 1681. I have used one of the two Cambridge University Library copies (shelf mark R.2.27): the book is extant in a variety of bibliographic states. Two scholars have previously discussed aspects of Pett's work and I am indebted to them. [J. R.] Jacob, 'Restoration, Reformation [and the origins of the Royal Society]', *History of Science* 13 (1975); Jacob, 'Restoration ideologies [and the Royal Society]', *History of Science* 18 (1980); [A.] Whiteman, 'The census that never was: [a problem in authorship and dating]' in *Statesmen, Scholars and Merchants*, eds A. Whiteman, J. S. Bromley, and P. G. M. Dickson (Oxford 1973) pp 1–13.

troops were used to break up meeting-houses, and prosecutions reached unprecedented levels. The raucous propaganda of the Tory press was, wrote Richard Baxter, designed to show all dissenters to be 'a crazed company of fanatics' and to prepare them 'for destruction'.[3] By the time of James's accession 'an exemplary pitch of conformity' was everywhere reported.[4] The position of Catholics meanwhile only marginally improved. Tory magistrates and divines prided themselves on a *via media* in judicial terror against the agents of both Rome and Geneva. As Captain Alford put it, there 'hath been of late two horrid plots; the one by the Papists, and the other by the Presbyterians'.[5] The prevailing conviction was that only by the most disciplined loyalty in Church and State could England weather the coming storm of the popish prince, avoiding the Scylla of the fires of Smithfield and the Charybdis of sectarian anarchism.

The administration which presided over this reaction was dominated by a group of Tory high churchmen who felt they had the Catholic heir where they wanted him: sufficiently frightened by whiggery never to dare more than to practice his religion privately. This clique included James's brothers-in-law, the Hydes, earls of Clarendon and Rochester, together with the archbishop of Canterbury William Sancroft, and those impeccable symbols of Anglican rectitude, the duke of Ormonde and Sir Leoline Jenkins.

One or two voices of restraint did, however, retain a foothold. The most famous of these was the marquess of Halifax. The Whigs hated him for opposing Exclusion, but he was not a natural Tory either, for he was too sceptical and anticlerical, and given to quasi-republican schemes. He advocated projects for liberalising the Church, and a statute of Limitations of the Crown's prerogatives as an alternative to Exclusion. When he was in the ascendant in 1681–82 the Tory reaction was held in check. He deplored what followed. His fortunes briefly waxed again at the turn of 1684–85, at which juncture he circulated in manuscript his celebrated tract *The Character of a Trimmer*, for which he has earned immortality as the philosopher of Tory pragmatism. He defended Crown and Church, but also appealed for tolerance and an end to the travesties of judicial due process. The trimmer sought 'a mean between the sauciness of some of

[3] *Reliquiae Baxterianae* (London 1696) pp 196–7.
[4] Denis Granville to Archbishop Sancroft: Bodl[eian Library], MS Rawlinson, d. 103, fos 2–6.
[5] *Mercurius Tibicus* 24 March 1680. I owe this reference to Tim Harris.

the Scotch Apostles and the indecent courtship of some silken divines'. He deprecated the 'mistaken devotion' by which 'a devouring fire of anger and persecution breaketh out in the world'.[6]

A less renowned trimmer was the earl of Anglesey, Lord Privy Seal from 1673 until brought down in a quarrel with Ormonde in 1682. He had been a Parliamentarian in the Civil War and after 1660 was regarded as a Presbyterian peer, although outwardly conforming. He trimmed with each government and for twenty years was able regularly to ameliorate the plight of victims of the penal laws, both Catholic and dissenter. His friendship with papists and simultaneous distaste for popery has been taken to be emblematic of the Englishman's 'schizophrenic' attitude to Catholicism.[7] A contemporary critic accused him of being a friend 'to the Romanists, to the Lutherans, to the Calvinists, to the Arians, Anabaptists, Antitrinitarians, &c'.[8] In March 1686 James interviewed him and it was reported that, but for his untimely death, he would have become Lord Chancellor or Lord Lieutenant of Ireland. James told him he wanted him because 'I would not be priest-ridden'.[9] Anglesey wrote a trimmer's apology, in memoranda of 1682 and 1686, the latter of which was intended to be appended to Pett's *Happy Future State*. He argued for acceptance of the popish prince's reign and the desirability of a united protestant church, yet he sought a tolerant and moderate alternative both to Sancroftian Anglicanism and the imprudence of James's Jesuit advisers.[10]

These trimmers needed a more substantial treatise which, whilst defending the utmost loyalism, put the case for latitude and tolerance. It would express their vision of how the English state should come to terms with religious plurality and a Catholic king—in short,

---

[6] Halifax, *Complete Works* ed J. P. Kenyon (Harmondsworth 1969) pp 70–4; (the 'Scotch Apostles' are the presbyterians and by implication the dissenters generally). See H. C. Foxcroft, *The Life and Letters of Sir George Savile, Bart, First Marquis of Halifax* (London 1898); J. P. Kenyon, *Robert Spencer, Earl of Sunderland* (London 1958) ch 3.

[7] B. Coward, *The Stuart Age* (London 1980) p 272, out of [J.] Miller, *Popery and Politics [in England, 1660–1688]* (Cambridge 1973) p 16.

[8] *Great News from Poland* (London 1683) p 1.

[9] [Earl of] Anglesey, *Memoirs*, ed P. Pett (London 1693) sigs A2r, A8r; [A.] Wood, *Athenae Oxoniensis*, ed P. Bliss (London 1817) IV p 185; *Ellis Correspondence*, ed G. Ellis (London 1829) I pp 95–6.

[10] *The Earl of Anglesey's State of the Government and Kingdom* (London 1694); Anglesey, *Memoirs*. See D. G. Greene, 'Arthur Annesley, First Earl of Anglesey, 1614–86' (unpub PhD thesis, Chicago 1972).

a treatise of sceptical Toryism.[11] Sir Peter Pett was their man for the job. He was a natural courtier, a gentleman civil servant, a scientific adviser. His career moved in three orbits: the navy, the Royal Society, and the government of Ireland. He was a lawyer from a family of shipbuilders and naval administrators. As a Fellow of All Souls, Oxford, in the 1650s he had met Robert Boyle, with whom he struck up a life-long friendship, and through whom he came to know the luminaries of the early Royal Society. He met two people with whom his career would intertwine: Arthur Annesley, the future earl of Anglesey, and the statistician Sir William Petty. The Boyles and Annesleys were well established in Irish affairs. With alacrity they switched from Henry Cromwell's to Ormonde's viceregal entourage. In the 1660s Pett, their protégé, was appointed Advocate General of Ireland, sat in the Irish Parliament, benefitted from Ormonde's shower of knighthoods, and lined his pockets from the tax farm and from confiscated Dutch property.

In the 1670s Pett was in London, practising at Gray's Inn, acting as Anglesey's man of business, and politicking on the fringes of the earl of Danby's administration, which crashed in 1679 in the Exclusionist storm. When Halifax engineered Danby's release from the Tower in 1684, Pett was amongst the welcoming party, along with Sir Thomas Meres and Danby's son Lord Latimer. They all belonged to 'the loyal society or club in Fullers Rents', a group of anti-Exclusionist supporters of the fallen earl. In James's reign Pett came closest to the centre of things. With Petty and Pepys he discussed naval finance and ship design; together they plied the king with schemes for commerce, revenue, defence and Ireland. Pett acquired some influence. In 1685 his friend Bishop Barlow was threatened with suspension by Sancroft, because he never went to his cathedral at Lincoln and so was nicknamed 'the bishop of Buckden'. In a letter bewailing his plight, Barlow looked to the intercession—the 'prudence and diligence in managing this affair'—of Halifax and Pett. In 1688, in conjunction with the Catholic Lord Powys, Pett won a battle against Clarendon, a long-standing and now fallen enemy, concerning a patent for control of the Thames waterfront. In May a loyal address of the seamen and naval manufacturers was orches-

[11] The phrase draws a parallel with Duncan Forbes's notion of the sceptical Whiggism of David Hume and Adam Smith, who were Whig in politics but not given to the conventional shibboleths of Whig ideology. See, e.g. his 'Sceptical whiggism, commerce and liberty' in *Essays on Adam Smith*, eds A. J. Skinner and T. Wilson (London 1975).

trated: Powys presented it and Pett discoursed on the king's—Pepys's—improvements to the navy. Pett, like Pepys, was now badly tarred with the brush of popery.[12]

Meanwhile, he prepared his *Happy Future State*. For Halifax's and Anglesey's practical purposes Pett was, it must be said, useless. Controversialists, like journalists, must submit their copy on time. Pett began his book in 1681 but did not publish it until the turn of 1688. Because of its long gestation, the book's history is complicated.[13] He started in January 1681 after the dissolution of the second Exclusion Parliament and it took the form of a letter to Anglesey vindicating both him and 'that great man' Halifax from the charge of popery brought against them by the Whig leader in the Commons, Sir William Jones. A subsidiary section, called *The Obligation Relating to the King's Heirs and Successors*, is dedicated to Halifax, who is shown to be the nation's saviour from the Whigs. Pett quoted the lines of Dryden's *Absolom and Achitophel* which would clinch for later generations Halifax's place in the pantheon of Parliamentary orators.[14] Pett scorned the profligacy of the Whigs in not accepting Halifax's proposals for Limitations. In 1681 Pett's book was privately circulated but not published. Soon the influence of Anglesey and Halifax faded. At the turn of 1685, when the *Trimmer* was circulated, Pett brought his book up to date with a long preface full of confidence for a regime of humane protestancy under a tolerant Catholic king. Anglesey's trimmer essay was composed shortly after. But again events overtook them. Halifax was dismissed in October 1685 and

---

[12] For these and other biographical details see: DNB; Wood, *Athenae Oxoniensis*, IV pp 576–80; Pett's Memoir of Robert Boyle: B[ritish] L[ibrary] Add MS 4229, fols 33–48; Pett's letters: BL, Add MSS 17017, fol 96; 28015, fol 312; 28053, fols 390–1; Bodl MS Ballard 11, fols 28– 30, 211–12; and in *The Rawdon Papers* ed E. Berwick (London 1819) pp 136–66. See also: [T.] Barlow, [*The Genuine*] *Remains*, ed P. Pett (London 1693); *Calendar of State Papers: Ireland: 1663–5* and *1666–9*; *The Petty-Southwell Correspondence*, ed Marquis of Lansdowne (London 1928) *passim*; C. Leslie, *An Answer to a Book Entitled The History of the Protestants in Ireland* (London 1692) Appx pp 31–6; [C.] Webster, *The Great Instauration* (London 1975) p 167 and *passim*; D. Allen, 'The political clubs of Restoration London', *Historical Journal* 19 (1976) pp 574–8; and n 34 below.

[13] The following summary of the bibliographical history of the *HFS* has been pieced together from various copies, and from: Anglesey, *Memoirs*; BL Add MS 28053, fols 390–1; Bodl MS Ballard 11, fols 211–12.

[14] 'Jotham of ready wit and pregnant thought, / Indew'd by nature, and by learning taught / To move Assemblies, who but onely try'd / The worse awhile, then chose the better side; / Nor chose alone, but turn'd the balance too; / So much the weight of one brave man can doe.': Dryden, *Absolom and Achitophel* (London 1681) pp 27–8; *HFS* p 215; 2nd pag[ination] p 57.

Anglesey died in April 1686. James changed course and in April 1687 published his Declaration of Indulgence. Halifax and Boyle, and most Anglicans, drew the line.

Pett, however, moved with the times and supported the Indulgence with a new tract called *The Obligation Resulting from the Oath of Supremacy to Assist and Defend the . . . Dispensative Power*. This he dedicated to two Catholic peers, the moderate Powys and the immoderate Melfort. At last, at the close of 1687, he set about publishing *The Happy Future State*, only to meet with the disapproval of the chief minister, Sunderland, for the book offended the extremer papists. Sunderland permitted publication on condition that Pett's Indulgence tract was republished with it. For good measure Pett added a grovelling dedication to Sunderland, applauding the 'glories' of James's reign. So Pett's book, strewn with several incongruous dedications, went on sale as James's reign moved towards its crisis. Appearing at that time and with that title it was a spectacular piece of bad timing. The book was a flop, 'lying dead on the bookseller's hands'. After the Revolution he tried to make another go of it. He dropped the preface, the Indulgence tract and the offending dedications, and gave it a new title, *A Discourse of the Growth of England*, designed to emphasise its scientific and utilitarian value.[15] He turned his hopes to Danby, to whom he sent a copy in February 1689, a few days after the earl's appointment as Lord President in William III's government. But to no avail. He remained in the wilderness, in mutual commiseration with Pepys. Pett's treatise, in its successive guises, is a sad palimpsest of the politics of the 1680s. It was a large book—a third of a million words—for a brief moment, and that moment came and went in 1685, the confident dawn of James's reign.

II

In *The Happy Future State* Pett's first preoccupation was to account for the antipopish frenzy and for the way it rebounded on the Whigs. He began to write during 'the turbid interval of the kingdom, the interval of panic fears, . . . when the air of man's fancies was generally

---

[15] The new title was 'A discourse of the growth of England in populousness and trade since the Reformation. Of the clerical revenue . . . Of the number of people of England . . . and political observations thereupon. Of the necessity of future public taxes . . . Of the advancement of the linen manufacture . . .'.

infected', a period he dubbed the 'Martyrocracy', an 'empire of the Witnesses', when innocent Catholics died at the hands of half-crazed informers. Protestants were 'valuing themselves as the best of men upon their believing what was sworn by the worst', and demagogue politicians were 'purchasing . . . adoration from the people on such easy terms', for 'a zeal against popery is a remedy so cheap and so easy to be had'. Pamphlets like Marvell's *Account of the Growth of Popery* whipped up hysteria and each election 'produced patriots more zealous for . . . the extermination of popery'. Pett found the 'purgatory' of the Plot years nauseating. It 'made the English nation appear somewhat ridiculous abroad'. It had threatened to destroy his friends Pepys, Powys and Anglesey. England was a 'bedlam': he had heard a teacher 'who seeing his scholar reading a learned book of geometry writ by a Jesuit, did with great gravity advise him to read only protestant mathematics'. *The Happy Future State* was written to exorcise such nonsense.[16]

Pett detected that in some ways attitudes to Catholicism were improving in the Restoration. Earlier generations held that Catholic worship was intolerable because it was idolatrous. Transubstantiation was of course still ridiculed, but Grotius and the Anglican theologians Hammond, Thorndike and Taylor had exonerated Catholicism from idolatry. Pett was confident that 'the Grotian divines' had convinced thinking protestants that Catholicism was not guilty of the worst of spiritual obscenities. It was crucial to realise that, for all the heat and dust concerning 'host worship', the crisis really concerned popish sedition not theological superstition. The ground of fear was not metaphysical absurdity but the politics of papal supremacy. Even so, the political objections themselves seemed overwhelming. Most people were still convinced that the papacy would authorise any atrocity to quell heretics. The papacy claimed the right to depose heretical princes and to authorise Catholics to take the deposition personally in hand. To assert that a prince's fall from grace was sufficient to disqualify him from temporal rule was the dangerous doctrine that 'dominion is founded in grace'. Worse still, it could be shown that Catholics believed themselves released from the ordinary rules of morality in endeavouring to extirpate heretics, since 'faith need not be kept with heretics'. The massacres of St Bartholomew and of the Irish protestants were the standing examples. Since the canonists could be found to legitimise

---

[16] *HFS* ep ded; sigs A1v–A2v; pp 1, 19, 150, 153, 199, 229, 285.

the burning of heretic cities, many had no doubt of the papists' responsibility for the Fire of London. Accordingly, in 1678 almost everybody readily believed that the papists had a plot to kill the king, instal his Catholic brother and destroy protestantism.[17]

But the extraordinary paradox of the Exclusion crisis was that the Whigs quickly came themselves to be thought guilty of an equal and opposite 'popery'. Once the Whigs began recklessly to implicate James in the Plot and denounce opponents of Exclusion as popish fifth columnists, the suspicion grew that the Plot was fabricated by 'fanatic' protestants for their own revolutionary purposes. The Whigs aimed 'by outcries against the Church of Rome to bring in a Roman Republic'. As a result 'the deluge of the popular fears [against Catholics] did sensibly decrease after the year 1681.'[18] It was fundamental to Tory belief that Whiggery—'Presbyterianism' as it was significantly still called—was the protestant mirror-image of popery. The radical Calvinists asserted that princes could be deposed for ungodliness. On this ground they had executed Charles I and now endeavoured to exclude James. This was a protestant manifestation of the doctrine that 'dominion is founded in grace', and if the Whigs threatened political assassination then they too destroyed morality in the name of religion. The Presbyterians were as destructive as the Catholics because they used a religious principle to destabilise civil states. If the murder of Sir Edmund Berry Godfrey in 1678, the magistrate who first investigated the Plot, was the work of Catholics, so the murder of Archbishop Sharpe of St Andrews in 1679 was the work of fanatical Calvinists. Two crimes symbolised the revolutionary terrorism of Rome and Geneva. Halifax in his *Trimmer*, Sir Leoline Jenkins in his renowned Commons speech against Exclusion, Pett, and all the Tories, insisted that the Exclusion project was itself papistical because it invoked the principle that 'dominion is founded in grace', that is, it dangerously sought to rest civil rule on a religious principle. To depose a prince, even a Catholic one, for 'irreligion' was to court a bloodbath. The Whigs followed the pope, who is 'an Excluder-General of kings'. Thus the Tory attack upon Whiggery and dissent was a natural outcome of the Popish Plot fever: the 'popery' of revolutionary protestantism had to be stamped out as well as that of the Catholics.[19]

[17] *Ibid* sigs C2r, Flr, Q2v; p 173.
[18] *Ibid* ep ded; sig C1r; p 285.
[19] *Ibid* sigs A1v–A2r; pp 133–9, 326, 331, 357, 361; 2nd pag p 16; Halifax, *Complete Works* p 74. See also Barlow, *Remains* p 380.

Pett made explicit a concept of popery implicit in the Tory attribution of popery to the Whigs. The essence of popery was the specious use of a theological principle to undermine temporal sovereignty. Popery might be said to manifest itself in both Catholicism and protestantism, although it was not essential or faithful to either. Historically it had been manifested in both, but it was an empirical question as to whether it still did. Pett's advice to Catholics and dissenters was that they should convince the world of their renunciation of popery. He was himself convinced by recent Catholic denials of the papal deposing power—most Catholics 'have no Plot but to get to heaven'. The concept of 'popery' could therefore be detached from Catholicism. Catholicism was a creed, a set of theological opinions, a politically indifferent phenomenon. There was a vital distinction to be drawn between the 'religionary points' and the 'irreligionary' or pseudo-religionary, the latter being 'the anti-monarchical principles of the Jesuits and presbyterians'. There was no ground for punishing people merely for confessional or private opinions in theology, but every ground for suppressing sedition masquerading as religion. Early in the 1680s Pett felt that on balance the penal laws must stand for the time being. In 1687 he applauded the Indulgence with the claim that doubts had now been sufficiently assuaged. Certainly he squirmed on the hook when confronted by Sunderland and the Indulgence, but he always maintained an Erastian view that toleration was a pragmatic and circumstantial question. Wherever 'any papist [is] not only willing to change the name papist for catholic, but the thing papistry, for the principles of the Church of Rome under its first good bishops' then toleration of Catholicism should prevail, for they, agreed Anglesey, 'have a right and title to the free and undisturbed worshipping of God.' Any religion is entitled to toleration if it accepts the first principle of public peace: that nobody is warranted by religion to invade the right of sovereign princes.[20]

The apogee of papal temporal claims, all protestants agreed, was the decree of the Fourth Lateran Council of 1215 which laid down the duty of princes to exterminate heretics and their answerability to Rome in this duty. It was much cited by Exclusionist tracts. There was no question, Pett conceded, that for several centuries the papacy sought to effect a 'Universal Monarchy' in Christendom. But he in-

---

[20] *HFS* sigs A2r–v, B1r–v, C2r, K1v–K2v; pp 9–11, 16–17, 19–20, 131, 168–72, 283, 317; 2nd pag p 46.

sisted that protestants had failed to grasp that three epochal events
were changing the face of modern Catholicism and were beginning
the demise of Lateran popery. The first of these was the Treaty of
Westphalia, which had concluded the Thirty Years War in 1648. The
English, he said, were still mesmerized by the 'antique' preachings of
earlier generations and 'seem to have been asleep since the Munster
Treaty'. The treaty had dissolved the bigotry and warfare not only of
protestant and Catholic but also of Lutheran and Calvinist. Article
Seven had entrenched a principle of tolerance in the constitution of
Europe. 'On this rock of the Munster Treaty was the holy concord of
holy churchman, discordant in opinions, founded'. And if this 'perpetual pacification' was not wholly fulfilled, yet 'all Christendom
was embarked in that treaty and going with full sail, and favoured
with a strong gale of nature into its haven of rest'. The pope's condemnation of the treaty had been brushed aside, the princes agreeing
that no church decrees could stand against it. The pope's power
dimmed, 'the constellation of the great Roman Catholic kings shin-
ing in the Munster Treaty'. Pett did not believe that 'any Roman
Catholic prince now living in the world should favour the usurpation of the papal power'. Catholics are now 'under no obligation
by the Lateran Council to be either persecutors or disloyal'. The
modern principle of temporal sovereignty had superseded the papal
usurpation. Since civil supremacy was taking hold in Catholic states,
the Catholic church could be said to have begun its own Reformation. The account of Westphalian Christendom was necessary 'because the factum of that peace hath not by any writer since our late
fermentation (that I know of) been insisted on for the illumination of
people's understanding in the firm provision made there for mens
being secure in their religion by law established, whatever the religion of their lawful princes may be'. In 1680, he noted, a church of
'Holy Concord and Union' was dedicated at Fredericsburg in a joint
ceremony by Lutheran, Calvinist and Catholic divines, whilst in
England, Plot fever raged.[21]

The second event Pett dilated upon was the papacy of Innocent XI,
then reigning. His remarks are startling in the warmth of their
approval for Innocent. St Peter's chair had rarely been 'filled with a
person of so great morality and virtue as the present pope is'. In his
determination to reform abuses he had been called by 'many Roman
Catholics . . . the Lutheran pope' and by others 'the Jansenist pope'.

[21] *Ibid* ep ded; sigs Flr– Hlr; pp 275, 292, 325, 363; Anglesey, *Memoirs* pp 274–97.

A decree of 1678 had suppressed 'a multitude of Indulgences' and one clause 'did shake the whole body of Indulgences'. He had tamed the worst excesses of Mariolatry. The Bull *Sanctissimus Dominus* of 1679 was his greatest 'piece of Reformation' for it struck at the heart of the Jesuits. It was the Jesuits who, in their search for means to extirpate heresy, corrupted the laws of morality by their laxist doctrines of probabilism, and by their casuistical allowance of murder, lying and calumny. Probabilism was the doctrine that in a case of moral doubt a person may without sin follow any course of action which had some probability of being morally correct. It was the foundation of the legend that the Jesuits allowed the end to justify the means. The 'Christian heroical acts of this pope' had begun to clear 'the Augean Stable of the casuists'. The 'tendency of the Jesuits' principles to the very legitimating' of massacres, and the casuistical divinity which the English believed to have brought about the murder of Sir Edmund Berry Godfrey now stood damned by the pope himself. It was a pity, Pett concluded, that Innocent had not suppressed the Jesuits altogether, but their demise was now inevitable, particularly as one of Europe's most celebrated books, Pascal's *Provincial Letters*, had inflicted wounds from which 'they can never recover'. The English would be cured of their fears if they understood of what 'great moment to Christendom' this pontificate was.[22]

The third feature of European Catholicism which blind protestant zealots failed to understand was the tradition of eirenicism within Catholicism. Throughout his book Pett cited with approval those Catholic scholars whom earlier protestant ecumenists, like Grotius, Isaac Casaubon, John Selden and Robert Cotton, had befriended: Paulo Sarpi, the champion of Venice in its quarrel with the papacy and author of the antipapal *History of the Council of Trent*; Traiano Boccalini, Sarpi's friend, whose *Ragguagli di Parnaso* (Venice 1612–13) praised tolerance, confounded Trent and the Hapsburgs, and looked to France for Europe's 'general reformation', a tract which appeared in England in 1656; and De Thou and Peiresc, the Frenchmen who in the 1610s and 1620s were a principal focus in the republic of letters. Erasmus and More he cited too, noting the tolerance of *Utopia*. Seventeenth-century France he thought was es-

---

[22] HFS ep ded; sigs Blv–B2r, Ilr–I2r, O2v, Slv; pp 15, 42–53. The *Provincial Letters* were published in English translation in 1658 under the title *The Mystery of Jesuitism*. Innocent XI was beatified in 1956; the process of canonization was earlier halted in the 1740s because of French pressure and suspicions of Jansenism. The Jesuits were (temporarily) suppressed in 1773.

pecially important as a guide to the future. Although Pett shared
Halifax's and Danby's desire to contain French power, he also shared
the virtuosi's admiration for French intellectual progress. The
philosophers, the Jansenists and the Gallicans between them were
dissolving superstition and popery. Louis XIV's battle with the pope
for jurisdictional supremacy over the Gallican Church was at its
height, and in 1682 the Gallican clergy repudiated papal supremacy.

> The Roman Catholic church there doth so much swarm with
> New Philosophers there called Cartesians and Gassendists,
> whose new philosophy has been there by zealous catholics ob-
> served to have ruined the mystery of the Real Presence . . . tis no
> wonder if the growth of the *Messieurs les Scavants* increasing
> with the populacy of that realm, makes any man's belief in his
> [the pope's] infallibility pass for a degree of madness, accord-
> ingly as Mr Hobbes, Chap. 8 Of Man, well observes, that 'ex-
> cessive opinion of a man's own self, for divine inspiration and
> wisdom, becomes distraction and giddiness': and this probably
> may be the final result of the late fermentation about the
> Regalia, &c, and the pope be tacitly thought so as aforesaid, and
> his power there insensibly evaporate.[23]

The France of the 1590s and 1600s was instructive too. Henry IV,
who had converted from protestantism to Catholicism, had pacified
the religious factions and issued the Edict of Nantes, which De Thou
helped to draft. The Huguenots, unlike the English dissenters, did
not rebel against their king when he turned Catholic. Pett was especially fond of the writings of the tolerant and *politique* diplomat
Arnaud, Cardinal D'Ossat, Henry's agent at Rome and a friend of
De Thou. Boccalini had pinned his hopes on Henry IV, and moderates of both religions had anticipated a grand scheme for the pacification of Christendom. They all acknowledged that Henry's assassination in 1610 was an appalling disaster. Pett's moral was clear: Henry
IV, not Mary I of England, was the appropriate model for James II,
and the fires of Smithfield were an irrelevant memory.[24]

In his secularizing endeavours to dissolve the knot which tied religion and politics, Pett was powerfully influenced by Thomas

[23] *HFS* p 129.
[24] *Ibid* sig E2r; pp 70, 73, 206–9, 222, 232, 236, 242, 249; see Barlow, *Remains* pp 302–11. Anglesey, *Memoirs*, has much on French Catholicism, e.g. pp 278–81. On Boccalini see F. Yates, *The Rosicrucian Enlightenment* (London 1972) pp 133–6; on the circle of De Thou and Peiresc see K. Sharpe, *Sir Robert Cotton, 1586–1631* (Oxford 1979) pp 95ff.

Hobbes and the polemicists of the Royal Society. In his admiration for Hobbes Pett is about as unabashed as anyone could be in the Restoration. He called him 'a great philosopher of our nation', coupled him with Descartes 'those two great masters of wit and philosophy', and quoted regularly from *Leviathan* and *Behemoth*. The 'ingenious' history of the Civil Wars he took to be Hobbes's posthumous gift, 'a beneficial providence', to anti-Exclusion Toryism in its exposure of the Presbyterian rebels' war against Charles I. He used Hobbes's more notorious dicta about human psychology without a blush of embarrassment: 'it hath been well observed by a great enquirer into human nature, that a restless desire of power after power that ceaseth only in death, is the general inclination of all mankind'. He explained the enmity of politicians against his patron Anglesey, and the motivation of his lordship's friends, in terms of Hobbes's mechanics of power: 'Your lordship knows that fear in people is an aversion with an opinion of hurt from any object . . .'; 'Your very reputation for power is power, for that engageth those to adhere to you, who want protection'. Pett especially admired the chapters on religion in *Leviathan*, for Hobbes had vividly argued the necessity for ridding the world of all *jure divino* doctrines of jurisdiction. Hobbes had exorcised what Pett called the 'Manicheanism' of upholding an autonomous spiritual kingdom against the civil state.

> The *conclusum est contra Manicheos* . . . that is now *vox populi*, [and] doth with its full cry pursue Presbytery as well as Popery, for the making *duo summa principia* in states and kingdoms, and claiming an ecclesiastical power immediately derived from Christ and not dependent on the civil. There is no observation more common, than that Popery and Presbytery that seem as distant as the two poles, yet move on the same axle-tree of a church supremacy immediately derived from Christ; and Mr Hobbes his *Leviathan* might have passed through the world with a general applause, if no notion had been worse in it than in Chapter 44, the making his kingdom of darkness to consist of Popery and Presbytery.

Indeed the temper of the age was such that in their hatred of ecclesiastical 'manicheanism' people were 'too apt with Mr Hobbes to thrust the whole nation of spiritual beings out of the world'. Pett evidently believed that Hobbes's principles lead ultimately to toleration, for Hobbes's concern was to separate the wheat of religion, to which the magistrate should be indifferent, from the chaff of the pseudo-religionary pursuit of earthly power. 'Mr Hobbes saith in his *Behemoth* "I confess I know very few controversies among Christians of points necessary to salvation. They are the questions of authority and power over the church or of profit, or of honour to churchmen, that for the most part raise all the controversy" '. Having quoted this, Pett went on to say that it was not doctrines of transubstantiation or justification which mattered to the magistrate but 'papal power and the complication of the tenet of the plenitude of that power with those religionary tenets'. A Hobbesian hatred for the 'kingdom of darkness', of popery, was compatible with tolerance for Catholicism.[25]

Hobbes's other great importance was his contribution to the new philosophers' demolition of scholasticism. Hobbes was seen to be at one with Descartes, Gassendi and the Royal Society. 'In the dividend of our time little will come to the share of metaphysics'. It was an age bent on 'real knowledge' which finds 'very absurd' enquiries into universals and *entitas* 'which Mr Hobbes well Englished, the *isseness* of a thing'. The age owes a 'great obligation' to the Royal Society for its 'plantation of real knowledge'. Armed thus, the 'useless cobwebs' of scholastic divinity are abolished. 'A general disposition to believe nothing contrary to reason is the cutting of the grass under popery's feet'. The new age is equipped with the light of reason; 'neither popery's nor presbytery's kingdom of darkness can . . . overthrow our quiet'. The rise of rationalism from the Renaissance onward guarantees the eventual demise of the superstition that 'dominion is founded in grace'. Pett quoted two of the best known dicta in Sprat's *History of the Royal Society*, that 'the universal disposition of this age is bent upon a rational religion' and that 'experimental philosophy will enable us to provide beforehand against any alteration in religious affairs which this age may produce'. He recapitulated Sprat's Baconian account of the light of knowledge emerging from medieval darkness and giving people a power to vanquish irrational fears. The Reformation was 'the first blind step out of a blind chaos into a paradise of knowledge'. That Pett saw the influences of Hobbes and the Royal Society as comfortably interlocking needs underscoring, for Hobbes's relationship with the Society is still con-

---

[25] *HFS* sigs B2v, D1r; pp 21, 23, 24, 29, 37, 57, 66–73, 76, 133, 243, 314; 2nd pag pp 9, 13, 22, 31, 37.

troversial. Pett's view reinforces the case for saying that no deep ideological divergences excluded Hobbes from the Society.[26]

Pett's account of the birth of 'real learning' was redolent of the aspirations of the circle of Boyle, Wilkins, J. A. Comenius and Samuel Hartlib in the 1650s: on the one hand pragmatic and empirical, on the other, pansophist, optimistic and mildly Panglossian. It is 'as a philosopher' that Pett confidently predicted that the way of history led to the demise of popery. He wrote (from the Book of Daniel) of the dawning of 'a new heaven and a new earth' and cited J. H. Alsted, the pansophist teacher of Comenius and friend of Hartlib. Pett has been called a millenarian, but he was not so in any consequential sense. History had a discernible and progressive path, but the antics of the apocalyptic puritans he found contemptible. He was concerned to put aside 'the fantastic utopias, oceanas, and new atlantises that our late visionaries and idle santerers [sic] to a pretended new Jerusalem troubled England with'. The way forward is by empirical analysis and piecemeal social engineering, by what he himself calls 'the science of politics'. The emphasis is utilitarian, but like most proto-Enlightenment thought it was tinged with gnostic illuminism.

Where Pett differed from the mainstream of the Royal Society was in his generosity to Catholicism. James Jacob has shown that when the new generation of Fellows of the 1680s, particularly Pett's friend John Houghton, redeployed the ideology of the Society to defend the anti-Exclusionist state of the 1680s, they quietly dropped the anti-papist element, a lacuna which some protestant Fellows deplored. Yet it is clear that Pett did not ignore the issue. He shared the Society's sense that 'real learning' will be a bulwark against popery, that the new science will consummate the Reformation, but he was careful to allow that Catholicism might itself be successfully purged of popery. What was crucial, as we have seen, was that popery was a phenomenon detectable in protestantism as well as catholicism, and extinguishable from both. This was the sceptical science of a Tory, a natural philosophy for an English state which must come to terms with its Catholic prince and be rid of Whig revolutionism. In this, Pett was seconded by another of the Society's apologists, Joseph Glanvill, another of the Oxford Group of the 1650s and latterly a royal chaplain. Shortly before his death in 1680 Glanvill wrote a tract

---

[26] *Ibid* pp 57, 66–76, 243, 251, 272. See Q. Skinner, 'Thomas Hobbes and the nature of the early Royal Society', *Historical Journal* 12 (1969).

called *The Zealous and Impartial Protestant*. He argued that there was
nothing to fear from James's succession. James well knew that any
attempt to impose popery 'would hazard the ruining him'. The
antipopish frenzy was a crazy hysteria, and he feared that 'the time is
near . . . when every friend to the king and church shall be [called] a
papist'. The magnifying of the popish threat is an excuse for 'other
plots of as dangerous a nature as theirs'. Glanvill's tract was another
work of sceptical trimmer Toryism and Pett much admired it.[27]

III

When we turn to Pett's attitude to protestant dissent we find it was
a paradoxical one but one by no means uncommon in the 1680s. His
tolerance is bounded by the strict parameter of conformity to the
Church of England. He took for granted that the Church should be a
single church, the nation at prayer, and that there were no worthy
grounds for separation. Moreover, he added the weight of scientific
'prediction' to Tory confidence that dissent will soon disappear
altogether. 'The numbers of our nonconformists are daily decaying,
and the names of their tenets will probably be in a short time forgotten'. By 1685 Pett was even more enthusiastic for uniformity: 'the ebb
of their numbers is at this time so apparent'. Dissent was not a living
force but the decaying remnant of the Presbyterian and Independent
zealots of the 1640s, for 'it is . . . observable that most of the race of our
old Presbyterian and Independent divines having become extinct . . .
scarce any new ones . . . have since . . . propped up the credit of their
party'. In short, 'dissentership is languishing under its old age'. Pett
imprudently argued that the fashion for 'liberty of conscience', begun
in 1641, had had its last fling in the Declaration of Indulgence of 1672,
words which he swallowed in his applause for James's Indulgence.
Nor did Pett refrain from vilifying dissenters as heartily as any Tory
divine. They would have foisted on England a Genevan dictatorship;
they had shown no clear evidence of renouncing the 'intolerably
seditious' doctrine of the 1640s that 'if the magistrate will not reform
the world, they may'. With a catholicity of citation, he recommends
Bramhall's *Fair Warning* (1649) against the Scotch discipline,

---

[27] *HFS* sigs D1v–D2r, F2r, Klv; pp 66, 73–4, 130–2, 140–1, 185, 237, 243, 251, 272,
320; Glanvill, *The Zealous and Impartial Protestant* (London 1681) pp 45–56; Jacob,
'Restoration, Reformation', *passim*; J. I. Cope, *Joseph Glanvill, Anglican Apologist*
(St Louis 1956); on Alsted see Webster, *Great Instauration* pp 22–3.

Tillotson's notorious 'Hobbesian' sermon of 1680 which asserted that it was better to have no revealed religion than have the fanatics' religion, and Hobbes's notion of a clericalist 'kingdom of darkness'.[28]

At first sight, Pett seems no tolerationist. But much the same position was adopted by the well-known theological 'liberal' Edward Stillingfleet, whose *Mischief of Separation* (1679) and *Unreasonableness of Separation* (1681), which Pett approved, were the most famous of contemporary assaults on dissent. Stillingfleet was the latitudinarian who had produced the celebrated *Eirenicum* (1661), and his reputation for liberalism exacerbated the anguish of dissenters like Richard Baxter who published replies to Stillingfleet. Stillingfleet, and Glanvill, held that the worst threat of popery came from dissent: not only did its persistence weaken the Established Church and the unity of protestantism, but its ground for schism, or worse still for political resistance, was itself popish for it set up *imperium in imperio*. Schism was a denial of the cardinal tenet of the Reformation, the civil magistrate's supremacy in religion. Here was the core of Stillingfleet's latitudinarian ecclesiology, its Erastianism. The way forward for peace and tolerance was seen to lie in the growth of liberal theology *within* the church and not sectarian schism outside it. Liberal comprehension rather than plural toleration was the ideal. The latitudinarians were 'tolerant' in a specific sense and only by appreciating the strength of the ideal of comprehensive uniformity (and by putting aside our knowledge of its permanent failure in the Act of Toleration of 1689) can we make sense of Stillingfleet's and Pett's combination of genuine liberalism with aggressive hostility to dissent. The same paradox subsists in Hobbes's ecclesiology. It is not accidental that Stillingfleet was widely accused of Hobbesianism and that Pett plainly was a Hobbesian.[29]

The latitudinarians were also impatient with the intransigence of Anglican high churchmen who thought the church's establishment, episcopacy in particular, was *jure divino*. Little of this theme emerged in Pett or Stillingfleet—or in *Leviathan*—because in the 1640s and 1680s the worst danger seemed to come from Presbyterianism. Nonetheless, Pett's Erastianism and indifferentism marks him out from the high churchmen. Pett had no objection to bishops, but like

---

[28] *HFS* sigs Blv, D2r–v, E2v, Hlr, I2v–K2v; pp 29, 133–7, 280–1.
[29] I am indebted to John Marshall's forthcoming article, 'The ecclesiology of the latitude-men, 1660–89: Stillingfleet, Tillotson and Hobbism'.

the latitudinarians he built his hopes on 'Ussher's Reduction', Archbishop James Ussher's scheme for episcopacy moderated by presbyterial synodical forms. In 1660, in the interval before the Act of Uniformity, Pett and his friends had publicly called for the institution of Ussher's broad church. They feared 'a vindictive retaliation' by the rigid Anglicans. Although from Pett's pen, the *Discourse Concerning Liberty of Conscience* was the outcome of collaboration between Boyle, Barlow and John Dury, one of the most energetic idealists for religious union in the Interregnum. The tract was one of the half-dozen which Locke had in his library under the heading 'Tolerantia'. alongside his own *Letter on Toleration*. Pett's argument was characteristic of latitudinarian indifferentism. Beyond the obligation that God be soberly worshipped, nothing is *jure divino*, and the civil magistrate is empowered to institute any form of worship and jurisdiction. The ruler is entitled to coerce acceptance of rigid impositions, and nobody had grounds for sectarian objection, but it would be an impolitic move on the ruler's part. In the broad domain of 'things indifferent' the sovereign is free to make a prudential calculus for the common good. In this tract Pett was the mouthpiece of Boyle and the virtuosi. Like Hobbes and Stillingfleet, they shared the Erastian paradox: they were liberal and anticlerical, yet capable of intense distaste for sectarianism. In the 1680s Pett harked back to Ussher's Reduction. He pointed out that it had been offered early in the 1640s, before the outbreak of the Civil War; the Presbyterians' unforgivable crime was their fanatical insistence on the fullness of Genevan theocracy, which had had its outcome in bloody war. Anglesey's part, as a 'Presbyterian' MP in the Long Parliament, in thwarting the *jure divino* Scotch discipline earned Pett's highest praise: Anglesey had been more Erastian than Presbyterian.[30]

Whilst Pett harked back to Ussher's scheme, he also, by the 1680s, came to regard the restructuring of the Church by comprehension schemes as now unnecessary. The increasing recognition of the indifference of rubrics, creeds and jurisdictions meant that dissenters

[30] *HFS* pp 29, 138; 2nd pag pp 9, 13. See Pett's Memoir of Boyle: BL Add MS 4229, fos 33–48; Jacob, 'Restoration, Reformation', pp 157–61; J. R. Jacob, *Robert Boyle and the English Revolution* (New York 1977) pp 134–54; G. H. Turnbull, *Hartlib, Dury and Comenius* (Liverpool 1947) pp 292, 316; *The Library of John Locke*, eds J. Harrison and P. Laslett (Oxford 1965) no 2820. On the religious outlook of the early Royal Society generally see B. J. Shapiro, 'Latitudinarianism and science in seventeenth century England', *PP* 40 (1968), and the many writings of Margaret and James Jacob, esp. 'The Anglican origins of modern science: the metaphysical foundations of the Whig constitution', *Isis* 71 (1980).

would naturally drift back into the Church, despite 1662. Within the Church, ecclesiastical punishment for heresy would lapse. Hierarchies and rubrics would become the uncontroversial fabric of good order; theologies would be diverse, private and unmolested. The tendency of history was towards theological latitude. 'The old way of arguing about speculative points in religion with passion and loudness . . . is grown out of use, and a gentlemanly candour in discourse of the same with that moderate temper that men use in debating natural experiments has succeeded in its room.' The midwives of this trend were 'that breed of rational divines our Church of England hath been blessed with since the king's Restoration'.[31]

Pett noted that the most striking evidence for this latitude was the way in which in his own lifetime the tenets of Arminianism 'have ceased to ferment the state': the quarrel of Calvinists and Arminians 'seems lately to be retired to its eternal rest'. He predicted that the next major doctrine which would cease to be controversial was the Trinity. This was a shocking thing to say and it was said on the eve of decades of the Arian or Socinian controversy, which got under way with the appearance in 1687 of Stephen Nye's *Brief History of the Unitarians*. Pett blithely asserted that beliefs about the Eucharist or Justification or the Trinity were merely matters of opinion, that Christendom was coming to see that Christ's mission was not an 'errand from heaven to set the world right in speculations of philosophy', and that the doctrinal quarrels of the day would soon seem as trivial as ancient quarrels over the date of Easter. 'Heresy' was gradually returning to its original meaning, the taking of a speculative opinion, a point which Pett probably derived from Hobbes's essay on heresy. As for Socinianism, Pett could not see why the holding of Biddle's tenets—John Biddle had been condemned and punished by parliament in the 1650s—should trouble the magistrate, and that it would not matter if the heir to the throne were a Socinian rather than a Catholic. In the 1680s few would have dared to say this. It is not surprising that Pett was denounced for Socinianism, and he may once have been a member of Biddle's circle, but there is little evidence that he cared much about the theological issue. His point was that anything could be tolerated so long as it has no leaven of popery in it. Socinus had denied that

---

[31] *HFS* sig E1r–v; pp 68, 241–3; Anglesey, *Memoirs* p 161.

'dominion was founded in grace': that was all the magistrate—or a people contemplating their king—needed to know.[32]

When James came to the throne, Pett's friend Petty prepared some papers outlining the articles of a minimalist 'natural and universal religion': God was the first cause; the soul was immortal; there were rewards and punishments after death; sovereigns were God's lieutenants within their own states; and national churches provided for public religious rituals. Beyond this, credal speculation and private worship were unexceptionable.[33] James's circle of sceptical Tories believed that in time Christianity would be reduced to a deistic civil religion—much as Rousseau would describe at the end of *The Social Contract*. And since religion was the cause of most persecution and violence, the secular future would be a peaceful future.

IV

One of the main purposes of *The Happy Future State* was to demonstrate the contribution which empirical social science could make to government policy. In 1685–86, in the confident beginning of James's reign, we can envisage an embryonic scientific civil service intent upon rationally planned economic, naval, fiscal and demographic growth. Pett and Pepys had several interviews with the king concerning their schemes and Pett presented a memorandum on the economy and revenue of Ireland. His brother Sir Phineas and colleague Sir Anthony Deane were appointed navy commissioners. Among this group we can also number the mathematician Robert Wood, FRS, another friend of Pett from Oxford days, whose interests lay in currency reform and the Irish economy; John Houghton, FRS, who published tracts on agricultural improvement;

---

[32] *HFS* sig E1r–v; pp 168, 171, 241–3; T. Hobbes, *An Historical Narration Concerning Heresy* (London 1680); H. Brougham, *Reflections on a Late Book Entituled The Genuine Remains of Dr Thomas Barlow* (London 1694) pp 10–11. Pett's *HFS* has been used as evidence for Biddle's Socinian circle in the 1650s: J. Toulmin, *A Review . . . of . . . John Biddle* (London 1791) p 64; R. Wallace, *Antitrinitarian Biography* (London 1850) III pp 186–7; E. M. Wilbur, *A History of Unitarianism* (Harvard 1952) p 200. Pett's catholicity did not stop with the Unitarians. In 1680 he proposed a scheme to regularise the legal position of the Jews by enlarging their immunities and establishing them in a ghetto (as some Jews themselves desired). Pett was to be Justiciar of the Jews, to manage their relations with the king and farm their taxes. Anglesey raised the matter with the king, but Charles had more pressing matters on his mind. See *HFS* 2nd pag p 46; L. Wolf, 'Status of the Jews in England after resettlement', *Jewish Historical Society of England Transactions 1899–1901* (London 1903) pp 192–3.

[33] *The Petty Papers*, ed Marquis of Lansdowne (London 1927) I pp 130–2.

and Thomas Hale, a projector and member of the Danby club, who worked with Pepys and Pett to persuade the government to introduce the lead sheathing of ships, and whose *Account of Several New Inventions* (1691) is full of praise for the Pett family, for Wood and for Sir Peter's *Happy Future State*, a book 'full of the most useful inventions and discoveries in politics'.[34]

The term 'political arithmetic' was first used by Petty in a letter to Anglesey in 1672 but it did not gain currency until the 1690s when the fiscal demands of warfare made pressing the need for accurate assessments of revenue yields.[35] Pett was an energetic propagator of the manifold benefits of 'political calculations' for modern government—an ideal of 'pantometry' rather than pansophism.[36] The perfection of political calculations 'is the height of human wisdom in the political conduct of the world'. Its keystone was demography. His book would 'lay open a new scene of thought'. The main spur was for him not fiscal requirements, but the need for a therapy for national religious dissension. Statistical research would henceforth be crucial for 'an inquisitive or philosophical statesman' and those who proceed to public policy without it were 'but state-enthusiasts'.[37]

Pett honoured the pioneers in demography. He drew upon John Graunt's work of the 1660s on the population and mortality of London. 'The thanks of the age are due to the Observator on the bills of mortality, for those solid and rational calculations he hath brought to light, relating to the number of our people'. Pett had discussed these matters with Graunt and Petty and had employed Graunt to procure Walloon craftsmen for migration to Ireland.[38] Pett also ad-

---

[34] Among this circle should also be included Andrew Yarranton, Thomas Sheridan and the Catholic Robert Plot. See esp. Jacob, 'Restoration ideologies'. Also: Hale, *An Account* (London 1691); M. Hunter, *Science and Society in Restoration England* (Cambridge 1981) ch 5; [S.] Pepys, *The Tangier Papers*, ed E. Chappell (London 1935) *passim*; [S.] Pepys, *Naval Minutes,* ed J. R. Tanner (London 1926) *passim*; E. Fitzmaurice, *The Life of Sir William Petty, 1623–87* (London 1895) ch 9.

[35] *Ibid* p 158; [*The*] *Economic Writings of* [*Sir William*] *Petty*, ed C. H. Hull (Cambridge 1899) I p 240.

[36] The term is Sir George Clark's: *Science and Social Welfare in the Age of Newton* (Oxford 1949) p 131; see ch 5 generally.

[37] *HFS* ep ded; pp 91, 123; Barlow, *Remains* sig A4r.

[38] *HFS* pp 112, 142–3, 149, 155, 157, 189, 248–9; Barlow, *Remains* p 273; Pepys, *Naval Minutes* I p 115; T. Carte, *The Life of James, Duke of Ormond* (Oxford 1851) pp 283–4. *HFS* has been used as evidence in the lengthy debate over Graunt's authorship of the *Observations*: see e.g. D. V. Glass and D. E. C. Eversley, *Population in History* (London 1965) pp 159 seq; S. Matsukawa, 'Origins and significance of political arithmetic', *Annals of the Hitotsubashi Academy* 6 (1955).

mired the *Observations on the United Provinces* (1673), the work of Sir William Temple, another pioneer social scientist and trimmer politician who began his career in the Irish service. Pett's greatest debt was unquestionably to Petty. Often his book is no more than a mouthpiece for Petty's opinions, and an impatient one, for Pett used Petty's unpublished manuscripts and constantly pressed Petty to publish. The new opportunity of 1685–86, and Pett's urgings, did result in a crop of Petty tracts on population growth and Ireland. Petty 'never writ anything for the press but what he informed Sir Robert [Southwell] and me of and gave us manuscript copies of'. In *The Happy Future State* Pett often uses Petty's slogan that the new science was one of 'number, weight and measure'. Of special interest to Pett was Petty's admiration for Hobbes, his concern to minimise religious conflict, to measure the sects and regulate clerical wealth and power. His book is a working out of one item in Petty's list of the purposes of political arithmetic: 'From the knowledge of the number of the professors of all religionaries . . . may be understood the means and difficulties of bringing all to conformity'.[39]

For Pett the most pressing question was the size of England's population. Demography was the groundwork for economic, fiscal, religious, colonial and foreign policy. 'It is much to be pitied' that a census of population had not been undertaken for 'the knowledge whereof is the substratum of all political measures that can be taken as to a nation's strength or riches, and the part whereof is spareable for colonies, and the value of the branches of the public revenue, and the equality in proportioning any taxes or levies by act of parliament, and the satisfying the world about the value of our alliances'. Pett had in mind not just the mercantilist point that population meant power, nor just the Baconian point that knowledge was power, but also the Hobbesian point that *reputation* for power was power, for he was angered that ignorance laid England open to the barrage of French and Dutch propaganda which asserted that the British Isles had only half the population of France, or that England had only two million people. Pett's chief concern was to demonstrate that England's population was much in excess of figures put forward by foreigners or by 'cautious calculators'. If England's international standing was

---

[39] *HFS* sigs A2r, G2r, O1r; pp 106, 122, 130, 166, 186, 192–3, 196, 245; Barlow, *Remains* p 321; Bodl MS Wood F43, fol 217; *Economic Writings of Petty*, I pp xxx, 100, 124, 237; *Petty Papers* I pp xxiii, 116–43, 172–5, 181–4, 193–8, 253–65, 272–3; II, 47–58, 201, 253–65; *The Petty-Southwell Correspondence* pp 60–1, 176.

one motive for his efforts, the other was the problem of religion. If the population could be shown to be large, then the Catholic and dissenter communities could be shown to be utterly outnumbered. Once the population was known, the dissenters would be forced to stop exaggerating their influence and the protestants to cease being frightened of Catholics.[40]

We cannot here examine the details of Pett's statistical efforts and his assessments of the strengths and weaknesses of the hearth and poll tax returns and the Compton Census of 1676. His analysis of the Census, which he made available to James, has been a valuable source for historians. In 1676 Danby and the bishops had wanted to demonstrate to Charles that his endeavours on behalf of dissent, culminating in the 1672 Indulgence, were an impolitic pandering to a small but self-inflating minority. Bishop Compton surveyed the parishes of the province of Canterbury in order to measure the denominations. That Danby sought to shape policy with social statistics earned Pett's fulsome praise: his lordship was 'as great a master of the science of numbers as perhaps ever any that acted in that high sphere of state'. Pett had discussed the figures with Danby when he visited him in the Tower. As a prime minister who fell victim to the Plot fever and whose release depended on the waning of the fever, he had good reason to impress upon Pett the importance of publishing the Census figures in order to quell popular fears. In analysing the figures Pett came to the conclusion that the population of England and Wales was at least seven million and conceivably as high as twelve million. This is considerably higher than the present day estimate of five million for 1676 and Gregory King's estimate of five-and-a-half million.[41]

Having demonstrated the populousness of England, what conclusions followed for Pett? The first was that France was not to be feared. Neither obeisance nor war was necessary, for it was impossible for France or any nation to attempt a 'Universal Monarchy'. France's strength could be successfully combatted by demographic and economic competition and a powerful navy. This coincided with Petty's scheme of 1687 for enforced fecundity to double the population within twenty-five years and create such economic and

---

[40] *HFS* sigs N2v, O1r; pp 112, 116.

[41] *Ibid* sig O1r; pp 113–9; BL Add MS 28053, fol 390; Hale, *An Account* pp xl–xli; Barlow, *Remains* pp 321–3. See esp. Whiteman, 'The census that never was'. Compare: G. S. Holmes, 'Gregory King and the social structure of pre-industrial England', *Transactions of the Royal Historical Society* 27 (1977) pp 49–53.

state power that 'the king will be the greatest in Christendom without war or bloodshed'. The second conclusion was that republican scheming in England was 'ridiculous' in modern times, for republics are only feasible in small states. Admiration for classical Greek models was anachronistic, and 'a fantastic Oceana' or Whig 'projecting' of commonwealths was chimerical. 'Sober political virtuosi' will see that populousness correlates with monarchy and that as population increases the drift of European progress would be towards centralised monarchies.[42]

The next conclusion was that the proportion of Catholics was small. At most it was 1:150. The Catholics' own estimates were therefore plausible: he cited Lord Castlemaine's 1679 estimate of fifty thousand. These are close to modern assessments, which suggest about one percent of the population. Pett's use of the Compton Census to diffuse antipopish paranoia was anticipated in Glanvill's tract, which Pett cites. It was plain to them that a Catholic attempt at domination, let alone a successful armed uprising, was out of the question. What is more, James and his ministers were well aware of the conclusions of their statistical advisers. Pett and his circle hoped James would see the necessity of working with moderate protestants, and that the nation would be loyal to James, confident that a popish despotism was structurally impossible. In assessing James's intentions, it is important for modern historians to recognise that he knew the demographic evidence, and it underscores the unlikelihood of his aiming at anything more ambitious than toleration and access to office for his co-religionists.[43]

The fourth major conclusion Pett drew was that the proportion of dissenters had been inflated by their promoters, although he recognized that the Compton Census was less accurate here than in the measurement of Catholics. The Census gave 4.4 percent for Canterbury Province, 7.3 percent for the diocese of London. This he thought was probably fairly accurate, and it ought to restrain the dissenters' friends from the temptation to 'magnify their numbers'.[44]

---

[42] *HFS* pp 124–30, 186, 192– 6, 252–3; see *The Petty Papers* II pp 56–7.

[43] *HFS* sigs D1v–D2r; pp 97, 104, 128–9, 140–1, 148–9, 199; Barlow, *Remains* pp 316, 320–1; R. Palmer, Lord Castlemaine, *Compendium* (London 1679); Miller, *Popery and Politics* pp 9–11; Glanvill, *The Zealous and Impartial Protestant* pp 45–9; *Economic Writings of Petty* I p xxx.

[44] *HFS* sig D2r.

Finally, Pett placed his work on population into a broader historical and socio-economic framework. The multiplication of mankind was to be understood as having a necessary relationship to economic development, scientific progress, and the passage of the world from popery towards reason and liberty. Much as Pett disliked the republicanism of Harrington's *Oceana*, he followed its attempt to analyse the relationship between economic substructures and political and ideological superstructures. The steady increase in the world's population—Pett could not imagine that it was stable or declining—was a fact which 'must of necessity be fatal to the papacy', both because it made 'Universal Monarchy' impossible and because it generated ever larger bodies of superstition-resistant intellegentsias. It was 'a known truth' that the policy of the medieval church was 'to depopulate' states and thereby to subordinate them. This was a common contemporary view and Pett makes two familiar points: that depopulation had been partly secured by the institution of celibacy and by the excessive numbers of clergy (he reckoned 120,000 on the eve of the Reformation, ten times the 1680s figure); and that the present occupiers of the abbey lands (he estimated three million of them) created an immovable interest against restoring the Medieval Church.[45]

Pett improved on the conventional account of clerical depopulation by relating it to the agricultural system. The characteristic agriculture of the monasteries was pastoral sheep farming, which maximised clerical income whilst minimising the land's capacity to support population. The monks were 'wolves in sheep's clothing' who took too literally the injunction to 'feed my sheep'. He cited approvingly the testimony of More's *Utopia*, a book not written 'at the pope's feet', and quoted the famous remark that 'sheep do eat up men', and the passage where the Utopians are said to have few priests, who are chosen by the civil magistracy and who marry. Forms of agriculture, Pett maintained, are the economic determinant of a commonwealth's capacity to support populacy, trade, the arts and sciences, and the revenue and armies of the prince. He described three distinct stages of agricultural development: pasture, tillage, and market-gardening. It is the increasing intensity of cultivation which is the motor of demographic growth and in turn of civility, progress and national virility.

---

[45] *Ibid* pp 77–81, 87, 92–5, 101, 108–11, 128–9.

When through the divine blessing England shall arrive at the
state of being fully peopled, and being got beyond pasture, that
first improvement of a thin peopled country, shall likewise have
completed that second of tillage, that our being better peopled
will occasion, there will be a third in our view to employ the
labours of our consummate populacy, namely that of gardening, and to oblige us that the earth shall produce nothing but
what is exactly useful: and instead of going back from tillage to
pasture, we must naturally go forward from tillage to gardening, whereby one acre may be made to maintain twenty
persons.

It was foolish to think that popery could be restored in a country
'going on so fast towards the exactest culture by gardening'. A
model for market-gardening could be seen in Jersey and Guernsey
and there is a 'pleasant and profitable prospect of such improvement
near our metropolis and other great cities'; before long England will
be 'the garden of the world'. Pett's praise of Lord Anglesey's recrea-
tion of 'tillage and planting and gardening' on his estates was thus an
emblem of his patron's protestancy. It was a theme partly borrowed
from the horticultural propaganda of his friend John Houghton.[46]

Pett's discussion was fragmentary, its details seem now factitious,
and he never lost sight of his polemical endeavour to convince the
English that a Catholic king was safe. He was of course right to insist
that Catholicism in the 1680s could never be like the Medieval
Church and that a sense of history revealed as much.[47] This insight
encouraged him to detach the concept of 'popery' from that of
'catholicism'. 'Popery' was a combination of superstition and clerical
despotism which depended upon certain social and demographic
formations. In short, popery meant clericalism—and protestants
could be guilty of it. For instance, he believed that the economic fact
that the capital value of the episcopal and capitular lands in the 1640s
was £6 million had motivated the fanatical Presbyterians to devise
the superstition of *jure divino* Presbyterianism in order to legitimise
the transfer of those lands and revenues into their own grasping
hands. To effect it, they had invented a godly duty to overthrow the
state. This was why the Presbyterians could literally be called

[46] *Ibid* pp 94–5, 100–2. See J. Houghton, *A Collection of Letters for the Improvement of Husbandry and Trade* (London 1681–83); J. Thirsk, 'Seventeenth century agriculture and social change' in *Land, Church and People, Agricultural History Review Supplement* ed J. Thirsk (London 1970) pp 162–4, 171.

[47] See J. Bossy, *The English Catholic Community 1570–1850* (London 1975).

popish, for they copied the Medieval Church's conjunction of economic interest, superstitious doctrine, and exorbitant clericalism.[48] As mankind progressed the clerical interest declined, so also the motivation to invent self-serving 'popish' superstitions, and so too the need for people to be apprehensive of the intrusion of religion into politics. The popish and Whig 'plots' and the frenzies of fear in the 1680s were superficial eruptions, 'turbid intervals', on the surface of a secular trend.[49]

When a sceptic in the late seventeenth century reflected historically upon the political impact of religion—when, that is, he added the insights of Harrington to those of Hobbes—he began to formulate theories of progress, of stages of development, and of the relationship between what we now call ideology and the socio-economic structure. It was a prefiguration of the Enlightenment and of modern social science, but it was wrought within a distinctively protestant consciousness.

Churchill College, Cambridge

---

[48] *HFS* sig D2v; pp 88–9, 108–9. See pp 81–6, and Barlow, *Remains* pp 271–80 on clerical revenue. Also *The Petty Papers* II pp 227. In June 1683 Pepys reported that 'About religion, Sir P. P. did quote somebody, I think Sir W. P., and he is of the same mind, that it will of religion shall be any profit to anybody.': *The Tangier Papers* p 317.

[49] *HFS* pp 64–6, 102, 199, 252.

THE POLITICS OF 'PERSECUTION':
SCOTS EPISCOPALIAN TOLERATION
AND THE HARLEY MINISTRY, 1710–12*

by D. SZECHI

R ELIGION WAS the ideological motor of politics in the first age of party. Though the distinction between the Whig and Tory positions on religious issues was often small compared to their internal divisions on other matters, religion was felt to be the only real justification for both parties. The Whigs stood for a cosmopolitan Erastianism embracing protestant dissent, the Tories for a stronger, national Church for which religious uniformity was still a worthwhile goal. The Church was inextricably caught up in these national political divisions, and its own internecine warfare between high and low church mirrored them exactly.[1] It naturally followed from this that religious issues were the most passionately upheld by the Whigs and the Tories, and were those which had most impact on national politics. Hence the Tories put themselves out of office in 1704–5 by the zeal with which they tried to push the Occasional Conformity Bill through, even though it was certain to create a constitutional crisis which would paralyse the British war-effort against France. And the Whigs seized the opportunity to 'roast a parson' afforded by Henry Sacheverell's high church ranting on the theme of 'the Church in Danger' by trying to impeach him. Their partial success only served to validate and refresh the 'Church in Danger' preaching they had hoped to silence, and they were crushed by an avalanche of outraged Toryism in the 1710 election.[2] Since religious issues were the most keenly felt and constituted the central dynamic

* I would like to thank Anthony Fletcher and Dr L. M. Kirk of the University of Sheffield for their advice and criticism on this article. This study is based on my thesis which should be consulted for a more detailed account of contemporaneous political manoeuvres and events. See: D. Szechi, 'Parliamentary Jacobitism and its Influence in the Tory Party, 1710–14.' Oxford Bodleian MS D.Phil c 1485 pp 74–154, 193–9.
[1] G. S. Holmes, *British Politics in the Age of Anne* (London 1967) pp 97–106, 'Religion and Party in Late Stuart England', *Historical Association Pamplet*, (1975) *passim*.
[2] G. S. Holmes, *The Trial of Dr Sacheverell* (London 1973).

275

of the party battle, the translation of religious conflict from the nation at large to Westminster gives us a glimpse of the real strength of religion's hold on the concept of party, and hence its influence in contemporary politics.

The struggle to secure religious toleration for Episcopalian Dissenters in Scotland was one such case. Because of its chronology it has been over-shadowed by other dramatic political events, so it gives us an opportunity to approach some old problems from a new angle.

Scotland's political establishment was in a nervous state for most of 1710. The Kirk was understandably upset by the wave of anti-dissenting riots sweeping England in the wake of the Sacheverell impeachment, and alarmed by the welter of rabid polemic and sermonising directed against the English nonconformists by the many imitators of Sacheverell who had arisen among the Anglican lower clergy. As the sequence of dismissals and manoeuvres which preceded Robert Harley's return to power began to unfold, Scotland's rulers also began to feel uneasy. Scotland had been under the control of two Whiggish groups since the Union of 1707, both having established themselves as the 'Revolution interest' during the negotiations and Parliamentary battles which had accompanied its passage. Queensberry's Court Whigs were faithful allies of lord treasurer Godolphin, while the Squadrone Whigs looked to the English junto for leadership.[3] Though theirs was an uneasy alliance, punctuated by bouts of faction-fighting, both felt equally threatened by Harley's stealthy approach to power in London during the spring and summer of 1710.[4] This atmosphere of alarm and apprehension among Scotland's political establishment combined to produce a minor spate of anti-prelatic preaching (aimed at both Anglicans and Catholics), and some repressive legal action against both sets of Scots dissenters by overzealous Presbyterian magistrates.[5]

Of the two sets of Scots dissenters the Episcopalians were the most important because they were protestants. The Episcopal Church of Scotland was a relic of the Revolution of 1688. William III was forced to reinstate the Presbyterian church-order displaced in the 1660s because, like the English Nonjurors, the Episcopalian hierarchy

---

[3] [P. W. J.] Riley, [*The Union of England and Scotland*] (Manchester 1978) pp 293–8.

[4] C. Jones, 'Godolphin, the Whig Junto, and the Scots', *ScHR* 58 (1979) pp 158–74.

[5] W. F. Leith, *Memoirs of Scottish Catholics During the Seventeenth and Eighteenth Centuries* (London 1909) pp 264–73; Oxford, Christ Church, Wake MSS XVII, fol 246.

refused to accept him as king. Unlike the Nonjurors though, the Episcopalian hierarchy commanded considerable support among the lower clergy, particularly in the north of Scotland, which determinedly went into schism with the new order. Separation in teaching followed separation in allegiance, and Episcopalian doctrine steadily became more high church in tone due to the influence of Nonjurors and high churchmen south of the border. Rejection of William III and the Revolution also inevitably led to the Episcopalian Church becoming thoroughly imbued with Jacobitism.[6] Kirk presbyteries usually only took notice of Episcopalian dissent when it was forced upon them, but Presbyterian zealots did periodically initiate local bouts of legal persecution. These allowed the Episcopalians to present themselves as martyrs for the Anglican liturgy with some modicum of conviction and truth. English high church Tories were predisposed anyway to see them as simple Scots Tories persecuted by Presbyterian Whig fanatics, and the Episcopalians used occasional instances of legal persecution to maintain this perception of their situation in Scotland. As both sides there knew, the Episcopalians' views on politics, society and the religious order were generally far more extreme than those of the English Tories, and they looked to the exiled Stuarts at St Germain for both temporal salvation and political direction.[7]

The Harley ministry which was installed in stages during the summer of 1710 faced some delicate political problems in Scotland. Harley's moderate political position was made necessary by the circumstances of his coming to power and his own temperament. The queen's aversion to the outgoing Whig ministry stemmed from its political partisanship towards every office in Church and State, so he had to avoid extensive purges of the administration if at all possible. The attitude of the administration however often proved crucial in elections, particularly in Scotland, so that leaving Whigs in office there threatened an electoral upset. On top of the queen's dislike of political purges, Harley was constrained by the inbuilt Whig majority in the Lords to keep a small group of Court Whig peers attached to his government. The need not to offend their political sensibilities thus

[6] B. Lenman, 'The Scottish Episcopal Clergy and the Ideology of Jacobitism', in *Ideology and Conspiracy: Aspects of Jacobitism 1689– 1759*, ed E. Cruickshanks (Edinburgh 1982) pp 36–48.

[7] Riley pp 9–10; B. Lenman, *The Jacobite Risings in Britain 1689–1746* (London 1980) pp 102–3.

reinforced his initial disinclination to make extensive changes. Maintaining control of the Lords even with the support of Court Whigs required consistent support from the sixteen elected Scots Representative Peers too. At the same time Harley wanted no extra-Parliamentary problems with Scotland either, and so wished to leave the religious situation there much as he found it. The only change he wanted was the lessening of religious tension in Scotland, which he achieved even before he officially came to power in August by having the Scots administration drop its support for legal actions against Episcopalians and Catholics, and having his Scots adherents soothe the Kirk's fears about what his return to office portended.[8]

Faced with an election, Harley and his Scots political managers, the duke of Argyll and the earls of Mar, Kinnoull and Islay, had to make some difficult decisions. There were three major alignments among the Scots peers, any two of which could outvote the other: the Court party (including Queensberry's Court Whigs); the Squadrone; and the duke of Hamilton's Episcopal cum nationalist party. Harley's Scots managers quickly decided that the Court party should ally with Hamilton's party, reasoning that alliance with Hamilton would guarantee the election of sixteen peers of which the Court would get the lion's share, and though Hamilton's followers who made up the rest were not certain to be reliable, they offered a better prospect of it than the same number of Squadrone peers. The problem with such an alliance was that it laid up trouble in store, as it would reawaken all the Kirk's carefully soothed fears and the Episcopalians were liable to be troublesome and hungry after so long in the political wilderness. Harley accordingly tergiversated while his Scots managers were more and more alarmed by tentative signs of a deal between the Episcopalians and the Squadrone, based on cold-blooded *realpolitik*. Eventually he gave in and the Court-Episcopalian alliance carried the day handsomely in the Representative Peers' election. The Court tried to prevent further Episcopalian political gains by standing neutral in the Commons' elections, but they still managed to win about a third of the forty-five Scots seats.

One of the many characteristics of contemporary political parties displayed by the Episcopalians in this election was that they fought it on the basis of a broad electoral programme designed to draw in as much support as possible. Overtly it had two elements: compensa-

---

[8] Oxford, Christ Church, Wake MSS XVII, fol 262; *HMC, Mar and Kellie MSS* pp 483–4.

tion for the Scots peers transported to London in the aftermath of the failed Jacobite invasion attempt of 1708 and the securing of a legal toleration for Episcopalianism. Covertly, it was mooted 'that now or never was the time to do something effectually for the king [the Old Pretender], and by restoring him dissolve the Union.' Politically moderate voters could be persuaded of the merits of the ostensible platform and unreconstructed Episcopalian nonjurors could be persuaded to take the oaths required to vote for the secret platform.[9] So when Parliament assembled in November 1710 it included a small, cohesive group of political outsiders intent on a radical reordering of affairs both within Scotland and outside it. Securing a legal toleration for Episcopalianism was technically only part of their programme, but it was the most politically practicable. Compensation for the prisoners of 1708 was unlikely to attract much English support, and doing 'something effectually for the King' was so nebulous as to require no specific action. On the other hand, an appeal for relief on behalf of suffering fellow Anglicans persecuted by wicked Presbyterian bigots was far more likely to succeed.

The religious excitement and extensive war-weariness characterising the electorate's mood in the 1710 election particularly favoured high church Tory candidates in England because of their extrovert zeal for the Church of England and their passionate denunciations of the Whigs as war-profiteers. Consequently, a substantial proportion of the Tory majority in the new Parliament consisted of such zealots. They arrived at Westminster determined to secure the Church against nonconformity, purge all Whigs from office, impeach Marlborough, Godolphin and the junto and to make peace with France as soon as possible.[10] Harley had done his best to minimise the number of high church Tories returned, and hoped to dissipate their enthusiasm with a few palliative measures. Instead, these merely served to whet the appetites of these 'Country' Tories. Having viewed the installation of the Harley ministry with something akin to millenarian fervour, they expected to be led by the ministry in fortifying the Church of England and crushing their enemies forever. Harley's abruptly calling a halt to anti-Whig Parliamentary action and offer-

---

[9] [*The*] *Lockhart* [*Papers*, ed A. Aufrere] (2 vols London 1817) 1 p 319; Edinburgh, Scots Catholic Archives, Blair Letter: James Carnegy to Bishop Nicolson, 20 Sept 1710.

[10] E. Gregg, *Queen Anne* (London 1980) p 324.

ing little by way of greater security for the Church duly left his backbenchers angry and frustrated.

Ministries had disappointed their backbenchers before and would do so again. Where the 1710 Parliament was exceptional in this respect was that such behaviour galvanized the government's backbenchers into forming a Country Tory alliance designed to force the ministers to accede to their demands: the October Club. From the end of January 1711 this growing group of backbench zealots hammered through a series of measures dear to Tory hearts despite the united opposition of the Whigs and the ministry.[11] Very few Episcopalian MPs formally joined the October Club, but a secret steering committee directed most of their Parliamentary activity so as to be in effective alliance with it.[12] As high church Tories, the October Club's members were automatically sympathetic to Episcopalian grievances and, unlike the ministry, they cared little for the political quiet of Scotland when religion was at issue.

Leading members of the Kirk had become uneasy about the prospect of Parliamentary action against the religious settlement in Scotland ever since the Court-Episcopalian alliance had proved so successful in the 1710 election. William Carstares, Moderator of the General Assembly, was moved to write to Harley in December 1710 seeking assurances that this was not the case.[13] The ministry's attitude was unchanged, and around the same time Mar was optimistic that judicious pressure on the Episcopalians' English sympathisers and some douceurs for selected Episcopalians would vitiate any agitation they might be planning.[14] Meanwhile, the Episcopalians had been casting around for support for the Greenshields appeal from the time they arrived in London. This appeal to the Lords by James Greenshields, an Episcopalian clergyman, was against a decision to imprison him by the Edinburgh magistrates, as upheld by the Lords of Session, in response to a complaint against him by the Edinburgh presbytery after he refused to stop using the English Book of Common Prayer.[15] Patently an attempt to test the legal and political climate of opinion in England, news of the appeal aroused considerable alarm in Scotland and even rumbles of discontent from the usually docile

---

[11] K. G. Feiling, *The First Tory Party, 1640–1714* (Oxford 1924) pp 430–3.

[12] *Lockhart* 1 p 388.

[13] [*HMC*], *Portland* [*MSS*], 4 pp 629–31, 646–7, 650–1, 10 pp 351–2.

[14] *Ibid* 10 p 352.

[15] [*The London Diaries of William*] *Nicolson*,[*1702–1718*, ed C. Jones and G. S. Holmes] (Oxford 1983) Dec 1710 and Jan to Mar 1711 *passim*.

General Assembly. This spurred the ministry into greater efforts to obstruct the Episcopalians' search for allies at Westminster, but with no success.[16]

Given the Whigs' strength in the Lords, the Episcopalians had to divide them on the issue to get the appeal through. They did this by bringing over almost the entire body of Whig bishops by the skilful presentation of the atypical Greenshields as an unexceptional Episcopalian clergyman.[17] Greenshields was unusual in that he was willing to abjure the Old Pretender and attest his fidelity to the protestant succession. This ploy made the Whigs and the Scots Presbyterian peers appear simply to be mouthing party-political cant when they asserted that Episcopalianism was synonymous with Jacobitism in Scotland. The appeal was heard on 1 March 1711 and the bishops' support proved decisive. The legality of the appeal was agreed *nem.con.*, despite the articles of Union, and the only division came on a motion to adjourn just after this. This was defeated by sixty-eight votes to thirty-two, with only two bishops dividing with the Whigs' and Scots Presbyterian peers' minority. Argyll and Islay then walked out in disgust and the Court mooted another adjournment on the grounds that their knowledge of Scots law and the case was indispensable. This was angrily rejected and the appeal upheld without a further division. Lord North and Grey and the earl of Abingdon wanted the sentence declared illegal so that the Edinburgh magistrates could be sued for damages, but this was legally too dubious even for the Tory zealots and the proposal was dropped.[18]

The Scots Presbyterians were outraged by the Greenshields decision, and rumours about the Episcopalians' next step turned their anger into near-hysteria. One story had the October Club, the Episcopalians and the high churchmen in Convocation plotting to overturn the religious settlement in Scotland *in toto*. Toleration and Patronage Bills were said to be being prepared. Argyll predicted imminent civil war.[19] The ministry intervened to calm the situation by asking the Episcopalians to drop any further measures they might be planning, only to be rebuffed. The Episcopalians were planning

[16] *Portland* 4 pp 652–3; *Lockhart* 1 pp 346–8.

[17] *Lockhart* 1 p 348; *Nicolson* 27 Feb 1711; [Edinburgh] S[cottish] R[ecord] O[ffice] Dalhousie Papers GD 45/14/352/2.

[18] *Nicolson* 1 Mar 1711; [Edinburgh] N[ational] L[ibrary of] S[cotland] Wodrow Letters Quarto 5, ep 110; SRO Dalhousie Papers GD 45/14/352/5.

[19] *Portland* 4 pp 663–5; NLS Wodrow Letters Quarto 5, epp 96, 106, 110; BL Additional MSS 17677 EEE, fols 110–12.

to introduce either a Toleration or a Patronages Bill, and refused to be put off. Only when the ministry prevailed with the queen personally to request that any such proposals be shelved did the Episcopalians agree, and then only on condition that the ministry would help to get a Toleration Bill through next session. Harley then wrote a mendacious letter to Carstares denying that rumours of a Toleration or Patronages Bill had any truth in them, and the situation in Scotland duly calmed down.[20]

The ministry was already on the retreat over the Episcopalian toleration issue. The Episcopalians in Parliament had made effective use of the appeal of their case to Anglican sentiment to force the Greenshields appeal through despite the Court's opposition. Moreover, they had been prevented from going further only by the ministry's last desperate trump: the queen. Harley almost certainly did not intend to honour his promise to aid the Episcopalians next session, but it was a measure of his difficulties that he had to make it at all.

British politics underwent serious upheaval in December 1711. During November, peace preliminaries which the ministry had secretly negotiated with France first became public knowledge. They were not well received by either party as Britain and the allies' gains by them looked distinctly meagre. After an initial near-disastrous defeat in the Lords on the question of the peace, and ominous signs of forthcoming trouble in the Commons, the Government retrieved the situation by winning back the support of the Tory rank-and-file and mass-creating twelve peers. Winning over the October Club was the most important part of the exercise, and the alliance had its price. As well as promises of extensive purges when the peace was completed, the ministry had to let the October Club have its way with regard to certain measures which the Club wanted carried on, one of which came to be Episcopalian toleration.

For all that it could not openly aid the Scots Presbyterians' efforts to stop the Scots Toleration Bill, the ministry did its covert best by trying to convince the Bill's backers not to introduce the measure at all. Oxford[21] enlisted the services of the place-hunting Greenshields and sent him round the Episcopalian leaders lobbying against a Toleration Bill on the grounds of 'unseasonableness'. When George

---

[20] *Lockhart* 1 pp 339–40; SRO Mar and Kellie MS GD 124/15/1020/14; [*HMC*] *Laing* [*MSS*] 2 p 61.

[21] Robert Harley was created earl of Oxford and Mortimer in May 1711.

Lockhart, Sir Simeon Stuart and Sir Alexander Areskine began to prepare the Bill for the Commons the ministry tried to persuade them to drop it. When they refused, the queen was persuaded to have a 'politick gout' during which illness she asked that the Bill be not introduced. They reluctantly agreed, but this only delayed the introduction for a week, and once the Bill began its passage the ministry gave up the fight and confined itself to expressions of sympathy to the Kirk's delegation based in London to lobby against the measure, while tacitly supporting it in Parliament. The government undoubtedly regarded the whole business as stupid mischief-making, but its alliance with the October Club and its already strained relations with the Scots Episcopalian peers in the aftermath of the Brandon patent case, forced it to back the measure.[22]

The Scots Toleration Bill was finally introduced into the Commons on 23 January 1712, with the full support of the October Club and the grudging support of the ministry.[23] Its passage then proceeded with a high-handed disregard to the constitutional niceties of any opposing case. George Baillie and John Pringle's objection that the Bill contravened the articles of Union (which it did) was dismissed. When Presbyterian MPs argued for the insertion of oaths of loyalty to the established order in Church and State, Lockhart threatened to put in one against the Solemn League and Covenant to be taken by all Scots clergymen. An amendment requiring Scots officials to be conforming members of the Church of Scotland, just as English officials were required to be conforming Anglicans, was rejected without a division. A motion to hear a petition from the Kirk against the Bill was summarily thrown out. The only amendment which did pass was one requiring all clergymen wishing to benefit from the Act to pray expressly for Queen Anne and the Electress Sophia at each religious service.[24] Even this amendment so offended some of the Episcopalians that they either boycotted the Bill's final reading or voted against it, thus contributing to the minority of seventeen who opposed the final passage after the Whigs walked out

[22] *Portland* 10 pp 379–80; *Lockhart* 1 pp 379–80; [*The*] Wentworth [*Papers, 1705–39*, ed J. J. Cartwright] (London 1882) pp 251–2; Stafford Staffordshire Record Office Dartmouth MS D 742/U/1/97; NLS Wodrow Letters Quarto 6, ep 104.
[23] *Wentworth* pp 247–51, 264–5; BL Portland Loan 29/143/3, 22 Mar 1712; NLS Wodrow Letters Quarto 6, ep 57.
[24] NLS Wodrow Letters Quarto 6, epp 56, 57, 65; [*House of*] C[*ommons'*] J[*ournals*] 17 pp 53–4; *Laing* 2 p 162.

in protest at the way the October Club had bulldozed the measure through. The majority for the Bill was 152.[25]

Getting the Toleration Bill through the Commons was relatively easy, but the Lords presented more difficulties. Whig, Presbyterian and moderate Tory numbers there were proportionately greater, and the Bill was liable to be substantially amended. The amendment the Episcopalians most feared was the addition of an abjuration oath. Because of their Jacobite sympathies a toleration dependent on such an oath would have been unacceptable to the overwhelming majority of the Episcopalian clergy. Lockhart therefore made a bargain with Carstares and Islay while the measure was in the Commons, agreeing to drop a clause removing the Kirk's power to oversee the morals of Episcopalian members of the community, in return for opposition being restricted to the whole Bill in the Lords. In essence the Presbyterians agreed not to put in wrecking amendments in the Lords. Once there, however, Islay and the Whigs reneged and put in an abjuration clause on second reading, claiming it was not an abjuration oath *per se*, but just resembled one.[26] This left the Episcopalians in an unenviable quandary. The abjuration clause was politically impossible to remove, and, faced with the appalling prospect of a Toleration Act excluding them, the Episcopalian clergy frantically beseeched the Bill's sponsors to drop the whole measure.[27] The Episcopalian MPs responded by altering the wording of the offending clause when the Bill returned to the Commons, making it unacceptable to Presbyterians as well as Episcopalians. This was done without the usual procedure of a conference with the Lords on the reamendments, so the Presbyterians felt confident the Lords would reject both the changes and the Bill. Instead, after extensive lobbying, the Episcopalians persuaded the Lords to accept the alterations after a division of fifty-six to forty, with nine bishops favouring the Presbyterian case.[28]

The Episcopalians followed up the passage of the Toleration Bill with a measure restoring ecclesiastical patronage to the control of lay owners from Kirk synods, and set up an investigation of the uses

[25] BL Additional MS 17677 FFF, fol 49; *CJ* 17 p 73.
[26] *Lockhart* 1 pp 379–80; *CJ* 17 p 69; BL Additional MS 17677 FFF, fol 56; NLS Wodrow Letters Quarto 6, epp 67, 70.
[27] NLS Wodrow Letters Quarto 6, epp 72, 74.
[28] *Lockhart* 1 pp 380–3; *CJ* pp 103–4; NLS Wodrow Letters Quarto 6, epp 75, 78; [Reading], B[erkshire] R[ecord] O[ffice] Trumbull Additional MS 136/3: Ralph Bridges to Sir William Trumbull, 3 Mar 1712.

made of former episcopal lands as a prelude to a resumption. The Presbyterians were demoralised by their experiences fighting the Toleration Bill, and offered no serious resistance to either. The Scots Toleration Act enforced an armed truce on both churches. Only about half of the Presbyterian clergy would take the oath, and then with an illegal preamble. Only fifteen of the Episcopalian clergy had taken it by November 1712. Local meetings of clergy of both communions unanimously refused the oath in some areas, notably in Glasgow.[29] By summer 1712 a schism that was to last until 1718 had split the Kirk between juring and nonjuring, 'Cameronian' clergy, with mass field-meetings, mutual excommunications and a bitter propaganda war waged on both sides.[30] This made both churches' friends in the magistracy reluctant to prosecute the other's nonjuring clergymen for fear of retaliation against nonjurors in their own church. Public opinion in Scotland was offended by the whole business. There were serious riots in Edinburgh in June 1712 during which one of the rioters' slogans was 'No abjuration'.[31] Moderate Presbyterian opinion in the political nation was alienated by these and subsequent developments, and decisively swung over to the Squadrone in the 1713 election, giving the Court interest in Scotland one of the few electoral defeats it was to suffer there before the 1832 Reform Act.

The Episcopalian campaign to obtain an acceptable legal toleration for their church offers a wide range of insights into the workings of contemporary politics. Religion dominated the parties' self-image. The October Club was in a state of incipient fragmentation in January 1712, yet it acted determinedly and unitedly to rescue fellow Anglicans from their Presbyterian foes. The Scots Episcopalian peers had their own quarrel with the rest of the Tory party as a consequence of the Brandon patent decision, but they reunited with them to ensure the Toleration Bill passed. Religion was the only issue which transcended all the internal divisions of the first Tory party. Even the earl of Nottingham, who angrily split with the rest of the party over the peace preliminaries in December 1711, vigorously

[29] BRO Trumbull Additional MS 136/3: Bridges to Trumbull, 21 Nov 1712; *Lockhart* 1 pp 384–5; *Portland* 5 pp 230–1; NLS Wodrow Letters Quarto 6, ep 103; SRO Breadalbane Papers GD 112/40/8/2/2.
[30] *Portland* 5 pp 217, 218–9; NLS Wodrow Papers Folio 35, ep 114; *Statutes at Large* 5 pp 23, 159–61.
[31] BL Additional MS 17677 FFF, fol 260; Oxford Bodleian Carte MSS 238, fols 233–5.

supported the Greenshields appeal and the Toleration Bill. Because of its hold on the imagination of the Tories, religion could mobilise the party in a way nothing else could, and at the same time bring out the growing ruthlessness of party ethics which had religion at their core. The numbers moved to act in Lords and Commons on Episcopalian issues from 1711 to 1712 demonstrates the power of the subject. In the same way the cynicism with which constitutional propriety and simple justice were ignored during the Toleration Bill's passage shows the dialectical development of the parties' willingness to abuse their Parliamentary strength, thus leading towards a one-party state. The behaviour of the bishops could be taken as evidence that party lines were not absolute, but they were in a uniquely invidious position. As spiritual leaders of the Anglican communion they could hardly justify condemning fellow Anglicans to continued legal penalisation (however rarely applied) at the hands of a Presbyterian state. The interesting aspect of their behaviour is how some bishops could not even ignore the call of party loyalty in such a case. Two bishops voted against the Greenshields appeal, nine against the Toleration Bill in its final form.

If the passage of the Toleration Bill gives us an insight into the essence of party, Presbyterian opposition to it demonstrates the hold that the concept of religious uniformity still had on many people. One of the main objections to the Toleration Bill was that it would be 'a seed of a perpetual division'. Exactly the same kind of argument was put forward two years later by Tories justifying the draconian Schism Bill of 1714. This has usually been seen as a reactionary aberration by the Tory party, but given that religion formed the central dynamic behind the concept and practice of contemporary parties, perhaps it was implicit in their nature to produce such measures. By regarding the Whig's aggressive extension of the basis for legal nonconformity as progressive, we may have lost sight of quite how much of a religious statement it was too, making Tory behaviour appear reactionary and aberrant when in context it was not.

One facet of contemporary politics clearly brought out by the events of 1711 and 1712 was the limited ability of political management to control party politics. The Harley ministry was consistently on the defensive against the Episcopalians' manoeuvres. It could not prevent them bringing in either the Greenshields appeal or the Toleration Bill, despite the fact that Harley was well aware that both would create problems in Scotland. All the Government could do in such cases was procrastinate in the hope that the problem would go away of its own accord. When both measures continued despite them the ministry had little choice but to go along with whatever the mass of the party demanded or risk being identified with the 'enemy'. Its powers seem to have been limited to little more than delaying matters and softening some of the more unpalatable aspects of their backbenchers' proposals. This weakness could be argued to be a feature only of measures which fired the religious zealotry of the parties, but if religion was central to political conflict then some reconsideration of the real powers of the great men of the time may be in order. An appropriate visualisation of the relationship between the political managers and their backbenchers may not be that of a shepherd and his sheep, but that of a huntsman with a pack of fierce mastiffs whom he must feed lest they devour him.

University of Sheffield

THE PERSECUTION OF FRENCH JESUITS
BY THE PARLEMENT OF PARIS 1761-71

by D. G. THOMPSON

IN THE 1760s the parlement of Paris undertook to destroy the Society of Jesus in the central one-third of France which it controlled, and to use its influence to gain the destruction of the order elsewhere.[1] Its immediate victims were the 1,200 Jesuits resident in 42 colleges and other institutions in its own territory in 1761, but it also claimed authority over any of the other 2,200 French Jesuits who had been born in its territory or might enter it.[2] By this time four French Jesuits in five were priests or future priests whose primary functions were preaching and teaching; the remaining one in five was a temporal coadjutor, often an administrator of property. This ratio prevailed in the groups with whom the parlement dealt.[3] The parlement viewed all Jesuits as enemies and regarded as a Jesuit any man who had ever made vows in that order. Then, as now, members of the Society of Jesus not only made the usual three religious vows but also owed complete obedience to their superior-general in Rome and were bound by the special vow of obedience to the sovereign pontiff taken by the professed of the order. The unique nature of the Jesuit institute was widely understood in France in the 1760s and was a reason for the respect shown to Jesuits by the privileged classes from which many Jesuits came and which they served so well.

Knowledge of the strength of their support in aristocratic and administrative circles and at the king's court encouraged the French Jesuits to remain firm in their vocation whatever the parlement

---

[1] Grants from the University of New Brunswick and the Canada Council made the research for this article possible. See Dale Van Kley *The Jansenists and the expulsion of the Jesuits from France, 1757-1765* (New Haven 1975) on factions within the parlement of Paris and the political-religious motivation of the policy-makers.

[2] [Paris] A[rchives] N[ationales] X^{1b}8953 Omer Joly de Fleury, advocate general, report in minutes [of the parlement of Paris] 8 May 1767; [Alexandre] Vivier [*Status Assistentiae Galliae Societatis Iesu 1762-68*] (Paris 1899) p xiii; and A[rchivum] R[omanum] S[ocietatis] I[esu] Gallo-Belge 23 fols 1-73; Fl–Bel 42 fols 262-71^v; also Rhin Sup 23 and Germ Sup 40.

[3] When the noun 'Jesuit' is used in this article, that ratio, confirmed by Vivier, obtains, unless otherwise indicated.

might do to them and caused it to proceed with caution lest by violent action it encourage the Jesuits' friends to rally to their defence. Thus, although the parlement wanted to destroy the Jesuit order by dealing harshly with the loyal members, it refrained from enacting all aspects of its anti-Jesuit policy at once. Instead, it introduced the policy piece-meal, as events rendered such a policy acceptable to a basically pro-Jesuit ecclesiastical and lay establishment. Even so, the crown did intervene to delay the implementation of the parlement's legislation. As a result of all these considerations, in the decade 1761–71, Jesuits subject to the parlement of Paris were dispersed, then banished, then tolerated and then banished under harsher conditions than before. As all this happened, French Jesuits experienced uncertainty, mental anguish and physical hardship which must have seemed interminable. This essay examines the parlement's implementation of its anti-Jesuit policy and the Jesuits' experience during the decade of persecution.[4]

The parlement argued that the continued existence in France of an order whose members pledged absolute obedience to a foreign superior-general constituted a danger to the established political order. Jesuits who remained loyal to the general could never be loyal subjects of the king of France or loyal servants of the Gallican church. To destroy the Jesuit order it would not be enough merely to expel Jesuits from their houses. Even dispersed Jesuits who remained loyal to their institute and general might one day resurrect the order in France. Such men must therefore be prevented from associating with one another and from exercising any public functions or influence. Individual Jesuits willing to renounce the Roman connexion might live normal lives. The parlement's officials in the *bailliages* and *sénéchaussées*, and police officials ensured that, in every corner of its territory and at the centre, the law should be obeyed.[5]

The first stage in the implementation of the parlement's anti-Jesuit policy began in August 1761, when the parlement issued legislation

---

[4] See *Les Etablissements des jésuites depuis quatre siècles* ed Pierre Delattre 5 vols (Enghien 1949–57) descriptions of the dispersal in 1762–4; also Ludwig von Pastor *History of the popes from the close of the middle ages* trans E. F. Peeler 40 vols (London 1950–3) 36 pp 415–19.

[5] For the execution of anti-Jesuit legislation the *procureur du roi* of the *bailliage* or *sénéchaussée* was responsible to the procurator general of the parlement of Paris, Guillaume Joly de Fleury, brother of the advocate general, who employed rigorous standards in judging the admissibility of evidence. See BN Coll[ection] Joly de Fleury 1617–29 and especially 1624 fols 134, 171.

condemning the Jesuit institute.[6] As a result, the parlement's Jesuits had to dismiss their novices, refrain from making religious vows, give up their revenues, send their pupils home and close their colleges by the beginning of April 1762. By then some 80 or 90 Jesuits, including 40 novices, resident in Jesuit institutions during the previous summer had gone home.[7] Between April and August 1762 the parlement's officials assumed control of the Jesuits' real property and the Jesuits stayed in their houses but got ready to leave.[8] Superiors reported that men were in a state of extreme agitation, not knowing what they would do in the future; superiors worried about finding the means to feed so many men.[9]

Dispersal officially occurred in August 1762. The Jesuits' religious vows were declared null and void. All Jesuits, now referred to by the parlement as the 'former, so-called Jesuits', had to give up their habit and leave their houses as soon as travel allowances and subsistence pensions for the first year could be paid by a parlementary official. Jesuits too ill to leave were to stay where they were and be treated by the court's doctors until well enough to travel. To Jesuits who wanted to go on teaching and preaching and performing other public functions, the parlement offered the opportunity to make the oath of August 1762, whereby they would forswear their constitutions and institute, their connexion with the general and the 'pernicious' morality allegedly taught by the Jesuit order regarding the person of kings. They would also swear to be loyal subjects of the king of France and to hold and profess the Gallican liberties and the Four Articles and to obey all aspects of the anti-Jesuit legislation issued by the parlement. Non-jurors might perform no public functions. For the moment there was no time limit for taking the oath.[10]

Any Jesuit over the age of 33 with little or no other income might request a subsistence pension of up to 400 livres a year for priests and up to 200 livres a year for temporal coadjutors.[11] There was no

---

[6] AN X^{1b}8940 *arrêts* [of the parlement of Paris] of 6 Aug 1761, 7 Sept 1761.

[7] See ARSI Hist Soc 273 fol 73 and Vivier, especially pp 136–8, 164–6; also AN X^{1b}8942 and X^{1b}8944 *états* [of Jesuits resident in the parlement's territory in Apr 1762].

[8] AN X^{1b}8940–2, especially *arrêt* of 23 Apr 1762. See also D. G. Thompson (unpub PhD thesis, University of British Columbia 1972).

[9] See for example ARSI Franc 49 fols 359, 430 and Hist Soc 273 fols 68–71, 75.

[10] AN X^{1b}8942 *arrêt* of 6 Aug 1762.

[11] Jesuits over 33 were in a state of civil death and unable to inherit or bequeath property. See also AN AD XVII, 23 act of *conseil d'état du roi* of 18 Aug 1773 on pensions.

allowance for young Jesuits. Pensions were paid by a royal official[12] on the parlement's recommendation, with the result that the parlement retained powers of compulsion over Jesuits dependent on pensions. On leaving their houses in the late summer and autumn of 1762, Jesuits were allowed to take with them a limited supply of personal property consisting mainly of linen.[13] They were ordered to withdraw to any part of the kingdom they chose and to live separately and privately in obedience to the king and the ordinary. They were not to communicate with one another.[14]

One thousand, one hundred and ten Jesuits were subject to the laws of August 1762.[15] Of these 457 gained royal pensions, but during the next 18 months only two or three took the oath of August 1762.[16] During the same period 844 of the 1,110 Jesuits of 1762 withdrew from the parlement's territory, most of them definitively.[17] In August 1762 it was still legal to be a Jesuit in most of the rest of France and at least 653 of the Jesuits then resident in the parlement's territory had not been born there. They had no reason to stay. In the following years the parlement dealt mainly with Jesuits born in its territory, though the harshness of its policy[18] meant that many in that category but resident elsewhere in 1762 never returned. Since the parlement required that its Jesuits stay within the kingdom, those who actually left France in 1762–4 rendered themselves ineligible for pensions. Jesuits with private incomes enjoyed freedom of movement and some established small communities in such places as Fribourg,

---

[12] BN F 23627 (127) *Actes royaux, lettres patentes du roi* of 2 Feb 1763.

[13] AN X^{1b}8942 *Arrêts* of 13 Aug 1762, 7 Sept 1762.

[14] *Ibid arrêt* of 6 Aug 1762.

[15] This is the total of the numbers cited in AN X^{1b}8942 and X^{1b}8944 *états*.

[16] AN X^{1b}9842 *état*, which lists Jesuits resident in the parlement's territory who had applied for a pension by 22 Feb 1763, cites 471 Jesuits who applied for pensions, including 14 who were refused them. See also BN Coll Joly de Fleury 1621 fol 106 and AN X^{1b}8946 *arrêt* of 9 Mar 1764, preamble.

[17] To arrive at the quantity 844 and, unless otherwise indicated, at all quantities cited hereafter in this article, I have compiled statistics based on the information in AN X^{1b}8942 and X^{1b}8944 *états*, BN Coll Joly de Fleury 1631 (the parlement's efforts to make sense of all the local officials' reports) and, above all, Coll Joly de Fleury 1617–29, local officials reports to the procurator general of the parlement. Comparisons have been made with *arrêts* dealing with oath-takers and Jesuits seeking to be declared legally infirm in AN X^{1b}8946–7 *arrêts* of Feb 1764 to Jun 1764. Totals have not always coincided exactly but have not diverged by more than ten percent. In cases of disagreement I have cited the more conservative figure.

[18] See Jean Egret 'Le Procès des jésuites devant les parlements de France (1761–1770)', *Revue historique* 204 (1950) pp 1–27.

NUMBERS OF JESUITS IN THE TERRITORY
CONTROLLED BY THE PARLEMENT OF PARIS
1761–1771*

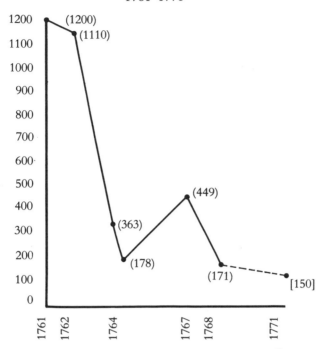

* Based on BN Collection Joly de Fleury 1617–31 and AN X^{lb} 8942 &
8944 *états* of Jesuits present in the territory of the parlement of Paris
23 Apr 1762.

Liège and Câteau-Cambrésis.[19] There were not many such men.
Most of the 639 who had not applied for pensions did not come from
wealthy families but were simply unwilling to seek a pension. Some
of these men went to Jesuit communities in Lorraine and Avignon.[20]
But it is likely that most withdrew to other parts of the kingdom and,
under the patronage of sympathetic bishops, took up ecclesiastical
positions, however humble, in which they remained unless affected
by harsh legislation promulgated by other parlements.[21]

---

[19] François Ducrest 'Séjour à Fribourg de trente-six jésuites français exilés, 1762–68',
  Annales fribourgeois 1 (1913) pp 254–69. Also ARSI Franc 49 fol 492 and BN Coll
  Joly de Fleury 1622 fol 356.
[20] Vivier pp 41–116, 175–99.
[21] See AN X^{lb}8953 Omer Joly de Fleury report in minutes 8 May 1767.

Those who remained within the territory of the parlement of Paris had few alternatives. Denied the right to live together or associate with each other, a few found bishops willing to employ them in public priestly functions until the parlement's officials put a stop to that.[22] Many took up life with their families again. A handful of temporal coadjutors and scholastics not yet ordained as priests chose to marry and to found their own families. Other Jesuits returned to elderly parents or younger relations. A new phenomenon developed. Jesuits in receipt of royal pensions lived in family homes and shared their pensions with otherwise indigent families. Jesuits became heads and pillars of families.[23]

The second stage in the application of the parlement's anti-Jesuit policy began in February 1764. Apparently disappointed that Jesuits had not taken the oath of August 1762, the parlement claimed that pro-Jesuit publications of the previous two years were proof of a plot to resurrect the institute in France. It therefore issued legislation which altered the conditions under which Jesuits born or resident in its territory might remain in France. The new legislation was harsher than that of 1762. All Jesuits now had to take a new oath against their constitutions, institute and general and against allegedly 'pernicious' Jesuit beliefs. Failure to take the oath of February 1764 would result for all except those judged too ill or too old to travel, in expulsion from France.[24] Pensions would be paid abroad.[25] Those who took the oath of February 1764 had four years in which to take the one of August 1762 and resume a normal life.[26]

The anti-Jesuit legislation of February reinforced by that of March 1764 affected at least 363 Jesuits resident in the parlement's territory, of whom 266 had been there in 1762 and 97 had entered the territory since 1762. No able-bodied Jesuit, however influential, could escape the major provisions of the new legislation.[27] Those with wealthy patrons could avoid exile from France by withdrawing to territories controlled by less unfriendly parlements.[28] But only those judged to be infirm were allowed to remain in the parlement's territory. A hundred and eighty-eight Jesuits applied to be exempt from the new

---

[22] Compare BN Coll Joly de Fleury 1625 fol 4; 1626 fol 92; 1627 fols 5, 12, 221.
[23] BN Coll Joly de Fleury 1617–29 *passim*.
[24] AN X^{lb}8946 *arrêts* of 22 Feb 1764, 9 Mar 1764.
[25] As by AN AD XVII, 23 act of *Conseil d'état du roi* of 27 Jul 1764.
[26] *Ibid* 23 *arrêt* of 13 May 1768.
[27] See for example BN Coll Joly de Fleury 1629 fols 165–7^v.
[28] See for example *ibid* 1625 fol 292.

legislation on grounds of ill-health, advanced age, or both. Virtually all were examined by the court's doctors who recommended that the court exempt 26 from the provisions of the legislation. The court ordered at least 149 Jesuits claiming to be infirm to obey the legislation and to leave the kingdom.[29]

Now, in significant numbers, Jesuits did take the oath against their institute and general. Of the 363 Jesuits resident in the parlement's territory in early 1764, 139 took the oath of February 1764. Half of them had been under 33 in 1762 and were therefore without pensions, and 17 were old men unable to accept the prospect of another move. Twenty-six who took that oath, took the oath of August 1762 at the same time.[30] Some 30 other Jesuits undertook to make declarations of loyalty to the king which they hoped would suffice in place of the oath and were found liable for expulsion.[31] By the end of April 1764, the 139 jurors, along with the handful of men judged to be infirm, were the only Jesuits allowed by the parlement to stay in France. Even for jurors the future would be difficult. The 113 who had taken only the second oath had managed to maintain the living arrangements they had established since August 1762 and could continue to live on their pensions. But they also had to live with troubled consciences in greater isolation from other Jesuits than before. Several of the 26 who had taken both oaths and looked forward to the end of isolation and penury were disappointed. On the grounds that they had betrayed their institute, bishops refused to employ them.[32] Three Jesuits who took the oath in fear in March retracted it in the course of the next eight months and were pursued and threatened with imprisonment.[33] Men who refused to obey the law ran the same risk and the authorities did not hesitate to arrest, imprison and question anyone identified as a Jesuit who stopped in the parlement's territory. In this way the parlement gained detailed information about the activities of French Jesuits in other locations.[34] Any news of French Jesuit achievements elsewhere excited the parle-

---

[29] AN X^lb8946 *arrêts* of Mar 1764 and Apr 1764 and BN Coll Joly de Fleury 1631 fols 176^v–80^v.
[30] AN X^lb8946 *arrêts* of Mar 1764 and Apr 1764 and BN Coll Joly de Fleury 1631 fols 43–6, 173–5. See also AN X^lb8946 *arrêt* of 9 Mar 1764, preamble. The 139 jurors included 93 priests and scholastics and 42 temporal coadjutors, a higher than usual proportion of the latter.
[31] *Ibid arrêts* of Mar 1764 and Apr 1764 and BN Coll Joly de Fleury 1623 fols 209, 279.
[32] *Ibid* 1622 fol 115; 1627 fol 221.
[33] *Ibid* 1631 fols 193–5.
[34] *Ibid* 1622 fol 356.

ment to new determination to crush the loyal Jesuits over whom it had power.

For non-jurors, things were much worse than for jurors in the period after February 1764. To avoid harassment and possible imprisonment, non-jurors had to leave the parlement's territory as quickly as possible. To continue to receive pensions, they had to establish their residence outside France. They received no *viaticum* this time, but could wait for the payment of the next instalment of their pension before leaving.[35] Often travelling on foot and sometimes on horseback, French Jesuits, including some in poor health, spilled over the frontiers at the points closest to their previous homes. They went to Flanders, the German states, Lorraine, Switzerland, north Italy, Avignon and Spain. Sometimes they joined established small French Jesuit communities. As their numbers increased they became the object of host authorities' suspicions and sometimes found borders closed to them. Some lived as fugitives in foreign places.[36]

Besides the physical hardship of leaving, being alone and having to provide for all their needs from their pensions, exiled Jesuits suffered the mental anguish of having had to abandon families with whom they had so recently made new lives and who had become dependent on their pensions and skills. One Jesuit with a dependent niece obeyed the law despite his infirmities and had to live in a barn.[37] Another with a dependent mother and physical complaints of his own was expelled despite his petition to be allowed to stay.[38] And there is no sadder story arising from the expulsion than that of the temporal coadjutor in his fifties who thought that by marrying he had proved that he had abandoned his old way of life but who, though he bore his wife great friendship, could not bring himself to take the oath. Instead, he took the long road to Avignon.[39]

By November 1764, when the king issued an edict whose effect was to undo much of the parlement's legislation passed earlier in the year, the 178 jurors and men legally judged to be infirm together with those who had evaded the law were the only Jesuits left in the parlement's territory. The royal edict suppressed the Society of Jesus in all parts of France except Lorraine and the region of Avignon and

---

[35] AN X^{1b}8946 *arrêt* of 13 Apr 1764.
[36] See ARSI Hist Soc 273 fols 75, 82 and BN Coll Joly de Fleury 1620 fols 9–10.
[37] See BN Coll Joly de Fleury 1622 fol 176.
[38] *Ibid* 1628 fols 118–27.
[39] *Ibid* 1626 fols 211–18.

guaranteed the French Jesuits' right to live privately in France.[40] The parlement of Paris registered it with serious provisos in December 1764; it required the non-jurors to live separately in obedience to the king and ordinary in the diocese of their birth and to report to officials of their *bailliage* or *sénéchaussée* at six-monthly intervals. Non-jurors were to avoid going within ten leagues of Paris; those born in or near the capital were to arrange with the parlement's officials to live elsewhere.[41] Any Jesuit who had taken the oath of February 1764 might live where he chose; any who had taken both oaths might live and perform public functions wherever he wished.[42] During the following 28 months, 271 Jesuits born in the parlement's territory returned to that territory or appeared there for the first time since 1762, and five jurors who had suffered anxiety since taking the oath of February 1764 came forward to retract it.[43]

The new law of December 1764 enabled Jesuits to return to the parlement's territory, but many found it inconvenient to live in the diocese of their birth and to report, as the parlement required, at six-monthly intervals. Jesuits whose families no longer lived in the place where they had been born asked to join their families.[44] Elderly and sick Jesuits returning to France and seeking to live in the place, other than their birthplace, where they had been cared for prior to March 1764 petitioned the court.[45] One temporal coadjutor wanted to live with a non-Jesuit friend at some distance from his own home because the friend promised to find him work to supplement his inadequate pension.[46] All such requests were refused. And the parlement sent its officials to be sure that the law was obeyed. The parlement was slightly more ready to grant requests from elderly, infirm Jesuits to be allowed to report to a more convenient location than the one decreed by the parlement, but it exempted no one from the responsibility for reporting at six-monthly intervals to officials answerable to the parlement.[47]

The Paris authorities tried to enforce as rigorously as possible the

[40] AN AD XVII, 23 *édit du roi* of Nov 1764.
[41] AN X¹ᵇ8948 *arrêt* of 1 Dec 1764.
[42] BN Coll Joly de Fleury 1624 fol 206; 1625 fols 92–3.
[43] *Ibid* 1631 fols 193–5.
[44] See *ibid* 1617 fol 385; 1618 fols 159–61.
[45] See *ibid* 1618 fol 351; 1620 fols 311–2.
[46] *Ibid* 1620, 336–41.
[47] AN X¹ᵇ8949–51 *arrêts* of May 1765 to Mar 1766 and BN Coll Joly de Fleury 1628 fol 6.

requirement that Jesuits not live in or near the capital. The police spy system kept the authorities informed of rumours regarding the presence of an influential or powerful Jesuit in Paris but was not always able to produce the man. Nevertheless, between December 1764 and May 1767, the *lieutenant général de police* apprehended some 21 Jesuits whom he obliged to leave the capital.[48] Jesuits born there had some say in where they were relocated.[49] By the end of April 1767, probably because the situation of Jesuits elsewhere in France had deteriorated, there were at least 449 Jesuits in the territory of the parlement of Paris, 254 of whom had been there in 1762 and 195 of whom had lived elsewhere in French territory that year. Until May 1767 they lived under the parlement's law of December 1764.

These, then, were the men who experienced the third stage in the application of the parlement's anti-Jesuit policy. In May 1767 the parlement took stock of the Jesuit's behaviour over the previous five years. It observed that since 1761 very few of the original 1,200 Jesuits had done anything to prove their loyalty to their sovereign and their country. French Jesuits were unworthy of the grace granted them in the king's edict of November 1764. The pope should be encouraged to suppress the Society of Jesus through the world. In the meantime, French Jesuits were guilty of the same sort of crimes and deserved the same treatment as the Spanish.[50] The parlement therefore restored the law of March 1764 with harsh modifications. This time no man who had previously refused to take one or both oaths could take either. Any Jesuit who had not previously taken the oath of February 1764 had to leave France.[51] Royal pensions would be paid to exiled Jesuits provided they established a foreign residence and used the services of specially appointed Paris notaries.[52] Again there was no *viaticum* but Jesuits without the necessary resources could wait until a portion of their pension was paid before leaving France.[53] Jesuits too old or ill to travel were to be exempt from the law and the court's doctors recommended this status for 62 Jesuits. The king did not intervene to undo this legislation, which was in force until the suppression of the parlement in 1771–4.

---

[48] *Ibid* 1629 fols 187–90.
[49] AN X^{1b}8949 *arrêt* of 8 Mar 1765.
[50] AN X^{1b}8953 Omer Joly de Fleury report in minutes 8 May 1767.
[51] *Ibid arrêt* of 9 May 1767.
[52] AN AD XVII, 23 *arrêt* of 4 Aug 1767.
[53] BN Coll Joly de Fleury 1622 fols 73–84; 1631 fols 109–17.

In the months after the promulgation of the parlement's anti-Jesuit legislation of May 1767 some 261 Jesuits disappeared from the parlement's territory; including 15 who died, at least 207 non-jurors or retractors of the oath and some who, though ill, were too proud to ask permission to stay.[54] Some were being exiled for the second time. Again the authorities pursued Jesuits who disobeyed the law and after May 1767 arrested and imprisoned a number of Jesuits for retraction of the oath and other offences. The parlement still sought information about French Jesuits abroad and imprisoning and interrogating likely travellers was one way to get it. Other Jesuit prisoners were unable to provide information. One, who had previously suffered remorse for taking the oath, retracted it and went mad. He was interned in the Bicêtre and died there.[55]

The second expulsion brought even greater suffering than the first to Jesuits who had resumed family life. Several Jesuits were the sole support of their family; their departure would mean its ruin and great suffering for an elderly parent.[56] Two Jesuit priests wanted to stay to help their widowed sister-in-law adminster their nephews' property and oversee their nephews' education.[57] Another priest who took refuge in Switzerland had provided a home for a young niece who, like so many others, had become dependent on the pension he shared with her. Knowing how cruel the coming winter would be to her, he beseeched the court to allow him to return to attend to her affairs.[58] A temporal coadjutor who was ill wanted to be left with his family, who had looked after him in return for a share of his small pension.[59] The parlement denied all these requests. In this exile, which had no official end, Jesuits were able to go to fewer places of refuge than before. Flanders and Spain were already closed to them and other places soon would be.

In 1768 the Jesuit order was suppressed in the border regions of France previously exempt from the king's edict of November 1764.[60] The parlement reopened the question of who might remain in France. Seventeen of the 62 Jesuits recognized the year before as infirm, now had to leave the kingdom. Then, late in 1768, the court

[54] *Ibid* 1620 fol 324.
[55] *Ibid* 1628 fols 63–74; also 1624 fols 22, 91–6, 354; 1625 fols 149, 156; 1626 23ᵛ–32.
[56] *Ibid* 1617 fols 84–5, 94; 1619 fol 441; 1622 fols 300–2.
[57] *Ibid* 1621 fols 81–9.
[58] *Ibid* 1622 fol 341.
[59] *Ibid* fol 7.
[60] Vivier pp xxi–xxiii.

received a report on the number of Jesuits in its territory. Probably no more than 171 were still there at that time. These included 112 who had taken the second oath, 45 judged to be infirm and for that reason allowed to stay and 14 whose status was still undecided.[61] The infirm were removed from their families and placed individually in hospitals where security was assured.[62] Then, between 1768 and the parlement's own suppression in 1771, old age and illness took their toll. Probably no more than 150 Jesuits remained in the parlement's territory at the beginning of 1771.[63] They were too old or too sick or too anxious to forget their association with the Jesuit order to be in evidence. This remnant of the order could never have reestablished the Society of Jesus in France. The parlement had ensured that the Jesuit order should not be resurrected by eliminating from its territory all able-bodied Jesuits who had remained loyal to their institute and general.

To achieve this end, it had submitted the Jesuits who had refused to renounce their Roman connexion to three exiles from established residences in France, prevented them from practising their sacred ministries or other public functions, hounded them out of its territory and out of their country, reduced them and sometimes their families to indigence, imprisoned them or assigned them to hospitals from which there was no release and prevented them from communicating with their friends. Above all, it had denied them the right to pursue their chosen vocation and had condemned them to enforced idleness with all its ills at home and caused them to live in extreme poverty in uncertain refuges abroad. By maintaining an administration which constantly pressed individual Jesuits to obey its harsh laws, the parlement succeeded in gaining its end without employing physical violence against its victims. So long as it pursued that policy, there was no significant outcry against its methods or perceptible complaint about the results. The Jesuits subject to the parlement of Paris disappeared from public view almost without leaving trace, and no public authority decried their loss. By persecuting French Jesuits in 1761–71 the parlement of Paris attained precisely the ends it desired. And by retaining the full series of docu-

---

[61] BN Coll Joly de Fleury 1631 fols 27–61 and AN AD XVII, 23 *arrêt* of 6 May 1768.
[62] *Ibid arrêt* of 6 May 1768.
[63] Compare Yves Blayo, 'La Mortalité en France de 1740 à 1829', *Population* (special issue (Nov 1975) pp 123–42 at p 126.

ments on the administration of its anti-Jesuit policy, the parlement also assured that the record of the Jesuits' sufferings at its hands should not be entirely lost.[64]

University of New Brunswick, Canada

[64] BN Coll Joly de Fleury 1609–31, especially.

'NO LAW WOULD BE GRANTED US': INSTITUTIONAL PROTESTANTISM AND THE PROBLEM OF CATHOLIC POVERTY IN ENGLAND 1839–42*

by GERARD CONNOLLY

FTER THE Rebellion (of 1745) a soldier, on return from Manchester, called at Stretford and tarried at a public house. A man who was a bitter enemy to my parents because they were Papists, dropt into the soldier's company, and they drank till they were intoxicated. The man told the soldier that if he would go to my father's house, and demand a sum of money he might have it because we were Papists and no law would be granted us. The soldier came and without apology entered the house. Providentially my father was from home, or it would have cost him his life. The soldier having loaded his fire-lock, clapped it to my mother's breast and demanded money. . . . As the soldier was putting the money into his pocket my mother laid hold of the fire-lock, and giving it to me, I immediately ran away and hid it. She then seized the robber by the collar of his coat and shook him, tho' he was a lusty man and thrusting him out of the door locked it. My father came home and procured a constable to apprehend the soldier and he was brought to our house; but upon acknowledging his fault and returning the money, he was dismissed.[1]

This extract is taken from the autobiography of John Morris, born in 1734 to spend his childhood amongst the Catholic community gathered around the Trafford family's estate between Salford and Manchester. Recalling his youth, Morris provided a moving account of the trials likely to beset a dissenter growing up in rural England on the eve of industrialization.

One day I went with my brother to bathe in the river. We found upon the bank a man whom I knew to be an inveterate enemy to

* I am indebted to the Leverhulme Foundation for financial support during the writing of this short paper.
[1] *Arminian Magazine* 17 (Jan 1795) p 19 (quotation abbreviated). *Ibid* pp 18–23, (Feb) pp 71–6, (Mar) pp 122–6 for Morris's Life.

my father on account of religion. When we had stript to go into a shallow part of the river the fellow seized us both by the hair and thew us into a hole where the water was two yards deep. He then left us, swearing that papish children were like witches, they would never sink. We rose again and the stream carried us to the other side from whence we crossed the river in a shallow part to our clothes.[2]

Hair raising though these incidents may seem, I doubt if either demonstrate much beyond a tolerable level of mutual disrespect between otherwise preoccupied sections of English society. While technically speaking Catholics continued to be religious outlaws until 1778, more searching enquiry has, of late, questioned whether this meant their being any more disadvantaged than any other nonconforming community. That Catholics remained at risk from the determined is, of course, undeniable. In the end, however, Morris's experiences seem more an appropriate reminder of the contrary quality of village life and its precariousness in an age when interpersonal relationships probably counted for at least as much as the intentions of legislators.

Interestingly, Morris, later propelled towards guilt, conversion and Methodism by a combination of signs, dreams and a spine-chilling visitation from something oddly resembling Marley's ghost, himself attributed his subsequent life of public harrassment not to the notion that the law afforded him no remedy, but rather to a lack of understanding emanating from society compounded by the behaviour of individuals who ought to have known better. It is somewhat ironic that, after witnessing the likes of John Nelson, Peter Jaco and John Wesley given short shrift by the mob and subjected to popular abuse himself, he had particular cause to rue the 'torrent of persecution' visited upon him by his own Catholic relations and former friends. A quote from scripture constantly before his mind, 'And a man's foes shall be those of his own household' probably says as much about religious mentalities in this respect as anything.[3]

Catholics were able to obtain a considerable measure of helpful legal freedom in the second half of the eighteenth century, prior to nineteenth-century admittance to full rights—and it seems worth adding here, obligations—of citizenship by the English state. In

---

[2] *Ibid* (Jan) pp 19–20 (quotation abbreviated).
[3] *Ibid* (Feb) pp 71–4.

common with most dissenters this lengthy process was progressively accompanied less by gratitude than by a rising tide of self-righteousness, further grievances and a chorus of discontent at the preferential status of the Established Church. Yet despite the collective nature of this experience Catholics were perhaps unique both in the vigour with which by the mid nineteenth century they had begun to seek satisfaction by pursuing a separate existence from mainstream English society, and in the depth of their conviction that English law was the instrument of a vendetta directed unmistakeably against them.[4]

The reasons behind an intensification of ill-will towards their native legislature—so much so that 'no law would be granted us' looks more at home as a cry of mid-nineteenth-century Roman Catholic chagrin—are varied. Some appear obvious, the situation of Irish Catholicism, for example; others less so, such as the ambitions of the Catholic clergy and that subject an aspect of which I intend outlining here: namely the tense relationship which came to exist between the Catholic citizen and emerging agencies of governmental policy. For as the Catholic population grew disproportionately at the economic level most dependent upon forms of assistance or public opportunity, then too were Catholics thrust into contact on an extensive scale with those institutions of central government regulation which were to lay the foundations of modern interventionism, yet which still reflected the character of a self-consciously Protestant state. Education, enlistment, detention and welfare cover most eventualities. And as fewer places demonstrate their workings better than the towns of Morris's boyhood, I have chosen partly to investigate the last in Manchester and Salford as representative of progress, or lack of it, in this relationship. Also, since, if one choses to leave aside health services, welfare must be taken here to involve almost exclusively mitigation of the effects of destitution, then it presents Catholics facing arguably their least voluntary association with the problem in general.[5]

Institutional Protestantism, a title under which I have previously

---

[4] For two early attempts to assess such legislation, C. Butler, *An historical account of the laws respecting Roman Catholics, etc.* (London 1795) and J. B. Brown, *An historical account of the law enacted against Catholics* (London 1813).

[5] As far as I am aware public hospitals never gained the notorious reputation for religious sharp practice amongst Catholics as did the Workhouse network. I attribute this to their broadly independent status and a possible Irish disinclination at first to exploit in-patient treatment.

introduced this topic, would seem a self-explanatory definition.[6]
Moreover, ruling out unequivocal private enterprise, the scope of interpretation in effect extends only to the Poor Law and even then, precluding Out Relief, to none but those *confined* to its premises.[7] In short, concern here is with indigence at its most constraining.[8]

In spite of the restrictive scope of the definition, in Manchester and Salford there were a substantial number of baptised Catholics whose personal liberties were circumscribed by incarceration in one of the Poor (later Work) Houses. Under the old 'autonomous' system a House was erected in Manchester in 1754, and replaced in 1792; while another was put up in Salford the following year. Later, with some reservations, both adopted the provisions of the Amendment Act of 1834; Salford in 1839 and Manchester in 1840.[9] In 1842 when a first approximate survey of establishments and inmates becomes possible, the Manchester Union ran three, possibly four, Houses, at least two of them branch houses with schools for children; Salford two, one a branch house and school. The Chorlton Union, formed from the townships to the south of Manchester in 1837, possessed a single Poor House with schooling facilities. Together, the total number of internees as an annual average stood at around 2,000 in what was admittedly a boom time for pauperism. Of these it seems likely that a third were baptised Catholics.[10] I say here baptised Catholics as a predicament likely to exacerbate any Catholic distrust of Poor Law authorities was that of a growing percentage of Irish immigrants whose notions of Catholicism made them unaware of

---

[6] [G. P.] Connolly, 'Catholicism in Manchester [and Salford 1770–1850',] (unpublished PhD thesis, vols 1–3 Manchester University 1980), see here 2 pp 178–247 especially p 193 et seq. Also [J. Morris (no relation), *The] English Poor Laws [and the Catholic Poor]* (London 1860).

[7] See *Reports of the Manchester and Salford District Provident Society* (Manchester 1833–58) and *Rules and By-Laws of the Manchester and Salford Asylum for Female Penitents* (Manchester 1823) as examples of the 'private enterprise' to which I refer. Compare here *Rules for the Government of the Poor House in Manchester* (Manchester 1800).

[8] The comparison with the overworked concept of institutionalized violence is tempting, Connolly 'Catholicism in Manchester' 2 pp 193–4, though I now think less convincing.

[9] [G. B.] Hindle, [*Provision for the Poor in Manchester 1754–1826*] (Manchester 1975) pp 1–39, and Connolly 'Catholicism in Manchester' 2 p 196 et seq. Also D. A. Farnie, 'The Establishment of the New Poor Law in Salford 1838– 50', (unpub BA dissertation, Manchester University 1951) p 5 et seq, and J. R. Wood, 'The Transition from the old to the new Poor Law system in Manchester', (unpub BA dissertation Manchester University 1938) pp 1–97 esp. pp 8–16. Compare here N. C. Edsall, The *Anti Poor Law Movement 1834–44* (Manchester 1971) pp 105–218.

[10] Connolly 'Catholicism in Manchester' 2 pp 212–14.

the necessity to practice their religion regularly and publicly by frequenting Mass and the Sacraments.[11] Just why this should have proved pertinent to a breakdown in relations can be seen by considering the opportunities afforded to Catholic clergymen for access to inmates.

Under the terms of the old Poor Law in Manchester and Salford the priest's right of access to Catholics within the House looks to have been established early through tacit exemption from religious obligations arising from the strong Protestant flavour of House rules. Precisely what this, a relationship dependent upon goodwill on both sides, offered Catholic clergymen can be deduced from the frequent visits of the resident missioner Rowland Broomhead to the House, and provision for Catholic children to attend Catholic Sunday Schools and to allow Mass on the premises.[12] Though the Catholic priest, as with other dissenting ministers, retained no official status within the House comparable to that of the Anglican chaplain, whose duties theoretically encompassed all religious activities conducted in the establishment, there appears to have survived no complaint nor tradition of sour feeling on the part of self-styled Catholic chaplains and their community. Quite plainly the relationship was one of an acceptable *modus vivendi*.[13]

The initial outcome of the intrusion of the law of 1834 upon many such customary practices was, as one might expect, counter productive. Clause XIX of the act provided that:

no rules orders or regulations of the said Commissioners nor any bye laws at present in force or to be hereafter made, shall oblige any inmate of any workhouse to attend any religious service which may be celebrated in a mode contrary to the religious principles of such inmate, nor shall authorize the education of any child in such workhouse in any religious creed other than that professed by the parents or surviving parent of such child, and to which such parents or parent shall object or in the case of an orphan to which the godfather or godmother shall object; provided also that it shall and may be lawful for any licensed minister of the religious persuasion of any inmate of such work-

---

[11] [G. P.] Connolly, ['"With more than ordinary devotion to God": The] Secular Missioner of the North [in the Evangelical Age of the English Mission'] *North West Catholic History* 10 (1983) pp 8–31.

[12] Connolly 'Catholicism in Manchester' 2 pp 200–1 and also *Manchester Poor House Book*, (1790) pp 122– 3, M3/3/5, City Archives, Manchester.

[13] Connolly 'Catholicism in Manchester' 2 pp 201–4.

house at all times in the day, (and night), on the request of such
inmate to visit such workhouse for the purpose of affording religious instruction to such inmate and also for the purpose of instructing his child or children in the principles of their
religion.[14]

Brave Whig idealism. Before long, however, conflicting interpretations of what had seemed quite unambiguous English forced those
Commissioners to intervene, not least to prevent the workhouse
from becoming the battleground for religious enthusiasts claiming a
right to proselytize there as licensed under clause XIX.[15] A minute
was necessary to settle the Catholic clergyman's equality of opportunity with other dissenting ministers, and orders had to be made to
force incoming clergy to comply with household discipline. Soon
also legal opinion upheld the privilege of Anglicans solely to occupy
the official post of chaplain, resulting in the proviso of parental consent being waived when the chaplain acted in his official capacity.[16]
Thus the Established minister was restored to his prerogatives in the
hope that he would continue not to abuse them. For the rest it seems
it was a case of *plus ça change, tout le meme*, and access to religious dissenters reverted to reliance upon working relationships within a
stricter legal framework.

Readjustment was well under way when the Manchester Union
was formed, and within three years the Board of Guardians was able
to inform the Commissioners that in the house,

Provision is also made for Roman Catholic inmates; their priests
to hold two regular services on the Sabbath and render such
attentions on the week days as to them may appear necessary.[17]

These arrangements were made since it was at first thought to be a
contravention of the intent of the new legislation to allow paupers to
leave the House for any purpose, particularly on a Sunday. And despite minor hiccups Catholics, originally suspicious of the new code,

[14] See 1834 4 & 5 Will. iv c 76. (*An act for the better Administration of the laws relating to the Poor in England and Wales*).
[15] *Fifth [Annual] Report [of the Poor Law] Commissioners*, 1839 (239) xxi. Appendix A pp 43–6. Also *Seventh [Annual] Report [of the Poor Law] Commissioners*, 1841 (327) xi. Appendix B pp 134–5, and *Eighth [Annual] Report [of the Poor Law] Commissioners*, 1842 (389) xix. Appendix A p 50.
[16] *Fifth Report Commissioners* pp 43–6. Also Connolly 'Catholicism in Manchester' 2 pp 214–5. Here compare [O.] Chadwick, [*The Victorian Church*,] (3 edn London 1971) 1 pp 95–8.
[17] *Seventh Report Commissioners* p 136, and also Hindle p 41; Connolly 'Catholicism in Manchester' 2 pp 202–4.

appear to have settled down to resume reasonable access on an amicable basis. In Salford in 1841 the diplomatic qualities of their non legal chaplain Roger Glassbrook brought a generous measure of assistance for their special problems. On his respectfully indicating that he knew of Catholic children present at Protestant services, leave was granted for children in the Pendleton branch House to attend the Catholic school on Sundays. Doubtless a smooth dialogue here owed something to the election of a Catholic Guardian, John Leeming. Even so, compromise with 'Popery' in this enclave of popular anti-Catholicism was no foregone conclusion, as proved by subsequent protests from Salford's Protestant sentinel, Hugh Stowell.[18]

Inexplicably Glassbrook was removed only months after arriving by the very man who had assigned him his commission, George Brown who,[19] much against his inclination, had been bishop and Vicar Apostolic in Lancashire since 1840. A tenacious, foul-tempered clericalist, Brown had begun a series of tough administrative reforms which had the effect of stamping the Catholic community there with some greater semblance of Tridentine orthodoxy.

One of the obstacles to such a reorientation was the far from uniform hold of modern religious conformism amongst immigrant Catholics to which I have alluded. In Liverpool in 1842 clergymen estimated that scarcely one-tenth of baptised Catholics practised.[20] Growth in the number of institutionalized Catholics therefore—and in Manchester by 1833 the Irish and their dependants in receipt of relief had increased fivefold over the preceding decade,[21]— must have represented a singularly worrying trend. Industrial priorities, easy settlement, and unfortunate legal marital stipulations of Catholics before 1837 all combined with a high level of parental neglect amongst Irish paupers so that the local institutions were increasingly peopled by those very baptised Catholics the missioners were des-

[18] Connolly 'Catholicism in Manchester' 2 pp 204–5, and [*Salford Union*] *Minute Book*, (1841) pp 42, 89, 250. L/GS/AM/2 [Metropolitan Council Archives, Salford]. Also here [L.] Woodward, [*The Age of Reform, 1815–70,*] (Oxford 1979) pp 454–5.

[19] For Brown, Connolly 'Catholicism in Manchester' 3 pp 437–45.

[20] W. Gillespie *The Christian Brothers in England 1825–1880* (Bristol 1975) p 97, and see Connolly 'Secular Missioner of the North' pp 12–14, 18–21. It seems likely that standards of Catholic practice recovered only slowly and with fluctuations in Liverpool. Gillespie's sources may have exaggerated totals, but not necessarily proportions.

[21] [*Royal Commission on the condition of the Poorer Classes in Ireland Appendix G, The State of the*] *Irish Poor in* [*Great*] *Britain*, 1836 (40) xxxiv. pp 44, 45–50.

perate to reach, but who were hardly likely to seek their services *un-prompted*. This was especially true of children literally dumped on the leypayers by adults decamping elsewhere.[22] Though these children were in urgent need of instruction, the priest was continually thwarted in his approach to such inmates by the requirement of parental consent. In the twin town this impasse had been made that much worse by overwork and a crippling mortality rate amongst the Catholic clergy themselves who, during the crucial formative years of the new Poor Law between 1839 and 1841, seem to have been precluded from anything more than at best cursory visits to the institutions in their care.[23]

It was to help remedy this that Brown had charged Glassbrook with full-time chaplaincy faculties, *a latere*, dispatching him to Manchester and another missioner to Liverpool to cover institutional demands.[24] The situation required the mending of broken fences and thus tact and patience; virtues which by 1841 look to have been running short among Catholics in England. It does then seem ominous that Glassbrook, having made a promising start, was summarily replaced by a man as near as possible his complete antithesis.

Andrew McCartney[25] was an Irish convert, previous to his ordination a professional soldier and an Orangeman. The individual talent he brought to his new job was seemingly a practised skill in shooting from the hip to back up a suitably inverted attitude of what later became known by the slogan 'no surrender'. He assumed his position on 10 October 1841 and barely a month later the Salford Union received from him the first of a series of brash complaints and some undisguised petty-fogging, directed at virtually every local internment institution.[26] He denounced the accommodation afforded him, criticised in-House services, objected to buildings being inconveniently sited, berated parental safeguards which he insisted were manipulated against him, took umbrage when asked to cooperate with internal procedures, demanded parity with the Anglican chaplain, and derided almost everyone connected with the management of institutional law at both local and national level.

[22] *Ibid* pp 44–5. *See also List of Children sent to the Poor School at Swinton* (1846–64), M4/20/1, City Archives, Manchester.
[23] Connolly 'Catholicism in Manchester' 2 p 206.
[24] (George Brown) *Status Religionis* (Lancashire District 1840–1?) p 5, Wiseman Papers, Archives of the Archdiocese of Westminster.
[25] For McCartney, [*The*] *True Tablet* 10 June 1843 p 360; T. Curley, *A Catholic History of Oldham* (Market Weighton 1911) p 13.
[26] Connolly 'Catholicism in Manchester' 2 pp 201–26.

It is the public aspect of McCartney's behaviour which casts doubt upon his professed earnest to seek a solution to Catholic problems through goodwill on all sides. His early engagements at Salford's New Bayley gaol soon led to embroilment in a bitter altercation with the resident chaplain, the Evangelical, Charles Bagshaw.[27] Preferring not to exhaust normal channels of grievance, he showed an unseemly haste in appealing over the heads of the prison authorities against what he construed as Bagshaw's misconduct in allegedly obstructing the wishes of Catholic internees. This on heresay evidence from a partisan source.[28] His claim to have uncovered a nationwide scandal involving the quiet persecution of Catholics taken straightaway to the House of Commons as ammunition for T. S. Duncombe and, predictably, Daniel O'Connell, looks premature to say the least. Even if the ailing, rather sad Bagshaw, subsequently exonerated by the Prison Visitors, was guilty of some indiscretion, McCartney's readiness to exploit what amounted at worst to excess of zeal in the absence of regular visits by the Catholic missioner, does him scant credit as an advocate of fair play.

The hint that exploitation may serve as an appropriate description of McCartney's approach to his job seems confirmed in his dealings with the Manchester Union. For whatever reasons—and one is tempted to assume lack of good manners—McCartney, neglecting authorization, presented himself at the Blackley branch House, about fifteen miles from Manchester, in February 1842. The Governor was out; but on acquainting the schoolmaster with his status and requirements he was promised cooperation in keeping with Union policy.[29] The following week he made a similar journey to Prestwich branch House, intending the same. This time, instead, he found his entrance barred by order of a Board of Guardians simply aghast at his impudence, though familiar with his reputation; they had probably gone to some lengths already to meet his criticisms of the Manchester House. On this occasion, however, with an election pending, they may have felt it advisable as well as justifiable to demonstrate mastery in their own house.[30] The outcome, as

---

[27] *Ibid* pp 205–6.
[28] *Ibid* pp 206–8, and *True Tablet* 19 Mar 1843 pp 51–2. See also *Manchester Chronicle* 19 Mar 1842, and *Manchester Guardian* 2 Apr 1842, and *Hansard* (Third series) 60 (Feb– Mar 1842) col 1284, 61 (Mar–Apr 1842) cols 598–604.
[29] Connolly 'Catholicism in Manchester' 2 p 219.
[30] *Ibid* pp 219–23.

McCartney and the Guardians squared up to each other in a test of intransigence, was another public wrangle.

In this confrontation McCartney procured a powerful ally in a fellow convert and later M.P., Frederick Lucas.[31] Lucas, ordinarily editor of the London based *Tablet*, had troubles of his own, locked in dispute with his erstwhile partner, John Cox.[32] Deprived of his title and forced to adopt the rival styling of the *True Tablet* for his publication, he was waging a destructive circulation war with the continuing *Tablet* under Cox's replacement editor, Michael Quin. Ultimately the feud transferred itself on to the streets, and in Manchester Lucas found himself competing for the support of the expanding Catholic population and, more to the point, the approbation of its clergy.[33] To this one time Quaker of radical sympathies, disdainful of the Established Church, McCartney's quarrel must have appeared as a gift of providence. Just as the Catholic chaplain was keen to broadcast the wrongs which he was convinced the law deliberately inflicted upon the Catholic poor, so too the beleaguered Lucas saw it his happy duty to abet him in every way.[34]

Throughout the spring of 1842 the *True Tablet* had carried reports of developing acrimony between McCartney and the institutional authorities. By the summer, thanks to Lucas's journalistic skills, local friction in Manchester had become a question of broad principle threatening the religious liberties of all Catholics in England.[35] The issue: whether Catholics should expect impartial treatment from the English law, soon prompted spontaneous meetings, petitions and agitation nationwide amongst Catholics, aroused to a sense of profound injustice by a combination of McCartney's repeated charges of persecution within the institutional system and Lucas's inflammatory rhetoric.[36] 'The starving, emaciating, robbing, hardening, unsocialising, uncharitable, unchristian, inhuman (poor) law',[37] was, according to Lucas, framed 'to violate the rights of the existing

---

[31] For Lucas, [E.] Lucas, [*The*] *Life* [*of Frederick Lucas, MP,*] 2 vols (London 1886) which does not mention this contretemps save in passing at 1 p 78. But see also 1 pp 45–57, 114–22.

[32] *Ibid* 1 pp 72–7 and *The Tablet* 24 July 1982 pp 737–8.

[33] Connolly 'Catholicism in Manchester' 2 p 209, and *True Tablet* 14 May 1842 pp 193, 194–5.

[34] See *True Tablet* 23 April 1842 p 131 for McCartney's invaluable approval against Cox.

[35] As, for example, *ibid* 11 June 1842 p 253 and supplement, 2 July 1842 pp 306–7.

[36] *Ibid* 11 June 1842 p 253 and supplement, 25 June 1842 pp 290–2, 20 Aug 1842 p 421.

[37] *Ibid* 25 June 1842 p 292.

Catholic population, to ruin the religious faith of our poor adults, to pervert their offspring to heretical and schismatical courses'.[38] The executive of this would-be campaign of malice was the 'hierling' Anglican chaplain,

> . . . at liberty—distinctly and unequivocally—to torment with his religious heresies all paupers who are too feeble, too careless or too much afraid of the vexations power of the master of the workhouse to raise a positive objection to such torment.[39]

Even discounting the near hysterical language with which Lucas, who was also a barrister, whipped up passions for a crusade against institutional law, the objections he advanced on the testimony of McCartney seem conspicuously lacking in less prejudicial corroboration. His ranting against an imagined anti-Catholic direction of the law betrayed an obsessive preoccupation with Protestant persecution.[40] McCartney, for all his huffing and puffing in the press and on the public platform, was hard pressed even to uncover evidence of bad faith by his own institutional authorities. This at a time when Evangelicals filled almost all the official chaplaincies.[41] On the other hand the local Guardians, despite or because of vilification by Catholics countrywide, displayed an embarrassing willingness to afford Catholics all facilities in keeping with the letter of the law and beyond (including in Salford use of the Protestant chapel), and later extended concessions to comply with article 33 of the Commissioners advice, given in an appendix to their Eighth Annual Report of 1842, to permit internees to leave the House on Sundays for worship in addition to services and instruction on the premises.[42]

It may have been true that the attitude of some institutional officers towards the priest left a good deal to be desired. But this was a cross Catholics had borne in the past, some might argue with profitable resignation, and were likely to have to do so for the forseeable future. There were even Catholics, shouted down by Lucas *et*

[38] *Ibid* p 290.

[39] *Ibid* p 291.

[40] *Ibid* pp 290–2. His insinuations against the Methodist Governor of the Manchester Poor House, p 291, seem near libellous. McCartney, by contrast and in more sober mood, took the trouble to exonerate the House schoolteachers, 'kind and human', *ibid* 2 July 1842 p 306.

[41] Connolly 'Catholicism in Manchester' 2 pp 203–4, 205, 217. All named clergy belonged to known Evangelical societies in the towns. Compare also here Chadwick 1 p 96 and especially at note 3 which unfortunately provides ammunition for Lucas.

[42] *Minute Book* (1841) L/GS/AM/2 pp 229, 233–4 and *Eighth Report Commissioners* p 50. See also *True Tablet* 25 June 1842 p 291. Want of consecrated altars made in-House Catholic services a problem, though apparently not an insurmountable one.

al., correspondingly certain that, given the chance, the law could and would be made practicable.[43] Rather tellingly, however, voices of moderation came mainly from among traditionalist English laity, a section of the Catholic population by 1842 suffering a downturn, giving way to a clergy I have elsewhere depicted growing in that self-esteem arising from the solidarity of a reinvigorated profession.[44]

In the long run it is my guess that any historian drawn to this topic in order to replace the by now dog-eared assessment of the problem by the other John Morris in 1860 might usefully link it with a discussion of contemporary clerical fortunes.[45] An illustration, mercifully at its least excruciating, of Lucas's renowned medievalist nostalgia perhaps makes the point succinctly. In an editorial of June 1842, 'Proselytism and Persecution in Workhouses: Horrible injustice in Manchester', which tends to speak for itself, he concluded: '. . . we Catholics . . . ought to have almshouses of our own in which to shelter Christ's poor from physical necessity and spiritual destitution.'[46] Numerous Catholic clergy whose approval Lucas finally won would have agreed, confident that it was odds on them to hold power in any parallel Catholic establishment. Of course, even then this could never have been a wholly realistic solution. Yet for nineteenth-century Catholics, led by the nose to appreciate the virtues of voluntary separation from society, any reservations were probably set aside by duty.

The majority of the Catholic clergy undoubtedly followed their best instincts when taking the offensive against what they interpreted as the pernicious shortcomings of the law. Regrettably, by 1842 these same instincts were fast becoming intolerant of the priest's *de facto* status within English society, minister to a 'variety of

---

[43] Connolly 'Catholicism in Manchester' 2 pp 224–5, and *True Tablet* 20 Aug 1842 p 421.

[44] See here [J.] Bossy, [*The English Catholic Community*] (London 1975) pp 349–50. By 1842 George Brown was probably already determined to curtail the activities of the lay orientated Catholic Institute; though McCartney had some praise for its contribution, *True Tablet* 27 Aug 1842 p 440. But see too his comments *ibid* 19 Mar 1842 p 241. Also here G. P. Connolly, 'Vocation or Profession? English Catholics and the origins of clerical ascendancy 1790–1840', paper read before the Catholic Record Society conference, Oxford 1983, forthcoming.

[45] Morris predictably sees the issue wholly in pastoral/political terms, *English Poor Laws* pp 3–48.

[46] *True Tablet* 25 June 1842 p 292, and also Lucas *Life* pp 45–57. Here compare R. K. Donovan, 'The denominational character of English Catholic charitable effort 1800–65' *Catholic Historical Review* 62 (1976) pp 200–23.

nonconformity'.[47] Some years before matters came to a head in Manchester, Nehemiah Gardiner, Directing Overseer and later clerk to the Board of Guardians, lamenting the disproportionate rise in Irish cases relieved, rounded upon Catholic clergymen whom he considered substantially to blame.[48] According to Gardiner their irresponsibility in encouraging the faithful to flaunt the 1753 marriage act, one labelling its procedures 'perfectly nugatory', and thus at a stroke multiplying potentially chargeable bastardy, exacerbated no end the precariousness of the situation. In fairness counsels of extremity such as this from the Irish missioner Daniel Hearne,[49] McCartney's host at St Patrick's Manchester, are more indicative of Irish insensitivity towards the conventions of the English Mission than anything else. In public, at least, many English clergy would have deplored this kind of advice. Privately, however, Catholic clerical attitudes towards the messy question of the solemnization of marriage on the British mainland before 1837 represented a sufficient state of ambivalence to make Gardiner's outburst far from unwarranted.[50] Answering McCartney as the spokesman of the Board, this pious scriptural Christian may well have had cause to reflect upon the pertinent irony of his inserting into their icy correspondence a line bidding his opponent meditate upon the text 'as you sow, so shall you reap'.[51]

Gardiner's indignation is worth taking seriously. Access to detainees drew much of its urgency from indirect complications, and possibly none more so than the specifically *Catholic* problem of the inconsistent state of religious instruction amongst those Irish poor liable to incarceration. Even Lucas faced up to this; though without drawing quite the same conclusions.[52] The inmate unacquainted with regular sacramental observance could not be trusted automatically to forward his or her name or those of dependants to receive the priest. Under such circumstances, the position of the Anglican chap-

---

[47] Bossy pp 323–63, 391–401.

[48] *Irish Poor in Britain* p 47.

[49] *Ibid* p 62 for the above declaration (concerning the calling of Catholic banns in Protestant churches and others). Hearne certainly fits Gardiner's inditement. For Hearne G. P. Connolly, 'Little brother be at peace: the priest as Holy Man in the nineteenth century ghetto', *SCH 19: The Church and Healing*, ed W. J. Sheils (Oxford 1982) pp 191–206.

[50] See J. Bossy 'Challoner and the Marriage Act' in *Challoner and his Church*, ed E. Duffy (London 1981) pp 126–36 for the gist of clerical objections.

[51] Connolly 'Catholicism in Manchester' 2 pp 220–1.

[52] *True Tablet* 25 June 1842 pp 291–2.

lain was quickly made to look crucial and the law to be his accomplice. To what extent this development suited Catholic clergymen, and, if so, what might follow from this, implies a debate too complex to be settled here. Though perhaps it is worth mentioning that there is also a pastoral argument yet to be heard. By 1848 there were allegedly 50,000 children in the institutional system nationally, perhaps a third of them of baptised Catholic parents.[53] As this was only the beginning of paternal state custody, no priest could afford complacency.

What does emerge, however, is a slight boost for the image of the English law, attempting to balance even-handedness with propriety in an area of conscience. It must at least be exonerated on the more jaundiced accounts of pigsticking levelled at it by Catholics and which have shadowed its reputation with them down to this present day. And while it would be over optimistic to envisage rehabilitation of its reputation, I hope I have done enough to suggest that the frame of mind which accepted that 'no law would be granted us' was not necessarily that of the maligned, and that there remains the serious possibility that historians may be able to make out a respectable case for the English law having, in one respect, discharged its obligations to Catholic subjects without prejudice.

Kent

---

[53] Woodward p 455. See also Connolly 'Catholicism in Manchester' 2 pp 226–9, and *English Poor Laws* pp 5–32. A sympathetic assessment of pastoral constraints can be found in S. W. Gilley, 'English Catholic Charity and the Irish Poor in London, part 1: 1700–1840' *Recusant History* 11 (January 1972) pp 179–95.

BISHOP ALEXANDER AND
THE JEWS OF JERUSALEM

by PATRICK IRWIN

THE *Devastation* reached Palestine on 20 January 1842. She brought with her Michael Solomon Alexander, first Anglican bishop in Jerusalem. The bishop was originally to have been transported to Palestine in HMS *Infernal*. At this his Lordship demurred and the Admiralty obligingly thought again. So it was that HMS *Devastation* was the carrier of the bishop to the Holy Land. The Admiralty's assistance was supplemented by Mr Arthur Guinness, who in the first of his firm's timely benefactions to the Anglican church had provided without charge a supply of stout.

So began Alexander's episcopate in Jerusalem.[1] The Anglican bishopric of 1841 is chiefly remembered today as the third blow which finally shattered Newman's faith in the Anglican church.[2] It deserves a better press. The years which followed were to witness profound changes of emphasis within the bishopric. Of all the periods the first is perhaps the least known. The four years of Alexander's episcopate have a particular interest, however, for in these years alone the Jewish mission reigned supreme. Subsequent bishops would concentrate their energies in various ways on improving the lot of indigenous Christians. Alexander, on the other hand, was principally interested in the Jews, and it is with his relationship with the Jews of Jerusalem that this paper will deal.

Alexander was himself a Jew. Born in 1799 at Schoenlanke in the Grand Duchy of Posen, he was the son of a rabbi. On his father's death he emigrated to England and served as rabbi in Norwich and later in Plymouth, where he and his wife were converted to Christianity in 1825. Alexander moved to Ireland where he studied at Trinity College, Dublin, and was ordained deacon and priest in Anglican orders. In Dublin he assisted a leading Evangelical, Archdeacon Henry Irwin, at Sandford church as well as ministering

---

[1] Jerusalem and the East Mission Private Papers box 1 files 1–3 in the Middle East Centre, St Antony's College, Oxford, contain a typed biography and correspondence of Alexander. I wish to acknowledge the Jerusalem and Middle East Church Association's generosity in granting me access to them.

[2] J. H. Newman, *Apologia pro Vita Sua* (London 1864) p 245.

to the local Jews at the German chapel. Alexander went on to work as a missionary to the Jews in Danzig and in 1832 became Professor of Hebrew at King's College, London.

Here then was a Hebrew of Hebrews, born under the Prussian flag and in Anglican orders; a Hebrew scholar well versed in converting Jews. Surely Alexander would be the obvious choice to be first Anglican bishop in Jerusalem. Actually he was not. The post was offered first to the Irish Hebraist Alexander McCaul, a leading member of the London Society for Promoting Christianity amongst the Jews (LJS), whose immense knowledge of Judaism was to be condensed into *The Old Paths*. McCaul, however, declined on the grounds that it would be better to appoint a Jewish convert.[3] Lord Ashley, so Bunsen relates, accordingly suggested Alexander's name.[4] The suggestion was immediately taken up with enthusiasm. The prospect of a Jewish successor of Saint James was an entrancing one. Moreover, the appointment of a Jew to this important position would demonstrate both the respect with which the house of Israel should be treated by Christians and the opportunities in the Church open to converts. A Hebrew Christian would have a unique advantage in preaching to the Jews. Alexander's journey to Jerusalem was seen as a Jew's return to the land of his fathers. Alexander indeed went to Jerusalem not to die, but to live and work. Thus in a sense he can be seen as a standard-bearer for *aliya*.

That the bishopric should be employed to further the Christian mission to the Jews was very much an English idea. The originators of the scheme, King Frederick William IV of Prussia and his minister Bunsen, emphasised the benefits for Protestant prestige and Christian unity which would be acquired by the establishment of a Protestant bishopric in Jerusalem. They did not consider the needs of the Jews. It is significant that the instructions of Frederick William to Bunsen for the negotiations to be undertaken in London, which resound with high hopes and expectations, mention the mission to the Jews only *en passant* near the end. There the king gives permission for Prussian clergy and missionaries to 'connect themselves with this episcopal foundation, on behalf of such converted Jews as may speak the German language, as well as of Protestant Christians of German

---

[3] [W. T.] Gidney, [*The History of the London Society for Promoting Christianity amongst the Jews, from 1809 to 1908*] (London 1908) p 207.

[4] [E.] Hodder, [*The Life and Work of the Seventh Earl of Shaftesbury, KG*] (London 1886) 1 pp 371–2.

extraction.'[5] There is nothing here of the restoration of Israel. When Bunsen uses the phrase in his diary in referring to Alexander's appointment he is merely echoing the enthusiasm of his friend Ashley.[6] At that time the road to Jerusalem lay for Germans (such as Ewald) through London and the LJS. It was Gobat's work among indigenous Christians that would bring to Jerusalem German missions and a pastor to care for them.

For Ashley and other supporters of the LJS, men with millenarian fervour coursing through their veins, the appointment of Alexander was seen as a triumphant affirmation of the Society's principles and a sure indication that the last days were approaching. They saw the dogged efforts of a few zealous missionaries now officially blessed by the two Protestant Great Powers. Now the restoration of Israel was at hand. Their joy knew no bounds. In his sermon at Alexander's consecration McCaul placed the event within the perspective of prophecy. 'Signs such as these proclaim that, if the set time to favour Zion has not yet fully arrived, it can hardly be far distant.'[7] With these sentiments in his ears and in his heart Alexander set sail for Jerusalem. We will now turn to the Jews to whom he came.

Who were the Jews of Jerusalem in Alexander's time? The Montefiore census of 1839 reckoned that there were 3,000 Jews there, of whom 83% were Sephardic Jews. Ashkenazim from Europe had only been there since 1812, though their numbers were to swell until they formed the majority of Jews in Jerusalem by the 1880s. Mortality was high. The English surgeon Sandford reckoned in 1847 that 'the ordinary (Jewish) mortality was that of plague or pestilence in Europe.'[8] Forty-nine per cent of all Jewish women in the Montefiore survey were widows. This remarkable statistic combines the high mortality of husbands with the practice of widows migrating to Jerusalem for religious reasons or to receive support from public funds. The Jewish population of Jerusalem would have declined had it not been for constant immigration. As two Scottish observers reported in 1839, 'There is, without doubt, a constant influx of Jews into this country. Yet not so great as to do more than

---

[5] B. Bertheim, *The Protestant Bishopric in Jerusalem: its Origin and Progress* (London 1847) p 41.

[6] Hodder 1 p 372.

[7] S. C. Orchard, 'English Evangelical Eschatology, 1790–1850' (Unpub Cambridge PhD thesis 1968) p 236.

[8] E. A. Finn, *Reminiscences of Mrs Finn* (London 1929) p 74.

supply the annual deaths.'[9] In the 1839 census 41% of Jewish men in Jerusalem were immigrants of less than ten years' standing.[10]

These Jews came for religious reasons to an otherwise unappetising minor Ottoman town. They came to be buried in holy ground. Death and not commercial opportunities was the lure that brought a steady flow of Jews to join their co-religionists in Jerusalem. A few Jews were merchants but most were supported financially by *haluka* (public charity) obtained from Europe. The *haluka* had gradually decreased during the late 1830s, with a consequent effect on the community's wellbeing.[11]

The Jews of Jerusalem were thus a small group of devout believers. They were to a great extent under the influence of their rabbis. The Sephardic Chief Rabbi was recognised by the Turkish authorities as the legal head of the Jewish *millet* (community). Robinson wrote of these Jews that 'they are of all others the most bigoted, and the least accessible to the labours of Christian missionaries.'[12] (He explained 'bigotry' as meaning 'strong attachment to their ancient faith'.) Robinson was not alone in this assessment. Comparatively few Jews were being converted to Christianity in England or Germany. How many could one reasonably expect to be converted in the unique surroundings of Jerusalem? So mused visitors such as A. F. Strauss.[13]

Alexander's responsibilities were laid down in the authoritative *Statement of Proceedings Relating to the Establishment of a Bishopric of the United Church of England and Ireland in Jerusalem.* This stated succinctly that 'his chief missionary care will be directed to the conversion of the Jews, to their protection, and to their useful employment.'[14] (Conversion of anyone else, of course, would have been against the Ottoman law of the time.) Alexander set about his Herculean task with vigour. He was responsible for the establishment in 1843 of three institutions to cater for the needs of the nascent Hebrew Christian Church. In May he opened 'The Hebrew College'

[9] A. E. Boner and R. M. McCheyne, *Narrative of a Mission of Enquiry to the Jews from the Church of Scotland in 1839* (Edinburgh 1846) p 148.

[10] U. O. Schmelz, 'Some Demographic Peculiarities of the Jews of Jerusalem in the Nineteenth Century' in *Studies on Palestine in the Ottoman Period*, ed M. Ma'Oz (Jerusalem 1975) pp 120, 131, 140.

[11] PRO, F[oreign] O[ffice] 78/368 no 13, Young to Palmerston 25 May 1839.

[12] E. Robinson, *Biblical Researches in Palestine, Mount Sinai, and Arabia Petraea* (London 1841) 2 p 87.

[13] A. F. Strauss, *Sinai und Golgotha. Reise in das Morgenland* (Berlin 1850) p 286.

[14] [*The Jerusalem Bishopric* (Documents) ed W. H.] Hechler (London 1883) p 110.

as indicated in the *Proceedings*, 'a College . . . under the Bishop, whose chaplain will be its first principal. Its primary object will be, the education of Jewish converts . . .' The College began with four students, but it was not to last much longer than Alexander himself. His successor, Samuel Gobat, whose priorities were different, closed the College on the grounds of lack of funds. Funds were not lacking, however, for the Bible schools he was to establish for indigenous Christians.

The other two institutions were under the control of the LJS missionaries and so survived the change of bishop. 'The School of Industry' was established as a hostel in which converts could be housed and fed while they were trained or employed to do such work as carpentry and joinery which the mission required. Such employment was indeed a novelty for the Jews of Jerusalem. Thirdly, 'The Enquirers' Home' was opened to accommodate Jews interested in Christianity whilst they underwent observation and initial instruction before being admitted to 'The School of Industry'.

In 1844 a Bible depot was opened to make available the Holy Scriptures in Hebrew, Arabic, Greek, Italian, French, German, and Spanish. Also provided were such works as McCaul's *Old Paths* and Bunyan's *Pilgrim's Progress* in Hebrew, as well as a Hebrew edition of Holy Communion. In this venture there was close cooperation with the British and Foreign Bible Society. The Jerusalem rabbis responded to this new threat by excommunicating all Jews who entered the building.

Alexander and the LJS missionaries were hard-working and devoted to their cause, but the number of converts remained small. In 1842 eight Jews were baptised. Next year the number was fifteen.[15] On the bishop's death in 1845 thirty-one converts signed a letter of condolence to his widow.[16] Such was the modest size of the Hebrew Christian church. Its existence, however, is its most remarkable feature. The missionaries were accused of seducing Jews from their ancestral faith with financial inducements, but it is difficult to see what appeal board and lodging whilst learning a trade would have for someone who had come to Jerusalem to prepare prayerfully for death. Since converts would be ostracised by the Jewish community and deprived of *haluka*, it was necessary for the missionaries to pro-

---

[15] Jerusalem, Israel Trust of the Anglican Church register of baptisms p 1. I wish to acknowledge the Israel Trust's generosity in granting me access to its archives.

[16] *Jewish Intelligence* (1846) p 128.

vide for their maintenance. More attractive, no doubt, was the prospect of British protection, for the Damascus Affair of 1840 (in which prominent Jews were arrested and tortured) was still fresh in Jewish minds. Alexander made no attempt to correct the impression that baptism into the United Church of England and Ireland somehow brought with it British citizenship, but Her Majesty's consul was on hand to do so. (Ordination was deemed even more efficacious than baptism in this respect. The first convert ordained by Alexander, E. M. Tartakover, appeared in Beirut and requested a British passport on the grounds that he was 'a British subject by spirit'. Alexander held that the oath of allegiance to the Queen sworn by the ordinand made him a subject of the British Crown.)[17] Aberdeen had clearly instructed Consul Young to 'abstain from affording to persons who may associate themselves to Bishop Alexander's congregation any protection, as British Dependents, to which, under other circumstances, they could not properly claim.'[18] British policy on the amount of protection to be accorded Jews was to fluctuate considerably after Palmerston's instruction in 1839 'to afford Protection to the Jews generally',[19] but Anglican baptism was never to be a decisive point.

Relations between bishop and consul steadily deteriorated. The most spectacular collision occurred in October 1842 with the arrival of three Russian rabbis at the house of Ewald, one of the LJS missionaries. They claimed to be prospective converts and to be in flight from the Jewish religious authorities. Alexander accepted their story and agreed that the mission should harbour them. Rabbi Bordaki, the Russian consular agent in Jerusalem, wrote to Consul Young to say that the trio were fugitives from justice and to demand their return. Young sought to achieve this and a lively correspondence with Alexander ensued.[20] What to the consul was a matter of civil order was to the bishop a question of religious persecution. The three Jews solved the problem by returning of their own free will, but two of them later resumed their attendance at the mission and were baptised the following May. They were to form half of the Hebrew College's first batch of students.[21] Young was invited by Alexander to act as their sponsor; he declined, but attended the baptism service.[22]

[17] PRO, FO 78/537, Rose to Aberdeen, 26 December 1843.
[18] *Ibid* 501, Aberdeen to Young 3 May 1842.
[19] *Ibid* 368 no 2, Bidwell to Young 31 January 1839.
[20] *Ibid* 501 no 7, Young to Aberdeen 11 October 1842.
[21] Gidney p 237.
[22] PRO, FO 78/540 no 26, Young to Aberdeen 22 May 1843.

In their zealous attempts to build up the Hebrew Christian church Alexander and the missionaries were to draw criticism from Protestant observers as well as the local Jews. Constantin Tischendorf (the discoverer of Codex Siniaticus) had occasion to visit the Jerusalem mission. He was not impressed. He found in the sermons a new Pharisaism which suggested that only Jews could be fully Christian. The Jews, he felt, were invited to retain their inherited privileges. Tischendorf noted that other Protestants in Jerusalem objected to this line of the LJS missionaries and that one had even publicly complained to the preacher and ceased to attend his sermons.[23] In the circumstances an emphasis on the values of Judaism in the missionaries' sermons was scarcely surprising. Their utterances formed an unexceptionable part of a wider movement to restore to Christian tradition its Jewish heritage and to recognise the theological importance of the Jewish race. Only under Alexander, however, were such views to be officially promulgated by the Anglican bishopric.

Anglicans in Jerusalem were not restricted in their concerns to the conversion of Jews and the edification of the faithful. The LJS medical work played an important role in the city, and it was under Alexander that its significance first became plain. The LJS had maintained a medical service in Jerusalem since 1839. Dr Macgowan had come out to run it in 1841. (In 1825 the LJS missionary Dalton had arrived in Jerusalem to establish a medical centre, but he died within a month.)

At the time the LJS establishment was the only source of reliable medical aid in a city where such aid was greatly needed. The impetus given to its work by Alexander's arrival and interest, as well as the publicity surrounding the creation of the bishopric, encouraged the Jews to improve their own medical facilities. In 1842 there was an appeal published in the German Jewish press for the establishment of a Jewish Missionary Society 'to further Jewish interests, and strengthen Jews in their faith.'[24] This aroused considerable interest and in September came the first response. A Jewish community in Turkey contributed 100 ducats to start a Jewish hospital in Jerusalem. The following year Montefiore sent out a Jewish doctor, Simon Fraenkel, to care for poor Jews. The Muslims also responded to the challenge. In 1847 the Turkish authorities opened a free clinic under the auspices of the garrison doctor.

[23] C. Tischendorf, *Reise in den Orient* (Leipzig 1846) 1 p 49.
[24] Hechler p 70.

In 1842 Macgowan reported 'that the Medical Department had succeeded in accomplishing the main effects of its establishment, viz. the relief of suffering Jews, and the awakening of a grateful and friendly feeling in the Hebrew population in general.'[25] After reporting the arrival of Fraenkel in Jerusalem, Macgowan remarked that there was room enough for both of them, and expressed his regret, not that a rival had entered the field, but that the amount of sickness and distress was more than their united exertions could successfully cope with.

The picture painted by Macgowan, however, was too rosy by far. The rabbis were suspicious of the Christian medical service and indeed regarded it as a tool of proselytisation. They strenuously sought to prevent Jews from attending it. Montefiore had been alarmed to discover that Jews were attending the Christian missionaries and in a letter to Jerusalem rabbis in 1843 expressed the hope that the arrival of Fraenkel would remove the risk of missionary influence.[26] That it did not do.

In December 1844 Macgowan opened the Hospital for Poor Sick Jews. The following month a Jewish patient died and the Chief Rabbis refused him burial, unless Macgowan undertook to dismiss all his Jewish patients and servants and not to admit them in future. Naturally he refused and the dead man was buried in the British burial ground 'after having been duly washed and prepared by members of the Jewish Community, according to their own customs'.[27] The Chief Rabbis now pronounced sentence of excommunication on all Jews who attended the Christian hospital. All eight patients and the Jewish servants accordingly left. The storm soon blew over, however, for within a fortnight four Jewish patients had been admitted and others soon followed. A second excommunication, issued in March, produced very little effect. The rabbis, indeed, were not always unbendingly hostile. In 1851 the Chief Rabbi, accompanied by other Jerusalem rabbis, was to visit Macgowan. He would pronounce a blessing on arrival and thank him for the good that he had done for Israel.[28] Such appreciation, though, was exceptional.

Was the Christian hospital a centre for proselytism as the rabbis feared? Dr Aiton visited Jerusalem in 1845 and reported that

[25] *Ibid* p 70.
[26] A. M. Hyamson, *The British Consulate in Jerusalem* (London 1939) p 62.
[27] PRO, FO 78/625 no 3, Young to Aberdeen 31 January 1845.
[28] Hechler p 73.

Both in the Hospital and in the House of Industry plenty of New Testaments in the Hebrew tongue are laid on the tables. But while every facility is given to the reading of the Gospels, there is nothing like compulsion, or any indication that the conversion of the inmates is the sole but disguised object of these institutions. On the contrary, everything is done, so far as the funds will admit of it, for the benefit of the Jews in Palestine.[29]

Aiton's combination of the two institutions here is extremely misleading, for in the House (or School) of Industry Christianity was *de rigeur*, but his comment is a fair description of the hospital. There medical care was genuinely offered to poor Jews without any pressure being placed upon them to become Christians. Macgowan was styled a medical missionary and was naturally gratified by any Jewish conversion to Christianity, but in his hospital he worked with the hands of a philanthropist and not a proselytiser. The hospital was an attempt to mitigate the appalling conditions in which the Jews of Jerusalem lived, and as such it was to be the fore-runner of a distinguished line of medical institutions. That Jewish imitation was spurred on by fear of proselytism does not reduce the value of the example.

In 1845 the Jerusalem rabbis produced a remarkable document for distribution to European Jewry. This was a vitriolic attack on the Christian missionaries, and it included a remarkable section on medical care.

They have occasioned our distress. For we are compelled to give of our substance and of our money to build and repair an hospital. For they have opened the eyes of the needy among us. Formerly from time immemorial, since a settlement has again been established for us in the Holy City, such a thing as a hospital for the sick of the people of Israel, has not been seen. Every one was clean in his own house, his wife attending him in his sickness—the poor was cherished in his affliction, the Doctor attending him gratuitously, being paid out of the chest of the Society for visiting the sick, and giving him medicine without pay. As for an hospital its name was not known.[30]

Such language scarcely did justice to the grim reality of life for the Jewish poor of Jerusalem, but it was typical of a fierce conservatism which did not restrict its attacks to matters of medicine or indeed to

[29] J. Aiton, *The Lands of the Messiah* (London 1852) p 319.
[30] PRO, FO 78/625 no 7, Young to Aberdeen, 4 March 1845.

Christian enterprises. Jewish attempts to introduce western 'improvements' were resisted with equal vigour. Even Montefiore ran foul of the local rabbis. As Consul Finn was to report in 1858,

> The difficulty experienced by Sir Moses in promoting European education among the Jews of Jerusalem, has equally affected the intentions of the great Jewish families of Paris and Vienna: for all have been obliged to modify their plans on account of the fanaticism of the Rabbinical authorities, who will not suffer their people, especially in the holy city, to 'learn the ways of the heathen'. Sir Moses was even excommunicated by some of the synagogues, and insulted by the population in the street.[31]

Thus the attacks of the rabbis were not reserved for Christian missionaries. Consideration of their opposition to the Christian hospital would be incomplete if restricted to the religious point of difference. European culture was seen by the Jerusalem rabbis to be as much of a threat to the traditions of their community as missionary Christianity. The Jews who sought to bring the benefits of European civilisation to their co-religionists in Jerusalem were impelled by the knowledge that the Christians had already arrived with them. This lent a certain urgency to the matter. Fraenkel was brought to Jerusalem by the work of Macgowan; Alexander's School of Industry was responsible for Montefiore's windmill.

In November 1845 Alexander died in the desert whilst on his way to visit Egypt. (That country formed part of his diocese.) His episcopate had lasted for a mere four years and the Anglican community in Jerusalem felt cruelly bereaved. Despite the shortness of his time in the Holy Land Alexander had made a notable contribution both to the Church and to the city in which he had made his home.

For the Church Alexander had created something of lasting worth. His modest and hard-won success so beset by controversy in establishing a Hebrew Christian congregation in Jerusalem ensured that Christian Jewry would have a share in the development of the Holy Land. He had established foundations on which others could build. Mission to the Jews would no longer be the principal activity of the Anglican bishopric, but Alexander's episcopate had bound it securely to the Anglican church.

The Jews of Jerusalem too were Alexander's debtors. In his encouragement of the medical mission he had demonstrated that his

---

[31] *Ibid* 1383 political no 1, Finn to Clarendon 1 January 1858.

love for the Jews was not dependent upon their accepting Christianity. Alexander can with justice take his place among the Jews of the nineteenth century who sought to raise up the Jews of Jerusalem from their state of degradation. The activities of these Jewish philanthropists can indeed be regarded as a response to the challenge provided by the pioneer Christian enterprises of Alexander's episcopate.

Thus as Christian pastor and Jerusalem pioneer Alexander has two distinct claims on posterity's regard. They have survived the evaporation of the unrealistic expectations of 1841. The restoration of Israel was delayed and the link with Prussia faded, but Alexander's modest achievements remain. Perhaps most appealing, though, is Alexander the man, the convert with a passionate concern for the Jewish people that transcended all difficulties. An innocent abroad he may have been, but his generosity of spirit is singularly refreshing. The Holy City has never lacked energetic defenders of the faith. Alexander was something rarer in Jerusalem, a tolerant divine.

Pembroke College, Cambridge

POPE PIUS IX AND RELIGIOUS FREEDOM

by PETER DOYLE

THE LIBERAL outcry occasioned by the publication of the *Syllabus of Errors* in 1864 concerned in large part the apparent condemnation by Pius IX of religious liberty and freedom of conscience.[1] Lord John Russell quoted practice in Mexico to show that the Pope meant that Roman Catholicism should be maintained to the exclusion of every other form of worship, while the *Saturday Review* argued that Pius had defended the duty of the Church and the State to persecute those who worked against Roman Catholicism.[2] The main problem for these and other critics was constituted by articles 24, 77 and 79 of the *Syllabus*: how could these be interpreted except as condemning religious toleration and liberty of speech?[3] A few years later, Gladstone, in attacking the Vatican decrees on the Church, argued that the *Syllabus* had not only denied the principle of toleration but had also positively favoured persecution, and referred to article 78.[4]

Some Roman Catholics also felt that the *Syllabus* was unfortunate, or that, at least, it needed very careful handling to avoid the above interpretations. Liberal Catholics like Acton, of course, condemned it: it was a 'damnable document' precisely because it justified intolerance;[5] others went to great lengths to temper its apparent harshness.

[1] H. Denziger, C. Bannwart, *et al*, *Enchiridion Symbolorum Definitionum et Declarationum de Rebus Fidei et Moram* (30 ed Freiburg 1955); reference is to DB and section number. The *Syllabus* is DB 1701–80. [L.] Brigué, [*DTC*, vol 14, cols 2877–2923] gives history, text and commentary.

[2] [D.] McElrath, [*The Syllabus of Pius IX: Some Reactions in England* (Louvain 1964)] pp 36, 71. Also, E. Papa, *Il Sillabo di Pio IX e La Stampa Francese, Inglese e Italiana* (Rome 1968) and [N.] Blakiston, [*The Roman Question*: Extracts from the Dispatches of Odo Russell from Rome 1858–1870 (London 1962)].

[3] DB 1724: *Ecclesia vis inferendae potestatem non habet neque potestatem ullam temporalem directam vel indirectam*; DB 1777: *Aetate hac nostra non amplius expedit, religionem catholicam haberi tanquam unicam status religionem, ceteris quibuscumque cultibus exclusis*; DB 1779: *Enimvero falsum est, civilem cuiusque cultus libertatem, itemque plenam potestatem omnibus attributam quaslibet opiniones cogitationesque palam publiceque manifestandi conducere ad populorum mores animosque facilius corrumpendos ac indifferentismi pestem propagandam.*

[4] [W.E.] Gladstone, [*Rome and the Newest Fashions in Religion* (London 1875)] pp xxvii–xxix, liv, 75–8. DB 1778: *Hinc laudabiliter in quibusdam catholici nominis regionibus lege cautum est, ut hominibus illuc immigrantibus liceat publicum proprii cuiusque cultus exercitium habere.*

[5] McElrath p 214.

Even Antonelli, the papal secretary of state, claimed that the Pope had condemned only what was evil in modern movements and ideas and had not been discussing what was good or acceptable in certain circumstances.[6] Dupanloup, the bishop of Orléans, quickly published a pamphlet defence which was to furnish papal apologists with their stock response.[7] He proposed a distinction between the 'thesis' and the 'hypothesis', where the thesis represented the ideal, or the principle, and the hypothesis represented what might exist in a particular set of circumstances. Accordingly, the Pope could be taken as having supported, as a principle, the idea that only Roman Catholicism should exist in the perfect human society, without being taken to have condemned any situation in which more than one religion existed and was tolerated in practice. Ideally, in other words, a state should only allow the true religion (Roman Catholicism) and should take positive steps to extirpate heresy; if this ideal could not be realised, then the state might allow liberty for all or some other forms of worship.

The Pope thanked Dupanloup for his efforts, but without commenting on the actual interpretation; he does not seem ever to have adopted it as his own. Some people complained that the bishop had explained the *Syllabus* away altogether, and Russell was sure that he had misinterpreted the Pope.[8] But the explanation was accepted gratefully by *The Tablet*,[9] and was expounded at length by Ward in *The Dublin Review*: the Pope denied that citizens had any right to liberty of worship, but did not deny toleration in those countries where hereditary Protestantism had existed for a long time. It could hardly ever be right, Ward continued, to give immigrants to a country a freedom of public worship which would not otherwise exist there: 'religious unity, where it prevails, is so unspeakable a blessing, that a signal benefit is conferred . . . if non-Catholic immigrants are prevented, through the prevalent intolerance, from there settling.'[10]

Toleration, then, might be a matter of expediency, it could never be a matter of principle. As Pius himself put it on one occasion, 'The

[6] [R.] Aubert, [*Le Pontificat de Pie IX 1846–1878*], FM 21 (Paris 1958) pp 256–7; Blakiston p 320; F. J. Coppa, *Pope Pius IX: Crusader in a Secular Age* (Boston, Mass. 1979) p 146.

[7] Aubert p 257. See also his 'Mgr Dupanloup et le Syllabus', RHE vol 51 (1956) pp 79–142, 471–512, 837–915, and DHGE vol 14 (1960) cols 1070–1122.

[8] McElrath p 36; Aubert pp 257–8; D. McElrath, *Richard Simpson 1820–1876, A Study in 19th Century English Liberal Catholicism* (Louvain 1972) p 127.

[9] McElrath p 97.

[10] Quoted in McElrath p 103, from *The Dublin Review* vol 4 (April 1865) pp 441–99.

Pope indeed wants liberty of conscience in Sweden and Russia, lest Catholics suffer, but he does not want it in principle'.[11] It is interesting that Newman, also, in answer to a request from Dupanloup for theological authorities against persecution, concluded that, 'the great question is expedience or inexpedience', and that the state had the right to inflict punishment for religion as religion.[12]

Another justification of the *Syllabus* was also put forward. Each article or error had attached to it a reference to a speech or letter of the Pope in which the condemnation had originally appeared, and the articles had to be understood strictly according to the accepted principles of interpretation, that is, in the context of the original statements; they should not be applied universally.[13] If, for example, the statement had been prompted by particular events in Italy (as many of them had), then the condemnation referred only to what had been considered evil in those events in the first place. By the nature of the *Syllabus*, the articles were very terse summaries, and one should not expect a full theological statement in them.

Too much weight should not, however, be put on this terseness, as though the whole document was the result of a rapid culling from previous condemnations put together in the heat of the moment to meet a crisis. Probably no papal document has ever been longer in preparation, and it went through a number of re-draftings in its thirteen-year gestation.[14] Moreover, it was accompanied by a full encyclical letter, *Quanta Cura*, which allowed a thorough exposition of papal thinking and gave an opportunity for the invocation of principles and a delimitation of the extent of the condemnations, if that was intended.[15] The encyclical was largely ignored at the time—the terse summaries of the *Syllabus* gave opponents ample ammunition in a much more deadly form—but it calls for some analysis.

The letter has the same air of doom and gloom as most of Pius' encyclicals: the whole of the Christian religion and of civil society is under threat if the outstanding errors of the time are not condemned and rejected. Those who promise liberty are themselves the slaves of

[11] Aubert p 252.
[12] [W.] Ward, [*William George Ward and the Catholic Revival* (London 1893 repr. 1969)] p 268.
[13] McElrath pp 283, 301.
[14] Brigúe col 2877. Also, M. Buschkühl, *Great Britain and the Holy See 1746–1870* (Dublin 1982) pp 100–7, and his bibliography p 226; I owe these references to the kindness of Dr S. Gilley.
[15] [*Pii IX Pontificis Maximi*] *Acta* 9 vols (Graz 1971) 3 pp 687–701.

corruption; they are evil men with wicked designs and they 'spew out their confusing notions like the billows of a raging sea.'[16] In particular, he condemns those who assert that the best condition of society is one in which the civil authority does not acknowledge its duty to punish those who violate the Catholic religion; such an assertion is said to be against the doctrine of the Scriptures, but no references are given to support this. There is no indication that it is not intended as a universal condemnation; indeed, to interpret it otherwise would be to go against the whole tenor of the document. The Pope goes on to quote with approval his predecessor's letter *Mirari vos* which had described the idea of liberty of conscience as a madness (*deliramentum*).[17] If liberty of conscience were allowed, he continues, then that would be the end of all religion in society: justice would disappear, material power become all important and nothing would be left but to amass riches and satisfy one's own desires and comforts. Those who argued for such liberty wished to destroy not only public religion but private family religion too, for that is what Communism and Socialism teach.[18] This type of argument by *reductio ad extremum*, whereby those who advocate religious liberty are equated with Communists and Socialists, is typical of much of Pius' approach. The whole of the encyclical, and especially the general condemnation with which it ends, gives no indication of being a reasoned attack on errors which had arisen in particular circumstances.

These comments on the language of *Quanta Cura* illustrate a difficulty with the second justification outlined above, that the condemnations in the *Syllabus* are to be interpreted strictly according to theological principles. Most of the letters and speeches referred to as sources are made up largely of accounts of the undoubted evils perpetrated against the Church by various regimes, and the Pope was clearly right to defend the Church against such attacks. But there is no careful use of language nor concern for the technicalities of theological argument. Indeed, there is little argument at all: the points made are put forward as self-evident to all right-thinking men. Only truth has rights and only Roman Catholicism is true. Any contrary position is derided, and its authors are men of evil intent, enemies of the light, out to destroy the Church and civilisa-

---

[16] *Ibid* 3 p 688.
[17] *Ibid* p 690. *Mirari vos* had been issued in 1832.
[18] *Ibid* pp 691–2.

tion itself. To the example quoted above from *Quanta Cura* may be added another which occurs more than once in Pius' letters and speeches: to advocate liberty of conscience is to support indifference in religious matters; the two are taken to be synonymous although, again, no justification is given for this stance. In his very first encyclical, *Qui Pluribus*, of November 1846, he wrote that those who favoured indifferentism removed the distinction between virtue and vice and held that 'men could attain eternal salvation in the practice of any religion'.[19] No allowance was made even for the possibility that those who wanted religious freedom were sincere in their own beliefs. On another occasion, he replied to a suggestion that Protestants might be allowed some freedom of worship in the Papal States with a mixture of horror and scorn: how could he possibly think of allowing such a thing when it could only be a cover for bringing in Socialism and Communism, which follow from permitting private interpretation of the Scriptures?[20]

It is hardly practicable, then, to interpret the letters and speeches of the Pope as carefully weighed theological pronouncements; they are, rather, evidence of a mind which interpreted the world according to pre-conceived and simplistic models of evil and good. In contrast to their looseness of language is the legal crispness of another set of papal documents, the concordats, and these are worth examining to see if they reveal anything different about Pius' attitudes to religious liberty.

The Pope signed seventeen concordats between August 1847 and September 1862. They ranged from an agreement with the Emperor of Russia to those with Latin American countries such as Ecuador and San Salvador.[21] Basically there were two types: one for countries where Roman Catholics were in a minority, the other where they were the only recognised religious group or were in a large majority. Of the seventeen concordats, eleven were between the Holy See and former colonies of Spain or Spain itself. All the concordats raised the obvious, basic issue of the relations between Church and State, an issue which the Pope dealt with on a number of occasions.[22]

---

[19] *Ibid* 1 pp 12–24. For an excellent analysis of this approach in Gregory XVI's writings, see P. Hegy, *L'Autorité dans La Catholicisme Contemporaine du Syllabus à Vatican II* (Paris 1975) pp 45–8.

[20] *Acta* 1 pp 201–2, December 1849.

[21] [A.] Mercati, [*Raccolta di Concordati su Materie Ecclesiastiche Tra La Santa Sede e Le Autorità Civili*] 2 vols (Vatican 1919 enlarged ed 1954) for full texts and some relevant documents.

[22] For example, speech on New Granada, September 1852, *Acta* 1 pp 383–6.

For Pius, two powers existed in the world, one charged with caring for secular society and its affairs, the other charged with looking after man's eternal salvation. The latter power, the Church of Christ, was by its origins and purpose superior to the former and was in itself a perfect society, with its own rulers, rights and laws. It was always separate and independent of all civil authority, and no civil power had any right to issue laws dealing with church affairs. If such laws were issued, the Church retained the right to declare them null and void, a right which Pius exercised frequently.[23]

The strongly medieval flavour of this teaching is worth noting. Another way of expressing Dupanloup's original thesis/hypothesis dichotomy would be to say that the thesis or ideal equalled the vanished medieval world, while the hypothesis or reality equalled the modern, nineteenth-century world. But this needs an essential qualification: for Puis IX the ideal had not vanished and was not merely a nostalgic desideratum; it still existed and could be offered as a practical model for governments to copy. Indeed, concordats were designed to reproduce the ideal conditions of Spain or San Salvador in other countries.

Where concordats were signed with countries in which Roman Catholics were a minority, there was no mention, of course, of Catholicism being the only religion. With the Emperor of Russia, for example, Pius was concerned to obtain what little protection he could for his harrassed flock, and most of the concordat dealt with the rights of diocesan bishops to make ecclesiastical appointments.[24] In the concordat with the king of Württemberg, it is agreed that the education of Catholic children should be entirely under episcopal direction; no other exclusive rights are mentioned.[25] A similar point about education was made in the agreement with the Emperor of Austria of November 1855.[26] It is interesting that this last-mentioned concordat does not say that Roman Catholicism was to be the only religion in any part of the Empire; its concern was for the Church's rights, and it should be seen as the end of the long battle over Josephism.[27] As was usual, however, the concordat was fol-

[23] *Acta* 2 p 544 (Mexico); 6 pp 253–73, general letter of November 1873, *Etsi multa luctuosa*. For a detailed discussion, M. Nedoncelle, R. Aubert, *et al.*, *L'Ecclésiologie au XIXe Siècle* (Paris 1960).

[24] Mercati 1 pp 751–61.

[25] *Ibid* pp 853–62.

[26] *Ibid* p 822.

[27] Aubert p 75, says this is also true of the concordat with Tuscany of 1855; see Mercati 1 pp 767–9.

lowed by a papal letter to the hierarchy of the country concerned on how it should be implemented. In this the Austrian bishops were warned that two evils in particular were to be avoided; one was rationalism, the other the deadly damage to Church and State from the 'most putrid error of indifferentism'.[28]

The contrast is striking when one turns from these concordats to those signed with officially Roman Catholic countries. In these cases, the first article was usually as follows: 'The Catholic, Apostolic and Roman religion is the religion of the state in . . . and will always be kept intact there with all the rights and privileges which it ought to enjoy by the law of God and the sacred canons'.[29] In the concordat with Spain of 1851 the wording was stronger: 'The Catholic, Apostolic and Roman religion, which continues to be the sole religion of the Spanish nation to the exclusion of every other cult . . .'[30] The second or third article dealt with education and instruction: at every level this was to be supervised and controlled by the bishops, who were to ensure that nothing was taught contrary to the Catholic religion and good morals. A further article dealt with the bishops' right to examine and, if necessary, censor all books and writings which in any way concerned matters of belief, church discipline or public morals, and with the civil government's duty to support the bishops in this task.[31] Another duty usually laid on the government was that of providing financial support for the Church.[32]

While it is true that most of the articles in these concordats concerned rights of appointment and rights of property, the opening articles were not just formalities. That the Pope attached great importance to them is clear from two sources. Firstly, there are the accompanying letters to the bishops of the country concerned, which usually picked out one or two points for specific comment. For example, the Pope stressed to the Spanish bishops that the concordat gave the Catholic religion the unique position which had allowed it to flourish and be dominant in former times in their country, so that every other cult was clearly done away with and forbidden. To the Costa Rican bishops he pointed out that according to the

---

[28] *Acta* 2 pp 512–5.
[29] Mercati 1 pp 800–9, concordat with Costa Rica, 1852.
[30] *Ibid* pp 770–96.
[31] *Ibid* p 801, Costa Rica 1852; pp 949– 50, Nicaragua 1861; p 961, San Salvador 1862.
[32] *Ibid*.

concordat the Catholic religion would continue to be for ever the state religion.[33]

Secondly, there are a number of letters and speeches which express papal concern either with governments which are deemed to have broken concordats or with events in particular countries. In a letter of August 1847 to the president of New Granada (Colombia) the Pope condemned the freedom of public worship which had been granted to 'dissident minorities'.[34] By 1855 he was complaining that the Spanish concordat of four years earlier was being broken: one of the main reasons for entering into it had been to ensure that Catholicism should be the sole religion in that country, but new laws had broken the first two articles; the laws were declared void.[35] A later letter to the Spanish bishops spoke highly of their attempts to 'avert the deadly evil of such toleration'; they should make known to the faithful that they rejected such liberty, and should work with all their strength to keep safe that unity of religion handed down by their ancestors which was so closely linked to the glory of their country.[36] In 1856 it was events in Mexico which were worrying Pius: the detestable and dreadful pest of indifferentism was one of the worst evils, and, in order to overthrow 'our most holy religion', the free practice of any religion was being permitted. Everyone was allowed to put forward openly and publicly whatever ideas he liked, and when the Mexican bishops had begged the government that 'at least' the law allowing the free exercise of other religions should not be passed, they had been ill-treated. Again the offending laws were declared void.[37] Some years later, in 1868, it was the turn of the Austrian government to be reprimanded for breaking the concordat. The 'Fundamental Law' of December 1867 had decreed freedom of 'belief, conscience and doctrine', and had given the right to members of any religion to set up schools; this law was to bind even in those regions of the empire where Catholicism was the only religion. Along with a later law of May 1868 this was described as abominable and was condemned; both laws were declared to be void, and their

---

[33] *Acta* 1 pp 295 (Spain), 450 (Costa Rica).

[34] [G.] Martina, [*Pio IX, 1846–1850* (Rome 1974)] p 121; see also his *Pio IX, Chiesa e Mondo Moderna* (Rome 1976).

[35] *Acta* 1 pp 441–2.

[36] *Ibid* 7 pp 182–6 (March 1876).

[37] *Ibid* 2 pp 538–49 (December 1856).

authors and anyone who attempted to carry them out were told that they should keep in mind the Church's penalties.[38]

For some liberal Catholics it was not a question whether concordats worked or not; they were uneasy about the policy of making them at all. In the early years of the pontificate they could point to Belgium as an alternative model: no concordat existed between that country and the Holy See, and yet the Church enjoyed all its rights and was not interfered with—it was a working example of a free church in a free state. But events there after 1855, and the growth of anti-clerical power, seemed to the supporters of the papal policy to prove that Pius was correct in thinking that only concordats could prevent the spread of the principles of 1789, with a subsequent weakening of the moral and religious foundations of society.[39] The liberals were more in tune with the times, for rulers and governments were becoming increasingly unwilling to bind themselves in such a formal way to opposing the growth of toleration and pluralism. The Pope refused to recognise the growth as anything other than the fruit of evil intentions directed against the Catholic religion; it was to be opposed, not by argument, but by increasingly strident reiteration of so-called obvious first principles and by relying on what has been called a regime of privileges and external prestige in the bosom of officially Catholic states.[40]

In such an atmosphere the liberal Catholics had no chance of success. When Montalembert published his Malines speeches of 1863 as a pamphlet entitled, *L'Église Libre dans L'État Libre*, it was immediately answered by one entitled, *L'Erreur Libre dans L'État Libre*, and the demand for a full condemnation of Montalembert was one of the immediate factors in the publication of the *Syllabus*. He had argued strongly against the concordat mentality: it was a tactical mistake, he claimed, to look for privileges, and the Church's freedom would be far better safeguarded by the general freedom of all the citizens of a country than by a 'fickle grant of privileges'.[41] Opponents of his position fastened on to his espousal of religious toleration as a principle. He argued that the modern state's toleration of error was more preferable to the old systems of intolerance in countries like Spain, Italy and Portugal. 'The bonfires lit by a Catholic

---

[38] *Ibid* 4 pp 407–9 (June 1868).
[39] Aubert p 246, for Belgium.
[40] R. Aubert, *L'Église dans le monde moderne*, Vol 5 of *Nouvelle Histoire de l'Église* (Paris 1975) p 42.
[41] [J. C.] Finlay [*The Liberal Who Failed*] (Washington DC 1968) pp 124–35.

hand', he wrote, 'horrify me just as much as the scaffolds on which the Protestants have killed so many martyrs.'[42] Ward regarded this as a disparagement of the Church's legitimate authority and an attack on the medieval (for him the ideal) system of relations between Church and State. He was willing to accept that 'modern liberties' were practically necessary in the nineteenth century, but not that the medieval system had been wrong in principle to refuse toleration.[43] Others went further than Ward. Veuillot refused to accept that a distinction could be made between what was good in the liberal approach and what was false: 'it is as if one wished to distinguish between good and bad Protestantism', he wrote. The Abbé Gaume put Montalembert among those hypocrites who, like the Jansenists, wanted to remain in the Church without belonging to it.[44]

Pius did not associate himself with these extreme views, and hesitated to condemn formally one who had done so much for the Church. In the end, two private letters were sent, one to Montalembert and one to the bishop of Malines. The liberals made a last attempt to hold up the publication of the *Syllabus* on the grounds that it would play into anti-clerical hands in Belgium; Antonelli, although he had pushed for a full condemnation of Montalembert, was won over to the idea that publication would do more damage than good. Pius, however, finally went along with the Holy Office and the group of cardinals who had been urging publication for some time, and the *Syllabus* was issued.[45] He later argued that it was not to be taken as a condemnation of Montalembert, for, as he explained to Monsell (Newman's friend and sometime contributor to the *Rambler*), he had not even read Montalembert's pamphlet.[46] While this was a sound technical point, it raises some doubts about the earlier two letters sent in response to the pamphlet, and does not weaken the fact that the leading supporters of the *Syllabus* saw in it a condemnation of all that was assumed in Montalembert's approach, while he and his friends also thought that they had been condemned.[47]

Non-catholic critics of the *Syllabus* also saw it in this light. Papal apologists could, indeed, score technical points against them,

[42] *Ibid* p 133.
[43] Ward pp 158–9.
[44] *Ibid* pp 242–3 for both quotations.
[45] Aubert pp 251–4.
[46] Ward p 243.
[47] Finlay pp 187–8.

because of a lack of expertise in dealing with such documents, but given the general context of the Pope's pronouncements they could hardly be blamed for their hostile reactions. A clear message from the Pope was that Catholics were asking for a toleration for themselves which they would not always give to others; that he would continue to campaign against the introduction of any freedom of worship in countries like Spain, and that Catholics were urged, if they should return to power in countries where a certain pluralism had developed, to re-impose their previous monopoly.[48]

Neither Manning nor Newman, for example, had any difficulty in finding technical weaknesses in Gladstone's arguments, but Gladstone was not far from the truth when he described Pius as 'a Pontiff who has condemned free speech . . . the toleration of nonconformity, (and) liberty of conscience'. He used the example of the lack of freedom in the Papal States, 'where no opinion could be spoken or printed but such as (the Pope) approved', and concluded, on the basis of the Pope's attitude to the Church's right to use force, that the 'extreme claims of the Middle Ages have been sanctioned and revived'.[49]

It is obvious that Pius saw himself as defending the traditional rights of the Church against a hostile world. What needs to be stressed is that this outlook did not develop after the troubles of 1848, nor as a result of the increasing anti-Roman activities of the Piedmontese government. In his very first encyclical letter of 1846, when he had been pope for only a few months, he appealed to princes to defend the Church, and spoke of the struggle between Christ and Belial. The tone is already extremely pessimistic: the times were deplorable, and a bitter and terrible war was being prepared against the Church.[50] The letter dates from Pius' so-called liberal period, but, as he himself pointed out in the following year, it was a mistake for people to have interpreted his early political reforms as a sign of liberal inclinations, as though he thought so kindly of everyone that he might believe that even those who were not members of the Church could gain eternal salvation.[51] The pessimism, and the sense of persecution, remained throughout his pontificate, and did not need particular crises or anti-clerical activity to bring them to

---

[48] *Acta* 2 pp 538–49, to Mexican bishops, December 1856; 7 p 185, to Spanish bishops, March 1876. Also, Martina p 477, to President of New Granada, August 1847.
[49] Gladstone pp liv, 21–4, 75–8, 109, 128; McElrath pp 283, 300–4.
[50] *Acta* 1 p 23, '*Qui Pluribus*', November 1846.
[51] *Ibid* p 73, '*Ubi Primum*', December 1847.

the fore. When, for example, several hundred bishops met in Rome in 1862 to celebrate the canonisation of the Japanese martyrs, and were addressed by the Pope, he quickly passed from a brief mention of the joy which the occasion brought to him to a long account of the most deadly war being waged against everything Catholic. This was followed by a diatribe against freedom of worship and all the other errors of 'our most unhappy age'.[52]

A recent biographer of the Pope has commented on the contrast between his sense of persecution, with its accompanying harshness, and the strong human warmth which was evident on other occasions, and suggests that there was a deep contradiction in the Pope's mental make-up.[53] Whatever the truth of this, there is no doubt that Pius made capital out of persecution. He played on it to win sympathy and support, using language at times which is frightening in its exaggeration. In 1871, for example, he said to a group of ordinary pilgrims to Rome:

> It is not, however, true that on my Calvary I suffer the pains which Jesus Christ suffered on His; and only in a certain sense can it be said that in me is renewed in figure all that was in fact accomplished on the Divine Person of the Redeemer.[54]

He also used the sufferings of bishops affected by anti-clericalism to bind them more closely to himself. He and they were fellow sufferers in the struggle against the powers of darkness. In 1863, for example, he wrote to the Italian bishops, quoting Saint Leo to the effect that he accepted their sufferings as his own. The triumph of the Church over all its present troubles, he went on, was already apparent in the faith, love and obedience which bishops throughout the whole world showed towards the Pope and the see of Peter. He also picked out for praise their outstanding constancy in safeguarding religious unity.[55]

Pius' attitude to religious toleration reflected a number of different, although interdependent, positions: political, linked to a fear of what might happen to the Papal States if democracy was accepted in principle; psychological, arising from a desire for the security, certainty and clarity of the medieval system, and theological, based on a belief that the Church as an institution had inalienable rights, as

---

[52] *Ibid* 3 pp 451–4, June 1862.

[53] Martina pp 121–2.

[54] Quoted in Gladstone p 146, from *Discorsi del Summo Pontefice Pio IX*, 2 vols, ed P. de Franciscis (Rome 1872/3) which he reviewed for *BQR* 1875.

[55] *Acta* 3 p 611.

had the truth which she alone taught. He could not, therefore, accept nineteenth-century developments, and did all he could to perpetuate the last remnants of medievalism, wherever they might be found. This is not to deny the undoubted wrongs and the sufferings inflicted by the regimes which the Pope attacked, nor the need for an outspoken defence of the right of the Church to exist and function freely. Whatever was wrong, however, with the liberal model of society which was developing, the papal model was not acceptable as an alternative. Only by ignoring the obvious meaning of his words can his statements be interpreted as other than a universal condemnation in principle of religious toleration and freedom of worship. It was, in part, to let Catholic bishops everywhere know that this was the only acceptable view that the *Syllabus* was issued.

Bedford College of Higher Education

TOLERANT BISHOPS IN AN
INTOLERANT CHURCH:
THE PUSEYITE THREAT IN ULSTER

by S. PETER KERR

I T IS surely ironic that while the 'spoiliation' of the Irish Church
in 1833 provided the initial rallying cry for the Oxford Movement, neither Tractarian spirituality, theology nor its later liturgical innovations ever really took any serious hold on that Church. It
is perhaps even more paradoxical to note that though Alexander
Knox, one of the forerunners of the movement[1] was a lay member of
the Church of Ireland, other sons of that Church, notably Robert
Dolling, the notorious ritualist slum-priest; Dowden, the high-
church bishop of Edinburgh; and Tyrell, the Catholic modernist, all
made their careers outside Ireland. As Bishop Alexander was to
comment, perhaps with the more colourful ritualists like Dolling in
mind, the Church of Ireland had never to bear the cost of discovering
that the liturgy had 'lips of fire';[2] though perhaps that is not quite
accurate, for, as I hope to show, fear of the heat from those 'lips of
fire' was to be a major disruptive influence in the life of the Established, and disestablished Church in Ulster.

The reaction to Tractarianism—or Puseyism, as it was popularly
referred to—in the two united dioceses which cover the indus-
trialised north-eastern corner of Ireland, Down Connor and
Dromore, and, Derry and Raphoe is important because it is in this
area that Anglicanism was, and is, numerically strongest and where
intolerance of Tractarianism, if not quite leading to persecution, certainly radically affected the future character of the Church's ministry
in the northern province. Understanding the reaction, admittedly
extreme, in the north of the country may also give some insight into
the question of why Tractarian principles were more generally rejected by the Irish Church.

---

[1] J. H. Newman, *Apologia pro sua vita* 1864 (Everyman edn) p 105. The question of
the dependence of the Oxford Movement on Knox is discussed by Y. Brillioth in
his *Anglican Revival* (London 1933) Appendix 1.
[2] *Journal of the general synod of the Church of Ireland,* 1905, p lxvii. Cited in [R. B.]
McDowell, *The Church of Ireland [1869–1969* (London 1975)] p 25.

I want first to consider the attitudes of two of the bishops of Down Connor and Dromore, Bishop Mant and Bishop Knox, and Bishop Alexander of Derry and Raphoe (roughly covering the counties of Londonderry and Donegal). Both Knox and Alexander were subsequently archbishops of Armagh and the three bishops between them span a period of eighty-seven years (1823–1910) which should afford some insight into episcopal reactions both to events in Oxford between 1833 and 1845 and to the more long-term reverberations of the Tractarian movement in English church life. I will also discuss the attitudes of the lower clergy and laity to what they saw as the threat of Puseyism and finally try to come to some assessment of why Tractarianism was tolerated by the bishops and yet met with such intolerance by the rank and file members of the clergy and laity.

Bishop Richard Mant, Englishman, scholar and hymn-writer was translated to the diocese of Down and Connor in 1823 from the diocese of Killaloe, whose financial provision had not quite come up to what he had been led to expect! This is not to imply that he was a career bishop. Anyone who accepted a bishopric in the 'wild west' of Ireland during those troubled times could only be doing it out of a sense of Christian duty![3] Further, his biographer maintains that he was free from any suspicion of political time-serving in that his preferment to a more important, peaceful and remunerative diocese was delayed on account of some inopportune remarks on Romish errors, (in a charge to his clergy in 1820), which were considered politically unhelpful at that particular time, for, as he darkly alludes, 'the days were the days of conciliation'.

At the heart of Mant's new diocese lay Belfast which was to mushroom into a typical Victorian industrial city sharing more common interests with a Liverpool or Glasgow than with other Irish conurbations like Dublin, save for its increasingly bitter sectarianism. As the Protestant and Catholic workers were sucked into the city by the manning requirements of the new industries, they inevitably brought with them their centuries-old suspicion and hatred of each other, and in the cramped living conditions of a nineteenth-century industrial city this hatred was, in later years, to erupt into periodic rioting, a feature of the city's life which was not unconnected with many of the Anglican clergy's and laity's intolerance of Puseyism.

---

[3] 'It was the expressed opinion of one of his friends: "I think that he would never have gone to Ireland, had he not been impelled . . . by a sense of duty"'. [W.] Mant, [*The*] *Memoirs* [*of the Right Reverend Richard Mant* (Dublin 1857] p 113.

When called to account, Bishop Mant constantly asserted his anti-Tractarian pro-Protestant pedigree. During a Tractarian scare in the late 1830s—about which I shall go into more detail later—when the bishop was openly accused of having links with Oxford, he stated his loyalty to 'our National Church' in no uncertain terms:

> Against the Romish corruptions, I have again and again raised my voice . . . Against the modified form of Popery to which you advert, I also have not been wanting in bearing my testimony . . .[4]

He further pledged himself to continue to conscientiously oppose

> . . . every effort, however innocently or undesignedly made, for introducing amongst my brethren of the Protestant Established Church, any institution which even remotely savours of those false doctrines and teachers, whose evil ways are now so manifest elsewhere.[5]

Later, in 1842, when the Tractarian controversy was at its height, he published a critique of several of the Tracts.[6] Detailed attention was given to Tract XC and also to a letter from Dr Pusey to the archbishop of Canterbury commending what Mant described as the 'devotional provisions of Rome'. His biographer comments favourably on this defence of Protestant orthodoxy claiming that of all the bishops who commented on the tracts at this time 'none did so more energetically than the Bishop of Down and Connor'.[7]

But despite his protestations of orthodoxy, Mant also unequivocally owned his high-church allegiance: 'Wherever I am known' he wrote, 'I apprehend my high-churchmanship must be tolerably well known also'.[8] And indeed his writings and the character of his episcopate reveal him to be much more than merely tolerant of high-church principles, and therefore, it follows, of some of the central emphases of Tractarianism. In his Bampton Lectures which he delivered in Oxford in 1812, before going to Ireland, he argued that the doctrine of baptismal regeneration was both scripturally based and crucial to the Church's teaching.[9] Episcopacy was the lynch-pin of

---

[4]   "*Ecclesiologism Exposed*": the letters of the Rev'd William McIlwaine as published in the *Belfast Commercial Chronicle* 1843 pp 62–63.

[5]   *Ibid.*, p 57.

[6]   R. Mant, *The Laws of the Church* (a collection of the Bishop's charges reprinted in one pamphlet. See W. Mant, *Memoirs* p 410).

[7]   W. Mant, *Memoirs* p 411.

[8]   Quoted in the *Irish Ecclesiastical Gazette*, May 1857.

[9]   'And he undertook "to show, by the adduction of several passages in the Liturgy of

his ecclesiology. He readily concurred with Ignatius that 'without the bishop nothing should be done in the church'.[10]

Mant's concern about the conduct of public worship might also be said to indicate a mind in sympathy with some of the most important emphases of at least the second-generation Tractarians. The importance he attached to liturgical rectitude comes out very clearly in his writings and charges to his clergy. In *Horae Liturgicae*,[11] he inveighs against liturgical error, 'popish or puritanical', and goes so far as to list 'seventy-two discrepancies' in the performance of the Church's liturgy in his diocese. The discrepancies include infrequent communion; 'extemporaneous prayer', which not only endangered 'the purity of God's worship' but also threatened to 'compromise the character' of the national Church; private baptism and baptism 'out of a moveable common household basin' or 'a glass tumbler'.

However, his concern about public worship did not only manifest itself in the issuing of detailed regulations and instructions to his clergy. His interest in church architecture and in hymn writing must also set him loosely in the Tractarian High Church tradition. Some of his hymns are well-known. Perhaps not so well known is that he was a patron of the Cambridge Camden Society and was responsible for organising a society with similar objectives ('to add dignity and majesty to the houses of God in our land') under the title of The Church Architecture Society in his own diocese, a decision, as we shall see, which was not well received.

As one who was normally shy of public controversy, Bishop Mant was naturally suspicious about the direction in which Tractarianism seemed to be moving in the late 1830s and early 1840s. But this cannot disguise his tolerance for much of what the Oxford Movement stood for. Perhaps he, like Blomfield, Samuel Wilberforce and even John Keble are simply illustrative of the point that Tractarianism was not something which Newman, Froude and Pusey attempted to graft on to the Church of England and Ireland, but was indeed the flowering of a deeply rooted tradition within classical Anglicanism.

Though tolerant of different emphases within Anglicanism, Bishop Mant, as a typical 'zealous high-churchman', had still a rather

the Church . . . that the doctrine of regeneration by baptism is most clearly asserted by her", see W. Mant, *Memoirs* p 87.
[10] R. Mant, *Some Particulars in the Ministerial Character and Obligations examined and enforced* (Charge 1824) p 47.
[11] R. Mant, *Horae Liturgicae* (1845).

narrow view of the Church.[12] His successor, Robert Bent Knox, was, by all accounts,[13] a more liberal man of a much broader churchmanship. The son of an Irish archdeacon, a man of few scholarly pretensions, he was bishop of Down and Connor from 1849 until 1886 when he was translated to the archdiocese of Armagh. His breadth of vision is witnessed to by his support for a National System of Education in Ireland,[14] despite the opposition of most of his clergy, his encouragement of ecumenical prayer meetings[15] and his inauguration of annual conferences for his clergy and laity to discuss topics of concern to both Church and society.[16] It comes, then, as no surprise that his tolerance was also extended to those Churchmen with Tractarian or ritualist tendencies. In 1891, after complaints had been made by an organisation calling itself the Protestant Defence Association about the conduct of worship at two Dublin churches, Knox, now Primate, was very critical of the narrow-mindedness evinced by the complainants and of what he called their efforts 'to coerce and denounce certain incumbents and congregations, simply because they do not carry on their services with the same dull, solemn monotony which delights and no doubt edifies many'.[17] As a member of the court of the general synod, he also dissented from a judgement which upheld an appeal from the Dublin diocesan court against the dismissal of a complaint against the erection of a cross in St Bartholomew's church in Dublin.[18]

A bishop, then, who was tolerant of ritualist innovation. It was no easy tolerance born of apathy. On the contrary, it was the tolerance of a deeply principled man, who, while sharing his fellow-churchmen's antipathy towards Rome, nevertheless was unafraid to

---

[12] He was accused of bigotry by the Presbyterian historian W. D. Killen, *Ecclesiastical History of Ireland* (London 1875) p 474.

[13] One of Knox's opponents in the National Education controversy, Thomas Drew, said of him '. . . I learned that no man is more ready to give full and perfect toleration of the opinions of others who differ from him'. [A.] Lee [(ed)] *Report [of the Proceedings of the Conference of the Clergy and Laity of the United Dioceses of Down, Connor and Dromore* (Belfast 1862)] p 101.

[14] *Dublin Evening Mail*, 29 Apr 1862, quoted in the *Irish Ecclesiastical Gazette* 15 June 1862.

[15] I. Nelson, *The Year of Delusion* (1860) p 208.

[16] A. Lee, *Report*. Topics discussed at the conferences included 'Church and State', 'State Education' and 'Movements of Religious Thought in our Church'.

[17] *Journal of the General Synod of the Church of Ireland, 1890, xliv*, quoted in R. McDowell, *The Church of Ireland* pp 87–88.

[18] Royal commission on ecclesiatical discipline, minutes of evidence (Cd 3096) pp 231–40, H.C. 1906, xxxiii; also cited by R. McDowell, *The Church of Ireland* p 86.

go against prevailing opinion, whether it be with regard to the Church's policy on education[19] or disestablishment (he alone, among the bishops, supported Gladstone's bill in 1869), if he thought it was misguided. Knox would never be accused of being a Tractarian sympathiser as his predecessor was, but that is certainly not to say that he was intolerant of the movement's later ritualistic developments in the Irish Church.

William Alexander was probably the nearest that the Irish Church had to a Tractarian bishop, with perhaps the exception of Archbishop Trench. The son of an Irish country clergyman, he went up to Oxford in 1841 at the height of the Tractarian controversy, and fell under the spell of John Henry Newman. Indeed he was only prevented from following him to Rome by a chance meeting with 'a gentle Quakeress' whose 'very presence brought calm and soothing' with the result, concludes his biographer triumphantly, that 'never again was he tempted to forsake the faith'![20] However, despite his biographer's confidence in his subsequent protestant orthodoxy, and despite his own gentle repudiation of his 'old Oxford teachings' in 1869,[21] both he and his wife—the hymn-writer C. F. Alexander—kept in constant touch by both letter and visit with such men as Keble,[22] Pusey[23] and even Manning.[24] Safer, more central high-churchmen such as Samuel Wilberforce[25] were also amongst Alexander's friends.

His stance in the controversy over the proposed revision of the Book of Common Prayer which troubled the recently disestablished Church in the early 1870s also indicated his definite Catholic preferences. He sided with the Archbishop of Dublin—'Puseyite Trench', according to the pro-revisionists' graffiti—and against many of the laity in opposing a protestant purge of the Prayer Book. What is more, in his opposition to any revision, he laid great stress on the authority of the unchanging inheritance of the Christian tradition,

[19] In a speech at school opening in Belfast he commended the National System of Education as being '. . . the only system suited to the want and requirements of this country . . .' *Dublin Evening Mail*, 29 Apr 1862.

[20] E. Alexander, *Primate Alexander, Archbishop of Armagh* (London 1913) p. 69. Alexander himself writes of how Newman's sermons showed him 'the hidden things' of his own soul, though he later 'found many drawbacks in his paragon of other years', p 71.

[21] *Ibid* p 300.

[22] *Ibid* p 125.

[23] *Ibid* p 158.

[24] *Ibid* p 140.

[25] *Ibid* p 152.

'the dogmatic faith from which the Christian Church had for ages looked upon whole generations passing away'.[26] He also aired grave doubts about the 'stability' which a 'state establishment' gave to the Church, very much in the style of Keble in 1833. As late as 1895 he was planning to invite the notorious Father Dolling to a Church congress in Derry, the heartland of rugged puritanism. Fortunately he was dissuaded from such a course of action by a more sensitive layman of the diocese.[27]

The bishop of Derry's Tractarian predilections were no secret from the Church at large. On his appointment to Derry and Raphoe in 1867 the Lord Lieutenant of Ireland, a fervent evangelical wrote to him:

> I may venture to say what I am sure no one is better aware of than yourself, that even a very moderate amount of High Churchism would be more out of place in the Diocese of Derry amongst the somewhat severe and rugged people than perhaps in any other diocese in the kingdom.[28]

Even his daughter admits that he was rarely invited to preach in Ireland for fear of what he might say as a 'High Churchman', though she hastily adds that his sermons were in great demand in Oxford, Cambridge and all the English Cathedrals.[29] There is little doubt then about Alexander's sympathy with and tolerance for not only Tractarian principles, but also some of the leading members of the movement. Though, it must also be noted that his Tractarian leanings were not sufficiently blatant or provocative to prevent him being chosen as Primate of the disestablished Church of Ireland in 1896—surely in some sense an indigenous vote of confidence in his protestant pedigree.

The tolerance of the bishops in Ulster towards Tractarian principles was not generally reflected in the attitudes of the lower clergy and laity. There were isolated instances of Tractarian practice,[30] but certainly not on the same scale as in Dublin.

[26] H. Patton, *Fifty Years of Disestablishment* (APCK 1922) p 43.
[27] E. Alexander, *Primate* pp 277–8. Alexander was particularly grieved by the Canon forbidding the placing of a cross on the Communion Table, *Ibid* pp 185–188.
[28] *Ibid* p 147.
[29] *Ibid* p 262.
[30] Bishop Mant's warnings against a mixed chalice, the singing of creeds and excessive kneeling may indicate the presence of some High Church practices in his diocese. R. Mant, *Horae Liturgicae* p 14, The Revd William Henn was the first clergyman in the Diocese of Derry to give 'full assent to the propaganda' (from Oxford), E. Alexander, *Primate* p 73. The Revd William McIlwaine, one of Bishop

Opposition to the Puseyites was much more common. We have noted how Bishop Alexander regretted his opposition to 'so many of the laity' in his refusal to entertain a protestant revision of the Prayer Book and how he was prevailed upon by a prominent layman (and in response to synodical hostility) to cancel his invitation to Father Dolling to speak at a Church congress. The hostility aroused in Belfast amongst laymen in the early 1900s by suspicions that the government was going soft on ritualists has been described elsewhere.[31] Perhaps not so well known is that it was intolerance towards suspected Puseyite tendencies which was responsible for bringing about the postponement of the first organised church extension programme in Belfast in 1843.

The Church Accommodation Society had been founded in 1838 to facilitate the building of additional churches for the growing population of industrial Belfast. It ceased operations in 1843, apparently according to plan. However, things were not quite as they seemed, for, according to one observer:

> Many regretted the dissolution of this society . . . but the harmony and confidence exhibited at the 1838 meeting no longer existed. Romanising influence had sadly increased to the perversion from the truth of many among both clergy and laity.[32]

Since the society had originally been founded amidst concern about, and to strengthen the Church against, the 'enemies' of the Church in the 'University of Oxford', the suspicion that such enemies had infiltrated the society itself was bound to excite hostility.

But what was the substance of these allegations? What was the nature of this 'Romanising influence' which was apparently on the increase? It seems that several members of the Church Accommodation Society, including Bishop Mant, were also inaugural members of the Down Connor and Dromore Church Architecture Society, founded to encourage 'whatever tends to add dignity and majesty to the houses of God in our land.'[33] That the society became affiliated to the Cambridge Camden Society, of which Mant was also a patron, did nothing to promote its popularity in the diocese at large. William

Mant's most hostile critics, was to become 'the sole representative of the moderate High Church party' according to his obituary in *The Irish Ecclesiastical Gazette.*

[31] R. McDowell, *The Church of Ireland* p 88.

[32] A. Dawson, *The Annals of Christ Church, Belfast, from its foundation in 1831.* Unpublished papers, Northern Ireland Public Records Office, T 1075/11.

[33] W. Mant, *Memoirs* p 421.

McIlwaine, the acerbic vicar of St George's, Belfast (later, according to his obituary in *The Irish Ecclesiastical Gazette*, to be converted from his extreme evangelicalism to become 'the sole representative of the moderate High Church party . . .') spearheaded the attack in a series of letters to the *Belfast Commercial Chronicle*, attempting to prove the connection between 'the rise and progress of Puseyism and the new-fangled rage of Church Architecture'. He described the Church Architecture Society as that '. . . young and sleeky cub', which the 'Protestants of Belfast and Ulster' will 'have no fancy for fondling' especially

> when they see it drawing its milk, and receiving and returning the carcasses of the parent lioness, whose sojourn is Cambridge, and den on the banks of the Isis.[34]

McIlwaine concluded that that 'originally noble institution, the Church Accommodation Society', because of its connections with the Church Architecture Society was now tainted by Puseyism. Once the red rag of Puseyism had been waved, the outcome of the controversy was inevitable, quite apart from the fact that McIlwaine was unable to produce any real evidence to link either the Church Architecture Society or the Cambridge Camden Society with Puseyism. The Church Accommodation Society ceased operations and organised church extension was delayed for another nineteen years, for, as the curate of Christ Church, Belfast later observed:

> It was not to be expected that the great body of clergy would give their counsel, or the laity contribute their means, to the furtherance of a work which might . . . be perverted to the intro-duction of Romish error into their pure and scriptural church.[35]

The most significant aspect of this affair was not so much the impact it had on church extension in the diocese, important though that was, but, as Mant said, the placing of the bishop 'under the dic-tation and the ban of his clergy'. Diocesan policy had been radically altered by the intolerance of the laity and lower clergy towards so-called Puseyite tendencies. This was not as in England, the reaction of the mob to ostensibly Roman practices in their local parish church. It was the considered response of informed church people, lay and ordained, not to ritualism as such, but to unsubstantiated insinuations of Tractarian influence in high places.

---

[34] W. McIlwaine, *Ecclesiologism Exposed* p 38 (Letter XII).
[35] A. Dawson, *Annals*.

Why such intolerance and hostility amongst churchmen, when the bishops' attitude towards the general thrust of Tractarianism, if not the more extreme manifestation, was so tolerant? Further, why does such intolerance remain so central a feature of church life in Ulster?

One answer might be that the bishops, certainly Mant and probably Alexander, could not communicate their tolerance because they were not close enough to their people. They could not appreciate the depths of feeling aroused by the spectre of Puseyism. To the bishops the Romanising tendency associated with the Tractarians was a theological issue rather than a possible threat to political identity. Being well versed in the Anglican tradition they were able to distinguish between what was of Rome and what was of Cranmer, Taylor, Hooker, Bramhall and others. This seems to be clearly implied by a comment of Archbishop Alexander to his diocesan synod in 1898:

> One naturally often asks oneself the origin of the Romeward tendency which developed itself in the Oxford Movement.[36]

The Protestantism of Mant, Alexander and of Knox, though in the case of the latter to a lesser extent, was more theological than political, more English than Irish. And this is not surprising, for Mant and Alexander, scholar and poet, both Oxford educated and constantly in contact, by visit and letter, with the English establishment, appear as fish out of water, as 'English' bishops in an Irish Church. It is not wholly surprising then, that Bishop Mant in response to criticism of the Cambridge Camden Society admitted that minds which nursed such grievances were possessed of a 'sensitiveness' in which he could not easily participate.[37] Alexander's invitation to Father Dolling also seems less out of character, when viewed in this light.

Bishop Knox, a naturally more liberal man, did work much harder at getting the clergy and people on his side, though, while he won their respect, he did not really succeed in softening their attitudes. His ability to get alongside his clergy may not be unconnected with the fact that he was educated in Dublin rather than Oxford. But it would be far from the truth to suggest that it was only the bishops' insensitivity which prevented them from communicating their own more tolerant attitude towards Tractarianism. There were much more fundamental factors involved.

The susceptibility of the Church, certainly in Belfast, to revivalist

---

[36] E. Alexander, *Primate* p 75.
[37] W. McIlwaine, *Ecclesiologism Exposed* p 63.

spirituality was certainly important in the formation and sustenance of minds who would have no truck with Puseyism. If Tractarianism gave the English Church a new sense of mission and a rich source of spirituality in the nineteenth century, it might also be argued that the Irish Church, particularly, though not exclusively in the North, was correspondingly influenced by evangelicalism, strongly tinged by revivalist tendencies.

The 1859 revival affected the Established Church in Ulster much more deeply than the Church on the mainland. It did not encourage people to leave the Church for the sake of some new sectarian ideal, but rather confirmed and enlivened their commitment to the beliefs and liturgy of the Established Church. Bishop Knox himself welcomed the 200% increase in confirmees and took it as evidence of 'the truly spiritual character of this great work'.[38] Incumbents spoke of a rise in attendance at church and the Lord's table and an 'increased seriousness at public worship'; they also noted the comparative absence of the hysteria usually associated with revivals.[39] Church life was being revitalised and nurtured by revivalism. Perhaps even more significant, the revivalist tradition was being incorporated into the life of the Established Church. This meant that the Church not only received the undoubted spiritual stimulus of revivalist theology, but also the strongly anti-Roman bias of that theology, which encouraged the conviction that 'if the Evangelical Protestants of Ireland were united together in one firm band, by God's blessings Popery's advances would be checked.'[40] In such an atmosphere there was little hope of tolerance towards Puscyism.

But perhaps the basic cause of intolerance towards Tractarians had to do with the question of political identity. To the Anglicans of Ulster particularly, Protestantism was, historically, as much about political identity as religious allegiance, an identity which was thrown into greater relief in the growing industrial city of Belfast where they lived alongside Catholics whose religion was taking on an increasingly nationalist aspect. Further, this Protestant identity seemed to come increasingly under threat as the century progressed from revitalised and aggressive Catholicism on the one hand, and

---

[38] *Irish Ecclesiastical Gazette*, July 1859.
[39] W. Gibson, *The Year of Grace* (1860) p 408; C. Seaver, *The Ulster Revival* (Belfast 1859) pp 7–8; R. Knox, *Charge to Diocese of Down, Connor and Dromore* 1858 Appendix. A. Dawson, *Annals*.
[40] C. Seaver, *The Ulster Revival* p 22.

government attempts to appease Irish nationalist aspirations on the other. This intertwining of political identity and religious commitment was deeply ingrained in Church life at all levels. An editorial in a Church newspaper blithely stated:

> . . . we feel that Popery with all its connextions and appendages is actually the chief cause of all the misfortunes of Ireland.[41]

While the Reverend Thomas Drew, vicar of Christ Church, Belfast, in a sermon immediately preceding some serious rioting in 1857, exhorted all Orangemen to hold together till the laws were impartially administered and 'the parliament is purified' of 'incompetent Romanists'. He further reminded his congregation that they were 'enjoying the liberty purchased' by their Protestant forbears, and, he recalled that, 'we call the land of William's victory "Protestant Ireland" . . . .'.[42] Even Bishop Knox described Gladstone's Home Rule bill of 1893 as 'a bill to suppress the protestant faith'.[43]

It is not surprising that this clash of identities surfaced periodically in the form of sectarian rioting. Perhaps a little more unexpected is the direct involvement of some of the Anglican clergy in the instigation of these riots.[44] When these factors are taken into consideration, it is not difficult to understand why Puseyism met with such intolerance. It would have had difficulty enough in taking root where only religious sensibilities were threatened, as in some English parishes, but intolerance was inevitable where political identity was also at stake.

The bishops did not share the intolerance of the wider Church towards the Puseyite threat. They would certainly have drawn back from the ritualistic excesses of the Tractarians' successors, as did many English churchmen. But they were tolerant of much of Tractarian teaching because they considered it to be firmly rooted in the Anglican tradition. They could not appreciate the intolerance of their clergy and laity because their political identity was not threatened by the seemingly Romeward trend of the Tractarians, at least to the same extent. Though it is true that even their political

---

[41] *The Christian Examiner.*

[42] *Commission of Enquiry into the Riots in Belfast, 1857 & 1864* (1864) pp 250–53.

[43] *Journal of the general synod* 1893, pp xiv–lii; also cited in R. B. McDowell, *The Church of Ireland* p 99.

[44] The Rev'd Thomas Drew and the Rev'd William McIlwaine were particularly singled out for the part they played in inciting Protestants to riot. *Commission of Enquiry.*

allegiance was somewhat shaken by Disestablishment,[45] and, as we have seen, by the Home Rule bill, all in all, they rested secure in their identity as 'English' bishops in an Irish Church.

Lincoln Theological College

---

[45] Alexander of Derry wrote of the passing of the bill for the Disestablishment and Disendowment of the Irish Church: 'I can never forget the summer night just after the decision when I reeled out into the cool air almost hearing the crash of a great building', E. Alexander, *Primate* p 173.

PERSECUTION AND TOLERATION IN PRE-COLONIAL AFRICA: NINETEENTH-CENTURY YORUBALAND

by JOHN ILIFFE

WHEN CHRISTIAN missionaries penetrated sub-Saharan Africa during the nineteenth century, three main persecutions of their converts caught the attention of Europe. The earliest took place in Madagascar between 1837 and 1857, when several hundred converts attached to the London Missionary Society were killed.[1] The last of the three occurred in the Buganda kingdom of East Africa and culminated on 3 June 1886 when some 26 Baganda Christians were burned on a single pyre.[2] Both these persecutions took place in autocratic and expanding kingdoms whose modernising rulers had initially welcomed missionaries for their skills. In both kingdoms the missionaries converted younger members of the ruling class. In both, the deaths of the modernising rulers precipitated traditionalist reactions in which converts were killed more to discourage and control Christianity than to extirpate it. Both persecutions were bounded in time. Both failed, leading only to further Christian expansion, the capture of power by Christian modernisers, and their use of the authoritarian political institutions to create overtly Christian kingdoms.

Between these two cases of triumphant martyrdom, a third instance of persecution was also famous in its day. It took place among the Yoruba people who today inhabit south-western Nigeria.[3] The centre of persecution was Abeokuta, the chief town of the Egba section of the Yoruba. Yet the Egba persecution which caught

---

[1] See [William] Ellis, [*The*] *martyr church* (London 1870); Bonar A. Gow, *Madagascar and the Protestant impact* (London 1979) cap 1.

[2] J. F. Faupel, *African holocaust: the story of the Uganda Martyrs* (London 1962) p 198. The best account is J. A. Rowe, 'The purge of Christians at Mwanga's court', *Journal of African history* 5 (1964) 55–71.

[3] The outstanding modern account of missionary work in this area is [J. F. A.] Ajayi, *Christian missions* [*in Nigeria 1841–1891* (London 1965)]. The most detailed account of the persecution is P. R. McKenzie, *Inter-religious encounters* [*in West Africa: Samuel Ajayi Crowther's attitude to African traditional religion and Islam* (Leicester 1976)] pp 26–31. See also Peter McKenzie, 'The persecution of early Nigerian converts', *Orita* (Ibadan) 11, 1 (June 1977) 3–14.

European attention in 1850 was entirely different from those in Madagascar and Buganda. Neither Abeokuta nor Yorubaland was an autocratic or expanding kingdom; both were fragmented, pluralistic polities engulfed in a century of civil war. Yoruba did welcome missionaries for their skills, but the missionaries did not make converts among the ruling class; their few adherents were mostly of low social standing. It is not certain that even one Christian was killed for his faith. The persecution was not bounded in time but continued throughout the second half of the nineteenth century. It did not result in Christians capturing power. And Yorubaland did not become a Christian country; it is today evenly divided between Christians and Muslims, many practising much eclecticism.[4]

Yet although events in Yorubaland were less dramatic than in Madagascar or Buganda, they reveal much more about persecution and toleration in pre-colonial Africa. One reason is that the sources for Yorubaland are especially good. There the Church Missionary Society in particular employed numerous African clergymen and evangelists who were required to keep daily journals. These are the main sources for this paper.[5] The other reason why the Yoruba case is especially instructive is that they possessed perhaps the most sophisticated intellectual and religious ideas of any African people who still held mainly to an indigenous faith.

Yoruba religion was a complicated and unsystematised body of beliefs and practices which often contradicted one another.[6] There was a supreme, life-giving God known as Olorun, the Owner of the Heavens. He was the ultimate source of spiritual power and recipient of worship, but he had no institutionalised cult or priesthood. Religious life focused chiefly on subordinate divinities (*orisha*) who included cosmological figures, personified natural forces, and tutelary divinities. *Orisha* were objects of cults with temples, festivals, priests, and initiates. In addition, each descent group venerated its ancestors and there were quasi-secret societies and a divination system, Ifa, whose practitioners were the intellectuals of Yoruba society

[4] J. S. Eades, *The Yoruba today* (Cambridge 1980) pp 128, 143.
[5] The records of the Church Missionary Society (cited as CMS) are in the Birmingham University Library, those of the Wesleyan Methodist Missionary Society (cited as MMS) are in the Library of the School of Oriental and African Studies, London. I am indebted to the librarians of both institutions and also to the Executive Director of the Historical Commission of the Southern Baptist Convention for a microfilm of the papers of T. J. Bowen.
[6] See E. Bolaji Idowu, *Olodumare: God in Yoruba belief* (London 1962).

and perhaps the only people who reflected on the relationships among the heterogeneous religious elements.[7] The diversity of the indigenous religion provided a wide range of resources for those responding to Christianity, which partly explains why responses were so varied. The multiplicity of cults had also accustomed Yoruba to religious choice and co-existence, although this had limits: in 1884 the cult of the smallpox god was temporarily prohibited in Abeokuta and Ode Ondo during an epidemic.[8] Yoruba also had experience of Islam, which had arrived by the seventeenth century. The first Christian missionaries in Abeokuta held that the Muslim presence was 'one practical proof of religious toleration',[9] but Muslims had experienced much persecution during the early nineteenth century. The supreme value of Yoruba culture was not so much toleration as harmony.[10] Their way of thought appeared clearly in their legal system, which made family heads chiefly responsible for keeping order. In extreme cases a family might execute an uncontrollable member, while the authorities might censure someone taking a relative to court or refuse to interfere in a dispute unless it bred actual violence.[11] If wronged, a man might first retaliate and then wait for chiefs and elders to restore harmony.[12] As a missionary described one case, 'The palaver was, as it is done in most cases, settled in favour of all parties, and to the justice of neither party'.[13] If public order was gravely threatened, however, the authorities might intervene ferociously. This pattern of family autonomy and low-level disorder, balanced by attempts to preserve harmony and punctuated by violent interventions from the authorities, was precisely the experience of Christianity in nineteenth-century Yorubaland.

[7] See [William] Bascom, *Ifa* [*divination* (Bloomington 1969)].

[8] Lahanmi, journal, 14 March 1884, CMS G3/A2/0/1884/208; Young, journal, 29 July 1884, CMS G3/A2/0/1885/7; A. K. Ajisafe, *History of Abeokuta* (2 edn Bungay 1924) p 142.

[9] Townsend, journal, 25 September 1846, CMS C.A2/0.85/233. For Islam, see T. G. O. Gbadamosi, *The growth of Islam among the Yoruba, 1841–1908* (London 1978).

[10] See, for example, Robert Farris Thompson, 'Yoruba artistic criticism', in Warren L. d'Azevedo ed, *The traditional artist in African societies* (Bloomington 1973) pp 58–9.

[11] W. S. Allen, journal, 24 August 1869, CMS C.A2/0.19/8; Lahanmi, journal, 20 August 1884, CMS G3/A2/0/1885/45; Meakin, journal, 15 September 1858, CMS C.A2/0.69/10.

[12] Wood to Lang, 12 November 1885, CMS G3/A2/0/1886/4.

[13] Hinderer, journal, 23 March 1851, CMS C.A2/0.49/101.

The first resident missionaries, Henry Townsend and Samuel Crowther of the Church Missionary Society, reached Abeokuta in 1846. Their journals and those of other missionaries show the Yoruba using their indigenous religious resources to locate Christianity in their world without disturbing its harmony. One resource was prophecy, in which Ifa diviners were skilled. If Ifa could be shown to have foretold the coming of Christianity, its arrival would positively validate old beliefs. Six years after the missionaries settled in Abeokuta, a diviner explained 'that Ifa foretold them that Obbatala [the *orisha* closest to Olorun] would have two children, the youngest of which would hereafter disobey him (meaning the European to be the child) because they do not bow down as to worship after the heathens.'[14] Those more welcoming to the missionaries preferred to quote a prophecy that white men would come to bring peace to Yorubaland.[15] Yoruba also had a notion of enlightenment, *olaju*, which was to be achieved by gaining access to the secret knowledge possessed by the rich and powerful, especially foreigners.[16] The missionaries' possessions and skills demonstrated such knowledge and they had no inhibitions about exploiting its appeal:

> I then told them of the temporal blessings which resulted from true religion and its inseparable companion, civilization—improvements in arts, and scientific discoveries. Amongst other things I named rail-ways, steam-engines, and gas-light; which surprised them very much, and led one of the Chiefs to exclaim, with great emphasis, 'God make that nation!'[17]

In 1879 a diviner listened to an evangelist's account of the Christian God and then 'rose and prostrated before me [a common Yoruba gesture of respect], and said, "Truly you have a superior knowledge".'[18] This search for enlightenment could breed disillusionment:

> I had a long conversation with a Babalawo [diviner]. He acknowledged that they (the heathens) had long missed the way; but it is now impossible for them to give up their ancestral customs. He said he had made enquiries about our books

---

[14] C. Phillips, journal, 24 October 1852, CMS C.A2/0.77/3.

[15] Crowther to Acland, 22 September 1852, CMS C.A2/0.31/23.

[16] J. D. Y. Peel, '*Olaju*: a Yoruba concept of development', *Journal of development studies* 14 (1977–8) 139–65.

[17] Annear, journal, 7 August 1844, MMS 260/F/6.

[18] S. Johnson, journal, 4 July 1879, CMS G3/A2/0/1880/160.

from the converts, in hopes to find in them a clearer means for divination than the Ifa. But he was disappointed to find that they contain only historical records.[19]

The idea that it was too late to abandon ancestral customs drew on another element in Yoruba thought. The strongest unit of Yoruba society was the descent group and its clients, often living in a single compound which might occupy half an acre and contain scores or even hundreds of people bound together by collective interest in property, collective responsibility in law, and collective representation in their town's politics through their senior male member.[20] In such a society, heredity was the core of identity. A man was literally the reincarnation of an ancestral spirit. His social position and even the marks cut into his face were inherited. How then could a man possibly change his religion? One evangelist failed to convert his parents because 'they are so blindfolded that they think it to be against nature to exchange one religion for another'.[21] A convert from another family was warned that 'he cannot be happy in heaven, for he will go there alone'.[22] The claim that God had given Yoruba their religion just as He had given Christianity to white men was the most common objection to missionary preaching. Yet it could also facilitate co-existence, much as the Roman Empire could often tolerate Judaism.[23] In 1877 an evangelist conversed with two devotees of Shango, the god of thunder:

> Both of them, one after another would make me to believe that after God had made them being unable to care for them all, distributed them among the gods, some to Mohammed his messenger, and others, few in number he reserved for himself to be serving him truly; and this latter are the bookpeople [Christians]. Therefore, continued they, we are quite right to serve Shongo, and we would never venture to turn your mind from your book, since God alloted you to that.[24]

This view did not allow for an individual to adopt a new faith, but for this he could draw on another strand in the generous inconsis-

[19] C. Phillips, journal, 1 October 1888, CMS G3/A2/0/1889/56.

[20] See [N. A.] Fadipe, [*The*] *sociology* [*of the Yoruba* (Ibadan 1970)] pp 97–118. Family-based compounds were especially predominant in new towns like Abeokuta and Ibadan: see J. D. Y. Peel, *Ijeshas and Nigerians* (Cambridge 1983) p 36.

[21] Wright, journal, 6 August 1866, CMS C.A2 PP 0.97/4.

[22] S. Johnson, journal, 24 December 1877, CMS C.A2/0.58/9.

[23] G. E. M. de Ste. Croix, 'Why were the early Christians persecuted?' *PP* 26 (1963) p 25.

[24] Doherty, journal, 9 October 1877, CMS C.A2/0.35/13.

tency of Yoruba belief. Each individual, it was held, had a personal destiny which he must fulfil in order to gain happiness:

> Before a child is born (or reborn), the ancestral guardian soul appears before Olorun to receive a new body . . . a new breath, and its fate or destiny . . . during its new life on earth. Kneeling before Olorun, this soul is given the opportunity to choose its own destiny, and it is believed to be able to make any choice it wishes, although Olorun may refuse if the requests are not made humbly or if they are unreasonable.[25]

This belief enabled an individual to claim that his choice of Christianity or Islam was the fulfilment of his destiny. By the late nineteenth century some Muslims were claiming that their destiny to join Islam had been revealed by Ifa, and it was said that a diviner had told Samuel Crowther's parents that his son would worship Olorun.[26] Moreover, popular belief held that happiness itself was proof of having correctly identified one's destiny:

> They said, there is one by the name Odubiro who had forsaken his Idols and embraced Christianity; and from that time since, he had been blessed with children, whereas before his conversion, he had been living with a child. So some of them said, it is because the religion of the white man agrees with him.[27]

Popular thought also considered it essential to remain loyal to such a commitment once made. In 1873 evangelists rebuked a Christian who had relapsed under persecution:

> An Ifa priest who met us in the street, confirmed our conversation and advised him to adhere to the Christian religion which he once embraced, upon which, he said, his prosperity depends, as he has never ceased from experiencing troubles after troubles since he has given up Christianity.[28]

This notion of destiny is peculiar to certain West African religions and is not found elsewhere in black Africa.[29] It could support much religious pluralism:

> One of the men replied, it was no matter, whether one was a Mahomedan, or a pagan, he had seen people professing all sorts

[25] Bascom, *Ifa* p 115.
[26] Gbadebo Gbadamosi, '"Odu Imale": Islam in Ifa divination and the case of predestined Muslims', *Journal of the Historical Society of Nigeria* 8, 4 (June 1977) 88–92; McKenzie, *Inter-religious encounters* pp 14–15.
[27] Anonymous journal (from Ikorodu), 27 February 1872, CMS C.A2/0.29/9.
[28] D. Williams, journal, 14 November 1873, CMS C.A2/0.90/23.
[29] Meyer Fortes, *Oedipus and Job in West African religion* (Cambridge 1959) p 19.

of religion during his travels in Africa, but he found this was the chief thing to be attended to, to be kind and gentle; as for the devil every body had his own maker, who after having formed a person, gave him a certain spirit, 'esu' (devil) to be his companion, and what this companion tells us, he said we must do, adding, if we do not do so, our maker will be vexed.[30]

Yet these approaches to toleration are recorded only occasionally in the mission journals. A more common response was to absorb Christianity (or Islam) as one more cult into the immense complexity of Yoruba religion. Muslims and Christians invited this by using the name Olorun—the Owner of the Heavens—as the name for Allah and Jehovah. Since Olorun had no indigenous cult or priesthood, the missionaries filled a gap in Yoruba religion. Olorun's supreme position gave his new cult undeniable authority. 'We ought to worship God, is it not so?' an African pastor asked two listeners. 'Both replied in the affirmative.'[31] In 1859 a priest of another cult 'came out to us in the street, and on reaching us fell flat with his face to the ground before saluting us; he called us children of God . . . He said though he and all in the place were worshipping idols yet they look to God for help'—exactly the relationship which Yoruba believed to exist between *orisha* and Olorun.[32] Moreover, Christians often behaved like a cult group. Townsend had to dissuade his converts from wearing 'some badge of Christianity in their mode of dress', as was the normal practice of cult members.[33] 'I made him to understand', an evangelist recorded of one conversation, 'that as Pricilla is a Communicant, no body else ought to bury her . . . As a heathen, he dares not do it; just as the Ogboni Club would never permit any other Club to perform the funeral ceremony of any one of their members.'[34] 'Here! Man of God I give up my daughter for the book religion', one Yoruba declared, thereby dedicating her to Olorun in place of her previous dedication to Shango.[35] A common reason for devotion to an *orisha* was the advice of a diviner consulted

---

[30] Maser, journal, 13 September 1864, CMS C.A2/0.68/130. Eshu, the messenger between Olorun and men, was commonly misinterpreted by missionaries as the Devil.

[31] D. Williams, journal, 12 February 1873, CMS C.A2/0.90/21.

[32] W. Allen, journal, 27 December 1859, CMS C.A2/0.18/17.

[33] Townsend to Secretary, 17 May 1853, CMS C.A2/0.85/16.

[34] Doherty, journal, 20 August 1881, CMS G3/A2/0/1882/29.

[35] J. Johnson, 'A visit of inspection to Ilaro and itinerancies', January 1879, CMS C.A2/0.56/52.

in misfortune. Such distress became the most common reason for adopting Christianity, which in the early period was essentially a cult of affliction. Unsophisticated evangelists exploited this mercilessly. 'I . . . promised to attend her', one wrote, 'and that my fee would be, that she become a convert to the Christian Religion as soon as she is well.'[36]

As one among many cults, Christianity could be patronised by rulers alongside all their subjects' other religious activities. Laying the foundations of a church, a ruler declared, 'Why should I not build a house for the God who made us all, when we used to build for our orishas'—and in the evangelist's journal the words 'used to' were inserted as an afterthought.[37] Moreover, if Christianity was one among many cults, it must in the general interest take no more than a proper place among them, lest the *orisha* be offended. In 1853 a chief enquired 'whether it was not enough for all Egbas that now some of them have become Christians'.[38] Yoruba saw religion not as an 'either/or' but a 'both/and' matter. Their most common desire was to co-exist with the new cult of Olorun in their habitually eclectic manner. Ibadan's chief physician expressed this view in 1859:

> As soon as our Church was built, he said, he would be the first to attend it. At last he carried me to an Orisa (Idol) grove of his own planting, there he said, when I have learnt your worship of God, there I will put it, by the side of all my other Orisas.[39]

Thoughtful Yoruba pondered the religious plurality surrounding them. In 1856 a missionary in Abeokuta 'noticed for the first time the people saying: why has God given us so many modes of worship, meaning the heathenism, the muhamedan and ours'.[40] Yet the eclectic mind remained astonishingly absorbent. Nothing is more striking in the religious history of nineteenth-century Yorubaland than the lack of paranoia in indigenous views of Christians, despite the fact that many psychiatrists regard persecutive delusions as especially common in Africa.[41] Only one accusation of witchcraft against

---

[36] Savage, journal, 24 February 1896, CMS G3/A2/0/1896/159.

[37] Doherty, journal, 19 February 1875, CMS C.A2/0.35/8.

[38] Maser, journal, 20 July 1853, CMS C.A2/0.68/112.

[39] Hinderer, 'Half yearly Report of the Ibadan Station ending April 1859', CMS C.A2/0.49/116.

[40] Maser, journal, 16 May 1856, CMS C.A2/0.68/122.

[41] See, for example, Marie-Cécile and Edmond Ortigues, *Oedipe africain* (new ed Paris 1973) cap 4.

a Christian is recorded, and he was declared innocent.[42] Beliefs in cannibalism were common, but no Christian is recorded as having been accused of it, as Christians were (among other unnatural horrors) in Buganda.[43] Nor were Christians ever blamed for the terrible fires which devastated Yoruba towns every dry season, although there were occasional grumbles that fires had grown worse since Europeans arrived.[44]

Many Christians responded positively to the warm embrace of eclecticism. They continued to fear witches, observe as much as possible of the ancestral cult, and believe that each misfortune was a divine punishment for sin.[45] Some, including schoolteachers, belonged to the Ogboni society which, apart from political and judicial functions, was also guardian of the earth cult.[46] Yet full religious eclecticism was surprisingly rare among Christians. 'It is seldom we detect any one in idolatry except under great fear of man', Townsend reported in 1853.[47] The main reason was the extreme hostility towards Yoruba religion inculcated by the missionaries and especially their African agents, who saw the world in the purest shades of black and white. One wrote in his journal:

> A young man remarked in the course of our conversation that it was impossible for them to forsake their gods, whom their mothers had served in their old age, but that they were willing to serve God at the same time. I told him that God was a God of light and the day, and the Idols, Gods of the night and that both could never be brought together.[48]

An uneducated evangelist put it more bluntly: 'So as you never in one day eating with dog in dunghill, the same the Great God never eating with any Idols, for God hated it.'[49] Towards Yoruba customs, too, the missionaries were uncompromising. They required converts to abandon charms, destroy 'idols', renounce polygyny, bury their dead in Christian cemeteries, and absent themselves from their

---

[42] Lahanmi, journal, 9 February 1888, CMS G3/A2/0/1889/125.
[43] Walker to Baylis, 13 March 1894, CMS G3/A5/0/1894/116.
[44] Barber, journal, 10 March 1858, CMS C.A2/0.21/20.
[45] J. Smith, journal, 5 April 1859, CMS C.A.2.0/83/16; Olubi to Committee, 26 June 1871, CMS C.A2/0.75/3; White, journal, 28 May 1874, CMS C.A2/0.87/84.
[46] 'Report of C. A. Gollmer for the halfyear ending September 25th 1861', CMS C.A2/0.43/136.
[47] Townsend to Secretary, 17 May 1853, CMS C.A2/0.85/16.
[48] Maser, journal, 7 November 1856, CMS C.A2/0.68/124.
[49] Vincent, journal, 13 August 1884, CMS G3/A2/0/1885/8.

relatives' polygynous marriages and any indigenous rite which included sacrifice. A missionary in Ibadan reported:

> In going to town I found almost before every house broken pots and calabashes heaped up. I asked what it mean and received the answer, they do it that nobody in the compound may die. I tried then to show them the foolishness of such a custom and smashed some of the pots etc to pieces.[50]

Townsend rejoiced when a protégé 'stamped upon the devils altar in the street'.[51] An African minister was encouraged by 'the contemptuous views which the young ones have for the gods of their fathers'.[52]

Yoruba were shocked and saddened by the intolerance of Christians. 'Everything the Christians speaks of as sinful', ran a popular song.[53] 'I visited the headman of the hamlet', a schoolteacher recorded,

> and asked him how he would like missionaries among his people. He said, it would depend upon how the missionaries come. I asked what he meant by 'how the missionaries come'— he said, if they come and remain quiet disturbing nobody about his own peculiar mode of serving God—leaving the Sango-worshippers go on with their Sangoes, and the Ifa-worshippers with their Ifas, then they can live together in peace. I told him that the duty of missionaries is to turn people from all these false gods to the one true and living God. He and his friends present entered into a long argument to show that everybody ought to be left undisturbed as to his peculiar mode of serving God, since they do not deny His existence.[54]

An African minister ended his account of a disputation with the words: 'They persisted in opposing me, but a few men who sat under a tree called them away and told them that it was of no use to oppose me.'[55]

To Yoruba, Christians were intolerant intruders into a tolerant society. And just as Christians in the Roman Empire were persecuted because their 'monotheistic exclusiveness' seemed to threaten the whole society by endangering its relations with the gods,[56] so

[50] Kefer, journal, 7 August 1854, CMS C.A2/0.59/6.
[51] Townsend to Straith, 20 July 1852, CMS C.A2/0.85/12.
[52] Moore, journal, 21 June 1864, CMS C.A2/0.70/51.
[53] S. Johnson, journal, 26 April 1879, CMS C.A2/0.58/11.
[54] Macaulay, journal, 22 November 1855, CMS C.A2/0.65/93.
[55] White, journal, 5 July 1856, CMS C.A2/0.87/51.
[56] Ste. Croix, 'Why were the early Christians persecuted?' p 24.

Christians were persecuted because they threatened the harmony of the pluralistic Yoruba world. Yet the interesting point about persecution in any society is the form it takes. That was true in Yorubaland. Only twice, in 1849 and 1867, was persecution launched by the authorities in Abeokuta, and even then the statement requires severe qualification. By contrast, most persecution took place within the family-based compounds. The significance of this appears when persecution in Yorubaland is compared with that in Buganda and Madagascar. Baganda Christians were seldom persecuted by kinsmen, except occasionally by die-hard conservatives after Christians had gained power.[57] During the state-directed persecution of 1886 Christians were frequently protected by non-Christian kinsmen.[58] The main reasons for the absence of family persecution in Buganda were the power exercised by the monarch and the structure of the family. At marriage Baganda left their parents' villages to establish independent elementary households.[59] Great men had great households, but their male followers were generally attached by political or personal ties and could join other chiefs if they wished. Moreover, households had few religious functions and the first Christians were mostly people at court detached from family backgrounds.[60] This social organisation differed greatly from the corporate descent groups of the Yoruba. In Madagascar, on the other hand, social organisation was closer to that in Yorubaland, with a strong family structure and ancestral cult. Some Imerina families protected Christian members, but others reproached them and even delivered them up to death.[61] What distinguished the Malagasy persecution was the control exercised by the state, which until 1837 protected Christians even against the hostility of conservative kinsmen, then at intervals encouraged families to hand over their Christian members, and finally ended the persecution in 1857. By contrast, the authorities in Abeokuta neither favoured nor disfavoured the new religion but concentrated instead on preserving harmony when it was threatened by conflicts within the compounds.

Forms of persecution in pre-colonial Africa were thus closely correlated with political and social organisation. That is the main point

---

[57] See, for example, CMS Unofficial Papers 84, F/3/1, book V, p 19.
[58] Michael Wright, *Buganda in the heroic age* (Nairobi 1971) pp 22–3.
[59] John Roscoe, *The Baganda* (2 edn London 1965) p 96.
[60] See John V. Taylor, *The growth of the Church in Buganda* (London 1958) pp 32–4.
[61] Ellis, *Martyr church* pp 68, 78, 138–40; William J. Townsend, *Madagascar: its missionaries and martyrs* (London n.d.) pp 65, 81–2.

of this paper. It must now be illustrated in detail in the Yoruba case. The first missionaries settled in Abeokuta in August 1846. Their earliest report of persecution was written just over a year later. It was a classic case of family persecution and the authorities met it with a firm defence of toleration:

> One of the first persons that joined our class of candidates was a man called Aina on doing which he threw away his god. His wife missing the god in the place that it used to occupy and that her husband had cast it away was greatly enraged against him and backed by her mother used every means to torment him, to induce him to abandon his intention of becoming a Christian; they proceeded so far as to summon him before their chief court of law to answer for despising the country gods; but Aina pleaded his own cause boldly defending himself on two grounds, that of the liberty that is given to all to worship what they pleased, and also of the right that he had of doing what he would with his own, from the former he pleaded his right to worship the true God and from the latter his right to throw away a false one having purchased it with his own money. He obtained judgment in his favour.[62]

During the following months sporadic family persecution occurred, especially in Igbore township, where Crowther's church stood. The township was dominated by warchiefs at odds with the Sagbua, the chief magistrate of Abeokuta. It was also a trading centre whose interests were threatened by British actions against the slave trade.[63] Early in October 1848 an influential man of Igbore put his younger brother, a Methodist member, into the stocks at the township's Ogboni council house for refusing to take part in ancestral veneration. Crowther successfully begged the convert's release,[64] but a week later one of his own baptismal candidates, Oguntolla, was also put in the stocks by his relatives. Crowther decided to let Oguntolla 'weather it out' in order to show that Christians 'are governed by better principles'. After three days the Ogboni elders, perplexed by Oguntolla's firmness, debated 'whether it was right to confine a man for so long a time for what he conscientiously believed would do him

---

[62] Townsend, journal, 12 December 1847, CMS C.A2/0.85/239. The case was previously mentioned in Crowther to Greenway, 15 September 1847, CMS C.A2/0.31/2.

[63] Earl Phillips, 'The Egba at Abeokuta: acculturation and political change, 1830–1870', *Journal of African history* 10 (1969) pp 120–1.

[64] S. A. Crowther, journal, 4–6 October 1848, CMS C.A2/0.31/104.

good'. Some insisted that a young man must not 'defeat the object of the whole council', but the meeting broke up 'in vexation and disappointment'. Public opinion was swinging in Oguntolla's favour and next day, after failing to frighten him into recantation, the elders initiated him into the Ogboni society (presumably as a means of discipline) and released him. 'His leg which was thrust through a perforated wall for five days were swollen and painful.' He was baptised a month later.[65] A period of relative tranquillity followed. In July 1849 a woman persecuted by her husband and relatives for attending church appealed to the Sagbua and won a resounding declaration in favour of pluralism and toleration:

> Sagboa now speakes. With a prudent and calm speech he drew the minds of all to his subject. Then he began to ask: 'Did the Egbas ever know of so many country-fashions [indigenous cults] as they now do? No. Whether Sango had ever injured any of such people, who do not worship him, and who of late have forsaken him? No. Are there not among us worshippers of Obbatala, Ifa, Orisako and of hundreds of Gods? And have we not many Mahomedans in the Land? Yes. Well then, did people ever express any illwill towards those differences? If we tollerate the one, we must of necessity tollerate the other also. Therefore my advice is this: that ye permit this woman to worship whom and what she pleases without the least infererence.' And with this advice all agreed.[66]

Yet in the compounds, as a Methodist evangelist put it, 'the fathers are rising up against their children, and the mothers against their children, the father-in-law against his son-in-law, the brothers are against each other, because they become Christians'.[67] The crisis came in October 1849. What appears to have escalated family persecution into concerted action was that the warchiefs and merchants of Igbore, Igbein, and Itoku townships found an issue which moved the Ogboni elders. That issue was the first Christian burial of a convert on 10 October 1849. This offended the Ogboni, who, as guardians of the earth cult, claimed to supervise funerals. The convert belonged to Itoku township. On 10 October, following the funeral, several Christians in Itoku were arrested and chained in the Ogboni council house:

[65] *Ibid.*, 13–17 October and 19 November 1848, CMS C.A2/0.31/104.
[66] Müller, journal, 3 July 1849, CMS C.A2/0.72/11.
[67] Bickersteth, quoted in Martin to Secretaries, 18 July 1849, MMS 261/A/25.

The people bored the wall of the house and have the converts feet fastened in the wall. And besides this, they beat them severely, all because, simply, they renounced the custom of their forefathers, and became the followers of the meek and lowly Jesus.[68]

The elders complained that the converts were disobedient and that Christianity should be confined to Europeans and those Yoruba who had lived in the British colony in Sierra Leone, but on 16 October the converts were beaten, fined, and released.[69] Four days later the persecution shifted to Crowther's congregation at Igbore and for the first time the urban crowd, a potent element in Yoruba history, was called into action:

Oro the executive power of the nation was called out in Igbore town, the Ogboni drums were beating in fury, and a great multitude were armed with billhooks, clubs and whips, catching and dragging our converts to the council house where they were unmercifully beaten and cruelly tormented . . . As they could not get a denial of their faith in Christ, they shaved the heads of them all in order to shave baptism off, purchased a pigeon and wrung the blood upon the heads of the women.[70]

Some seventy or eighty Christians were imprisoned in Igbore and apparently smaller numbers elsewhere, although Ake, the senior township, resisted pressure to persecute. After three days, compound heads and relatives secured the release of individual prisoners by making valuable presents to the elders. On 24 October the last prisoners were released, although they were fined heavily and forbidden for a time to go to church.[71] Just over a year later another outbreak of persecution followed the burial of a Christian who had also belonged to the Ogboni society. The elders complained of Christians 'refusing to worship their gods, refusing to go to war, corrupting the town, using European dress, revealing secrets to women &c &c.' On 2 December 1850 the town crier proclaimed 'That whosover has thrown away his Ifa and Orisa should no more go into the house of God'. Seven days later the wives of Christians were forbidden to trade in the market.[72] Early in 1851, however, the crisis

[68] Bickersteth, journal, 13 October 1849, MMS 261/A/32.
[69] Hinderer, journal, 10–16 October 1849, CMS C.A2/0.49/96.
[70] Crowther to Venn, 3 November 1849, CMS C.A2/0.31/8.
[71] Hinderer, journal, 20–28 October 1849, CMS C.A2/0.49/96.
[72] S. A. Crowther, journal, 21 November–9 December 1850, CMS C.A2/0.31/112.

was forgotten when Abeokuta was attacked by its great enemy, Dahomey. The British Consul visited the town, presented four boxes of ammunition, and insisted that persecution of Christians must cease. The chiefs agreed and Crowther's congregation immediately increased.[73]

There was no further concerted attack on Christianity in Abeokuta until 1867. Despite occasional alarms, the 1850s and early 1860s were, at the public level, a time of great toleration. 'We enjoy almost unbounded liberty among this people', an Anglican missionary reported in 1855.[74] His Methodist counterpart agreed: 'We can preach in any market, or street in Abbeokuta, without fear of being troubled, except by a noisy woman, or giddy young man now and then.'[75]

Within the compounds, however, conflict between Christians and their relatives continued. Death remained an important focus of dispute. So did sickness, for not only might Christians be blamed for illness among their relatives but, as the mission journals present it, sick Christians might be abandoned by non-Christian relatives and friends.[76] Yet the distinctive feature of family persecution—and of persecution in Yorubaland generally—is that it weighed most heavily on the weakest family members: women, the young, and slaves. In the fine account which he published in 1965, Ajayi argued that the chief obstacle to Christianity in nineteenth-century Yorubaland was the solidarity of the community and especially of the family compound. He scarcely mentioned persecution.[77] Since he wrote, historians have realised that family solidarity in Africa often meant in part the domination of weaker family members by mature men.[78] That was certainly so in Yorubaland. Although mature Yoruba women enjoyed much independence, for example, young women did not. At Ijaye in 1853 'The husband of Gbade, the best classwoman, entered Church during service, armed with a rope, to tie his wife,

---

[73] *Ibid.* 10–19 January 1851, CMS C.A2/0.31/113; [Earl Harold] Phillips, 'The Church Missionary Society, [the imperial factor, and Yoruba politics, 1842–1873' (unpub PhD thesis, University of Southern California 1966)] pp 157–66.

[74] Smith to Venn, January 1855, CMS C.A2/0.82/30.

[75] Champness to Hoole, 29 January 1862, MMS 263/C/7.

[76] See, for example, Morgan, journal, 20 August 1857, CMS C.A2/0.71/33.

[77] Ajayi, *Christian missions*, pp 4–5, 15, 39, 226.

[78] The seminal work is Claude Meillassoux, *Anthropologie économique des Gouro de Côte d'Ivoire* (Paris 1964). For the changing historiography, see John Lonsdale, 'States and social processes in Africa: a historiographical survey', *African studies review*, 24 (1981) pp 139–225.

should he find her here.'[79] In this case, as in others, the husband was under pressure from his wife's family to discipline her. In another case a husband complained of his wife's Christian practices to her family, who bound and beat her and then scarified her breast and rubbed in 'a kind of powder for the purpose of counteracting the injurious effect of the drug supposed to be given her by the white man, which made her so bold and obstinate'.[80] The numerous victims of persecution recorded by the missionary Anna Hinderer in Ibadan in the mid 1850s all seem to have been young women.[81] Of course, not all Yoruba men tyrannised over their womenfolk. There are recorded cases of wives persecuting their husbands into abandoning Christianity, daughters trying to force their mothers to give up the new religion, and adult children seeking to stop their fathers becoming Christians.[82] Normally, however, adult men escaped direct persecution and could claim the protection both of the law, as in Aina's case,[83] and of male solidarity. When a man sought in 1853 to force his younger brother to abandon Christianity, 'the war chief of his town sent to the brother to trouble him no more, stating that it was folly to take steps with a man of age and sound judgment'.[84]

The young had no such protection. Yoruba law gave parents almost total authority over children, whose upbringing was very severe.[85] A missionary wrote from Abeokuta in 1856 of a young woman who 'had been chained since the day she had been delivered by the King into the hands of her mother, and . . . had been much beaten of which the stripes were still to be seen'.[86] In 1860 a girl was whipped for refusing to marry any but a Christian husband. Two years earlier Townsend had redeemed a boy sold into slavery for persisting in attaching himself to a mission station.[87] A case from Ode Ondo in 1890 illustrates the predominant rationale:

[79] Mann, journal, 2 December 1853, CMS C.A2/0.66/80.
[80] White, journal, 25 March 1867, CMS C.A2/0.87/70.
[81] *Seventeen years in the Yoruba country: memorials of Anna Hinderer* (London 1872) pp 131–7.
[82] Maser, journal, 9 July 1858, CMS C.A2/0.68/125; S. Crowther, journal, quarter ending 25 December 1856, CMS C.A2/0.32/65; J. Johnson, 'From Ibadan to Oyo and Ogbomoso', n.d. [1877] CMS C.A2/0.56/51.
[83] Above, p 368.
[84] King to Straith, 25 April 1853, CMS C.A2/0.61/3.
[85] See Fadipe, *Sociology,* pp 108–9.
[86] Maser, journal, 9 July 1856, CMS C.A2/0.68/123.
[87] J. Smith, journal, 6 July 1860, CMS C.A2/0.83/18; Townsend, journal, 17 July 1858, CMS C.A2/0.85/263.

Today we have the first instance of open persecution. An old man rudely entered the church while I was preaching, to force out his son (a lad about 18 years old) from the church. He failed to carry out his intention, being evidently overawed by the sight of the reverent congregation. But when the young man returned home, he bound him and flogged him severely. The following day Mr Coker and I went to remonstrate with him. But we found him as obstinate as ever. He said he had permitted a nephew of his to attend Christian instruction, but he could not permit the young man who is his own son, for if they both became Christians, he would have no one after his death, who will keep up the worship of the Osonyin [god of medicine] which he had inherited from his ancestors, and regard as indispensable to the well being of his family.[88]

Apart from women and the young, those most often persecuted were slaves. They were numerous in nineteenth-century Yorubaland and their treatment ranged from brutality to almost complete adoption into their master's family.[89] That many Christians were slaves indicates that they often enjoyed much independence, although some were slaves of Christian masters who brought their households with them into the church. On the other hand, slaves were obviously vulnerable to persecution, especially in the later nineteenth century when the British colony at Lagos became a haven for escaped slaves, whose masters naturally resented Europeans and their faith. In 1893 Ode Ondo saw a persecution which illustrated the methods of deterring slaves from conversion:

> one was loaded with chains from the farm for refusing to partake of the sacrifice; another, a woman, was tied to a post and there chastised for several days . . . ; a third, from being an adopted daughter and the pet of her mistress, was not only degraded to the usual servitude, but forced to swear that she will never attend the Church again.[90]

Even during the relative tranquillity from 1850 to 1867 the Christians of Abeokuta knew themselves to be surrounded by violence and threatened with domestic persecution. Occasionally they went to church armed, although they never had to use their weapons. Many

---

[88] C. Phillips, journal, 16 February 1890, CMS G3/A2/0/1890/166.

[89] The most comprehensive (and perhaps somewhat idealised) account is E. Adeniyi Oroge, 'The institution of slavery in Yorubaland with particular reference to the nineteenth century' (Unpub PhD thesis, Birmingham University 1971).

[90] Lijadu, journal, 18 February 1893, CMS G3/A2/0/1893/132.

reduced the occasions for conflict with their neighbours by building separate quarters around the mission stations. These settlements were known as *wasimi*, 'come and rest'. Christians in Abeokuta also formed a separate military force and a civil company 'for purposes of mutual protection against the oppressions of the Chiefs.'[91] Congregations sometimes accepted legal responsibility for members, paid fines or compensation collectively, or clubbed together to redeem a slave convert.[92] With less success they tried to assert a separate law. In 1889 the Abeokuta Church Council resolved:

> All the Christians of this place should unite to a man, to resist heathen interferance with the property of a Christian, whenever a 'will' is made, and that the Christians should not interfere with the property of heathen relations: and that Christians should no more allow their daughters to be given to heathen in marriage.[93]

In Yoruba towns other than Abeokuta there was no clear parallel to the persecution of 1849. The nearest approximation occurred in 1879 in Ogbomosho, where conflict over the burial of a convert led to intervention by the chiefs and the crowd in which the church and much Christian property was destroyed.[94] Certain towns banned Christians entirely, notably Ife (the spiritual capital of Yorubaland, whose ruler excluded missionary work until 1899) and Ijebu (whose middleman position close to the coast made it especially hostile to European penetration until defeated by British troops in 1892).[95] By contrast, in Ibadan, the most powerful and warlike of Yoruba towns, the severe family persecution which afflicted the first Christian enquirers during the mid 1850s later gave way to resigned contempt. 'Christianity is at a discount', a Yoruba minister reported from Ibadan in 1877, 'and Christians hold a low social position and are accounted and spoken of as a lazy, idle and coward people because of their refusal to go out with war and slave making expeditions and their steady pursuit of Agriculture'.[96] Yet given Ibadan's

---

[91] Tugwell, 'Abeokuta: re Companies', n.d. [September 1898] CMS G3/A2/0/1898/150. Generally, see Maser to Venn, 15 May 1867, CMS C.A2/0.68/75.

[92] Wood to Lang, 10 June 1887, CMS G3/A2/0/1887/143; Olubi to Committee, 17 January 1872, CMS C.A2/0.75/4.

[93] Minutes of Abeokuta Native Church Council, 1 July 1889, CMS G3/A2/0/1889/115.

[94] Olubi to Fenn, 19 February 1880, CMS C.A2/0.75/47.

[95] 'Bishop Phillips's account of work in the Ondo Mission District from Decr. 1899 to March 1900', CMS G3/A2/0/1900/89; Robert Smith, 'Nigeria–Ijebu', in Michael Crowder (ed), *West African resistance* (London 1971) pp 170–7.

[96] 'Report from Revd. J. Johnson', August 1877, CMS C/A2/0.56/50.

militarism, it is remarkable that it tolerated the despised Christians at all. The main reason was political. From the 1850s, as the British established themselves in Lagos and interfered in Yoruba politics, Ibadan sought their aid against the Egba and Ijebu who stood between Ibadan and the coast.[97] To tolerate Christians was a very small part of the price which Ibadan paid for British friendship. Political motives also encouraged toleration of Christians in Ondo, which strove to remain neutral in the Yoruba civil wars. 'It is their desire that we should remain here for our presence serve as a sort of protection for the town', the minister in Ode Ondo reported.[98] Similarly, the Alafin of Oyo, struggling to regain his ancient status as the premier Yoruba ruler, needed British aid and protected Christians even at their most provocative:

> We took the whole of the congregation out into the market place one morning, and for two hours we were singing and preaching the way to Jesus. This caused some opposition as some people went to the king to complain that the white men and the Christians were in the market telling the people to leave their idols. The king asked if we were using clubs to make the people believe? and being told that we were using no force he said whoever wishes to become a christian let him do so.[99]

Yet in the last resort toleration and persecution were family matters. Neither chief nor fellow-Christian could do much to restrain a family that was bent on collectively persecuting a Christian member. In 1874 the senior chief of Ibadan—the most powerful man in Yorubaland—'wondered, that he was not listened to' when he tried to stop a family persecuting one of its young women.[100] 'Such combined malice of Elders and a family, nobody can hinder, even not the King', it was observed in Abeokuta.[101] And when the local evangelist reported two cases of family persecution to the Alafin of Oyo in 1874, the incumbent of the most distinguished Yoruba throne told him 'that though he have no objection to any of his peoples embracing Christianity yet he has no power to prevent

---

[97] See. B. A. Awe, 'The rise of Ibadan as a Yoruba power in the nineteenth century' (unpub D. Phil Thesis, Oxford University 1964) cap 6.
[98] C. Phillips Jr., journal, 8 August 1879, CMS C.A2/0.78/22.
[99] Harding, circular letter, 30 September 1892, CMS G3/A2/0/1892/192.
[100] Olubi, journal, 15 June 1874, CMS C.A2/0.75/30.
[101] Maser, journal, 21 May 1855, CMS C.A2/0.68/119.

family persecution that every man is at liberty to do what he likes in his family in religious matter'.[102]

Defence of the patriarchal social order was a major priority for Yoruba rulers.[103] Only urgent political considerations ranked higher. Their role appeared most clearly in Abeokuta in October 1867 during the second major outbreak of religious conflict surrounding Christians: the Ifole or 'house-breaking'. Its roots lay in the deterioration of relations between Abeokuta and Britain following the British occupation of Lagos as a colony in 1861, which led the Egba to fear British aggression against them.[104] When regular troops from Lagos landed on the mainland in October 1867, the Egba authorities closed all churches in order to oblige the missionaries to explain to Queen Victoria the need to recall the provocative Governor of Lagos. That in fact crowds of men looted and destroyed the mission stations was not the chiefs' intention, so they claimed, but 'the act of a lawless rabble'.[105] The Christian accounts of the looting do not suggest that it was the spontaneous work of the crowd,[106] but the attack was specifically against missionaries rather than converts. The missionaries left Abeokuta and did not return to settle there permanently for another thirteen years. For the Christians who remained, Christianity was officially prohibited for several months, but congregations met in private houses. The Methodist chapel was reopened on 9 August 1868 and the central Anglican church at Ake on 3 January 1869.

The public position of Christians in Abeokuta eased again during the last third of the century, mainly because relations with Lagos improved. Christianity spread geographically within Yorubaland, but in Abeokuta the converts became a distinct segment of the population with little missionary zeal. In 1872 Ake church had 312 communicant members; in 1878, 306; in 1890, 302.[107] When a European missionary settled there again in 1880 he found 'almost everything in

---

[102] Moore to Hutchinson, 5 May 1874, CMS C.A2/0.70/28.

[103] For a vivid example, see R. H. Stone, *In Afric's forest and jungle, or six years among the Yorubans* (Edinburgh 1900) p 59.

[104] See especially Phillips, 'Church Missionary Society' pp 697–718.

[105] Saburi O. Biobaku, *The Egba and their neighbours 1842–1872* (Oxford 1957) p 90.

[106] W. Allen, journal, 13 October 1867, CMS C.A2/0.18/20; Maser, 'The second persecution of the Abeokuta Mission, Octr. 1867', CMS C.A2/0.68/163; Grimmer to Boyce, 4 November 1867, MMS 263/E/91.

[107] Williams to Secretaries, 11 December 1872, CMS C.A2/0.90/30; Williams to Fenn, 7 March 1879, CMS C.A2/0.90/36; *Proceedings of the Church Missionary Society* (1890–1) p 26.

a most delapidated condition'.[108] In many fields the Christians achieved a working compromise with indigenous society. Christian participation in 'heathen' funerals became more common and they also began again to pay bridewealth at marriage, which the first Christians had abandoned as a 'pagan' custom. In 1883 fewer than a quarter of Ake's communicants were males; the other men in the congregation were barred by polygyny.[109] The Methodist church in Abeokuta, chronically neglected by the mission authorities, was in no better state. In 1870 it had 147 full members; in 1878 there were only 99 and headquarters feared 'that for Abeokuta the day of grace is past'.[110]

Although organised persecution of Christians ceased after 1867, the obstacles to conversion remained. 'Though new enquirers meet with no such persecutions as those in the early days of Christianity in Abeokuta', a schoolmaster wrote in 1884, 'yet they do punish enquirers in such a cunning way'.[111] Young men who became Christians might still be accused of betraying male secrets or deprived of their fiancées. The sick and bereaved might still be neglected or ostracised. Women and the young might still be assaulted. In the Roman Empire public fear and hostility towards Christians decreased with time, so that persecution became increasingly political, but there is no similar evidence in Yorubaland, where family persecution continued vigorously well into the twentieth century.[112]

Family persecution, long sustained, was much more damaging to Christianity in Yorubaland than were the relatively brief and politically-motivated persecutions in Madagascar and Buganda. Admittedly, it would be wrong to ascribe the limited success of Christianity in Yorubaland to persecution alone. The sophistication of their indigenous religion left Yoruba with less need of Christianity than most Africans, in the sense that this might also be said of Muslims or Buddhists. Moreover, nineteenth-century Yoruba showed little interest in literacy or Christian education, a curious fact

---

[108] Faulkner to Fenn, 28 January 1881, CMS G3/A2/0/1881/35.

[109] Tugwell, 'Regarding burials, heathen and Christian', n.d. [September 1898] CMS G3/A2/0/1898/149; 'Abeokuta Divorce Court. August 1898', CMS G3/A2/0/1898/151; Lamb to Lang, 8 May 1883, CMS G3/A2/0/1883/88.

[110] Marshall to Boyce, 31 October 1870, MMS 264/B/36; Thomas to Kilner, 2 December 1878, MMS 272/A/34; C. P. Groves, *The planting of Christianity in Africa* (4 vols London 1948–58) 2 p 235.

[111] Green, journal, 25 March 1884, CMS G3/A2/0/1885/44.

[112] Ste. Croix, 'Why were the early Christians persecuted?' pp 26–7; Peel, *Ijeshas*, pp 169–70.

which has never been explained but contrasts strongly with the enthusiasm in Buganda and Madagascar. Nevertheless, the daily suffering of family members at the hands of those closest to them was a most effective restraint on conversion. 'Many are hindered in hearing the truth thro' fear of persecution in their own family', Townsend reported in 1850, 'and few indeed can join us without encountering some opposition somehow'.[113] 'In my class of Candidates today', a missionary wrote from Ibadan in 1855, 'on the question "What is the greatest evil in the world"? expecting the answer "it is *Sin*" one of them entirely betraying the thoughts of their hearts answered "*Persecution*".'[114]

This pattern of persecution also shaped the future character of Yoruba Christianity. Within their own families Christians were as authoritarian and intolerant as their parents.[115] But whereas in Buganda and Madagascar persecution by the state bred authoritarian Christian orthodoxies, its absence from Yorubaland left Christians without the drive or the means to dominate their neighbours. Western Nigeria today is a place of outstanding tolerance.[116]

St John's College, Cambridge

[113] Townsend to Secretaries, 8 November 1850, CMS C.A2/0.85/3.
[114] Hinderer, journal, 27 October 1855, CMS C.A2/0.49/113.
[115] P. C. Lloyd, 'The elite', in P. C. Lloyd and others (ed), *The city of Ibadan* (Cambridge 1967) pp 139–43. For individual accounts, see T. A. Adebiyi, *The beloved bishop: the life of Bishop A. B. Akinyele* (Ibadan 1969); Wole Soyinka, *Aké: the years of childhood* (London 1981); Carlos Moore, *Fela, Fela: this bitch of a life* (London 1982).
[116] I am indebted to Dr J. S. Eades and Dr J. M. Lonsdale for their comments on a draft of this paper, and to Professor J. A. Crook and Dr P. H. Linehan for advice on comparative reading.

TOLERATION AND PERSECUTION
IN COLONIAL NATAL

by J. B. BRAIN

NATAL WAS the second acquisition of the British Empire in Southern Africa. While the Cape Colony was acquired permanently in 1814, and the Orange River Sovereignty temporarily in 1848 only to be abandoned in 1854, Natal was annexed reluctantly but permanently, for mixed strategic and philanthropic reasons, in 1844. The White population at this time was a few thousand, the Black about eighty thousand. The only missionary work that had taken place up to this time was that of the American Board of Commissioners for Foreign Missions, which had established two stations in Zululand in 1835, and the Church Missionary Society. In the period before the annexation they had had little success among the Zulus in Natal, and none at all in Zululand because of Dingane's attitude to them. All left Zululand in 1838 and the missions were not reopened until the 1860s.[1]

The decision to annex Natal was followed by the approval of a number of emigration schemes in a decade in which large scale emigration, particularly to North America, was in full swing. Despite the energetic propaganda being disseminated in England to encourage emigration to Natal, the 189 migrants in the first scheme were Germans who arrived under the leadership of Jonas Bergtheil to grow cotton. Bergtheil, who had been in Natal since 1846, had had some success with this crop and had successfully sold his products in Manchester; he had been unable, however, to persuade any of the local inhabitants to accompany him back to Natal. He therefore turned to Germany, and after a great deal of difficulty persuaded forty-seven families to return with him. These German immigrants settled outside Durban in what is now the industrial area of New Germany, where they were joined by Pastor C. W. Posselt, a Lutheran from the Berlin Missionary Society.[2]

---

[1] J. M. Sales, *The Planting of the Churches in South Africa* (Grand Rapids 1971) pp 112–3.

[2] R. E. Ralls, 'Early immigration schemes in Natal, 1846–1853' (unpub. M.A. thesis Natal 1934).

In 1848 the first British settlers began to arrive in Natal, some individually and others as part of emigration schemes such as those of Byrne and Irons. They brought with them their English culture, including the religious beliefs and attitudes prevalent in England at the time. Altogether about five thousand arrived from the British Isles between 1849 and 1852, three thousand of them under the Byrne scheme. William Irons, a Wesleyan minister at St Albans, was the chairman of the Christian Emigration and Colonisation Society, and his well-organised party arrived in Natal in 1848–49 to settle at Verulam, named after a sponsor, on the coast north of Durban. The third group of 248 came in 1849 from Yorkshire and is known as the Boast party, although in fact, as a result of Boast's unexpected death, it was financed by Joseph Smith, his father-in-law. They settled in the York district of inland Natal. Many of these, and also of those who settled in Durban and Pietermaritzburg, were Methodists.[3]

There were also a number of French speaking immigrants from Mauritius, who arrived in small parties after 1847. Many were Roman Catholic sugar or cotton planters who settled along the coast. Norwegian Lutherans settled at Marburg on the south coast. Among the Byrne settlers were people of various Protestant sects— Anglicans, Presbyterians, Methodists, and Congregationalists—and the British regiments stationed in Pietermaritzburg also included members of these denominations together with a sprinkling of Catholics. Although the Boers who had formed part of the Great Trek and had settled in Natal in 1838 had begun to leave as soon as the British annexation was announced, some nevertheless remained permanently, especially in northern Natal, so that the Dutch Reformed Church also had its adherents. The members of these various Christian denominations, whether from Europe or from the Cape Colony, brought with them all the prejudices, intolerance and bigotry that prevailed in those places at the time. Distance from Europe and slow communication tended to petrify these antipathetic attitudes, change being slow to reach Natal. In addition there was a tendency for members of each sect to fight among themselves over what must appear from a distance of a hundred years to be rather trifling issues. The local press, which has been described as 'vitriolic',[4] added fuel to the flames.

[3] A. F. Hattersley, *British settlement of Natal; a study in imperial migration* (Cambridge 1950) pp 94–148.
[4] B. B. Burnett, *Anglicans in Natal* (Durban 1953) p 57.

Thomson, describing the mid-Victorian period, states that the most generally accepted and practised form of Christianity at the time was that which may be broadly called evangelicalism, with its emphasis on moral conduct as the test of the good Christian.[5] It transcended all barriers of sect. Among the Natal settlers were many with this evangelical outlook, and, as in England, it was the Anglo-Catholic movement connected with the names of Newman, Keble, Pusey and Froude that was particularly disliked by the evangelicals. The Evangelical Alliance was formed in England in 1846 to oppose the Roman Catholic church and all its influence. Any hint of ritualism aroused strong emotions in both England and Natal. It was into this atmosphere of religious intolerance that John William Colenso arrived in 1854.

The government of Natal, however, sticking carefully to its guarantee of religious toleration, gave grants of land in urban areas for the erection of places of worship without prejudice; each denomination was also allocated land for burial on request. Unlike the situation in the Cape Colony in the 1820s, when Colonel Christopher Bird, colonial secretary to Lord Charles Somerset, had been forced to resign when he refused to take the oath of office in the days before the Catholic emancipation act,[6] there was no such problem in Natal. The first bishop, M. J. F. Allard (1853–74), sensed that Governor Pike disliked Catholics[7] but received courteous treatment at his hands. Nevertheless John Bird, surveyor, acting colonial secretary and colonial treasurer, believed to the end of his life that it was because of his Roman Catholic faith that he had been denied promotion to the high position his talents deserved, as his father had been.[8] Later, in 1888, some anti-Catholic prejudice was shown by J. C. Bodley, the so-called historian of France, but it seems to have been related more to social class than to religious doctrine:

> As the R.C. bishop is a Frenchman, I thought perhaps Benediction would give me a reminiscence of the past, but I might as well have gone to the Salvation Army as to the Papist cathedral, filled with Irish dragoons and niggers, where half a dozen loud-voiced Colonial girls bawled round a harmonium.[9]

[5] D. Thomson, *England in the nineteenth century* (Harmondsworth 1955) p 107.
[6] W. E. Brown, *Catholic church in South Africa from its origins to the present day* (London 1960) p 10.
[7] J. B. Brain, *Catholic beginnings in Natal* (Durban 1975) p 45.
[8] *Ibid* p 45.
[9] J. E. C. Bodley, 'Unpublished journal' in A. F. Hattersley, *The Natalians; further annals of Natal* (Pietermaritzburg 1940) pp 163–4.

Among the first missionaries to enter Natal were James Archbell and James Allison. Both were Methodists, and the latter brought a considerable group of followers to settle at Indaleni and at Edendale, a highly successful missionary enterprise near Pietermaritzburg. Both had disagreements with their church leaders and broke off official contact.[10] The Presbyterians were first represented in Natal by the Rev. William Campbell, who built a church for the community in Pietermaritzburg in 1854. The number of adherents was small, yet within a few years, as a result probably of personality clashes, a second Presbyterian church had been built a few hundred yards away under another minister. The adherents were bitterly divided between the two, refusing all attempts at reconciliation for the next eighty years.[11] In addition the Norwegian Missionary Society was split round the personality of Bishop Schreuder, both groups continuing to work among the Zulus; and the Hermannsburg Missionary Society, which was established in Natal in 1853, was divided by dissension in Germany and formed a splinter group in Natal, the Hanoverian Missionary Society.[12] Again both groups continued their missionary work among the Zulus.

Religion played a central role in the Colony and with the large number of denominations—Dutch Reformed, Anglicans, Congregationalists, Methodists, Lutherans from three nations, Roman Catholics and Presbyterians, later reinforced by the Swedish Holiness Union mission, the Scandinavian Alliance mission, the Scandinavian Baptist mission, the Salvation Army, the Free Methodists, and the South African General mission—it is not to be wondered at that Natal was described as 'one of the most over-occupied mission fields in the world.'[13] And this proliferation of sects, with their internal dissensions and personality clashes, led both to the persecution of individuals for their beliefs or mission methods and to toleration in the rare cases where sects were prepared to work together, or at least to desist from attacks on one another. Nevertheless the effects of the presence and the teachings of these numerous divisions of the Christian church cannot but have confused the indigenous peoples and the non-Christian immigrants who arrived in considerable numbers from India after 1860.

[10] Sales, *Planting of the Churches* p 115.
[11] A. Petrie, *Presbyterian church of Pietermaritzburg centenary review* (Pietermaritzburg 1950) pp 14–32.
[12] Sales, *Planting of the Churches*, pp 113–15.
[13] *Ibid* p 120.

The most interesting and most controversial of the churchmen in nineteenth century Natal was Colenso, who was consecrated at Lambeth in 1853 as first Bishop of Natal. Before taking up his post Colenso paid a ten weeks' visit to Natal during which he was escorted by Theophilus Shepstone, the secretary for native affairs, who acted as interpreter when Colenso called on the more important Zulu chiefs.[14] Colenso's name was well known in Britain in the last century; far better, in fact, than the name of Natal, of which many people heard for the first time because he was its bishop. Colenso was described as 'belonging to the liberal wing of the broad church group', while his metropolitan, Bishop Robert Gray, and the Dean, James Green, were high churchmen.[15] Colenso was a man of considerable intellect and determined character, and the years of controversy which followed his arrival in 1854 until his death in 1883 influenced not only religious but also political affairs. He has been variously described as 'a great missionary with an immense love for the Zulu' and as 'a wilful heretic who would stoop to any action, however mean',[16] and the storm he caused in colonial Natal was certainly without parallel in that small outpost of empire. His first brush was with missionaries of all denominations, some of whom had been at work in the colony for ten or fifteen years before Colenso paid his initial ten week visit in 1854. The cause of the disagreement was his decision to use the Zulu name for God, Nkulunkulu, in his translation of the Bible into Zulu and for services. Missionaries of other denominations had already decided, as had their colleagues in the Eastern Cape Colony, that this word had too many pagan associations, and had agreed in consultation to use the word Uthixo (creator), which had no tribal overtones.[17] The essence of the dispute lay not in the use of the word but in the whole question whether the Zulu was a 'noble savage', with an element of nobility in all his customs (the toleration view) or a child of Satan, whose entire culture had to be rooted out and replaced with the ideas of a Christian and Western civilisation (the persecution view).[18] Colenso's tactical error was to pronounce upon this complex issue after a brief visit to Natal, and without consultation with his fellow Christian mis-

---

[14] Burnett, *Anglicans in Natal* pp 36–40.

[15] *Ibid* p 68.

[16] P. Hinchliff, *Anglican church in South Africa; an account of the history and development of the Church of the Province of South Africa* (London 1963) p 64.

[17] Burnett, *Anglicans in Natal* p 40.

[18] Hinchliff, *Anglican church in South Africa* pp 67–8.

sionaries. In fact, history has justified his decision, and Nkulunkulu, or Umvelinqangi, is the word used by Christian Zulus today.

The second clash was over the treatment of polygamy. Zulu social structure allowed a man several wives if his financial position permitted him to pay the *lobolo* or price in cattle which confirmed the contract between the father of the girl and the male party. Christian missionaries were almost universally opposed to polygamy on Biblical grounds, thus preventing many well-disposed Zulu men from accepting the Gospel. Those who were baptised had to send away all their wives except one, and since the bride-price ensured that the children of the union belonged to the man's kraal in case of death or separation, the unfortunate women affected by a conversion lost their children also. It was the humanitarian aspect that influenced Colenso, and he determined to accept polygamists for baptism, though he forbade the man from taking further wives in the future. The children, having become Christians, would marry only one wife apiece and thus eradicate polygamy in the second generation. Even Dr Callaway—one of Colenso's own party—was unable to accept this decision, which gave rise to a flood of pamphlets. The toleration shown by Colenso was, of course, as much concerned with social as with theological matters, and while the religious saw it as a disregard for the Biblical injunction, the non-religious approved of its human aspects. Abbot Pfanner, an essentially practical man who founded Mariannhill monastery in 1882, insisted on the polygamist putting away all his wives but one, but at the same time he provided refuge and occupation for the discarded women in an attempt to solve both problems.[19] In modern times the Church of the Province of South Africa allows baptism to the wives but not to the polygamists themselves, the men joining a special guild 'until such time as they shall be in a position to accept the law of Christ.'[20]

Colenso's attempts to enforce his episcopal authority were to lead to a storm in Durban, where the lay wardens of St Paul's church had, in their years without a bishop and sometimes without a minister, deviated from some of the rubrics laid down. Colenso, who had had to come to the financial assistance of the churchwardens, appointed Archdeacon Mackenzie, who was to rectify these departures from orthodoxy and at the same time to confiscate pew rents and replace them with an offertory. The wearing of surplices was also in dispute,

---

[19] Brown, *Catholic church in South Africa* p 250.
[20] Hinchliff, *Anglican church in South Africa* p 68.

as it was in Cape Town. Assisted by the press, the churchwardens of St Paul's, among whom were some of the most influential citizens of Durban, came out in open defiance of the bishop.[21] The *Natal Mercury* published the following rallying call, which reveals the fanaticism of the writer and the misplaced patriotism to which at least some of the Anglican citizens responded:

> Civil despotism is bad. Military despotism is worse, but spiritual despotism is worst of all and this, it would seem, is the despotism under which we live. The Bishop is practically our ruler. His word is law. People of Natal who love your Queen and the glorious constitution which elsewhere, wherever the sun shines, guarantees liberty of conscience and the right of self-government, will you in this little corner of Her Majesty's Dominions, few and feeble as you are, will you suffer your Sovereign's honour to be tarnished and your dearest rights to be crushed under the iron hoof of a petty, despicable despotism, skulking under a Bishop's lawn while it wields the tyrant's sword? No, never, never, never. Rouse ye. Quit ye like men— like free-born Englishmen.[22]

The result was an outbreak of noisy behaviour in which the bishop was burned in effigy in the market square amid banners calling for NO POPERY, DOWN WITH THE BISHOP, and so on.

Colenso had succeeded in upsetting the missionaries with his decisions on polygamy and the Divine titles, as well as in his toleration of Zulu culture. The laity of Durban had reacted so strongly to his authority as to border on persecution. The new bishop of Natal had a tempestuous beginning in his ministry which was to continue in the same way. By 1858 his theology was causing great concern to Dean Green. Colenso adopted what has been described as 'virtually the Zwinglian position' as regards the Eucharist, namely that the sacrament was not much more than an aid to devotion, while Green stood out strongly for the orthodox position as defined by the Council of Trent.[23] Eventually Green wrote to Bishop Gray, then in England, accusing Colenso of heresy. In his reply, in which he was influenced by Bishop Wilberforce, Gray apportioned some of the blame to each of the parties and came to no decision. Shortly afterwards Colenso fell out with his clergy over the question of laymen sitting with the

[21] Burnett, *Anglicans in Natal* pp 56–7.
[22] *Natal Mercury* 30 Nov 1855.
[23] Hinchliff, *Anglican church in South Africa* pp 82–3.

clergy as equals on the church council, instead of the traditional separation by 'houses'. Colenso apparently wanted to gain the support of the laity, particularly in Pietermaritzburg; in Durban he was still regarded as a 'Popish autocrat', and a Church of England Defence Association had been formed to resist him. In both places, however, there were people who disapproved of what they perceived as Tractarian views held by some of the clergy, and were willing to support Colenso against Green. The Church of England, both clergy and laity, was split down the middle. In Pietermaritzburg open conflict developed between Green and his bishop, with a series of unedifying events in which water was brought in to flood the cathedral, garbage was dumped into it and the doors were locked against whichever of the parties happened to be outside at the time.

In the next decade the Church of England in Natal was again in the centre of controversy, this time concerning Biblical interpretation. In 1861 Colenso published his commentary on the Epistle to the Romans 'explained from a missionary point of view'. In this he followed F. D. Maurice, who had had an important influence on his theology from the beginning, in denying that Christ died to placate an angry father; but Colenso went further. He suggested that Christ's death had redeemed all men everywhere, so that from the moment of birth every man was reborn, part of the new Adam. Both conversion and baptism were in the last resort meaningless. The missionary was to preach the Gospel in order to show the heathen the pattern of Christ and the example of his love, and to assure him that he is already redeemed. Although in our time this interpretation would perhaps not cause an eyebrow to be raised, 'its inadequate teaching on the atonement, conversion, the Church and the sacraments', and the statement that this was the proper way to preach the Gospel, forced Gray to take action. He begged Colenso to withdraw the commentary from circulation and to consult with his friends and advisers in England. When he refused, Gray handed the whole matter over to the Archbishop of Canterbury. Before any decision was made *The Pentateuch and the Book of Joshua Critically Examined* appeared, in which Colenso, applying the so-called Higher Criticism, challenged the fundamentalist belief in the Mosaic books. In this he was far ahead of his time and more in line with Continental theological thought than English; he was quite out of place in the Colony. Thereafter Archbishop Longley called a meeting of the

English, Irish and Colonial bishops, and twenty-nine of the thirty-three bishops present refused to receive Colenso as a preacher in their dioceses.[24] The charges against Colenso, who was accused of heresy, were that he denied the divinity of Christ and maintained that the Bible *contained* the word of God but was not a record of God's revelation of himself to man. In saying that the Old Testament could be matched by Zulu legend, he meant that God had spoken equally 'in Cicero, Lactantius and the Sikh Gooroos' as through the prophets.[25] The Colenso controversy occurred at a period when such events were not uncommon, when Tractarians and Evangelicals were in open conflict, and men like Pusey were forbidden to preach at Oxford while F. D. Maurice was dismissed from his professorship on theological grounds. But when one considers that the entire White population of Natal at this time was only about fourteen thousand and that missionary endeavour was aimed, as much in Natal as in Central Africa, at the conversion of the heathen to Christianity, it is obvious that Colenso, his ministers and his people had lost sight of their goal while becoming embroiled in petty local disputes at home and lofty theological discussions abroad.

Colenso was tried for heresy and deprived of his see and his stipend. He appealed to the Privy Council on technical grounds as the Queen's bishop; his salary was reinstated, and in a case in the Natal supreme court he was given possession of church property. Returning to Natal in 1865 after a four year absence, Colenso preached in Durban despite the protests of the minister and the churchwardens. He then proceeded to Pietermaritzburg where he ignored the objections of Green and others and declared that he had come 'to discharge in this church and Diocese the duties committed to me by the Queen'. While he was speaking the Registrar read out in a loud voice from the chancel the sentence of deposition. Finally, in 1866, having ignored Gray's advice to him to appeal to the highest ecclesiastical authorities, Colenso was excommunicated.[26] The Chuch of England was now, as a result of these legal disputes and particularly of the Romilly judgment, declared to have no existence outside England. Gray, like other colonial bishops, was obliged to draw up a constitution and work out the relationship between the

---

[24] *Ibid* pp 82–110.
[25] J. W. Colenso, *The Pentateuch and the Book of Joshua critically examined* (London 1862–72) I p 154.
[26] Burnett, *Anglicans in Natal* pp 75–7.

'unestablished' church in the colonies and the Church of England. The result was the Church of the Province of South Africa, which came into existence in 1870. Colenso returned to Natal and continued his work as Bishop of Natal in the Church of England, while Gray appointed William Macrorie as Bishop of Maritzburg. Until 1883, when Colenso died, the two bishops existed side by side, their congregations split irreconcilably, their missionary work at a virtual standstill since neither had enough clergy to fill even the urban livings, and both suffering from shortage of funds which might otherwise, in a united congregation, have enabled the educational and religious work of the missions to have continued and prospered. The two factions were finally reconciled in 1910, although a small evangelical body, the Church of England in South Africa still exists. The latter part of Colenso's life was spent in campaigning on behalf of the Hlubi chief Langalibalele, and, after the Zulu war, on behalf of Cetshwayo;[27] the affection in which he is generally held in Natal today rests largely upon his search for political and social justice for them.

Yet another kind of persecution existed in nineteenth century Natal. This was the treatment of the Amakholwa or Christian Blacks by their traditional families and clans. Conversion to Christianity had far-reaching effects upon the convert, since such customs as initiation, polygamy and ancestor worship might no longer be practised and the convert was therefore out of step with his community. Although Colenso could see much good in the Zulu tribal and social system, 'seeing the rejection of the whole Zulu mode of life as barbarous and utterly depraved . . . as a false judgment',[28] many missionaries were less tolerant and objected to many aspects of it. The Zulu chiefs felt that conversion to Christianity alienated their subjects, undermined tribal discipline, and, in elevating the status of women, made their girls into women of the street.[29] To their shame the White colonists preferred the non-Christian Black and gave no encouragement to the Amakholwa.[30] The literature quotes cases where children, especially girls, were dragged away from mission schools or beaten,[31] and in one case at least it seems that a young con-

[27] Hinchliff, *Anglican church in South Africa* pp 100–6.
[28] Burnett, *Anglicans in Natal* p 40.
[29] Natal Archives, S.N.A. Papers 1/1/196: 1621/1894, case of ill-treatment of certain native girls for professing Christianity.
[30] *Times of Natal* 12 Apr 1894.
[31] J. B. Brain, *Catholics in Natal II* (Durban 1982) p 141n.

vert was poisoned when he insisted on returning to school.[32] Mission experience in this regard is similar in Lesotho, Zimbabwe and other parts of Africa.

In 1860 the first groups of indentured Indian immigrants began to arrive in Natal, and before the system was halted in 1911 a total of 152,184 had come. Of the indentured migrants, 1.4% or 2,150 were Christians, about 15% were Muslims, and the remainder were Hindus from north and south India. In the earliest groups the Christians were mostly Roman Catholics or Syrians of the Roman rite; after 1900 a number of Baptists from Kurnool and Ongole migrated, and the existing missionaries in the colony took care of their spiritual needs.[33] Hindus, who made up the bulk of the Indian population, soon began to apply for and receive grants of land for the erection of temples,[34] and the Brahmins among them served as priests. In 1904, for example, an application was made to the Durban municipal authorities for the transfer of a priest, one Chettysingh, from their employ as an indentured labourer to temple duty, since he was accustomed to serving in this capacity.[35] In addition to indentured workers, Indian traders, known as passenger Indians since they had paid their own passages, began to arrive about 1875; they were Muslims and Hindus with a sprinkling of Christians. In 1877 an official application was made for a mosque site in Durban and this was granted,[36] as were other requests for sites or for cemeteries in the urban areas. Hindu religious worship tended to be informal in the early years, with shrines built of clay and reeds and situated near the place of work. Only when a considerable number of free (ex-indentured) Indians formed a settled community did they begin to raise money for a substantial temple. Examples of these can be found at Umzinto,[37] the most southern sugar growing area at the time, and at Verulam in the north.[38] The only case I have traced where a temple site was refused occurred in 1885 when a man named Subrareddy applied to the Ladysmith municipal council for a site, claiming to be a Brahmin priest representing the Hindus of the district. The Protec-

---

[32] Burnett, *Anglicans in Natal* p 53.
[33] J. B. Brain, *Christian Indians in Natal, an historical and statistical study* (Cape Town 1983) pp 193, 222–5.
[34] Natal Archives, G.H. 1070: 1889, pp 193–203.
[35] Natal Archives, Indian Immigration Papers II/1/124: 115/04, 13 January 1904.
[36] *Ibid* II/1/2: R 87/77, 21 March 1877.
[37] *Ibid* II/1/160: 1837/08, 4 August 1908.
[38] *Colonial Indian News* no 29, 6 Dec 1901.

tor of Indians wrote a long explanation of the functions of the Brahmin priest or guru and suggested that the applicant, since he was not a Brahmin, might be a pujari, able to offer propitiatory sacrifices and to decorate the altar. Since, however, the attorney-general had declared some time earlier that Subrareddy's statements were 'not to be implicitly relied on', and taking all the facts into consideration, the application was turned down, not because of Hindu religion but because 'he is not a proper man to be recognised as the spiritual guide of any body of Indians, notwithstanding that he appears to have a standing among them.'[39] The first substantial temple, described as the first in Africa, was built on the Umbilo River at South Coast Junction in 1875.[40]

An indication of the toleration shown by the authorities towards the Indian immigrants can be seen in the efforts made to understand and apply justly the regulations for Indian marriages. The records contain many requests for rulings on marriages between Hindus and Christians or Hindus and Muslims, as well as on divorce procedures and the minimum age at which girls might marry.[41] Indian religious holidays too were treated with understanding from the earliest times, both Hindus and Muslims celebrating the Shiite festival of Mohorrum. Employers granted a holiday to their workers and colourful processions took place in the larger centres. Only in 1910 did a Hindu swami request that employers of Hindus be instructed to prevent their taking part by cancelling the holiday.[42] The Protector refused, and there was never interference with either Mohorrum or the Hindu festival of Lights. At the present time both communities celebrate their festivals and Mohorrum is kept in Durban with both groups attending.

A source of friction between Muslims and Hindus was the use of tom-toms and other noisy instruments by the latter when celebrating any religious occasion. In Natal the police in Durban and Pietermaritzburg were instructed to suppress tom-tomming on several occasions,[43] and on one a petition was presented to the Legislative

[39] Natal Archives, CSO 1018:2041/1885: Protector to Colonial Secretary, 3 Aug 1885.
[40] Durban's notable buildings (Durban 1974).
[41] Natal Archives, Indian Immigration Papers II/1/44: 446/88: statement by J. B. Stephens on Hindu marriage and II/2/9: 13 Aug 1908 on Muslim–Hindu marriage.
[42] Ibid CSO 1883: 299/1910: Protector to Colonial Secretary, 18 Jan 1910.
[43] Pietermaritzburg Corporation: Police committee minute book, 1901–2. pp 136, 142.

Council complaining that this interfered with religious freedom.[44]
Indian Christians also expressed their enthusiasm in this way and as
early as 1861 Father Sabon, the Catholic priest who had welcomed
the first arrivals, wrote:

> knowing that there was to be midnight Mass, these dear chil-
> dren, without telling me, went and borrowed the biggest drum
> in the town, and about midnight, to the astonishment of the
> Protestants, they wended their way to the chapel to the beating
> of the drum . . . After Mass they were joined by another band,
> together with two men playing violins, and all spent the night in
> the church, singing hymns.[45]

There is no recorded comment from the townspeople!

Toleration was extended, then, to all, including the Muslims and
Hindus, by the colonial government; but what of the colonists? In
1860, when the first Indians arrived, the Colenso controversy was
reaching its peak, while dissension weakened not only the Church of
England but also the Presbyterians and the Norwegian and
Hermannsburg mission groups. There were relatively few Indians—
only 6,445 in the first fourteen years of the scheme—and most were
allocated in small groups to sugar, coffee and cotton plantations, or
individually to farmers and householders. The colonists expected
that they would all return to India at the expiration of their contracts
and their religious customs are barely mentioned in the archives at
all. After 1874, when a large number of indentured workers began to
arrive, it was the cultural differences in sanitary, health and housing
customs that led to complaint. By 1885 there were as many Indians as
Whites in Natal, and agitation centred around political and economic
rather than religious competition. To the evangelical Protestant the
monotheistic Muslim, who was often a businessman or trader and
fairly affluent, was closer to the Protestant ethic and easier to understand than the Hindu with his pantheon of gods, temples and statues
and his exotic way of life. The colonists made no effort to understand
Hinduism, and the missionaries involved with the conversion of the
Hindu complained that the colonists showed no interest in their
work, though giving generously to the Zulu missions.[46] The whole

---

[44] Natal Archives, Natal Parliamentary Papers 645: Petition 18 of 1886.
[45] Sabon to Fabre, 28 March 1862 in M. Ferragne (ed), *Records from Natal, Lesotho, the Orange Free State and Mozambique concerning the history of the Catholic Church in South Africa* (Roma nd) I p 78.
[46] Brain, *Christian Indians in Natal* p 217.

cultural and religious way of life seemed to the colonist, who was insular in the extreme, to be too strange and foreign to be considered seriously as a threat to Christianity.

For a colony as small and underdeveloped as Natal there was an unusual amount of religious controversy. This can, I believe, be attributed to the large number of denominations and sects, many of which were in competition in the mission field and jealous of one anothers' successes, however limited. The colonists, on the whole, retained their prejudices and intolerance towards people with different views within the same group and towards foreigners, while rationalism and the new scientific ideas were slow to infiltrate from Europe. The physical difficulties of climate, poor transport, the shortage of helpers and the nature of work among people of alien culture put a strain on missionaries which only those of resolute and determined character could survive. And these were the qualities that nourished controversy.

The press played an important part in stirring up argument within the colony, publishing letters from eccentrics and troublemakers which would not have found their way into print in Britain. There were no institutions of higher education and few of the colonists were able to present a balanced, well-informed view on theological matters and so stop the emotive and ill-considered statements that appeared almost daily on one subject or another. The unfamiliarity of the Hindu and Muslim religions and the absence of social contact did not encourage the white settlers to learn more about them. They preferred to continue the old disputes with their fellow Christians, leaving the adherents of Eastern religions to worship where and how they wished.

University of Durban-Westville

THE RELIGIOUS BACKGROUND
TO MAX WEBER

by NORMAN STONE

IT IS easy to vulgarize Max Weber. His assertion that 'the Protestant Ethic' was related to capitalism could be, and was, taken to mean that Protestantism was about money whereas Catholicism was about parasitism. Weber himself stoutly denied that any such vulgarization was legitimate. He himself could not see any sense in going through religious documents of early modern Europe with a view to finding out what the various divines had to say on economic subjects: on the contrary, he stressed that 'Of course our concern is not with what was officially and theoretically laid down in moral compendia of the age . . . but rather with something quite different—the secular translation (*Ermittlung*) of the psychological forces, created by religious beliefs and practices, which gave directions for the conduct of one's life and held the individual to them'.[1] Did Protestantism and Catholicism vary on the ground, in daily life, and especially in economic affairs? It was a good question, and, for the literature and research it generated, one of the most important ones of this century.

As with most vulgarizations, the suggestion that Weber was somehow anti-Catholic did, despite his denials, have an element of truth: where, in the sixteenth century, the religious contenders waged their wars over religious and textual matters, in the later nineteenth century they did so over the conduct of daily, communal life. The economic argumentation subsequently became rather broader, in the hands of Troeltsch and Tawney; nowadays, we appear to be arguing as to whether Protestants had a different conception of the State than Catholics. On the whole, the historical argument seems to have gone largely against Weber, at least in England, where the contours of religious differences can be *nuancé* almost out of existence, and where a recent well-known book, Quentin Skinner's *Foundations of Modern Political Thought*[2] has taken

[1] Max Weber, *Die Protestantische Ethik und der Geist des Kapitalismus* (München-Hamburg 1973) p 117.
[2] Quentin Skinner, *Foundations of Modern Political Thought* (2 vols Cambridge 1978).

a very ecumenical line. My purpose in the present paper is not to discuss the applicability of the Weber Thesis as regards early modern Europe, but rather to suggest how that thesis came to have such resonance in Weber's own time and place. To put forward an immediate instance: in the few years before the First World War, British headlines were preoccupied with the Irish Question. Was it purely coincidental that, in 1911 and 1912, there were political conflicts—even, general strikes—over the rôle of Catholicism in public life in Bavaria, in Baden, and in Belgium?[3] The Catholic Question was well to the fore in other places as well: it provided the stuff of politics in the Third Republic and in Liberal Italy until the first years of this century. In Austria, the emergence of Karl Lueger's *Christlichsoziale Partei* in the 1890s broke the Habsburg system; in Ireland, Catholic Home-Rulers dominated Irish—and English—affairs. Everywhere in Europe, from Galway to Lublin, the 1890s saw a new force emerging. How did this shape the Weber Thesis?

Lord Salisbury, looking back, remarked accurately that the 1880s had been the greatest decade of change he had ever experienced. It began with discussions between conservatives and liberals of an old-fashioned kind: parliaments, elected by very limited franchises, met seldom and spent most of their time on small budgetary matters, or on discussion of *l'ordre moral*—the slogan of French monarchists and aristocratic Catholics, opposing such matters as divorce or relaxation of censorship. But the decade was a time of very considerable economic change. 'The Great Depression' was a time of rapidly-falling agricultural prices, which wrecked a great part of old agriculture. The counterpart of cheap food was of course a great growth of the cities; everywhere, there was a 'flight from the land', and most cities in Europe reveal, at a glance, that in the 1880s huge parts of them must have been building-sites. As the 1880s closed, the politics of most European countries began to follow a recognizably parallel course: on the whole, there were parties of Property which faced parties of non-Property, as the towns produced socialist groups, and trade unions, the activities of which unquestionably scared the older parties.

It is curious to note how the dominant political mood in various

---

[3] See Karl Bosl, *Handbuch der bayerischen Geschichte* 4 (München 1976) E. Huber, *Deutsche Verfassungsgeschichte* 4 (Düsseldorf 1973) and W. Kossmann, *The Low Countries* (Oxford 1978).

countries was much the same at much the same time in this period.[4] For instance, around 1900, governments of forthright imperialists were in the seat: in 1896 came Crispi's attack on Abyssinia, in 1897 Marchand's advance on Fashoda, in 1899 the Boer War, in 1898 Tirpitz's battle fleet, in 1904 the Russo-Japanese War. Around 1905, came a reaction to this: the Liberal landslide in Great Britain, universal suffrage-riots elsewhere, or the left-leaning Bloc government in France. For present purposes, two such trans-European parallels may be of use: the confused politics of the 1880s and the period immediately before war broke out in 1914. The 1880s are a period of extraordinary confusion for anyone to follow, even at a very superficial level: try and follow the disintegration of Germany liberalism in that era (it split into three, then four groups); try even to puzzle out what R. C. K. Ensor says about British politics in the middle-1800s, when Gladstone, Parnell, Salisbury and Chamberlain performed their complicated mid-eighties dance over the Irish Question; or try to sort out what on earth General Boulanger, or Count Taaffe, or Agostino Depretis were doing. The fact is, that in each case the confusions came from much the same cause: the disintegration—largely under fiscal and social pressures—of mid-nineteenth century liberalism, and the rise, in one form or another, of the political power of the Church: whether with the Home Rulers in this country (in 1884, Archbishop Walsh made what amounted to a concordat with Parnell, the upshot of which was a clear moderation of the Land League);[5] or, in Germany, the arrival of the Catholic *Zentrumspartei*, which held the balance of power in the *Reichstag*; or, in Italy, the recovery of Catholic political confidence in the 1880s—which stopped Italy from having that law for divorce which practically every other country in Europe has had since the 1880s; or, in France, the two-fifths of the Chamber won by Catholic candidates, operating, for the first time in 1885, as a *bloc*. This Catholic factor led to a great number of political problems, in all countries. For anyone in continental Europe, the Catholic factor was omnipresent; in the 1880s, and in many respects beyond, it was more important than the socialist menace of which so much, at the time and later, was made.

---

[4] These issues are discussed in Norman Stone, *Europe Transformed 1878–1919* (London 1983).

[5] E. Larkin, *The Roman Catholic Church and the Plan of Campaign in Ireland (1886–1888)* (Cork 1978) which argues that the bishop's adhesion to Parnell, and his agreement to give them control of education, made for a one-party *'de facto'* Irish state'.

In the Italian case, Indro Montanelli says—though with characteristic exaggeration—that 'Liberals and Catholics spoke the same language, but said opposite things; Socialists and Catholics spoke different languages, but were saying much the same thing.[6] When, in 1903, Max Weber wrote his famous book on *The Protestant Ethic and the Spirit of Capitalism*, it was not simply an historical exercise.

To put it bluntly, Weber could, like many liberals in Europe, regard political Catholicism as a terrible enemy—anti-semitic, hostile to education, absurdly indulgent towards peasants' fantasies, anxious to penalize the enterprising through taxation, and endemically bureaucratic in spirit—in other words, quite hostile to the spirit of capitalism, as then understood. He himself was not given to moral judgements in his scholarly work, at least after 1898, and there are not many records known to me of his attitude to political Catholicism. However, in 1906, writing to his friend Naumann, he did complain that the Catholic *Zentrumspartei* was deeply corrupting parliamentary life: 'as the key party in parliament it has furthered and supported the system of sham constitutionalism' and as its main aim it had 'maintenance of parliamentary client-systems behind the wings'.[7] For Weber, political Catholicism was a party of bureaucracy, which, as a good individualist, he detested in principle. How appalling it was, he thought, that 'the world would be composed only of these little cogs, of people who stick to a little job and strive for a bigger one'. Save us, he thought, from this *Parzellierung der Seele*. True, he did distinguish Catholic piety, which he admired, from the 'virtuoso *Maschinerie*' of Mother Church, but he thought that clerical machinations would win in the end over piety, and for him it was 'a human commandment' to resist that.[8] I wonder if, at bottom, Weber would not have formally endorsed what was written, this time of the early modern era, by one of his exegetists, the Swiss historian Herbert Lüthy: that the Calvinist work-ethic did not simply mean a huge work-house, but, on the contrary, 'created the legal and moral framework for a free and egalitarian society, in which work was no longer simply a corvée for a ruling-class of parasites, and its fruits were no more to be merely a prey for the

---

[6] Indro Montanelli, *L'Italia di Giolitti* (Milan 1975) p 64.
[7] Marianne Weber, *Max Weber. Ein Lebensbild* (Heidelberg 1950) pp 441 seq.
[8] [Wolfgang J.] Mommsen, *Max Weber* [*und die deutsche Politik 1890–1920* (Tübingen 1959)] p 138. From this book, and Marianne Weber's, I take my account of Weber's life and politics.

powerful'.[9] Catholics, maybe, saw in their Church a point of warmth in a cruel world. Protestants and anti-clericals saw, often enough, only Tammany Hall.

J. M. Keynes, looking back, called the world before 1914 'an economic Eldorado', in which there existed citizens 'content with their lot' and enjoying 'an almost absolute security of property and person'. I believe that he took too rosy a view of these last years before the First World War. For anyone with a brain, it was a very difficult time indeed—consider the extraordinary changes in the arts and sciences that came in the few years after 1900—and for a political economist, as Weber was, the orthodoxies of liberalism had ceased to count.

Weber's own process of maturation—it took a long time—led him eventually into a left-liberal position, in which he argued for better accommodation with socialism; he was associated with the formation of the Weimar Republic. However, his youth and early middle age were much less tolerant. His father was a well-known right-wing Liberal, a follower of Bismarck, with most of the prejudices that that entailed; and young Max, having done brilliantly in his studies, followed rather faithfully in his father's footsteps. In particular, he wrote his first serious work on trading societies in the Middle Ages (for which he had to learn Spanish and Italian) and in 1891–2 he published the results of a lengthy, and still very useful, inquiry into *Die Lage der Landarbeiter im ostelbischen Deutschland.*

That sounds purely statistical. In fact, it was inspired by considerations far from the scientifically-sociological. At this time, the early 1890s, there were loud complaints that German civilization was being eroded in the east by constant inroads of semi-civilized Poles or Russians—the Poles, being Catholics, with a much higher birth-rate. Good German land was being sold up to these Poles, who multiplied and spread out into the cities: Poznania, Silesia, West Prussia were being Polonized. German agricultural workers would not face the competition of low wages paid to the Poles, and they moved out in droves. The heart of this problem, for Weber, was another good National Liberal target, the Junker lords of east-Elbian Germany, who brought the Poles in as cheap labour.[10] Then, their

---

[9] Herbert Lüthy's contribution in Constans Seyfarth and W. M. Sprondel eds, *Seminar: Religion und gesellschaftliche Entwicklung. Studien zur Protestantismus-Kapitalismus-These Max Webers* p 122.

[10] The best introduction to this subject is Gordon Craig, *German History 1867–1945* (Oxford 1981) but there is an immense list of works on the Prusso–Polish prob-

farming methods being slovenly, and the times being depressed, these lords would sell up to the Poles, who farmed in families, and so had lower costs. One way and another eastern Germany was facing ruin. Weber wished for state intervention: it was a matter not of economic interest, but *Staatsräson*: 'the maintenance of a large, strong and patriotic rural population, as a reservoir for the national armed forces and peaceful defence of the eastern marches'.[11] Be it added that, by 1895, Weber had become a forthright German imperialist. His famous professorial inaugural lecture argued for 'a future on the waves'. Germany needed foreign markets, and places to send her surplus proletariat: then there would be class-harmony inside Germany. It was all good liberal-imperialist stuff, of a kind to be heard, in one form or another, in this country or in France. In 1899, Weber even resigned from the Pan-German league on the grounds that it would not opt for expelling the Polish rural population altogether. The most that the Prussian government would do was to set up a fund to settle Germans on bankrupt land, though in 1908 the *Lex Miquel* also allowed straightforward expropriation of Polish farms and estates. By that time, Weber himself had grown up. He had got to know many Poles; he had also visited Scotland, with its wildernesses brought about by the Clearances, and Ireland, with its plethora of tiny peasant plots, and its rapacious landlords. By the time he wrote his *Protestantism and Capitalism*, the original, rather fanatical impulse to all of his work had died away, and—after a long nervous breakdown—had become abstract. In the end, he rather liked the Catholics, and he set about learning Polish.

Still, no observer of the German scene around 1900 could fail to see that there was a very great difference between Catholics and Protestants; and, more generally, that difference could be detected in virtually every other European country, though with variations along the way. When Max Weber aligned (rather than equated) Calvinism with the spirit of capitalism, he was talking what appeared, for his contemporaries in Germany, to be sense. There, capitalism and enterprise appeared to be an almost completely Protestant and Jewish phenomenon; political Catholicism aimed either to frustrate its operation or to live, parasite-fashion, off it.

The very terms in which this issue is to be discussed are difficult. In

---

lem generally. H.-U. Wehler, *Krisenherde des Kaiserreichs* (Göttingen 1970) devotes a lengthy, thorough and well-written essay to this issue.
[11] Mommsen p 150.

the first place, it is not a question of the official doctrines of the churches themselves. Holy Scripture could allow a range of economic ways of doing; clergymen were not very well qualified to discuss economics in any detail; and—a point frequently made in objection to Weber's thesis—a great number of the really successful capitalists were not particularly religious. In social doctrines, the churches spoke with many voices once they came away from the level of generalities.[12] There were liberal Catholics like Charles Périn, a Belgian professor famous in his day, who combined ferociously ultramontane opinions in religious and political matters with ferociously Nassau-Senior or 'Manchester' views in economics; the stiff *Staatskatholiken* who deposed Ludwig II of Bavaria, and who ran that country in the subsequent *Prinzregentenzeit*,[13] were impeccably national-liberal in their economic opinions, to the point of defying a political-Catholic majority in parliament. In Italy, political Catholicism could barely get going, because of the Pope's *non expedit*, and when it did get going, after 1900, the divisions of Corporatists (grouped around Toniolo), 'Red priests' in Murri's *Lega*, and moderate, Giolitti-supporting middle-class liberals associated with Meda and the bulk of the Catholic *buona stampa* were such that the chief Catholic organization, the *Opera die congressi* split into warring factions and was closed down by Pius X.[14] In France, political

[12] On these questions generally, see J. Winckelmann, *Die protestantische Ethik* (2 vols Hamburg 1972); E. Shils, *The Methodology of the Social Sciences* (London 1949); H. Lüthy, *Le Passé présent* (Paris 1965); K. Samuelson, *Religion and Economic Action* (London 1961) which strikes me as quite misunderstanding what Weber said—to take Scotland, the homeland of Tennants, Youngers, Runcimans, Carnegies and how many others, as evidence of Weber's inapplicability requires no little ingenuity; Philippe Besnard ed, *Protestantisme et capitalisme. La controverse postweberienne* (Paris 1970); Oskar Lange, *Politische Oekonomie* (Frankfurt a.M. 1963); P. L. Berger, *The Sacred Canopy* (Garden City 1967); A. Giddens, *Politics and Sociology in the Thought of Max Weber* (London 1972); E. Gellner, *Thought and Change* (Chicago 1964).

[13] [Karl] Möckl, [*Die Prinzregentenzeit. Gessellschaft und Politik während der Aera des Prinzregenten Luitpold in Bayern* (München 1972)]. Hertling, a late but characteristic representative of the *Staatskatholiken*, who became Bavarian Minister-President and, in 1917–18, *Reichskanzler*, regarded 'corn-laws and compulsory guild-co-operatives' (*Innungen*) as the (quite wrong-headed) demands of the populist Catholics as distinct from the high-liberal ones like himself (and, later, Brüning) (p. 200).

[14] Giorgio Candeloro *Storia dell'Italia moderna 6* (Milano 1979). p 59 displays General Bava-Beccaris at Milan, during the *Fatti di maggio* of 1898, bombarding the Capucin monastery in the via Malaparte in Milan, on the grounds that Catholics were concealing anarchists there. He had in fact seen some friars doling out soup to a crowd of waiting beggars. 80 people were killed, and 450 wounded, in this affray, during

Catholicism divided between the moderate *ralliés* of 1892 and the Republic-hating, and, later, Dreyfus-persecuting bulk of the higher clergy in the *Union de la France chrétienne*.[15] True, the famous Encyclical, *Rerum Novarum*, of 1891, did speak a language curiously close to that of the Marxists: 'The social struggle has indeed been ignited. It is the consequence of progressive industrialization, the modernization of technology, the altered social relations between owners of the means of production and wage-earners . . . and of moral decline'; there would soon only be a few vastly rich owners of property, and 'a broad mass of people without property, held in almost slave-like dependency'. But what did Leo XIII wish to be done? In concrete terms, Catholics disagreed. Some wanted socialism; others welfare-capitalism; others some form of mediaeval commune, with guild well to the fore. In Germany, the Catholic social thinker Wilhelm Hohoff thought Marx 'the greatest economic genius of all time'; Franz Hitze said 'We must have "socialist" association of social forces, as against the social disintegrativeness of liberalism; but we want a corporatist "association" of society, as against the faceless sameness (*Unterschiedslosigkeit*) of the socialist *Volksstaat*'.[16] Earlier Catholic writers, whether Albert Maria Weiss (1844–1925) or the famous Vogelsang seem to have looked to the co-operative movement: in both cases, Jewish usurers and pawn-brokers were the target, and Vogelsang, who led the Austrian Christian Social movement, simply pronounced that, according to canon law, loans for productive purposes were just as bad as straightforward usury.[17]

which the ladies of Milan fed cake to the gunners. Murri attacked '*una borghesia di Formazione anemica e parassitaria, a cui gli avvenimenti d'Europa hanno dato uno sviluppo precoce*'. . . (etc).

[15] A. Sedgwick, *The Ralliement in French Politics* (Cambridge Mass. 1965) and M. Ozouf, *L'École, L'Église et la République* (Paris 1962) are convenient accounts. For more recent works, see J.-M. Mayeur, *Les débuts de la Troisième République* (Paris 1976) which has a very good bibliography and which handles the religious issue with much sensitivity. A recent short English work makes a good attempt to survey the clerical and religious aspect of politics: Hugh McLeod, *Religion and the People of Western Europe* (Oxford 1981). It has a good bibliography.

[16] [Helga] Grebing ed, [*Deutsches Handbuch der Politik* 3 eds W. Gottschalch *et al*, *Geschichte der sozialen Ideen in Deutschland* (München-Wien 1969)] pp 387–8 (this section, by Franz Josef Stegmann, covers Catholic political thought in the modern era, pp 325–561, and also gives a German text of *Rerum Novarum*).

[17] *Ibid* pp 386 seq. Vogelsang, though by origin a *reichsdeutsch* Protestant, became very influential in Austria as a Christian Socialist. A recent introduction for the English-language reader is G. Lewis: 'The Peasantry, Rural Change and Conservative Agrarianism in Lower Austria' in *PP* 81 (1978), though it makes the common error of supposing that conservatism and agrarianism are much the same thing. In Central Europe, it has been aptly said, *christlich* meant 'anti-semitic'.

After 1900, Catholic social and economic doctrine began to settle down more or less to its present form, of steered market-economy, but, in the era when Weber wrote, political Catholicism spoke with many tongues.

Max Weber was attacked for suggesting that the economic ways of the two religions could be deduced from clerical texts. If he had ever made that suggestion, he would of course have been quite rightly annihilated, both as regards the period of the later Middle Ages and the Reformation, and in view of the official disunities of the Catholic world in his own day. A straight-forward equation of Calvinist writings and early capitalism is of course preposterous—it is characteristic that the permission to charge interest on loans given for productive purposes was issued, in Geneva, not by Calvin, but by a bishop a century and a half before him. However, Weber never suggested anything so obviously silly. Just the same, there was no lack of Catholic anti-capitalists in his own day for him to use in pursuit of his thesis, had he chosen to do so. The Dominican Albert Maria Weiss (1844–1925) who was professor of *Sozialwissenschaft* at Fribourg, wished to forbid *all* interest-taking; in 1884, Vogelsang announced that canon law forbade *all* interest, whether usurious (*Wucher*) or 'productive' (*Darlehensvertrag*) as in Weber's distinction. They were, Vogelsang said, 'identical', and condemned by Natural Law.[18]

Maybe this is very vague—a charge that Weber certainly has to answer, though less in the *Ethic* than elsewhere—and maybe, too, evidence one way or another is almost bound to be incoherent or meaningless. But, for anyone concerned with the leading thought of a society, or the broad terms of its economic life, Weber's idea seems to be to be worth considering. Religious ideas—more narrowly, ideas of morality—obviously affect people's economic conduct. To take a very simple case, and one much-discussed in Germany at the time, that of inheritance-rules in farming. Are all children to inherit equally, regardless of the damage done to the property by parcelliza-tion of it, or is primogeniture to rule, or is the extended family to carry on as before, as in the world of Orthodoxy? What is the proper attitude to labour? The hanging of sturdy beggars, as in many Protestant countries after the Reformation, or the construction of elaborate charitable enterprises, together with vast public works, high taxes, and pawn-shops (*monts de piété*) as in the legendary

[18] Grebing p 389.

Counter-Reformation world? How far must individuals accept the State, with its bureaucracies that have to be paid for by people of enterprise?

I am not qualified to discuss these matters in the centuries to which Weber referred. However, in the Germany of his time, and specifically in the southern part where he taught (he was at Freiburg and Heidelberg), there were very clear differences between Protestant and Catholic. The individualistic, liberal world in which Weber grew up, and which he always greatly respected, was clearly coming to an end, and one of its inheritors was political Catholicism. Weber began his book with the *Berufestatistik* of his own region to display his arguments. There was no doubt that Catholics were poorer and less educated. In 1908, in Prussia, they paid less than a sixth of all income tax, whereas they numbered a good third of the population; in Aachen, the non-Catholic twenty-sixth paid one third of the income tax. In Baden, almost two-thirds Catholic, just over a third of students were Catholic; in Bavaria, under half of the university professors were Catholic, though Catholics made up 71% of the population.[19] Such figures could be multiplied almost indefinitely for any area with a population mixed in religion: they hold as true for Latvia as for northern Ireland around 1910, where Protestant incomes were, on average, four times the Catholic ones. The contrast between Catholics and Jews, in these respects, was greater still, and it is not altogether surprising to find *bien pensant* France, in the early 1880s, shrill with complaint at the predominance of Protestants and Jews in the ranks of the *Opportuniste* republicans.

What lay behind this difference? In southern Germany, there was quite an easy answer. The Catholics had left the land later than the Protestants, so that, even in 1912, their third of Prussia supplied only one quarter of the dwellers of large cities. Protestant families, it is argued, sub-divided their plots in inheritance, whereas Catholic families kept them together, as family farms. In the circumstances of the 1840s, tiny Protestant farms collapsed, whereas larger Catholic ones survived; by 1860, in the Catholic Oberland district of Württemberg, 56.3% of farms were over 35 acres in size, compared with 13.8% in the Protestant Neckarland nearby. By 1870, the countryside of Württemberg had become largely Catholic, the towns largely Protestant; and there was a further twist, in that the

[19] [David] Blackbourn [*Class, Religion and Local Politics in*] *Wilhelmine Germany* [(Yale 1980)] pp 28–9.

Protestants, owning small plots, had been driven towards artisan-trades, which could be adapted. The upshot of the flight from the land in Württemberg was a number of flourishing small concerns—one third of the German corset-manufacturing trade; one-quarter of the cigarette-lighters on the one side; Daimler and Mauser on the other.[20] In Bavaria, the Protestant parts responded in much the same way, as Franconia and the Wormser Ecke produced far more than their share of capitalists, engineers, and artisans of all sorts—'sourfaces', as the Irish journalist D. E. Moran (no doubt with justification) called their equivalents in Ireland.[21]

The Catholic flight from the land came only later—the late 1880s and 1890s, when the Depression of commodity-prices, and the pressures of over-competition caused a rash of Catholic bankruptcies and foreclosures. All accounts of German politics, whether at *Reich* level, or at *Bundesstaat* or even municipal levels, agree that, around 1890, there was a dramatic change; a re-making of politics.

There was a much higher degree of 'populist' Catholic attacks on the reigning Protestant liberals, on the one side; on the other, there was a considerable change within political Catholicism itself. You can see this all over Europe—happening everywhere, seemingly for altogether unrelated reasons, but with parallel outcomes. I know, for instance, that the fall of Parnell as leader of Irish Home Rule, in 1890, is supposed to be an accident, brought about by Gladstone's refusal of further confidence on the grounds that Parnell's adultery offended his nonconformist supporters. But Parnell's fall, and the 'catholicizing' of Home Rule as a result, goes together with other changes—the Papal Encyclical, *Rerum Novarum*, in 1891; the French *Ralliement* in 1892–3; the 'social Catholic' conference at Liège in 1890; the foundation of the *Volksverein für das katholische Deutschland* in 1890—much of it, obviously, a response to the mass-organization of socialism at the same time (the Second International was founded in 1889, on the centenary of 1789).

Throughout the 1880s, as 'mass-politics' came into existence, the older, staid and upper-class Catholics were supplanted. In the 1860s and 1870s, political Catholicism had been just what it claimed to be: a defence of the Church, led by aristocrats and cardinal archbishops, some of whom, even in Catholic countries, had to go to prison in defence of their religious privileges in, say, educational matters, as

---

[20] *Ibid* pp 42, 79–80, 128 seq.
[21] C. Cruise O'Brien *States of Ireland* (London 1972) p 77.

did the archbishop of Gniezno, Ledóchowski, at the hands of Bismarck, or the archbishop of Salzburg, Cardinal Prince Schwarzenberg, at the hands of Franz Joseph. Then, as the 1880s went ahead, such figures were replaced by men of much humbler origins. For the greater part, they were lawyers or school-teachers: Josef Wirth or Matthias Erzberger, for instance, whose origins were very modest (in Erzberger's case, illegitimate son of a postman). One of the curiosities of French political Catholicism is that this did not really occur. On the contrary, the French Catholics were caught by the upper classes, and the *Ralliement*, there, failed to become a mass-movement. Instead, the Radicals made all of the running in politics, though their equivalents everywhere else were in clear decline. In most countries, the arrival of mass-politics meant that upper-class Catholics became identified with the conservatives, rather than with the middle-class political Catholics. In Germany, the Westphalian and Silesian magnates of the 1870s—Lichnowsky, Hatzfeld, Schorlemer-Alst, Ballestrem—followed this path.

In Bavaria, there was an odd development. There, and in some other countries (Belgium being a good instance) there had been an alliance of liberals and liberal Catholics, who were usually associated with the Wittelsbach Court, and whose views on the Papacy were condemnatory: they had encouraged the *Altkatholiken*, the oppo-nents of Infallibility whom Acton knew and liked, a first version of that reasonable, moderate and sometimes 'modernistically' inclined Catholicism that seems pretty well doomed any time it tries to achieve anything substantial. In Bavaria, where Catholics formed over 70% of the population, politics took a strange shape, in which the Protestants survived, more or less in charge, because of their association with liberal Catholics—a process again complicated by Munich's link with Berlin. Bismarck found it all pretty well incom-prehensible, and remarked that 'a Bavarian is a cross between an Austrian and a human being'. By 1890, as Karl Möckl observes in his *Prinzregentenzeit*, the challenge of populist Catholicism was felt. Local priests resented the superior ways of the Court Catholics; in a famous instance, the parish priest of Oberammergau even allowed the nuncio, Agliardi, to get out at the station, with a small party, and trudge through the rain to find his own carriages for the journey: the priest later explained that he had not obtained coaches for the party because there were always plenty of coaches at the station, so many that they were usually forced to do a fare for less than the fixed price.[22]

The new populist Catholicism stood for much more than the simple defence of Catholicism and of particularist interests. It gained much of its electoral strength because it voiced the complaints of the very many people who found the vast changes of the later nineteenth century working against them. In areas where there were minority-languages, for instance, the priests made a serious and usually successful effort to capture the cause: Poles in Prussia, Bretons in France, Catalans in Spain, Slovaks in Hungary, Slovenes in Austria, Flemish in Belgium—in all cases, a strong priestly leadership for the minority people, against the tyrannous majority with its insistence on the virtues of one, centralizing nation with a supposedly superior language. Priests interpreted for peasants who found bureaucratic and legal language beyond them. In Belgium, it was common enough, in elections, to see the priest simply leading his village to the polls; in Glasgow, at elections for the School Board, in the 1880s, there was a great deal of resentment because priests used diagrams, like cross-words, to show their illiterate parishioners where to put their fifteen crosses, so as to unify the Catholic slate and defeat the reigning Protestants.[23]

In Germany, such political Catholicism gained a powerful constituency in the small farmers and artisans. As cheap food came in, as chemists came up with substitutes for butter ('margarine') or sugar ('saccharine'), and as ways were found for bottling beer and keeping it, local farmers and brewers demanded protection: they went bankrupt in droves, and complained to the priests. Political Catholicism argued their cause, and gained for them such measures as the decree, in Württemberg, that no 'vending machines' should be set up in stations. A similar proposal, at Reichstag level, was that margarine should be coloured a revolting gentian, the colour of the Reichstag skirting-board, and also given a horrible name, *Oeltalg*. There was one final way in which political Catholicism appealed: it

[22] Möckl pp 327–8.
[23] James Roxburgh *The Glasgow School Board* (Glasgow 1970) p 44. No doubt similar stories could be told of other religiously-mixed cities in the British Isles (in Glasgow, relations were for some reason better than in Liverpool: their poor state emerges from P. J. Waller, *Democracy and Sectarianism. Liverpool 1868–1939* (Liverpool 1981). G. Barnich, *Le régime clérical en Belgique* (Brussels 1911) is one instance of parallel trends on the Continent. There are a great many others.

became very useful indeed in the expanding municipal bureaucracy of early twentieth-century Europe.[24]

In Max Weber's world, municipal bureaucracy was very thin on the ground. In the 1870s, most towns were still small, and could still be run by a fairly small bureaucracy. In this country, towns depended on volunteers, and mayors had only a few dozen helpers on salary; while both the rate-payers and the State tended to be very stingy. After 1890, but particularly after 1900, the pressure for more bureaucracy was irresistible—municipal services of many kinds were set up (Water Boards, Electricity Boards, telephones, transport, schools, hospitals and much else). The result was a great growth of the civil service in all countries. I have only ever found these figures collated, for various European countries, in Hermann Finer's *Government*. In Prussia alone, the advance, from 1901 to 1911, was from 152,000 to 542,000; but in this country, from 153,000 to 644,000. It was the beginning of a bureaucratic explosion, which Weber noted, and which has gone on until our own day. In that world, of curious municipal favours, of appointments to minor and even miniature jobs in public concerns, priests were good at placing their own people. In Munich, even before the First World War, the old idea of *Parität* between Catholic and Protestant was translated at the level of municipal transport: Catholics became bus-conductors, and socialists, as a result of this strange pact, became bus-drivers. Later on, council housing followed this pattern.

In politics, Catholic parties tended to stand on the Right, provided that establishments supported their claims in education and in other matters. It came about, in Germany at the level of the Reichstag, that the Catholic deputies, roughly a fifth of the Reichstag, held the balance of power between the old Bismarckian *Kartell* parties, and the rising Left of socialism and democratic liberalism. Whenever it came to a test—as over the Zabern affair in 1913, or over the Prussian franchise in 1910, or over the Peace Resolution in 1917—the *Zentrumspartei* would never firmly tread the path of reform. In Saxony, the Catholics even voted to re-arrange the franchise in such a way that socialists lost most of their seats in the local parliament, even although this also meant that the Catholics lost many of theirs

---

[24] The development of the European 'Tammany Hall' is, for recent-day historians, a new subject. Blackbourn, *Wilhelmine Germany* is an important beginning. E. N. and P. Anderson, *European Political Institutions and Social Change* (Berkeley 1967) and Hermann Finer, *The Theory and Practice of Modern Government* (4 edn New York 1961) may be read with profit.

as well. Later on, the votes of Catholic parties were not used in a very positive sense: nowhere, before 1945, was the record a very good one. The rise of inchoate interest-groups, in the name of political Catholicism, was a feature visible throughout Europe in 1900, and it forms the background to Max Weber's remarks on capitalism and the Protestant Ethic. I have to say, it sends me back to the Reformation Era with a new interest.

Trinity College, Cambridge

INTOLERABLE TOLERANCE:
THE CANADIAN BISHOPS AND THE 1912
'APPEAL ON BEHALF OF CHRISTIAN UNITY'

by RICHARD E. RUGGLE

THE CONVOCATION of Bishop's College, Lennoxville, was gathered in the chapel. In 1910 an honourary doctorate was being conferred on the bishop of Fredericton. In his convocation sermon, Bishop Richardson confided that the most disquieting thing he saw about the religious life of his day was its attitude of sheer indifference. The foe was seen in impatience with doctrinal sermons and in undenominational religion, but most of all it stood 'naked and unashamed in countless arguements for Christian union.' It was not the indifference of the masses outside the Church but of the faithful within it that disturbed him. The Christian world was 'coming to mistake looseness of belief for liberality of thought.' He conceded a grudging acceptance of the modern view of 'the duty of toleration as the characteristic temper of the religious life', while warning against the 'danger of being so wide awake to the value of every other man's opinion as to fail to form any strong intellectual convictions for oneself.' Although the Inquisition and the fires of Smithfield were hideous, 'behind all the cruel intolerance of persecution there was something that is lamentably lacking in the Church to-day,—a magnificently stern sense of responsibility for the safe-keeping of a sacred trust.'[1] The Canadian bishops would soon exhibit their stern sense of stewardship.

Toleration suggests an ability to withstand threatening or unpleasant forces. The Canadian church had weathered a number of storms, and in the process had come, as Bishop Richardson reluctantly did, to accept liberality of spirit as a positive virtue. The earlier nineteenth century witnessed a gradual erosion of Anglican claims to a favoured place in the eyes of the state. Her bishops could no longer claim by right a seat on the colonial executive councils, the reserves of land set apart for the support of her clergy in Upper Canada were being abolished and her claim to special consideration in public and

[1] J. A. Richardson, "*Contending for the Faith*" (Lennoxville 1910).

409

university education were being denied.[2] The Church of England as by law established was a commodity unfit for export. She had become one of many denominations contending, and co-operating, to influence a developing Canadian society; and she had to accept those denominations as her equals legally and numerically, even if she questioned their ecclesiastical propriety.

Not being an established church, she could not resort to the state to enforce her discipline. Although she was disturbed by disputes over churchmanship during the latter part of the century, no one could become a martyr to ritualism by suffering trial or imprisonment; and it was questioned whether British legal decisions on ritual bound the Canadian church. In eastern Canada, an evangelical laity regarded the bishops, with notable exceptions, as being overly sympathetic to ritual. Diocesan synods, formed to encourage lay involvement as financial support from the imperial government waned, became with vestries the battlegrounds for disputes over churchmanship.

The partisan strife exhausted the church. The formation of a General Synod in 1893 to bring together the isolated dioceses of the emerging nation coincided with a desire to unify the disparate views within the church. A small and widespread population could not afford the luxury of division, and a new inclusiveness in church activities fostered a tolerant spirit.

The *Dominion Churchman*, founded by Frank Wooten in 1875, had been suspected of a high church bias which prompted the establishment of the *Evangelical Churchman* the following year. Wooten became convinced that a party organ would not survive, changed the name of his paper to the *Canadian Churchman* (1890), and bought out what competitors he could. He greeted the expiry of the *Evangelical Churchman* (1900) with an editorial entitled 'The Survival of the Fittest.' But his determination to avoid controversy, excising 'withering sarcasm or insulting epithets' from letters to the editor, won a broad readership.[3] By the start of the century a common Sunday school curriculum, adhering closely to the catechism so as to avoid controversial matters, provided further common ground for Canadian Anglicans.

In 1908 the General Synod approved a *Book of Common Praise*, whose guiding principle was 'unity by inclusion and not by exclu-

[2] John S. Moir, *Church and State in Canada West* (Toronto 1959).
[3] Obituary notice of Wooten in the *Canadian Churchman* 4 April 1912.

sion'.[4] A few evangelicals found it too inclusive in its choice of communion hymns, but the book quickly gained acceptance. At the same time, churchmen of all party backgrounds were working together to compile the conservative first Canadian revision of the prayer book. Divisions over churchmanship persisted, most conspicuous in the maintenance of rival theological colleges in both Toronto and Vancouver. By the early years of the twentieth century, however, the Canadian church had gone far to practice an inclusive tolerance.

The gradual acceptance of biblical criticism provided a further lesson. When *Essays and Reviews* questioned the Christian's right to hope for the everlasting punishment of the damned, it was disliked by the Canadian bishops and clergy,[5] and the desire of Canadian bishops for an authoritative body to protect the colonial church from heresy was an important factor leading to the first Lambeth Conference. About the turn of the century it was dangerous to be a liberal biblical scholar. H. P. Plumptre left Wycliffe College when his classes so offended Principal Sheraton that the latter refused to speak to him.[6] F. J. Steen was forced from Montreal Diocesan College; and Herbert Symonds lost his post at Trinity College in 1892, as did John Todd as late as the 1920s. Todd returned to England, to a lectureship at Oxford and a vicarage nearby, where he kept two pigs fondly named for the Provost and the Dean of Divinity.[7] But in each case, the departing scholar was soon replaced by one of similar views. The church was learning to live with and accept new ideas.

The church found it difficult, however, to deal in practical terms with new ecumenical ideas. Canadians have constantly struggled with problems of unity. The confederation of British North American colonies in 1867 was followed by a period of vigorous nation-building, forging links of rail to join together a vast continent and to bring settlers to the western prairies. Regional and racial tensions, and rural suspicions of industrial cities, have made unity a continuing preoccupation. The churches exhibited a similar concern; and the Methodist unions of 1874 and 1884, with the Presbyterian

---

[4] *Book of Common Praise* (Oxford 1908) p ix.

[5] *Church Chronicle* (June 1864) p 47.

[6] [Archives of Ontario, Toronto, H. J.] Cody papers; H. P. Plumptre to Cody, 7, 18 May, 23 June 1903. Professor D. C. Masters, whose father had been a student at Wycliffe, indicates that Plumptre's liberalism was the cause of the principal's coldness.

[7] G. N. Luxton, *The Reluctant Anglican* (Toronto 1965) p 3.

union of 1875, long pre-dated the corresponding unions in Britain. As the denominations consolidated their resources, they began to catch the vision of wider reunion. The Church of England played a leading part in promoting this interest, and at her invitation a Conference on Christian Unity took place in 1889.

After the initial enthusiasm, the participating denominations continued to appoint committees on unity, but no one took the initiative to call a further conference. After a lapse of over a decade, the Methodist, Presbyterian and Congregationalist churches began conversations that eventually led to the formation of the United Church of Canada in 1925. The Church of England was invited to join in the discussions, but her committee on unity managed to procrastinate enough to avoid having to take part. For the first quarter of the twentieth century, however, there was always a threat that the Church of England might be called to act in furtherance of the ideal of unity which she so eloquently espoused.

Many within her ranks felt that she should take positive steps, if not toward reunion, then at least toward a closer relationship with other churches. Such was the attitude of George Wrong, an Anglican cleric who was hesitant about schemes of union which would glide over differences, but supportive of co-operation. A founder of the history department at the University of Toronto, Wrong's *Rise and Fall of New France* reflects his ideals. He suggested that French settlement went well in Canada until the revocation of the Edict of Nantes, after which the church in the colony lapsed into intolerance and worldliness. Meanwhile England had learned the secret of religious toleration and parliamentary liberty, which allowed the harnessing of the nation's moral energies and helped make inevitable British victory in North America.[8] The respect or lack of respect for the traditions of others, which had shaped the nation's past, would help determine the church's destiny.

The most ardent advocate of a broader outlook was Herbert Symonds. When Anglican involvement in the official negotiations toward union seemed unlikely, Symonds, now vicar of Christ Church Cathedral in Montreal, wrote an open letter to the Bishop of Huron proposing a conference to see what could be done at the moment.[9] Although the *Canadian Churchman* admitted that he might

---

[8] Alan F. Bowker, 'Truly Useful Men: Maurice Hutton, George Wrong, James Mavour and the University of Toronto, 1880–1927' (unpub PhD thesis, University of Toronto, 1975) p 183.

[9] *Canadian Churchman* 13 September 1906.

reflect the lay mind, Symonds' letter sparked little response. The following year, a Toronto clergyman urged that provision be made for non-Anglican clergy to be permitted to preach in Anglican churches.[10] That specific step would be embodied in proposals five years later which would cause great enthusiasm, and consternation, in the church. In that same year, 1907, the American church passed a canon allowing a bishop (as some already did) to 'grant permission to Christian men who are not ministers of this Church to make addresses on special occasions.' The canon was carefully worded, referring to 'men' rather than 'ministers', and avoiding the words 'preach' or 'sermon', but it provoked a massive protest, and was the occasion of sixteen clergy going over to Rome.[11] In England, an extensive public correspondence took place in 1911 about the desirability of Anglicans exchanging pulpits with nonconformists.[12]

The climate for unity seemed to become warmer for Anglicans. The 1908 Lambeth Conference dealt sympathetically with the subject, and the Canadian General Synod dutifully repeated Lambeth's sentiments in 1908 and 1911. In the latter year the Edinburgh Conference, echoed by a campaign of the Laymen's Missionary Movement in Canada, stressed the importance of unity in the churches' missionary work. A pastoral from the House of Bishops recognized that a multitude of almost antagonistic sects hindered missionary outreach and asserted reunion to be essential, though the bishops added the caveat that 'reunion purchased by the sacrifice of principle can have but short duration.'[13]

The time seemed ripe for some practical step, however, and in the autumn of 1912 there appeared 'An Appeal on behalf of Christian Unity.' It suggested that the need and mood for unity might be promoted in two ways:

> A. By the admission of Ministers of other Churches, under certain restrictions and by rightful authority, to the pulpits of our Churches.
>
> B. By permission being given to members of other Communions—being members in good standing in their Com-

---

[10] *Ibid* 4, 18 April 1907.
[11] *The Gazette* Montreal, 9, 10, 16 January 1913.
[12] The correspondence took place in the Westminster Gazette and was collected by the Dean of Ripon in *Church Unity*.
[13] *Quebec Diocesan Gazette* January 1912.

munion—on occasion and with consent of the Ordinary, to Communicate in our Churches.[14]

These measures would 'put into practice the sentiments of brotherly love so often expressed by our lips'. The Appeal was signed by Symonds, by H. P. Plumptre, who was now rector of Saint James' Cathedral in Toronto, and by one of the most prominent of Canadian preachers, A. P. Shatford. Within little more than a month they had attracted the endorsement of over three hundred clergy, roughly a quarter of the clergy in the church. But they also attracted bitter opposition. It would not be expressed in physical or legal ways, for this was an age of assaults by 'the sneer rather than the sword'.[15] The proposals would be dismissed as the musings of unrealistic men, and met with the self-fulfilling assertion that they would lead to strife rather than concord.

One of the first to react was the chairman of the church's committee on Christian Unity and Co-operation, the bishop of Quebec. A. H. Dunn's father was a Congregationalist, but the boy attended the Church of England with his mother. When the vicar invited anyone who was unconfirmed to attend classes out of a sense of British fair play, the young man went along and, contrary to his expectation, received the laying on of hands. He regarded confirmation as the turning point in his life, and felt that it set a course which would admit no deviation.[16] Dunn was a busy pastor, not a scholar, and his ideas lasted him a lifetime. He wrote little, although typically he did produce a devotional booklet, *A Few Earnest Words Addressed to Those Who Have Been Confirmed*.[17] His attitude to dissenters was to encourage friendly personal contact, which might win them to the church, rather than to engage in abstract discussions. His clergy were advised that visiting was the touchstone of a successful ministry, and that they should include 'those who differ from us' in their annual visitations.[18]

Canadian bishops were expected to deliver words of wisdom in their synod charges, and when they visited England, as they frequently did, to solicit aid for their dioceses. Although Dunn felt

[14] General Synod Archives, Toronto, *An Appeal on behalf of Christian Unity* (1912).

[15] George Whitaker, *Sermons Preached in Toronto; for the Most Part in the Chapel of Trinity College* (London and Toronto 1882) p 251.

[16] [Percival] Jolliffe, [*Andrew Hunter Dunn, Fifth Bishop of Quebec: A Memoir* (London 1919)] p 42.

[17] The original would have been printed *c*1892; a new, unchanged edition was published by the SPCK in 1907.

[18] Jolliffe p 93.

that the diocese of Quebec had matured to the stage where it should support itself, he did visit England in 1897 for the Pan-Anglican Conference. At his *alma mater*, Cambridge, he delivered the University Sermon, on the 'Re-Union of Christendom'; and his synod charge on the same topic seven years later repeated much of what he had said then. He feared his programme would be considered too radical, when he suggested that as long as he could get the quadrilateral, he should be quite glad to accept a large diversity of service.[19]

The bishop's stand on one of the questions raised by the Appeal was somewhat inconsistent. In 1894 he had forbidden the evangelical rector of Holy Trinity Church, Quebec, to allow a non-Anglican lay evangelist to preach there. The rector rejected his bishop's demand for canonical obedience, writing that he had 'never given an unconditional and unlimited pledge to any man, and by the Grace of God he never would', and signed himself 'Your obedient servant'.[20] When the bishop retaliated by announcing his intention not to visit Holy Trinity for confirmation, the rector thought he gave a 'good imitation of the ecclesiastical thunder of the Middle Ages'.[21] The vestry supported their rector, the metropolitan disclaimed any power to intervene, and the impasse was only resolved the following year when the rector resigned. But more recently Dunn himself had allowed a Presbyterian layman, the local secretary of the Laymen's Missionary Movement, to preach in his cathedral.[22]

It was the other proposal of the Appeal which worried Dunn more, and he sent a pastoral letter to his clergy, warning them not to yield to the temptation to sign. For the proposal threatened his touchstone of confirmation. Where the church required her children to prepare for communion by the apostolic laying on of hands, the Appeal 'would exempt those without her Communion from the qualifications which she demands from her own children.'[23] The pastoral further claimed that the Appeal would hinder union because it did not see episcopacy as essential, and it asserted (rather than argued) the role of bishops. A columnist in the *Canadian Churchman* coolly commented that the episcopate has never inaugurated great

---

[19] *Ibid* p 133.
[20] General Synod Archives, Toronto, W. J. Noble and A. H. Dunn, 26 February 1894. The archives contains a series of printed copies of correspondence between the rector and his bishop.
[21] *Ibid* W. J. Noble to A. H. Dunn, 3 March 1894.
[22] *Canadian Churchman* 12 June 1913.
[23] *The Gazette* Montreal, 9 December 1912.

movements, like the evangelical, or missionary, or Oxford movements. From the nature of their office, bishops are a restraining and balancing power rather than a propelling one.[24]

The desire to restrain was not confined to bishops. To give it added weight, the Quebec pastoral had also been signed by the Cathedral Council. One of its members, Richmond Shreve, was probably instrumental in having the Appeal condemned by the deanery of Sherbrooke. Another, F. G. Scott, vigorously rejected the proposals from his pulpit,[25] and complained in the *Church Times* that there was a crusade to undermine the catholic faith. He acknowledged that a large group of laity favoured the proposals, and that the economic appeal was strong, but this he interpreted as laxity caused by materialism.[26]

In Montreal, Canon John Almond warned his congregation against the 'Attempt to foist Protestantism on the Church of England', using as his text the story of the devil offering Jesus the kingdoms of the world if He would worship him. The church should refuse to be tempted by bigness—unless it were the bigness caused by the return of the protestant denominations to its fold.[27]

When the diocesan synod met, the preacher of the synod sermon threw cold water on the Appeal with a remark that people 'must not think to solve the problems of reunion by taking a sentimental attitude.'[28] Bishop Farthing had lost for a while his initial enthusiasm to quash the Appeal,[29] and was restrained in his comments. The wisest course, he felt, was to prepare for the future, and to co-operate in social and moral work.[30] The diocesan seminary was already part of a pioneer experiment in co-operative theological education. During the debate on the college, the Reverend Arthur French asked whether the other denominations acknowledged that the Church of England 'had a place in the stalls while the other bodies were down in the pit',[31] and Dr Symonds rose to express a more charitable view. The Appeal was not debated.

Two weeks later the new Saint Giles Presbyterian Church was

[24] *Canadian Churchman* 19 December 1912.
[25] *Ibid* 2 January 1913.
[26] Quoted *ibid* 30 January 1913.
[27] *The Gazette* Montreal, 2, 3 December 1912.
[28] *Montreal Churchman* I, 5 (May 1913) pp 7–9.
[29] Cody papers; S. P. Matheson to Cody, 3 January 1913.
[30] *1913 Montreal Synod Journal* p 47.
[31] *The Gazette* Montreal, 31 January 1913.

opened, and Dr Symonds accepted an invitation to preach. He had obtained permission from the rector of the parish in which Saint Giles was situated,[32] but when the select vestry protested the rector withdrew his permission, two days before the visit was to take place. Bishop Farthing advised against the action, but did not forbid it. In the ensuing controversy, Symonds cited a number of precedents, including Hensley Henson's visit to Erskine Presbyterian Church when he was in Montreal the previous year.[33] A. P. Shatford confided that scores of Symonds' brethren would hound him out of the church for accepting the invitation, and only two or three had the courage to stand up for him. 'We have not apparently got beyond the ecclesiasticism which nailed Jesus to the Tree!'[34]

The archbishop of Ottawa, Charles Hamilton, rarely expressed his feelings about Christian unity. At his synod in mid-January, he did affirm his hope that Our Lord's desire for one church would be realized. But he urged years of patient study rather than immediate action, and would rather wait for some suggestion proposed by the nascent World Commission on Faith and Order than adopt an isolated policy in Canada to pursue the ecumenical goal.[35] Hamilton may have felt personally as well as theologically defensive. His son, a former lecturer at Bishop's College, had just published an enquiry into Christian origins.[36] Two weeks before the synod, a review in the Montreal *Gazette* described the author's insistence on episcopacy. Symonds wrote the next day, branding the theory of apostolic succession as being 'without basis in Scripture, contrary to reason, lacking in charity and a weakness to the Church of England.' His plain words sparked a discussion which lasted a week.[37]

The most enthusiastic laity for the Appeal, in Symonds' opinion, were in Ottawa.[38] The synod did not reflect that enthusiasm. It met in private, as it had to discuss delicate financial matters. The high

---

[32] In 1905, Dr Barclay of Saint Paul's Presbyterian Church read the lessons and took communion in the cathedral on Christmas Day. In return Barclay invited Symonds to preach for him, but the rector of Saint George's parish refused to grant him permission. Cody papers; Symonds to Cody, 30 December 1905, 14 September 1912.

[33] [Richard] Ruggle, ['"Better no bread than half a loaf", or "Crumbs from the Historic Episcopate Table": Herbert Symonds and Christian Unity',] *Journal of the Canadian Church Historical Society* XVIII, 2–3 (1976) pp 68–71.

[34] Cody papers; Shatford to Cody, 22 February 1913.

[35] *1913 Ottawa Synod Journal* pp 35–6.

[36] H. F. Hamilton, *The People of God* 2 vols (Oxford 1912).

[37] Ruggle pp 67–8.

[38] Cody papers. Symonds to Cody, 27 April 1913.

church rector of Cornwall, T. J. Stiles, proposed a memorial to General Synod, that the changes advocated in the Appeal be not authorized. Stiles was a man whose frankness and good humour impressed even his opponents,[39] and his motion carried with only two dissentients.

The Primate, S. P. Matheson, regretted the episcopal fulminations. The bishop of Montreal had urged him to 'issue a Pastoral on the subject and even offered in the goodness of his soul to prepare such a Pastoral for me!!'[40] Archbishop Matheson emphatically declined to do so, preferring as little public comment as possible. The bishops of eastern Canada were unwilling to keep silent, and issued a pastoral which uttered a death sentence on the Appeal:

> While recognizing the right of every Churchman to hold and maintain his own views on things non-essential, they regard the specific proposals of the circular as calculated to subvert the Church's historic order, to imperil her internal harmony and to retard the progress of her legitimate work.

Not only did they reject the proposals, they thought it wrong even to discuss them:

> While earnestly desirous of promoting the visible unity of the Church, they deeply regret the publication of the circular in question, believing that such unauthorized action will inevitably hinder rather than promote the cause of real unity.[41]

Of those who signed the pastoral, the bishop of Niagara was the newest member of the bench. W. R. Clark had been elected to the see in 1911, after serving eight years as secretary-treasurer of the diocese. Surviving letterbooks suggest that the demanding tone he used with the church's delinquent creditors was carried over into his episcopate. He regretted that the canon on discipline had been rescinded before his elevation, because of its looseness. Clark claimed that he had always tried to preserve order and harmony, 'not by the action of external authority, but by the exercise of personal influence', but in a few cases he felt 'obliged to resort to severe measures.'[42] One such case was that of E. A. Eddy, a Methodist minister who converted and took a teaching post at Ridley College. Eddy wondered whether he had made the right decision, and made the mistake of confiding

---

[39] See 'Spectator' (James Elliott's) obituary tribute in the *Canadian Churchman* 24 July 1919.
[40] Cody papers; Matheson to Cody, 3 January 1913.
[41] *Canadian Churchman* 1 May 1913.
[42] *1923 Niagara Synod Journal* pp 32–3.

his doubts to his bishop. Clark replied that he could not have his clergy 'halting between two opinions' and asked Eddy to return his letters of orders.[43] Yet Clark professed liberal views: 'Toleration for the opinions of others and generous recognition of their work, so abundantly blessed by God, can be rendered without abandoning principles'. The key principle was episcopacy, 'of all experiments in church government the most proven, of all actual forms the best, and of all theories the most in accord with the Divine revelation of Holy Writ.'[44] That principle, he felt, was threatened by the Appeal.

The pastoral was also signed by the archbishop of Ottawa as metropolitan; by the bishops of Quebec, Algoma and Nova Scotia, who shared his high view of the episcopate; by the bishop of Fredericton, an avowed opponent of union;[45] by the bishop of Ontario, who did not expect visible unity 'this side of eternity';[46] by the vacillating bishop of Montreal; by the moderate bishop of Huron and by the worried bishop of Toronto. This last, James Sweeny, feared the Appeal as part of the ecclesiastical spirit of the age, crying 'Launch out into new and untried movements', urging new born agitations. The church might find her walls trodden down, her thought chaotic, if her people did not help their properly appointed leaders 'to steady the ship as she bounds over the billows of the world's tempestuous sea towards the haven where she would be'.[47]

The absence of the bishop of Moosonee's name on the pastoral was noted, while the bishop of Keewatin broke ranks and declared his hopes for the Appeal.[48] In the west, the bishop of Calgary rejected the proposals, speaking of unity as a matter of drawing 'others to us',[49] while his dean, preaching at the first synod of the new diocese of Edmonton, said that despite differences between eastern and western Canada, no action toward unity should be taken that would not be acceptable to the whole Anglican communion.[50]

The intensity of the episcopal statement shocked many. Correspondents to the *Canadian Churchman* regretted the use of the term 'unauthorized' for so tentative a document as the Appeal, and noted

---

[43] Diocese of Niagara synod office, Hamilton, Clark letterbook, 10 February 1919.
[44] *1915 Niagara Synod Journal* p 30.
[45] H. J. Morgan, *The Canadian Men and Women of the Time* (Toronto 1912) p 939.
[46] *1913 Ontario Synod Journal* pp 41–3.
[47] *1913 Toronto Synod Journal* p 56.
[48] *Canadian Churchman* 12, 19 June 1913.
[49] *1913 Calgary Synod Journal* p 24.
[50] *1913 Edmonton Synod Journal* p 35.

that the best way to oppose a move is to do nothing.[51] Symonds thought the pastoral timid and unjust, 'a mean attempt to crush our expression of opinion, which they know to be growing in strength, in the bud.'[52] But he confessed that he did not expect 'the strong, in some cases, violent opposition of the majority of the Bishops.'[53] Under the circumstances, he felt it would be foolish to court defeat by pursuing the matter at General Synod.[54]

The proposals of the Appeal were quietly dropped. In their place, a Church Unity League was formed with the broad goal of encouraging the study of unity, and the Canadian Church Union came into being as a counter blast.[55] With the coming of the First World War, interests were focused elsewhere, and the League lapsed. One of the effects of the war, as Plumptre expressed it, was to make people more intolerant of divisions.[56] When General Synod met in 1921 in the wake of the Lambeth Appeal for unity, it gave support for bishops to give occasional authorization for Anglican and other clergy to preach in one another's churches.[57] The change in attitude from the hostility of 1912–13 to the more tolerant sympathy of 1921 owed much to the persistent efforts of those who had promoted the Appeal on behalf of Christian Unity.

Trinity College, Toronto

[51] *Canadian Churchman* 8, 15 May 1913.
[52] Cody papers; 27 April 1913.
[53] H. Symonds, 'The Movement towards Church Unity in the Anglican Church' *Canadian Congregationalist* 1913 (undated clipping in Cody papers).
[54] Cody papers; Symonds to Cody, 11 May 1913.
[55] *Montreal Churchman* II, 7 (May 1914) p 5.
[56] Toronto *Star* 15 September 1917.
[57] *1921 General Synod Journal* pp 152–3.

THE PERSECUTION OF GEORGE JACKSON: A BRITISH FUNDAMENTALIST CONTROVERSY

by D. W. BEBBINGTON

THE DEBATE surrounding the appointment of George Jackson to a chair at Didsbury College in 1913 has been the chief theological controversy of the twentieth century in British Methodism. It forms an instance of an effort to extinguish alleged theological error, an attempt at persecution within rather than outside the church. It was, as contemporaries complained, a heresy hunt, comparable in some respects to the suppression of Modernism in the Roman Catholic Church in the previous decade and in other respects to the outcry over the appointment of Hensley Henson to the Anglican episcopate four years later. The issue was, in fact, most similar to controversies over the legitimacy of biblical criticism that took place in Scotland in the later nineteenth century and in America over a much longer period. Fundamentalists argued that Jackson was unsuitable for the appointment because he was prepared to doubt the historical accuracy of the Bible. The debate and its aftermath raised questions about the limits of toleration, revealed the balance of forces on the propriety of doctrinal discipline and contributed to shaping the destiny of evangelical Protestantism.

George Jackson was a man of highly organised mind, an external London graduate and a great lover of books. His most notable achievement was the creation of a flourishing Methodist Central Mission in Edinburgh, a city that before his arrival in 1888 at the age of twenty-three had supported only a single Wesleyan congregation, and there he became known as a preacher to young men. They appreciated his zeal, his clarity and his frank treatment of Bible difficulties.[1] In 1906 he was invited to the pulpit of Sherbourne Street Methodist Church, Toronto. In Canadian evangelical circles there was already acute dismay about departures from received views of the Bible. When Jackson declared his acceptance in principle of the

---

[1] Annie Jackson, *George Jackson: a commemorative volume* (London 1949) pp 7, 15, 18–19.

higher criticism, he was denounced by eminent Canadian Methodists for denigrating scripture. In 1909 he moved within Toronto from Sherbourne Street to the chair of English Bible at Victoria University, and over the next four years carefully avoided public discussion of biblical criticism.[2] Although the Canadian controversy attracted relatively little attention in Britain at the time, Jackson was marked out as a man with 'advanced' views on the Bible.

At the 1912 Wesleyan Conference Jackson was chosen by a substantial majority and without controversy to occupy the chair of Homiletics and Pastoral Theology at Didsbury College, Manchester, one of the four Wesleyan theological colleges in England, with effect from September 1913.[3] But at the same Conference he delivered the annual Fernley Lecture, published simultaneously in much expanded form, on *The Preacher and the Modern Mind*. Initially there was a deceptive calm, with reviews that merely expressed reservations over omissions or points of emphasis.[4] The storm broke in March 1913, when a pamphlet was issued by W. Shepherd Allen, a distinguished layman and ex-MP, attacking Jackson for abandoning biblical infallibility. The impact of Allen's pamphlet was reduced by an astonishing blunder: a sentence that he singled out from Jackson's book for particular censure as a 'most offensive passage' was a quotation from John Wesley himself, and presented as such by Jackson.[5] Nevertheless the pamphlet roused a feeling that Jackson must be prevented from teaching students for the ministry. District synods debated, though none of them passed, resolutions urging Conference to reconsider the choice.[6] At this juncture *The British Weekly*, the leading Free Church journal, published extracts from a farewell address by Jackson to his Toronto men's Bible class. 'The first eleven chapters of Genesis are antiquarian lumber', he was reported to have said. 'Why not throw them out?'[7] Such statements fanned the flame of protest to white heat. The following issue of *The British Weekly* carried an explanation that the extracts had been copied from a grossly inaccurate report in the Toronto press: the remark about 'antiquarian lumber' was put by Jackson in the mouth of an

[2] *Ibid* pp 26–33. [*The*] B[*ritish*] W[*eekly*] (London) 5 June 1913 p 242.
[3] [*The*] M[*ethodist*] R[*ecorder*] (London) 1 August 1912 p 10.
[4] MR 8 August 1912 p 3; 5 September 1912 pp 3, 4; 31 October 1912 p 4.
[5] MR 13 March 1913 p 3.
[6] MR 22 May 1913 p 7; 29 May 1913 p 6; 12 June 1913 p 6.
[7] BW 29 May 1913 p 226.

imaginary objector so that he could repudiate it.[8] But this piece of sensational journalism had drawn much wider attention to the Fernley Lecture. Letters poured into the denominational press; rumours circulated about a conspiracy to foist Jackson on Didsbury; and the Rev. George Armstrong Bennetts circulated a reputed ten thousand leaflets on *The Doctrinal Crisis in Wesleyan Methodism*.[9] Men began to take sides and a sharp conflict was expected at the Plymouth Conference.

The issue arose twice at Conference. The first occasion was on 21 July at the Representative Session, when laymen were present alongside ministers. There were feverish preparations, with Gipsy Smith, a well-known evangelist, taking the laymen in his hotel to hear Jackson preach and so satisfy themselves of his orthodoxy.[10] At the Conference session Jackson's hour-long speech in his own defence was masterly—low-key, detailed but carefully controlled. His position on the Bible, he argued, far from being radical and extreme, was conservative and moderate. After his contribution, the outcome was assured. When it was proposed that, having heard Jackson, Conference should take no further action, the resolution had only seven opponents.[11] Four days later at the Pastoral Session, consisting of ministers only, a committee report largely exonerating the Fernley Lecture from a charge of doctrinal unsoundness was accepted by 336 votes to 27.[12] George Jackson took up his duties at Didsbury two months later.

Controversy, however, did not end there. On the contrary, the more intransigent of Jackson's opponents banded together before the year was out to form a permanent organisation standing for their convictions, the Wesley Bible Union. The moving spirits were Armstrong Bennetts, who from 1917 to his death in 1925 acted as president, and Harold Morton, who was secretary and editor of the Union's monthly *Journal* from soon after its creation until his death in 1936.[13] Supporters organised local gatherings, wrote to the press, tried to exclude Modernist preachers from their pulpits (with little

[8] *BW* 5 June 1913 p 242.

[9] *MR* 12 June 1913 p 3; [*The*] *M*[*ethodist*] *T*[*imes*] (London) 26 June 1913 p 3.

[10] [W. F.] Howard[, 'Didsbury, 1900–14',] *Didsbury* [*College Centenary, 1842–1942*, eds W. B. Brash and C. J. Wright] (London 1942) pp 127–8.

[11] *MR* 24 July 1913 pp 15–19, 26–27.

[12] *MR* 31 July 1913 pp 8–10, 19–20.

[13] [*The*] *J*[*ournal of the*] *W*[*esley*] *B*[*ible*] *U*[*nion*] (Gloucester) January 1926 pp 1–5. Elizabeth Morton and Douglas Dewar, *A Voice Crying in the Wilderness: a memoir of Harold Christopherson Morton* (London 1937).

success in a connexional system), condemned sermons in official
meetings, spread pamphlet literature, held Bible studies on Fundamentalist lines and wrote in protest to men giving 'false teaching'.[14] Although they broadened their attack to include anything
deemed subversive of the Bible, whether Darwinian evolution or international socialism, their main target remained the higher criticism
(what Bennetts dubbed 'guess-criticism') and Jackson was their *bête
noire*. But the grand aim of the Union was to press home some
prosecution for heresy at Conference. In 1915, for instance, there
was an unsuccessful attempt to condemn the Rev. S. T. Bosward's
Man the Glory of God for its acceptance of evolution and its rejection
of eternal punishment, the visible return of Christ and the resurrection of the body; to bring to book *The Wesleyan Sunday School
Magazine* for explaining away Old Testament miracles; and to censure *The Methodist Times* for printing an article approving prayers for
the dead.[15] The apocalyptic atmosphere of war-time seconded its
efforts, not least by raising suspicions of anything which, like the
higher criticism, could be labelled 'made in Germany'. In 1916, as a
result of a memorial from the Tonbridge Circuit, Conference resolved that synods should ensure that there was fidelity to the connexional standards,[16] and in 1917 a Committee on Unity of Doctrine
was appointed to examine the limits of Methodist orthodoxy. Despite the presence of Bennetts and Morton on its crucial sub-committee, this body reported two years later that Wesleyan ministers
should be expected only to give hearty assent to 'the general system
of Evangelical truth' contained in the connexional standards. The
word 'general' was dropped when Conference accepted the report,
but the remaining formula clearly permitted a great deal of latitude in
belief.[17] 1919 marked what Morton later called 'the doctrinal
Rubicon'.[18] In the following year an attempt to condemn Frank
Ballard, the best-known Wesleyan speaker in the field of Christian
apologetics, made little headway. The Wesley Bible Union, recognising the futility of bringing heresy charges in a denomination that
had set its face against defining orthodoxy now altered direction. It
began to foster links with extreme conservative groups in other denominations, in due course changed the title of its journal to *The*

[14] *JWBU* May 1921 p 117.
[15] *JWBU* October 1915 p 220.
[16] *JWBU* September 1916 pp 193–4.
[17] *JWBU* August 1917 pp 169–70; November 1917 p 249; August 1919 pp 169–78.
[18] *JWBU* February 1927 p 29.

Fundamentalist and in 1931 became the undenominational British Bible Union.[19] This later trend was a confession of the defeat of the persecuting temper in Wesleyan Methodism.

The justifications offered by the Fundamentalists for their campaigns can be summarised under three headings. First, they appealed to the connexional standards of belief, the forty-four sermons and notes of John Wesley. At their ordination ministers avowed their conviction that the 'system of doctrine' in the sermons and notes was a true reflection of scripture; and each May they publicly affirmed at synod that they preached 'our doctrines'. The problem for those who wished to enforce right belief was that in 1882 Conference had elucidated that the 'system of doctrine' was not to be equated with the statements in Wesley's sermons and notes, but consisted of the principles underlying the statements. Consequently ministers were bound only by whatever the Conference interpretation of the 'system of doctrine' might be.[20] Furthermore, the nature and effects of inspiration, a central issue in the controversy, were not defined in Wesley's sermons and notes. Hence Fundamentalists had to argue that scriptural infallibility was implicit in the standards. It is hardly surprising that, however powerful as a spur to action might be the belief that some ministers were repudiating their ordination vows, this line of argument had little force for those who had no initial inclination to impose doctrinal discipline. Secondly, the militants contended that the higher criticism in particular led to heresy over the person of Christ. Critics who denied the Davidic authorship of Psalm 110 were forced to admit that Christ, who treated David as its author, was mistaken. Jackson explicitly surrendered belief in the omniscience of Christ.[21] For critics like Jackson, this was to deepen our appreciation of the humanity of Christ.[22] The reaction of Fundamentalists was very different. 'It almost made his heart stand still', declared Morton at the Conference of 1913, 'to find a man saying that their Lord made mistakes.'[23] Just as during the uproar in the Church Missionary Society over biblical criticism in 1922,[24] the ultimate issue for the conservatives was christological. Heresy on a

[19] *JWBU* September 1921 pp 214–6; [*The*] *Fund*[*amentalist*] (Taunton) August 1927; October 1931 p 224.
[20] *MR* 13 February 1913 p 12; 20 February 1913 p 3.
[21] George Jackson, *The Preacher and the Modern Mind* (London 1912) p 166.
[22] George Jackson, *Studies in the Old Testament* (London 1909) pp 50–1.
[23] *MR* 31 July 1913 p 10.
[24] G. W. Bromiley, *Daniel Henry Bartlett, M.A., D.D.: a memoir* (Burnham-on-Sea 1959) pp 42–7.

subject at the heart of the Christian faith could not be tolerated. Thirdly (and this followed from the second point) it was argued that Methodists had a plain duty to eliminate so deadly a peril. Controversy might be distasteful, but it was an obligation. Contending for the faith was the only way to avoid Methodist apostasy. Their quarrel, they claimed, was not with individuals, even Jackson, but was with their views. Since those views did not have to be searched out, for they had been published to the world, their campaign was no heresy hunt.[25] Others had a different impression. But those who harried Jackson had no doubt of where their duty lay.

The case for toleration was more pluriform, but it contained three main strands. The first focused on the principle of free inquiry. Only if scholars were allowed free scope for research would the right answers to modern questions be established. The position adopted by Bennetts and his friends put the student of the Bible in fetters. Further investigation was essential if the critical problem was to be solved to the satisfaction of faith. In any case, newer methods of biblical study were entirely compatible with fervent evangelism. There should be no restriction on intellectual exploration so long as a man accepted central Christian doctrines.[26] Secondly, a small number held the very different view that development of doctrine, in substance as well as form, was highly desirable. The notion of a definite body of truth given in the past had been transcended by 'a higher and more vital conception of religion, viz., that of an unending, increasing Divine revelation'.[27] It was the task of men like Jackson to drag Methodist theology into the twentieth century. To this way of thinking, persecution of a man for his beliefs was utterly retrograde. Thirdly, a much broader section of Wesleyan opinion deplored heresy hunting because it disrupted the peace of the connexion. Minister was set against minister, lay preacher against lay preacher and time was wasted on fruitless recrimination. The only result of controversy was the banishment of Christian love. 'When we are tempted to kill George Jackson with our fountain pens', wrote one correspondent, 'shall we read over 1 Cor. xiii. vv. 1, 2, 3?'[28] Toleration, as well as persecution, could be the result of deeply felt Christian convictions.

[25] *MR* 24 July 1913 p 15.
[26] *MT* 26 June 1913 p 3.
[27] *MT* 26 June 1913 p 10.
[28] *MR* 19 June 1913 p 5.

Toleration gained the victory, however, for reasons other than the strength of its arguments. The two sides were ill-matched. Jackson possessed far more skills as a controversialist than any of his opponents except Morton. In his original lecture Jackson could be accused of having made too few concessions to the susceptibilities of the Methodist public, but his frankness was essential to his purpose. The other side could sometimes be vitriolic. 'To poison the well of truth', wrote Henry Marsden, a Derbyshire circuit steward who was to sit on the first Wesley Bible Union committee, 'is a worse sin than any in the Decalogue.'[29] Again, years later, when Bennetts and Morton were privately discussing the question of inspiration on the sub-committee on Unity in Doctrine, they were entirely humourless. 'When the rest of us laughed', noted a young participant, Robert Newton Flew, 'they protested it was no laughing matter!'[30] Their attitude is explained by the fact that far more hung on the issue for Fundamentalists than for their opponents: if they failed, their church would cease to be Christian. But such deadly earnestness won few friends. Nor did the image of the two sides, a connected matter, help those who stood for doctrinal firmness. They seemed fuddy-duddy, drawing support from those like the Rev. William Backhouse, who was grieved at the thought of Methodist theatre-going,[31] and from the cultural backwaters of Cornwall.[32] The proposer of the motion against Jackson at the 1913 Conference, was 'thin, grey, elderly', his seconder 'bent and frail', Bennetts himself (in the eyes of the secular press) 'the very type . . . of the old-time Methodist preacher'.[33] The early members of the Bible Union, Morton recalled, were 'mainly people of mature years'.[34] In sharp contrast, Jackson was seen as the champion of young folk and their aspirations. 'The younger generation of Methodists', wrote one of them to the press, '. . . wish to assure him that we look to him as one who is honestly and bravely facing difficulties of which we are only too painfully aware.'[35] It seemed pointless to encourage children of Methodist families to attend public schools and universities and then leave them with no

---

[29] *MR* 3 July 1913 p 5.

[30] G. S. Wakefield, *Robert Newton Flew, 1886– 1962* (London 1971) p 42.

[31] *MR* 18 December 1913 p 6.

[32] *JWBU* July 1921 p 161.

[33] *BW* 24 July 1913 p 412; *MR* 24 July 1913 p 26; *The Daily News* (London) 22 July 1913 p 5.

[34] *Fund* February 1928 p 43.

[35] *MR* 12 June 1913 p 6.

guidance in relating faith and learning. Jackson represented scholarship. Methodists who saw education as the chief path to rising social status were unlikely to range themselves against him. Fundamentalists might clamour about the traditions of the fathers, but George Jackson symbolised the future.

Despite their manner, the Fundamentalists could have made a much greater impact on Wesleyan policy, both in 1913 and afterwards, had they enjoyed more support. Only one ex-president of Conference, the Rev. Silvister Whitehead, declared openly against Jackson, and only two others, both deeply conservative in taste, temperament and politics, backed the Wesley Bible Union—Dr W. L. Watkinson and Dr Dinsdale Young.[36] What the cause lacked in weight it might have enjoyed in breadth. Membership figures of the Bible Union were not disclosed, but some indication of the meagreness of its support is given by the figures for total regular income in 1917–18 and 1918–19: £258 and £382 respectively.[37] The most glaring failure was to rally the most obvious bloc of likely supporters, the holiness wing of Methodism. Belief in entire sanctification, that is, the possibility of perfect holiness in the earthly life, was a tradition that went back to Wesley, but it had been tacitly abandoned by most Methodists and was now associated with a particular journal, *Joyful News*, and a particular institution, Cliff College, a centre in Derbyshire for training Christian lay workers.[38] Readers of *Joyful News* were theologically conservative and likely to resent any apparent undermining of the Bible. In fact two of the three reviews hostile to Jackson's Fernley Lecture appeared in this newspaper.[39] The journal of the Bible Union was itself an advocate of entire sanctification, yet it failed to touch more than the fringe of those who looked to Cliff for leadership. The explanation is that the Rev. Samuel Chadwick, who had previously been a tutor at Cliff and took over as principal in the year of the Jackson controversy, wanted no part in a heresy hunt. Chadwick, like Jackson, had for many years been superintendent of a Central Mission, and must have wished to avoid criticising a man who had successfully tried to communicate the Christian message to the masses of a great city. At the 1913 Conference Chadwick's dictum was that he believed in Jackson, but not

[36] *JWBU* February 1917 p 28; January 1915 p 4; May 1916 p 103.
[37] *JWBU* May 1920 p 98.
[38] J. I. Brice, *The Crowd for Christ* (London 1934).
[39] *MR* 24 July 1913 p 17.

in his book.[40] In 1915 Chadwick deplored the campaign of the Bible Union as a cause of bitterness and a diversion from the work of the gospel.[41] In 1919 he called for an end to 'wrangling and haggling'.[42] The whole spirit of the Bible Union was anathema to him. Chadwick was a conservative evangelical rather than a Fundamentalist. Biblical criticism, in his view, could not be ignored, as the Fundamentalists tried to do.[43] And he believed in the positive work of preaching the gospel, not in negative campaigns that stirred up animosity. Chadwick's stance was incomprehensible to Morton, who frequently sniped at items in *Joyful News*.[44] Morton was alienating his best potential friends. Conservative evangelicals in Methodism, as opposed to the Fundamentalists, showed no disposition to persecute.

Bennetts, Morton and their circle were therefore a tiny minority in the denomination, but they might hope, at least initially, to arouse concern in high places. The Methodist authorities, the permanent office-holders who dominated Conference, might be expected to uphold traditional views. They had been notorious in the previous century for their willingness to call to heel any minister who strayed from the narrow path of theological, ecclesiastical or even political duty. As recently as 1902, in the controversy over Joseph Agar Beet's repudiation of eternal punishment, the authorities, although declaring 'some freedom of opinion' to be permissible on the subject, carried a Conference resolution forbidding Beet to teach or publish his views.[45] Orthodoxy was reaffirmed. The best strategy for Jackson's opponents in 1913 was to win the backing of the denominational leadership through tactful representations behind the scenes. Bennetts' populist campaign, involving the breach of etiquette of using the pulpit to denounce Jackson,[46] was a serious mistake, and a strange one for a man who, as temperance secretary, had been a connexional official for fourteen years. Yet drumming up mass support did raise the spectre of laymen losing confidence in the theological colleges and withdrawing their financial support. It was then possible to claim that the welfare of the colleges must dictate the

---

[40] *MR* 31 July 1913 p 9. I am grateful to Dr S. P. Mews for this point.
[41] *Joyful News* (Stockport) 29 July 1915 p 6.
[42] *JWBU* August 1919 p 177.
[43] N. G. Dunning, *Samuel Chadwick* (London 1933) p 193.
[44] *JWBU* July 1916 p 165.
[45] [R. M.] Pope, [*The Life of Henry J.*] *Pope* (London 1913) pp 207–8.
[46] *MR* 26 June 1913 p 3.

exclusion of Jackson from the chair.[47] Again it was argued that the volume of antagonism stirred up by Jackson revealed that he lacked the discretion needed in a theological professor. On these grounds *The Methodist Recorder*, the official Wesleyan organ, at one point doubted the prudence of the appointment.[48] This was a sign of the direction of the official mind. The trend of thought was arrested, however, by John Scott Lidgett, the editor of the other Wesleyan weekly, *The Methodist Times*. Lidgett had experienced the pain of having his teaching questioned when his own Fernley Lecture for 1897 on the atonement had been officially censured.[49] In a series of strong leading articles, publicly at Conference and no doubt privately beforehand, he strove vigorously for liberty of thought. The man who had held the ascendancy in the Edwardian Conference and had formulated the resolution on Agar Beet's teaching, H. J. Pope, had died in the previous year,[50] and so Lidgett was coming forward as the leading figure he was to remain into the 1940s. It was folly for the Wesley Bible Union, if it wished to make any impact on Conference, to attack Lidgett, as it did in the following year for the publication in his newspaper of a favourable review of an outspokenly Modernist work.[51] The Union was giving vent to its resentment against Lidgett as the individual who did most to secure Jackson's position. Wesleyan officialdom had come down on the side of toleration.

In some ways circumstances seemed to favour a campaign against doctrinal slackening. Between 1906 and 1911 the Free Churches had been disturbed by the 'New Theology' of R. J. Campbell, the minister of the City Temple. Not far removed from pantheism, Campbell's teaching was the more worrying to many for being linked with socialism.[52] Jackson's opponents exploited the fear that though his own conclusions might be Methodist doctrines, his premises could lead ministerial candidates toward the New Theology.[53] The trouble with this charge was that it was entirely hypothetical and that Jackson's preaching was so different from

[47] *MR* 12 June 1913 p 6.
[48] *MR* 26 June 1913 p 3.
[49] J. S. Lidgett, *My Guided Life* (London 1936) p 157.
[50] Pope, *Pope*, pp 218–19, 260.
[51] *MR* 6 August 1914 p 6.
[52] Keith Robbins, 'The Spiritual Pilgrimage of the Rev. R. J. Campbell', *JEH* 30 (1979).
[53] *MR* 24 July 1913 p 15.

Campbell's as to make the risk highly implausible. Again, since 1907 Methodist membership figures had been falling relentlessly, and so alarmists could assert that the pulpit had been robbed of its certainties by biblical criticism. This became received opinion in the Bible Union, but *before* the Jackson controversy the decline in membership had been explained in a different way, as the fruit of worldliness, and especially of the cult of amusements. Even Morton and Bennetts subscribed to this view in 1912 rather than attributing the decline to any theological weakness.[54] Consequently Methodist opinion had not grown accustomed to the belief that the fall in membership was due to doubting the Bible, and was disinclined to agree. Most telling among the circumstances was the widespread acceptance of higher criticism. The series of debates in the Free Church of Scotland beginning in 1876 with the Robertson Smith case familiarised the British public with the issues, and by the opening of the new century there was no doubt that higher criticism had come to stay.[55] What is more, by 1895 it had become established among Wesleyan scholars, even though they tended to greater caution than their colleagues in the other English Free Churches.[56] At Didsbury itself there was no single view. Dr J. S. Simon, whom Jackson replaced, was suspicious of the whole enterprise ('When they began to sharpen their knives on the Old Testament I foresaw that before long they would use them to cut up the New.'), but R. Waddy Moss, Simon's colleague and successor as principal, accepted good biblical criticism without reserve.[57] Consequently the newer attitudes to the Bible had spread in the ministry. 'He was taught these things fifteen years ago', declared the Rev. Benjamin Gregory, a young supporter of Jackson in 1913, 'and their students were being taught them to-day. "You can't stop the dawn . . . by wringing the neck of the crowing cock".'[58] That was the greatest problem of all for those who wished to discipline Jackson. They were simply too late.

It is possible to draw a number of conclusions about Fundamentalism and Methodism from this episode. The work of the Primitive Methodist biblical scholar A. S. Peake, the editor of the famous com-

[54] *MR* 21 March 1912 p 6, 25 April 1912 p 7.
[55] A. C. Cheyne, *The Transforming of the Kirk: Victorian Scotland's religious revolution* (Edinburgh 1983) pp 44–57.
[56] W. B. Glover, *Evangelical Nonconformists and the Higher Criticism in the Nineteenth Century* (London 1954) pp 205–11.
[57] Howard, *Didsbury,* pp 126–7, 118–19.
[58] *BW* 29 May 1913 p 226.

mentary, has often been given credit for the avoidance in Britain of a public Fundamentalist controversy like that of the 1920s in America.[59] The Jackson case and its aftermath, however, form one illustration—to which can be added the C.M.S. division in 1922 and Baptist dissensions over the work of T. R. Glover[60]—that American-style controversy was not in fact avoided in Britain. There was the same doggedness, the same passion, the same venom in defence of biblical infallibility on both sides of the Atlantic. What distinguished Britain from America was the *smallness* of Fundamentalism, a smallness which prevented it from creating a greater stir. That was not the achievement of Peake, whose popular commentary did not appear until 1919. In the Wesleyan case the weakness of Fundamentalist efforts was the result of tactical failures, unpropitious circumstances and the refusal of conservative evangelicals to adopt the persecuting temper of the extremists. People like Chadwick were conservative over the Bible but liberal over toleration. To them, and their equivalents in other denominations, should go some of the credit for the marginal nature of public strife over the Bible in early twentieth-century Britain. That the impact of the Wesleyan Fundamentalists was so slight is also a consequence of the issue they chose to fight on. They might have persuaded the Methodist authorities to act against some of the instances of doctrinal relaxation that became evident after 1913 if they had not in that year branded themselves as unreasonable fanatics. But in the Jackson case there was no chance of securing the condemnation of an attitude to the Bible that was already entrenched in the ministry as well as in the colleges. As it was, the Fundamentalists merely drove the authorities in due course to redefine loyalty to the standards in a looser sense. Wesleyan Methodism effectively renounced its traditional commitment to the maintenance of 'our doctrines'. The vindication of Jackson in 1913 and the virtual end of doctrinal discipline in 1919 gave free rein to the tendency of the main body of Methodism towards a more liberal attitude to belief—towards, in fact, a form of 'liberal Evangelicalism'.[61] The mild heterodoxies of Donald Soper over the virgin birth and of Leslie Weatherhead over the atonement

[59] J. T. Wilkinson, *Arthur Samuel Peake: a biography* (London 1971) p 195.
[60] Gordon Hewitt, *The Problems of Success: a history of the Church Missionary Society, 1910–1942*, 1 (London 1971) pp 461–73; H. G. Wood, *Terrot Reaveley Glover: a biography* (Cambridge 1953) pp 155, 159–63.
[61] J. M. Turner '1900–1932 Methodism in England'. *A History of the Methodist Church in Great Britain* (4 vols London 1983) 3 p 319.

became possible. In inter-war Methodism, as in most other Protestant churches, Christian theology was to seek an accommodation
with secular thought rather than trying to challenge it.[62] The efforts
of the would-be persecutors of George Jackson, that is to say, were
counter-productive. Their virulence helped on the liberalisation they
wished to resist.[63]

University of Stirling

[62] A. D. Gilbert, *The Making of Post-Christian Britain: a history of the secularization of modern society* (London 1980) pt 3.

[63] I am glad to acknowledge the support from the British Academy and from the Carnegie Trust for the Universities of Scotland that made possible the research on which this paper is based.

THE POPE AND THE JEWS IN 1942

by OWEN CHADWICK

THIS PAPER runs from the Wannsee Conference of 20 January 1942 to the Pope's Christmas message of 1942. The final solution of the Jewish problem was planned at the Wannsee Conference under the chairmanship of Heydrich. On 24 December 1942 the Pope believed that he protested publicly against it. On 20 January no one outside the secret inner Nazi ring knew that such a plan was even contemplated. By Christmas 1942 all the world new in outline what was going on. So this paper is partly a study in information: how much did they know in the Vatican, how soon, and by what means did they know it? And partly it is a study in pressure. As the knowledge grew, so grew the pressure on Pope Pius XII to do something, say something, tell the world, condemn. Naturally the effectiveness of all such pressure depended on the extent of the knowledge, and the belief that the knowledge was reliable.

At the outset we need to beware of an illusion to which are prone otherwise quite good scholars who know nothing about the Vatican. This illusion is that the services of information are excellent; that every priest stationed through the world is a likely source of accurate news. Walter Laqueur, a learned man on the Second World War and after, can write these sentences about 1941–4: 'The Vatican was better informed than anyone else in Europe. There were tens of thousands of Catholic priests all over Poland, Slovakia and other countries . . . There were many millions of practising Catholics in Germany, and again tens of thousands of priests—not a few of them serving with the German armies in the East . . . The Vatican had direct or indirect channels of communication with every European country but Russia.' And elsewhere he writes: 'The Vatican had an unrivalled net of informants all over Europe.'[1]

This portrait of the information services certainly gives ground for consideration. That was not how it felt, I do not say, to the Pope and his men, but to the diplomats accredited to the Vatican and during the war inside Vatican City. They kept being surprised how little the

[1] W. Laqueur, *The Terrible Secret* (London 1980) pp 55–6, p 201.

435

Vatican knew, what inadequate sources of information it could find. Our British envoy in the Vatican, d'Arcy Osborne, spent hours a day listening to the BBC, making summaries of the news reported and getting it into Italian to lay before the Pope. He found this occupation hard work and boring. But he came to regard it as of the first importance, for he soon came to realize, even if he had not been so assured by members of the Vatican staff, that this was the only information, or almost the only information, which came to the Pope's eye from sources which were not under Axis control. Later this was supplemented. The Polish underground got messages to the Poles in London, London told Casimir Papée the Pole in the Vatican, Papée told the Pope. But Papée had news only on Poland and not much of that. Osborne was far more important, because he was the agent through whose ears the Pope could listen to the broadcasts of the BBC, and therefore through whom he gained his only non-Axis information about the general course of war.

Casimir Papée was a fine person with a strong historical bent. He spent much time in the Vatican Library during his wartime incarceration inside Vatican City. His papers are in the Polish Institute on the southern edge of Hyde Park London. Of all the foreign agents inside the Vatican he was the person with the best chance of getting reliable news out of Poland. He was in regular touch with the Polish government exiled in London which tried to maintain its own secret source of information.

In France and most of the Balkan countries the nuncio in each capital was able to communicate fairly freely. With the commitment of Italian troops to the Russian front, an occasional eye-witness reappeared on leave in Rome. But the information was always scanty and inadequate. It was very seldom better than what was known by the belligerents in London and Washington, and very frequently it was much worse, for both London and Washington were reading German codes. The idea of a news-sender in every priest is wide of the mark.

This erroneous view is bound to lead to a charge of bad faith against those who edit Vatican documents. If the Vatican had such good information at its disposal, why do the Vatican's published Acts and Documents of the Second World War say so little? Walter Laqueur went to Cardinal Casaroli the Secretary of State and asked to see the other materials not published in the Acts and Documents. Cardinal Casaroli assured him that such materials, so far as they concerned his theme, do not exist. Walter Laqueur patently thought this must be a lie. 'if so' he wrote ironically 'it must be assumed that the great majority of the notes, reports, letters and memoranda etc. exchanged between the Holy See and its own representatives on one hand and foreign governments on the other have been lost: one can only hope and pray that the loss is not permanent.'[2] And then he added a footnote to the charge that the Cardinal must have lied. 'Such attempts to keep Vatican knowledge of events secret are politically and psychologically understandable, but not very far-sighted, for sooner or later some of the facts will become known'.

I would not trouble you with this if Walter Laqueur was a mere antipapal pamphleteer. But this is a serious historian who has much helped the study of the subject. Certainly it is at first sight hard to believe that an organization with tentacles across the world and with a spy in every parish was so culpably ignorant. I can only say this: the archives of which I have knowledge are the archives of the various diplomats immured like prisoners in the Vatican City—British, French, American, Polish. Their documents are of a perfect consistency with the Vatican documents.

Later in this paper we shall find another charge of bad faith made against the Vatican editors. But I shall meet that in its proper chronological place.

Let us take another instance. Carlo Falconi[3] says this: 'Subsequently the language employed by the *Osservatore Romano* became increasingly cautious; so much so that in the article commemorating the death of Fr Kolbe (14 August 1942) there was no mention of the circumstances in which it had occurred—namely at Auschwitz in the starvation bunker where that friar had taken the place of one of his companions so as to save his life'. Every fact in that sentence is correct. The entire implication is false. Falconi assumed that the Vatican must know where and how Kolbe died and only dared not say so out of prudence. The fact is, the Vatican had no idea how Kolbe died, even by August 1943 a year after the death. They thought that he died in the concentration camp at Dachau. This was a reasonable guess because most Polish priests were sent to Dachau. The only bit of information which the Vatican received was from their Polish ambassador Papée, who told them erroneously that Kolbe died in a German concentration camp. In fact, by August 1942 no one knew of the importance of

---

[2] *Ibid* p 57.
[3] [C.] Falconi, *The Silence of Pius XII* (Eng. trans. London 1970)] p 211.

Auschwitz as a death-camp. What interests is Falconi's anxiom that the Vatican was over-cautious because it dared not say what it knew, and his refusal to credit the idea that it did not know.

In using the printed Vatican documents we need to have a different kind of caution. We need to remember that the paper now in the archives of the Secretary of State was not everything that happened. We need to be aware that they read Italian newspapers, and talked, and received verbal messages, and heard rumours passed by conversation. There is one astonishing illustration of the contrast between what the Vatican knew if one looks at the paper, and what it must have known; the wreck of the *Struma*.

The Jews wanted to flee from anti-semitic Romania. At exorbitant prices they bought passages to Palestine on a wretched and unsafe tub, about 240 tons, under the flag of Panama. They had no visas for Palestine and the British asked the Turks to stop the voyage. This unpleasant ship arrived at Constantinople on 15 December 1941 with 769 Jews in loathsome conditions, a broken engine, one lavatory aboard, and no fresh water. The Turks refused to allow anyone ashore. The local Jewish community fed them till permits could be got, and meanwhile tried to negotiate leave for an overland journey by train to Palestine. This ended when the British government said that it would not let them into Palestine because their arrival would disturb the Arabs. The British asked that this ship of 'illegal immigrants' should be sent back into the Black Sea. They suspected it of being the first load of a series of illegal ships for Palestine, and further suspected that Nazi agents might be aboard. The Turks, confronted with a ship which no one wanted, ordered it to sea. Its engine was still broken, and after a fight between Turkish police and passengers it was towed into the Black Sea on 23 February and early next morning blew up with the loss of every soul aboard except a single male. No one knew whether it was an accident or a torpedo. The Vatican received a report on this terrible tragedy, for which the British were not exempt from blame, during July, nearly five months later; in a letter written by Monsignor Roncalli's secretary in Istanbul. If we had only the Vatican papers to go by, we should suppose the Vatican only to know of it in July. If so, the news service of the Vatican was the worst in the world. But that is unthinkable. The European newspapers were full of it, at the end of February and beginning of March. The sinking did irretrievable damage to the relations between the Zionists and the British government.

Let us be clear on one thing: everyone knew in 1941 that many Jews from Germany were being deported eastward. They were believed to be destined to supply a labour force. Germany made no secret of the plan. By later October 1941 the terrible drama began; Jews moving eastward to already overcrowded and filthy eastern ghettoes; sanitation designed for five coping with five hundred; epidemics and squalid air; little Jewish bosses strutting in ghettoes; suspicion by Germany that Jews spirited away their valuables into ghettoes; governors and mayors protesting; bureaucrats tearing their hair; trains dumping their human cargo—and what then? Everybody longed for the peace treaty with Britain and France and so the opening of Madagascar as the future Jewish homeland. By the end of the year 1941 everyone knew that to be deported was a bad fate; that the conditions of transport, especially in winter, were cruel; that the conditions of work and of rations in the camps were killing. No one knew much about it but everyone wanted to avoid deportation and with more fear than just fear of a compulsion to leave one's historic home.

Father Tacchi-Venturi was the Jesuit whom Mussolini trusted and whom the Vatican used as its link with the Italian government. On the very day of the Wannsee Conference, 20 January, he wrote a letter to the Secretary of State in the Vatican Cardinal Maglione, saying that his efforts for the Jewish children in Croatia had failed to keep them from *orribile deportazione*.[4]

So the deportations to Poland were already known to be *orribile*, and those who endured them to be wretched. No one believed that they were sent to Poland to be murdered. They were sent to Poland to work. That very month the authorities in the Vatican still struggled to get passports and permits for Jews to emigrate to Latin America, or to prise the Lithuanian rabbi and his family out to Lisbon.

Everyone knew that the fate of Jews in Poland was not likely to be happy. In a screaming voice Hitler said so on the radio. Eleven days after the Wannsee Conference, on 30 January 1942, Hitler made such a screech. Osborne, immured behind the Vatican walls, read the speech next morning in the Italian translation printed in the *Messagero* newspaper. The sentence of Hitler which caught his eye was this: 'The Jews will be liquidated for at least a thousand years!'

---

[4] *Actes et Documents du Saint-Siege relatifs a la Seconde Guerre mondiale* [hereafter ADSS] (Vatican City 1965–71) 8 p 416.

On a foul cold wet day Osborne walked to see the Vatican Secretary of State Cardinal Maglione; and Maglione had also taken the phrase, because he remarked to Osborne on 'Hitler's new outburst against the Jews' (*Osborne's Diary*—hereafter OD—31.1.1942). Everyone knew that it was bad to be a Jew and deported to Poland. They knew that in the Vatican just as clearly as anywhere else. Hitler said so. No one knew how bad.

On 9 March 1942, came the first of a sinister series of messages. It came from Slovakia. Slovakia was an independent but satellite State since the incorporation of Bohemia into the Reich, and it happened to be strongly Catholic. Its president Father Tiso was a priest. The Vatican chargé d'affaires in Bratislava had free communication with the Vatican.

After the war on June 15, 1948, a member of the German delegation in Bratislava, Hans Gmelin, declared under oath that in February 1942, the nuncio in Bratislava sent two notes to the prime minister, Tuka, saying that it was 'inexact' that Jews were sent to Poland to work. They were sent to be exterminated. This evidence from the Nuremberg documents has been widely accepted. Yet it is impossible to believe that Gmelin's memory had the date right. At a date much later than February 1942 the nuncio at Bratislava had obviously little idea what was happening.

On 9 March the chargé Burzio reported that the Slovak government was advanced in a plan to send all its Jews, of all ages, from Galicia and the district of Lublin, into Poland. Males, females and children would be deported separately. There is no pressure from Germany to do this, Burzio had gone to the prime minister Tuka who said that he saw nothing inhuman or unChristian in the proceedings. Burzio added 'The deportation of 80,000 people into Poland at the mercy of the Germans is the equivalent of sending a large number to certain death'.

This was the first formal intimation, from a pair of eyes near to the event. Notice that not even those eyes have any idea of what was decided at Wannsee. These people will be sent, under inhuman conditions, into Poland; will be made to work under inhuman conditions, and a lot of them will die.

On the very next day a body of orthodox Jews in Switzerland approached the nuncio at Berne, Monsignor Bernardini, to tell him that the deportation of the Slovak Jews, 135,000 in number, would begin on 23 March. They, the Swiss Jews, had the opinion that the

Vatican was their only hope; especially because Slovakia was a Catholic country. Monsignor Bernardini kept asking them whether they were sure that the information was true. They assured him, there could be no doubt whatever.

Three days after that, 13 March, the nuncio in Hungary passed on a Hungarian appeal to the Pope on behalf of the Slovak Jews. The Pope was begged to approach the President of Slovakia Father Tiso, who, said the appellant, was a very good priest. This report said that the number to be deported was about 90,000.

The Vatican Secretary of State, Cardinal Maglione, summoned the Slovak minister to the Vatican, Karl Sidor, on 14 March 1942 and gave him a note with the information. On 25 March a letter arrived from the chargé Burzio that a rumour was running to the effect that the deportations were suspended. The letter nevertheless shocked the Vatican by a story that Jewish girls of ages 16 to 25 were kidnapped last night, probably to serve the sexual needs of the German army on the Russian front. Cardinal Maglione summoned Karl Sidor again, in the effort to stop such a horror.

Burzio's information was wrong. The deportations started the same day (25 March). 'Madness!' noted the deputy secretary Monsignor Tardini in the Vatican when he heard. 'And the madmen are two in number: Tuka who orders it, and Tiso who lets it happen—and Tiso is a priest!'

Notice the situation, 26 March 1942.

1 No one doubted that a lot of Jews died in being deported to Poland, either on the way or in the conditions of work.

2 No one supposed that Jews or anyone else were sent to Poland simply to be murdered.

3 No one had any evidence that anyone but Slovaks deported Jews as a whole people rather than as individuals however numerous.

4 The policy of getting Jews out of Germany, to Lisbon or to Latin America, was still thought possible though very difficult.

5 No one had evidence that the Germans ordered the Slovaks to do what they did.

6 The ignorance, and the amazing illusion about the whole nature of German racial theory, is shown by the Vatican belief in the story from Bratislava, that young Jewish girls were exported to satisfy the sexual needs of German soldiers.

7 In the documents is little sign of the Pope being involved. All is

done by Cardinal Maglione or his deputies, Tardini or Montini.
But we have evidence of some of the documents being shown to
the Pope. We cannot doubt that he was kept continuously informed. He was certainly informed of the rumour about the
Jewish girls for German soldiers.[5]

8 Not the least of their problems was the Catholic nature of the
government of Slovakia; headed by a Catholic priest as president; with the only bishop on the Council of Ministers saying
that the Jews were enemies of Slovakia and he approved of this
action; and with the bishops issuing a corporate protest which
nevertheless declared that the Jews were chiefly responsible for
the massacre of Christians in Russia and Spain, and had a
pernicious influence on Slovakia, in the economy, in culture,
and in morality.[6]

9 They received an assurance from the Slovak government that
the deported would be treated humanely and that families
would be reunited. This the Slovak government had reason to
believe. We know, what the Vatican did not, that all this started
with an offer from the German Foreign Office to take 20,000
strong young Jews as a work force and as a contribution to solv-
ing the Jewish problem; and from the German point of view the
offer seems to be perfectly genuine, that is, it did not come from
the implementation of Wannsee but as a continuity of the old
policy. The Vatican did not say whether it believed this
assurance of humane treatment. It already had strong reason to
doubt.

For another month and a half they had no more worth-while
information.

Father Pirro Scavizzi was the chaplain to an Italian hospital train
bringing wounded from the Russian front. We do not know the
movements of himself or his train. We find him in Rome in
November 1941. We next find him in the Polish town of Cracow on
15 April, for on that day he called to pay his respects to the
archbishop Monsignor Sapieha—incidentally he may easily have

---

[5] *Ibid* pp 453–5, 475, 479. For the story of the girls heard by a Red Cross visitor to
Hungary and Rumania in March 1942, see Laqueur *The Terrible Secret* p 61; so the
Vatican was not the only responsible body to believe it. For the evidence of Hans
Gmelin, see [Saul] Friedlander, [*Pie XII et le IIIe Reich: Documents* (Paris 1964)] p
103; for the documents of the Swiss Jews, *ibid* pp 104–5.
[6] *ADSS* 8 p 519.

met a future Polish Pope who was in the archbishop's retinue at that time. Father Scavizzi found that the archbishop had, waiting to be delivered as opportunity served, a letter to the Pope, which he had written six weeks before on 28 February.

Sapieha's letter was written in Latin. It thanked the Pope for his good wishes, a letter which the Pope sent out on 6 December 1941, urging the clergy and faithful of the diocese of Cracow to stand firm and sending them his blessing. Then it described their 'tragic condition'; deprived of human rights, at the mercy of cruel brutes, living in continual fear of deportation or imprisonment in a concentration camp ('from which few return alive'): camps where thousands and thousands of good men are kept without trial though they are innocent of any crime; among them many priests. We have not enough food to live on, typhoid is upon us, we have no drugs. It is no wonder in such conditions that men go Communist. They remain good Catholics. But 'I cannot deny that lately there has grown pernicious agitation against the Holy See. The sufferers of atrocities want to hear it condemn those atrocities. They do not hear it and so listen to the agitators'. 'Still, the people are strong and full of faith . . .' So the Archbishop thanked the Pope for his messages and gifts of money and wished that communication with Rome were not so difficult and asked the Pope's blessing.[7]

Father Scavizzi took this letter with him for the Pope. But next day, before he left Cracow, he was called on by a Dominican Father, who begged him in the archbishop's name to burn the letter, because if it fell into the hands of the Germans they would shoot all the bishops and perhaps others. Father Scavizzi obeyed the request. But first he made a copy, and this is the copy which now we have. We do not know when Scavizzi arrived in Rome and the Pope saw the letter; but it was not before the middle of May; perhaps 18 May but possibly not till the end of the month when Cardinal Maglione sent Archbishop Sapieha a letter.

Sapieha did not mention the Jews in his letter. On 22 May 1942 the Polish ambassador Casimir Papée pleaded with the Vatican to act on behalf of Poland.[8] Cardinal Maglione said that he had no proof; and that experience showed that the intervention of Rome was counter-

---

[7] *Ibid* 3 p 539.

[8] So Harold Tittmann's Mss, s.v. Atrocities p 7; no record in *ADSS* 3; but *ADSS* 3 p 572 has a letter from Cardinal Maglione to Orsenigo in Berlin trying to do what he can for Poland.

productive. We have a letter of the Pope at the end of the month, to exiled Cardinal Hlond, in which he says that he does know about Poland; though he also does not mention Jews (30 May 1942).

'We know exactly' he told Cardinal Hlond, 'and hear with deep distress, the news of what is happening in Poland. That country is suffering a horrible fate and yet does not flinch under every sort of persecution'.[9]

Simultaneously the Slovak minister to the Vatican Karl Sidor revealed the extent of the German plan. He wanted to justify (23 May) what his government did and therefore wanted to push away part of the responsibility. He said that the Slovak deportations were part of a grand design. A community of half a million Jews would be created in the East; Occupied France would send, and Belgium, and Holland, and the Protectorate (Bohemia) and the Reich; and Hungary was ready to send 800,000. The Slovak Jews will be given permanent homes near Lublin; the Aryan population will be moved; it will be a Jewish area with a Jewish administration. Families will remain united. The German government has promised that Christians of Jewish origin will be put somewhere else. They have promised that the Jews will be treated humanely. The story of the girls for harlots is false. Some German soldiers who slept with Jews have been shot. This letter of Sidor was shown to the Pope. It was encouraging, if they could believe it. The deportations were causing terrible suffering, they knew in Rome. But perhaps things would come to settlement. 'What damage it does' soliloquized Monsignor Tardini

> that the President of Slovakia is a priest. Everyone realizes that the Holy See cannot get anywhere against Hitler. But that it cannot control a priest who can understand?[10]

On 7 June 1942 this question struck much nearer home. The newspaper *Il Messagero* published a picture with the caption *Jews at work on the banks of the Tiber*. The diplomats in the Vatican were disturbed by this picture. Harold Tittmann the American went to Montini. 'It seems' he said 'all the more appalling that this could exist within the shadow of St Peter's, the foundation of Christian charity'. He argued that it was a pollution, incompatible with the sacred character of the city of Rome as laid down in the Lateran Treaty. Osborne said 'It is very shaming to Italy, as I think most Italians would agree. I hate Italy to be so degraded herself by Gestapo methods' (4 June 1942).

---

[9] Falconi p 199.
[10] *ADSS* 8 p 598.

Montini talked to Maglione and Maglione talked to the Italian ambassador to the Vatican, who said that he would do what he could; a few days later Maglione also approached Father Tacchi-Venturi. Tacchi-Venturi took it up with the Director-General of Demography and Race who assured him that the Jews in the labour force on the Tiber were indeed labourers and not professional men ill-equipped for such work.[11] The reply dissatisfied but they never had to complain again of any similar incident until after the Germans occupied Rome, when for more than one reason they could not dare to complain.

They were still under illusions. Almost the same day Cardinal Maglione (6 June) asked Monsignor Orsenigo to do what he could to get exit permits for some German Jews. It was the last time of illusion. The Final Solution was already in movement but the Cardinal Secretary of State had as yet no understanding whatever of what was happening. He only knew that horrid things were happening, to nearly everyone and not only Jews. On 24 June Orsenigo replied from Berlin that he could do nothing, that his interventions might do harm to the persons concerned and could not possibly do good.[12]

As the news filtered through, bit by bit, it began to disturb the diplomats in the Vatican. They were not uniquely disturbed about Jews. They were disturbed about everything, especially in Poland, but in France too; and in Greece or Yugo-Slavia; and the Jews were only one ingredient in a wider horror. Gestapo chief Heydrich was wounded by assassins sent from England on 27 May and died on 4 June. The systematic shooting of Czech hostages thereafter was announced in German news bulletins, Osborne grimly recorded and added the numbers. On 11 June Daluege wiped out a whole Czech village for sheltering Heydrich's assailants, executing all men and seizing all the women and children. Osborne had been gently chiding since the beginning of hostilities. The desks at the Foreign Office, at least since Eden succeeded Halifax as Foreign Secretary, were not displeased with his criticisms, and turned them, *moribus suis*, into fierce reproaches. But these Czech murders outraged Osborne in Rome. He said he wanted to strangle Germans with his bare hands. On 13 June he visited Cardinal Maglione and afterwards recorded his feelings:

The courtyard of San Damaso was full of little First Com-

---

[11] *Ibid* p 556 p 560.
[12] *Ibid* pp 569–70.

munion boys and girls, an appealing sight. But unfortunately the moral leadership of the world is not retained by mass reception of Italian first communicants and all others. The Führerprinzip demands more than the benevolence of a Pastor Angelicus and moral leadership is not assured by the unapplied recital of the Commandments.

The American Harold Tittmann was also outraged. He only came into the Vatican after Pearl Harbour and was not six months old within the walls.

On 12 June 1942 Tittmann sent Sumner Welles a personal letter telling him of a conversation with d'Arcy Osborne. Osborne had said how unpopular was the Pope in England at the moment, how unlike the Pope of 1939 and earlier months of 1940. The British government believed that the Pope was insuring against an Axis victory; thought that the whole Curia was at bottom Italianate; that this could hardly be other in so tiny a state, nominally independent but actually dependent. 'This unpopularity' Tittmann recorded Osborne as saying 'had reached such proportions that it was only with the greatest difficulty that Osborne was able to elicit a message of felicitation from His Majesty the King of England to the Pope for his Jubilee. . . .'[13]

Four days later Tittmann sent a report to the State Department. He said that a stream of criticism was directed at the Pope from pro-Allied sources. 'It was felt that the Holy Father was occupying himself with spiritual matters, charitable acts and rhetoric, while adopting at the same time an ostrich-like policy towards atrocities that were obvious to everyone.' People think that the great moral authority won for the Papacy by his predecessor Pope Pius XI, was being dissipated. In Poland they have reserves about him, some are even hostile. The criticisms are particularly violent over the treatment of hostages in Poland and Czechoslovakia. Tittmann had asked Cardinal Maglione whether the Holy See could not say something about the massacres that happened every day in Bohemia and Moravia (as a reprisal for Heydrich's murder). Maglione had shaken his head sadly and said that an intervention by the Pope could only make things worse.

Why, asked Tittmann, does the Pope take this attitude? Is it a policy of appeasement, resting on a conviction that the Axis is bound to win the war? Others say that he really believes that in the long run

[13] Harold Tittmann's Mss, s.v. Atrocities p 13.

the Allies are bound to win; if the Nazis are going to be destroyed there is no point in subjecting antiNazis to more severe persecution.

Others say that his silence is caused by a fear of immediate reprisals. Those who want him to be bold admit that the result might be the seizure of the Vatican and himself by the Gestapo. But they were happy that this fate should befall because the moral stock of the Papacy would rise startlingly.

The impression is growing that the Pope still hopes to play the part of a mediator between the enemies. Therefore he has to refuse to say anything which could compromise his impartiality. He probably thinks it is better to displease his friends than his enemies; they are more likely to forgive, in the end, his sins of omission.[14]

So wrote Harold Tittmann (16 June 1942). Still no information about the Jews. All Europe was in travail and the Pope said nothing and yet he knew because everyone knew—that is what is being argued.

Three days later (19 June 1942) Casimir Papée talked with Cardinal Maglione on the same question. Maglione said 'The Holy Father cannot always be explicit; but all his public utterances about persecution where the victims are the Catholics and their families, are to be applied to Poland. Everyone really knows that the Holy Father is always referring to Poland'.[15]

On 25 June and 30 June the *Daily Telegraph* began to mount publicity on the extermination of Jews. The material was provided by Ziegelboim, one of the Polish National Council; who later committed suicide because of what he felt to be western indifference.

This was only newspaper material. Most people received it with a large touch of scepticism. But it was broadcast on the BBC and therefore included in Osborne's reports of European news for the Pope's eye. For example:

> *25 June* 'In recent months the Germans have been carrying out a new and systematic pogrom against the Jews. In Vilna alone 60,000 had been killed during the past few months'.
>
> *27 June* 'It is announced that since October 1939 the Germans have killed 700,000 Jews in Poland as part of their deliberate extermination policy; mass shooting, drowning and gas'.

Osborne said he was quite prepared to believe this. But by saying

---

[14] Tittmann, paraphrased in Di Nolfo, *Vaticano e Stati Uniti 1939–52* (Milan 1978) p 170. Di Nolfo uses '*ostrica*' ('oyster-like policy').

[15] Casimir Papée, *Pius XII e Polska*; Falconi p 207.

that he was quite prepared to believe this he showed that some people did not believe a word of it and that he had to work hard to screw it up to credibility.

> *30 June* 'The Germans have killed over a million Jews in all, of whom 700,000 in Poland. Seven million more have been reported or confined in concentration camps'.

Osborne liked to remind the Vatican what other ecclesiastics were saying.

> *9 July* 'Cardinal Hinsley has delivered an eloquent address in condemnation of the German terror in Poland and the other occupied countries, in which he referred to the utter bestiality of German methods,
>
> *10 July* 'According to an official report of the Polish government the Germans have exterminated, by execution or otherwise, 900,000 Poles . . . women and children have been hanged and gassed'.

On 15 July Osborne got hold of the *Tablet* for 20 June and found in it an article called *The Slaughtering of Europe*. This was really on the massacre of Czechs after Heydrich's murder. Osborne drew marks on the article and gave the copy to Cardinal Maglione and expressed the hope that it might be shown to the Pope. He had a talk with Cardinal Maglione and complained, though gently as was his way. 'The reaction' Osborne told London

> was unsatisfactory. He (Cardinal Maglione) said that the Germans would say that the stories of alleged atrocities were untrue. To this I replied that their own wireless retailed their threats to exterminate whole populations and announced mass executions and deportations. He also said that the Pope had already spoke clearly. I agreed he had, for instance, declared that the blessing or curse of God upon an occupying Power would depend upon its treatment of the population of an occupied country, but pointed out that this was over a year ago and that something more strong and specific was called for by the mounting score of massacres of individuals and of whole peoples. But nothing further emerged except that the Cardinal reminded me of his own representations to the Italian, Hungarian, Slovakian and other authorities. I think that it is true that he does all he can himself. But he has to defend the policy of the Pope, whether he approves of it or not.[16]

[16] Osborne to Howard, 12 July 1942, PRO, FO 371/33426.

When this letter came into the Foreign Office more than a month later R. J. Meade commented on it (12 August 1942) 'Papal timidity becomes ever more blatantly despicable'. But this was not fair because by mid August everyone knew or suspected a bit more than in early July.

More information now came from Croatia. The new state of Croatia suffered a communal war, Catholic Croats versus Orthodox Serbs, which was a religious war or rather a series of forced conversions under threat of massacre. The apostolic visitor in Zagreb was Monsignor Marcone; and as early as 21 February 1942 Cardinal Maglione had sent him a message praising the Croat bishops for trying to get humane treatment for the Jews. Rome liked the new Catholic State but was not at all pleased about the forcible conversions which stained its course. 'Is it possible' asked Montini of a visiting Croat priest who was an envoy of his government, 'that so many crimes have been committed?' Crimes or not, 240,000 Serbian Orthodox became Catholic. Whether the bishops did as much as they should for the Jews is more than open to doubt; for Archbishop Stepinac, when he visited Rome in May 1943, 'justified in part the methods used against the Jews, who in our country are the greatest defenders of crimes of this kind (he means abortion) and the most frequent perpetrators of them'.

On 17 July 1942 Monsignor Marcone in Zagreb wrote to Rome that he had seen the police and military chief General Kvaternik. The Croat explained how the Germans had ordered him to send all Jews in Croatia to Germany; and Kvaternik told Marcone that in Germany lately two million Jews had been killed. 'It appears' he said 'that the same fate awaits the Croat Jews, especially if they are old and cannot work'. The Croat Jews got wind of this plan and several approached Marcone for help, among them the chief rabbi of Zagreb.[17] Kvaternik said that he would do what he could to delay the execution of the order, and that he would be glad if the Vatican could intervene to get the order withdrawn, or a least to propose that the Jews be allowed to gather on an island in the Adriatic, or to a special region of Croatia where they could live in peace. The chief rabbi also said that Turkey had agreed to accept 50 Croatian Jewish children. These could not travel by Serbia, they must pass through Bulgaria, Hungary and Rumania. Bulgaria had given leave but Hungary and

---

[17] Report of Lobkowitz to Zagreb, in Falconi pp 315–6; cf pp 306, 308, 312.

Rumania refused. Could the Vatican intervene with Hungary and Rumania?

All these requests Tardini fulfilled. These efforts for Croatian Jews were still going on into October. They were not without success. The Croat government behaved like the Slovak. They assured Rome repeatedly that the Jews must leave the country but it was not at all the intention that they should be treated inhumanely.

If the head of police in Croatia said that two million Jews had lately been murdered in Germany did he know anything or was it rumour like everything else? We can see from the way it is formulated that it was rumour.

Maglione was still sanguine enough to approach Orsenigo in Berlin. Orsenigo reported that he had been approached already about two young Jews who were being held in a synagogue before being sent to Poland. He thought that he could do no good but went in conscience to the Vatican desk at the German Foreign Office. The occupant of the Vatican desk had lately changed—to Werner Picot, who was one of Himmler's men. Picot refused to receive Orsenigo's request and said that he would regard the request as not made.[18]

Maglione had also written about a Jewish woman who wanted to go into Germany to save her family property. Orsenigo replied to this astonishingly naive enquiry—rather naive at the time, very naive in relation to what we now know—'I'll do what I can; but with very little hope indeed; the Jewish situation here has no kindness in it. If she is not Aryan it would be better to advise her not to try the journey. She would hardly get a hearing here'.

It will be observed that by 20 July 1942 neither Orsenigo nor Maglione have any idea of what is going on. The police of Zagreb has told Marcone, and Marcone has told the Vatican, that two million Jews have been murdered in Germany. They did not believe it, and we know that we were right not to believe it. But it is clear that they did not believe it to be even a wild approximation to the truth; or they would not be concerning themselves with leave for a Jewish woman to make an expedition into Germany to look after the property which she had inherited. Archbishop Sapieha of Cracow got a letter to Rome in only three weeks, an amazingly short time, and it arrived on 1 July. But it did not mention Jews or massacres, only the dangers to the Church.[19]

---

[18] 20 July 1942, *ADSS* 8 p 604.
[19] *Ibid* 3 pp 604–5.

The Pope and the Jews in 1942

On 21 July there was a mass for the Jews in Madison Square. The rumour of millions dead was incredible, it looked like one of those atrocity stories for the sake of propaganda, which the First World War made ridiculous. And it was sometimes accompanied by stories which were incredible and untrue—but which happened to be no more untrue than things which happened. The evidence of massacre might also tell of Jewish girls as harlots for German soldiers, which was absurd; or it might tell of Jewish bodies being used to make soap or fertilizers, which was absurd and happened to be untrue but not more absurd than what was true, feminine Jewish hair being used to make felt. But such stories were felt to be impossible and helped to discredit the witnesses. But then mere numbers tended to discredit the witnesses. If someone said that two million Jews were killed he was met by a wall of scepticism. How could any witness know about two million? There was strong propaganda reason to exaggerate, or invent. After a time the secret agents of the Polish underground who began to know quite a lot, found that they were not believed if they told what they thought was truth. So, absurdly, they started to record numbers which were much fewer than they thought to be truth, in the hope that these numbers at least would be believed.

Osborne's Diary, 25 July.

> I had a very pleasant lot of letters by Bag today, including a letter from Bridget on the Pope's attitude—or lack of attitude towards the German wholesale massacres in Europe. I am thinking of showing it to His Holiness, as the views of one of the faithful in England.

We have no evidence that he did show the letter to the Pope.

On 28 July Orsenigo wrote a more sinister letter. Montini had asked him (4 July) whether he could find out information on Jews who had gone to Poland because naturally their relatives wanted to know where and how they were. Probably this was caused by the European publicity at the end of June, as we have seen it in the *Daily Telegraph*. Orsenigo said that in Berlin no one could find out anything; that the deportations seem to be arranged so that the trail vanished; and that it was inadvisable even to enquire, because now it was dangerous even to stop in the street and to be seen to talk to someone wearing a Jewish star. He had heard from a Jesuit Father in Vienna, Father Ludger Born, that this inability to get information applied also to Vienna. Because no one can get any news, said Orsenigo, there is place for the most macabre rumours. There are rumours of mass massacres; we have no possible way to test these rumours. The Germans refuse any exceptions for baptized Jews. They say that they are defending Germany not from a religious creed but from a race. We hear good things from Holland, how a Protestant and Catholic protest has kept baptized Jews from being deported. We hear also that a heroic Polish priest has got leave to enter the ghetto at Litzmannstadt (Lwow) to minister to the Catholic Jews.

End of July: uncontrollable but very improbable Croatian rumour of massacre in Germany: uncontrollable rumour of massacres from Berlin—but still, a Polish priest gets into the ghetto at Lwow so a Jewish city exists and they can have sacraments.

Out of the Warthegau on 28 July wrote the Franciscan administrator, Father Breitinger. It was a letter like Sapieha's from Cracow, all the bad things that were happening to the Church in the Gau; and very bad things were happening, because this was an area annexed to the Reich and therefore the Polish race must be suppressed and therefore their Catholic Churches must be suppressed. They wondered whether the Pope had forgotten them. But the letter did not mention the Jews.[20]

Osborne's Diary, 31 July.

When I went for my evening walk I found the band of the Palatine Guard marching round and round the little path surrounding the bronze statue of St Peter on the top of the hill looking down on the back of St Peter's and the Vatican. I suspect that it was for a film which I heard today is being made, for world distribution, entitled *Pastor Angelicus*. I find this very regrettable and much too reminiscent of Hollywood publicity. It is a great pity that the Irish monk—Malachi, I think, though maybe he never existed—selected the name Pastor Angelicus for the 262nd Pope. If he had chosen *Leo Furibondus* or something of the sort the position of the Papacy in world estimation might be higher than it is. For I fear His Holiness sublimates his frustration in overdoing the *Pastor Angelicus*, thereby, incidentally, weakening his health and his morale, and also reducing the Papacy to the role of Patriarchate of Rome. Though this is not his fault, for I have no doubt that, if it were possible, he would expend his sympathies on other peoples. Only why, then, does

[20] *Ibid* 3 p 608.

he not denounce the German atrocities against the populations of the Occupied Countries?

Two days before he recorded this about the Palatine band and the film, he went down to have a meeting with the Brazilian ambassador Accioly and the American chargé Harold Tittmann. They agreed on a plan to make the Pope speak about atrocities, but it would take time to mature.

Something at least was being achieved where it could be achieved. The Slovak deportations were slowing down, and that was not for want of Jews still to deport. A lot of the Croatian Jews were in miserable camps but they were still in Croatia. Father Tiso defended the deportations in a radio broadcast, in which he said that love of the self is a commandment of God, and the report of this remarkable utterance came to the Vatican.[21] The Balkan situation was bad; from where they were in Rome they did not see how it could very well be worse; but we from our hindsight of perspective can see that it might have been much worse.

And now the Jews hit the headlines of the world. On 29 July 1942 the nuncio at Vichy, Valerio Valeri, reported the rounding up of Jews in Occupied France, with the aid of the French police. It was true that they were mostly foreign Jews, Czechs, Poles, Slavs. But this rounding up was not done amid the darkness of the eastern war where all news could be controlled, but in the west where no one could hide what was done. The rounding up was brutal, especially by separating children over the age of two from their parents. The bishops discussed a public protest but thought it best for Cardinal Suhard of Paris to write a letter to Marshal Pétain. 'Your Eminence will see', wrote the nuncio to Cardinal Maglione, that 'it is a purely Platonic protest.' (He meant that Pétain had no authority whatever in Occupied France.)

On 7 August the nuncio reported from Vichy that the deportations now extended to Unoccupied France. Two trainloads left from Gurs, it was thought to the General-Government, or into the Ukraine. The load included old and ill with young and fit, and therefore the plan cannot be to send them all to work. Pétain was grieved but said that he could do nothing, it was forced on them by Germany. Laval said that he approved of ridding France of Jews. The story reached London that Pope Pius XII had condemned, via the nuncio Valeri, the deportation of the French Jews. It was in the

[21] *Ibid* 8 p 664.

London newspapers. The Apostolic Delegate in London telegraphed Rome to find out if it were true. Cardinal Maglione telegraphed the reply that they had received no report of any such conversation between the nuncio and Marshal Pétain.[22]

The news was pouring in—but only of deportations. The inter-nuncio to Holland, who happened to be in Rome, reported (13 August) a letter from the Dutch priest dated Amsterdam 16 July in which he reported deportations of Jewish girls—('it is said to Poland')—and suicides of girls who threw themselves into canals rather than go.

The Swiss police received instructions to turn back Jewish refugees at the frontier.

In mid-August came a situation where the Vatican could help. The one government which it could influence was the Italian. Jewish Croats, to escape deportation, fled to the coast which was the area occupied by the Italian army. There they existed on very inadequate food until suddenly a new agreement between Italians and Croats meant that they must be again in Croat territory. The Yugoslav lega-tion to the Vatican appealed to Maglione who did all he could and, it seems, not without success. On 28 August, Hungary, at Vatican re-quest, agreed to let those 50 Croat Jewish children pass through Hungary on their way to safety.[23]

On 29 August a committee of some ten men, concerned over refugees, met in Geneva and considered what they could do to help the French Jews. They decided that they could do nothing for the adults, but that they might be able to do something for the children. The vicar-general of the diocese of Fribourg was present. A Swiss observer had an eye-witness account of the ghastly scenes when some 20,000 non-French Jews were deported in cattle-trucks. Should they try to get the children under the age of 16 to the Americas and as a first stop get them to Portugal? Then the Swiss committee turned to the vicar-general and asked him to ask the Berne nuncio to ask the Vatican to get into touch with the nuncios in Portugal and the Latin American countries and persuade bishops to prepare public opinion there to receive 'children separated from their parents; parents whom, without any doubt, they will never see again'. But we have to act fast. It is a matter of days, even hours.

The official line was still encouraging. Laval told Valeri (23

---

[22] Maglione to Godfrey, 11 August 1942, *ibid* 8 p 616 note.
[23] *Ibid* 8 pp 622–3, p 629.

August) and Valeri told Rome next day, that Hitler said how all Jews should be gathered into one region because that would mean that they could no longer hurt Germany by their propaganda. Valeri showed Rome that he suspected the story. On 26 August Laval demanded that Rome remove from his see Archbishop Saliège of Toulouse, the most courageously outspoken bishop on behalf of the French Jews.

We have now a far too optimistic letter from the American Harold Tittmann inside the Vatican to Washington.[24]

1 The nuncio at Vichy reported to Cardinal Maglione that the results of his démarche on behalf of the Jews of Unoccupied France were not encouraging. Thus recent press reports to the effect that the nuncio had asked Laval to ease the severity of his anti-Jewish measures were thus confirmed by the Cardinal Secretary of State. It was learned from the same source that Pétain had been approached earlier on the same matter by the nuncio.

2 Several weeks ago the nuncio mentioned to Laval his anxiety for the fate of 12,000 Jewish women and children concentrated in Paris and in that instance arrangements were made by Laval that families should not be divided.

3 In Italy the Vatican's intervention on behalf of the Jews has been much more successful, according to Cardinal Maglione, because the feeling of the people was strongly opposed to persecution and German pressure not so effective.

4 The information outlined above should be treated in the most confidential manner at the request of the Cardinal Secretary of State. The Vatican fears that their channels for the alleviation of suffering might be closed to them if their various démarches became generally know and talked about.

We notice the very strong desire of the Vatican not to say anything public because it could hurt all it said in private. We shall come in a moment to a very strong move by the diplomats to make the Pope say something public.

It was true that even into the end of August no one knew anything for certain. But now they all assumed the worst, whatever they might hope.

For example, the South-Italian camp of Jews at Ferramonti-Tarsia was unsettled. They got news of the deportations from Unoccupied France. They knew nothing about it but the bare fact. Panic ran

[24] Hyde Park, Myron Taylor Papers, Box 10, 31 August 1942.

through the camp. They were sure that the same fate was planned for themselves. No one could reassure them. They now had news from Slovakia, Germany, Holland, Occupied France—and now Unoccupied France—they feel the wave of persecution advancing relentlessly. 'It is natural' reported a priest attached to the camp 'that they fear for their own deportation and condemnation to death'.[25] They appealed to the Vatican as their only hope. They did not know, but they all assumed, as everyone else was beginning to assume, that if they were deported they would die.

At this point of time we must ask the question, *when* occurred the most famous of all interviews during the Final Solution; the interview between the SS man Kurt Gerstein and the nuncio in Berlin Monsignor Orsenigo. We know that on 17 August Gerstein, under orders to provide the gassing chemical Zyklon-B, went to the extermination camp at Belzec. There a train-load of Jews were disembarked and after undressing were driven staight into the gas chamber packed ultra-tight like some black hole of Calcutta; that the 'humane' killing was to be by carbon-dioxide pumped in from a diesel engine; that the diesel refused to work, according to Gerstein for two hours forty-nine minutes while Gerstein thought about the people suffocating inside. The other eye-witness (Pfannerstiel) says the diesel took eighteen minutes. We next find Gerstein travelling on the night train to Berlin on 20 August, already evidently suffering nervous breakdown because he burst into tears as he talked to the secretary of the Swedish embassy, Baron von Otter, whom by chance he met on the train, and with whom he stood in the corridor all night; wanting the neutral world to know the dreadful thing that was done. Whatever the state of his nerves, he was able to tell von Otter details; transport, arrangements, collection of jewelry and gold teeth, behaviour of Jews and guards. He was also clear of his aim in telling von Otter. He believed that if neutral countries spread the news, so that it could not be dismissed as enemy propaganda, the German people would cease to support Hitler.[26]

Thereafter we have no evidence of the timing. Gerstein appears to have called on Otto Dibelius, formerly Protestant Bishop of Berlin, and according to von Otter Dibelius believed what Gerstein told. Gerstein certainly called on Monsignor Orsenigo. We shall probably

[25] *ADSS* 8 p 642.

[26] Laqueur, *The Terrible Secret* p 49. Laqueur examined the von Otter file at the Swedish archives.

not be far out if we suppose this call to have taken place during the last days of August but we have no certainty. He called without any appointment and heavily bribed an underling to get him into the house—it sounds vaguely improbable, the nuncio would hardly have tried to keep out an SS man in uniform. Gerstein and Orsenigo talked in French. Gerstein described what he had seen at Belzec. There was silence. The nuncio seemed to be scarcely listening. Until suddenly he cried, '*Get away! Get out!*'[27] And so Orsenigo descended into history as the infamous type who represents the betrayal of the suffering Jews by the Churches.

No report went from Orsenigo to the Vatican about this meeting. The first time any of the extermination camps was mentioned in the Vatican, according to our evidence, was four weeks later on 26 September, when Belzec was mentioned though it was spelt wrong. The Vatican learnt nothing about Belzec through Orsenigo though Orsenigo had just had a macabre eye-witness describing what happened on a specially awful day.

Why this silence? Orsenigo was a weak man, in the thirties at least he quite liked the Nazi regime, he was a worthy running-mate for the British Sir Nevile Henderson. The Catholic Bishop of Berlin thought him a deplorable nuncio and wanted him recalled. Nevertheless he was not a nothing of a person. We can postulate three aspects of his mind at this moment—first, that the diplomatic bag is tampered with; second that the witness is in a high state of nerves and not to be relied on; and thirdly, the evidence of an SS man could easily be a trap into which to ensnare the entire Catholic hierarchy if it were believed. We also know, what has been proved time and again by the historians, that the truth was incredible in the strictest sense of the word. Rational people refused to believe in the possibility of what was done even when they were offered evidence. And incidentally Orsenigo knew that if he sent a report it would be equivalent to his passing sentence of death on Gerstein. To tell the Vatican could make no difference to the course of events. It still left them without a scrap of controllable evidence. Gerstein was naive. He imagined that if the Pope, or the Swedish government, told the world what happened at Belzec the world would believe them on his

---

[27] Jeffrey *Gerstein* (Eng. trans. 1971) pp 169–72. Gerstein apparently gave a report to the legal adviser (Dr Winter) of von Preysing, Catholic Bishop of Berlin. See 'Augenzeugenbericht zu den Massenvergasungen' in *Vierteljahrshefte fur Zeitgeschichte*, 1 (1953) p 193; Friedlander p 123.

word alone and then the Germans would believe the world and the Germans would desert Hitler. Orsenigo and the Swedes were not naive and knew better.

Let us consider what Baron von Otter did with Gerstein's evidence. He reported what he had heard to the head of the German department of the Swedish Foreign Office, Soederblom, who did nothing with it. He regarded it just as one of many uncontrollable stories that came out of Poland. As for telling the Allies, he said afterwards that to pass information from one belligerent country to another was too risky for a neutral.[28] Just like Orsenigo, the Swedes did nothing.

On 27 August Rabbi Wise wrote to the American State Department about extermination. The State Department took the line that this news was unconfirmed, and they believed that the Jews were put to labour.[29] On 2 September there was a great meeting of protest in Caxton Hall, Westminster.

That September Mr. Mander, a Liberal MP, drafted a question to ask the Secretary of State in the House of Commons whether he had any statement to make about the use by the German government of gas to murder a large number of Jews in Poland in mobile gas chambers? and if steps could be taken to inverview the three grave-diggers who escaped? Early in January 1942 three Jews ran away successfully from Chelmno and in Warsaw told what they saw happen to Jews in touch with the Polish underground. The information was brought to the West by courier, doubtless through the Swedish travellers whom the Polish underground could use until the summer of 1942. American newspapers had it in late July. The Foreign Office asked the Polish government in exile to check. The Pole of whom they enquired was sceptical, and said that he could not check the authenticity. The Poles preferred nothing to be said in the House of Commons, lest it risk lives in Poland.[30] The Foreign Office officials asked Mander to withdraw the question on 'humanitarian grounds'. The British government, like the Pope, preferred silence for the sake of the Jews.

The Vatican diplomats' idea to make the Pope say something went back to the end of July. It started with the Brazilian ambassador

---

[28] Laqueur, *The Terrible Secret* p 49. Friedlander p 123 believes that Bishop von Preysing must have sent Gerstein's report (to his legal counsellor) to Rome at the end of 1942.

[29] *Ibid* 224.

[30] *Ibid* pp 220–1.

Accioly, who was the senior ambassador immured inside the Vatican. He was not influential because Brazil was not influential in the war. But he was liked, and respected. He started to approach his colleagues to persuade them to approach their governments to allow them to join in the united démarche. All the diplomats consulted their governments and got a favourable response. They all agreed that they would leave their démarche with Cardinal Maglione in mid-September. Casimir Papée of Poland jumped the gun, and sent a long memorandum on 27 August begging the Pope to say something about Poland[31]—'the voice of the Holy Father, lifted for the sake of Poland, would not make the plight of the Poles worse, but would do the opposite, it could put a check on the fury of the Germans—if not of all the Germans at least some of the Germans' . . . 'The Polish government begs the Holy Father to speak in defence of the most fundamental and sacred principles of Christian morality' . . . The Germans are spreading the lie that the Pope is indifferent to the fate of the Poles . . . 'Even fervent and educated Catholics cannot account for the refusal of the supreme moral authority to defend the Poles in the moment when they are being exterminated' . . . 'The Polish government pleads with the Holy Father that he will lift up his voice for Poland; that voice will be heard throughout the world; it will carry succour to the tormented spirit of the Poles; it will destroy the impious weapon which the Germans use to sow doubt among the Poles; and it will put a curb on the senseless murders which destroy the Polish Nation'. Papée did not mention the Jews.

The other diplomats kept to a more or less common démarche of 12 to 14 September. Most of the démarches did not mention the Jews. But the British included it—'the merciless persecution of the Jews throughout Europe'. At that moment Osborne's new assistant, Hugh Montgomery, arrived and presented his credentials (11 September). He also joined the pressure. He said to the Pope that 'the Poles had hoped for some further expression of sympathy from the Holy See'. The Pope looked very concerned, and said 'But I have already done so much!'. He mentioned his broadcast of 13 May 1941. He said that this broadcast was suppressed in Germany—which showed that the Germans knew what it meant. The Poles, he said, did 'not know what difficulties faced the Vatican'. Messages to Poland from the Vatican were stopped by the Germans. 'If he were

[31] *ADSS* 5 p 657.

to go with details and mention names, it would only harm the victims'.[32]

On 11 September, then, the Pope's attitude was: (1) I have already spoken generally, and the Germans understand what I mean, (2) I cannot speak particularly because it would hurt the people I am trying to help, (3) I cannot get much through the barriers of censorship.

The Curia was angry at the common démarche. It thought that it was a plot. They believed, and continued to believe, that public protest must make the lot of the Poles and Jews worse, and that a public protest must cancel the effectiveness of what they could now do by private protest; that if they were required to denounce all the immoralities committed in a Great War the job would be a major industry and would touch others besides the Germans; that it was still widespread rumour rather than hard fact; that already the Pope had condemned such formalities in general terms and everyone will understand to what these generalities refer in particular.[33]

'It may perhaps be objected' said Osborne in his démarche, 'that His Holiness has already publicly denounced moral crimes arising out of the war. But such occasional declarations in general terms do not have the lasting force and validity that, in the timeless atmosphere of the Vatican, they might perhaps be expected to retain . . . A policy of silence in regard to such offences against the conscience of the world must necessarily involve a renunciation of moral leadership and a consequent atrophy of the influence and authority of the Vatican; and it is upon the maintenance and assertion of such authority that must depend any prospect of a Papal contribution to the reestablishment of world peace'.[34]

On 17 September arrived in Rome Myron Taylor, Roosevelt's personal representative to the Pope, on a visit of a few days. He drove through Rome in a closed car. It was extraordinary that Mussolini let him come. The German government thought it extraordinary and made its vexation plain to the Italians. His principal mission was to persuade the Pope that the Americans could not lose the war and that they meant to win and that their determination to win had a moral basis against villainy and that this moral basis the Pope could not help but approve. Therefore he wanted to stop the

---

[32] PRO, FO 371/33414; cited [A.] Rhodes, [*The Vatican in the Age of the Dictators* (London 1973)] p 291.

[33] cf Tittmann's Papers, s.v. Atrocities p 22.

[34] *ADSS* 5 p 676.

Pope making proposals for a compromise peace (though of this there was at that moment no danger whatever). But he also, almost as a side-issue, gave the Pope American information about the maltreatment of the populations of occupied Europe. The information told of the French deportations, with very reasonable statistics though a little out of date.

In this personal interview with the Pope he made only a suggestion of a papal utterance. In an interview with Monsignor Tardini (22 September 1942) he was more outspoken. Tardini's notes of the meeting heave a sigh thus: 'Mr. Taylor talked of the opportunity and the necessity of a word from the Pope against such huge atrocities by the Germans. He said that from all sides people are calling for such a word. I assented with a sigh, as one who knows the truth of this all too well! I said in reply that the Pope has already spoken several times to condemn crimes by whomsoever they are committed. I added that some people want the Pope to condemn by name Hitler and Germany, which is an impossibility. Taylor said to me "I don't ask this. I have not asked that he condemn Hitler by name". I said again, "The Pope has already spoken". Taylor said, "He can repeat". And I could not but agree'.[35]

Three days later Myron Taylor had a last interview with Cardinal Maglione, and we have the record of the interview made by the American priest Carroll, though his record was made from notes after the conversation. This ranged over the various subjects discussed by Myron Taylor when in Rome; and among them the atrocities. 'Mr. Taylor said that there was a general impression both in America and Europe—and he said that he could not be wrong in reporting this impression—that it was necessary now for the Pope again to denounce the inhuman treatment of refugees, hostages, and above all the Jews in the Occupied countries. Not only Catholics want the Pope to speak but also Protestants. Cardinal Maglione replied that the Holy See is continually at work trying to help the sufferers . . . In the different countries various representatives of the Church have openly denounced the maltreatment of the people and have done everything they can to help the oppressed. The Pope has condemned the oppressors of the peoples and has said that governments will be blest or curst by God according to the way they treat the occupied countries. That is a pretty strong statement; as strong as is possible without descending the particulars which would involve

[35] *Ibid* p 705.

the Pope in political questions and have to be supported by documentation, reports, etc. Obviously the Pope cannot do this. Mr. Taylor showed that he agreed but insisted on the opportunity for an appeal of a high character. The earlier declarations were some time ago. It is time for another. Certainly it would please everyone. Individuals as well as peoples have poor memories. Many want the Pope today to denounce these evils. Cardinal Maglione assured Mr. Taylor that at the first possible opportunity the Pope would not fail to express anew his thought with clarity'.[36]

Here then Myron Taylor extracted from the Secretary of State a promise; the Pope shall speak, as soon as he gets the chance, and shall speak clearly.

It was not easy. On the same day, 22 September when Myron Taylor saw Tardini a regrettable Italian clergyman handed Tardini a note from the German ambassador to the Vatican asking the Pope to condemn the air bombing of German cities. On 26 September the Pope signed a letter appealing for pity and charity to all the innocent victims of bombs from the sky. Tardini told the Italian ambassador Guariglia knowing that he would pass it to the Germans and so it would reach Berlin, and the Vatican would gain a little credit in Berlin; the subject which he chose to link with this credit was the worsening treatment of the Church in Warthegau; which indeed grew terrible; it concerned Catholic Poles and not non-Catholic Jews.

'I am not clear' wrote Myron Taylor, uncompromisingly in a note for his consequent conversation with Montini, 'whether the Holy See has condemned the bombing of London, Warsaw, Rotterdam, Belgrade, Coventry, Manila, Pearl Harbor, and places in the South Pacific'.[37]

And now Taylor supplied some hard information about something that till now was rumour.

We know that on 22 July 1942 began the process of emptying the Warsaw ghetto into the extermination camps. Despite the need of the German army for trains, one train a day with 5,000 Jews aboard left Warsaw for Treblinka. No one in the ghetto at first knew where they went or why. Since the trains returned in 12 to 14 hours they got some idea of the distance. Then a Polish railwayman brought back a description of Treblinka. Before the end of August 1942 the Jews in-

---

[36] *Ibid* pp 721–2.
[37] *Ibid* pp 723–4, p 729.

side the ghetto, or some of them, were aware of Treblinka, and what could happen there. The Jewish administrators of the ghetto still cooperated totally.

The news got out to the Jewish agency in Palestine. On 30 August this sent a report to Geneva, saying that they had two eye-witnesses. On 24 September Washington sent it off to Myron Taylor in Rome. On 26 September Myron Taylor laid what he knew before Cardinal Maglione. The liquidation of the Warsaw ghetto is in progress. Without distinction of age or sex they are taken away to be killed. Their bodies are used to make fertilizers. The mass executions are not in Warsaw but in special camps, one of which is said to be at Balzek (*sic*). The Jews deported from Germany, Belgium, Holland, France and Slovakia are sent to be massacred while the Aryans are deported to work. The Poles are stirred up by the Germans against the Jews. Taylor added a lot more detail some of which was very vague—'it is said'—'one story says'—. It did not provide the Vatican with the documentation which alone could, in its eyes, justify intervention.[38]

Cardinal Maglione stood firm. He took several days to reply. We have the office draft for an answer.[39] Harold Tittmann walked into the Secretariat on 1 October and asked for a reply. The draft reads: 'The Holy See has had reports of Jews being severely treated. We have not been able to test the accuracy of all of them. We have done all we can to help the Jews whenever we have the chance'.[40]

On 3 October Casimir Papée the Pole, who naturally plugged away at this more deperately than anyone else, wrote a report.

Everyone knows about German massacres in Poland; the means are various but they include gassing in specially adapted places.

He illustrated with figures the reduction of ghetto populations, including Warsaw.

It appears that the Jews are sent to camps where they are killed. It is certain that their families have absolutely no news of them afterwards.[41]

Notice how much is certain. There are vast falls in ghetto populations. But where do the people go? No one can trace them, they

---

[38] *Foreign Relations of the United States, 1942*, 3 p 775.
[39] *ADSS* 8 p 669.
[40] *Foreign Relations of the United States, 1942*, 3 pp 777–8; Cf *ADSS* 8 p 679; and Sumner Welles to Myron Taylor, Hyde Park, Myron Taylor Papers, Box 10, 21 October 1942.
[41] *ADSS* 8 p 670.

vanish totally. And someone has reported a gas chamber in one of the camps. It is not yet certain that the existence of the gas chamber is connected with the most mysterious disappearances. But the connexion is becoming probable.

On 7 October Pirro Scavizzi the chaplain with his hospital train on the eastern front wrote a report. We have no idea when this report reached the Vatican. The mass killing of Jews includes babes at the breast. When they are alive they cannot live a civil life—cannot go into a shop or travel in a bus or go to a Gentile house. Before they are deported or killed they are forced to labour, even if they are of the educated classes. It is said that about two million have been killed. Poles can find housing in ghettoes emptied by the systematic killing of Jews. Casimir Papée had another go on 9 October. He said to Cardinal Maglione (notice that he did not mention Jews) 'In view of the vast extent of the persecution of the Church in Poland, could not the Holy Father speak out in defence of the country?' Cardinal Maglione answered with great 'liveliness and emphasis': 'We have done our whole duty and whatever was necessary . . . For the moment we must wait and not raise the question again just now'.[42]

It should not be forgotten that some of the Jews in the Polish ghettoes knew a lot less than the outside world. When the ghetto at Lodz was almost empty the Jewish president of the community escorted the march of the children to the railway station quite confidently.[43] The date was then September 1942.

The American information was not the only information, as Maglione said. On 18 September Count Malvezzi came to see Monsignor Montini. Malvezzi reported terrible things in Poland: Russian air attacks on Polish cities, and systematic massacres of Jews, massacres which have reached monstrous proportions and happen every day. 'It seems that by the middle of October they want to empty entire ghettoes of hundreds of thousands, to make room for all the Poles driven from their houses to make room for the Germans evacuated after air-raids'.[44]

From Istanbul on 18 September Monsignor Roncalli wrote to the Vichy nuncio Valeri to interest him in a little band of Jews stuck at Perpignan near the Spanish border.[45] Roncalli did not think that

---

[42] Papée to Foreign Minister of Polish Republic, London, 12 October 1942; Falconi p 163.
[43] G. Reitlinger, *The Final Solution* (London 1953) p 266.
[44] *ADSS* 8 pp 665–6.
[45] *Ibid* p 647.

Valeri would succeed but hoped that he would try. 'It can do no harm'.

19 September: The President of the Dominican Republic Trujillo offered via the Vatican to accept 3,500 of the Jewish children left behind in France, and offered to organize the voyage and pay the cost.

21 September: The Vichy counsellor Pacini reported that the Vichy press was prevented from saying anything about the French Jews; that some Communists placarded on the walls the protest of Archbishop Saliège of Toulouse; and that the Vichy radio attacked the Church, including the nuncio and the Holy See, for its critical attitude.[46]

23 September: Cardinal Maglione approached the nuncio in Bucharest, Cassulo, to do what he could for the Transylvanian Jews ordered to be deported across the river into Transnistria. But the tone of this approach was weak. 'Among them are 3,000 or 4,000 Jews converted a good while ago to Catholicism and some of them deserved very well by generosity in supporting Catholic schools and institutions, especially in the diocese of Timisoara . . . You will represent what a very sad situation it would be for citizens who are Jewish by race but became Catholic some time ago and are strong supporters of the Church'.[47]

We have a letter dated 29-31 August 1942 from the Ruthenian metropolitan at Leopol telling of the massacre of 200,000 Jews in his area and other massacres especially in Kiev. But we do not know when or whether the letter got through, for we have no record of any reply.[48]

Maglione was not inventing when he pleaded that they did all they could. That 3 October he approached Father Tacchi-Venturi to persuade Mussolini to get the Italian descendants of mixed (i.e. half-Jewish) marriages cleared for marriage under Italian law.[49]

By October 1942 non-German Europe was full of press reports. In Switzerland a Protestant newspaper talked of poison gas. In Stockholm a report was published that some trains of deportees went straight to death camps. The executives of the Red Cross met in Geneva on 14 October and like the Pope decided to issue no state-

---

[46] *Ibid* p 658.
[47] *Ibid* p 659.
[48] *Ibid* 3 p 625.
[49] *Ibid* 8 pp 662-3.

ment, because any statement would violate the neutrality that was necessary to the work of the Red Cross.[50]

Osborne recorded for the Pope (29 October) how big a meeting was held in London to protest against the extermination of the Jews, and how the Archbishop of Canterbury spoke and Cardinal Hinsley was represented.

Meanwhile the news began to change. Stalingrad held; everyone still expected its fall to be only a matter of time; but incredibly, the siege went on, seventy days, eighty days, a hundred days. There began to be faint signs of Allied morale rising, visible even in Rome. Then the news of El Alamein began to come in; and then the American landing in North Africa.

Osborne did not yet expect this dramatic change to make a difference to what it might be possible for the Pope to say. If the Germans are going to win the war, that makes a difference to what it is prudent to say; and if the Allies have after all a chance of winning the war, the motives for prudence might at least shift in balance. That was not at first seen. All Osborne was still doing was to record for the Pope the Jewish atrocities as reported by the B.B.C.; especially on 30 November when the deputy Polish Prime Minister gave details. And Osborne commented:

> From all I hear it is quite true that Jews are crowded into trains, the floors of the carriages being covered with disinfectant in the form of chlorine or chloride or whatever it may be. The heat from the sun and the overcrowding results in poison gas. They are hermetically sealed goods wagons. The result is that after a long journey the great majority of the unfortunate Jews are dead. Those who survive are finished off on arrival. Italians have seen this. There seems every reason to credit the incredible report that Hitler and Himmler have decreed the extermination of the Jews in Poland if not in all Europe . . .

Notice that the report is still called *incredible*, only there is reason to credit it.

Meanwhile the Pope and Maglione were working very hard to prevent Rome being bombed. They tried every sort of diplomatic channel to extract an undertaking from the British. The British could not see why they should refrain from bombing an enemy capital and in any case, even if they never bombed Rome, were determined not to tell the Italians that they were not bombing Rome. This problem

---

[50] Laqueur, *The Terrible Secret* pp 62–3.

had given Osborne much work for months and months. But it was only in this December 1942 that the battle at last got him down; and what got him down was the ardent activity of the Vatican to prevent an 'atrocity' in Rome while it showed no signs of activity about atrocities in the rest of Europe.

Sunday, 13 December 1942; 'The more I think of it, the more I am revolted by Hitler's massacre of the Jewish race on the one hand, and, on the other, the Vatican's apparently exclusive preoccupation with the effects of the war on Italy and the possibilities of the bombardment of Rome. The whole outfit seems to have become Italian'.

This almost became Osborne's normal defence against pleas that the British should promise not to bomb Rome. 'I urged' he wrote of a talk with Cardinal Maglione on 14 December, 'that the Vatican, instead of thinking of nothing but the bombing of Rome should consider their duties in respect of the unprecedented crime against humanity of Hitler's campaign of extermination of the Jews, in which I said that Italy was an accomplice as the partner and ally of Germany'.

He collected all the factual information he could about the pogrom and handed it to Monsignor Tardini on 18 December, in the effort to make the Pope say something about it in his Christmas Eve broadcast. He asked Tardini, when he handed him the dossier, whether the Pope was not going to say something. 'But he said that the Pope could not take sides! It is very unfortunate. The fact is, I think, that His Holiness is clinging at all costs to what he considers to be a policy of neutrality, even in the face of the worst outrages against God and man, because he hopes to be able to play a part in restoring peace. He does not see that his silence is highly damning to the Holy See and is entirely destructive of any prospects of his being listened to'.

19 December: 'I went to see the Cardinal and had a quiet and amiable talk with him. I didn't want to go back again to my aggressive talks about Vatican policy and the Jews etc. He seemed deeply moved by my only reference to the Jewish atrocities'.

This day, 19 December, was the day when the Polish envoy Casimir Papée gave the Vatican the most famous letter of the whole affair. That day Papée told the Secretariat of State that he had authentic information about the Jews in Poland. The Germans suppress the entire Jewish population; first the old, the sick, women and children; and this proves that they are not deported for work. Information shows that the deported are put to death by different methods in places specially prepared. Young and strong men are often forced to work in such a way as to drive them to die from overwork and undernourishment. We reckon that the number of deaths is more than a million. In the ghetto at Warsaw there were about 400,000 Jews in mid July; 120,000 ration cards on 1 September; 40,000 ration cards on 1 October. The same liquidation goes on in the other cities of Poland.

It is evident that despite the evidence from the Warsaw ghetto no one knew by December much more than they knew in September.

This information of Papée caused another modern charge of bad faith against the Vatican editors. In 1974 Gitta Sereny published the book *Into this Darkness* on the extermination camp at Treblinka and got from Polish sources the letter of Papée and could not find it in the Vatican volumes as then published, and stated in her book (p 330) that the omission 'raises the gravest doubts as to the integrity of the Vatican publications'. That was a severe charge which an author would only make if she already had the axiom that something was likely to be concealed. I complained of this charge as unwarranted, and pointed out that the best defence of the editors was their publication of Papée's letter in its proper place in the volume which came out almost simultaneously with Sereny's book. The revised 1977 paperback edition of Sereny's book has not altered the statement in the text but added a footnote: 'As of 1973 when the book originally went to print. The document . . . has now (1976) been included in one of the latest volumes'. I regard this amendment as less than full, because although it is true and much better than nothing, readers could still think that the editors tried to conceal a vital text, and only printed after the existence of the document was made public by Sereny.

But from early in December telegrams began to flow into the Vatican from Jewish communities all over the world; the Jews of Costa Rica first; mostly from Central America, but also from Egypt and from Canada. The Chief Rabbi in London besought the Pope, invoking the Fatherhood of God and the brotherhood of man, to save a suffering people; and Montini took orders from the Pope that they were quietly to reply that the Holy See is doing all that it can.

By 3 December the British Foreign Office possessed at last information that must be substantially true; descriptions of the emptying of the Warsaw ghetto; the report of a Polish policeman inside the ghetto; a more doubtful report on Belzec. They had nothing on Chelmno or Auschwitz. It is extraordinary that no one yet had anything on Auschwitz. What they knew about was the Warsaw ghetto.

A day or two later Count Raczynski laid before Anthony Eden some of the Polish evidence. Churchill saw the note and asked for more. There was talk of a common declaration by the Allied Powers on behalf of the Jews. The State Department was not friendly: the reports are unconfirmed, we can do no good, the only way to help Jews is to win the war.[51] The London Foreign Office drafted a joint statement, with a phrase which the Russian ambassador Maisky added, that the number of victims was 'many hundreds of thousands of entirely innocent men, women, and children'.

On 17 December the Allies issued from London, Washington and Moscow their joint declaration on the German persecution of the Jews; and Osborne brought it to the Pope, suggesting that the Pope might endorse it in a public statement.

Cardinal Maglione gave his negative a little more clearly, with reasons. The Holy See could not mention particular atrocities. It had frequently condemned atrocities in general. Privately it had done everything possible to help. He deplored the cruelties. He said that they could not verify Allied reports on the number of Jews exterminated.

The diplomats were beginning to watch this Christmas broadcast, but in their different ways pessimistically.

22 December Harold Tittmann, telegram to Washington, No. 212: 'It is rumoured that the Pope, in his Christmas broadcast, will take a strong line on the subject. Any deviation from the generalities of his previous messages is unlikely, I am afraid'.

22 December Osborne's Diary: 'Having been reliably assured that the Pope was going to speak out this Christmas, I am now equally reliably assured that he is not. The Vatican will be the only State which has not condemned the persecution of the Jews'.

The Pope said something at last in clear. He appealed to all good men to make a vow to bring back society under the rule of God; it is a duty we owe to those who lie dead on the battlefields; to the mothers and widows and orphans who have lost their men; to the exiles torn from their men; to the exiles torn from their homes by war; to 'the hundreds of thousands of innocent people put to death or doomed to slow extinction, sometimes merely because of their race or descent'; to the many thousands of noncombatants who have lost life and

[51] R. B. Reams, in Laqueur, *The Terrible Secret* pp 225–6.

everything else by those air raids which we have never ceased to denounce from the beginning.[52]

Even in this utterance the Pope was very careful to guard against exaggeration. The story was, two million Jews killed for their race. The Allied Declaration had not believed it, and said hundreds of thousands. The Pope says, some hundreds of thousands. The story was that they were all killed just for their race and this was true. The Pope says they were sometimes killed only for their race, *talora*, on occasion. Like the minds of most of western Europe, the mind of the Pope was not bad enough to believe the truth. Like the high officials of the British Foreign Office he thought that the Poles and the Jews exaggerated for the sake of helping the war effort.

The phrase was not trivial. It displeased Mussolini, who called it contemptuously, 'a speech of platitudes worthy of the parish priest of Predappio'.[53] Some people said that it was made possible by the changing war—El Alamein, the Americans in North Africa, the German failure in the Caucasus, and Stalingrad—it really looked as though the Germans might not win the war. Ribbentrop wondered whether the Pope was deserting his neutrality and ordered Diego von Bergen, his ambassador in Rome, to threaten physical retaliation. Von Bergen obeyed. The Pope stayed quite silent. Then, very calmly, he said that he did not care what happened to him; that if there were a struggle between Church and State, the State would lose. 'Pacelli' reported Bergen to Ribbentrop 'is no more sensible to threats than we are'. German security studied the broadcast and defined it as 'one long attack on everything we stand for'. . . . 'God, he says, regards all peoples and races as worthy of same consideration. Here he is clearly speaking on behalf of the Jews . . . He is virtually accusing the German people of injustice towards the Jews, and makes himself the mouthpiece of the Jewish war criminals'.[54]

Harold Tittmann's telegram to Washington of 28 December took a more moderate line. '. . . The message does not satisfy those circles which had hoped that the Pope would this time call a spade a spade and discard his usual practice of speaking in generalities. The message is described in Vatican circles however, as "candid and forceful"'. The French ambassador, the Vichy man Leon Bérard, asked the Pope directly why he had not used the word Nazi in his

---

[52] Text in *ADSS* 7, p 161.
[53] *Ciano's Diary*, ed M. Muggeridge (London 1947) p 538.
[54] Ribbentrop to von Bergen, 24 January 1943; von Bergen to Ribbentrop, 26 January 1943, RHSA report on the broadcast; Rhodes pp 272–4.

condemnation. The Pope replied to Berard that if he had mentioned the Nazis by name he would have also had to mention the Communists by name.

In Poland Archbishop Sapieha heard the broadcast and welcomed the speech as what he had waited for.[55]

The Pope himself told several ambassadors that this speech was the condemnation which they had all been demanding.[56] He took this for granted when he talked to Tittmann. He seemed surprised when Tittmann told him that not everyone thought the same. Tittmann reported to Washington what he said:

> He said, that in his opinion, it was obvious in the eyes of all that when he spoke of hundreds of thousands of innocent people killed or tortured, and at times solely because of their racial or national origins, he had in mind the Poles, the Jews, and the hostages.

> He told me that, in speaking of atrocities, he could not have mentioned the Nazis without also mentioning the Bolsheviks, and this would surely not have pleased the Allies.

> He also said that he feared that Allied information on atrocities was, alas, only too true, though he gave me to understand from his attitude that, as he saw things, they contained a small element of exaggeration for the sake of propaganda. Taken as a whole, he said that he thought that his message would be well received by the American people and I said that I agreed with him.

Listening to the broadcast, Osborne thought it useless. ('He has produced the inevitable Five Points, this year on the special social problem or social problems'). When he had his New Year audience on 29 December he spoke very frankly about the Jews and the Pope listened with kindness and understanding. To London, after reflexion, Osborne began to make the best of it. On 5 January he reported to London that the Pope considered his broadcast 'clear and comprehensive' and that it 'satisfied all demands recently made upon him to speak out'.[57] But he also reported (31 December) that this was not the opinion of all his colleagues, and that the reaction of some at least of the other diplomats 'was anything but enthusiastic. To me he

---

[55] Papée to his government, 24 January 1943, in Falconi p 209.

[56] Papée to his government, 30 December 1942; Tittmann to Cordell Hull, 5 January, 1943; in Falconi pp 208–9.

[57] 5 January 1943, PRO, FO 371/34363; cf Martin Gilbert *Auschwitz and the Allies* (London 1981) p 105.

claimed that he had condemned the Jewish persecution. I could not dissent from this, though the condemnation is inferential and not specific, and comes at the end of a long dissertation on social problems'.[58]

The President of the Polish Republic in London, Wladislaw Raczkiewicz, thought nothing of the broadcast and on 2 January 1943 sent off to the Pope another desperate appeal for his people.[59] When this appeal was brought personally to the Pope by Casimir Papée, Pius XII for once was disturbed and accused the document of ingratitude.[60] On 3 February Cardinal Maglione sent a message to the Polish President in London which was tough:

> It would have been a good moment to say a thank you to the Pope. The President's message contains not a line of gratitude for all the various help and representations which the Holy See has made for the sake of the Poles; not only does it lack gratitude, it does not even deign to notice that anything has been done.[61]

And with that final protest from the Pope's side we may leave the tragedy of 1942.

Selwyn College, Cambridge.

---

[58] *ADSS* 9 p 71; cf B. Wasserstein, *Britain and the Jews of Europe* (Oxford 1979) p 175; S. Friedländer, *Pius XII and the Third Reich* pp 132–4.

[59] Text in *ADSS* 7 p 179; partly translated in Polish in Papée, *Pius XII a Polska 1939–49* pp 63–4, partly translated in Falconi p 218.

[60] Tardini's note, *ADSS* 7 p 180.

[61] Maglione to Godfrey, 3 February 1943, *ADSS* 7 pp 215–6.

RELIGION AND SOCIAL CONTROL IN THE SOVIET UNION 1945–1964

by GAVIN WHITE

W HY HAVE churches in the U.S.S.R. been harassed in recent years? It has been supposed by many that if Stalin stopped most persecution during the Second World War, then things under Khrushchev could only improve. Instead they deteriorated, and all liberties of Soviet citizens received more respect except the religious.

A common answer has been that the Soviet authorities were horrified by the continued hold of religion which they considered to be a threat to Marxism. Such a view is quite popular in the west where a clash of ideologies, with Christianity triumphing over Marxism, consoles churchmen who cannot find such a triumph in their own society. But this assumes that the Soviet rulers consider Christianity to be a religion based on certain tenets, and as Marxists they cannot be expected to do so. For them religion is primarily an instrument of social control.

Most of us tend to smile at this theme in such writers as E. P. Thompson,[1] or in the more recent writer who started, 'Much religious teaching of the nineteenth century contained no social or political message', and then ended an intelligent survey of social control as if this really were the critical element in English religion.[2] The church historian knows only too well the unsuitability of a Church for the task of imposing unwelcome social ideas. But the Marxist considers that religious faith is either a sham or a delusion, and that a religion is basically a device for social control which has been constructed by a feudal or bourgeois society, but which can be utilised by Soviet authority for controlling societies which lie outside the committed mainstream of Soviet life.

That this was so for the Second World War has been accepted by English-speaking readers since the publication of Struve's study in

---

[1] E. P. Thompson, *The Making of the English Working Class* (Harmondsworth 1968) pp 385–440.
[2] Jennifer Hart, 'Religion and Social Control in the Mid-nineteenth Century', A. P. Donajgrodski ed, *Social Control in Nineteenth Century Britain* (London 1977) p 108.

1962.[3] This showed that the 1940 extension of Soviet borders to the west also saw the Russian Orthodox Church, then on the verge of extinction as an organised force, sending three of its few bishops to head churches in the newly invaded lands, and being used again in 1943 and after as the lands were re-conquered from the Germans. The subject was explored in more detail by Fireside in 1971, and he observed with some surprise that Orthodoxy was ill-suited to being the instrument of any regime since, 'Services emphasise ritual, and sermons are as a rule devoted to purely spiritual, other-worldly topics.'[4] Alexeev and Stavrou studied the same subject but, as diasporan Orthodox, knew that even while the state exploited the weakness of the Church, the Church also exploited the weakness of the state, and particularly the state's naïveté on the subject of religion.[5]

But it was not only religious bodies which could be used for social control. National groupings could be employed in the same way, and if a nationality did not exist where it was needed, then it could be created. In the 1920s, after the Soviet war with Poland, the northern boundary between the two powers ran through an area given national status by the Soviet Union with what has been called an artificial language, Byelorussian, in order to draw the border peoples to Moscow rather than to Warsaw.[6] But having once created this nationality, the Soviet authorities found that it came too much to life and were obliged to damp it down with programmes of russification in the 1950s.[7] The Moldavian and Karelian languages are similarly artificial. And behind all this lies the philosophical notion of men as 'hollow', merely pushed by external stimuli, so that the state is able to 'treat language as an instrument of social control.'[8] And this was especially so with the peasant population; it was only after the personality was admitted to exist in the post-Stalin period that social control ceased to be respectable.[9] And once social control was ideologically doubtful, it was more difficult to justify toleration of religion.

[3] Nikita Struve, *Christians in Contemporary Russia* (London 1962).
[4] Harvey Fireside, *Icon and Swastika: The Russian Orthodox Church under Nazi and Soviet Control* (Cambridge Mass. 1971) p 191.
[5] W. Alexeev, T. G. Stavrou, *The Great Revival: the Russian Church under German Occupation* (Minneapolis 1976).
[6] [Hélène] Carrère d'Encausse, *L'Empire Éclaté* (Paris 1978) p 232.
[7] *Ibid* p 333.
[8] [Robert C.] Tucker, [*The Soviet Political Mind: Stalinism and Post-Stalin Change*] (London 1972) pp 161, 165.
[9] *Ibid* p 167.

But it had never been respectable to use social control in Soviet society, and its use with peasants was only justified by their being outside Soviet society. It was Herzen who wrote of the 'two Russias', regime and peasants, existing from the eighteenth century,[10] and this concept was developed by Preobrazhenski of the 'left opposition' in Lenin's day as the relationship between a colonial power and its colony.[11] But if colonialism is the analogy, then it is the colonialism of Leopold and the Congo in the days of red rubber, with armies of city workers sent out to confiscate foodstuffs, both in the period of war communism under Lenin and in that of collectivisation under Stalin, with the millions of deaths which ensued.[12] In imperial Russia there was never any pretence of peasants having the normal rights of citizens, and it was not until 1906 that they were given a more generous form of passport for internal travel.[13] In the Soviet Union peasants have, with some exceptions, had internal passports only since 1976, though the process has continued since then.[14] Until 1964 collective farm workers had no system of social security, and even when they did receive a system of pensions these were lower than for the country as a whole.[15] Most astonishingly, collective farms were not even allowed to purchase power from the national electricity grid until 1954, as if to make it clear that they were not really part of the nation.[16] As for income, collective farm income rose rapidly from 1953 until 1958 when agriculture flourished, but then fell in relation to fixed wages.[17] In general, workers in urban areas received half as much again as workers on state farms who received half as much again as workers on collective farms, and it is significant that Khrushchev expressed astonishment when he heard of a few collective farm workers who were actually paid more than urban workers.[18]

Yet this division was never intended to be permanent. It has been said that in 1945 Stalin had no choice but to leave agriculture in ruins

[10] *Ibid* p 125.
[11] [Lazar] Volin, [*A Century of Russian Agriculture: from Alexander II to Khrushchev*] (Cambridge Mass. 1970) p 193.
[12] *Ibid* p 234.
[13] *Ibid* p 108.
[14] [Hélène] Carrère d'Encausse, *Le Pouvoir Confisqué* [: *Gouvernants et Gouvernés en U.R.S.S.*] (Paris 1980) p 397.
[15] Volin p 428.
[16] *Ibid* p 478.
[17] *Ibid* pp 420, 427, 528.
[18] *Ibid* p 422.

if he was to re-build industry with the resources available, and industry must come first for any regime which was 'urbanist and anti-peasant'.[19] Agriculture was to be used to feed the cities in the knowledge that peasant revolts had always been too isolated to be dangerous in the past and would be so in the future,[20] while the continuing peasant revolts in the Ukraine could be put down at leisure.[21] Agriculture was still a wealth to be used for the cities; agricultural weakness had not yet become a drain on the whole economy.[22] And if agriculture was to be left alone, so was the Church which maintained the relatively strong position it had achieved during the war and which was expected to keep the peasants quiescent.

But Stalin did not entirely neglect the agricultural problem. He no longer tried to apply Marxist doctrine to the peasants, perhaps recognising that Michurin's notion of directing evolution was extremely chancy when applied to people.[23] Instead he left the peasants alone and tried to change their environment. Though the 'agrogorod', the agricultural worker's urban dwelling unit which would make peasants think like workers, only reached fruition in Khrushchev's day, it was under Stalin that it began.[24] And Stalin, far more than Khrushchev, did try to change agriculture by Michurinist direction of biological evolution. The ideas of T. D. Lysenko not only wrecked Soviet scientific progress, but they did immense damage to agriculture, and even forestry, with his programme of planting trees in groups since 'some trees would voluntarily die out, sacrificing themselves for the sake of the other seeds in the interest of preservation of the species. According to Lysenko, competition took place only between species, not within'.[25] Of course we in the west have heard something not dissimilar from the sociobiologists, but not as an indirect means of changing human nature.

Religion, however, probably meant more to Stalin than just a means of controlling peasants until science could change them. It has been ably argued that after the terrible losses of the Second World War there was very little left of the communist party, which was out-

[19] [William O.] McCagg, [*Stalin Embattled 1943–1948*] (Detroit 1978) pp 247, 248.
[20] Volin p 164
[21] Martin McCauley ed, *Communist Power in Europe 1944–1949* (London 1977) p 44.
[22] Carrère d'Encausse, *Le Pouvoir Confisqué* p 396.
[23] Tucker p 152.
[24] [Edward] Crankshaw, [*Khruschev*] (London 1966) pp 166, 179.
[25] [Werner G.] Hahn, *The Politics of Soviet Agriculture 1960–1970* (Baltimore 1972) p 68.

flanked by a bureaucracy inspired by Malenkov and his 'metal-eaters'.[26] Statistics on party membership do not entirely bear this out, and even if it is accepted that most party members were non-ideological promotions from the battlefield we must still consider that the Party had been so constantly purged in the 1930s that a weak Party was nothing new.[27] Nonetheless, Stalin may well have felt threatened by the industrialists and it is quite possible that he did respond by building up not one counter-weight but two, Party and Church. In Soviet Russia it has been customary to see Leningrad as a Party centre but Moscow as a national centre, with the Church as an element in the national identity, and if swift action against the industrialists was needed then party and Church could both be encouraged.[28] Almost certainly the Party was so used but got out of control and became a threat to Stalin, thus leading to the bloody purge of the otherwise mysterious Leningrad affair in 1949.[29] That the victims were Marxists is a reminder that the faith which has been most dangerous to its devotee in the Societ Union has not been Christianity but Marxism. In fact there is another theory of the Leningrad affair, that it was Stalin's purge of the moderate Zhdanov faction,[30] but like the Kirov affair of 1934 it may always be a mystery. Yet the counter-weight theory does give the best explanation of why Stalin may have kept the Church in case he needed it in the future, though it must be admitted that a Stalin who ran his empire with the secrecy and night habits of a Howard Hughes cannot be easily submitted to rational analysis.

All changed with Khrushchev. The reign of terror ended, though subtler repression did not. It has been stated that this was necessary if anyone was to be found willing to work in a bureaucracy hitherto so dangerous, though genuine humanitarian impulses existed in Khrushchev who may have had his colleagues' blood on his hands but disliked it.[31] But as Roy Medvedev has written of him, 'there was one freedom that he would not tolerate: that formerly extended to the Orthodox church'.[32] Repression of religion became general, but without recourse to violence.

[26] McCagg pp 21, 86, 98, 120.
[27] Carrère d'Encausse, *Le Pouvoir Confisqué* pp 55, 94.
[28] McCagg pp 93, 131, 179–180.
[29] *Ibid* pp 118–120.
[30] Werner G. Hahn, *Postwar Soviet Politics: the Fall of Zhdanov and the Defeat of Moderation 1946–53* (Ithaca 1982) p 122.
[31] Roy Medvedev, *Khrushchev* (Oxford 1982) pp 90, 91.
[32] *Ibid* p 213.

The religious policy of Khrushchev, like every other policy of Khrushchev, must be seen in relation to his agricultural ambitions. And it should be noted that the life of Khrushchev by the Medvedev brothers refers to his religious policy only twice, once when his closing of churches drove older peasants from the villages and thus harmed agricultural production, and once when his successors allowed churches to re-open and thus halted the drift from the land.[33] If Stalin's farm policy allowed religion, Khrushchev's did not, and for him this would not have seemed repression but deliverance. Peasants were to be brought into the mainstream of Soviet life and thus no longer needed religious solace and could be freed from superstition and the priests. In fact collective farm personnel were being made 'more aware politically' even before Stalin's death,[34] and attempts were now made to supersede the old rural sense of community. The new ideal was not that of the farm but of the grain factory,[35] and in this ideal mechanisation was seen as 'an essential attribute of a socialist farm enterprise, contributing mightily to that Marxist desideratum, the erosion of the gap between agriculture and industry'.[36] Scattered villages were to be replaced by urban-style apartment houses,[37] and even the Communist Party was divided into urban and rural sections so that peasants might receive attention which had never been theirs before.[38] By 1958 when it seemed that all Khrushchev's agricultural policies would triumph, he felt confident enough to dissolve the machine tractor stations which were virtual colonies of city workers providing technical guidance and political guidance for the rural population.[39] Peasants were now to provide both for themselves. There was some movement towards collective farms being absorbed into state farms which were ideologically preferable and turned peasants into salaried workers, but this did not have much impact in most areas.[40] And if Khrushchev's virgin lands campaign, like his corn campaign, was undertaken with such pellmell enthusiasm that it led to a degree of catastrophe, from

---

[33] Roy A. Medvedev, Zhores A. Medvedev, [*Khrushchev: The Years of Power*] (London 1977) pp 150–181.
[34] *Ibid* p 37.
[35] Volin p 199.
[36] *Ibid* p 476.
[37] Hahn, *The Politics of Soviet Agriculture 1960–1970* p 190.
[38] Carrère d'Encausse, *Le Pouvoir Confisqué* p 157.
[39] Roy A. Medvedev, Zhores A. Medvedev p 85.
[40] Carrère d'Encausse, *Le Pouvoir Confisqué* pp 140, 141.

his point of view it had the virtue of uprooting whole populations and, in theory, leaving their old ideas behind them.[41]

We know a good deal about Khrushchev's aims in agriculture but very little about his motives in religious policy. Yet what we know of his rural aims suggests that it would be logical for him to discontinue religious activity in the countryside, and to him this would not be so much persecution as the winding down of some 'quango' or quasi-autonomous non-governmental organisation which had outlived its usefulness. And if Marxists in general regard churches as agencies of social control, Khrushchev in particular had good reason to do so. He had been sent into Poland at the time of the partition in 1939, and with the deportations and the shootings there had also been the imposition of a Moscow bishop to control the Church.[42] And yet his partially Ukrainian background may have been as much a factor as any in turning him against religious activity, for religion in the Ukraine was traditionally divisive. It is in some ways difficult to reconcile the view of religion as social control with anti-religious propaganda, and yet Khrushchev's first independent decree in 1954 concerned a modernisation of anti-religious activity as if religion was an objective force.[43]

But after the removal of Khrushchev in 1964 there was no change in his religious policy. It did not progress; it just drifted. Perhaps this was because nobody knew what to do with agriculture, and religion went with it. Perhaps nobody really cared about religion anyway. But it may also be that the ability of the Church to use the concept of social control was fading. For twenty years churchmen could demand the minimum freedom to be a Church on the grounds that otherwise they would not look like a Church and could not impress peasants, or impress foreigners, and since the state considered that the religious side of religion was unimportant, that freedom was given. The Church would then act as a Church while making gestures to convince the state that it had social significance, which foreigners sometimes took too seriously—though some foreigners helpfully pretended to be impressed by what Russian church leaders said in order to give them more leverage in their manipulation of the state.

But there is a paradox here. Churchmen could only take advantage

---

[41] Roy A. Medvedev, Zhores A. Medvedev pp 118–121.
[42] Crankshaw p 135.
[43] *Ibid* p 200.

of the Marxist blinkers of the state as long as the state was Marxist, and if the state or part of it should become more pragmatic then the Church will lose out. The old game of Marxists using religion in the conviction that their history is inevitable so concessions do not matter, and Christians using Marxism in the conviction that their history is inevitable so concessions do not matter, may not work in the future. Each deceiving the other was profitable in its day, but if the Soviet Union becomes less Marxist, which is improbable for the immediate future, or merely becomes a more homogeneous society less concerned about controlling anyone, then the Church may be redundant.

But toleration may be bought for a number of prices. Ethnic Russians worried about the Soviet Union's Asian birthrate tend to retreat into their Orthodox past,[44] and there may be some role for the Church there. Alternatively, there is the threat of modern science. Marxism is tied to the climate in which it began to a far greater extent than is Christianity. Newtonian certainties applied to human history made an attractive ideology as long as Newtonian certainties were certain, but when Heisenberg's uncertainty principle escapes from the laboratory and is applied to history, then Marxism suffers.[45] It may be that religion may be brought into the system to provide an external point of reference, though it is hard to see this being done with official approval. But if toleration must be sought and a price must be paid, this is not only so in the Soviet Union. Churches which seek toleration or even privilege are accustomed to exaggerate their social utility, and churchmen who do this frequently come to believe their own exaggerations. And yet there is a question which defies analysis about social control and social utility. This concerns the extent to which religion, even if ineffective in imposing unwelcome social ideas, is effective in imposing welcome ones. Ultimately the function of religion in social control may be greater than we believe, but the process may be more one of society seeking sanction for what it wants than being bullied into accepting what it does not want.

University of Glasgow

[44] Edward Allworth ed, *Ethnic Russia in the U.S.S.R.: The Dilemma of Dominance* (New York 1980) pp 46, 78, 111; Carrère d'Encausse, *L'Empire Éclaté* p 341.
[45] Tucker p 150.

AASRP	*Associated Archaeological Societies Reports and Papers*
AAWG	*Abhandlungen der Akademie [Gesellschaft to 1942] der Wissenchaften zu Göttingen* (Göttingen 1843–)
AAWL	*Abhandlungen der Akademie der Wissenschaften und der Literatur* (Mainz 1950–)
ABAW	*Abhandlungen der Bayerischen Akademie der Wissenschaften* (Munich 1835–)
Abh	Abhundlung
Abt	Abteilung
ACO	*Acta Conciliorum Oecumenicorum,* ed E. Schwartz (Berlin/Leipzig 1914–40)
ACW	*Ancient Christian Writers,* ed J. Quasten and J. C. Plumpe (Westminster, Maryland/London 1946–)
ADAW	*Abhandlungen der Deutschen* [till 1944 *Preussischen*] *Akademie der Wissenschaften zu Berlin* (Berlin 1815–)
AF	*Analecta Franciscana,* 10 vols (Quaracchi 1885–1941)
AFH	*Archivum Franciscanum Historicum* (Quaracchi/Rome 1908–)
AFP	*Archivum Fratrum Praedicatorum* (Rome 1931–)
AHP	*Archivum historiae pontificae* (Rome 1963–)
AHR	*American Historical Review* (New York 1895–)
AKG	*Archiv für Kulturgeschichte* (Leipzig/Münster/Cologne 1903–)
AKZ	*Arbeiten zur Kirchlichen Zeitgeschichte*
ALKG	H. Denifle and F. Ehrle, *Archiv für Literatur-und Kirchengeschichte des Mittelalters,* 7 vols (Berlin/Freiburg 1885–1900)
Altaner	B. Altaner, *Patrologie: Leben, Schriften und Lehre der Kirchenväter* (5 ed Freiburg 1958)
AM	L. Wadding, *Annales Minorum* 8 vols (Rome 1625–54); 2 ed, 25 vols (Rome 1731–1886); 3 ed, vol 1–, (Quaracchi 1931–)
An Bol	*Analecta Bollandiana* (Brussels 1882–)
Annales	*Annales: Economies, Sociétés, Civilisations* (Paris 1946–)
Ant	*Antonianum* (Rome 1926–)
APC	*Proceedings and Ordinances of the Privy Council 1386–1542,* ed Sir Harris Nicholas, 7 vols (London 1834–7)
—	*Acts of the Privy Council of England 1542–1629,* 44 vols (London 1890–1958)
—	*Acts of the Privy Council of England, Colonial Series (1613–1783)* 5 vols (London 1908–12)
AR	*Archivum Romanicum* (Geneva/Florence 1971–41)
ARG	*Archiv für Reformationsgeschichte* (Berlin/Leipzig/Gütersloh 1903–)
ASAW	*Abhandhungen der Sächischen Akademie [Gesellschaft to 1920] der Wissenschaften zu Leipzig* (Leipzig 1850–)
ASB	*Acta Sanctorum Bollandiana* (Brussels etc 1643–)
ASC	*Anglo Saxon Chronicle*
ASI	*Archivio storico Italiano* (Florence 1842–)
ASL	*Archivio storico Lombardo,* 1–62 (Milan 1874–1935); ns 1–10 (Milan 1936–47)
ASOC	*Analecta Sacri Ordinis Cisterciensis [Analecta Cisterciensia* since 1965] (Rome 1945–)
ASOSB	*Acta Sanctorum Ordinis Sancti Benedicti,* ed. L. D'Achery and J. Mabillon (Paris 1668–1701)

ASP	*Archivio della Società [Deputazione* from 1935] *Romana di Storia Patria* (Rome 1878–1934, 1935–)
ASR	*Archives de Sociologie des Religions* (Paris 1956–)
AV	Authorised Version
AV	*Archivio Veneto* (Venice 1871– —): [1891–1921, *Nuovo Archivio Veneto*; 1922–6, *Archivio Veneto-Tridentino*]
B	Byzantion (Paris/Boston/Brussels 1924–)
Bale *Catalogus*	John Bale, *Scriptorum Illustrium Maioris Brytanniae Catalogus*, 2 parts (Basel 1557, 1559)
Bale, *Index*	John Bale, *Index Britanniae Scriptorum*, ed R. L. Poole and M. Bateson (Oxford 1902) *Anecdota Oxoniensia*, medieval and modern series 9.
Bale, *Summarium*	John Bale, *Illustrium Maioris Britanniae Scriptorum Summarium*, (Ipswich 1548, reissued Wesel 1549)
BEC	*Bibliothèque de l'Ecole des Chartres* (Paris 1839–)
Beck	H-G Beck, *Kirche und theologische Literatur im byzantinischen Reich* (Munich 1959)
BEFAR	*Bibliothèque des écoles françaises d'Athènes et Rome* (Paris 1876–)
BEHE	*Bibliothèque de l'Ecole des Hautes Etudes: Sciences Philologiques et Historiques* (Paris 1869–)
Bernard	E. Bernard, *Catalogi Librorum Manuscriptorum Angliae et Hiberniae* (Oxford 1697)
BF	*Byzantinische Forschungen* (Amsterdam 1966–)
BHG	*Bibliotheca Hagiographica Graeca*, ed F. Halkin, 3 vols + 1 (3 ed Brussels 1957, 1969)
BHI	*Bibliotheca historica Italica*, ed A. Ceruti, 4 vols (Milan 1876–85), 2 series, 3 vols (Milan 1901–33)
BHL	*Bibliotheca Hagiographica Latina*, 2 vols + 1 (Brussels 1898–1901, 1911)
BHR	*Bibliothèque d'Humanisme et Renaissance* (Paris/Geneva 1941–)
Bibl Ref	*Bibliography of the Reform 1450–1648, relating to the United Kingdom and Ireland*, ed Derek Baker for 1955–70 (Oxford 1975)
BIHR	*Bulletin of the Institute of Historical Research* (London 1923–)
BISIMEAM	*Bulletino dell'istituto storico italiano per il medio evo e archivio muratoriano* (Rome 1886–)
BJRL	*Bulletin of the John Rylands Library* (Manchester 1903–)
BL	British Library, London
BM	British Museum, London
BN	Bibliothèque Nationale, Paris
Bouquet	M. Bouquet, *Recueil des historiens des Gaules et de la France, Rerum gallicarum et francicarum scriptores*, 24 vols (Paris 1738–1904); new ed L. Delisle, 1–19 (Paris 1868–80)
BQR	*British Quarterly Review* (London 1845–86)
Broadmead Records	*The Records of a Church of Christ, meeting in Broadmead, Bristol 1640–87*, HKS (London 1848)
BS	*Byzantinoslavica* (Prague 1929–)
Bucer, *Deutsche Schriften*	*Martin Bucers Deutsche Schriften*, ed R. Stupperich and others (Gütersloh/Paris 1960–)
Bucer, *Opera Latina*	Martini Buceri Opera Latina, ed F. Wendel and others (Paris/ Gütersloh 1955–)
Bull Franc	*Bullarium Franciscanum*, vols 1–4 ed J. H. Sbaralea (Rome 1759–68) vols 5–7 ed C. Eubel (Rome 1898–1904), new series vols 1–3 ed U. Höntemann and J. M. Pou y Marti (Quaracchi 1929–49)
BZ	*Byzantinische Zeitschrift* (Leipzig 1892–)

CA	*Cahiers Archéologiques. Fin de L'Antiquité et Moyen-âge* (Paris 1945–)
CaF	*Cahiers de Fanjeaux* (Toulouse 1966–)
CAH	*Cambridge Ancient History* (Cambridge 1923–39)
CalRev	*Calamy Revised*, ed A. G. Mathews (Oxford 1934)
CalLP	*Calendar of the Letters and Papers (Foreign and Domestic) of the Reign of Henry VIII*, 21 vols in 35 parts (London 1864–1932)
CalSPD	*Calendar of State Papers: Domestic* (London 1856–)
CalSPF	*Calendar of State Papers: Foreign*, 28 vols (London 1861–1950)
Calvin, *Opera*	*Ioannis Calvini Opera Quae Supersunt Omnia*, ed G. Baum and others *Corpus Reformatorum*, 59 vols (Brunswick/Berlin 1863–1900)
Canivez	J. M. Canîvez, *Statuta capitulorum generalium ordinis cisterciensis ab anno 1116 ad annum 1786*, 8 vols (Louvain 1933–41)
Cardwell, *Documentary Annals*	*Documentary Annals of the Reformed Church of England*, ed E. Cardwell, 2 vols (Oxford 1839)
Cardwell, *Synodalia*	*Synodalia*, ed E. Cardwell, 2 vols (Oxford 1842)
CC	*Corpus Christianorum* (Turnholt 1952–)
CF	*Classical Folia*, [*Folia 1946–59*] (New York 1960–)
CGOH	*Cartulaire Générale de l'Ordre des Hospitaliers de St.-Jean de Jerusalem (1100–1310)*, ed J. Delaville Le Roulx, 4 vols (Paris 1894–1906)
CH	*Church History* (New York/Chicago 1932–)
CHB	*Cambridge History of the Bible*
CHistS	*Church History Society* (London 1886–92)
CHJ	*Cambridge Historical Journal* (Cambridge 1925–57)
CIG	*Corpus Inscriptionum Graecarum*, ed A. Boeckh, J. Franz, E. Curtius, A. Kirchhoff, 4 vols (Berlin 1825–77)
CIL	*Corpus Inscriptionum Latinarum* (Berlin 1863–)
Cîteaux	*Cîteaux: Commentarii Cisterciensis* (Westmalle 1950–)
CMH	*Cambridge Medieval History*
CModH	*Cambridge Modern History*
COCR	*Collectanea Ordinis Cisterciensium Reformatorum* (Rome/Westmalle 1934–)
COD	*Conciliorum oecumenicorum decreta* (3 ed Bologna 1973)
Coll Franc	*Collectanea Franciscana* (Assisi/Rome 1931–)
CR	*Corpus Reformatorum*, ed C. G. Bretschneider and others (Halle, etc. 1834–)
CS	*Cartularium Saxonicum*, ed W. de G. Birch, 3 vols (London 1885–93)
CSCO	*Corpus Scriptorum Christianorum Orientalium* (Paris 1903–)
CSEL	*Corpus Scriptorum Ecclesiasticorum Latinorum* (Vienna 1866–)
CSer	*Camden Series* (London 1838–)
CSHByz	*Corpus Scriptorum Historiae Byzantinae* (Bonn 1828–97)
CYS	*Canterbury and York Society* (London 1907–)
DA	*Deutsches Archiv für [Geschichte, -Weimar 1937–43] die Erforschung des Mittelalters* (Cologne/Graz 1950–)
DACL	*Dictionnaire d'Archéologie chrétienne et de Liturgie*, ed F. Cabrol and H. Leclercq (Paris 1924–)
DDC	*Dictionnaire de Droit Canonique*, ed R. Naz (Paris 1935–)
DHGE	*Dictionnaire d'Histoire et de Géographie ecclésiastiques*, ed A. Baudrillart and others (Paris 1912–)
DNB	*Dictionary of National Biography* (London 1885–)
DOP	*Dumbarton Oaks Papers* (Cambridge, Mass., 1941–)
DR	F. Dölger, *Regesten der Kaiserurkunden des oströmischen Reiches*

	(Corpus der griechischen Urkunden des Mittelalters und der neuern Zeit, Reihe A, Abt I), 5 vols: 1 (565–1025); 2 (1025– 1204); 3 (1204–1282); 4 (1282–1341); 5 (1341–1543) (Munich/Berlin 1924–65)
DRev	*Downside Review* (London 1880–)
DSAM	*Dictionnaire de Spiritualité, Ascétique et Mystique,* ed M. Viller (Paris 1932–)
DTC	*Dictionnaire de Théologie Catholique,* ed A. Vacant, E. Mangenot, E. Amann, 15 vols (Paris 1903–50)
EcHR	*Economic History Review* (London 1927–)
EEBS	Ἐπετηρὶς Ἑταιρείας Βυ3αντινων Σπουδων (Athens 1924–)
EETS	*Early English Text Society*
EF	*Etudes Franciscaines* (Paris 1899–1938, ns 1950–)
EHD	*English Historical Documents* (London 1953–)
EHR	*English Historical Review* (London 1886–)
Ehrhard	A. Ehrhard, *Uberlieferung und Bestand der hagiographischen und homiletischen Liberatur der griechischen Kirche von den Anfängen bis zum Ende des 16. Jh,* 3 vols in 4, *TU* 50–2 (= 4 series 5–7) 11 parts (Leipzig 1936–52)
Emden (O)	A. B. Emden, *A Biographical Register of the University of Oxford to 1500,* 3 vols (London 1957–9); *1500–40* (1974)
Emden (C)	A. B. Emden, *A Biographical Register of the University of Cambridge to 1500* (London 1963)
EO	*Echos d'Orient* (Constantinople/Paris 1897–1942)
ET	English translation
EYC	*Early Yorkshire Charters,* ed W. Farrer and C. T. Clay, 12 vols (Edinburgh/Wakefield 1914–65)
FGH	*Die Fragmente der griechischen Historiker,* ed F. Jacoby (Berlin 1926–30)
FM	*Histoire de l'église depuis les origines jusqu'à nos jours,* ed A. Fliche and V. Martin (Paris 1935–)
Foedera	*Foedera, conventiones, litterae et cuiuscunmque generis acta publica inter regis Angliae et alios quosvis imperatores, reges, pontifices, principes vel communitates,* ed T. Rymer and R. Sanderson, 20 vols (London 1704–35), 3 ed G. Holmes, 10 vols (The Hague 1739–45), re-ed 7 vols (London 1816–69)
Franc Stud	*Franciscan Studies* (St Bonaventure, New York 1924–, ns 1941–)
Fredericq	P. Fredericq, *Corpus documentorum inquisitionis haereticae pravitatis Neerlandicae,* 3 vols (Ghent 1889–93)
FStn	*Franzikanische Studien* (Münster/Werl 1914–)
GalC	*Callia Christiana,* 16 vols (Paris 1715–1865)
Gangraena	T. Edwards, *Gangraena,* 3 parts (London 1646)
GCS	*Die griechischen christlichen Schriftsteller der erste drei Jahrhunderte* (Leipzig 1897–)
Gee and Hardy	*Documents illustrative of English Church History* ed H. Gee and W. J. Hardy (London 1896)
GEEB	R. Janin, *La géographie ecclésiastique de l'empire byzantin;*
CEM	1, *Le siège de Constantinople et le patriarcat oecumenique,* pt 3 *Les églises et les monastères* (Paris 1953);
EMGCB	2, *Les églises et les monastéres des grands centres byzantins* (Paris 1975) (series discontinued)
Golubovich	Girolamo Golubovich, *Biblioteca bio-bibliografica della Terra Santa e dell' oriente francescano:*
	series 1, *Annali,* 5 vols (Quaracchi 1906–23)
	series 2, *Documenti* 14 vols (Quaracchi 1921–33)

series 3, *Documenti*, (Quaracchi 1928–)
series 4, *Studi*, ed M. Roncaglia (Cairo 1954–)

Grumel	V. Grumel, *Les Regestes des Actes du Patriarcat de Constantinople*,
Regestes	1: *Les Actes des Patriarches*, 1: 381–715; II: 715–1043; III: 1043–1206 (Socii Assumptionistae Chalcedonenses, 1931, 1936, 1947)
Grundmann	H. Grundmann, *Religiöse Bewegungen im Mittelalter* (Berlin 1935, 2 ed Darmstadt 1970)
Guignard	P. Guignard, *Les monuments primitifs de la règle cistercienne* (Dijon 1878)
HBS	*Henry Bradshaw Society* (London/Canterbury 1891–)
HE	*Historia Ecclesiastica*
HistSt	*Historical Studies* (Melbourne 1940–)
HJ	*Historical Journal* (Cambridge 1958–)
HJch	*Historisches Jarhbuch der Görres Gesellschaft* (Cologne 1880–, Munich 1950–)
HKS	Hanserd Knollys Society (London 1847–)
HL	C. J. Hefele and H. Leclercq, *Histore des Conciles*, 10 vols (Paris 1907–35)
HMC	*Historical Manuscripts Commission*
Holzapfel	H. Holzapfel, *Handbuch der Geschichte des Franziskanerordens*
Handbuch	(Freiburg 1908)
Hooker, *Works*	*The Works of . . . Mr. Richard Hooker*, ed J. Keble, 7 ed rev R. W. Church and F. Paget, 3 vols (Oxford 1888)
Houedene	*Chronica Magistri Rogeri de Houedene*, ed W. Stubbs, 4 vols *RS* 51 (London 1868–71)
HRH	*The Heads of Religious Houses, England and Wales, 940–1216*, ed D. Knowles, C. N. L. Brooke, V. C. M. London (Cambridge 1972)
HS	*Hispania sacra* (Madrid 1948–)
HTR	*Harvard Theological Review* (New York/Cambridge, Mass., 1908–)
HZ	*Historische Zeitschrift* (Munich 1859–)
IER	*Irish Ecclesiastical Record* (Dublin 1864–)
IGLS	*Inscriptions greques et latines de la Syrie*, ed L. Jalabert, R. Mouterde and others, 7 vols (Paris 1929–70) in progress
IR	*Innes Review* (Glasgow 1950–)
JAC	*Jahrbuch für Antike und Christentum* (Münster-im-Westfalen 1958–)
Jaffé	*Regesta Pontificum Romanorum ab condita ecclesia ad a. 1198*, 2 ed S. Lowenfeld, F. Kaltenbrunner, P. Ewald, 2 vols (Berlin 1885–8, repr Graz 1958)
JBS	*Journal of British Studies* (Hartford, Conn., 1961–)
JEH	*Journal of Ecclesiastical History* (London 1950–)
JFHS	*Journal of the Friends Historical Society* (London/Philadelphia 1903–)
JHI	*Journal of the History of Ideas* (London 1940–)
JHSChW	*Journal of the Historical Society of the Church in Wales* (Cardiff 1947–)
JIntH	*Journal of Interdisciplinary History* (Cambridge, Mass., 1970–)
JLW	*Jahrbuch für Liturgiewissenschaft* (Münster-im-Westfalen 1921–41)
JMH	*Journal of Modern History* (Chicago 1929–)
JMedH	*Journal of Medieval History* (Amsterdam 1975–)
JRA	*Journal of Religion in Africa* (Leiden 1967–)
JRH	*Journal of Religious History* (Sydney 1960–)
JRS	*Journal of Roman Studies* (London 1910–)

JRSAI	*Journal of the Royal Society of Antiquaries of Ireland* (Dublin 1871–)
JSArch	*Journal of the Society of Archivists* (London 1899–)
JTS	*Journal of Theological Studies* (London 1899–)
Kemble	*Codex Diplomaticus Aevi Saxonici*, ed J. M. Kemble (London 1839–48)
Knowles, *MO*	David Knowles, *The Monastic Order in England, 943*–1216 (2 ed Cambridge 1963)
Knowles, *RO*	, *The Religious Orders in England*, 3 vols (Cambridge 1948–59)
Knox, *Works*	*The Works of John Knox*, ed D. Laing, Bannatyne Club/Wodrow Society, 6 vols (Edinburgh 1846–64)
Laurent,	*V. Laurent, Les Regestes des Actes du Patriarcat de Constantinople,*
Regestes	1: *Les Actes des Patriarches*, IV: *Les Regestes de 1208 à 1309* (Paris 1971)
Le Neve	John Le Neve, *Fasti Ecclesiae Anglicanae 1066–1300*, rev and exp Diana E. Greenway, 1, St Pauls (London 1968); 2, Monastic Cathedrals (1971) *Fasti Ecclesiae Anglicanae 1300–1541* rev and exp H. P. F. King, J. M. Horn, B. Jones, 12 vols (London 1962–7) *Fasti Ecclesiae Anglicanae 1541–1857* rev and exp J. M. Horn, D. M. Smith, 1, St Pauls (1969); 2, Chichester (1971); 3, Canterbury, Rochester, Winchester (1974); 4, York (1975)
Lloyd, *Formularies of faith*	*Formularies of Faith Put Forth by Authority during the Reign of Henry VIII*, ed C. Lloyd (Oxford 1825)
LRS	*Lincoln Record Society*
LQR	*Law Quarterly Review* (London 1885–)
LThK	*Lexicon für Theologie und Kirche*, ed J. Höfer and K. Rahnes (2 ed Freiburg-im-Breisgau 1957–)
LW	*Luther's Works*, ed J. Pelikan and H. T. Lehman, American edition (St Louis/Philadelphia, 1955–)
MA	*Monasticon Anglicanum*, ed R. Dodsworth and W. Dugdale, 3 vols (London 1655–73; new ed J. Caley, H. Ellis, B. Bandinel, 6 vols in 8 (London 1817–30)
Mansi	J. D. Mansi, *Sacrorum conciliorum nova et amplissima collectio*, 31 vols (Florence/Venice 1757–98); new impression and continuation, ed L. Petit and J. B. Martin, 60 vols (Paris 1899–1927)
Martène and Durand	E. Martène and U. Durand, *Veterum Scriptorum et Monumentorum Historicorum, dogmaticorum, Moralium Amplissima Collectio,*
Collectio	9 vols (Paris 1729)
Thesaurus	*Thesaurus Novus Anedotorum*, 5 vols (Paris 1717)
Voyage	*Voyage Litteraire de, Deux Religieux Benedictins de la Congregation de Saint Maur*, 2 vols (Paris 1717, 1724)
MedA	*Medium Aevum* (Oxford 1932–)
Mendola	*Atti della Settimana di Studio*, 1959– (Milan 1962–))
MF	*Miscellanea Francescana* (Foligno/Rome 1886–)
MGH	*Monumenta Germaniae Historica inde ab a.c. 500 usque ad a. 1500*, ed G. H. Pertz and others (Berlin, Hanover 1826–)
AA	*Auctores Antiquissimi*
Ant	*Antiquitates*
Briefe	*Epistolae 2: Die Briefe der Deutschen Kaiserzeit*
Cap	*Leges 2: Leges in Quart 2: Capitularia regum Francorum*
CM	*Chronica Minora 1–3* (= *AA* 9, 11, 13) ed Th. Mommsen (1892, 1894, 1898 repr 1961)

Conc	*Leges* 2: *Leges in Quart* 3: *Concilia*
	4: *Constitutiones et acta publica imperatorum et regum*
DC	*Deutsche Chroniken*
Dip	*Diplomata in folio*
Epp	*Epistolae* 1 *in Quart*
Epp Sel	4: *Epistolae Selectae*
FIG	*Leges* 3: *Fontes Iuris Germanici Antique*, new series
FIGUS	4: , *in usum scholarum*
Form	2: *Leges in Quart* 5: *Formulae Merovingici et Karolini Aevi*
GPR	*Gesta Pontificum Romanorum*
Leges	*Leges in folio*
Lib	*Libelli de lite*
LM	*Ant* 3: *Libri Memoriales*
LNG	*Leges* 2: *Leges in Quart* 1: *Leges nationum Germanicarum*
Necr	*Ant* 2: *Necrologia Germaniae*
Poet	1: *Poetae Latini Medii Aevi*
Quellen	*Quellen zur Geistesgeschichte des Mittelalters*
Schriften	*Schriften der Monumenta Germaniae Historica*
SRG	*Scriptores rerum germanicarum in usum scholarum*
SRG ns	, new series
SRL	*Scriptores rerum langobardicarum et italicarum*
SRM	*Scriptores rerum merovingicarum*
SS	*Scriptores*
SSM	*Staatschriften des späteren Mittelalters*
MIOG	*Mitteilungen des Instituts für österreichische Geschichtsforschung* (Graz/ Cologne 1880–)
MM	F. Miklosich and J. Müller, *Acta et Diplomata Graeca medii aevi sacra et profana*, 6 vols (Vienna 1860–90)
Moorman, *History*	J. R. H. Moorman, *A History of the Franciscan Order from its origins to the year 1517* (Oxford 1968)
More, *Works*	*The Complete Works of St Thomas More*, ed R. S. Sylvester and others Yale edition (New Haven/London 1963–)
Moyen Age	*Le moyen âge. Revue d'Histoire et de philologie* (Paris 1888–)
MRHEW	David Knowles and R. N. Hadcock, *Medieval Religious Houses, England and Wales* (2 ed London 1971)
MRHI	A. Gwynn and R. N. Hadcock, *Medieval Religious Houses, Ireland* (London 1970)
MRHS	Ian B. Cowan and David E. Easson, *Medieval Religious Houses, Scotland* (2 ed London 1976)
MS	Manuscript
MStn	*Mittelalterliche Studien* (Stuttgart 1966–)
Muratori	L. A. Muratori, *Rerum italicarum scriptores*, 25 vols (Milan 1723–51); new ed G. Carducci and V. Fiorini, 34 vols in 109 fasc (Città di Castello/Bologna 1900–)
NCE	*New Catholic Encyclopedia*, 15 vols (New York 1967)
NCModH	*New Cambridge Modern History*, 14 vols (Cambridge 1957–70)
nd	no date
NEB	*New English Bible*
NF	*Neue Folge*
NH	*Northern History* (Leeds 1966–)
ns	new series
NS	New Style

Numen	*Numen: International Review for the History of Religions* (Leiden 1954–)
OCP	*Orientalia Christiana Periodica* (Rome 1935–)
ODCC	*Oxford Dictionary of the Christian Church*, ed F. L. Cross, (Oxford 1957), 2 ed with E. A. Livingstone (1974)
OED	*Oxford English Dictionary*
OMT	*Oxford Medieval Texts*
OS	Old Style
OHS	*Oxford Historical Society*
PBA	*Proceedings of the British Academy*
PG	*Patrologia Graeca*, ed J. P. Migne, 161 vols (Paris 1857–66)
PhK	Philosophisch-historische Klasse
PL	*Patrologia Latina*, ed J. P. Migne, 217 + 4 index vols (Paris 1841–64)
Plummer, Bede	*Venerabilis Baedae Opera Historica*, ed C. Plummer (Oxford 1896)
PO	*Patrologia Orientalis*, ed J. Graffin and F. Nau (Paris 1903–)
Potthast	*Regesta Pontificum Romanorum inde ab a. post Christum natum 1198 ad a. 1304*, ed A. Potthast, 2 vols (1874–5 repr Graz 1957)
PP	*Past and Present* (London 1952–)
PPTS	*Palestine Pilgrims' Text Society*, 13 vols and index (London 1896–1907)
PRIA	*Proceedings of the Royal Irish Academy* (Dublin 1836–)
PRO	Public Record Office
PS	Parker Society (Cambridge 1841–55)
PW	*Paulys Realencyklopädie der klassischen Altertumswissenschaft*, new ed G. Wissowa and W. Kroll (Stuttgart 1893–)
QFIAB	*Quellen und Forschungen aus italienischen Archiven und Bibliotheken* (Rome 1897–)
RAC	*Reallexikon für Antike und Christentum*, ed T. Klauser (Stuttgart 1941)
RB	*Revue Bénédictine* (Maredsous 1884–)
RE	*Realencyclopädie für protestantische Theologie*, ed A. Hauck, 24 vols (3 ed Leipzig, 1896–1913)
REB	*Revue des Etudes Byzantines* (Bucharest/Paris 1946–)
RecS	Record Series
RGG	*Die Religion in Geschichte und Gegenwart*, 6 vols (Tübingen 1927–32)
RH	*Revue historique* (Paris 1876–)
RHC	*Recueil des Historiens de Croisades*, ed Académie des Inscriptions et Belles-Lettres (Paris 1841–1906)
Arm	*Historiens Arméniens*, 2 vols (1869–1906)
Grecs	*Historiens Grecs*, 2 vols (1875–81)
Lois	*Lois. Les Assises de Jérusalem*, 2 vols (1841–3)
Occ	*Historiens Occidentaux*, 5 vols (1844–95)
Or	*Historiens Orientaux*, 5 vols (1872–1906)
RHD	*Revue d'histoire du droit* (Haarlem, Gronigen 1923–)
RHDFE	*Revue historique du droit français et étranger* (Paris 1922–)
RHE	*Revue d'Histoire Ecclésiastique* (Louvain 1900–)
RHEF	*Revue d'Histoire de l'Eglise de France* (Paris 1910–)
RHR	*Revue de l'Histoire des Religions* (Paris 1880–)
RR	*Regesta Regum Anglo-Normannorum*, ed H. W. C. Davis, H. A. Cronne, Charles Johnson, R. H. C. Davis, 4 vols (Oxford 1913–69)
RS	*Rerum Brittanicarum Medii Aevi Scriptores*, 99 vols (London 1858–1911). *Rolls Series*

RSCI	*Rivista di storia della chiesa in Italia* (Rome 1947–)
RSR	*Revue des sciences religieuses* (Strasbourg 1921–)
RStI	*Rivista storica italiana* (Naples 1884–)
RTAM	*Recherches de théologie ancienne et médiévale* (Louvain 1929–)
RV	Revised Version
Sitz	*Sitzungsberichte*
SA	*Studia Anselmiana* (Roma 1933–)
sa	sub anno
SBAW	*Sitzungsberichte der bayerischen Akademie der Wissenschaften*, PhK (Munich 1871–)
SCH	*Studies in Church History* (London 1964–)
ScHR	*Scottish Historical Review* (Edinburgh/Glasgow 1904–)
SCR	*Sources chrétiennes*, ed H. de Lubac and J. Daniélou (Paris 1941)
SF	*Studi Francescani* (Florence 1914–)
SGra	*Studia Gratiana*, ed J. Forchielli and A. M. Stickler (Bologna 1953–)
SGre	*Studi Gregoriani*, ed G. Borino, 7 vols (Rome 1947–61)
SMon	*Studia Monastica* (Montserrat, Barcelona 1959–)
Speculum	*Speculum, A Journal of Medieval Studies* (Cambridge, Mass., 1926–)
SpicFr	*Spicilegium Friburgense* (Freiburg 1957–)
SS	*Surtees Society* (Durham 1835–)
SSSpoleto	*Settimane di Studio sull'alto medioevo*, 1952– , Centro Italiano di studi sull'alto medioevo, Spoleto 1954–)
STC	*A Short-Title Catalogue of Books Printed in England, Scotland and Ireland and of English Books Printed Abroad 1475–1640*, ed A. W. Pollard and G. R. Redgrave (London 1926, repr 1946, 1950)
Strype, *Annals*	John Strype, *Annals of the Reformation and Establishment of Religion . . . during Queen Elizabeth's Happy Reign*, 4 vols in 7 (Oxford 1840)
Strype, Cranmer	John Strype, *Memorials of . . . Thomas Cranmer*, 2 vols (Oxford 1824)
Strype, *Grindal*	John Strype, *The History of the Life and Acts of . . . Edmund Grindal* (Oxford 1821)
Strype, Memorials	John Strype, *Ecclesiastical Memorials, Relating Chiefly to Religion, and the Reformation of it . . . under King Henry VIII, King Edward VI and Queen Mary I*, 3 vols in 6 (Oxford 1822)
Strype, *Parker*	John Strype, *The Life and Acts of Matthew Parker*, 3 vols (Oxford 1821)
Strype, Whitgift	John Strype, *The Life and Acts of John Whitgift*, 3 vols (Oxford 1822)
sub hag	subsidia hagiographica
sv	sub voce
SVRG	*Schriften des Vereins für Reformationsgeschichte* (Halle/Leipzig/Gütersloh 1883–)
TCBiblS	*Transactions of the Cambridge Bibliographical Society* (Cambridge 1949–)
Tchalenko	G. Tchalenko, *Villages antiques de la Syrie du Nord*, 3 vols (Paris 1953–8)
THSCym	*Transactions of the Historical Society of Cymmrodorion* (London 1822–)
TRHS	*Transactions of the Royal Historical Society* (London 1871–)
TU	*Texte und Untersuchungen zur Geschichte der altchristlichen Literatur* (Leipzig/Berlin 1882–)

VCH	*Victoria County History* (London 1900–)
VHM	G. Tiraboschi, *Vetera Humiliatorum Monumenta*, 3 vols (Milan 1766–8)
Vivarium	*Vivarium: An International Journal for the Philosophy and Intellectual Life of the Middle Ages and Renaissance* (Assen 1963–)
VV	*Vizantijskij Vremennick* 1–25 (St Petersburg 1894–1927), ns 1 (26) (Leningrad 1947–)
WA	*D. Martin Luthers Werke*, ed J. C. F. Knaake (Weimar 1883–) [*Weimarer Ausgabe*]
WA Br	*Briefwechsel*
WA DB	*Deutsche Bibel*
WA TR	*Tischreden*
WelHR	*Welsh History Review* (Cardiff 1960–)
Wharton	H. Wharton, *Anglia Sacra*, 2 parts (London 1691)
Whitelock, *Wills*	*Anglo-Saxon wills,* ed D. Whitelock (Cambridge 1930)
Wilkins	*Concilia Magnae Britanniae et Hiberniae A.D. 446–1717*, 4 vols, ed D. Wilkins (London 1737)
YAJ	*Yorkshire Archaeological Journal* (London/Leeds 1870–)
Zanoni	L. Zanoni, *Gli Umiliati nei loro rapporti con l'eresia, l'industria della lana ed i communi nei secoli xii e xiii, Bibliotheca Historica Italica*, 2 series, 2 (Milan 1911)
ZKG	*Zeitschrift für Kirchengeschichte* (Gotha/Stuttgart 1878–)
ZOG	*Zeitschrift für osteuropäische Geschichte* (Berlin 1911–35) = *Kyrios* (Berlin 1936–)
ZRG	*Zeitschrift der Savigny-Stiftung für Rechtsgeschichte* (Weimar)
GAbt	*Germanistische Abteilung* (1863–)
KAbt	*Kanonistische Abteilung* (1911–)
RAbt	*Romanstische Abteilung* (1880–)
ZRGG	*Zeitschrift Religions- und Geistesgeschichte* (Marburg 1948–)
Zwingli, *Werke*	*Huldreich Zwinglis Sämmtliche Werke*, ed E. Egli and others, *CR* (Berlin/Leipzig/Zurich 1905–)